Huế
1968

Also by Mark Bowden

Doctor Dealer

Bringing the Heat

Black Hawk Down

Killing Pablo

Finders Keepers

Road Work

Guests of the Ayatollah

The Best Game Ever

Worm

The Finish

The Three Battles of Wanat

Huế
1968

A Turning Point of
the American War in Vietnam

Mark
Bowden

Grove Press UK

First published in the United States of America in 2017 by Grove/Atlantic Inc.
First published in Great Britain in 2017 by Grove Press UK, an imprint of Grove/Atlantic Inc.

Copyright © Mark Bowden, 2017
Map copyright © Matthew Ericson, 2017

The moral right of Mark Bowden to be identified as the author of this work has been
asserted by him in accordance with the Copyright, Designs and Patents Act of 1988.

An excerpt from "Cheating the Reaper" is reprinted from *Praying at the Altar*
by W. D. Ehrhart, Adastra Press, 2017, by permission of the author.

"Ballad of the Green Berets," words and music by Barry Sadler and Robin Moore,
copyright © Music Music Music Inc., 1963, 1964 & 1966. Permission given by Lavona Sadler.

Photo credits are as follows: Photo 1.1 (Che Thi Mung): Courtesy of Che Thi Mung. Photos 1.2
(Frank Doezema), 2.1 (Jim Coolican): Courtesy of Jim Coolican and Fred Drew. Photo 1.3
(Nguyen Dac Xuan): Courtesy of Nguyen Dac Xuan. 1.4 (President Johnson and General William
Westmoreland): Bettmann/Getty Images. 2.2 (Gordon Batcheller): Official Marine Corps Photo. 2.3
(Chuck Meadows): Courtesy of Chuck Meadows. 2.4 (Alfredo "Freddie" Gonzalez): Official Marine
Corps Photo A419730, courtesy of the Marine Corps History Division. 3.1 (MACV press pass):
Courtesy of Gene Roberts. 3.2 (Jim and Tuy-Cam Bullington): Courtesy of Jim and Tuy-Cam
Bullington. Photos 3.3 (Tran Cao Van Street), 5.4 (raising the American flag): Rolls Press/Popperfoto/
Getty Images. 3.4 (Mike Downs): Courtesy of Mike Downs. 4.1 (Ernie Cheatham): Courtesy of
John Salvati. 4.2 (Catherine Leroy): Photo by François Mazure, published in LIFE Magazine
(February 16, 1968). 4.3 (Ray Smith): Courtesy of Ray Smith. 4.4 (Bob Helvey): Courtesy of Charles
Krohn and Robert Helvey. 5.1 (Civilians in Hue): Photo by Kyoichi Sawada, UPI. 5.2 (Ron Christmas):
Courtesy of Ron Christmas. 5.3 (Andy Westin): Courtesy of Andy Westin. Photo 6.1
(Walter Cronkite): Everett Collection Inc/Alamy Stock Photo. 6.2 (Bob Thompson): Courtesy of
John Olson, source unknown. Photos 6.3 (Dong Ba Tower), 7.2 (the Citadel): © John Olson.
Photo 6.4 (Steve "Storyteller" Berntson): Courtesy of Steve Berntson. Photo 7.1 (James Vaught):
Photo Courtesy of James J. Wilson, Sgt. E 5, B Co., 5/7 Cav. 1967-68.

1 3 5 7 9 8 6 4 2

A CIP record for this book is available from the British Library.

Grove Press, UK
Ormond House
26–27 Boswell Street
London
WC1N 3JZ

www.groveatlantic.com

Text Design by Norman Tuttle

This book was set in Dante MT with ITC New Baskerville
by Alpha Design & Composition of Pittsfield, NH

Hardback ISBN 978 1 61185 625 5
Trade paperback ISBN 978 1 61185 510 4
Ebook ISBN 978 1 61185 939 3

Printed and bound in Great Britain by Bell and Bain Ltd, Glasgow

For Gene Roberts

Wisdom comes to us when it can no longer do any good.
—Gabriel García Márquez

Contents

PART ONE: The Infiltration   1

PART TWO: The Fall of Hue   93

PART THREE: Futility and Denial   155

PART FOUR: Counterattack in
the Triangle and Disaster at La Chu   215

PART FIVE: Sweeping the Triangle   293

PART SIX: Taking Back the Citadel   395

Epilogue   519

Acknowledgments   541

Vietnamese Glossary   545

Source Notes   563

Index   595

Southeast Asia

CHINA

NORTH VIETNAM

Hanoi

LAOS

Thanh Hoa

Gulf of Tonkin

Vinh

Vientiane

Dong Hoi

DMZ

17TH PARALLEL

Khe Sanh

Hue

THAILAND

Da Nang

HO CHI MINH TRAIL

CENTRAL HIGHLANDS

Bangkok

Siem Reap

SOUTH VIETNAM

CAMBODIA

Phnom Penh

Cam Ranh Bay

Saigon

Gulf of Thailand

Can Tho

South China Sea

100 MILES

Hours before daylight on January 31, 1968, the first day of Tet, the Lunar New Year, nearly ten thousand North Vietnamese Army (NVA) and Viet Cong (VC) troops descended from hidden camps in the Central Highlands and overran the city of Hue, the historical capital of Vietnam. It was an extraordinarily bold and shocking move, taking the third-largest city in South Vietnam several years after America's military intervention was supposed to have shifted the war decisively in Saigon's favor. The National Liberation Front,[1] as the coalition of Communist forces called itself, had achieved complete surprise, taking all of Hue save for two embattled compounds, one an Army of the Republic of Vietnam (ARVN) base in the city's north, and the other a small post for American military advisers in its south. Both had no more than a few hundred men, and were surrounded and in danger of being overrun.

It would require twenty-four days of terrible fighting to take the city back. The Battle of Hue would be the bloodiest of the Vietnam War, and a turning point not just in that conflict, but in American history. When it was over, debate concerning the war in the United States was never again about winning, only about how to leave. And never again would Americans fully trust their leaders.

PART ONE

The Infiltration

1967–January 30, 1968

Frank Doezema, the army radioman who
manned the guard tower at the MACV
compound when Front troops attacked.

Che Thi Mung (left) and Hoang
Thi No, village teenagers with the Huong
River Squad who fought American and
ARVN forces.

President Johnson and General William
Westmoreland in the Rose Garden during the
general's November 1967 spizzerinctum tour.

Nguyen Dac Xuan, the Buddhist
poet who became a propagandist and
commissar for the Front.

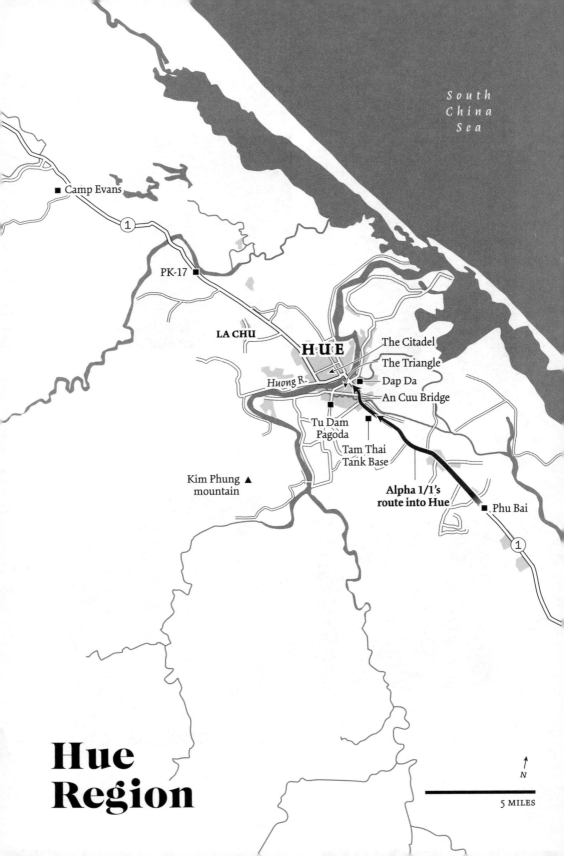

South
China
Sea

■ Camp Evans

①

PK-17 ■

LA CHU

H U E

The Citadel

The Triangle

Huong R.

Dap Da

An Cuu Bridge

Tu Dam
Pagoda

Tam Thai
Tank Base

Kim Phung ▲
mountain

**Alpha 1/1's
route into Hue**

■ Phu Bai

①

Hue
Region

↑
N

5 MILES

1

The Huong River Squad

IN THE AFTERNOON along Le Loi Street, uniformed children spill from school yards like flocks of freed birds, swinging backpacks, running or on bicycles, the boys in white shirts and shorts, the girls with their long black hair and the white flaps of their *ao dai* flying.

The street is Hue's center. It runs along the south bank of the Huong River and is planted at intervals with plane trees that lean out over the busy flow of scooters and cars. On the street's north side, along the riverbank, is a wide green promenade, and on the south side is a row of imposing stone buildings behind high walls painted in pastels of green, yellow, red, brown, and pink. Across the water rise the mottled, forbidding stone walls of the Citadel, a monumental fortress from another era. The river's name, Huong, evokes the pleasing scent of incense or the pink and white petals that float downstream in autumn from orchards to the north. The Americans called it the Perfume River.

In 1968, there were more bicycles than scooters and cars beneath the trees on Le Loi Street. The image of a pretty girl on a bike in an *ao dai*, the traditional tunic with flaps in front and back, and a traditional conical hat—*non la*—was on the cover of the pocket guide GIs were issued on their way to the war in Vietnam.[2]

One of those cycling girls in January of that year was Che Thi Mung. She was eighteen and as pretty as the picture on the handbook. Che was a village girl with little schooling. Riding her bike in Hue, she was the picture of innocence: slender with a round face, big eyes, and high cheekbones. She worked with her family in the rice paddies and helped weave palm leaves from village trees into *non la*, which she sold on the city streets. She would stack the hats and strap them to the back of her bike.

But Che was neither as innocent nor as friendly as she looked. She knew nothing of the global clash of ideas that brought American soldiers to Vietnam, but the war was her life. Her position in it was dead certain. With all the passion of youth, she hated the Saigon regime, the Republic of Vietnam. This enmity was largely an inheritance. Before she was born, her father had fought with the Viet Minh against the French, and when she was a child he had been imprisoned for years by the Saigon regime, which had followed the French. In her mind they were the same, only now the shadow behind the local oppressor was not France, but the United States. Her father, a bricklayer, had been fighting his whole life. For Che, the war had turned even more personal two years earlier, when the ARVN killed her big sister, a leader in the VC underground. She knew the regime's soldiers as *nguy* (fake), a word that in Vietnamese suggested a familiar Asian face masking an alien soul.[3]

After her sister was killed, the *nguy* had come looking for collaborators in Van The, her village, a small community of farmers and tradesmen in the Thuy Thanh district southeast of the city. It was off the main road and surrounded in all directions by well-tended rice fields, a flat and outwardly placid landscape. The weather was damp through most of the year but especially during the coastal region's wet months from December through February, which were filled with cool days shrouded in gray mist. Far to the west were the stark green peaks of the Central Highlands; to the east, just a few miles distant, were beaches and the South China Sea. About three of four people in Van The shared Che's feelings about the Saigon regime, so it was friendly ground for the VC. Her father was hidden by friends after Che's sister was killed. They knew that once the *nguy* figured out who she was, they would unearth his record and come looking for him.

When they came, they found empty bunkers beneath Che's house. Such shelters were common. Villagers dug them to hide from bombs or shells, and sometimes they were used to hide weapons or the VC. Sometimes village boys were sheltered there to avoid impressment by either side. So the ARVN could make what they wished of the bunkers.

In Che's case, they were suspicious enough, weighed with the actions of her sister and the absence of her father, for her arrest. She was taken to an ARVN post in the city with her mother and paternal grandfather. Interrogators poured soapy water down her nose and throat until she choked and her ears rang and head and throat stung. They demanded she tell them where her father had gone and the names of the VC fighters from her village.

She cried and pleaded. She was just a girl! She told them she knew nothing. Why were they tormenting her? Did they think the VC confided in sixteen-year-old girls? Didn't they have daughters? Sisters? For the rest of her life she would be proud of how tenaciously she protected her secrets. She told the *nguy* nothing.

She had joined the Viet Cong herself four years earlier, its Young Pioneer Organization.[4] She was fiercely proud of her martyred sister, heartbroken over her death, fearful for her father, and determined to live up to their example. When she and her family were released, martial law was imposed on Van The. Most deeply resented was a curfew that confined the villagers to their homes after seven in the evening. But the *nguy* did not live in the village. They could not be there all the time, and they could not know which neighbors to trust. It was easy for fighters like Che to avoid the patrols and to attend nightly meetings and training sessions. As for the rest of the village, the crackdown just generated anger—and recruits.

Che would sometimes see Americans with the ARVN troops. They wore similar uniforms but the Americans were easy to spot even from a distance because they looked so different. For one thing, most were bigger. At night she and her family listened to stories on the radio of American bombing in North Vietnam, imagining the death, destruction, and misery, but she did not fear or hate the Americans so much as she did the *nguy*, who seemed to her much worse. They had sided with foreigners against their own people. They spoke her language and were Vietnamese in all respects except the most important.

For the two years after her arrest and interrogation, she lived a double life, a committed revolutionary at night, and a law-abiding citizen of South Vietnam during the day. She found work at the same ARVN post where she had been tortured, cleaning and doing odd jobs. She had been cleared and released, and so many were subjected to this treatment that even if suspicions about her lingered, she little feared being remembered. She would bicycle into the city, selling her hats and working at the post, and most evenings she would ride home and attend meetings where she and other village girls sharpened bamboo spikes for booby traps. She would stand watch and spread the alarm whenever the *nguy* or Americans approached.

The cadre she supported, her sister's, took portions of the village harvest and carried it up to the hidden jungle camps in the highlands, what the troops referred to simply as *xanh* (the green). Mostly it was boys who did this work. The girls encouraged children to join the revolutionary youth groups, and tried to recruit villagers to the cause. Che would remind them of the onerous curfews, the rudeness of the soldiers who swept through periodically, and the arbitrary arrests and invented charges. She told them that the peace and freedom promised by the *nguy* and their American controllers was illusory. Their country was at war and would remain at war until the invaders and traitors were gone. The real Vietnam would rise she said. It would be united. She envisioned a future where the free Vietnamese people worked together to improve life for all.

She was eager to fight for it. When she turned seventeen, a year after her arrest, she was admitted to the Youth Union,[5] where she began working directly with the commune guerrillas. In their nighttime sessions, they now learned to break down, clean, and rebuild automatic rifles like the AR-15 and AK-47; how to shoot them and bazookas, B-40 rocket launchers; and how to handle grenades. These grenades took seven seconds to explode after you pulled the pin, so you had to count calmly to five before throwing them. Che took part in a hit-and-run attack on a *nguy* outpost one night that year and fired her weapon at the enemy for the first time.

Then, in October 1967, the most thrilling thing happened. She was selected to join ten other girls in a special squad. It would be led by Pham Thi Lien, a twenty-year-old native of their village who had fought with Che's sister. During the raid when Che had been arrested, Lien had been outed. She had escaped to North Vietnam, where she had received formal political and military training. On her return, she picked only the most committed young women from several villages in the area. Along with Che she chose Hoang Thi No, whose parents were already living underground with the VC. Hoang was so small and thin she looked even more harmless than Che, but she had worked with her on recruiting and also maintaining underground shelters. When the two girls from Van The met with the others in their new squad, Lien told them their mission was to prepare for a great push to be called Tong-Tan-cong-Noi-day (General Offensive, General Uprising). It would take place during Tet, which in 1968, according to the Chinese calendar, was to be Mau Than, the Year of the Monkey. Its most important part would be an attack on Hue, from which they would expel, once and for all, the Americans and the *nguy*. From the north would come thousands of well-armed, well-trained soldiers who would join with the VC and with other local patriots. The people would rise up. The war would end. The promised day of self-rule was at hand!

Lien's group, later called the Huong River Squad, was one of many mobilized in secret during those months. The girls felt part of something on a grand scale, and it was not just talk. Lien told them they would have to leave their families. Four specific missions were assigned: to spy on the *nguy* and American forces in the city; to recruit civilians to join the uprising and provide support; to train them with weapons and tactics; and to build a committed core who, when the battle began, would carry the wounded to medical stations in the rear and help feed the army. Weapons, ammo, food, and medical provisions all would be smuggled, stockpiled, and made ready. Pretty girls were not perceived as a threat in the city. They moved around freely. They could watch the military and police posts, mapping entrances and exits, defenses, and gun positions, and noting the enemy's numbers and routines. They could document the homes and habits of Westerners living in Hue. There were scores of American and European civilians living and working there, everyone from undercover CIA officers to peace activists. They could record the home addresses and routines of traitors, prominent officials in the Saigon regime, police and military leaders, and even lesser citizens whose loyalty was suspect. For all of these there would be a reckoning.

The girls were given money to rent homes in Hue. Che left to live with a family in Dap Da, a south bank neighborhood where the Nhu Y River emptied into the Huong, a short walk east of the city's center. The family she joined lived in a run-down house of brick and stone that was owned by a teacher who lived there with his son, a tailor; and his granddaughter, a schoolgirl. During the day, setting up on the sidewalk, Che would weave and sell hats, and she would watch. At intervals she would pick up her wares and bike west down Le Loi Street, past Hue University, the city hospital complex, the police headquarters, the prison, and the province headquarters. She kept a close eye on the river landing across from the university at the foot of the Truong Tien Bridge where American navy vessels came and went. Che's comrade Hoang sold hats and kept an eye on the Americans' favorite Huong Giang Hotel, among other spots. Along with the other girls, working over months, they drew a detailed portrait of Hue's military and police posts.

One of Che's targets was the busy American post, the Military Assistance Command Vietnam (MACV) compound, just two blocks south of the bridge. It was a rectangular enclosure formed by nondescript two- and three-story buildings and fencing. Inside was a large courtyard with a parking lot and a tennis court—used mostly for barbecues. The lot was filled with olive-colored Jeeps and six-by-six trucks. A high steel fence—topped with barbed wire and studded with flares and mines rigged to detonate if disturbed—surrounded the perimeter. There were only two gates, guarded by high towers. Outside them on the sidewalk were sandbag bunkers. It was a small urban fort without especially heavy defenses. There was always at least one bored soldier with a machine gun in the front tower, gazing down blankly on the constant flow of bicycles, cars, rickshaws, and scooters. Daily, Che counted the men and vehicles that came and went, and noted entrances and exits, guard shifts, the number and kinds of weapons.

Because there was no running water at the house in Dap Da, she walked with other neighborhood girls every evening to a public water fountain where they filled containers to carry home. It gave them an excuse to be on the streets after the evening curfew. The line of girls in their colorful silk blouses at the water fountain was catnip for the *nguy*, who were plentiful in that neighborhood. Across the street from the fountain were a military school and a brothel. The girls chatted and teased and flirted with the soldiers coming and going from both places, and learned a lot. Flirting was particularly useful. Once a *nguy* soldier was in the proper mood, Che had only to ask when his guard shift ended. In time she developed a working knowledge of the schedules at all the posts she observed. She never took notes. She committed all the details to memory and reported them back to Lien.

The girls were not told exactly when the Tong-Tan-cong-Noi-day would begin, but when that day came—and it would be soon—they would be called back to the village. From there they would lead NVA and VC troops into the city in darkness for the surprise attack. Once the fight started, they would assist, carrying the wounded and supplies.

To Che and the other girls on the Huong River Squad, it would be the biggest moment in their lives.

2

Thirty-Nine Days

IT HAD BEEN a long year for Frank Doezema. He was heartily homesick. Each time he wrote home to Shelbyville, Michigan, near Kalamazoo, he would note the days left in his one-year tour in Vietnam. On January 21, he told his brothers: "It won't be long now. Look out world, here I come! When I say world, I mean the good ole USA or Michigan or Shelbyville or just plain home . . . Let's see, 55 days, that's eight weeks."

He knew exactly what he would do when he returned: work on his family farm and eventually run it, either alone or with his brothers. Cornfields and cows were all he wanted, careerwise. He'd collected his diploma from Kalamazoo Christian High in 1966, and that had closed the book on school. Like all young men with a clear vision of their future, Doezema was in a hurry. He had his eye on a girl he intended to marry, although she didn't know it yet. He'd have been well along already, with farm and family, if not for the draft.

Every healthy male high school grad in the United States in 1966 without college plans was immediately draft bait. It was a stubborn reality, like taxes. Nearly everyone had a father or uncles who had fought in World War II or Korea, or both, and many had grandfathers who had fought in World War I. War was stitched deep in the idea of manhood. It was portrayed heroically in popular films and TV shows, books, and even comic books: stories of men bravely defying death and besting foes in faraway places for God, family, and flag. Doezema was not eager to be a soldier, but he didn't question the call. In fact, knowing there was no draft deferment for farmwork, he'd sought out the most efficient way to meet his obligation. He took advantage of an army program— designed to meet the urgent need for men in Vietnam—that would halve his commitment from four years to two. And as he'd expected, he was in Vietnam within months of completing basic training.

He was an authentic Michigan cornstalk: tall and thin with a blond crew cut and a long square jaw. Trained as a radio operator, he spent the first six months in-country assigned to a marine captain named Jim Coolican, who worked as an adviser to an ARVN battalion. Coolican rejected Doezema at first. The captain stood about six foot five, and towered over the Vietnamese soldiers he advised. Enemy snipers targeted officers and Americans. An officer and his radioman had to stay close together—the radio was needed to call in artillery and air support—and Coolican worried that being with Doezema, who was nearly as tall as he was, would double the danger. It was especially dangerous for Doezema because a radioman carried the unit strapped to his back: it was bulky and had a high antenna. Coolican considered himself brave, but he wasn't stupid. Still, Doezema pushed. He liked the captain and he liked the idea of seeing real combat during his tour. And from what he'd heard, the ARVN airborne troops mixed it up with the enemy often. Coolican eventually gave in, and the two had worked together seamlessly.

They saw action often. Their battalion,[6] part of ARVN's First Division, was deployed in I Corps, the country's northernmost sector, which encompassed five provinces of South Vietnam and stretched from south of Hue all the way north to the demilitarized zone (DMZ) and the border with the North. This was the easiest place for NVA troops to infiltrate, and it was obvious that Hanoi was planning something big, because many soldiers were coming. In the fall of 1967, there had been frequent violent clashes in this sector, and contrary to the poor reputation of South Vietnam's forces, the men Coolican and Doezema served with were aggressive and competent. During those months, the two tall Americans saw far more combat than most of their countrymen, and despite their size, neither had been hit. In time, they felt lucky to be paired. They worked shoulder to shoulder in the field during the day, ate their meals together, and slept side by side, often softly talking into the night. They shared everything. At twenty-seven, Coolican was eight years older than his radioman, who always called him Captain or sir, but in time there was little barrier of rank between them. Coolican came to feel like Doezema's older brother.

Americans who landed in Vietnam were strangers in a strange land. Few of them knew the language, the history, the culture, or even, except in broad outline, the nature of the conflict, which actually differed from zone to zone. Coolican and Doezema were having a far different experience. They lived and worked with their Vietnamese counterparts. The captain had been given some language training, but neither he nor his radioman spoke the language well enough to say anything beyond a few necessary words. And yet they had both developed a strong respect and affection for their ARVN counterparts.

To most American soldiers, the local forces were known as Arvin, and the name was not applied kindly. It suggested a caricature: a small Asian man in an oversize American helmet and uniform (cast-off American sizes often fitted Vietnamese men poorly), inadequately trained, ignorant of basic infantry tactics, equipped with Korean War–vintage weapons, incompetent, reluctant to fight, and all too often given to thievery and desertion. Some of the South Vietnamese men pressed into service fitted this mold, just as some of America's more reluctant draftees fell short of the ideal. All too often, the officers who led them were incompetent and corrupt. It was an ongoing problem. Largely out of necessity, American combat soldiers were aggressively insular. When they were not on patrol they stayed behind defensive perimeters of barbed wire and mines. They ate American food, shopped for American products at the PX, watched American movies, and listened to American songs on the radio. Fraternizing with the locals was discouraged—although whorehouses did brisk business. So the only Vietnamese most soldiers encountered were scouts, translators, whores, workers hired to perform menial jobs on American bases, or those who peddled goods and services nearby—licit and illicit. Enterprising Vietnamese mixed basic mercantile lingo with simple GI slang, and added coinages of their own: "numbah ten" for the worst, "numbah one" for the best. The primitive dialect reinforced disdainful stereotypes, even if the peddler who spoke broken English had language skills that exceeded his customers'. And most Americans viewed the locals with suspicion. The contemptuous word "gook" was applied not only to the enemy; there were gooks who were the enemy and then there were "our gooks." And even those more kindly disposed were often patronizing, seeing the "good gooks" as worthy little people stuck in a primitive past. Racism colored the alliance from top to bottom.

Coolican's experience was the opposite of all that. With the ARVN troops he "advised," he was the ignorant and inexperienced one. The very idea of a college boy from suburban Philadelphia having something worthwhile to impart about combat was laughable. The Vietnamese officers Coolican served were far better soldiers than he was. They had been at war for years. The only important thing he had to offer them was Doezema's radio, the ability to dial up American air and artillery—a game changer. This was why he was important to them, not because he had knowledge to impart. Without his radio, he was nothing more than a tall marine who drew fire.

The realization was humbling. Coolican found himself defending the ARVN troops from knee-jerk American scorn. He had been an air force ROTC cadet at St. Joseph's College before he opted for the marines. Vietnam had been his goal. He was an idealist, and a true believer. He had grown up trusting his elders, and accepted that just as his father's generation had fought in Europe, Japan, and Korea to protect the American way of life, his generation had its own role to play holding the line against Communism. Kennedy's inaugural address, with its evocation of the "torch being passed to a new generation," had spoken to him. He completed boot camp and infantry training over summer vacations, and upon graduation he was commissioned a second lieutenant. His experience in Vietnam, coming up on a year now, had only deepened his commitment to the cause and his career. He was exactly where he wanted and needed to be.

He and Doezema split up toward the end of 1967. Coolican had sought and received a transfer to the Hac Bao (Black Panthers), an elite ARVN unit with a reputation for ferocity and skill. Hand selected, they wore distinctive black fatigues when they were not fighting in the jungles. General Ngo Quang Truong, commander of the ARVN First Division at Mang Ca, the military base in the northeast corner of the Citadel, used them as a rapid strike force.

For Doezema, the change meant his days of fighting were all but over. Parting from Coolican, he went first to a small American compound on the outskirts of Hue, and then to the MACV compound.

He still worked as a radio operator, but now was surrounded by other Americans. The streets outside were comparatively safe. In the heart of this bustling city it was easy to feel that the war was a minor conflict at the wild edges of a thriving South Vietnam. There were regular convoys back and forth from the marine combat base at Phu Bai, eight miles south, and beyond it to the larger one at Da Nang. American vessels came and went from the boat ramp on the Huong's south bank. The war had visited the old capital city so infrequently in the previous years that the compound was regarded as a rear post, well out of harm's way.

He had downtime, and with it he had things to do. There were curbside restaurants to indulge his new taste for Vietnamese food, bars, museums, parks, and even historical sites like the old emperors' tombs and the ornate royal palace. The beaches of the South China Sea were just a few miles east. Doezema tried out the smattering of Vietnamese he had learned with Coolican. He would sometimes use his radio to call the captain, still humping around the countryside with the Hac Bao, and they would chat at night like old times. The farm boy was coasting through the final months of his adventure, crossing off the days on his calendar until his real life resumed. He had friends who would stop by for two- or three-day visits, staying in his room. They noticed that the Vietnamese girl who cleaned up had a crush on the tall blond American who treated her with such respect and made an effort to speak her language.

Here was one more unusual thing about Doezema. He made Vietnamese friends. One was a twelve-year-old boy whose family had lived adjacent to his first post in Hue. The boy's name was Quy Nguyen, and he lived in a big house with a walled garden just outside the city. He was the eldest of seven children. Doezema and his buddies would drive out to the Nguyen house with candy and teach the children English phrases and give them rides in the Jeep. In return, they were treated to large Vietnamese meals that put the compound mess to shame. On one of those trips in January, Doezema told Quy that he would soon be going home. He put his camera and his watch on a table and told the boy he could have his pick. Quy chose the camera.

The letter of January 21 to his brothers Ardis and Bill displayed both his homesickness and his sense of humor:

Here it is Sunday again and I have to work all day. It's a pretty nice day too. The misquitos [sic] are getting pretty thick again. We still haven't had much of a monsoon season or cold weather either like everyone told us we would. It's OK with me though. I will be glad to get back to all that beautiful snow though.

Last Sunday afternoon Bob [Mignemi] and I went down to my friend's house in Hue & visited with them a while. Yesterday afternoon we had a practice alert in the compound. Only about 1/3rd of the people were there so it really wasn't very profitable.

It's 10:00 already & a lot of late reports are coming in from last night's activities. Just mostly small contacts like ambushes being ambushed while on their way to an ambush site. We've got a brigade from the 1st Air Cav in our area now. That should make the V.C. think twice. Phu Loc [an American base south of Phu Bai] still takes sporadic fire once in a while. They've got a lot of nearby mountains so it's hard to locate the enemy.

I made it to the movie last night. I sure get homesick when I watch a movie with "round eyes" in it. It won't be long now, though. Only forty-eight more days. A lot of new people are coming in & now it is my turn to laugh. I can't hardly imagine what it will be like to get back. Alls I know is that it's going to be great. I can hardly wait. I sure do dream about it a lot lately. I'm not the only one though. 3 guys in our hootch are going home soon & that's all we talk about. Ernie Barbush is from Pittsburgh & goes home February 20th. Bob Mignemi is from New York & he goes home March 1. I go home shortly after Bob. Ernie gets out of the Army in July but Bob and I get out at the same time. That will be a happy day also.

How is everyone doing these days? Fine I hope. I imagine the guys aren't doing too much in all that cold weather. Is the roof over the lot finished & if so how does it work? At least it will keep the snow off the lot in this weather. What else is new around there? Keep me posted, OK? I'm fine, just homesick that's all. That will be changed soon though.

Well I guess I'll close here. I'll see you <u>very</u> soon. Your brother, Frank.

On January 30, his countdown had reached thirty-nine days. That evening he was expecting a visit from his friend Coolican. The captain's Hac Bao unit was taking off a few days for the Tet holidays, so he planned to drive down to the American compound. There would be beer and barbecue and conversation. It was likely to be the last chance Doezema would get to see him before flying home.

3

Spizzerinctum

ON FRIDAY MORNING, November 17, 1967, President Lyndon Baines Johnson had taken breakfast in bed. A big man, he was imposing even in his bathrobe. Three TVs were going across the room, each tuned to one of the three networks. Phones rang. Aides brought messages and documents to be signed. At his bedside sat General William Westmoreland, also in his bathrobe, eating breakfast off a tray, chatting between bites.

Westy, as he was known, was enjoying himself. His long march up the ranks of the US Army had led him here, to the bedside of the president of the United States. He wasn't just LBJ's most important general; he had also become a vital ally, a confidant, or at least he felt like one. Johnson was good at that. He had been summoned from Saigon, where he led the American military effort, the MACV.

The general and his wife, Kitsy, and their twelve-year-old daughter, Margaret, had been assigned upstairs quarters in the White House. The fifty-three-year-old former Eagle Scout from South Carolina didn't drink, smoke, or swear; the most colorful expletive in his vocabulary was "dad gum."[7] He was a West Pointer and had been an artillery commander in World War II. After that his career had been a steady upward climb. Once he'd won the war, which he fully expected he would—and soon—there was even talk of his running for president. These were heady days. He and Kitsy had dined the night before with the president and Democratic congressional leaders. Afterward, Johnson had even come upstairs for a late-night chat, loosening his tie and propping his big feet on a coffee table. Before the Westmorelands finally turned in, the two beds in their room had been pushed together, and inadvertently the phone, which ordinarily sat on a table between them, had been left underneath. So when it rang with the president's unexpected breakfast invitation early that morning, the four-star general had to crawl down and answer it on all fours.

"Yes, Mr. President. Yes, I'm awake, Mr. President. Not at all, Mr. President. I'll be right down, Mr. President."[8]

Even in his bathrobe, Westy looked the way generals were supposed to look: ramrod tall and fit, square jawed. His close-cropped hair had gone regally white at the temples while his thick eyebrows stayed dark, so there was something positively eagle-like about his gaze. Johnson had met him at West Point, where Westy was superintendent. After the fateful decision was made in 1964 to ramp up America's presence in Vietnam, Johnson tapped the steely-looking general he'd met at the Point to take charge. Three years had passed, and throughout ups and downs—and steady requests for more troops—Westy had calmly and persuasively predicted victory. Despite a growing and unseemly chorus of opposition throughout the country, he never wavered. The war was difficult, but it was progressing according to plan, from triumph to triumph. This was in keeping with not just his own can-do personality, but also the can-do spirit of the entire US military, which had proved itself in World War II and in Korea and considered itself with some justification to be the finest fighting force in the history of man.

If you were to sculpt a general to command this force in battle, Westy was that man. Even without all the stars and medals and ribbons on his dress uniform, he looked the part, knew it, and put great store in it.[9] Leadership was partly showmanship, and Westy neglected no means of projecting confidence, strength, and moxie. This last quality was key in war fighting, but away from the battlefield it was harder to display. Westy found ways. When he was presiding at West Point, he'd hung a banner across the "poop deck," the balcony high over the cadets' mess hall from which important announcements were made, that read: SPIZZERINCTUM. The cadets squinted up at the word, scratched their heads, and consulted their dictionaries. It was a southern colloquialism for vim, vigor, or gumption. A man who stood firm in the face of adversity was said to have spizzerinctum. Superintendent Westy wanted his cadets to have it.

Firmness in the face of adversity had defined his performance as MACV commander. It was not the highest position in the US military, but because it was responsible for the war, it was the most important. Westmoreland reported to Admiral Ulysses S. Grant Sharp, the commander in chief, Pacific, in Hawaii, who reported to General Earle Wheeler, the chairman of the Joint Chiefs. These top commanders shielded Westy from the doubts and criticism in Washington, not that he needed shielding. The louder the opposition, the more certain he seemed to be of his course. In 1966, speaking in Manila, he summed up his progress by noting a great improvement in kill ratios—the number of enemy killed per allied deaths—and claimed success by every other measure: "The number of enemy soldiers who surrender in battle has also increased," he said. "The number of casualties he leaves on the field of battle, rather than carrying them off, is rising. The stream of refugees choosing government security over Vietcong domination continues to grow. The flow of information about the enemy from the people in the countryside increases weekly."[10] In July 1967: "We have made steady progress in the last two years, especially in the last six months."[11] On his way to this White House visit, he had stepped off the plane in Honolulu and told reporters that the war effort was "very, very encouraging. I have never been more encouraged in my four years in Vietnam."[12]

This invitation as the year drew to a close wasn't just about hanging out with the president; it was also about showcasing some of that spizzerinctum. Johnson felt America needed a strong dose of Westy's can-do. Protesters now dogged the president's every public appearance, and his critics in Congress had become relentless: movements were afoot in his own party to deny him a second full term. The goddamn Kennedys and their people were bailing on him over Vietnam—Senator Robert F. Kennedy was known to be weighing a run for the White House himself—and they were the ones who'd gotten him into it. *Pay any price, bear any burden, my ass!* One by one the Camelot crew was going soft on him, even Bob McNamara, JFK's (and LBJ's) wunderkind defense secretary, one of the prime theorists behind "limited warfare," and an early advocate of the war.

Johnson had had it. He was pushing back. He had in mind a week-long course of backbone stiffening. America was a country that still respected its generals. Westy's eagle countenance and steely optimism would be on display all week in interviews and speeches, most notably a major address in four days at the domestic enemy's inner sanctum, the National Press Club.

The president was privately wearying of the war. He felt trapped by it. It wasn't something he'd started, after all; it was an onerous inheritance from three previous presidents. In the early 1950s, Harry Truman had sent arms, military trainers, and advisers to the French (then colonial masters of Vietnam), who were battling a nationalist movement called the Viet Minh. As the French hold on the country slipped, Truman's successor, Dwight Eisenhower, declined to send American combat troops (his vice president, Richard Nixon, favored the idea), but upped the number of arms and advisers. The French were chased from the country in 1954 after a stunning military defeat at the northern outpost of Dien Bien Phu. They signed an accord with the Viet Minh in Geneva granting independence to Vietnam, but temporarily partitioning it at the seventeenth parallel. The Viet Minh, under their leader Ho Chi Minh, set their capital in Hanoi, and a separate French-backed government was established in Saigon. The Geneva Accords called for elections in 1956 to reunite the country. But as it became apparent that Ho's Communist government had over-whelming popular support—Eisenhower later estimated that if the elections had been held in 1954, Ho would have captured 80 percent of the vote [13]—South Vietnam's president, Ngo Dinh Diem, reneged on the election. The United States, which had not been a party to the Geneva Accords, continued to back Diem, while the Viet Minh, newly reconstituted as the Viet Cong, began a war of resistance, aided by North Vietnam's regular army. Most people didn't give Diem much of a chance in that fight, but since Hanoi was a single-party Communist state, and Saigon was ostensibly a democracy, this remote civil war in faraway Indochina assumed, for some, global import. Eisenhower's successor, John F. Kennedy, had famously begun his tenure with that ringing promise: "Let every nation know, whether it wishes us well or ill, that we shall pay any price, bear any burden, meet any hardship, support any friend, oppose any foe, to assure the survival and the success of liberty." Vietnam became the case in point. In a letter to Diem in 1961, Kennedy wrote, "We are prepared to help the Republic of Vietnam to protect its people and to preserve its independence."

Once begun, a military commitment is a hard thing to contain. Even a small number of American troops, no matter how limited their mission, had to be protected and supplied. Under Kennedy, the advisory force grew significantly, as bases, ports, and depots were established to safely house, feed, and support those directly engaged. Then came Kennedy's assassination and Johnson's presidency. As the nation grieved, LBJ shouldered the slain president's ambitious agenda and made it his own: economic policies, civil rights, the moon program—and Vietnam. How would it have looked to pull the rug out from under the martyred president's most ambitious stand against Communism? Johnson upped troop levels significantly in 1964, doubled the draft, and installed Westy as MACV commander. The following year he unleashed a vicious bombing campaign over North Vietnam, arguing that it was not "a change of purpose . . . it is a change in what we believe that purpose requires." Later that year, he for the first time authorized American troops to engage directly in ground combat, claiming this did not represent an expansion of the war effort—despite the fact that it obviously did.[14] Over fifteen years and four presidents the war effort had evolved from a peripheral support mission to a vital and binding national cause. Johnson said in 1965: "If we are driven from the field in Vietnam, then no nation can ever again have the same confidence in an American promise, or in American protection."[15] A year later, in 1966, there were 385,000 American troops in Vietnam. They were now doing the bulk of the fighting, and Johnson speculated that victory might ultimately require almost double that amount.[16]

The number, which included Jim Coolican and Frank Doezema, was up to a half million by the time Westy arrived in the United States for this spizzerinctum tour. American troops had for the most part fought valorously and well for three years. They were highly mobile and well trained, backed by overwhelming airpower, superior weaponry, and seemingly endless reserves of ammo, fuel, and men. Handling the logistics of the war effort alone—providing food, clothing, shelter, fuel, ammo, etc.—took over fifty thousand soldiers.[17] More than nineteen thousand Americans had given their lives. The Republic of South

Vietnam had become a de facto American colony. But despite this enormous investment of blood and treasure, the advance of Communist
forces had been merely stalled, not defeated. In April 1967, Johnson had
dispatched General Creighton Abrams to Vietnam as Westy's deputy.
Abrams, a famous tank commander in World War II, had more combat
experience than any other officer in the upper ranks of the US military,
and some saw his appointment as a hint that LBJ was not entirely satisfied with Westy's progress. The White House denied it.[18] To a swelling
chorus of war critics at home, the huge application of American force
had accomplished only one thing: it had greatly increased the killing.

This was an ugly truth, but one that Westy embraced. Battlefield
deaths were something you could count, and the general, like the thoroughly modern manager he was—very much in McNamara's mold—
placed great stock in data. He could dazzle an audience with charts
and numbers and well-ordered explications, arranging the messy work
of war into neatly quantified categories and crisply reckoned "phases."
Westy was a demon for phases. And the body count was his go-to
metric. It was stark and final, and it offered something that appeared
irrefutable, so much so that it became a substitute for strategy. Missions
were planned and their success was measured not by how they advanced
a well-defined goal, but by how many casualties were inflicted.[19] In that
1966 Manila speech he had said: "The ratio of men killed in battle is
becoming more favorable to our side. From a little better than two to
one last January, the ratio has climbed to more than six to one in favor
of our side."[20] Westy argued that the ratio so heavily favored allied
forces that in time the mounting toll would buckle Hanoi's resolve.

And Johnson was a convert. Body counts were the first thing he asked
for in regular war briefings. He bragged that his general in Vietnam
killed thousands of enemy personnel for every one man he lost: "He
has done an expert job; anybody that can lose four hundred and get
twenty thousand is pretty damn good!" the president told *Washington
Star* reporter Jack Horner when questions were raised about the general's performance in early 1968.[21]

What became increasingly clear, however, was that Westy's counts
were bogus. He believed them—he was not the first general to welcome statistics he wanted to hear—but the numbers emerged from
an intricate origami of war bureaucracy: South Vietnamese, North

Vietnamese, and American. The truth was bent at every fold for reasons that went beyond propaganda to self-interest, sycophancy, and wishful thinking. In Hanoi there was no pretense of truth whatsoever; "facts" were what served the party's mission. American commanders, on the other hand, supposedly embraced a more enlightened standard. Accurate information was essential to war planning, and, unlike Hanoi, the United States was dogged at every turn by an independent press. But, in practice, there was every incentive for field commanders to inflate or even invent body counts. It was how their performance was assessed, and it became one of the greatest self-reporting scams in history. Everyone knew it was going on. Some of the more senior commanders discouraged the practice, but it was so widespread—and so hard to disprove—that few if any field officers were ever disciplined for it.[22] No one in a position to know better took the numbers that emerged from this process seriously. But Westy was far enough removed to embrace them. He was the last man up the self-reporting chain. The absurd body counts and kill ratios were proof of his leadership. He sold them to LBJ, who in turn presented them as fact to the American people.

But what if the death toll—which despite the distortions clearly favored the Americans—was having the opposite effect? What if heightened punishment by US bombs and guns actually *fueled* Communist resistance, inspiring ten recruits for every dead enemy fighter? Harrison Salisbury of the *New York Times* wrote an influential series of stories in December 1966, reporting from North Vietnam, where he witnessed firsthand the extensive damage done by American bombs. Salisbury reported that the death and destruction seemed to have only a small impact on the country's economy, and had in fact spurred the people's will to fight on. In the final story in his series, Salisbury wrote, "The basic question would seem to be: Has all this hurt the North Vietnamese so much that they are ready to quit? Their answer is, 'By no means!' And they say that they expect their task to get a lot harder before it gets easier."[23]

Salisbury's insight came as no surprise to realists in the government. A secret Rand Corporation study for the Pentagon had concluded in 1966 that while the bombing had caused widespread hardship and even food shortages in the North, "there is, however, no evidence of critical or progressive deterioration or disruption of economic activity . . . As to the effects of the war on public morale and effectiveness of government control, the cautious guess should be that they have redounded to the regime's net benefit. The bombing specifically has probably produced enough incidental damage and civilian casualties to assist the government in maintaining anti-American militancy, and not enough to be seriously depressing or disaffecting."[24] A CIA report completed in 1968 found similarly: "The war and the bombing have eroded the North Vietnamese economy, making the country increasingly dependent on foreign aid. However, because the country is at a comparatively primitive stage of development and because the bombing has been carried out under important restrictions, damage to the economy has been small. The basic needs of the people are largely satisfied locally. Imports from Communist countries have enabled North Vietnam to make up for losses in industrial production and to take care of new needs created by the war."[25]

For war hawks like Curtis LeMay, one of the architects of successful World War II bombing campaigns over Europe and Japan, the answer was more and bigger bombs. He said the United States should issue Hanoi an ultimatum, and, if they refused it, "bomb them back into the Stone Age." Johnson was mindful that fully unleashing America's airpower risked drawing China or the Soviet Union into the war, but he was hardly squeamish. More bombs had been dropped in North and South Vietnam by the beginning of 1968 than had been dropped over Europe in all of World War II, three times more than were dropped in the Pacific theater, and twice as many as in Korea.[26] LeMay's prescription sounded right to those—perhaps even a majority of Americans— who felt it was high time Ho's nettlesome regime was simply erased from the planet.

McNamara resisted escalation for reasons quite apart from morality or even avoiding World War III. He was beginning to believe the war could not be won. For nearly a year, in private, he had been saying so. In a secret October 1966 memo to Johnson he recommended that further investment of troops be slowed and their number capped. He believed the previous year's enormous military investment had "blunted the communist military initiative," but his careful reading of even the tainted metrics had begun to reveal the truth. "This is because I see no reasonable way to bring the war to an end soon," he wrote. "Enemy morale has not been broken—he apparently has adjusted to our stopping his drive for military victory and has adopted a strategy of keeping us busy and waiting us out (a strategy of attriting our national will). He knows that we have not been, and he believes we probably will not be, able to translate our military successes into the 'end products'—broken enemy morale and political achievements by the GVN [government of Vietnam]." He noted approvingly high enemy losses, "allowing for possible exaggeration in reports," and called Hanoi's infiltration routes "one-way trails to death."

"Yet there is no sign of an impending break in enemy morale, and it appears that he can more than replace his losses," McNamara wrote, both by sending more NVA troops down those "one-way trails," and by recruitment in South Vietnam.[27]

The defense secretary also knew that more and bigger bombs accomplished nothing. He had pushed for the bombing campaign in 1964 because he believed it would slow the southward movement of the NVA and armaments and inflict enough pain on the North to force Hanoi to negotiate an end to the war. But beyond the immediate death and destruction, the bombs had changed nothing. The economy of the North actually *grew* in 1965 and 1966. There was a sharp decline in 1967, the bombings having taken their toll, but it was more than offset by aid from the Soviet Union.[28] Troop movements southward had not slowed; they had kept pace with America's escalation. McNamara, the supreme quantifier, could no longer fight his own data.[29] The numbers were in. Bombing had failed.

How do you bomb a nation into the Stone Age when, in modern industrial terms, they are not that far removed from it? North Vietnam was an agricultural society that lacked the vast energy, transportation, and industrial infrastructure of more developed nations. In military terms, it lacked targets. Blown-up roads and bridges were rapidly repaired. Downed power lines were restrung. Destroyed power plants were replaced by thousands of small generators. Manufacturing plants were so small that destroying them was literally not worth the effort. In a classified briefing of US senators in the summer of 1967, McNamara explained that well over two thousand targets had been bombed in the North so far, and that of the fifty-seven identifiable ones that remained, none were significant enough to justify risking a pilot and plane, or even the cost of the bombs. One of the targets was a rubber plant that produced only thirty tires a day. Systematic bombing on the triple-canopy jungle that hid the bulk of North Vietnam's armies was yielding an estimated mortality rate of only about 2 percent. And the cost was terrible. Well over nine hundred aircraft had been shot down over North Vietnam as of January 1968. Two hundred and fifty-five airmen had lost their lives and almost that many were now prisoners of war, held in brutal conditions. The cost-benefit analysis, the kind of thing McNamara did so well, was clear.

The failure of the air war was mysterious to those who had grown up proud of the world's most powerful air force. Representative George Andrews of Alabama questioned one high-ranking military officer. As journalist Don Oberdorfer reported it:

"Do you have enough equipment?" asked the congressman.

"Yes, sir," the officer responded.

"Do you have enough planes?"

"Yes, sir."

"Do you have enough guns and ammunition?"

"Yes, sir."

"Well, why can you not whip that little country of North Vietnam? What do you need to do it?"

"Targets—targets," came the reply.[30]

On a trip to an aircraft carrier to thank and encourage some of the aviators flying these missions, LBJ was within earshot of a young flier complaining bitterly in a staff meeting. "We are going through the worst fucking flak in the history of man, and for what?" the pilot said, not knowing the president and his entourage were in the next room listening. "To knock out some twelve-foot wooden bridge they can build back a couple of hours later?"[31]

There were also profound human costs. An estimated one thousand North Vietnamese civilians were being killed or severely injured by American bombs *every week*. The carnage appalled the world. In a moving speech against the war in April 1967, Dr. Martin Luther King Jr., the Nobel Peace Prize recipient and a figure of towering international repute, branded his own country "the greatest purveyor of violence in the world today."[32] Increasingly the United States found itself isolated.

Having for two decades enjoyed its status as champion of the free world, it was increasingly the target of bitter criticism abroad and at home, where a growing number of prominent intellectuals and church leaders denounced the bombing campaign as barbaric. The military might disdain the fickle nature of public sympathy, but a democracy cannot sustain a war effort without it, and moral revulsion was growing.

In that memo to the president, McNamara firmly dispatched the bombs-away fantasy: "It is clear that, to bomb the North sufficiently to make a radical impact upon Hanoi's political, economic, and social structure, would require an effort which we could make but which would not be stomached either by our own people or by world opinion; and it would involve a serious risk of drawing us into open war with China."[33]

McNamara was dismissed by the president in late 1967—eased aside would be the more appropriate term. He was appointed to head the World Bank. In Johnson's opinion, he had "gone soft."[34] The president dug in. As journalist Don Oberdorfer would write, "[He] took it personally. In private his critics were 'simpletons,' they were 'cut-and-run people' with 'no guts.'" The war having commenced with the goal of stopping the spread of communism, there was no way LBJ was going to fall short of that promise. Despite McNamara's convincing analysis, the bombing continued.[35]

If death and hardship did not dim spirits in Hanoi, American combat deaths certainly did at home, where every coffin seemed to inspire more opposition. As the new year of 1968 began, the story of the Vietnam War in America was barreling down two opposing tracks: one a steady upbeat from Washington and the MACV, and the other a steady downbeat from the press.

As LBJ saw it, the noble effort to preserve freedom and democracy in South Vietnam had been hijacked by reporters, and from that quarter, a verdict had already been reached. Vietnam was a slowly unfolding disaster. It was eroding America's soul. Richard Harwood—no pacifist, but rather a former marine who was wounded in the assault at Iwo Jima and later became a distinguished journalist and editor at the *Washington Post*—wrote a critique of body counts in a September column entitled "The War Just Doesn't Add Up." He noted growing doubts about the narrative Westy was spinning. "A substantial majority of the correspondents in Vietnam believe and are reporting that the war is going badly," he wrote, "that no victory is in sight, that the effort to pacify the peasantry has been unproductive."[36] His opinion was shared increasingly by those who followed the war closely, including some at the highest levels of Johnson's own administration.

In one of the more horrifying and influential reports, the *New Yorker*'s Jonathan Schell in August of that year had documented efforts to cleanse villages in two South Vietnamese provinces of Viet Cong influence. Schell reported that the strategy consisted largely of destroying the villages and herding their population into tightly policed camps. And it wasn't working. When he asked to visit a "pacified" village with his translator, Schell was told that none were considered safe enough. Schell also observed the casual racism of American soldiers, who boasted of torturing and killing prisoners, throwing suspected Viet Cong from helicopters, and taking potshots at civilians from the air claiming they could tell enemy fighters from innocent villagers from above. It was hardly an exact science even on the ground. There were idealistic and brave Americans in the story, too, who were trying to do the right thing. But Schell, who made it no secret that he opposed the war, concluded that the entire effort was a poorly conceived, brutalizing exercise in failure.

America was not accustomed to this kind of reporting from its war zones. When David Halberstam, a *New York Times* correspondent, arrived in Saigon in 1962 and began asking probing questions in his initial interview with then US ambassador Fritz Nolting, the ambassador leaped to his feet, took Halberstam by the arm, and threw him out of his office.[37] In past conflicts, correspondents had been considered part of the team.

This had been the expectation in Vietnam, too, and it helps explain why newsmen were free to visit anywhere to which they could arrange transportation. Reporters hitched rides on military transport to hot spots. What they found was frequently at odds with official accounts, not because they had greater wisdom than the military commanders, but because smart young officers on the front lines had the spizzerinctum to tell the truth. Many correspondents were contemporaries of the lieutenants, captains, and majors in the field, those who bore the brunt of the fighting and dying. Men in this position always have smart, hard questions about how they are being used, questions they rarely have the opportunity to raise with top commanders. America's roving reporters brought their pointed questions back to Saigon; Halberstam had been doing this when Nolting threw him out. In time, pushback from the brass grew more vehement and less believable. Here was born the "credibility gap." Daily military press briefings in Saigon were famously dubbed the Five o'Clock Follies.

And increasingly the war, as seen through the eyes of reporters, was shaping up as a tragic exercise in futility. The initial Strategic Hamlet Program, known as pacification, had wasted years and countless millions herding people from their ancestral homes into "protected areas." The hamlets were more like medium-security prisons than villages, surrounded by a moat and fencing, with a command post at the gates, patrolled by a self-defense militia. The idea had been to isolate the population from the Viet Cong, although in most instances they were one and the same. Anyone who understood Vietnam would have known the policy was self-defeating. It was an insult. Ancestors anchored most Vietnamese to a place. Families built elaborate shrines in their homes to beloved kin, departed fathers and mothers, grandparents, aunts and uncles. In a society like this, home and community were not just an accident of geography—as they frequently were in America—but an obligation and an identity. So it is little wonder that the forced relocations were despised, and enemy infiltration was rife in the "pacified" hamlets. Forcibly relocating people was the opposite of personal freedom. More than anything else the policy resembled the disastrous social engineering practices of Stalin and Mao. Task Force Oregon, the operation described by Schell, had devolved into a savage parody of the concept, leaving villagers to choose between being attacked in their own homes or escaping to what UPI correspondent Neil Sheehan would call "the certainty of hunger and filth and disease in the refugee camps."[38]

The policy was abandoned in 1963, and within five years most villagers had drifted home. In the meantime, the MACV had shifted tactics, creating an agency called Civil Operations and Revolutionary Development Support (CORDS), which sent roving teams of ARVN and Americans on targeted patrols designed to root out Viet Cong and win support from the much-abused citizenry. But carefully targeting and orchestrating these patrols grew harder as the scale of American involvement ramped up. Discernment eroded. In time, whole areas where local support for the VC was strong were simply classified as free-fire zones. When CBS reporter Morley Safer captured marines rounding up elderly villagers at Cam Ne in 1965, and then setting fire to their homes—150 of them—it shocked the nation. Johnson would call and complain, not to the marines, but to the head of CBS.[39]

Westy regarded such accounts as "sordid and distorted." He felt they were rooted in a "preconceived idea" of the war. He disdained reporters who after only a short visit to Vietnam "proceed to write authoritative articles on the situation, strategy, and tactics that should be pursued."[40] But his criticism ignored the fact that reporters like Schell, Safer, Sheehan, and others reflected the views of the men actually fighting, or simply showed them in action. These snapshots were unmistakably real and disturbing. Increasingly they became the public face of the war effort.

"Pacification is a bad disappointment," McNamara concluded in a secret October 1966 memo to the president. "[It] has if anything gone backward . . . We control little, if any, more of the population; the VC political infrastructure thrives in most of the country, continuing to give the enemy his enormous intelligence advantage; full security exists nowhere (not even behind the U.S. Marines' lines and in Saigon); in the countryside, the enemy almost completely controls the night . . . In essence, we find ourselves—from the point of view of the important war (for the complicity of the people)—no better, and if anything worse off."[41]

Reporters who went out into the fields could see it for themselves. For Vietnamese villagers, joining one side meant becoming a certain target of the other. The Viet Cong were not the idealistic warriors of American antiwar propaganda; they were vicious. They relied on terror. Even keeping your head down, trying to stay neutral, didn't guarantee safety, because suspicion, not to mention artillery shells and bombs, fell on everyone. If there was one ideological rationale that had broad appeal, it was nationalism, which for many boiled down to a fervent desire to be *left alone*. To the extent that North or South could lay claim to that banner, the edge clearly went to Ho, whose fight for independence had gone on for so long that most Vietnamese were too young even to remember its beginnings. At least the government in Hanoi was fighting its own war.

To counter Ho's superior nationalist credentials, South Vietnamese children were taught that he was set, not on creating an independent Vietnam, but on abolishing it as a sovereign state and making it subservient to some future world Communist government. Ho's future would be one of "Three Nos," they were told: no family, no state, and no religion. Some were persuaded by this, but it demanded more of a stretch than most were willing to make, especially in families—and there were many—who had allied themselves with Ho and the Viet Minh in the war with France. And the efficiency of the Viet Cong cadres stood in stark contrast to the blundering of the Saigon regime. A Rand study would find that popular support for the Viet Cong was growing by default, concluding that "the revolutionary war in South Vietnam is being fought and lost" by Thieu's government. The United States was backing the incompetent side. Robert Komer, then running the CORDS program, told American ambassador Ellsworth Bunker in early January 1968 that Thieu's forces might simply be unable to meet the Communist challenge.[42]

On a return visit to Vietnam in 1967, Halberstam, no longer a *Times* reporter, had been invited to dinner in Saigon at the residence of Ambassador Bunker. He was asked to share what he had learned during his visit about the progress of the war. As he would later write in a preface to his best-selling book *The Best and the Brightest*, Halberstam said that it had become a stalemate:

> But a stalemate which favored the other side, since
> eventually we would have to go home. What our military did
> not understand, I added, was that Hanoi controlled the pace of
> the war, and it could either initiate contact and raise the level of
> violence or hold back, lick its wounds, and lower it, depending
> on its needs at a given moment . . . His [Bunker's] generals were
> like all Western generals before them, starting with the French;
> not so much in the wrong war, but on the wrong planet. Their
> ability to calibrate this war was limited, their skills were tied
> to other wars in other places, and with very few exceptions
> they, like the French before them, tended to underestimate the

bravery, strength, resilience, *and the political dynamic which fed the indigenous force* they were fighting.

The United States may not have shared the old colonial ambitions of Europe but did share its racism. Johnson called North Vietnam a "raggedy-ass little fourth-rate country."[43] The United States of America was concerned with bigger things. Having dispatched its mighty armies, it could not contemplate failure. If a small investment didn't work, there was always more where that came from. And more. And more after that. More would eventually produce victory. It was about containing Communism. A substantial majority of Americans still supported it: polls in 1967 still showed strong public support for the war, but declining approval of Johnson's handling of it. Americans seemed to buy the necessity of the war but wanted it over as quickly and painlessly as possible.[44] The kinds of war crimes described by Schell and other reporters were dismissed by Westy as unavoidable in an effort of this size. He would later write that out of more than two million Americans serving in Vietnam, the vast majority of whom served honorably, there were bound to be some "crimes of violence against civilians."[45] The bleeding hearts were always going to play up these examples. In war, bad things happened.

By the end of 1967, the antiwar movement had become a powerful political force. In the beginning, resistance had come only from predictable quarters: hard-core pacifists, leftist radicals, and ban-the-bomb activists who were passionate and skilled at creating public theater. Philip Berrigan, a former Catholic priest, and three other radical pacifists were arrested in October of that year after they poured blood—a mixture of their own and some from animals—over draft records at the federal courthouse in Baltimore. That same month, an estimated four thousand people turned out for an interfaith service in New York, where, after listening to prominent "dove" William Sloan Coffin, eighty-seven young men publicly burned their draft cards. The draft forced young men to make a personal decision about the war, and accordingly spurred antiwar activism on college campuses. The broadly leftist Students for a Democratic Society (SDS), formed in 1962, had never inspired a mass following, but chapters sprang up on college campuses across the country when the draft started. Protests were not always well attended, but they were continual. Increasingly, top officials in the Johnson administration found themselves inside cordons of tight security when they appeared in public, and sometimes protesters were menacing. In November 1966, McNamara was accosted by violent protesters during a visit to Harvard University and had to be secreted off the campus through a food service tunnel. An SDS protest in Chicago in November 1967 during a visit by Secretary of State Dean Rusk brought out thousands of demonstrators and turned violent, and three weeks later Stop the Draft protests all over the country resulted in the arrest of six hundred people.[46] That same month, longtime Minnesota senator Eugene McCarthy declared he would challenge LBJ in Democratic primaries, although his chances were considered slim.

Opposition to the war was becoming fashionable. Popular figures—intellectuals, athletes, musicians—stepped up to announce their opposition. Muhammad Ali, the heavyweight boxing champion, was fined, stripped of his title, and sentenced to prison after refusing induction. Carl Wilson, a member of the Beach Boys, was indicted for the same reason. Dr. Benjamin Spock, guru to the parents of the baby boom generation, became a prominent voice against sending their children to war in Vietnam. Just a month before Westy's "spizzerinctum" visit, hundreds of thousands of protesters marched in Washington in the first of what would become a series of mass mobilizations against the war. The prizewinning novelist Norman Mailer was arrested at the Pentagon with hundreds of others in a partly serious, partly comical effort to levitate the massive military headquarters, a spectacle Mailer recounted in his acclaimed book *Armies of the Night*. The book would win both a Pulitzer Prize and a National Book Award—the accolades themselves reflecting widespread opposition to the war in literary and intellectual circles.

Westy disparaged all such efforts as unpatriotic, noting correctly that they gave aid and comfort to Hanoi.[47] Those who backed the war, "hawks," found it hard to imagine that a small, relatively powerless nation could fight America to a draw. Reports that said otherwise were considered wrong. In January 1968, pro-war columnist Stewart Alsop quoted "a leading presidential adviser on Vietnam"—probably Westy himself—as saying that "in a few months everybody—even the most cynical and skeptical reporter in Saigon—is going to have to admit that we are definitely winning this war."[48] The United States had complete control of the air over all of Vietnam, and could presumably deliver a decisive blow at will. The failure to do so was blamed on the very notion of "limited war." America was fighting with one hand—or so the story went.

After dining in his bedroom with Westy that November morning, Johnson offered an animated defense of his Vietnam policy in the White House Press Room. Looking hale and confident in a crisp dark suit, wearing wire-rimmed glasses, he stepped down from the podium to get closer to the assembled press. Proximity was an important part of his sales arsenal. He literally leaned into his remarks. He complained about the "hopeful people" and the "naive people" who believed the North Vietnamese would jump at the chance to negotiate for peace if only the United States would stop bombing North Vietnam.

"So all of these hopes, dreams, and idealistic people going around are misleading and confusing and weakening our position," he said.

A reporter stood to lob a softball: "Mr. President, in view of your talks this week with General Westmoreland, Ambassador Bunker, and others, what is your present assessment of our progress and prospects in Vietnam?"

"Well, I will repeat to you their assessment, because they are the ones who are in the best position to judge things locally," he said. "And I will give you my evaluation of what they have said. First, I think every American's heart should swell with pride at the competence and capacity of our leadership in Vietnam. I believe, and our allied people believe, that we have a superior leadership. I think it is the best that the United States of America can produce—in experience, in judgment, in training, in general competence. I have had three meetings with Ambassador Bunker and three with General Westmoreland. I had coffee with him at length this morning, just before I came here.

"Our American people, when we get in a contest of any kind—whether it is in a war, an election, a football game, or whatever it is—want it decided and decided quickly; get in or get out. They like that curve to rise like this," he said, raising his left arm high over his head. "And they like the opposition to go down like this," he went on, chopping his open hand down abruptly. "That is not the kind of war we are fighting in Vietnam . . . We don't march out and have a big battle each day in a guerrilla war. It is a new kind of war for us. So it doesn't move that fast . . . We are moving more like this," the president said, sweeping his left arm upward gradually. "And they are moving more like this," he continued, slowly sweeping his right arm down, "instead of straight up and straight down. We are making progress. We are pleased with the results that we are getting. We are inflicting greater losses than we are taking . . . We have a lot to do yet. A great many mistakes have been made. We take two steps forward, and we slip back one. It is not all perfect by any means. There are a good many days when we get a C minus instead of an A plus. But overall, we are making progress. We are satisfied with that progress. Our allies are pleased with that progress. Every country that I know in that area that is familiar with what is happening thinks it is absolutely essential that Uncle Sam keep his word and stay there until we can find an honorable peace."

He had pinned his hopes on Westy. Johnson did not just admire him; he also *liked* him. When he bestowed on the general an Oak Leaf Cluster to adorn his Distinguished Service Medal, an award given for exceptional service to the nation, he sent a warm personal note, handwritten: "Westy, I have never been so sure of any commendation I've ever given and am confident *none* has ever been more deserved—except perhaps for the one I'm giving in this note to your Kitsey [*sic*]—for her endurance tolerance and love for you and her willingness to continue to go along with her commander in chief in his personal assignments. My appreciation to you both." The general had become a key member of the president's team.

Westy's Press Club speech later that week was the featured event in LBJ's "Success Offensive." The Washington-based press club was a center of establishment journalism, steered by polite, generally elderly reporters, editors, and columnists who had worked their way up the ladder at newspapers around the country. A good many had reported from the front lines of previous successful American wars. And now here was the army's shining star, an organization man par excellence, to dazzle them with a display of how he was bullet-pointing the Vietnamese Communists to death. In droning bureaucratese, Westy began by ticking off the long list of achievements in Phase One and Phase

Two of the war. Among them: "Drove the enemy divisions back to sanctuary or into hiding," "Raised enemy losses beyond his input capability," "Completed free elections with South Vietnam," "Discovered and thwarted the enemy's battle plans before they could be executed."

In other words, so far it was a rout.

"With 1968, a new phase is now starting," he said. "We have reached an important point when the end begins to come into view."

He said Phase Three would be devoted to strengthening the ARVN, providing more training and more up-to-date weaponry, and gradually giving it more and more responsibility until, as he put it, "we become progressively superfluous." Westy reported progress on all fronts—indeed, he said, Phase Three was well along—noting a supposed loss of popular support for the Communists, and a presumed transformational impact of the fraudulent election that reinstated President Thieu.[49]

"We are making progress," he concluded. "We know you want an honorable and early transition to the fourth and last phase. So do your sons and so do I. It lies within our grasp—the enemy's hopes are bankrupt. With your support we will give you a success that will impact not only on South Vietnam, but on every emerging nation in the world."[50]

The invitations to the New Year's Eve party at the American embassy in Saigon would read, "Come see the light at the end of the tunnel."[51]

The *Washington Post* headline the next morning read: WAR'S END IN VIEW—WESTY.

There might, of course, still be a few hiccups on the way.

Westy approached the coming Tet holidays with supreme confidence. He had prepared a special holiday surprise for enemy troops.

"We are developing a plan to broadcast from ground and air PA systems sentimental Vietnamese music to the NVA during Tet," he cabled the Joint Chiefs just days before the holidays would begin. "The Vietnamese youth is quite sentimentally disposed toward his family, and Tet is a traditional time for intimate family gatherings. The Vietnamese PSY War [Psychological Warfare] people have recently written a highly sentimental Tet song which is recorded. The Vietnamese say it is a tear-jerker to the extent that they do not want it played to their troops during Tet for fear their desertion rate will skyrocket. This is one of the records we will play to the North Vietnamese soldiers in the Khe Sanh-Con Thien areas during Tet."[52]

His intelligence analysts had noticed a steady buildup of enemy soldiers and supplies down the Ho Chi Minh Trail in the fall of 1967 through neighboring Laos and Cambodia. To counter it, the general had begun shifting more American forces into I Corps, the northernmost of the military's four sectors of South Vietnam, anticipating a big offensive in Quang Tri Province early in the new year, most particularly against the small marine combat base at Khe Sanh. A series of North Vietnamese attacks in the region had mystified the American command, because they seemed to produce little more than casualties, mostly North Vietnamese. But Westy had figured it out.

The buildup meant the enemy was about to make an all-out attack on Khe Sanh. This conviction was based, in part, on his belief that Hanoi lacked the strength to attack farther inside South Vietnam, and was forced, in effect, to nibble at the edges of the country.[53] Khe Sanh was close to the DMZ and the Laotian border. He saw a distinct historical parallel. It was exactly the strategy the Viet Minh had employed against the French. In the finest tradition of preparing for the last war, the general had long believed the North Vietnamese would try to reenact their successful 1954 attack on Dien Bien Phu, a victory that had forced the French out of Vietnam and led to the country's partitioning.[54] He was determined to prevent history from repeating itself. When Khe Sanh was targeted by a major mortar bombardment on January 21, he saw the opening salvo of the coming big offensive.

"We think that the long-expected attack on Khe Sanh in South Vietnam has been initiated," McNamara told the president in a phone call the next morning. "Substantial artillery and mortar fire and ground action is taking place there. Westmoreland believes he is fully prepared to meet it. I have nothing further to add."

"What—do they have heavy casualties?" asked Johnson. "The enemy there—yesterday, I heard on the radio. I had four hundred and fifty Viet Cong killed and seventeen American killed, and—"

"Mr. President," McNamara interrupted. "I just—I'm very skeptical of that size. Our reports don't indicate—they, our reports indicate an extensive action, but they don't indicate that large a number killed."[55]

Within weeks Westy had concentrated almost 40 percent of his infantry and armored battalions in the North, both to defend Khe Sanh against a major attack and to prevent Hanoi from seizing the same northern provinces they had taken fourteen years earlier, when they forced the French surrender.

He was as prepared as ever a general could be to win La Guerre d'Indochine.

4

The Royal Capital

OCCUPYING HUE WOULD be a bold step, the most dramatic action taken by Hanoi so far in Chien-tranh Chong My (the Resistance War Against America). It would shock not just Vietnam, but the world. The attack Che Thi Mung and the other girls in her squad were helping to prepare, the Tong-Tan-cong-Noi-day, would be part of a countrywide effort, but Hue was its centerpiece. Years later, Oberdorfer, the definitive chronicler of the Tet Offensive, would write: "The plan of action—a simultaneous surprise attack on nearly every city, town, and major military base throughout South Vietnam—was audacious in its conception and stunning in its implementation. The repercussions were on a scale to match."[56]

It would begin early Wednesday morning, January 31, the first day of the Lunar New Year and of Tet. Ordinarily the holidays were honored by a cease-fire, the only respite from the bloodletting. Families gathered to take stock, pray, and plan for their future; to remember their departed; and to beseech Ong Tao (the Kitchen God) for good fortune. Those who could afford it stretched the celebration out for days, having stored food and drink and fireworks enough to celebrate well into the new year. Blossoming cherry trees and branches and colorful lanterns were displayed indoors, much as evergreen trees and boughs and glittering ornaments decked the halls at Christmas in America.

But this year would be known not for joy and hope, but for death. Hanoi had attached VC forces from the region to four full regiments of tough NVA regulars, each with more than one thousand men, who had spent months marching south along treacherous mountain trails to get into position. These numbers had been supplemented by militia troops recruited and trained from the city itself, locals like Che who knew their way around and who would give the invasion a local face. The idea was for the offensive to be seen as a popular uprising. Similar but lesser efforts were planned for cities from Saigon[57] to Da Nang to Can Tho and Nha Trang, and also to smaller cities throughout the South. Taking Hue would send an immediate sharp message—perhaps "warning" is the better word—to the citizens of South Vietnam and to millions in the United States who had begun to doubt the wisdom of the whole undertaking.

Hue was a city of both practical and symbolic importance. With a population of about 140,000, it was the third-largest city in South Vietnam, and arguably the third most important in both Vietnams, after the capitals of Hanoi and Saigon, in that it symbolically belonged to both. As a center of Vietnamese culture, it had a significance that transcended the divide. It was a former imperial seat and the major center of learning and worship. Set on a thick finger of land formed by a bend in the Huong River, Hue originally had been just the Citadel, the enormous fortress that enclosed nearly two square miles of flat land. Its walls were twenty-six feet high and impenetrably thick. They were actually two parallel ramparts about twenty to thirty feet apart, the space between them filled with earth—wide enough at the top for there to be homes and gardens and walking paths and guard posts behind the parapets. Although crumbling in places, it was still an enormously impressive sight, bordered all around by a moat that was spanned by only eleven narrow bridges. Each led to a gate before a passageway built long before the age of the automobile. From the air, the structure formed a giant square with an appendage in the northeast corner called Mang Ca.

Westerners regard Asian history as something vast and mysterious that reaches deep into the mists of time, and the brown, silver, and russet stains on the Citadel's black stone walls certainly conveyed that sense. Reporters would routinely refer to it as "ancient" or "medieval," but it was neither. Most of the truly ancient rulers of Vietnam had been based in the north, closer to Hanoi. Hue had not become the ruling seat until 1802 under the Nguyens, who would rule for 143 years, an impressive run but a mere eyeblink in the land's long history. There were far more important dynastic periods. The longest lived was the Hong Bang, which was truly ancient, ruling from its seat in the region of Hanoi from 2879 BC to 258 BC, before the advent of the Roman Empire. From the fifth to roughly the fourteenth centuries, which in Europe spanned the Middle Ages and Renaissance, the land was intermittently ruled by the Chinese. When the Nguyens seized power and decided to erect their capital in Hue, they adopted the military principles of French architect Sébastien de Vauban. Thomas Jefferson was president of the United States. The fortress was as Western as it was Asian, and was younger than the White House in Washington, DC—although in considerably poorer repair.

Still, it *looked* as ancient as Troy. Its walls rose startlingly from the Huong River's north bank, sheer and unassailable. About half of the city's population lived inside it in 1968, many in neatly appointed neighborhoods, some quite affluent. There were one- and two-story masonry houses with red-orange barrel tile roofs originally built for those employed by the royal government. The taller ones had ornate wrought iron balconies. Many were painted in bright pastels, and housed extended families, often several generations, a traditional village way of life imported to the city. They were surrounded by high stone walls that enclosed elaborate, lovingly tended gardens. Most things grew in the semitropical climate, and some of these floral displays were extraordinary, with small, sculpted trees, bamboo thickets, broadleaf plants with exotic flowers, enormous palm fronds, and ponds stocked with colorful koi. The city had outgrown the fortress. There were neighborhoods just outside the walls and along approach roads on both sides of the river.

At the south center of the fortress were the royal palace and its grounds, which were enclosed by an inner fortress. The emperor Gia Long had modeled it after China's Forbidden City, with a throne room constructed of intricately painted wood beams and panels and colorful gilded dragons. The palace grounds had larger homes and outbuildings arrayed around lush gardens, lakes, and canals. These had once housed the Nguyen emperors' wives and children, and their imperial court.

But the Nguyen dynasty was long gone. The clan had served as a figurehead for the French colonial authorities, briefly for the Japanese when they occupied Vietnam in World War II, and then for the French again immediately after the war, until the Viet Minh forced them out. The imperial heir in 1954, Bao Dai, was a nationalist who had abdicated after the Japanese occupation ended in 1945, giving his benediction to Ho Chi Minh. This conferred a legitimacy on Ho that proved troublesome when Bao Dai briefly returned to head the French-backed government of South Vietnam. From 1949 until 1955, the faux emperor failed to shake his image as an interloper. Ho had been designated the national leader, and Bao Dai was now seen simply (and correctly) as an agent of the French. Those who followed him to the leading office in Saigon, presidents Ngo Dinh Diem and then Nguyen Van Thieu, shared the same taint. They continued to be viewed as agents, or "puppets," the word Hanoi's propagandists preferred, only now for the Americans, the latest colonial pretenders. And the perception was true. While both Diem and Thieu had supporters in the south, neither was beloved nor widely respected enough to stay in power without stout foreign support.

Even as the grand imperial edifices, tombs, and palaces fell empty and into disrepair, the city of Hue grew and prospered. Uncle Ho himself had grown up inside the Citadel, and had received his earliest education just outside its walls. The neighborhoods inside the walls remained among the city's most well-to-do, while the modern business of the city moved south, across the Huong. All the major government offices and schools were in an area shaped like a triangle, bounded not by stone walls but by rivers and roads. The Huong River was its northern boundary. To the west was the Phu Cam Canal, which flowed southeast from the Huong until it intersected Highway 1, which spanned the waters on the An Cuu Bridge.[58] Just north of the bridge the highway reached the southern terminus of Ba Trieu Street, which angled northeast back up to the Huong. The triangle thus formed was roughly bisected by the highway, a road that in happier times ran all the way from Hanoi to Saigon, but that during war became a contested thoroughfare from one end to the other. In the French War, a northern stretch of the two-lane highway saw so much fighting it had been dubbed La Rue Sans Joie (Street Without Joy). Most of it was elevated enough to remain passable even when the rice paddies on either side were completely flooded. In the Hue area, Highway 1 stretched from the big American base at Da Nang up to Phu Bai, a drive of about an hour and a half, then from Phu Bai north to the city. It crossed the Huong over the Truong Tien Bridge, a graceful structure designed and built in 1897 by Gustave Eiffel, famous for the tower in Paris. Topped with six low arches of latticed steel, it was wide enough for two-way traffic and walkways. Beyond the bridge, the Citadel sat astride the highway. To proceed farther north meant either driving around it or passing through the Thuong Tu Gate on the lower right and navigating the narrow streets inside toward the upper left gate called An Hoa.

The Truong Tien Bridge was one of two that spanned the Huong. The other, farther west, the Bach Ho (railroad) Bridge, carried the rail line across. There were numerous other smaller bridges around the triangle, spanning canals and large drainage ditches that channeled river water to the rice paddies that sprawled away from the city in all directions.

Hue had the bustle and appeal of a modern city like Saigon, but it had retained some of the elegance of an older Vietnam. The city's pagodas and baroque dynastic tombs were architectural treasures. From the park that ran along the south bank of the Huong you could watch sampans and fishing boats moving lazily on the water before the stark wall of the Citadel, or enter the elegant Cercle Sportif, a colonial-era sports and social club with vintage French automobiles parked outside, which on the inside was still furnished and run as if the seven decades of colonial rule had never ended. On the other side of Le Loi Street were mansions, commercial buildings, the treasury building, the post office, a prison, and a Catholic cathedral—the Church of the Most Holy Redeemer. The city was small, but it was thriving and completely urban, home to an emerging commercial class that had been largely sheltered from the war.

In fact, Hue was the one place in all of Vietnam that the war had hardly touched. Its people were not especially supportive of either side in the conflict. Ho knew that Hue's Catholics, Buddhists, and intellectuals, while not necessarily friendly to his cause, were also cool to Thieu's government. The president had the backing of his fellow Catholics, but few others. The heavy-handed policies and corruption of the Saigon regime under Diem had provoked in 1963 the shocking self-immolations of Buddhist protesters—broadcast around the world— and stinging criticism and protests by Hue University's intellectuals.

These events led to Diem's assassination later that year. The protests had abated, but resentment lingered. Buddhists were systematically ostracized by the Thieu regime; only Catholics' villages were provided arms to defend themselves against Communist rebels. Buddhists and most intellectuals in Hue, even those opposed to Ho, saw Thieu and his government as a creation of the United States. So the city was a tough nut for both the North and the South. It had largely been left alone.

As a result, the military presence in Hue was light. In January 1968 there were fewer than one thousand ARVN troops stationed in the city and surrounding area, and a smaller number of Americans. As the holidays approached, a large portion of the former were looking forward to a long holiday furlough.

In this peaceful city, during Tet, it was traditional to send cups of paper with lit candles floating down the Huong like flickering blossoms, prayers for health, for success, for the memory of loved ones away or departed, for success in business or in love, and perhaps for an end to the war and killing. It made a moving collective display, a vast flotilla of hope, many thousands of tiny flames. They would wind down the wide water without sound, flowing past the bright lights of the modern city to the south, framed to the north by the fortress's high black walls. People would line both banks of the Huong to savor the spectacle, stepping up and bending to add their own offering. The ritual was Hue's emblem and signature, a gesture of beauty and calm, of harmony between the living and the dead, an expression of Vietnam's soul, a place far from the horrors of war.

Not this year.

5

Moonshine and
Half-Hatched Ducks

THE MISSION SCARED Nguyen Van Quang. He was not ordered to do it, just firmly asked. The highest-ranking Viet Cong official in his sector, Tran Anh Lien, sat him down and talked about the need to deliver weapons into the city.

"Do you think you can do this?" Lien asked.

There were secret police and informers everywhere in Hue. Quang[59] had been avoiding them for years, spreading the word about liberation and assembling an underground militia. Distributing leaflets or speaking critically of the regime could get him locked up; smuggling weapons could get him shot. He was proud of his service and success in recruiting a local militia, and it clearly did not make sense to leave his cell of fighters unarmed, but he never imagined he would be the one to smuggle in the weapons. He didn't answer at first.

Lien tried a different tack. He asked, "Do you have any organization that dares to bring these weapons into the city for you?"

Quang stood.

"My dear comrade," he said. "This is very difficult for me." He explained that his activities so far had exposed him to a great deal of risk, but that this was worse.

"I might be able to encourage some people to bring guns into the city, but as for me . . ." He confessed that he did not know how it could be done.

"If that's the case, can you go back into the city secretly . . . avoiding the people who know you?" Lien asked.

"Yes. It would be difficult, but I can do that."

"Then you go back and form a group to transport guns in for you," Lien said. "And you will receive the guns and participate in that mission, all right?"

Quang had fled Hue when he was a high school student. He had been in the eleventh grade, little more than a wisp of a boy—small even by Vietnamese standards—and wiry. But even at sixteen he possessed an abundance of boyish energy and charm. People were drawn to him. He came from a family of intellectuals who lived inside the Citadel in a neighborhood abutting the walls of the royal palace. His father was a teacher, and all eight of his uncles had also pursued learned professions. All were known nationalists who had joined the Viet Minh in 1945. Two had died in that struggle. Young Quang felt pressure to measure up.

In high school, he had been elected secretary general of the Student Union. In 1965, when American troops began to pour into the heart of Hue, when he had seen for the first time foreign tanks and military vehicles and heavily armed soldiers moving across the Truong Tien Bridge, it had given him the push he needed. Until then he had seen President Thieu's government as wrongheaded but at least Vietnamese. He saw the war as a conflict between two factions of his own people with different ideas about governance. When those allied with the liberation movement would urge him to join the fight against the Americans, Quang would say, "How can we resist the Americans when there are none?"

Suddenly there were Americans everywhere. It crystallized Quang's thinking. This was clearly not just a civil war, but a struggle for independence, a new chapter in the one his father and uncles had fought. It was his turn. When it was announced that still more American troops would be coming, he helped organize a student walkout in protest, and afterward he and his classmates held other peaceful demonstrations. When he saw that this accomplished little, he sought underground representatives of the VC, and joined.

He was sent south toward the Bach Ma National Forest, a stunning and rugged landscape of high green mountains and gracefully curving terraced farms just north of Da Nang. Quang expected the resistance camp to be hidden and remote, but instead found that it was right out in the open in a well-populated area. He shuttled between Dinh Mon and Duong Hoa, villages near the famous Gia Long Tomb.

Controlled by the rebels, these villages were working models of the future, as far as Quang was concerned. He was received as a valuable recruit. His schooling and his familiarity with the city were rare among the VC, most of whom came from rural villages. Having made up his mind to fully commit, Quang was swept up in the idealism and fervor of the cause. The men and women in the villages came from all over Vietnam, from the North as well as the South, and they not only shared his anger at the American presence but also had a clear idea of what their country would become. This shared vision was being practiced in the villages, which were models of communal living. Quang saw exactly what he was fighting for. Poorly supplied and often hungry, the rebels shared a commitment to long struggle and a conviction that they would ultimately prevail. He grew close to these who entered training with him. They received political instruction and were taught to use modern Russian and Chinese weapons as well as older ones that had been seized from the French and the Americans.

Life at the camp so inspired Quang that his heart sank when he was ordered for the first time, near the end of that year, to return alone to the city. He reappeared at his high school in the fall, now working as a VC recruiter. He was good at it. Soon he had ten of his classmates working with him. They started a patriotic newspaper called *Hoc Sinh* (the *Students*), aimed at young readers, and written carefully to avoid provoking the *nguy*. Their stories were copied on a Roneo machine, a mimeograph, and consisted of a single sheet of paper folded in half with printing on all four sides. They reported strictly "legal" news—an account, for instance, of a fight between Americans and the VC near Phu Bai. Such a story broke no rules, but the message it conveyed to Quang's fellow high school students was subtly subversive. Americans were shooting at and killing Vietnamese. This was a foreign occupation, and some of their countrymen were fighting it.

The newspaper attracted new recruits, including the workmen who helped them operate the Roneo machine. In his final year of high school, Quang had an underground cell of more than thirty. His success was noticed. By the summer of 1966, as he was preparing for his second round of exams for Hue University, he noticed for the first time that he was being shadowed by a policeman. When his like-minded older brother was arrested and imprisoned, accused of being a Communist sympathizer, Quang was warned by friends that he would be next. He fled back to the rebel villages.

This time he did not stay long. The local commissar asked him to return again to Hue, despite the danger of arrest. This time he would be given a different name and new identity papers, and he was to avoid his old school and neighborhood. He would go to the fishing village of Kim Do, northeast of the Citadel. The work he was asked to do was still dangerous. He had always lived in the city, and sooner or later he was bound to come across someone who knew him, but there was something big in the works, he was told, and the risks were necessary.

He moved in with the family of Nguyen Ngu, which raised ducks, thousands of them. Quang worked as a tutor to the Nguyen children, and slipped back into the city at night to meet with his cell and to find new recruits. He had a number of close brushes with the police, but he never came across anyone who recognized him. Armed with his natural charisma and his devotion to the cause, he had more success than either he or his superiors had imagined. His original cell members were encouraged to recruit on their own. Through them he made contact with some of his old friends at the university who regarded him now as a hero, and they, too, agreed to help. There were now many students who sympathized. His underground militia swelled to one hundred members.

At night he moved around the city on a scooter wearing a helmet and visor; he often took these trips with a girl riding behind him so they would look like a young couple on a date. Once he was in a coffee shop when police entered. One officer stood right beside him at the counter. Quang's heart pounded but the policeman took no notice of him. His organization was built in concentric circles. Few outside his original group knew him. Among his cell were students, teachers, monks, young laborers, and small shopkeepers; there was even one uniformed ARVN soldier. The most capable he sent to Bach Ma for political and military training.

Quang's was one of a number of such cells in the city. In November 1967, at the same time Westy was visiting Washington, Quang and a number of other cell leaders met at another mountain base, this one about twelve miles northeast in Phong Dien district. Here they learned for the first time about Tong-Tan-cong-Noi-day. Plans were well advanced. A reinforced battalion of the NVA, nearly one thousand men, had already been assembled in and around the village of La Chu[60] in an area that the Americans had earlier designated a "secure hamlet," and that had since been abandoned. It was equipped with American-made concrete bunkers and buildings—a perfect bombproof headquarters, compliments of Uncle Sam. It would serve as the nerve center for the attack on Hue.

Tong-Tan-cong-Noi-day was conceived as an attack from without and from within; it was both an "offensive" and an "uprising." The bulk of the invading force would be NVA. Mixed with them were battalions of VC, many led by NVA officers who had moved south. So the only truly local part of the National Liberation Front was these local militiamen. Because they knew the city, some of the cell leaders would serve as party representatives, or commissars, once the city was taken. This was a political war, they were told, so the uprising was more important than the offensive. Local cadre chiefs like Tran Anh Lien, who had groomed Quang, would have a big role to play. They would spark and lead the anticipated citizen revolt, and supervise the building of the new Vietnam.

All together the Front would number nearly ten thousand. The NVA's Sixth Regiment alone, for instance, consisted of three regular infantry battalions, each of which broke down to three companies of roughly two hundred men, which were further divided into three platoons. Supplementing the regular forces were elite commando units, an artillery battalion armed with 122-mm rockets, and various specialist companies armed with mortars, heavy machine guns, and bazookas (either B-40s or the newer B-41s, which had more penetrating power).[61] This combined army wore an assortment of uniforms: the regular NVA had dark green Chinese-made uniforms with distinctive metal pith helmets; the VC had khaki uniforms and tan pith helmets of an older vintage, if they had helmets at all; and many wore civilian clothes or black pajamas[62] and shorts, or some combination of the above. Most carried canvas backpacks, ammunition, and food tied up in cloth tubes they draped over their shoulders. Most wore sandals. The local militiamen generally wore civilian clothes or pajamas. They would all pin to their left sleeve torn strips of red cloth and blue cloth over a white backdrop. Backing the fighters were scores of civilian volunteers, an elaborate support and supply network staffed primarily by local men and women like the village girl Che Thi Mung, who would steer the army into the city, and then, when the fighting started, deliver food and ammunition, evacuate the wounded to field hospitals, dig bunkers and trenches, and bury the dead. The Front troops had nothing like the firepower of American and ARVN troops, and they lacked the ability to attack and resupply by air or sea, but they had deep roots in the community. With leaders who had been fighting for decades, they were more than a match for the Americans, many possessing infantry skills—defense, firing, and maneuver—that would impress even the most battle-hardened American veterans.

Planning had been meticulous. By the end of 1967, the Front had broken down its assault to hundreds of specific missions. An unusual one was assigned to a VC veteran, Sergeant Cao Van Sen, who was to make and deliver a special flag to be run up the 123-foot flagpole at Ngo Mon, the monumental three-story platform that stood just outside the royal palace, before the Citadel's southern wall. Set on the north bank of the Huong River, it was visible all over Hue.

Careful thought had been given to this flag. Because many in the city were not yet committed to the revolution, a flag that flew so prominently would have to send a careful message. The party wanted Tong-Tan-cong-Noi-day to be viewed not as an invasion or occupation, but rather as a liberation. The party flag, bright red with a large yellow star at the center, would not do. This was the symbol of North Vietnam, which many in Hue still saw as a faction in the civil war. Nor would running up the VC flag, two horizontal stripes, the upper one red, the bottom one blue, with a yellow star at the center. The rebels were a minority in Hue. What the planners had in mind was an ensign to inspire the uprising, a flag that purported to symbolize Hue's own aspirations. The idea was to recognize real political differences between North and South, and to establish a neutral, independent South Vietnam with which Hanoi could negotiate terms for unification. Since much of the city was home to secular intellectuals, Buddhists, and Catholics, a politically correct flag would herald an alliance of these groups. The final design featured the yellow national star at its center, against a backdrop that was still bright Communist red through the center, but with two wide blue horizontal stripes on the top and bottom. The blue stripes represented the intelligentsia and the city's religious factions—Buddhists and Catholics.

This vision was more wishful than real. The efforts of Quang and others had drawn volunteers from the university, but these were nearly all students, not the city's true intelligentsia. Rural recruits like Che and the other girls in her Huong River Squad were typical of the VC's peasant base. There was negligible support from Hue's Buddhist community, beyond the endorsement of one venerable monk, Thich Don Hua, a champion of reunification. There was outright hostility from the city's Catholics, who ordinarily fought or fled from the rebels. The great hope of the Tet Offensive was that its very size and daring would trigger a surge of nationalism that would transcend barriers of ideology, class, and faith.

Sergeant Sen was a good choice for the flag mission, even though he had never done a thing like this before. He was a short man with a broad face and dark skin, born in a village on the northern outskirts of Hue. He had a dark gray birthmark that colored the whole right side of his face. His father had held an official job in the royal palace, and both he and Sen's mother had fought with the Viet Minh. Now Sen's large family, like the country, was divided. Three of his brothers fought with the ARVN, something his father considered a disgrace. Sen himself had joined the fight against the French when he was just seventeen, in 1950. When the Geneva Accords ended the war four years later, dividing the country, Sen and the other men in his unit were disappointed, but they believed the promised election in three years would reunite the nation. The men would hold up three fingers to each other as a reminder of the promise. Sen remained a soldier, attending school in the North for two years, and when the South reneged on the elections, he had been ordered to don the black pajamas of the VC and go back to his old district. He had helped establish the base at La Chu, and had taken part in small firefights against the *nguy* and American forces. In the months before Tet, he and his platoon of commandos had been learning to cross rivers at night, to remain hidden, and to scale walls. They would form a human pyramid three men high. The top man would fling a rope over the top of the wall and pull himself up and over, then lower the rope for the others.

But Sen was relieved of these climbing exercises to assume the flag mission. He obtained a sewing machine and cloth, and found a woman named Le Thi Mai to make the flag. It was so large and heavy it took two men to carry. Sen was given a journalist and a cameraman to document its raising. They were to deliver the alliance flag to Ngo Mon once the Citadel was taken, and run it up the high pole so every person who awakened on the thirty-first of January would know the city had changed hands.

The entire Tet Offensive was a masterpiece of clandestine effort. One US Navy commander would later call it "a logistical miracle." [63] By late fall of 1967, the regulars had begun moving into position by the thousands, passing through rural villages and along roadways. Local recruits made regular night trips past villages on the city's outskirts just to make guard dogs bark, which became such a nightly occurrence that few paid attention to it anymore—either that or the dogs would grow so accustomed they no longer stirred. [64] Still, there was no way to completely hide such a large number of men. It was the kind of troop movement that could remain secret only if the citizenry supported it, or didn't care enough to sound an alarm.

In November, on the visit to Commissar Lien when Quang was finally apprised of the mission, he was told that his militia would help attack Chanh Tay Gate, the northernmost of two on the west wall. It and the other, Huu Gate, were critical, because the bulk of the NVA Sixth Regiment would be coming from that direction. Starting the previous winter, commandos had begun to explore alternative ways into and out of the fortress. There were flood-control canals that flowed through its walls in stone and plastic conduits, some of them six feet tall. By the beginning of the year these had been fully explored, and would afford another way of infiltration.

Quang's company would join with NVA regulars on the night of the attack. Commandos who had slipped into the fortress would first approach the well-guarded Chanh Tay Gate from the inside, attacking the guards there and opening the doors. Then the main force would pour in, enough to overwhelm whatever ARVN troops remained or responded. Quang's militia unit would join the fight from the inside, and then get to work fomenting the popular uprising.

But first Quang would need to arm them. He left his meeting with Lien burdened with worry. Smuggling weapons frightened him, and he had no idea how to do it. When he returned to the Nguyens, he spent days debating with himself how or even whether to proceed. Mr. and Mrs. Nguyen had become surrogate parents to him; he called them Uncle and Aunt. They had a boat they used to deliver ducks and eggs to the city for sale. They might be able to hide a substantial shipment of guns and ammo on their boat on one of these trips, but he could not bring himself to ask them. They were sympathetic to the cause but not active revolutionaries. How could he ask them to take such a risk? For days he could not eat or sleep. Finally, Mrs. Nguyen, seeing his distress, asked him to explain.

"Tell me," she said. "Maybe I can help."

He confessed to both Nguyens that he had accepted a mission he could not perform.

"I'd do almost anything to help you," Nguyen Ngu said. "But asking me to do this is no different than killing me."

There were ARVN checkpoints on the river where all shipments were inspected. When the guards were familiar with merchants, as with the Nguyens, often they just waved them past, but not always. The family sometimes prepared small delicacies—boiled ducks and *hot vit lon*, a local favorite, a duck embryo boiled and served inside the shell—and offered them with a small cask of moonshine. Still, it was no guarantee. There was no predicting when the guards would decide to poke through everything on board.

Quang backed off. There were not many comrades in his neighborhood and it would have been dangerous for him to range too widely. For purposes of secrecy, he was not allowed to travel to the VC base without being summoned, so he could not go back to beg Lien to relieve him of the task. He spent a week away from the Nguyens, wrestling with the problem, and finally gave up and returned, defeated.

"Where have you been?" Mrs. Nguyen asked.

"I was trying to find another way to bring armaments into the city," he said.

"Did you find one?"

Quang said he had not.

"It's too difficult," he said.

"I think we can help you," Mrs. Nguyen said. She and her husband had discussed it in his absence, and in short she had talked her husband into it. He would fashion a false bottom on his boat to stash larger things, the guns and rocket launchers. Smaller things, like ammunition, could be wrapped in plastic and placed deep in the baskets of eggs. The guards typically probed merchandise in boxes or baskets with long rods, but they couldn't do so with baskets of eggs.

"How can we get the stuff off the boat without attracting attention?" Quang asked.

The Nguyens had thought this through, too. Their goods were not off-loaded at a market. Ordinarily they just berthed at a spot along the river and their customers came to them. Quang need only instruct his men to stagger their approach to the boat, purchase some eggs or ducks, and then carry off the weapons and ammo piece by piece.

"This part would be easy for us to do," said Mrs. Nguyen.

Quang wrote up the proposal in code and sent it by courier to Lien. *We now have a plan and someone willing to carry it out.* A few days later Lien himself paid a visit to the Nguyens. He brought along the deputy commander for all the forces in Hue. They listened to the plan in detail, and then they feasted on the Nguyens' ducks. The next morning Ngu started building a false bottom in his boat.

On the appointed day, early in January, Quang left the city with Ngu to supervise the loading. Into the bottom went piles of AK-47s, bazooka tubes, and grenades. The egg baskets were planted with ammo. He stayed behind as Ngu set off. Quang could see how nervous he was, so he suggested that Ngu drink some of the moonshine.

"Not enough to get drunk," he said, "but enough to *look* drunk."

Ngu's face flushed whenever he drank even a little alcohol. So he looked the part as he approached the checkpoints, and played it up. He staggered and bellowed and waved to the guards, offering them his presents and pleading with them to let him pass quickly: "Because I am drunk and I'm worried I'm not going to get to Hue on time, and my wife will kill me."

Quang waited back in Kim Do through that entire day. He did not learn until the following afternoon that his "uncle" had made the trip safely, and that his men had picked up the shipment. His force now was ready, armed. He could hardly believe it. As he saw it, the miracle proved the truth of Ho's teachings, that the party and the army were not enough. Real victory could come only from the people. Here he had been handed a task beyond his ability, beyond his courage. And his friend Uncle Ngu had stepped up. The arms had been delivered by *nhan dan*, the people.

6

Nhan Dan

Aɴᴛɪᴡᴀʀ ᴀᴄᴛɪᴠɪsᴛs ɪɴ the States romanticized Ho Chi Minh and his cause, emphasizing its nationalist character and seeing a common enemy in LBJ, but the president and the hawks were right about one thing: Hanoi was Communist and authoritarian to its core. It was not about to become a satellite state to either the Soviet Union or, least of all, China. Instead, the reunified nation imagined by the Vietnam Workers Party[65] was modeled on the Soviet state and deeply influenced by Mao's ongoing Cultural Revolution. It was ruthless and doctrinaire. It promised a state-run economy and a society ruled by the party, where allegiance to the regime was absolute.

No nation is immune to wishful thinking. By its own implacable logic, the party was *nhan dan*, the people, so what the party dictated was by definition the will of the people. It also believed its own propaganda. When the plans for the Tet Offensive were drawn up, it meant the attack on Hue and those throughout South Vietnam would be an expression of the people's will, so it was only natural to believe that the people would rise up to support it. Westy's ramrod optimism paled next to the party's. Led by First Secretary Le Duan, over the objections of more realistic politburo members, Hanoi had convinced itself that victory was within its grasp.

The plan called for attacks leading up to Tet against American bases throughout the South—Khe Sanh, Da Nang, Con Tien, Pleiku, and others. It anticipated that Westy would move his troops to defend his own bases, which would leave Saigon, Hue, Can Tho, Nha Trang, and dozens of other South Vietnamese cities to be defended by much weaker ARVN forces. The combined NVA and VC army would be more than a match for most urban defenses. But the logistics, secretly moving the Front forces into place, were daunting, and in some cases, at least initially, poorly thought out. When the great military strategist who had chased the French from Vietnam fourteen years earlier, General Vo Nguyen Giap, was dispatched to outline the plan to VC commanders in March 1967, he proposed establishing a center for the push into Hue in the lowlands southwest of the city.

Dang Kinh, a local commander, told him: "You will all starve to death!"

He explained that the people who lived in the area proposed were fishermen, and that they grew no rice. To feed an army, they would need a steady supply of rice.

Giap asked how much of Thua Thien Province (which included Hue) the proposed force would be able to take. Kinh responded facetiously, saying, in effect: *Why ask me?* He pointed out that Hanoi liked to make such plans without consulting lowly field commanders.

"I'm just a tool," he told Giap. "Point me at a target and I'll attack it. I'm not capable of answering your question, sir."

Giap told the scrappy local commander that he was going to be given a full NVA regiment.

"Sir, our military region cannot handle another regiment," answered Kinh.

"You are a strange bird," said Giap. "All of our battlefield commanders are asking for more units, but when the high command offers you another regiment you refuse to accept it."

"I'm a guerrilla commander," said Kinh. "If you give me too many troops, I will not be able to command all of them."

Since Hue had never been the scene of much fighting, it was rarely thought of in military terms. But considered as such, it had significant value. Vietnam is a long thin stretch of land, covering more than two thousand miles of coast along the Gulf of Tonkin and the South China Sea. It widened at the northern end, which bordered China, and fanned out again at the far southern end into the swampy lands of the Mekong delta, but at its center it narrowed as if cinched by a belt. It was so narrow in the Hue region that a drive from the beach to the mountainous Laotian border took under an hour. Both Highway 1 and the nation's primary rail line connecting the giant American base at Da Nang with the DMZ to the north passed through Hue. The Huong River was wide and deep enough for vessels to deliver a steady stream of supplies to forces north and south. Control of Hue was the key to these transportation routes. And yet the thrust of the plan to take the city was never primarily concerned with shutting down the river, the highway, and the rails. The thrust of the effort was political. The real battlefield, as far as the party was concerned, was *nhan dan*. If they could be induced to rally behind the Front's forces, the war would be over.

Kinh never believed it would happen, but he was a good soldier, and if ordered to attack, he'd attack. In discussions with Giap over the following days, he agreed that the city could be taken and, if his forces were properly reinforced and positioned, it could be held for a few days. He estimated that even with ten thousand men, within days the ARVN and Americans could respond with seven times that many men, not to mention artillery, air support, tanks, etc. They could not long resist such an onslaught, and they would take heavy losses. As for the plans farther south, he told Giap that Hanoi was trying to stage a bonfire with barely enough fuel to burn a match. But the party leaders had an answer for that: with enough fuel, all you needed was a match. They expected the oppressed people of South Vietnam to rise up en masse once they saw the liberation army marching in their streets. The Thieu government would collapse! The Americans would have no choice but to go home.[66]

Hanoi's leaders were virtuoso songbirds of propaganda. They lived in a bubble. There were no voices of dissent in their society to check or challenge wishful thinking. And they were certain of their ultimate victory. Years earlier the songbirds had argued that the war could be quickly ended before the American buildup, but that had not happened. Things had gotten worse in the south, not better. There was evidence of good feeling in rural areas, but the big cities showed no such signs. VC casualties had gone up alarmingly, recruitment was down, and desertion was becoming more common. So while no one outside the party's cloisters dared question the big plan, some within did.

There were basically two competing views about the war. One preached patience and caution, knowing that for all its firepower America could not sustain a long war and would eventually have to bargain and leave. This approach was advocated by China and endorsed by Ho himself, who was nothing if not patient after a lifetime of struggle. He was now a frail and sickly man of seventy-seven with only a year to live. He was spending more and more time at a clinic in China. He was there from mid-September to late December 1967, and after a brief visit to Hanoi returned to the clinic in early January to stay until late April 1968. He was out of the country for most of the planning and all the fighting of Tet. He had outlived not only his enemies in the party, but also much of his influence. He remained invaluable as Uncle Ho, the father of the nation. He was universally respected in the North, and revered by many in the South. The short poems attributed to him, read aloud on ceremonial occasions, were composed by committees for propaganda purposes, and they sounded like it, but they were also easy to remember and encapsulated the goals of the struggle. One went like this:

Vi doc lap, vi tu do
Danh cho My cut
Danh chon Nguy nhao.

For our independence and freedom
Let's sweep the Americans out
And make the *Nguys* fall down.

His influence was substantial but soft. *Soft*, in the sense that his legend and manner softened the party's message. Ho was viewed as a nationalist first, only secondarily as a Communist. He had fully embraced party principles, for sure, but he was also known for his humility and benevolence. The party, on the other hand, was hard. Persuasion was not a priority; its critics and enemies were imprisoned or killed. Ho knew there were many in the South who opposed Hanoi not so much on ideological grounds, but because of its methods. They had seen the VC execute or imprison leaders who did not fall in line. Ho consistently preached to the party that victory and reunification required winning the support of their southern cousins. He believed the effort might take many years. It would probably not come in his lifetime.

So for Ho, the point of war was to force the United States to negotiate. He took advantage of every opportunity to remind the Americans of his willingness to work with them. His speech declaring Vietnam's freedom in 1945 had cribbed from the Declaration of Independence.[67] He offered to begin negotiations for peace anytime, and even to invite the Americans over for tea, but at the same time he warned that he would prevail even if it took "twenty years."[68]

Younger party leaders were in a bigger hurry. A faction headed by Le Duan advocated not just forcing the Americans to negotiate an end to the war, but also *winning* the war. It was determined to seize the initiative. The politburo argued out war plans for the coming year in the summer of 1967. The foreign minister, Nguyen Duy Trinh, predicted some kind of major American offensive before the Americans' election day in November 1968—perhaps even an invasion of the North. Such a move might strengthen Johnson's hand enough to dictate a quick end to the war on his own terms. Le Duan argued, "We must elevate our own military activities to a new level, to a level that the United States cannot bear and that will force it to accept that it has failed militarily and that it has become isolated politically. If we can accomplish that, the United States will be forced to withdraw from Vietnam."[69]

Turning up the heat was appealing in part because of the growing antiwar movement in the United States. The politburo did not expect LBJ to capitulate, but an escalation of the war could undermine his hopes for reelection. Militarily, the Americans were already a potent fighting force, and they knew that Westy, for all his talk about turning over war fighting to the ARVN, was continuing to build up his own command: he had requested hundreds of thousands of new soldiers in 1967, and had been granted an additional forty-seven thousand in July. The American threat was only going to grow, so waiting carried big risks. Acting first, delivering a decisive blow, might give Hanoi a critical advantage.[70]

"As long as we have not won such a victory, we cannot achieve success at the conference table," Trinh said.[71]

"Victory" was defined as inflicting "heavy casualties" on American forces, the destruction of the ARVN, and inciting a general uprising throughout the South. The more realistic, like Ho, knew that all this was unlikely, but Le Duan believed complete success wasn't necessary. He wrote, "If for some reason the uprisings in the cities run into trouble and we are forced to pull our forces out, that will not matter. That will just be an opportunity for us to practice and to learn lessons from experience in order to prepare to try again at a later date. Comrade Fidel Castro's armed forces attacked the cities three times before they finally succeeded. If we enter the cities but then are forced to withdraw, that is nothing to be afraid of, because the entire rural countryside and the mountain jungles all belong to us—our position and our forces are strong in those areas."[72]

Ho remained unenthusiastic. His opinion was echoed by the Chinese, who pointed to the protracted nature of Mao's struggle. They saw the planned Tet campaign as a nod to Soviet tactics, and, in effect, a sign that the party was leaning more toward Moscow than Beijing.[73] More significantly, the campaign was also opposed by Giap. Le Duan had bested the general in a power struggle for party leadership in 1957, and the two men had been at odds for years. But this was a nation ruled by commissars, not by generals: the guerrilla general Kinh's sarcasm about the strategy was rooted in a truth Giap knew well. When the Party Central Committee adopted Resolution 13 in January 1967, calling for a "decisive victory" in advance of reopening talks with the United States, it meant Le Duan was still in charge.

Giap's handle on the military was slipping, too. The death of Hanoi's commanding general of southern operations in the summer of 1967 elevated General Van Tien Dung, who had long served as Giap's subordinate. While still nominally less important than Giap in the chain of command, Dung began meeting directly with Le Duan to plan the Tet Offensive. Ambition for it grew. Together they decided, in the words of Vietnam War historian Merle L. Pribbenow, to "consider risking everything on one roll of the dice."[74] It called for an all-out attack on cities in South Vietnam while the NVA's main forces worked to pin down American and ARVN troops in rural bases. The rest would be accomplished by the people.

Giap began skipping planning meetings, and made it clear he believed the strategy would not work. When the final plan for the offensive, Resolution 14, was approved by the politburo in December,

the old general was out of the country. He was in Moscow on the eve
of Tet, and attended a performance of the ballet *Swan Lake*. Giap did
not wish to be seen attending the theater at the same time his troops
were launching their daring attacks, so he waited until the house lights
were turned down before entering.[75] Ho abstained from voting on
final approval for the plan,[76] although once it was clear it was going
forward, he gave his endorsement before returning to China.[77]

Acting on instructions from Hanoi, the regional party committee for
the Thua Thien–Hue district resolved on December 3 "to concentrate
all of our strength and intellect on urgently carrying out preparations."
The offensive would be "a secret surprise attack against specific targets,"
after which the people would "conduct uprisings to fight and support
combat operations, and *force a revolutionary government*." A major goal
would be to "inflict heavy losses on U.S. and satellite [allied] forces,"
and "defeat the American 'limited war' strategy."[78]

It was not until January 15 that the final decision was made to launch
the offensive on the eve of Tet. According to Pribbenow, the party had
begun purging military officers whose sympathies were with Giap.[79] All
dissension was silenced. The songbirds took over. The cities would fall!
The people would rise up! The war would end! As the song reached
down to the rank and file, it spurred fanatical hope and zeal.

To that end, hidden cadres of loyalists living in camps in the mountains west and south of Hue had been working and waiting, some
of them for years. Most were young men and women accustomed to
hardship and fired with idealism.

For Nguyen Dac Xuan, a poet and Buddhist, the cause was mixed
with his religious fervor.[80] He had fled the city in 1966 during President Thieu's violent suppression of Buddhist protests. After hiding in
temples to escape the secret police, he had been invited by a friend to
take shelter in a VC camp hidden in the forested hills. Xuan had ended
up living there, and while he still considered himself Buddhist—he
was a follower of the Hue monk Thich Nhat Hanh, a peace activist
who had fled to the United States—he was by no means committed
to the religion's traditional pacifism. What joy and sense of kinship
and purpose he felt with his new comrades! They were both hardened and buoyed by privation, rationing rice balls while dreaming of
feasts, sleeping huddled together against the cold, imagining a blissful

communal future. They were not blind to the odds against them; they were *inspired* by these odds. They believed the very purity of their devotion guaranteed success. What could the Americans do to them? Their death, if it came, would be not a loss but a glorious sacrifice, like a drop of fuel for the great flame. Together they wrote poetry and memorized and dissected Ho's inspirational verses. On a Roneo machine they produced a propaganda newspaper called *Liberation Flag*.

For all his zeal, Xuan had chafed under military discipline. With surveillance planes often overhead, it was important to avoid anything that might give away the camp. So when Xuan and his comrades decided to cut down a few trees to clear space for a crude newspaper office, they were chastised for creating a hole in the canopy of trees. There was a strict ban on lighting fires for fear of telltale smoke, but the nights were cold. Xuan was convinced that no smoke could escape the thick blanket of low clouds that smothered them in the rainy months like a wet blanket. After making a small experiment a good distance away from the camp, lighting a fire and noting how its smoke drifted off hugging the ground, he defiantly lit one at the newspaper office. This brought his immediate superior running in panic. Xuan told her about his experiment.

"I don't know any science, at all," she told him, angrily. "But I do know the ban on fires is a rule none can disobey."

Xuan missed his home in Hue, and he and his friends would sometimes climb high in the trees to gaze down at it in the distance. He would point out his old neighborhood of Dap Da, and the university. Growing up and attending school he had never felt especially attached to the city, but in exile he yearned for it. So when he was first told of plans for Tong-Tan-cong-Noi-day, he was overjoyed.

The politburo decreed: "All South Vietnam will simultaneously launch a general offensive–general insurrection to seize the reins of government and place it in the hands of the people. Principle of the offensive: simultaneous attacks, simultaneous uprisings, with insurrections being the prime effort and relying primarily on local forces and forces in the rears."[81]

According to Vietnam's official history of the war, they were "to annihilate or disperse the puppet army and puppet government, to liberate the rural countryside, to form a revolutionary government, to kill and wound large numbers of American troops, and to surround and isolate the American forces so that they would be unable to come to the rescue of the puppet army . . . fight off enemy counterattacks, to inflict heavy losses on the enemy, and to firmly defend and protect the new revolutionary government in order to create favorable conditions to allow us to move forward to gaining total victory." [82]

Creating those "favorable conditions" meant weeding out their enemies. A great score settling was in store. They would target South Vietnamese officials, soldiers, and police—"thugs," "traitors," and "criminals" in official parlance. Presumably those insufficiently motivated to embrace the party's vision would quickly see the wisdom of doing so. Hue was going to join the revolution, like it or not.

For Xuan it also would be a homecoming. He and the others wrote and printed pamphlets to be distributed when they arrived. The handouts would explain the goals of the offensive, and emphasize that it was not a Northern invasion but a countrywide uprising. They explained the tripartite nature of the Alliance of National and Peace Forces; it was composed of intellectuals, religious leaders, and the VC cadres. The pamphlets also explained that success depended on *them*, on *nhan dan*. They were the future, casting out the past, ending foreign domination.

With the new year would dawn a new, independent Vietnam.

Their excitement spilled out in a book of celebratory poems. Xuan went to sleep in those nights ticking off in his head which neighborhoods he would visit first, which traditional Hue dishes he would first eat, which houses of his family and friends he would first visit. He anticipated a great battle. Some had drawn up last wills. They vied to be chosen to lead the assault.

7

Andy and Mimi

LIEUTENANT ANDREW WESTIN knew he was headed for trouble when he and everyone else, in Charlie Company were issued flak jackets.

"There's only one place in Vietnam where people wear these things all the time," Westin wrote to his wife, Mimi. "That's the DMZ! I pray we don't go there, but it sure looks like we will. Have you read about the trouble the Marines have had up there?[83] I guess they want us to help out. I am scared now."

Westin wrote Mimi almost every day. He was one of the thousands of men caught up in Westy's grand Checkers strategy, a major reshuffling of forces throughout I Corps. In his letter home in October, Frank Doezema had mentioned "a brigade of the 1st AirCav." This was Westin's, the Third Brigade of the army's First Cavalry Division,[84] which given the vagaries of army nomenclature was known as the Seventh Cavalry. He was in its Fifth Battalion. The Seventh was a storied unit that had seen service in every American war that century. Originally formed at Fort Benning in Georgia, it had last been flagged in South Korea before being deployed to Vietnam. Its officers wore yellow scarves and black Stetson hats. On their left sleeves they wore a distinctive yellow patch: a shield with a diagonal black stripe and the silhouette of a horse head in the upper right corner. The horses were history; the AirCav now rode to battle on helicopters, usually Hueys,[85] which could carry a full squad; or on the newer, giant twin-engine Chinooks,[86] which could haul more than fifty troopers at a time. They were a key part of Westy's strategy. In a war with few clear front lines, and where the enemy was apt to pop up unexpectedly, the AirCav offered unmatched speed and flexibility.

Westin's Charlie Company, manned increasingly by draftees, had been at work in An Khe in the Central Highlands, doing the kind of patrol work called for in the CORDS program, which was described by reporter Denby Fawcett as "mean-spirited village sweeps."[87] She had gone to see for herself. A fearless young photographer and reporter who worked for the *Honolulu Advertiser*, Fawcett was petite and fit, with dark red hair that she wore in pigtails, certainly a welcome sight to homesick troops in the field. She had tagged along with one of Westin's heroes, a rifle platoon lieutenant named Winfield Beck, on a patrol in 1967. The Americans arrived to find, as usual, a community filled with children, women, and the elderly. No young men.

"You never find a military age male in the village," Westin wrote. "They're either VC or trying to stay out of the South Vietnamese army."

On Fawcett's patrol, the villagers were not helpful. Beck's men set fire to their hay supplies—a perfect place to hide men and arms—and roughly questioned the inhabitants through their Vietnamese interpreter.

"Two Vietnamese boys they were questioning said they were just farmers," Fawcett wrote. "No, they were not Viet Cong. No, the boys told the interpreter, they had never seen any Viet Cong in the village. Yes, they hated the Viet Cong."

One woman with children was threatened with decapitation if she failed to reveal the whereabouts of her husband. She furiously stared down her inquisitor, calling his bluff.[88]

Westin had joined the Seventh in late summer 1967, and so far his war was going well. The worst part was being away from Mimi—Miriam, née Peters, a fun-loving, petite blond woman he had married eleven months before shipping out. Westin was a cheerful, fair-haired, guitar-playing, wholesome Methodist from Benton Harbor, Michigan, son of a county judge. He had graduated from Adrian College, a small church-run school just outside Ann Arbor. With grades too low for grad school, even if he had wanted to go, and the draft looming, he decided not to wait. The army offered him a better chance to steer his own path, or so it said, and he set out to steer clear of Vietnam. He graduated from officer candidate school in 1966, a second lieutenant. He immediately married Mimi and they honeymooned as they drove to Aberdeen, Maryland, where he had been assigned to command a group of ordnance school candidates. Westin thought he'd done it, found himself a nice stateside berth where he could serve out his obligation living with Mimi.

That blissful sojourn—and blissful it was, because Andy was crazy about Mimi, and they both were crazy about sex—had lasted less than a year. The army abruptly ordered him to Vietnam. He was twenty-six, just weeks shy of his first wedding anniversary. The letter that arrived at his comfortable Maryland desk began: "Congratulations."

He went for two weeks of jungle training in Panama, where he began his habit of correspondence. Mimi went home to Ypsilanti to live unhappily with her folks. He sent her a turtle and she named it Andy. His letters captured the carnal withdrawal of youth plucked from the pleasures of newly married life. They were full of childlike professions of love—"I love you oodles and goodles and noodles!"—and nagging laments of bridled lust. He warned her that his anniversary letter "might be slightly pornographic, but I'll try to keep it nice." By the end of his first month in Vietnam he was so horny he drew a stick figure of himself at the bottom of one letter with great antlers sprouting from his head. A few weeks later he drew the same thing, only now the antlers filled the whole page, and his body became a tinier stick figure, forlornly labeled: "Me."

On the long flight to Cam Ranh Bay, the mood on his plane full of soldiers was somber. When they finally reached Vietnam, out the window he saw beaches and, to the west, row upon row of deep green hills shrouded in mist and low-hanging clouds. His one-year turn for war had arrived.

"I really got a funny feeling as the wheels came down," he wrote. "You could have heard a pin drop."

After a few boring days at Cam Ranh Bay, he flew to join his new unit. He was given headphones for the approach into Pleiku, and he heard the pilot ask the tower operator: "Hey, you got anything going on down there? Any incoming?"

"No," responded the tower. "Just outgoing."

Westin's heart sank. He thought, *Oh man, this is real.*

But after an initial adjustment, the war had turned out not to be as bad as he'd feared. He explained to Mimi that his battalion consisted of four rifle companies—Alpha, Bravo, Charlie, and Delta. Within each company there were three rifle platoons and one mortar platoon. The mortar platoon for Charlie would be his. A command! He had received a promotion to first lieutenant on his arrival. He was issued a weapon, the AR-15, which was mostly carried by officers. While Westin at first thought it might be better to just carry an M16 and "look like any other private" in the field, status won out. Gone was his ceremonial yellow bandanna. Westin now wore around his neck a mud-brown sling he'd cadged from a medic; he used it to wipe the sweat and grime from his face and to shield his eyes and nose when choppers kicked up storms of dust. He had led his mortar platoon on air assaults, arriving after defoliants and artillery had done their work. It was a rush, riding in the open window of a chopper with a cool breeze blowing over him, descending with all that unholy firepower aimed outward. He wrote, "They're a lot of fun."

Patrols were another story. It was hot and humid by day and cold at night. They walked for hours across rice paddies and through palm groves and in grass over their heads. Tension gave way to monotony. On one of their early walks they found a skull. His men propped it on a stick, put an NVA cap on its head, and stuck a cigarette in its teeth. It was macabre, but also reassuring. Soldiers feel better patrolling areas that are deadlier for the enemy than for themselves. Any sighting of suspected VC provoked gales of ineffectual gunfire and offered momentary relief. It didn't feel as if much was being accomplished. On a typical day, the entire division of over ten thousand men, in its wide-ranging sweeps, would report having killed two or three VC; they were now Charlie. Westin drily noted that at that pace they would wipe out an entire enemy battalion in about a year. In his first firefight he felt weirdly out of place, chucking hand grenades over a big rock and feeling like a character in a war movie. He thought, *What the hell am I doing here?* "I really didn't think about the fact that I was trying to kill another human being until it was over and the VC had headed for the hills," he wrote Mimi. "Honey, it didn't bother me. The fact that it didn't bother me bothers me, not the fact that I shot at him." It became more real when he lost one of his men. His letter to Mimi did not sugarcoat it: "He had the top of his head blown off."

They were in the An Lao Valley when, in one of those bizarre twentieth-century moments, the actor Charlton Heston appeared.

The platoon was at a muddy encampment when up came one of the world's most famous tanned faces. Heston, in clean combat fatigues and white cap, and with a dazzling smile, shook hands all around, offered words of encouragement and appreciation, and signed a post-card-size publicity shot of himself for Mimi.

The day after this encounter, Westin was transferred to a staff job at battalion headquarters. He began working long days in an underground bunker lined with maps coated with acetate, sitting in a cheap folding chair, directing the constant flow of supplies and ammunition. After a few manly protests about preferring to be out in the bush with his men, he was actively scheming to avoid being sent back. He found he preferred the rigors of his desk job, he wrote, to "being shot at." He'd had enough of a taste of combat to satisfy any itch about proving himself, and he had no intention of making a career in the army anyway, he explained to Mimi. So it mattered little to him to score "command time," which was vital for promotion, and he was annoyed that the rules demanded it.

"No way in hell will I stay in the army," he wrote. "I have no desire to ever again get into a situation where I can get shot at. I don't like it. I want out."

The day they handed out the flak vests, he realized with chagrin that ahead he had more chances of being shot at. He was in the field again weeks later, but not near the DMZ, as he had feared. The battalion was instead sent to the Que San Valley, southwest of Da Nang. Mimi received one rain-smeared letter, wherein Westin described fog and "sheets of rain," and explained again why he did not wish to stay in the army when his tour was over. He wrote that he liked "some comforts." In Vietnam he had "ZERO comforts." He was soaked to the bone, cold at night, and broiling during the day. He was still drawing pictures of himself with antlers.

In one letter, Westin described the vocabulary of his new world. An "LZ" was a landing zone for choppers, and it became a firebase when artillery was placed around it. New LZs were being established in the field all the time. Andy named one LZ Mimi.

On October 11, he had reason to feel lucky about having lost his desk job. A small VC raiding party emerged from a tunnel in the middle of their base camp—this was the initial story—and killed everyone except two men at the battalion command post before they, too, were killed.[89]

The man who replaced him had died behind the same desk, sitting in the same folding chair where Westin had sat for two weeks. He became a rifle platoon leader shortly after that when one of the other lieutenants was wounded and evacuated. His platoon used a lot of ammo, despite rarely seeing the enemy.

"This having a rifle platoon is a lot different from the mortar platoon," he wrote. "Instead of supporting the troops with the mortar, I'm now the guy who requests the mortar to help me."

He wrote to complain of boredom when he and his men were ordered to stay at an LZ for a few days. They bathed in a nearby river, the first bath he had taken in weeks. He scrubbed himself with soap and rinsed over and over, removing layers of grime, and wrote Mimi that when he finished he was surprised to find that his tan was not as dark as he had thought.

A new company commander took over in late October, Captain Mike Davison.

"He's an airborne ranger, West Point type," Westin wrote. This was not a good thing. He explained to Mimi: "The West Point type in the company is a real yo-yo. He doesn't know his head from a hole in the ground. I don't like him." Davison, however, "seems to be pretty good. I hope he isn't gung ho. That would mean a lot of walking. He seems to have a good head."

By now the war inhabited him. He wore it, smelled it, and lived it day and night. It was caked in his ears and nose and he could taste it. The fear of being under fire never went away, even when he slept. What shut-eye he got, curled on his leaky air mattress in a shallow hole, was more like a pause between wakefulness and sleep. But the routine grew on him. There was comradeship, and laughs, and a sense of shared effort. The smallest pleasure, like a mouthful of canned fruit or the chance to bathe in an ice-cold river, was a luxury, something to be savored.

After a month of nearly steady patrolling, Westin wrote, "My guys got a gook yesterday. The first one since I've had the platoon. Great. I took a picture of it. I mailed a roll of film yesterday." Against all expectation, he felt he had become a warrior. In December, the annual rains started to fall, and became a more insistent enemy than Charlie. When water pooled around his air mattress, however, he finally found and patched two small leaks that had bedeviled him for months. He noted one day with some pleasure that his platoon shot two female VC. "Only one died," he wrote. When his platoon was hit by a mortar barrage, he wrote, "I've never felt so helpless in my life." A few days later he got to take another bath in an ice-cold river, and loved it.

Then came R&R in Da Nang, the biggest base he'd ever seen.

"There [sic] guys don't even realize there's a war going on!" he wrote. A Las Vegas showgirl with impressive curves and minimal apparel stopped by to pose for packs of horny soldiers with cameras. There would be hell to pay with Mimi for those photos.

Westin celebrated the New Year by shooting off some hand flares. Orders were "no fireworks," but you couldn't expect several hundred thousand men in a war zone, armed to the teeth with explosive devices, to follow an order like that. From Westin's hilltop perch, he and his men watched a vast panorama of red and green tracers and the impossibly bright bluish glow of illumination flares that descended slowly from small parachutes, turning night into day. "It was wild," he wrote. "Any place where there were GIs, the place went off."

To round out his education, Lieutenant Westin was sent to work with a small group of ARVN scouts. Westin posed for a heroic portrait with four of them. When one, a former Charlie who had converted, was getting married, the men in his unit took up a collection to give the new couple a set of dishes from the PX in Da Nang. Westin wrote Mimi: "He and his new wife will probably be the envy of all the local gooks." Weeks into 1968, his tour rounded the corner into its second half. Days seemed endless. Patrols. More patrols. Sore feet. Rain. Occasional firefights. Horniness.

"We haven't seen any action lately," he wrote Mimi. "We did trap an NVA in a bunker and we told him to give up. He said he'd fight to the death. He did." The rain now came so hard it collapsed hootches. He wrote, "When I get home there's no way I will ever get wet (with my clothes on) again."

On January 22 his division moved north. He wrote to Mimi: "Get out your map and find Hue. It's about halfway between the DMZ and Da Nang. We'll be working in that area."

It was a big move. He explained to Mimi that for once the entire division would be together instead of being spread out. He was confident this was a good thing. They would all be safer.

8

Banh Chung and Gio Cha

Hᴜᴇ ᴡᴀs ʜᴜʀʀʏɪɴɢ toward its favorite holiday on Tuesday, January 30. There was no hint of the coming storm.

There were fishing boats and sampans and flatboats moving in the drizzle on the Huong River and the other smaller waterways that threaded through the city. All were swollen now with the January rains. Roadways on both sides of the river were thick with traffic, and the central Truong Tien Bridge was backed up with small cars, trucks, scooters, and thousands of bicycles. In the slow-moving lines were also the Jeeps and truck convoys of Americans. There were peddlers selling fresh greens, poultry, and fish from boats at the edge of muddy canals to people stocking up for the days of feasting ahead. On the wet sidewalks others sold *non la* and baskets and other homemade goods spread on blankets and covered with sheets of plastic. At Hue University, students moved through long wide halls between classrooms, or hunched over books in the large library on the first floor. At Catholic elementary schools, students in their white uniforms sat in neat rows, waiting for the final bell. The Lunar New Year celebration, the biggest holiday on the Chinese calendar used throughout southeast Asia, would start late that night as the clock approached midnight. In hundreds of narrow side streets families toiled in their first-floor shops, children at their feet, making or repairing shoes, selling clothes or radios or booze, or setting steaming bowls of spicy noodle soup out for customers at small tables that spilled out to the sidewalk. Pink-blossomed branches and small trees were tied to the back ends of many scooters and bikes on their way to decorate homes for the holidays. Behind the high walls of the grandest homes workers swept and weeded gardens, sprucing them up for outdoor gatherings. Maids tidied rooms in the Huong Giang Hotel, where mostly Americans and foreigners stayed. Trains moved slowly across the Bach Ho Bridge at the west side, which you could see from the windows of the hospital or the Thua Thien–Hue Province headquarters on Le Loi Street, seat of the local government. Across the street on the river's south bank bartenders poured at the Cercle Sportif, where the city's elite liked to gather after quitting work early. It grew dark in late afternoon—the short winter days and constant overcast skies brought night early—and the colored lights that were strung from trees and draped across streets switched on, illuminating festive banners and lanterns.

Waiting in traffic late that afternoon was Terry Charbonneau, a marine lieutenant, sitting in the rear truck of a convoy pointed north. They were out of Phu Bai, bound for Camp Evans, about thirteen miles northwest. As part of Westy's Checkers reshuffling, Camp Evans was being converted from a marine base to an army base. The army was migrating north, and the marines were migrating south. Charbonneau's convoy was on its way to pick up another load of marines. It was being led by a captain who rode in the first vehicle. Charbonneau got in the rear.

Helping to manage a transport battalion was not exactly what he'd had in mind when he'd been commissioned. He had volunteered for Vietnam the year before, after graduating from a liberal arts college in Illinois, inspired—he would be a little embarrassed to admit this years later—by the number one hit in America in 1966, Barry Sadler's "Ballad of the Green Berets":

Back at home a young wife waits
Her Green Beret has met his fate
He died for those oppressed
Leaving her his last request

Put silver wings on my son's chest
Make him one of America's best
He'll be a man they'll test one day
Have him win the Green Beret.

The marines were not Green Berets, an elite army unit, but Charbonneau had been in a hurry. He'd spent a college year studying in France, and fancied himself an internationalist. He saw military service as a form of public service abroad, much like the Peace Corps, which sought to spread the gospel of democracy and free enterprise across the world. Charbonneau saw the marines as just another means to the same end. The main action seemed to be in Vietnam, and the Marine Corps had offered him the fastest ticket there.

So far it hadn't been what he'd expected; this was more like working for a trucking firm. And what was romantic about a traffic jam? It looked as if most of the nation was heading home for the holidays; almost everyone had three or four days off. All traffic north and south funneled through the city and slowed to a crawl at the Citadel. Coming out of Phu Bai they'd taken on a rough-looking group of soldiers, a US Army Long Range Reconnaissance Patrol (LRRP, pronounced "lurp"), looking for a ride up to Camp Evans. He invited them to ride in his truck. It was a win-win. They got a ride, and the convoy got some extra protection. Charbonneau wasn't expecting any trouble, but he liked the idea of having them along. LRRPs were notoriously badass. When they came to a complete stop just outside the fortress, some of them, no doubt smelling the party gearing up all around, asked permission to hop off and look for some beer.

"Go ahead," said Charbonneau. "I don't care what you do, but when the traffic moves we're moving, and if you're not on the truck, that's your problem."

Several took off for a front yard where a Vietnamese family was seated at folding tables, and they asked if they could buy some beer. The young men in the family were happy to oblige, but an elder stepped in.

Working with limited English, the elder said, "No, no. We no sell beer. It is Tet. Beer numbah ten. Wine numbah one."

Large tumblers were filled with the family's best. The men brought back the gift and it was passed sacramentally around the back of the truck.

At another traffic stop, children threw candies to them, sugary rice wrapped in colored paper. Charbonneau was suspicious—there were stories of Americans being given candy laced with broken glass—but the LRRP unit's Vietnamese translator ate some and pronounced it safe.

Here and there in the happy crowds along the road Charbonneau noticed a glowering face—always a young man. Despite the wine and candy, not everyone out there was friendly. By the time they reached Camp Evans it was dark, and the LRRPs were fast asleep.

The party was just starting for the citizens of Hue. It was a time for homecomings. Tuy-Cam, a slender, fashionably Western young woman from Saigon, was overjoyed to see her younger brother, Long, a cadet at the South Vietnamese Air Force Academy in Yakang. The family had expected he would miss Tet because he was being sent to Texas for flight training, but at the last minute he had shown up. Tuy-Cam was the eldest of ten children. Her prosperous and well-connected family lived in a walled estate in southwestern Hue near the railroad tracks. Her father, who had died several years earlier, had been a high-ranking intelligence officer with Thieu's regime. He had foreseen, five years ago, that a big wave of Americans was going to hit South Vietnam, and that fluent English would be a sure way to catch it. He had sent Tuy-Cam to a language school in Saigon. When the Americans came, the wave had lifted her and the entire family. Now she worked at the US consulate in Da Nang. One of her other younger brothers, An, was an ARVN lieutenant just graduated from the nation's top military academy. For the first time in years the whole family would be together.

It was a particularly significant reunion for Tuy-Cam. Joining the family for their feast that night was her new fiancé, Jim Bullington. She had met him when she was working as a receptionist and translator at the US consulate in Hue three years ago. Beside the petite Tuy-Cam, Bullington was a giant, a big-boned, long-armed, long-legged foreign service officer who spoke with a gentle Tennessee drawl. He had a broad forehead and a receding hairline that made him look older than his twenty-eight years, and wore glasses with thick black rims, fashionable at the time, which gave him a brainy, bookish appearance—an Ivy League look popular with ambitious young men in what was still called the Kennedy era. But Bullington wasn't an Ivy Leaguer, and fitted no mold. Afflicted with polio as a child, trapped indoors, he had become a ham radio operator, and conversations with people around the world had broadened his opinions and whetted his appetite for foreign adventure. He was mortified by the overt racism in his state and throughout the South. He attended Auburn University in Alabama,

and as editor of its student newspaper, the *Plainsman*, he had kicked
up a storm in the cradle of the Confederacy with a front-page editorial
attacking the state's proud tradition of strict racial segregation. A cross
was burned on the lawn before his frat house. The school president
was pressured by Alabama governor John Patterson to expel him. The
controversy went national, and Bullington become a minor hero in the
civil rights movement. He had weathered the storm with the backing
of the American Association of University Professors.

The *Chattanooga Times* had taken him on as a copy editor for the
summers during his college years, but after graduating in 1962 he for-
sook journalism for the State Department. He moved to Washington,
where he had joined the March on Washington, and was in the crowd
for Martin Luther King Jr.'s famous "I Have a Dream" speech. He
brought that passion for changing the world to South Vietnam, where
he arrived in 1965 filled with enthusiasm for the American effort to resist
the spread of Communism. What he found, filing reports from Quang
Tri Province for the CORDS program, was a much more complicated
and compromised mission. A big part of his job now was evacuating
and relocating Vietnamese villagers from a large swath of the DMZ,
where McNamara wanted to build an electronic barrier to prevent
the infiltration of troops from the North, an effort that Bullington
and his colleagues considered foolish. The barrier wouldn't work, and
they were manufacturing a refugee crisis. They called it, derisively, the
McNamara Line, alluding to the infamously porous Maginot Line that
had failed to protect France in World War II.

In Saigon, Bullington gravitated toward the small circle of war correspondents at the Caravelle Hotel, and while his views of the war were
not as sour as theirs, his leaned in their direction. He and Tuy-Cam
were planning to be married in March, just before Bullington would
rotate back to the States. This would be their last visit with her family
before the wedding and their departure. He arrived that evening in an
International Scout, a Jeep-like vehicle he had borrowed from CORDS
headquarters, with his friend Steve Miller, who was a US Information
Service officer based in Hue, and one of Tuy-Cam's American colleagues from the Da Nang consulate, Steve Haukness.

The feast was bountiful, and a chance for Tuy-Cam's American
friends to experience a wide range of traditional Vietnamese dishes:

banh chung (glutinous rice cakes wrapped in dark green banana leaves), *cha lua* (ham sausage), *xoi lac* (a reddish-brown sticky rice with peanuts), *thit ga* (boiled chicken served the Vietnamese way, with the head still attached), and *mut* (candied fruits), all of it washed down with ample wine and beer. One of Bullington's friends had been unable to attend because he had been in Da Nang when that air base came under attack, and there was at least some ominous talk of more trouble ahead. But when one of his fiancée's uncles asked him about it, Bullington was dismissive. He said such talk was routine in Quang Tri and rarely amounted to anything. He said he had asked about the rumors at CORDS headquarters earlier that day, and while everyone had heard them, no one took them seriously. In general, Communist attacks tended to be more of a nuisance than a threat.

Bullington had been in plenty of danger during his years in Vietnam. Here in the midst of the holiday festivities, he was happy and comfortable. The official story was that the war was well in hand, particularly in urban areas like this. Besides, he said, he would be spending the night at a guesthouse on the grounds of a power plant across the river, where his friend Albert Istvie, a Franco-Vietnamese engineer, worked and lived.

"Where I'm staying," he said, "they could never find me."

9

Palace Soldiers

As the last light of the old year faded, Le Huu Tong was marching toward darkness on the outskirts of Hue dressed in a spanking new uniform. His NVA regiment, the Sixth, a body of nearly two thousand men, had camped at a mountain base for the last two days. They had taken a long and harrowing road there, and the days had provided welcome rest, good food, the new uniforms, and, finally, a clear mission. Like infantry everywhere, he lived a life of strenuous routine and uncertainty, never quite knowing what the big picture was, where exactly he was going, or why. Tong had always felt a sense of purpose, but missions had been harder to come by. He had been in the army for five years. He was twenty-two, a native of Ha Nam, a province immediately south of Hanoi. He had not been home in years.

The Sixth had been ordered south in July 1967 after fighting for some months in Laos. Tong's battalion, more than four hundred men, was the last to begin walking. American air strikes had destroyed most roads and bridges, so they made the trek on foot along forest and mountain trails, moving mostly at night without flashlights. Sometimes they were guided only by the fungi that glowed on tree branches, or men in the front would catch fireflies and hold them in their hands or crush them on their caps so they could be seen. In the rainy season small streams would rise before them suddenly, and become too violent to cross. Then the men who had already gone over would sit and wait, sometimes for days, until the waters ebbed and the rest could join them. They walked for months this way, dragging themselves over mountains that often took a day or more to summit—the Nguyen Chi Thanh Mountain pass was more than three thousand feet high—carrying everything on their backs. Tong's load weighed about eighty pounds. He was part of an antitank squad, and lugged a bazooka and ammo. Some carried more. Each soldier also carried a week's worth of food, two sets of clothes, mosquito netting, a small blanket, and a bundled nylon hammock. They wore rubber sandals made from tires, which, when the path was muddy, would sometimes be sucked right off their feet. Soon into the march Tong had discarded his long pants. Leeches would attach themselves to his legs, and with the long pants, he would not realize it until the slimy creatures were fat with his blood. The men would roll rice balls and carry them in their pockets, eating them cold, sometimes for days at a time before they rested and could cook. Rest came when they reached occasional camps along the trail where there were poles in the ground from which they could string their hammocks. Sometimes traveling propaganda troupes of performers entertained them at these stops, performing plays and singing folk songs that illustrated the party's ideals and goals. There were pretty girls in the troupes.

Tong's battalion moved in segments. One would march ahead, and the others would wait, sometimes for weeks, before following. Avoiding encounters with superior-armed American soldiers on search-and-destroy missions was critical. One such clash had forced them to take a weeks-long detour into Laos. There were other hazards. At points along the trail American agents had placed listening devices. These would trigger air raids out of nowhere, usually at night, when C-130s dropped flares and blasted away with powerful cannons and machine guns. Jets loosed terrifying splashes of napalm. There were also mines, about the size of a man's fist, which could blow off a man's legs. Many of the men in Tong's battalion were killed or wounded on the way. When they reached the Ben Hai River, which flowed along the demarcation line between North and South, the battalion was so depleted they set up camp and waited for reinforcement. It took them over four months of walking, with occasional stops like the one at the Ben Hai, before they reached Ba Long Province, rejoined the other battalions of the Sixth, and established a base camp to prepare for what would come next.

They were met at Ba Long by VC troops who welcomed them to their ranks. Tong officially became a member of the Front, trading the red star of the NVA, worn on his helmet, for one that was half red and half blue. Not long afterward they encountered helicopter-borne American forces, and engaged in a running battle with them for nearly a month before making it farther south. They had finally arrived in Quang Tri, just north of Hue, near the end of the year.

On the eve of Tet, Tong's battalion assembled to receive its orders. The commanders of each unit read out the mission for that night. All were taking part in a grand offensive to liberate the city of Hue, which Tong had never seen. Most of the Sixth was going to attack the northern half of the city, the Citadel. Tong's battalion would join elements of the Fifth, which was going south of the Huong River to take down an ARVN armored camp at the lower tip of the triangle, Tam Thai. They were read their formal orders at a large assembly. The opening words were: "Move forward to achieve final victory!" It called for combat by the army *and* population:

> And in compliance with the attack order of the Presidium, Central Committee, South Vietnam Liberation Front, all cadres and combatants of all South Vietnam Liberation Armed Forces should move forward to carry out direct attacks on all the headquarters of the enemy, to disrupt the United States imperialists' will for aggression and to smash the Puppet Government and Puppet Army, the lackeys of the United States, restore power to the people, completely liberate the fourteen million people of South Vietnam, and fulfill our revolutionary task of establishing democracy throughout the country. It will be the greatest battle ever fought throughout the history of our country. It will bring forth worldwide change but will also require many sacrifices. It will decide the fate and survival of our Fatherland and will shake the world and cause the most bitter failure to the imperialist ringleaders.

All of them raised their hands and pledged an oath: "All is for liberation of Hue; all is for liberation of South Vietnam." Then they were served a holiday feast of dumplings and Tet cakes. They were given canteens filled with tea. The propaganda troupes entertained them. Then, to underscore the historic nature of their undertaking, they were issued new khaki uniforms, made in China: a broad-brimmed cap, a gabardine shirt, clean trousers, and ankle-high boots. Bright strips of torn red and blue cloth were pinned on the left sleeves to signify that they were part of the Front.

The new uniforms were meant to impress. City dwellers in the South had been fed lies about the VC and the NVA for years. They were portrayed as uncivilized, even animal-like. So the Front was going to do more than liberate Hue; it was also going to *dazzle* it. They were given lessons in polite behavior, memorizing twelve rules of conduct. They were to take nothing, to help tidy the streets, to repair broken utilities like sewers or wiring, in other words, to make themselves useful. They would present themselves to Hue as a clean and disciplined professional army. This was to be the last battle, and they were going to win it. They wanted to look and behave like winners. Many of these young soldiers had never owned a suit of clothes as fine as the ones they now wore. It filled them with pride and a sense of importance.[90]

They were so certain of final success that they joyfully destroyed their camps. Living in the jungle was hard, and was at long last over. Le Kha Phieu, who years later would become the party's general secretary, joined in as members of his unit urinated on their camp stove before leaving. They were never coming back.[91]

The Sixth Regiment began the twelve-mile trek toward the city as the sun was setting behind them. It was cold and wet. They carried twice as much ammo as usual. It was two hours before midnight when they reached the swollen Ke Van River, which flowed outside the high western walls of the Citadel. On the opposite bank were blocks of residential neighborhoods, railroad tracks, and then the towering walls of their objective. There were four gates on that side—An Hoa, Chanh Tay, Huu, and Nha Do—and each was guarded by a small force of ARVN soldiers unlucky enough to have been assigned duty over the holiday.

They stripped to their underpants. Each man had been issued a nylon bag, into which went his new uniform and ammo. There were both plastic rafts and rafts made of lashed-together bamboo trees to carry the bags and weapons across. One by one they slipped silently into the cold river. It was nearly thirty yards wide at some points, and there was a swift current. Tong saw several men give up and slip under. No one, not even the drowning men, made a sound. On the other side they dressed again. Tong and a few hundred from his battalion turned south. Many hundreds more moved on toward the fortress.

General Kinh, the VC commander who had challenged Giap the previous spring, had evidently impressed the old strategist, because he had charged Kinh with drawing up plans for taking the city. The Front had been watching Westy's Checkers maneuver with interest, noting that 60 percent or more of American and ARVN forces were being concentrated in the northern part of Thua Thien Province, in the vicinity of Quang Tri and along Route 9, an east-west road just south of the DMZ that led out to Khe Sanh, reflecting the American commander's paramount concern. This had left Hue one of the most thinly defended spots on the map of I Corps.

For purposes of the war, the party divided South Vietnam into four geographic zones, each administered by a board of political commissars and senior army officers. Those for the two northernmost zones, Quang Tri and Thua Tien (which included Hue), were merged in the summer of 1967 to coordinate for the offensive. This new board broke its two districts down further. As an indication of their importance, Hue and its surrounding area were assigned to Le Tu Minh, deputy secretary for the entire northern zone. Le had a number of close associates, but Kinh was preeminent. Two nights earlier Kinh had hiked down from the hills with a small support group, moving on jungle paths and swimming across a small river to set up a command post on the west bank of the Huong, from where they could observe the attack. Artillery crews took up positions in the rock formations around it, and the general and his command group sheltered in a small grotto, where they worked, ate, and slept. They were just eight miles from the city's center.

Early that morning, American planes dropped defoliants on the mountain behind them. Then helicopters inserted American combat troops in the cleared zone. Kinh's men were alarmed, but he wasn't. He had contempt for the Americans. He told his men they were nothing but "palace soldiers."

"They will not dare to conduct searches down to the foot of this mountain," he said. "They won't go anywhere unless it is by motor vehicle or helicopter."

He sent a sniper team up to harass them. For the rest of the day, it crept close enough to shoot, and then raced back downhill. When choppers came to evacuate the wounded, the team climbed back up to shoot some more.

Late in the afternoon his men reported that another large group of helicopters had set down. Kinh said he believed they had come to carry the assault force away and told his men not to shoot at them anymore.

"Just let them pick up their bodies and withdraw from the hilltop. If you shoot anymore you'll make me go deaf."

Sure enough, the choppers loaded up the force and departed.[92]

One of the thousands closing in on the fortress walls was the recruiter and arms smuggler Nguyen Van Quang, who in the last days before Tet had been told he would not lead his militia inside the Citadel. He worried that he had done something wrong. His commanders reassured him.

"We have a lot of faith in you," said Party Committee Secretary Lien. "You have been assigned another important mission. You have to understand, we can have anyone command the team living in the Citadel because they already know their way around the city. But in order to lead a troop from outside, we need someone like you, someone who can lead those who know nothing about the city."

Quang would be at the fore of about four hundred who would attack the Chanh Tay Gate. There were a dozen men in the command group, most of them military officers. Quang was considered a "political officer," or commissar. He was also the youngest.

He had reported to the main forces in hiding late the previous afternoon dressed in his civilian clothes and was told that he would be in the vanguard. He was at first eyed suspiciously by the uniformed soldiers he would lead.

"This is your captain," the men were told by their commander. "He will lead this key company. You needn't worry. He may be young, but he is not an amateur."

Along with the other men, he had sworn an oath: "Let us die for our nation to survive."

Their approach to the gates was across a narrow bridge. Above was a guard tower with a machine gun. Once inside, Quang would lead one half of the group to the Tay Loc airstrip, while another would go to the royal palace, where the custom-sewn flag would be raised.

Afterward, Quang would have several even more important jobs. He was to orchestrate the civilian uprising, recruiting and organizing. He also would command a political cadre tasked with finding and removing enemies of the people, and at the same time build a new revolutionary local government.

As darkness approached, he took his position before the troops he would lead.

Behind him, among the thousands converging, was Nguyen Dac Xuan, the young Buddhist poet turned propagandist on the way to his homecoming. He and his company had also enjoyed a traditional Tet feast, and then shortly after sunset received the order to march. They moved silently beneath the groves of banana palms, their pace quickening the closer to the Citadel they came. Xuan heard only the occasional clanging of metal, pots suspended from backpacks hitting against weapons or bundles of ammo. Signal flares descending from American planes overhead, a nightly routine, offered dramatic strobe-like glimpses of the rapidly moving procession. Men carried rifles, mortar tubes, bazookas, machine guns, field glasses, knives, and other tools. He felt part of something powerful and right. He also felt a deep connection with the history of his country. The surprise attack reminded him of a similar ploy executed in the eighteenth century by Emperor Quang Trung against Chinese invaders. His own name, which he had hated as a child because it was traditionally associated with a class of servants, had two connections to this historic event. Xuan was what Hue had been called at the time of Quang Trung's attack. He felt a sudden surge of pride in his name for the first time. As they came closer, he could see the red lights of Hue's broadcast antennas.

When they reached a point just outside Chanh Tay Gate, they were all ordered to dig. Xuan and his company scraped out a trench just north of the Phu Cam Canal. Dogs from nearby villages barked loudly. A rocket whistled down suddenly out of the dark sky and exploded in their midst, wounding several soldiers. Xuan was covered with flying dirt.

At first they feared they had been discovered, but it had apparently been a stray, because no more came.

10

Hatred in Blood

CHE THI MUNG, the village girl who had spent months spying in the city, was leading troops across dark rice paddies. She had been summoned back to her village that afternoon. Che had started on her daily trip from the house in Dap Da to the water fountain when one of her squad stopped her. The moment had come. Che was too excited to be frightened.

She dropped her water container and bicycled the few miles to her village, only to be told when she arrived that she and the others had to go back. The Saigon authorities had declared a two-day armistice for Tet, which would begin that night. The normal patterns they had documented at targeted installations would likely change. The Huong River Squad's leader, Che's older sister's friend Pham Thi Lien, wanted her team back in the city to observe these last-minute changes. The declaration also meant that it was okay to be out after curfew. Ordinarily the girls would not have been missed in their Hue neighborhoods, where they had been living for months, because at night the residents were confined to their homes, but with people set loose for once on a cool January evening, Lien feared their absence might attract attention.

So the girls all biked back. At the house in Dap Da, Che dressed for a night out, donning her traditional *ao dai*, a long, tight-fitting silk tunic worn over flowing pants, and high heels. She and a girl from her city neighborhood went to see a Chinese movie, *Hatred in Blood*, but Che found it hard to concentrate on the story. When the movie let out, she and her friends heard loud popping noises and were stopped by ARVN soldiers who told them to hurry home: the cease-fire had been called off, and grenades were exploding in the streets.

Che knew the sound of an exploding grenade, and what she heard were just fireworks, but she pretended to be frightened and hurried as best she could in her heels. Back at the house she removed them, tied the flaps of her *ao dai* together, and ran in the darkness down familiar paths through the rice paddies to her assigned rallying point.

There, she donned work clothes and prepared to lead the assembled forces into the city. She was issued a weapon. Most of the Front soldiers she would lead had never been to Hue. It was a much bigger city than most had ever seen. Che and her comrades were split into three groups. Each would steer fighters to preordained launching points.

Che's group led a battalion, about four hundred men, across rice fields and into the city. Not a shot was fired, even as they moved from open country into crowded neighborhoods. The force was in position shortly after midnight in the Cho Cong sector, on the south bank of the Huong at the foot of the Truong Tien Bridge. Across the street was a military school. The Cho Cong force would attack and seize various targets here, and block movement from the bridge south. Along with all the other invading forces, they settled in to wait silently. The attack was supposed to begin at two thirty in the morning.

All these moves attracted little attention. There had been signs aplenty that something was coming. Despite the Front's stealth, and the general solidarity of the local peasantry, signs had trickled into MACV headquarters that something big was afoot. Jack Lofland, a marine sergeant embedded with ARVN troops, reported being attacked by a very large NVA force northwest of the city just weeks earlier. It was the largest concentration of enemy he had ever encountered. He also noted that villagers in the area had begun requesting sandbags to reinforce their safety bunkers, but would not explain why.[93] Another marine adviser with the redolent name Ty Cobb (no relation to the baseball player), working with the ARVN Second Airborne Division, had discovered the week before an enormous cache of weapons and ammo hidden outside the city.[94] But these clues had not triggered a general alarm. Two weeks earlier General Truong had reported to his American allies that the VC were capable of mounting only small attacks against the city. This estimate had been intercepted by the Front, much to the delight of General Kinh. It proved that his massing of forces had not been detected.[95]

But late on Tet Eve, Truong suddenly changed his mind. His sixth sense for trouble nagged at him. Skinny, short, stooped, and hollow chested, he was the opposite of Westy's model of a general. Truong walked with a slow, shuffling gait. He had a broad, rugged face. A Salem cigarette usually dangled from his lower lip, so he was always squinting from the smoke. When he screwed his head up from that stoop, with his squinty gaze, he seemed to view the world with a sneer. But he was one of the few ARVN top commanders fully respected by the Americans. Unlike many who led from the rear, who owed their position to family connections and demonstrated little military skill, who appointed relatives to key staff positions, and who enjoyed perquisites and amenities—homes, cars, offices—that became grander with their rank, Truong led his men from the front and seemed both shrewd and incorruptible. He lived like a soldier, sharing the conditions of his men, and had egalitarian manners that appealed to the leadership style of the American officers who worked with him. One of them, Major Norman Schwarzkopf Jr., who served as Truong's adviser and would become a celebrated four-star general, said the ARVN commander was "the most brilliant tactical commander I'd ever known."[96] Truong seemed to have an instinct for what his enemy planned to do.

The previous afternoon, lead elements of the Front had been spotted by a surveillance plane at a ferry crossing on the Ta Trach River, southwest of the city. They had made a mistake by arriving at the crossing before dark. Artillery fire zeroed in on the spot, and had continued intermittently until early the following morning, but apart from killing a dozen men caught in the open, it had not stopped the advance. Nor had the sighting betrayed the size of their force or its intentions. No ground forces had been sent to investigate. Nevertheless, this along with the other odd encounters and sightings finally alarmed Truong enough to make him call off the cease-fire at the last minute.

There had been a similar reversal in Saigon, although it's not clear whether Truong knew of it. Westy had urged Thieu to do it, and the South Vietnamese president had relented late Tuesday, but in keeping with the time-honored political practice of having things both ways, the president's staff never bothered to broadcast the order. As Westy would later write, "There was great consternation at the last minute and considerable disgust by all of us that the GVN [Government of Vietnam] would be so lackadaisical . . . that they would virtually abandon the store on the eve of the Tet holiday." [97] Truong's own order came too late to fully reverse course. Most in the city, like Che and the girls in her squad, never learned of it. Nor did most of the general's men. The small portion of his division that had not left Mang Ca stayed, but most had already scattered. Truong was able to rally three platoons of the Hac Bao, a few dozen men, to guard key locations in southern Hue, the provincial headquarters, the power station, and the prison. He sent small squads to beef up security at the eleven Citadel gates.

So the warning signs were not ignored. But no one imagined the scale of what was coming. None of the clues had registered a big alarm, because they did not fit the overarching narrative. The story American forces had told themselves about the war went like this: The enemy was weak. He had little or no popular support. He had no significant presence in South Vietnam beyond small bands of rebels capable of minor raids in rural areas. If Hanoi was going to launch a surprise attack, it would come at a remote outpost like Khe Sanh. In Westy's overconfident narrative there was simply no way his enemy could invade and occupy South Vietnam's second-largest city, or launch surprise attacks in cities throughout the country. It could not happen.

Truong's men interpreted the last-minute change as an excess of caution. By the time Lieutenant Tran Ngoc "Harry" Hue, the Hac Bao commander, received Truong's new order, he had only a handful of his two hundred men still with him. He dispatched those who remained to satisfy the general's new order, and then had his driver drop him at his home in the southwest sector of the fortress.

There he showered and changed out of his uniform. It was a rare chance to spend a few days with his wife and his children, to celebrate their ancestors, buried nearby, to say good-bye to the old year and welcome the new. At midnight Wednesday, the beginning of the new year, they would sit down to a big ceremonial meal.

11

A Pretty Night

CAPTAIN JIM COOLICAN had come back to Hue that afternoon with the Hac Bao, eager for a holiday break. He had been with the unit for months in Quang Tri Province in the northwest.

On the road south he had a vague sense that something was off. There seemed to be less traffic north of the city than usual. The children who ordinarily lined the streets when they passed through villages were nowhere to be seen. He was suspicious enough that when the convoy stopped at Camp Evans he directed the men to load their trucks with rocket launchers. They collected about three hundred of them.

But Coolican saw no further sign of trouble the rest of the way, and there seemed to be no sense of danger at Hac Bao's headquarters. Harry seemed unconcerned, and Coolican had learned to trust him.

Besides, Coolican wanted to put some distance between himself, Harry, and the rest of the unit over the holidays. One of Tet's superstitions held that the first person you encountered in the New Year would be a harbinger of your fortune for the next twelve months. So in Vietnamese homes every move was choreographed to ensure a lucky outcome. Coolican did not want to blunder into anyone's prospects. As soon as the Hac Bao camp cleared out that evening he headed for the MACV compound. There would be beer and barbecue, and some good friends, like Frank Doezema.

Just before midnight, he drove himself through the Citadel and out one of its southern gates. It was a pretty night, so he stopped his Jeep and took a walk along the north bank of the Huong River to savor it.

He admired the colorful lights draped across the streets, reflected in the river. Vietnam had been mostly hot and humid during the nine months of his tour, but this night the air was cool and pleasant. The city was at rest. You would have never known there was a war on. He felt a surge of affection for the country, and proud to be doing his part to protect it.

There is little doubt, in retrospect, that this solitary, strolling American was being watched by scores of disciplined enemy soldiers hiding along the riverbank, waiting for two thirty, when the attack would begin.

PART TWO

The Fall of Hue

January 31, 1968

The city is stormed, and taken. At the American base in Phu Bai, eight miles south, commanders with no sense of what has happened dispatch two companies of marines—just over three hundred men—against ten thousand enemy troops. The battle begins.

Marine Captain Jim Coolican, who helped coordinate the fight for the MACV compound and later fought in the Citadel.

Captain Gordon Batcheller, a marine company commander who was gravely wounded leading his men toward Hue on the first day of the battle.

Alfredo "Freddie" Gonzalez, the diminutive marine sergeant from Texas who would be awarded the Medal of Honor for his heroism.

Marine Captain Chuck Meadows, commander of Golf Company 2/5, who was ordered to lead a futile attack on the Citadel against overwhelming odds.

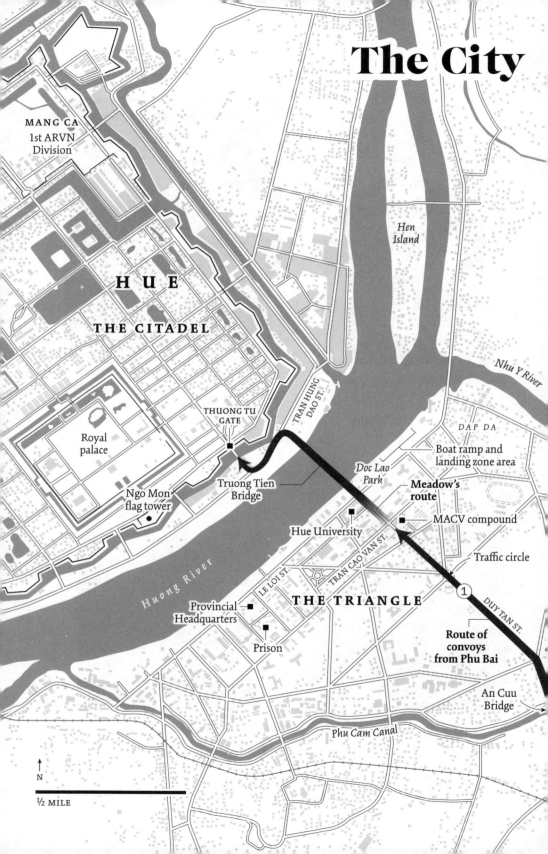

The City

MANG CA
1st ARVN
Division

HUE

THE CITADEL

Royal
palace

THUONG TU
GATE

Ngo Mon
flag tower

Truong Tien
Bridge

Huong River

Provincial
Headquarters

Prison

LE LOI ST.

TRAN CAO VAN ST.

THE TRIANGLE

TRAN HUNG DAO ST.

Hen
Island

Nhu Y River

DAP DA

Boat ramp and
landing zone area

Doc Lao
Park

Meadow's
route

MACV compound

Traffic circle

1

DUY TAN ST.

Route of
convoys
from Phu Bai

An Cuu
Bridge

Phu Cam Canal

Hue University

↑
N

½ MILE

1

Fireworks

THE FIRST BIG blow was struck by a five-man team of commandos, part of the NVA's Fifth Regiment that called itself Thanh doi Hue (the Hue City Unit). For weeks they had been living underground in the mountains west of the city, planning how to destroy the tanks at Tam Thai, an ARVN armored base less than two miles south of Hue's center.[1] Based there were more than two dozen M41 Walker Bulldogs, American-made tanks, which were parked behind four concentric barbed wire fences off Highway 1 just beyond the southern tip of the triangle. The small, antiquated tanks were no match for more modern antitank weaponry, but in the streets of Hue they could do a lot of damage to infantry armed mostly with rifles. Destroying them would be key to the attack's success.

As they prepared, Nguyen Quang Ha and his team had lived in a hole big enough for all of them with a thatched cover to make it invisible from the air. Camped with them were hundreds of comrades, a full NVA battalion, which would swarm the base after they blew up the tanks. Ha had heard a lot of talk about a battle that would end the war once and for all, but for him and the others in his squad, after months of living in the mountains or on jungle trails, it meant their days of living in the dirt were over.

Ha was not a career soldier. Until the year before he had been happily employed as a middle school math teacher in Bac Ninh, a village north of Hanoi. He was thirty years old, older than most of his comrades, and his maturity and education had marked him for special training.

Months of climbing, constructing bombs, slithering in wet ditches, and learning the fine arts of camouflage and infiltration had gone into his preparation. He had, for instance, learned to hide himself and move silently and invisibly across an open field. This involved smearing himself with mud from head to toe and inching his way forward, halting every few inches to remain as still as a lizard. To traverse a hundred yards might take most of a day. Working through the barbed wire barriers at Tam Thai without alerting guards would take all his acquired stealth. At sunset, the City Unit devoured all their remaining rice. They figured they would need their strength for the fight and, once they had taken the city, food finally would be plentiful.

Overall, the invading force was divided in two, one part for the north and the other for the south. The northern one would take and hold the Citadel and the areas around it, and the southern one would do the same in the triangle. Their combined strength was four NVA regiments (Nine, Eight, Five, and Six) and eight Viet Cong battalions, along with local militias (like the one created by Nguyen Van Quang). Each of these twenty-four battalions (in each regiment there were four, of varying sizes) had support companies for scouting, communications, special operations, artillery, and crew-served weapons.

The northern force was led by Major Nguyen Thu, a veteran NVA officer. He would command the Ninth and Eighth NVA Regiments, four VC battalions and their support companies, and the local militia troopers. The southern force was led by Major Than Trong Mot, who commanded the Fifth and Sixth NVA Regiments and four VC battalions.[2] His real name was Than Trong Thoan, and he had been fighting for his country's liberation for more than twenty years. He took the name "Mot," which means "first," because the combat unit he commanded in the French War was then the first of the MVA's 101st Regiment. Both of his parents had died in French custody, and were believed to have been tortured to death. Within both combined forces, north and south, were commissars responsible for sparking and steering the anticipated popular uprising.

The northern thrust was more difficult and important. The Citadel and its royal palace had tremendous cultural significance, and Mang Ca was the city's hardest military target. There was also the airstrip at Tay Loc, on the west side of the fortress, which had important tactical value—not the least of which was denying the enemy a place to land men and supplies. Major Thu was a twenty-two-year army veteran who had fought in the French War. He did not accept the party's grandiose ambitions for Tet. There was, in his opinion, zero chance that the people of Hue would rise up spontaneously, certainly not to the degree hoped. Like his commander, General Kinh, Thu knew they could take the city, but also that they could not hold it for long. Achievable goals, he believed, were to destroy the ARVN division at Mang Ca, and to violently uproot the local government by rounding up and punishing (by execution in some cases) those who represented the Saigon regime. This could be done in five days to a week. To inspire, recruit, organize, and lead a mass revolt was another matter. It would take much longer than a week even if they would not have to prepare for the coordinated American and ARVN counterattack he knew would come. When that came, it would be all they could do to hang on. He nevertheless believed the effort was worthwhile. Hitting Hue and other South Vietnamese cities would not bring the war to a swift end, but it would bring the war's violence to the doorsteps of the more well-to-do urban citizens for the first time. Fighting in city streets would erode confidence in Thieu's regime, and undermine the American effort, which, as Thu saw it, was already failing. The bombing in the north had not slowed Hanoi's war effort, and dealing the Americans a strong blow on the ground, in areas they supposedly controlled, would also undermine support for the war in the United States.[3]

Apart from Mang Ca, the primary targets inside the Citadel were the airstrip (where the tenacious Hac Bao unit was quartered along with an ARVN ordnance company), the royal palace, and Ngo Mon flag tower. In southern Hue, the primary targets were the armored base at Tam Thai, various large government buildings along or just off Le Loi Street—the province headquarters, the treasury, the hospital complex, the post office, the prison, and the radio station—and the sole American base, the MACV compound. There were long lists of smaller targets, mostly the homes of local South Vietnamese government leaders and regime supporters, who were marked for arrest and punishment. Small sapper units were assigned to blow up bridges—the Truong Tien, the Bach Ho Bridge about one mile to the west, and the An Cuu Bridge at the southern tip of the triangle. If these went down it would impede the inevitable American counterattack.

Some commandos had sneaked into the city the day before, moving through storm drains or among the crowds of citizens entering or leaving the city for the holidays. A few wore ARVN uniforms so they could approach the fortress gates from the inside and surprise the guards.

The low-lying fog, especially near the rivers and canals, helped hide the major troop movements. As the village girl Che Thi Mung led her contingent across open fields, she could not see far enough in the darkness to count how many followed her. She guided them across the rice fields of Thuy Thanh up to Thuy Van, then to Vi Da and into Dap Da, the neighborhood where she had stayed on her spying mission. They would set up a roadblock right in the middle of Ba Trieu Street, which formed the eastern edge of the triangle and led down to Phu Bai.

Mai Xuan Bao was part of that force. He was a veteran commando with a local Viet Cong battalion. They had been preparing for the offensive through most of the previous year, accumulating three tons of food and ammo in a warehouse. They had carried it there in small deliveries, floating it across rivers and canals at night on makeshift bamboo rafts. They had no vehicles, so they did it all on foot, carrying it cross-country on treks that sometimes lasted a week, moving at night. On those long marches, they had their own version of C rations; they carried live pigs, some of them weighing upwards of two hundred pounds, drugging them to keep them quiet and still. The animals were slaughtered and eaten along the way. On this night the men each carried two hundred rounds for their rifles and double the normal number of grenades and rockets—twenty grenades each and up to eight rockets, which were heavy. To fight in the city, they had practiced scaling walls and also how to blow holes in them. They had done all this without knowing exactly what they were preparing for. They had celebrated the holiday early, watching skits performed by the propaganda troupes. As they watched, they had sewn bandoleers and filled hand grenades with gunpowder, so absorbed in the performance that they kept sticking themselves with their needles. At the feast afterward they couldn't enjoy the food because the bitter taste of powder from the grenades had gotten into their mouths and noses.

They had marched out of their camp in the jungle late Monday night, January 29, toward Truong Ha, south of the city. On their way out, one of their units tripped a signal from an American sensing device—they called the devices *cay nhiet doi* (tropical trees), because their antennas were disguised to look like branches—and they were hit by an artillery barrage. Most had escaped unharmed. Bao's group had slept at homes in Truong Ha from three o'clock Tuesday morning until noon, and then prepared to move into Hue that night. Waiting now by the base of the Truong Thien Bridge, Bao could hear the *chug-chug-chug* of machines in a nearby ice factory.

Bao's battalion would attack the police headquarters. A handpicked group of commandos, including him, would blow a hole in the wall for the initial assault. After they had cleared the building, large numbers of others would follow to occupy and hold it.

Another battalion approached southern Hue from the west. With them was Dang Dinh Loan, a commissar, whose main work would begin after the city was taken. They had stayed the night before in fields near the Gia Long Tomb and had been delayed when an American plane dropped a bomb near their position, wounding several men. They had to cross the Ta Trach River, and Loan did not know how to swim, so his comrades threw together a raft made of banana trees and floated him across. Several times as they moved, the overcast night sky lit up with flares. Everyone would hit the ground and would lie very still. This slowed them, but no attacks followed. They did their best to move silently. Across open fields they heard sounds of worshipping: chants and the hollow percussion of the "wooden fish," instruments used to accompany Buddhist chants. They trampled through a field of coriander, which filled the moist air with a pleasing peppery odor. As the hours passed they fell behind schedule, so they began moving at a trot.

The offensive was to start with an artillery barrage fired from the western hills toward Mang Ca. The assault on Hue would, of course, be only one of many attacks throughout South Vietnam that day, attacks that would stun the world, but none was more important than this. Westy himself, years earlier, had been asked what move he would make if he were commanding Hanoi's war effort. He said, "Capture Hue."[4]

Nevertheless, the Front's leaders were confident their attack would come as a complete surprise. Truong Sinh, a VC commander, had carefully watched the busy reshuffling of American and ARVN forces in the previous weeks, and it was clear this had nothing to do with countering the surprise attack. That night, he and other Front leaders were at the command center at the base of Kim Phung Mountain, west of the city. They used a spare radio code to communicate with their forward observers without arousing suspicion, sending messages in coded three-letter bursts. They smoked cigarettes and played cards and ate ginger marmalade brought specially from Hanoi for the occasion. They also sampled Hue specialties—goose tea and sesame candy. Then they listened to the broadcast of Uncle Ho's Tet greeting before settling in to wait.[5]

Before the scheduled hour, Ha and other members of his City Unit crept up to the barbed wire fencing around the Tam Thai base. They propped up the bottom of the barbed wire fences and one by one crawled under. The base was quiet. There were a few guards posted, but the ARVN soldiers who had not gone home for Tet were inside two bunkers at the north end. The tanks were parked in neat rows. The commandos crawled from one to the next, placing two packs of dynamite under each, one wedged in the metal tread and the other just under its diesel engine. The explosives were armed with primers that could be detonated remotely. They then crawled back outside the fencing, awaiting the opening artillery barrage.

Part of the Sixth Regiment was spotted moving in a graveyard just north of the Citadel. These men were getting into position to scale the north wall near the Hau and An Hoa Gates. A small ARVN outpost started shooting at them, and inside Mang Ca, General Truong ordered flare rockets over the site. But the commandos had scattered and the flares lit up only headstones and tombs.[6]

Just a few miles southwest of the city, Terry Egan, an Australian Army adviser working with a small ARVN recon platoon, was startled to observe NVA regulars in what appeared to be crisp new uniforms moving stealthily toward the city. There were far too many for his force to attack. Egan hunkered down in the darkness to watch and to count. They kept coming and coming. Egan counted two full battalions, more than four hundred men. He radioed this information back to Mang Ca, and shortly before midnight General Truong ordered a spotter plane.

But the fog hid everything, and after two hours of looking the pilot reported he had seen nothing.[7]

From an observation point atop Chia Voi Mountain, at 2:30, a Front forward observer reported that all was still quiet.

"Electric lights are still burning," he said. "Vehicles continue to cross the Truong Tien Bridge. Red and green signal flares occasionally light up the sky."[8]

He said there were no disturbances in the areas where the bulk of the Front's forces were located, and apart from some scattered rifle fire, which was not unusual, there was no sign that these forces had been discovered.[9]

Fifteen minutes later, commandos reported that they had reached the top of the north wall of the Citadel and were in position to attack Mang Ca. Other units were waiting to move on the north and west gates. Loan's battalion in southern Hue had been delayed, but was now moving rapidly. The forces around Tam Thai were waiting to blow up the tanks.

Two thirty came and went. General Kinh, who had moved to the top of Kim Phung, reported back to the command center downhill every five minutes. Nothing. Inside the center, the Front's command group exchanged worried glances. Kinh reported next that there were two "old woman planes," propeller-driven surveillance aircraft, north of the city, which had dropped two green flares, and that five red flares had gone up in various places over the south side. Otherwise all was silent. The room was also silent. One assistant had a radio handset in one hand, a pencil in the other, and was staring at the luminous dial of his watch. The operations room commander stood up beside him. Ordinarily a calm, reserved man, he nervously directed his assistant to call their various forward observers for reports.

"Do you see anything yet?" the aide asked the first one. "Why haven't they opened fire? Are there any problems?"

"I am following the situation," the observer responded. "Wait. Wait a minute."

The aide called a second observer, who said, "I am awake. I am looking down at Hue. The lights of the city are still on. The sky is quiet. Nothing is happening."[10]

Tension built. Sinh worried, *Had something happened? Was the operation still secret and safe? Had the main forces lost their way? Are they being
blocked by the enemy?*[11]

Presently the boom of mortar shells was heard at Phu Bai, then at
Mang Ca, and then throughout the city arose the sound of gunfire.
Noise was scattered at first, and then, as if touched off by a fuse, it
rose rapidly to a din.

Simultaneously, the planted packs of dynamite went off under the
tanks at Tam Thai, scattering parts everywhere. The combined blast
was so loud it startled marines miles away in Phu Bai. One member
of the City Unit who had not moved back far enough was killed and
several others in the support battalion were wounded by hot shards
of flying steel. Vehicles erupted in tall columns of flame against the
night sky. Then the support battalion stormed into the base, moving
through gaps in the wire left by the commandos and past the flaming
vehicles. Among them were forty-six men carrying rocket launchers,[12]
including Le Huu Tong, who had come on the long and difficult march
from the north. All the ARVN troops outside the bunkers were gunned
down. Heat from the flames and the pungent odor of gunpowder and
burning fuel were so intense that for a few minutes the attackers had
to back off.

The view from Kim Phung was spectacular. Le Tu Minh, the top
commander, would later write: "The night blazed up like there were
fireworks erupting in the sky. It was extremely beautiful."[13]

It took an hour to root out and kill the bunkered ARVN troops.
Then the base was silent. As the men's ears adjusted, they could hear
gunfire and explosions in the distance to the north and south, but
there was nothing more to shoot at inside the base. They had suffered only a few casualties, and had dealt Hue's defenders a crushing
surprise blow. Just outside the gates near Highway 1 was a row of
flaming tanks that had somehow made it out, or had been parked
there before the raid started. They had been destroyed with rockets.
Their crews were dead. One crewman had been blown out of the
top hatch, legless. His blackened, scorched torso came to rest on the
vehicle's front. A short time later, when General Truong called for
tanks to help defend his base at Mang Ca, there was no one at Tam
Thai to respond.[14]

Eleven tanks and several armored personnel carriers had been away from Tam Thai, and their crews, startled by the sudden eruption of shooting around the triangle, started moving them north toward the Truong Tien Bridge. They came under heavy attack near the center of the triangle. Their commander's tank took a direct hit, and he was killed. Most of his column made for the nearby MACV compound. Some tanks drove to the bridge, where their crews parked and locked themselves inside. Others simply fled, leaving their tanks in the street, some of them still running.

The forces charged with seizing the southern half of the city moved into the triangle virtually unopposed. At police headquarters, Bao's squad blew a hole in the outside wall and stormed the building. They came so fast and in such numbers that after firing a few random shots the guard detail fled. Troops flooded into the building and the commandos moved on to their next target a few blocks away. On the way, they ran into a small ARVN squad rushing to help defend the prison, and a brief gunfight ensued before both sides broke off. Some of Bao's men were hit, including a local man who had been guiding them. Without him they were lost. None were from Hue, and all city blocks looked the same to them, especially at night. In their rush to press the attack, they had left wounded men behind, and without their guide they couldn't find their way back. It grieved Bao to abandon them, but they could go neither forward nor backward. They sheltered in houses a block south of the riverfront and waited.

Lieutenant Hoang Anh De's battalion, which had taken part in the attack on Tam Thai, moved north into the triangle completely unopposed. They were delayed by several ARVN tanks as they attempted to cross the An Cuu Bridge, and had to find boats downstream in order to cross over, surround, and destroy them. Sappers set explosives under the bridge that were detonated but failed to topple the structure.

Hoang was a veteran NVA officer, thirty-six years old, who had been sent south to lead a VC battalion. He wore simple black pajamas with the blue and red cloth strips pinned to his sleeve, with no sign of rank. He had lost two of his closest friends already: his unit's political commissar, who had accompanied the commandos on the tank raid and was killed there; and his scout, who had been killed at the bridge. Both men had been with him for years, and, like him, were more than a decade older than most of the men they commanded. Losing them hit Hoang hard. He had their bodies carried to the Tu Dam Pagoda in southwestern Hue that would serve as the Front's field headquarters so they could be buried with honors.

They arrived later than expected at the heart of the city, and found most of their objectives along Le Loi Street already taken. One exception was the radio station, where American communications officers, mostly air force men, held out for about fifteen minutes and then fled, retreating to hidden bunkers under an adjacent hostel. It wasn't until Hoang's men moved on the prison and east to the MACV compound that they ran into serious resistance. Hoang found that he lacked enough firepower to overrun either location because he had taken so much of the city so fast, and had had to leave men behind in the neighborhoods that he'd seized.

North of the river, in the Citadel, there were bigger fights. Major Thu's assault focused primarily on the northern and western gates. Mang Ca was subjected to an extended mortar bombardment and then attacked by forces that had come either over or under the north wall. The attack was bigger than General Truong had imagined, and bigger than any he had seen before. His reduced forces were outgunned and outnumbered. The fight there would rage well into daylight, with the ARVN base fending off waves of determined enemy assaults.

On the west side, six commandos dressed in ARVN uniforms and armed with rifles approached the guards at Chanh Tay Gate at the northwest corner, then opened fire. Explosives were used to blow open the doors, and Nguyen Van Quang, the militia recruiter, led the first wave through.

Shouting "Attack!" Quang ran through the dark passageway into the fortress, firing his rifle as he came. No one fired back. The commandos inside shone red flashlights to mark their positions. They said all the ARVN guards there either had been killed or had run away.

There were fights at each of the entrances, but by far the biggest was at Huu Gate, farther down the west wall from Chanh Tay. At Huu a forty-man assault company had to improvise an attack. It had originally planned to slip into the fortress through a water main just outside Mang Ca, but had been blocked by an impenetrable thicket of barbed wire. Before the attacks began, it had made its way around the northwest corner and down past Chanh Tay Gate. There was no assault force to attack Huu Gate from the inside, so the company had no choice but to assail it head-on. The tower machine gun covered the narrow bridge over the moat. It had walls on either side that were only knee-high. Surprise was their only hope, and surprise had been lost when the attacks kicked off citywide. The first group that tried to run across the bridge was mowed down. Two-thirds of the men, including their leader, were killed or badly wounded. Those remaining fell back and settled into a prolonged exchange of fruitless gunfire with the tower guards. More of the attackers were killed. Desperate, several bravely set off to crawl across the span, hugging the low walls. They made it all the way to the closed iron gate directly under the tower gun, which could not fire straight down. They placed a charge against the doors and retreated to both sides before the blast. The explosion blew open the gate, and they ran inside. The ARVN machine gun was now under attack from front and back. It was finally silenced by a rocket. Only fourteen members of the assault company remained.[15]

One of those fourteen was Nguyen Duc Thuan, an experienced NVA commando. He and his men, once inside, were lost. They had not planned to enter the Citadel there, and their local guide had been killed. They split into two groups, one for the airstrip, and the other, with Thuan taking the lead, for the palace and flagpole. They immediately came upon an old man carrying an umbrella and making his way to a family altar to offer his Tet prayers. Startled and frightened, he bowed repeatedly and pleaded for them to spare him.

"No, we are liberation soldiers," Thuan assured him. "We came here to liberate the people. You have nothing to worry about. Just lead us to the flag stand and to the royal palace."

So the old man started them through the streets southward. On the way, they surprised and grabbed an ARVN soldier who, hearing gunfire, was hurrying back to his ordnance company at Tay Loc. The old man was thanked and released. The prisoner's hands were bound and he was pushed forward to guide them. Thuan demanded that he lead them to the royal palace, which the old man had told them was nearby.

They went just a few blocks before gunfire started. Thuan felt a sharp blow to his knee and dived for the side of the street, pulling the prisoner with him. He could see they were nowhere near the palace. Their prisoner had led them into a trap.

"What the hell is this place?" Thuan asked angrily.

"This is my company," the man said.

"What company?"

"The ordnance company."

"We asked you to take us to the royal palace! Why did you take us to your company?"

It was an honest mistake. The words for royal palace in Vietnamese were *dai noi*, but because Thuan was from the North, his accent was slightly different, and his prisoner heard the words *dai doi*, which meant "company."

The firing stopped once they cleared the street. Thuan inspected his knee, which was bloody. A bullet seemed to have passed clean through its front, under the kneecap, without damaging the joint. He could still move it and even bear some weight on it. So he wrapped a cloth tightly around it and his little group continued south. They captured another man, a city guard, who understood their northern accent better, and he led them exactly where they wanted to go.

Quang's advance group was at the airstrip, where the Hac Bao were dug in. The nearby ordnance company was an easier target. Quang knew an ARVN soldier based there, who as a student had worked with him years earlier. The man had been drafted into the ARVN, but Quang had kept in touch and had written him a letter telling him that although he now wore the *nguy* uniform, he should "keep the revolution in his heart." He now called out the man's name with a megaphone, telling him to convince his comrades they were surrounded and should surrender, which they did.

Quang removed his friend from the prisoners, and handed him his pistol.

"No," the man said. "Let me take your AK. If you trust me, chief, I will fight alongside you and protect you."

He would stay with Quang throughout the battle.[16]

All over the city, residents were jarred by the fighting. Some were awakened, while others, still up, were just startled. They had stayed up through the night playing cards, drinking, and talking. Many at first mistook the explosions and pops of gunfire for Tet fireworks. But wherever the shooting was close, there was no confusion. Tran Thi Thu Van, a writer and poet[17] who had come to Hue from Saigon to attend her father's funeral and had stayed to offer prayers for him at Tet, was sleeping in her family home close enough to Tam Thai that there could be no mistake. Each blast snapped the wooden shutters on the windows open and then shut. In the small house with her was much of her extended family. Her ears ringing, she rolled out of her wooden plank bed and huddled terrified with her brothers, uncles, aunts, cousins, nieces, and nephews in the center of the room. The burning candles and incense at the family's ancestral alter were doused. The gunfire seemed to be coming from every direction at once.

Fifteen-year-old Le Ngoc Thinh hid with his family in a metal drainage pipe. A friend had come running past their house shouting that "they" were coming, and everyone knew what "they" meant. The drainage pipe was well over one hundred feet long and about four feet high. So many people were huddled there that it was hard to breathe. The adults talked in hushed tones about the VC and everyone listened to the sounds of gunfire.

Twelve-year-old Le Cong Thanh had been allowed to stay up late with the rest of his large family. They lived in the shadow of a Catholic church just outside the Citadel, near the Truong Dinh Gate—the northeastern passage that led directly into Mang Ca. Le's father, Le Van May, was a captain in the ARVN, but he was home to spend the holidays with his wife and nine children and an assortment of close relatives. The family had stocked up enough food for a week, and were gathered very early that morning around an altar to begin. The table was laden with offerings, flowers, food, sweets, and candles. But their prayers were interrupted by gunfire. Le saw green lines in the sky from tracer bullets, and gunfire and explosions that were close. He ran inside with his family, and his father locked the door. He told the children to crawl underneath a big wooden bed. It sounded as though a terrible battle was being fought at the police station nearby. After a while, Le crept to the door and peeked out the keyhole. He saw soldiers moving through his front yard, skinny men in black pajamas wearing round pith helmets. His father whispered, "VC." In school he had been told the VC were like monkeys who lived in the forest. Le was surprised that these did not have tails.

Tran Huy Chung was eleven. His family, now up late celebrating Tet, lived outside the Citadel near Mang Ca. Before the shooting started, some Front soldiers asked for directions to the ARVN base, which he gave. They wore shorts and carried backpacks and rocket launchers, and they spoke with northern accents. When the battle began, his family stayed in their house, but he ran to hide in a trench at a nearby construction site. He couldn't figure out what was happening. Early that morning he climbed a guava tree in his yard and watched bright flashes and fighting by the Tay Loc airstrip. Chung had heard that the Communist soldiers were cruel, and bad. But later in the day, when the shooting died down, some of the soldiers played games with him and the other children, shooting marbles and flipping coins. That day, the people in his ward who had worked for the local government were arrested.

Shooting also awakened Harry Hue, the Hac Bao commander, at his family home. Hue was stocky with a broad face and small, wide-set eyes. He was a fierce and extremely competent commander, one whose abilities outstripped his rank. To his battle-trained ears there was no mistaking the sounds, which were coming closer as the invading forces made their way down from the upper gates. Hue rounded up his three children and his parents, and herded them with his wife into the family bunker. He then jumped onto his father's bicycle, the sounds of the battle coming closer, and began pedaling furiously toward Tay Loc. He was shocked to see NVA soldiers—many of them—moving through the streets. He was not in his uniform, and the soldiers for the time being were ignoring him. He considered stopping and turning back. He would be safer, at least initially, as a civilian with his family, but it wouldn't take long for them to figure out who he was. Besides, his duty was to be with his men at such a dangerous moment. Thirty of them were staying in barracks at the airstrip. He slowed down to avoid attracting notice and finally fell in behind a group of NVA soldiers, following at a short distance. When he reached the outskirts of Tay Loc, he made a dash for it. Some of the encircling enemy troops shot at him, but missed. His own men recognized him even in the darkness.

They were surrounded and had been hit hard by mortars. Arranged in bunkers outside their barracks, they were armed with rifles and the rocket launchers that Coolican had thought to collect on the trip south the previous afternoon. Theirs was the only point of serious resistance on the west side of the Citadel once the gates had been breached. After a confusing hour, shooting had temporarily eased. Mortars continued to fall inside their perimeter and there was still some shooting, but it appeared the attackers were waiting for reinforcement. Given the numbers Hue had seen in the streets, it was likely a bigger attack would come. This was no isolated ambush. They could hear intense gunfire to the northeast, from the direction of Mang Ca. The smell and taste of cordite were in the air. When several enemy soldiers got inside the unit's perimeter, they captured two. The men's hands were tied and they were placed in a foxhole to the rear of their bunkers.

"Sit here in this foxhole," Hue instructed them. "Do what I tell you to do. We won't kill you if you obey us."

Not long afterward a rocket exploded in the foxhole, and both were killed.

The news from elsewhere was not good. The platoon sent to southern Hue to guard the prison was calling for help. In its last exchange, the lieutenant there asked Hue to look after his wife and seven children. By radio, General Truong ordered the Hac Bao to abandon the airfield and make their way to Mang Ca if they could. The general had armed cooks and clerks and workers at the division hospital to help man his beleaguered perimeter. Truong estimated he was under attack by two battalions. They had come over the base's high walls in a number of places, and at one point had fought to within sixty feet of Truong's own office before being driven back. Fighting was hand-to-hand, and desperate. The general was broadcasting calls for every unit in the area to come to his aid.

Not many could. Within hours of the initial assault, ten of the eleven gates into the Citadel were controlled by the enemy. The only way for allied troops to enter was through the Tria Gate at the northeastern corner, but that now had Front forces in neighborhoods immediately outside.

Lieutenant Hue realized his thirty men could not hold out much longer at the airstrip. Their only hope was to make it to Mang Ca and shore up that encircled corner until reinforcements could be flown in or could fight their way in. He assembled his men and rallied them as best he could. Nearly all, like him, were from the city. He did not minimize their plight. He reminded them that they were fighting not just for South Vietnam, but for their families and their homes. He told them they were the best of the First ARVN Division, and if anyone could save Hue, it was them and only them.

"Hac Bao!" he shouted.

His men cheered, and followed. Most knew the Citadel streets, and they had friends on nearly every block. Hue saw that the invading forces had not yet spread out evenly. They seemed to have focused instead on a few specific objectives, and once there, were digging in. For the time being this left whole neighborhoods open. Civilians who recognized the Hac Bao uniforms helped steer them around danger points.

As they approached Mang Ca, they surprised the enemy by coming up on them from behind. The Hac Bao fought its way through the headquarters' rear gate. Once inside, it tilted the balance of the struggle. Surprised by the sudden reinforcement, and perhaps overestimating its size, the attackers fell back.

The Front was hampered by delays down the line. Lieutenant Tang Van Mieu's battalion had gotten lost on the outskirts of the city after their local guide ran off. The diminutive battalion commander would arrive at the Citadel with his hundreds of reinforcements a full day late. So a combination of luck and determined resistance was enough to preserve General Truong's headquarters, for the time being.

At the opposite end of the Citadel, Nguyen Duc Thuan's bandaged knee was holding up. He was still too filled with adrenaline to feel much pain. They were joined by more men who had come through the Chanh Tay Gate. Outside the palace they split up. The two squads who had met them went for the palace itself, quickly breaking through the small guard detail outside. They took turns sitting on the ornate throne in the emperor's ceremonial room. Thuan and his men moved on to the flag stand.

The enormous pole was guarded by seven soldiers. A blast of machine-gun fire killed one of Thuan's men, but he and the others made it into the second floor of the structure. Guards fired down from the third floor. They crept nervously up the stairs, expecting at any moment to be gunned down, but when they reached the top it was empty. The guards had fled.

They found the yellow flag of South Vietnam in a heap at the base of the pole. Apparently it was raised every dawn and lowered every sunset, but the flag detail had not bothered to untether and fold it. Thuan and his men used their knives to cut it loose and then shredded it.

They then waited for their own specially designed flag to arrive.

It was more than an hour before Sergeant Cao Van Sen came, with the flag's two bearers. Sen also had a writer and a cameraman with him to witness and record the historic moment. It was eight in the morning when they hauled the flag up.

Few saw it at first. The morning was so foggy that the men standing at Ngo Mon could not see all the way across the Huong River. But soon enough the blue and red stripes and yellow star would be seen, not just in Hue, but all over the world.

2

The Compound

W HEN THE SHOOTING started, Frank Doezema was on guard duty in
the northwest tower of the MACV compound.

Ordinarily it was a dull business even in daytime, when the streets
below were busy. The tower had a circular platform about twenty feet
up surrounded by a wooden railing and topped with a tin roof. It offered
a good view of the downtown neighborhood. Below was Duy Tan
Street—the stretch of Highway 1 that passed through the city. To the
north on a clear night you could see past the white walls of the two-
story Hue University to the river, the Truong Tien Bridge, and across
the water the Citadel walls, but this was not a clear night. Beneath, just
outside the front gate on the corner sidewalk was a sandbag bunker
that during the day was manned. With so many advisers coming in
for the holidays, the courtyard inside had more parked vehicles than
usual. Jim Coolican had driven in a few hours earlier. He had greeted
his old radio operator warmly, and then Doezema had retaken his
place on the tower.

To practiced ears like Doezema's, there was no confusion about
fireworks. He knew the sound of an AK-47. It made a high-pitched,
more mechanical crack than the American rifle, the M16, which made
a deeper, rounder sort of pop. And there was no mistaking the *pock!*
of a launched mortar, nor the explosion when it hit.

At once Doezema could see NVA soldiers moving in the streets
below, hundreds of them. Most seemed to be congregated in the
shadow of Hue University. When they advanced with rifles and rocket

tubes, Doezema raked them with an ear-shattering blast of his machine gun.[18] Those who did not fall dragged the others back. A few minutes later they came again, he raked them once more, and once more he drove them back. He draped a white towel over his neck, checked his weapon, and waited.

The shooting shocked the sleepy compound awake. Some of the roughly four hundred men staying there were combat veterans like Doezema and Coolican, but most were not. They were nothing like a well-honed fighting force. The compound was considered a rear post, a transit stopover for the army and marine officers attached to ARVN First Division troops. Day to day, it was manned mostly by office workers, cooks, drivers, supply officers, and those serving on the staff of army colonel George Adkisson, who had taken command only days earlier. He was just learning the job, which was to coordinate the relationship between General Truong and the MACV. Weeks earlier, Adkisson had put the compound through the self-defense drill Doezema had mentioned in his letter. The previous afternoon the colonel had heard about Truong's order recalling his own men and putting them on alert, but if similar orders had been issued from American headquarters in Saigon they had not prompted extra precautions at the compound.

Men scrambled to their assigned positions. Adkisson stepped out of his quarters, having quickly dressed. Two mortars exploded overhead against a roof, and moments later two more struck in the courtyard. One ignited the gas tank of a Jeep, which became a ball of bright orange flame. The colonel stepped back inside. His first thought was that the soccer stadium across the street must be under attack and they were being struck by errant fire.[19] After those first mortars and the spasms of shooting by Doezema, it briefly grew quiet.

The roof had literally fallen in on Major Frank Breth, who crawled to his shower stall, clutching his rifle. A second blast sent down shattered ceiling tiles that opened a cut on his forehead. Partly buried and bleeding, Breth panicked for a moment until he realized he had not been badly hurt.[20]

Pulling himself out of the debris, he went into the courtyard, where he met Coolican. Both raced to inspect the perimeter, making sure all the defensive positions were manned and supplied with ammo. If another attack was coming, these were critical minutes. They directed a young lieutenant, Steve Lampo, to organize the marine advisers who were not ordinarily based at the compound into a makeshift company with a clear chain of command. Then Coolican ran to a bunker at the south end that had taken a mortar hit. Five chopper pilots inside had been wounded. He helped carry them on stretchers to the suddenly very busy dispensary. There was one doctor, Stephen Bernie, who was already hard at work. Coolican then joined Breth to continue making the rounds. Periodically, Doezema cut loose a stream of fire from his tower. Both towers were manned, but the threat seemed to be coming only from the front. Men had piled into the sandbag bunkers just outside the fencing. There was a large open field that stretched to the southeast, but otherwise the blocks outside the compound afforded an attacking force plenty of concealment. If the enemy came from several directions at once, the post could be easily overrun. They were hearing lots of shooting and explosions in the distance. It sounded as if all of Hue was under attack.

Doezema opened fire again. He was working hard when a rocket exploded against the tower's roof. His gun went silent.

Coolican ran to the tower and climbed up the narrow platform to reman the position. The grenade had sent shards of tin slashing straight down on Doezema. The marine captain found his friend badly sliced and bleeding heavily. One leg was nearly severed. When he tried to move Doezema, putting him over one shoulder to carry him down the ladder, the mangled leg prevented them from threading the opening. So Coolican laid him back down on the tower floor. He took the towel Doezema had draped around his neck and used it to tie a tourniquet. He then injected two shots of morphine, and with his combat knife cut through the remaining tissue attaching Doezema's leg. He then put him on his shoulders, threaded through the trapdoor, and carried him to the ground.

He put one hand on his friend's chest and leaned down. He wasn't sure, because of the morphine, that Doezema could even hear him.

"Frank, we are going to get you out of here," he said. "And when I get home I'm coming to see you in Kalamazoo. I've got to go."

He ran for one of the grenade launchers he had collected the previous day on his trip down to Hue, grabbed several bands of machine-gun ammo, and climbed back up the tower.

Breth made his way up to the roof of the main building on the north side. Below he could see enemy soldiers all over the streets a block away, and started squeezing off shots at them with his rifle. Guards in the bunker outside the main gate were shooting. They had plenty of targets. As Breth watched, too distant to shout a warning, one determined enemy soldier crossed the street, crept up behind the bunker, and dropped a grenade inside. The explosion silenced the bunker's guns. Breth started firing on automatic and threw down several grenades.

James Mueller had left his cot in such a hurry that he wound up in one of the inner sandbag bunkers in his underwear and shower sandals, wearing a flak vest and a helmet. To their north was a chain-link fence, and they were shooting at anything that moved outside it. One of their outward volleys touched off a flare in the barbed wire, which turned night into day at their corner of the compound. All around them there was shooting, explosions, flares, and the screams of the wounded. Mueller searched across the street for a target, and prayed.[21]

In a bunker at the southeast end of the compound, George W. Smith huddled in the dark trying to tell by sound what kinds of weapons they were up against. There were green tracers, a color associated with VC guns. A more experienced marine sorted out the sounds for him. This was all frightening and new to Smith, an army captain whose job was coordinating press releases and reporters' access to Adkisson and General Truong. He had not been in Hue for long. Staying in the bunker seemed like a bad idea. If the enemy got into the compound—and they were close—a grenade could kill them all. As he and the others discussed this, a rocket exploded very close and a man cried out in pain for a medic. Staying in the bunker also had its appeal. The matter was settled when they were ordered to move to specific defensive positions around the courtyard.[22]

Smith's was on the second floor in one of the compound's buildings with a marine captain. He had never been in combat, and, much to his surprise, he felt more exhilarated than fearful. He felt hyperalert, and worked at scanning the street and buildings below continually, as he had been taught in a training exercise at Fort Benning. It was still dark, and he saw no movement.

In fact, after the flurry of initial attacks, the enemy seemed to have backed off. The Americans knew it couldn't last—but it did. It amazed

Coolican, who could see how vulnerable they were. But he took advantage of the lull to turn the tower over to others and climbed back down to raise Phu Bai on the radio. For the time being, he told the command center there, the compound was secure. They needed help, but there was no immediate crisis. More urgent was the need to get some of the wounded men out, like Doezema. He wasn't going to make it if he didn't get to a hospital. Could they get a medevac chopper in? He was advised to keep checking back. With surprise attacks throughout the region, choppers were in short supply. One was promised as soon as it became available. He set to work finding a place for it to land. The compound itself was out. There was not enough room. He found a city map. Just two blocks north, on the south bank of the Huong, just east of the Truong Tien Bridge, was the boat landing. Between it and Le Loi Street was Doc Lao Park, a nice wide, flat space. The problem was that they had seen a lot of the enemy in the buildings and streets just outside. Could they safely move the wounded there?

Coolican didn't know what was going on beyond their immediate neighborhood, but there had been a lot of shooting. Some of the Americans scattered around the city, like those at the radio station, had called in desperate for help. If there were that many NVA and VC out there, where were they? Why were they not hitting the compound harder? It was the only American base of any consequence in the city.

The truth is that Lieutenant Hoang's overextended battalion, which had occupied the triangle with such ease, didn't dare. Two support battalions had failed to show up. One battalion had stumbled into a fiercely defended Montagnard post southwest of the city and was tied up there; it wouldn't arrive until sunrise. Another battalion had gotten lost. Success had been so rapid that Hoang had been forced to leave men behind to hold all the key positions they'd taken. With too few to launch a major assault on the compound, he moved his men into buildings and rooftops around it to set up firing positions. He saw no need to hurry. The whole point of the city invasion was to spark a citizen uprising. If that happened—and they would know soon enough—what hope would these surrounded Americans have? [23]

The standoff held until daylight, when much of the shooting around the city had died down. There was still gunfire in the distance to the north, but in the neighborhoods around the compound it had stopped.

The first day of Tet dawned gray, chilly, and wet over empty streets. The Americans who had spent a long night manning firing positions were tired, cold, and confused.

None of them knew what had happened. The city had been taken. Unlike most of the other assaults throughout the country, including a small abortive thrust into Saigon that would compel the world's attention for the next few days, Hue had fallen. General Truong and the heroic Hac Bao had held on, just barely, to Mang Ca, but the rest of the Citadel was in enemy hands. In the triangle, the Front owned the province headquarters, the radio station, the treasury, the post office, the hospital, the university, and every other major structure. They were near to finishing off the tough ARVN defenders at the prison, which, when it fell, would free thousands of inmates, many of them members or supporters of the VC. These men could be armed with weapons and ammo stored in warehouses the Front had seized.

Fred Drew, a wiry, towheaded army lieutenant with glasses, shared a bunker with three other men outside the compound on a narrow side street off its northeast corner. There had been no direct attacks on their position during the night, but they had received some gunfire from their left, in the direction of the main guard tower, and several times grenades had been hurled their way. No one in Drew's bunker had been hurt. They had returned fire, but most of the time couldn't see who was shooting at them. Drew had used a makeshift searchlight, a headlamp from a vehicle wired to a battery, to sweep the street, and had once or twice spotted someone standing up in the tall grass across the way firing toward the tower. They had shot at him. Now, as the gray sky brightened he saw bodies.

A boy stood up suddenly from the tall grass across the alley. He was drenched, standing in water up to his ankles. He looked to be about twelve. He held his hands behind his back.

Drew knew a little Vietnamese. He shouted across for the boy to raise his arms over his head. He did so. In one hand was a grenade. Drew told him to drop it, and when the boy didn't, the lieutenant fired a shot to his right. The boy then tossed the grenade off to his left, into the muddy water.

It exploded. The blast knocked the boy over, but he then stood up, dripping and apparently unhurt. It was an odd end to a frightening night.

3

A Mighty Python

THEY HAD COME on the run, some shouting party slogans, mostly men but also women, most of them young, by the thousands. They poured across the city's many bridges, through the fortress gates, swarmed up the wider avenues, and fanned out into side streets. Along the rivers and canals they came on sampans. The banks on the outskirts of the city were littered with the small plastic and bamboo rafts they had used to float their weapons and ammo across. They came on motorbikes and in Jeeps, the NVA in their clean, new green uniforms, the VC in khakis or worn black pajamas. All were armed.

Most believed they had come to stay. They were true believers, picturing the scenes in Hue playing out at the same time in cities throughout South Vietnam, the war's great and final act.

Liberation Radio, the voice of Hanoi, had broadcast throughout the country an appeal—and a warning:

> Compatriots, the hour to wash away our national dishonor and to liberate ourselves has come. Everybody must rise up and launch attacks against the hideouts of the Thieu-Ky clique [Ky was Vice President Nguyen Cao Ky] and topple the traitorous and sell-out government in various areas. We must set up at once a revolutionary government, build various revolutionary armed forces and patriotic organizations. Punish and arrest all the cruel lackeys of the Thieu-Ky clique and foreign nations, and help the revolutionary armed forces fulfill their duties.

We exhort the officers, soldiers, and the police forces of the Saigon regime to side with the ranks of the people and give their arms and ammunition to the revolutionary armed forces.

We exhort all those who have been going astray to quickly wake up. Those who recognize their faults and are willing to accomplish an exploit will be forgiven by the revolution. Those who willingly resist the revolution will be duly punished . . .

. . . Compatriots, we want to be delivered from slavery and from the dictatorial and ruthless regime. We do not want unemployment and bankruptcy. We do not want our national aspirations to be thwarted. We are determined to achieve our goals at any cost . . .

. . . Let's go forward together! The revolution will certainly be crowned with success! Long live an independent, democratic, peaceful, and neutral South Vietnam![24]

They had suffered losses at the Citadel gates and around Mang Ca, and some around the MACV compound, but otherwise the city had miraculously dropped into their hands. Le Tu Minh, their overall commander, estimated it had taken only about three hours. One VC battalion, making its way up Ly Thuong Kiet Street, which angled northwest through the center of the triangle, surprised six city policemen sitting in two cars. One of the cops, seeing uniformed men approaching, waved and called them over, evidently taking them for ARVN. The cops were placed in custody. They said most of their department had gone home for the holiday.[25]

The Front's primary command center was in the village of La Chu, to the northwest, but the field headquarters for Hue were set up in the ornate Tu Dam Pagoda, a famous seventeenth-century orange-brick, seven-story tower in the city's far southwest. The historical value of the pagoda meant it was unlikely to be bombed. Having taken the city, the leaders gathered there that morning to begin planning its defense. Despite their broad and rapid success, they foresaw trouble. In their excitement, the Front's legions had used prodigious amounts of ammo. They would need more fire discipline, and resupply became a big priority. Le sent an urgent request to Hanoi for more bullets. Having failed to take General Truong's relatively weak position with an all-out surprise attack, they were unlikely to do so now before he was reinforced. Likewise with the MACV compound, which by the end of the day would have doubled its defenses. Both were opportunities lost, but if things went well, they would not matter. He urged his men to press their attacks on the prison and to seize the Phu Cam Church, a Catholic center he said "would make trouble for us." He predicted that the American counterattack, when it came, would be difficult to withstand. Any plans for withdrawal, he advised, should be kept from the people, who then would be discouraged from rising up.[26]

Coming from this meeting, Major Than Trong Mot, the southern area commander, was invited to a celebratory feast at an elementary school by one of his battalions, flush with triumph. They had placed cafeteria tables end to end and covered them with white cloth. The long display was heaped with food "donated" by local residents. Another smaller table was filled with wine bottles that had also been "contributed."

Mot raised his walking stick and smashed at the wine bottles, berating his hosts and telling them to get back to their fighting positions.

"The upcoming fight will be your party!" he shouted.[27]

On the steps of the Ben Ngu Market, at the western edge of the triangle, Nguyen Dinh Bay (who went by the name Bay Khiem), the newly anointed head of security for southern Hue, made a speech to residents who had been assembled for the purpose. He was a middle-aged former railroad worker from Hue with a large family back in Hanoi, and he choked up as he pointed to the Alliance flag. He urged the people to help, to protect, and to support the liberation soldiers, and to assist with preparations for the coming American and *nguy* counterattack. He promised good things for those who did, and warned against failing to do so. He pleaded for them not to "disappoint the people." Propaganda leaflets were distributed. The crowd's response disappointed him. They listened quietly, as if receiving instructions. There was no cheering or applause. Then they returned to their homes.[28]

The South Vietnamese broadcast their own messages. Since the Front did not have planes or helicopters, even when they owned the ground they never owned the air above it. From a loudspeaker in an ARVN plane came the message that an enemy battalion had been defeated and its commander, Lieutenant Tang Van Mieu, captured.

Tang was standing with a group of his officers when the plane flew over. One reached out slowly and touched his arm, as if making sure he was still there. The others got a good laugh out of it.

Tang was, in fact, just arriving in the city with his battalion after getting lost early in the morning. He was just twenty-five, but he was a popular leader: charismatic, capable, and well-known. He had six years of experience fighting in Laos.[29] A tiny man, when gathered with his subordinate officers he looked like a boy giving orders to men. Although he and his troops had undergone weeks of political training, learning how to deal with city residents and to organize them into fighting units,[30] he had not helped create the broad design of the offensive. His thinking focused only on completing his mission. As he marched his men toward the city, he had been given three envelopes to be opened in sequence on appointed days. It was not until the last one, which he opened on Tet Eve, that he even knew their objective was the city. His battalion would play a central role in defending what the Front had just taken.

Radio broadcasts from Hanoi proclaimed the establishment of a new revolutionary government in Hue.

"Many people in Hue have come out openly to denounce the American-Thieu clique," the announcer said. Another broadcaster said, "We have started the fight, we are winning it, and we will completely win it." Clandestine broadcasts called on the population to rise up and join "the long-awaited general offensive."[31]

A broadcasting tower was erected at the post office inside the Citadel and speeches by cadre commissars blasted from it. In a northern accent that was distinct to Hue ears, one speaker proclaimed the city's "liberation." He warned that the Americans were "very stubborn," so to preserve their emancipation the people would have to rise up.[32]

There was enough positive response to these exhortations to thrill the poet/propagandist Nguyen Dac Xuan. He would later liken the army descending noiselessly from the hills to a "mighty python." He had arrived so soon after the breaching of Chanh Tay Gate that spent shells on the ground were hot under his sandals. He had expected to encounter heavy fire, perhaps even to be sacrificed, but no one shot at him as they entered. They passed through smoke and mist, past comrades killed in the initial assault, then past the bodies of ARVN soldiers. Xuan restrained an impulse to kneel and kiss the ground.

He saw signs of triumph everywhere. The streets teemed with armed fighters in their various uniforms. Those who were without new uniforms, or who had just stepped up to join the struggle, wrapped red bandannas around their heads or wore them loosely around their necks. Like him, most were young: Vietnam's youth had seized their fate, their future! For some of the VC veterans who had been in exile there were tearful reunions with their families and friends. The flag at Ngo Mon was especially meaningful to Xuan. The pole there had been a familiar reference point for him as a child. He had learned to tell the time of day by the position of the sun against it. Now the very sky seemed written with their victory.[33]

There was no sun this morning, just a brighter shade of gray. Xuan considered the new flag the first thing he'd encountered on Tet, and its portent could not have been more powerful. It foretold not just a great year but his nation's entire future. He was sure of it. His dreams were fulfilled. He would remember it as the happiest day of his young life. And he believed those feelings were widely shared. They stirred in the breast of every loyal soul in his liberated city. The strings of the puppet master had been cut! The people had triumphed!

He jumped into a commandeered ARVN Jeep with a comrade, and they drove toward his old neighborhood, which was near the Thuong Tu Gate. Eager to see his parents again, he anticipated a hero's welcome. Some who had known him were shocked to see him with the Front forces. As a member of the Buddhist movement years earlier, he had rejected Communism as forcefully as he did the Saigon government. He had been so devoted to his faith that at the height of the crackdown he had joined a "suicide squad." But Xuan in his shorts and black shirt and red armband, while still considering himself a Buddhist, was now first and foremost a disciple of Uncle Ho.[34] As he came closer to his old neighborhood he started to recognize some of the young men in the street. They wore red to show their support. He had not known them to be active in the revolution, but they now embraced him like a comrade. They had seen the light! One said there were rumors he had been killed, so it was as if he had returned from the dead. Xuan felt like he was dreaming.

But he also began to notice that the windows and doors of most homes were tightly shut. Some had hung flags to show their support for the victors—the North Vietnam red flag with a yellow star at the center, or Buddhist flags with six vertical stripes of blue, yellow, red, white, and orange to show their long-standing opposition to the Saigon regime—but there was little overt display. People seemed wary. The city's electricity and power had been cut off and water had to be collected from wells and springs, so there were people on the streets. But those Xuan saw avoided him and hurried about their business. The disciplined NVA battalions had already begun digging foxholes and trenches, and were erecting barricades across roadways. As they drove, Xuan used a megaphone to encourage people to come out. Those who had been working for the puppet regime would be welcomed and treated equally, he promised. If they had committed crimes and sincerely repented, they would be forgiven. They would be given a chance to perform heroic deeds to repay the people for their crimes. Xuan and his comrade stopped outside the royal palace, where the comrade gave a speech. A small crowd gathered. He said they would form a new government, and that the people would be allowed to choose their own leaders. He warned of the coming counterattack and encouraged residents to begin digging personal shelters under their homes.[35]

But Xuan felt in his bones that there would be no counterattack. The will of the people, once they were organized and instructed properly, would sweep everything before it. They would, in the coming days, shepherd forth such a wall of support that no power on earth could break it. Washington and Saigon with their armies and bombers and warships would simply back away in wonder. They would sue for peace.

4

An Afternoon of
Street Fighting

"Something is going on," said the marine who awakened Gordon
Batcheller early at Phu Bai.

Batcheller dressed quickly in the dark. He was annoyed. A marine
captain, he had recently assumed command of a company, Alpha 1/1,[36]
and like many young officers before him, he believed his unit was being
used all wrong. Batcheller was a striking man, a former football star
at Princeton University, tall and broad shouldered, with a shaved head
and a mustache that curled around the corners of his mouth. The son
of an admiral, he was a career marine. He was twenty-eight and this,
his first combat post, was the most important rung on that ladder.
He had volunteered for Vietnam, leaving his wife and two children in
Boston, and had then put in months as the battalion operations and
training officer, before getting his own company. But ever since taking
over a month earlier, he had been shuffled all around I Corps.[37] He and
his 160 men had mostly been up in Quang Tri, where they were used
to plug holes in defensive lines, guard bridges, and set up blockades
on roads or mountain passes. They rarely saw the enemy. Wherever
they landed, Batcheller would send small patrols to explore the surrounding terrain, looking for trouble, but they didn't know where to
look and were rarely in one place long enough to learn. Subjected to
the usual hit-and-run ambushes and booby traps, Batcheller felt the
enemy was just toying with him. He had been told they would stay
put in Quang Tri, which meant they could acquire some situational

awareness. Maybe do some damage. But no sooner had that prospect appeared than he was ordered to move again, this time to Phu Bai.

There was nothing at all wrong with Phu Bai, the big flat combat base off Highway 1 surrounded by rice paddies in all directions. His men were delighted. At Con Tien they had been sleeping in mud holes wrapped in ponchos. Here there were wooden hootches[38] with cots, warm food, and showers. Some days they even had cold milk and ice cream. In a few days, they would be driving up the road into Hue to guard the navy's busy boat ramp. The assignment was more appealing to the men than to their captain, because it promised to be a relatively quiet post in the middle of a city, which sounded like a better way to complete a one-year tour than pounding through marsh and jungle looking for trouble. They were promised a few days to rest up at the big air base during the first days of Tet, and then they'd drive north.

But the early morning attacks short-circuited that plan. The explosions at the Tam Thai tank base got everyone's attention, and there were reports of fighting all over the country. The first in their area arrived about the same time mortar rounds started crashing inside the base. These were scary but caused little damage. Just the usual negligible VC attacks. But the reports kept coming. Bad things were happening in the city itself.

A helicopter had been shot down over the Citadel that morning. It had crash-landed at Tay Loc. The crew survived with several wounded. They had taken shelter with the besieged ARVN ordnance company there, and when they called for help, Frederick Ferguson, flying a Huey, had jettisoned everything from his chopper that wasn't fastened down, then flown in low and fast over the river—swooping to the right at the flagpole and noting the surprising flag with the big yellow star. Under heavy fire he landed at the airstrip, barely able to fit his rotors in the small open space beside the downed crew's haven. On the ground only for seconds, he'd picked up the crew, and as he lifted back off nearly lost control. An exploding mortar spun the chopper halfway around. Ferguson kept it flying but raced away off course, heading over the west wall and disappointing his machine gunner, who had wanted to blast that new enemy flag on the way out. The chopper was riddled with mortar fragments and rifle rounds, and shook so violently that

Ferguson could no longer read his instruments. His transmission was shot and he had zero oil pressure when he narrowly cleared the barbed wire fencing at Phu Bai and skidded his wheezing machine to a stop in the sand.[39]

Clearly, Tet Mau Than was getting off to a fast start. The aptly named General Foster LaHue had only weeks earlier taken over at the base. He had been installed as commander of Task Force X-Ray, a newly created effort that combined the First and Fifth Marine Regiments[40] to muscle up the American military presence in the northernmost provinces. The chain of command went from Westmoreland to his deputy, General Abrams, and together they led five regional commands, with the northernmost, I Corps, under Lieutenant General Robert E. Cushman. In addition to Task Force X-Ray, Cushman's region had been bulked up by the deployment of the First Air Cavalry Division (the one to which Andy Westin belonged) to Camp Evans, under the command of Major General John J. Tolson. Both he and LaHue reported to Cushman.

LaHue had begun his career in 1942 as a platoon leader in the South Pacific, participating in island landings at New Georgia and Admiralty Islands, and had led a battalion in the Korean War. At fifty, he was a big player in the world's most powerful military, and accustomed to winning. He had every reason to believe that neither the NVA nor the VC could seriously challenge his marines—once they got up to speed, that is.

Task Force X-Ray was a work in progress. LaHue's permanent staff had yet to arrive, and with all the confusion over reassignments, some of the temporary ones had not received a paycheck in more than a month. There were lots of empty hootches—big parts of his command had yet to make it to Phu Bai. And while the base seemed resort-like to Batcheller's grunts, it was decidedly austere for a general's headquarters. On some days, lacking deliveries of fresh food, the mess hall just handed out C rations.[41] Task Force X-Ray was far from a well-oiled war-fighting machine. LaHue's intel operation was also less than ideal. When trouble came that morning, the general had only a sketchy notion of what was going on, but he was determined and confident he could regain the initiative with whatever forces were at hand.

Batcheller received an order to "saddle up" his company on trucks, pronto, and head south. So much for a few days of rest. They were to bring only essential gear. An ARVN unit on the way to Da Nang needed their help. John Ligato hadn't even had time to dry his socks. He was a private from South Philly who had gotten expelled from college for partying a little too heavily. Staring down the draft, he'd joined the marines after a long night of drinking shots with his buddies and had woken up with enlistment papers he had no memory of having signed. He'd been walking around with wet feet for days, so as soon as he got to a hootch he had taken off his boots, washed and wrung out his socks, and hung them up to dry. They were still moist. He was told he'd be back by noon, so he left them. He took only one bandolier of ammo.

They rolled out in darkness, a convoy of flatbed trucks filled with tired, disgruntled men, led and followed by two army Dusters: light armored vehicles with twin 40-mm guns that could fire hundreds of high-explosive rounds per minute.[42] The VC called them Fire Dragons because in action they appeared to be spitting flame. They also had two army M45 Quadmounts—the marines called them Quad-fifties—a standard two-ton truck with four .50-caliber machine guns inside a steel turret that could rotate a full circle and could fire an astonishing eighteen hundred rounds per minute. The men rode in "six-by-sixes," rugged six-wheeled trucks painted with green and brown splotches of camouflage, with a flat metal bed and removable wooden slats on both sides that offered little protection; the slats were there mostly to keep loads from rolling or bouncing off.

They drove for two hours in wet, cold darkness, and then stopped in the middle of nowhere. There was no sign of the needy ARVN unit. Batcheller wasn't even sure where he was. He had not been given a map.

Then his commanders in Phu Bai, in their wisdom, told him to turn around and head in the opposite direction, back through the base, and up Highway 1 through Hue to a point farther north, where they were to link up with an army unit. So they turned around and retraced their trip as morning dawned, eventually reentering the southern gate at Phu Bai. At about 8:30, more than four hours since they had been awakened to board the trucks and go south, they came barreling straight through the base and exited the north gate—confirming suspicion inside the trucks that no one in charge had a clue. Batcheller wasn't sure exactly where he was supposed to go, either, but he figured the South China

Sea was just a few miles east. If he kept that off his right shoulder they'd be going in the correct direction. When they got wherever it was they were supposed to go, he thought, somebody would certainly have a map.

Mike Anderegg was already farther up Highway 1. He was driving a Patton flame tank,[43] a Zippo,[44] which instead of a 90-mm gun mounted on the front had a powerful flamethrower. With him were another Zippo and two gun-mounted Pattons. They were on their way to the boat ramp in Hue, where they were supposed to be loaded onto boats and shipped north. Anderegg, an eighteen-year-old lance corporal from Ann Arbor, Michigan, had been stuck at Phu Bai for months, recovering from malaria and dysentery. When he wasn't convalescing, he'd mastered the art of building walls with sandbags, diving for cover when mortars rained. He had seen little of Vietnam, much less combat. He was glad to be going anywhere.

But as the tanks approached the southern tip of the triangle, they came upon the column of incinerated ARVN tanks just outside Tam Thai. The vehicles were just off the road. It was a sobering sight for the American, particularly the charred torso on the front end of one ARVN tank. They stopped to take it in and to consider their next step. A marine embarkation officer, Lieutenant Colonel Ed LaMontagne, who had hitched a ride with them, was in charge by default. He didn't like the look of those destroyed tanks, and had about decided to play it safe and return to Phu Bai when Batcheller's convoy rolled up. The officers consulted with LaHue's command center and were given yet another new, joint destination. They were now to proceed to the MACV compound, which was under siege. LaMontagne said he knew where it was.

They started north again, more cautiously now. Batcheller stood behind the turret on one of the tanks. He saw what appeared to be enemy soldiers in the distance moving parallel to the road. Tanks were vulnerable unless surrounded by infantry to prevent attackers from getting too close, so he ordered his men off the trucks—which offered little cover anyway. In the gray drizzle, lines of helmeted men in flak jackets and dirty green fatigues—the marines insisted on calling them "utilities"—began walking alongside, behind, and in front of the tanks. The captain swiftly changed his mind when several of them were hit by sniper fire. In the vehicles, they could move faster. So they reboarded the trucks. Some climbed onto the tanks, their guns pointed out. The convoy sped up.

A short distance ahead was the An Cuu Bridge. It had big holes in it from the satchel charges that had failed to bring it down. They drove across warily, and a short distance farther, in the city now, they approached a cluster of two-story houses built close to the road on both sides. It reminded Batcheller of a town in an old Western movie. They raced through, guns blazing, and were surprised when nearly the same volume of fire came back at them.

A rocket exploded against Batcheller's tank and he felt a stinging spray of shrapnel. When they reached the end of the gauntlet, his radioman, who had been right next to him, was gone. He must have been blown off. Leaning across the turret was one of his navy corpsmen,[45] who in addition to other wounds was missing both of his legs at the knees. His lower limbs had been sliced away cleanly by something hot enough to have cauterized the wounds, because they were not bleeding, but the man was dead. There were downed marines scattered behind on the road, and others trying to drag them to safety. One was missing both arms and both legs, still alive and screaming.

One of the marines on the street, James Brockwell, felt as if he had been hit with a large baseball bat. The impact knocked him over backward. When he checked himself, he found wounds on the sides of his legs, in his neck, and in his right arm.

"Can you go on?" Batcheller shouted to him.

"Yes," said Brockwell. He wondered, *What choice do I have?* Minutes later he got dizzy and fainted.[46]

Once they were clear of the gauntlet, the gunfire eased and the men again dismounted and spread out. More slowly, they advanced toward a big traffic circle. On the approach to it, Highway 1 straightened into a ridge about eight feet high bordered on both sides by a row of ornamental trees. The road itself was completely exposed, but there was cover downhill to either side, which was a good thing so long as you knew which way you were likely to be shot at. Flat green rice paddies stretched to the east and west. They saw no threats in either direction. So they walked on. Batcheller was behind the lead tank.

There was an Esso gas station on the left side of the traffic circle, and far beyond that, off in a field, a row of redbrick, two-story houses.

Arrayed around the circle were six ARVN tanks and an armored personnel carrier, remnants of the stray ARVN column. All of them were
empty. Most were badly damaged, but one was still running. Jack Rushing and Terry Strassburg climbed in.

"Can you drive a tank?" Strassburg asked Rushing.

"Hell, I can drive anything with a steering wheel," Rushing said, but
their sergeant ordered them out.

They were still in the traffic circle when shooting started from all
sides. A man walking behind Batcheller fell, clutching his leg, and the
captain did exactly what he had been trained not to do. Instead of
waiting to see where the shots came from and directing suppressing
fire, he ran directly to the downed man. He took hold of the collar
of his flak jacket and pulled him toward the closest tree. Then came
another burst of fire, killing the wounded man and knocking the captain off his feet.

He tumbled from the impact, and came to rest at the base of the tree,
tangled in a coil of barbed wire. He had been hit with three rounds in
his right arm and leg. The leg wound was the worst. A bullet had gone
straight through the leg, breaking his femur and leaving a great open
gash. Batcheller stared at the mangled interior of his limb. He saw no
squirting blood, but given the size of the hole he feared he would bleed
out quickly. His right forearm was sliced open from wrist to elbow
and was limp. Tangled in the wire, he could not move. He shouted to
his men to stay clear. He didn't want them making the same mistake.

A corpsman already had done that. Mike Fitzgerald of Dubuque,
Iowa, twenty-two, with a blond flattop crew cut and glasses in thick
plastic frames, was kneeling in the road, his butt back on his heels,
dead but still upright, a hole in his forehead.

Batcheller bellowed to his gunnery sergeant, John Canley, that Canley was now in command. Then it occurred to him there was nothing
more for him to do. He looked up through the tree branches at the
gray morning sky and prayed.

"Alpha Six [the company commander] is down," was the word spread
among the men strung out along the road. "Alpha Seven [Canley] is up!"

Most of the shooting was coming from the houses in the field, but
there were muzzle flashes in the rice paddies on either side, too. The
same force that had attacked them through the gauntlet had apparently

fanned out and moved up, and was now pressing from both sides. The Dusters and Quad-fifties were blasting away, but there were too many targets. The men of the Third Platoon were all flattened to the ground. Alfredo "Freddy" Gonzalez, a wiry twenty-one-year-old Texas sergeant, their acting platoon leader, stood beside a tree looking down at them. He signaled that they were going to charge.

Donald Floyd thought, *Oh, shit, I'm gonna die right here.* His rifle had jammed. He slammed the butt against the ground until the round ejected. Bill Purcell, a nineteen-year-old machine gunner, was so scared he felt his bowels about to give way.

The houses sheltering the enemy were to their left. Gonzalez was not going to charge straight at them; he wanted his men to get to the ditch on the far side of the road and then sprint north until they were outside the sweep of the machine guns. Then they could reach the houses' north flank by running across the field. Getting to the right side of the road and moving up would be the trickiest part. It seemed suicidal to Dan Winkel, who felt that just lifting his head at that point was enough to get him killed.

Gunny Canley joined them for the charge. He challenged them: "Do you want to live forever?"

Rushing thought, *In fact, yes!* But on Gonzalez's count of three, he and the other men got up and started running. Crossing the elevated road, Winkel felt like a duck in a carnival shooting gallery. When they got across and down the far side they were running in muddy water, which made for slow going. Purcell's boots sank deep with each step. When one of Rushing's legs sank up to the knee, he fell. Beside him Marty Marquez and Strassburg also went down. The two corporals faced each other, with Marquez between them, gone. He had been shot in the temple.

"We can't do anything for him," said Purcell.

Rushing shot and killed one NVA soldier off to his left, and then crawled to another downed marine, Donald Moore, who had been shot five times, including through both feet.

"Get the hell away from me," Moore said. "If they think I'm alive they'll shoot me again." [47]

Then Winkel was hit. He was running and then he went down. It felt as though someone had hit his right leg with a club. He splashed down into the gulley and, unable to stand, watched those still running leave him.

Despite these losses, fire from the Quad-fifties and the Dusters enabled most of Gonzalez's platoon to get across the field and around to the side of the houses. The sergeant was the first to enter the closest structure, and his squad must have taken the gunners inside by surprise, because he emerged with an armful of rifles and had a big grin on his face.

At this point, more than half of Alpha Company was dead or wounded. Anderegg watched out of the hatch of his tank in shock as marines fell to the left and the right. The tanks were stuck. If they rolled forward or backward, they would run over men on the road. The two machine guns on Anderegg's were kicking up a racket.

Then came help. From behind, in a Jeep, came Lieutenant Colonel Marcus Gravel, their battalion commander, with his operations officer, Major Walter Murphy; and a Catholic navy chaplain, Richard Lyons. Behind them was another long convoy of trucks. Gravel had thrown it together and headed north after hearing still more alarming reports from Hue.

In fact, not long after Batcheller's company had roared back through the base, it was dawning on the Task Force X-Ray command that this episode involved something more than isolated raiding parties. With Batcheller already on his way up to the compound, Gravel figured he and another company of marines ought to follow and proceed to reinforce General Truong in the Citadel. And just then, conveniently enough, Captain Chuck Meadows had walked in.

Meadows's Golf Company was not part of Gravel's command—it belonged to the Second Battalion, Fifth Marine Regiment, under the command of Lieutenant Colonel Ernie Cheatham—but it was available. Golf's 160 marines were returning from a night on a hilltop outside the base. Once the mortars started coming down, they had spent hours spotting firing positions and calling in artillery. They also did some patrolling in force, but, typically, had found nothing. Meadows's men had stripped off their gear and were headed for breakfast and then some rest while their captain set off to report in. He was meeting Gravel for the first time.

The colonel was a strikingly handsome man, with dark hair slightly graying at the temples, who carried himself with quiet dignity. There were plenty of marine officers who made a show of their strength. Cheerfully profane with crushing handshakes, they treated their own men and everyone else roughly. But this was not Gravel. He was kindly, religious—very Catholic—and sensitive. He expressed deep affection for his men. He would say, "Whenever one of my marines gets a scratch, I bleed." Unlike most battalion commanders, he made it a point to know each of their names—quite a challenge with nearly eight hundred under constant rotation. Gravel had held staff positions most of his career. First Battalion was his chance to command troops in combat.

The two officers shook hands, and Gravel said, "Chuck, I want you to get your company on these trucks." He gestured to the empty trucks lined up outside. "We are going up to Hue. We'll be back by this afternoon."

Even though they had been out all night, Meadows was happy to comply. The twenty-seven-year-old captain had sought command of an infantry company, and you don't do that without an appetite for combat. A native of Beaverton, Oregon, he had graduated from Oregon State University and planned to make the marines a career. He was disappointed on his first Vietnam tour in 1965 when he'd seen little action. Now, with his own company, he was eager to be put to use. His ears stuck out on either side of his high-and-tight and he wore US Marine Corps–issued glasses in thick black plastic frames. In his wallet, he carried a formal portrait of his wife, Missy, and daughter, Marianne, both wearing pink. The politics of the war didn't concern him at all. He was a marine; there was a war on.

His men took the news well. They had expected to be sent south, where there was heavy fighting. Instead they were going to the city, which sounded like a better option. After weeks in the bush they were going back to civilization! Hue was known to be a center for good food and pretty girls. There was some VC skirmish to put down, but after that they might have some time to look around. Gravel also seemed to consider the mission something of a jaunt. He collected his friend Murphy, a popular officer from Staten Island, a Wagner College grad, who had been a demolitions instructor at Quantico before volunteering for Vietnam; and Lyons, a Jesuit priest, asking, "You want to go to Hue for an afternoon of street fighting?"

Meadows told his men to travel light. Soon out of the gate he noticed something fishy. There were no people moving on Highway 1. Ordinarily during Tet the road by that time of morning was busy with people on bikes, or walking. There weren't even any chickens. Then they came across the burned-out ARVN tanks. Farther up there was blood on the road and bodies on the street where Batcheller's convoy had run the gauntlet. There was a dead woman stretched out on the side of the road already stiffened with rigor mortis, one hand reaching up.

They came to an abrupt halt when they caught up to Alpha Company under fire, stalled on the exposed road. Gravel's Jeep skidded crosswise, and everyone dived for cover. As Meadows leaped from his truck he saw a muzzle flash from a machine gun set against a low wall across a cane field. He arranged his men in the ditch on the far side of the road, and pointed out the position to his machine gunner. Then he jogged ahead to see what was going on.

Everywhere were the crack and pop of gunfire. The Dusters and Quad-fifties were still roaring. Most of the enemy fire seemed to be coming from the southwest. There were dead and wounded scattered about, some on the road and others off to the sides. As Meadows's company moved up to join the fight, Lyons went to work. He crawled in the mud at the bottom of the roadside ditch toward the downed men, stopping to offer solace and, in some cases, last rites. Up on the road it was still treacherous. When Lyons saw Batcheller, curled up and tangled at the base of a tree, badly wounded, he forgot his spiritual mission and lifted a discarded rifle. He began crawling toward the wounded captain, firing on automatic into the opposite rice paddy. Batcheller waved him back, warning, "You'll just draw more fire!"

Gravel sent his driver back for the Jeep and told him to move it up alongside the downed captain. This enabled four marines to finally reach him. Corpsman Michael Ker was horrified to see his friend Fitzgerald kneeling upright on the road with a hole in his head. He and John Ligato, the marine who'd left his socks behind, and two others knelt alongside the big captain and stretched out a poncho. Batcheller handed Ker his combat knife.

"Use this," he told Ker. "I'm not going to be needing it."

Ker cut the fabric of the captain's clothes to free him from the wire's barbs, and then they eased him onto the poncho, which curved with his weight. Batcheller felt sick to his stomach as his right leg sagged weirdly. It was now just a ruptured sack of blood and bone.

Ligato saw Batcheller go white and close his eyes. He thought the captain was dying. They lifted him and ran. One of the men buckled. A round had passed straight through his calf.

"Do not drop me!" Batcheller shouted.

Dying, but still giving orders, thought Ligato.

"Are you okay?" Ligato asked the marine who'd been hit.

"Yeah, I can make it," he said.

They set Batcheller down behind Gravel's Jeep, and Ker splinted the captain's right leg with a shovel.

Meadows took advantage of covering fire to race into the Esso station at the roundabout. He found a city map on a wall inside and grabbed it.

Enemy soldiers could be seen moving across the road behind them, and, worried that they might close it off, Gravel ordered all the wounded to be put on one truck, and all of the dead on another. Bloody men torn to pieces, missing limbs, conscious or just barely conscious, were hastily loaded. Gunny Canley, who had a shrapnel wound to his face, arrived carrying Patrick Fraleigh, a private whom he had dragged to cover, shielding him partly with his own body. He went to work packing Fraleigh's wounds, but despite his best efforts, the young man stopped breathing. "Good-bye, marine," Canley said. He wrapped him in a poncho and placed him on the truck with the other dead. One marine was shot in the ankle as he was helping to load the wounded, so he hopped in, too.

Canley stood outside the truck calmly looking around.

"Gunny, get down!" Ker told him. "You're going to get hit!"

"By the time I get down, I'll already be hit," he said. "So I may as well stand up here and see what the hell is going on."

As the trucks turned around, the tank driver immediately behind them, Anderegg, peeked around his vision block, the steel plate that protected him, and saw blood spilling thickly out of its back end as if it were being poured from a milk can. He felt his stomach turn. Then the commander of the tank in front of him, who had been up in the cupola with the upper half of his body exposed, was shot through the neck. Anderegg's tank swirled its turret in the direction of a Catholic shrine to their left, where they thought the shot had originated, and its machine gun blasted the shrine to rubble.

After making the U-turn, the two trucks made a run for it. When they barreled back through the gauntlet, the passengers who could still shoot fired on automatic. The battle was just beginning, but it was already over for Batcheller and many of the men he had led out of Phu Bai just an hour earlier. Every bump and turn of the drive was agonizing, and he expected at any moment they would be hit.

Gravel and Meadows watched the two trucks disappear into the distance southward. They were in a bigger fight than they had anticipated. Checking the gas station map, they saw that the MACV compound was close. Up ahead were the first urban blocks of Hue. But in the distance they could also see many uniformed enemy soldiers, men with helmets and weapons. For all his time in Vietnam, Meadows had only rarely laid eyes on even a single NVA or VC fighter. Those he had seen looked ragged, poorly dressed, and poorly armed. These were well equipped and clearly had plenty of ammo, because they were using it at a good clip.

As the convoy started forward once more, the level of resistance stiffened. One of the tanks took a direct hit, and when Ker and another marine, Jimmy Cook, climbed up to pull out wounded crew members, a shell nearly severed Cook's arm and sent him crashing to the road. One of his squad mates tied a tourniquet, strapped the limp appendage to his chest, and placed him on a tank.

Gravel kept them moving forward. He abandoned his Jeep—it made him too much of a target—and then, worried that the enemy would get its radio, he directed one of the Pattons to destroy it. A 90-mm shell weighed almost forty pounds and stood three feet high. One round exploded the Jeep.

As they approached a large intersection, the shooting suddenly surged. Men once more dived behind the tanks and trucks and off the road. An enemy machine gun was in a bunker on the right side of the road, which gave it complete command of the intersection. Two platoons were trapped in a gully, unable to move.

One of the men there, the sockless private from South Philly, John Ligato, figured he was dead. Rounds hit the water around him in the ditch and sent up sprays. He flattened himself farther into the mud, his bare feet cold and soaked inside his boots. A primal fear took hold. He thought there was nothing that could train men for this: the noise, the blood, the screams, the shattered bodies, the roaring of guns on all sides. He made himself still and small. Every inner alarm screamed, *Flee!* But where? Movement meant death. Even if he got lucky at first, raising himself, where would he go? To the east and back was the only conceivable retreat, but that meant standing up exposed in an open rice paddy—no cover for miles.

But at the same time, he saw something extraordinary. Some men still functioned. Canley and Gonzalez were creeping toward the machine gun. It seemed impossible for them not to be hit. Freddy Gonzalez in particular amazed him. How could you have predicted this about him? He was a wiry, cheerful, scrappy Texicano, who despite his small stature had played lineman for his high school football team. He had a strut Ligato had always considered a macho put-on, but it was clearly something more. He and Canley seemed immune to fear. During the earlier charge, Ligato had seen Canley pick up Fraleigh—both of them under heavy fire—and calmly drape him on his shoulders and carry him to safety. Ligato marveled, *How could anyone do these things?*[48] When Gonzalez and Canley were close enough to the machine gun they called for suppressing fire and then *stood* and hurled grenades. At the blast, they charged, firing their rifles on automatic, silencing the gun. Ligato would deeply admire both men for the rest of his life.

Still, the convoy was stuck. There was an enemy spotter and machine gun in the spire of a Catholic church to the west just raining fire down on them. Scattered off the road, Alpha and Golf companies did not dare remount the vehicles, but it was also too dangerous to stay where they were. One of the tanks slowly aimed its gun and took one shot, which removed the top of the spire. The tanks had been forbidden to fire in the city without permission. After placing the shot, the commander, Eddie Dailey, calmly got on the radio and asked if he might shoot at the spire. Permission was denied. He shrugged. His crew members were impressed.

LaMontagne, who recognized the increasingly urban streets and had been to the MACV compound before, recommended to Gravel that he be allowed to take two of the tanks and sprint ahead. They could bring back help.

A cheer went up inside the compound when LaMontagne and the tanks sped through the front gate. It was as if the cavalry had just ridden over the hill. But as he quickly explained to the compound's commander, Adkisson, it was the rescuers who needed rescuing.

Jim Coolican, Frank Breth, and Fred Drew commandeered trucks and with hastily recruited volunteers raced back down Highway 1 with LaMontagne, taking heavy fire as they went. It wasn't far to where Gravel and Meadows and the remnants of Alpha and Golf were pinned down. A big metal pipe ran under the road between the culverts to either side, where many of them had taken shelter. The additional suppressing fire enabled the marines to move again. The able-bodied heaved their dead and wounded aboard the vehicles and then climbed up themselves. Dan Winkel was among those pulled out of the ditch and thrown into the back of the truck. On the short drive to the compound they saw many bodies to the west of the road, where they had been directing most of their fire. It suggested an almost inexhaustible number of enemy soldiers, since shooting from that direction had hardly slowed. The convoy limped through the front gate of the compound, the shattered remains of the two convoys that had left Phu Bai hours earlier.

Meanwhile, back at Task Force X-Ray's headquarters, the two trucks Gravel sent back were also arriving. Captain Batcheller was off-loaded with the others at the base hospital, and then lost consciousness.[49] The marine whom Gunny Canley had tried to rescue, Patrick Fraleigh, was placed with the other dead outside the morgue, until an orderly happened by and the corpse spoke up.

"Good afternoon, marine," Fraleigh said.

"We've got a live one!" the man screamed, and Fraleigh was hurried into surgery.[50]

It was just past three in the afternoon. The bloodied marines of Alpha and Golf had seen more combat than any of them had ever before encountered in Vietnam. Bob Lauver, the army sergeant commanding one of the Quad-fifties, had expended ten thousand rounds. He had to replace the barrels on several of his guns.

And their day wasn't over.

An Idiotic Mission

THE TASK FORCE X-Ray commander at Phu Bai still did not get it. His frame of reference for enemy encounters did not include anything like this. Sightings of even company-size elements of NVA or VC, much less battalions or whole regiments, were so rare as to be almost mythical. And hit-and-run, by small bands of dead-end VC commandos, was the message they were getting from all over the country; news had also broken about a daring and predictably futile such attack on the US embassy in the heart of Saigon. So as the day wore on, General LaHue was increasingly disappointed to learn that the two rifle companies he'd dispatched to Hue had failed to bring the city back under control.

Marines do not hesitate in combat. If the Corps has a defining philosophy, that's it. In war, when the enemy is foolish enough to show himself, marines go right at him and kill him, risks be damned. LaHue wanted his troops to move. When Captain Coolican, after things had settled down around the compound—called to request air and artillery strikes—the thing he was trained to do for his Hac Bao unit—he was told, rather stingingly, that he was overreacting.

The general apparently saw no reason on earth why the more than four hundred men in that compound—reinforced now with well over three hundred fully armed US Marines accompanied by four Patton tanks and an assortment of ARVN armor, two Dusters, and two Quad-fifties, all of it being led by a certified marine lieutenant colonel—should not be able to flatten anything between them and the fucking

Citadel and rescue poor General Truong. What was needed was not more firepower, but a kick in the ass! So that's what he delivered. Gravel was instructed to do what he had been sent to do.

And he was willing, if mortified. The younger officers around him thought the order was crazy. Colonel Adkisson told him it was madness. The compound commander, a West Point graduate and a World War II combat veteran, believed his position was still in jeopardy. It was surrounded and apparently outnumbered, although no one knew for sure how many enemy soldiers were out there. He was not about to deplete its defenses to launch an attack on the Citadel.

Inside the sandbag bunker that served as a command post in the courtyard, Gravel and Adkisson, the ranking marine and army officers, had it out. Adkisson, a tall, stately looking officer with graying hair, told the marine colonel that his superiors with Task Force X-Ray had no grasp of the situation. Gravel knew this was true. No one at headquarters understood. His fight up Highway 1 had convinced him that there were a lot more enemy in the city than they imagined. But this was his first experience in combat—something he had trained for throughout his entire career—and, no doubt mindful of the toxic label of timidity under fire, he was loath to disobey a direct order, even when he considered it to be idiotic.[51]

Adkisson said Gravel was on his own. *His* men were going nowhere.

In their defense, the commanders at Phu Bai had gotten mixed messages. At one point, Adkisson himself had reassured them the Citadel was secure,[52] a report that found its way into an Armed Forces Radio broadcast later that day, slightly embellished: Hue, it reported, was free of enemy activity. This both astonished and amused the Americans huddled in the encircled compound. The truth was that no one knew exactly what was going on in the city, except that there seemed to be enemy forces everywhere.

But whatever awaited outside the compound, it had backed off for the time being. When Coolican got word that the medevac choppers he requested were inbound, he recruited Major Murphy and Gunny Canley and other marines from Alpha Company, and with two tanks running interference they carried the wounded two blocks to the south bank of the Huong. They found two more ARVN tanks there, with crews, part of the column that had failed to reach General Truong earlier in the day. The crews had locked themselves inside.

Once the marines had secured a decent perimeter, a navy Sea Knight chopper[53] landed, off-loading ammo and carrying away the worst of the wounded, including Doezema. A second chopper then landed and did the same.

After the second chopper lifted off, Murphy, Coolican, Canley, Breth, and a few other officers assembled behind one of the tanks to discuss how to more permanently secure the spot, at which point there was a loud blast from across the river. They turned in time to see a large black missile bearing toward them. It happened too fast for any of them to react, but slowly enough—the velocity suggested an older weapon—for them to see the rocket approach and then flash straight through them, chest-high, hitting no one, before exploding against the wall of a building across the street and taking an impressive bite out of it. A spasm of shooting erupted, with the Americans firing across the river in the general direction of the blast and the enemy shooting back. Neither side was close enough to do much damage, and the Front troops were shooting from inside buildings and behind walls. It was more a display, or a venting. Breth and one of his men climbed to the turrets of the ARVN tanks and manned the machine guns. Both had full boxes of ammo. Breth aimed at the opposite bank and could see the gun's effect about the time his ammo ran out. He hammered on the tank hatch, assuming there was more ammo inside, but the crew still refused to open it.

Drawn by the heavy fire, two US Navy patrol boats led by Jerry Irvine, a petty officer, sped down the river from the east and raked the north bank with machine guns. This provided cover for a third chopper to land and carry off the last of the severely wounded.

It was now late afternoon. The Americans had slightly expanded their toehold in southern Hue. They owned the compound, and this small space around the southern end of Truong Tien Bridge. It included the boat ramp, and their newly established LZ. Both positions would be critically important in the days ahead. The Americans also had a vital radio relay center in a nondescript building across the street from the compound, two blocks south, that the Front in all its careful planning had overlooked. It enabled uninterrupted and encrypted communications between General Truong in the Citadel, the compound, and Phu Bai. Marines began digging trenches and foxholes around the ramp and LZ. Tanks aimed their guns north, but there was no enemy to be seen across the river; there were just buildings and a park and the high, forbidding walls of the fortress.

Gravel had his orders to move. He was to bail out the Hac Bao platoon defending the prison, seven blocks west, and send another force across the Truong Tien Bridge and into the Citadel to help General Truong.

Gravel asked Coolican to lead the prison mission.

"Why would you want to do that?" the captain asked.

Gravel said it had to be done.

"I can guarantee you that the NVA now has the jail," Coolican told him.[54] "One of my platoon commanders [the Hac Bao unit dispatched there earlier] was on the radio with me. He told me they got hit with two attacks, that they were out of ammo, and that the NVA was getting ready to hit him again. He said after he got off with me he was going to destroy the radio. The NVA have the jail. So why would we go?"

"Because we're supposed to," said Gravel.

"Then tell me what's going to happen when I get down there and get cut off? Who is going to come and get me?"

Gravel had no answer. He appeared to Coolican to be floundering, somewhat undone by his experiences earlier that day. He had acted decisively under fire, but now he was struggling.

"Colonel," Coolican advised. "This is not a good idea."

"We have to."

"No, we do not."

"I am ordered to do it."

"Well, then, tell them you can't go, for chrissakes!" said Coolican.

Gravel tried. He got involved in a heated exchange on the phone with one of LaHue's staff officers. Any small American unit that strayed more than two blocks from the compound was in danger of being cut off and destroyed. They had no idea what kind of enemy strength there was farther out—across the bridge or inside the fortress. They knew the enemy was strong enough to have General Truong trapped and in trouble. To attempt two head-on assaults into the unknown was crazy. Gravel's protests were passed up the chain. He received a one-word response: "Proceed."

The prison mission was simply dropped. Coolican wasn't going to do it. Captain Meadows's company, on the other hand, would attempt the other. It meant crossing the bridge and trying to enter the fortress at the southeast corner, Thuong Tu Gate.

Gravel, Meadows, and Meadows's company rolled up in trucks to the park. To those who had witnessed the massed fire on the north bank, trying to cross the bridge seemed suicidal. They had seen everything from small arms to that big black shell, likely fired from a 57-mm recoilless rifle (a WWII-era rocket launcher usually mounted on a tripod). There was at least one heavy machine gun in a pit at the north end of the bridge. The Front was not contesting the bridge's south end, but it was poised to hammer anyone or anything that tried to cross.

As hastily drawn, the plan called for two platoons of Meadows's men, about one hundred marines, to cross the bridge behind a tank, and destroy the machine-gun pit. The remainder of the company would follow in trucks as the lead platoons pushed ahead and to the left along Tran Hung Dao Street, which paralleled the river on the north side. That would take them to Thuong Tu Gate Road, which led up to the gate itself. Once inside, the same road ran straight up to Mang Ca. On the map it looked like a clean shot, less than a mile of paved road.

But the plan began to unravel before it started. The enemy had attempted to blow up the bridge's central span that morning, and failed, but the explosions had left it badly damaged. There were holes in the span that opened straight down to the water. Gravel was worried that it would no longer support a Patton. He tried to enlist the smaller ARVN tanks, but the crews refused to budge. So Golf Company would have to cross on foot.

With the massed tanks and guns providing covering fire, Meadows and his men set off at a crouched trot. The captain went with his second platoon. The bridge crowned at the center, so on the upslope they could see only sky and the top of the gray fortress's southern ramparts. High above them to their left, above the setting sun, Meadows noticed for the first time the yellow star and blue and red stripes of the giant Alliance flag. The enemy withheld fire until the bulk of both platoons had crested the midpoint, and then started shooting. Bullets pinged off the steel superstructure and cracked against the pavement. Grenades skipped off the concrete and exploded, knocking down clusters of men. Ten of those in the lead platoon fell immediately, two of them dead; one marine was shot in the head, which appeared to just explode. The other marines kept moving.

Fred Drew and John Ligato watched this unfold from the south bank, aghast. Whose idea had it been? Fire from their distant position was nearly useless, but they blasted away.

A squad led by Barney Barnes was the first to make it all the way to the other side. These men set up a machine gun to exchange fire with the enemy bunker, but their gunner was immediately shot and killed. Another of the men, Lester Tully, got close enough to the bunker to hurl a grenade. It was an extraordinary throw, and the explosion silenced the gun.

Behind them, corpsman John Higgins encountered his first sucking chest wound. The marine he had stooped to help had a hole on the left side of his chest, which bubbled every time he breathed. Higgins rolled him over and felt for an exit wound on his back. There was none. He took out one of his C-ration packs, used the cellophane wrapper, smeared it with an antibiotic ointment, pressed it over the chest hole, and then wrapped a bandage around the man's torso as tightly as he could.[55]

Leaving some of his lead platoon to hold the north end of the bridge, Meadows sent Lieutenant Mike McNeil with the remainder into buildings across the street. It was a commercial district. There was a movie theater advertising the Italian Western *Tempo di Massacro* (*Massacre Time*)—a title that struck Meadows as both macabre and apt. For a few moments, the firing stopped.

Trailing Meadows's advance, Major Murphy came across the bridge with Father Lyons and more men. Both men—the officer and the priest—were a steadying influence. They were older than the platoon and company commanders, and projected an invaluable sense of calm and confidence under fire. The group they led was under heavy fire from buildings and bunkers on the land between the river and the Citadel. Five Front soldiers in the bunker Tully had destroyed had been mangled by the blast. One was still breathing, but when a corporal who spoke Vietnamese tried to question him, he died. The wounded and dead Americans on the bridge were lifted to a truck, and Father Lyons accompanied them back across the bridge.

Meadows pressed on west, toward the gate road. It was now late afternoon, and the sun was in their eyes. When they reached the road and turned the corner they came under heavy fire from the top of the south wall—rockets, grenades, machine guns, and small arms. The lead men tried to take cover in buildings on both sides of the road, but found the doors and windows nailed shut. Three more of Meadows's men were killed on the corner. A corporal squad leader with just ten days left on his tour, Glen Lucas,[56] lay motionless on the road. When corpsman Donald Kirkham made a move to help him, Lucas suddenly moved, waving him back. The corpsman ignored him, and then dropped, shot through the throat.[57]

On one corner of the intersection there was a pharmacy, to which Meadows sent a machine-gun team. He told them to get to the roof if they could. They crossed the street, broke down the door, and managed to make their way up. But from his spot behind a tree, the captain could see that the effort was hopeless. Before the big gate was a moat, spanned by a very narrow bridge. Over the gate there was a stone tower where he could see dozens of enemy soldiers. They could rain hell on anything that approached. He saw more enemy moving across the road to the southwest. Without supporting fire, either air support or artillery, there was no way this small force could assault this enormous fortress without being slaughtered. As they exchanged fire with well-concealed targets above, the captain reported to Gravel: "We are outgunned and outmanned."

There was some initial pushback from the hard-pressed colonel, but Meadows's mind was set. He was in the middle of disaster, staring at worse. His men continued to fall. Of the one hundred he had taken across, more than half were down: seven dead and forty-five wounded. Gravel knew what Meadows said was true. He could see downed marines all along the company's path.

Meadows said on his own authority he was pulling back to the bridge. First he had to account for all of his men. He tossed his smoke grenades up the street, and this allowed for the retrieval of two downed men, Lucas and Kirkham. Several marines who had been pinned down were able to retreat to his corner. There were too many wounded and dead to carry, so one of Meadows's enterprising marines hot-wired a flatbed truck parked on the street, and they piled men on that. Meadows and his gunnery sergeant Lou Heidel did a rapid count and found that one of the men was still missing. Gerald Kinny, an eighteen-year-old private with eight brothers and sisters back in Toledo, Iowa, was found lying on the street about fifty yards forward. Meadows ignored the heavy fire and sprinted toward him. His adrenaline pumping, with his rifle in one hand, he grabbed Kinny by the belt buckle and lifted him with one arm. Running for all he was worth, he half-dragged and half-carried him to the truck.[58] Kinny died on the way back.

From the south side of the bridge, Gravel could see that the retreat might be as bloody as the attack. There were too many downed men to carry off. He radioed Colonel Adkisson at the compound and demanded he send more trucks. None came. The army colonel had told Gravel that assaulting the bridge was folly, that his men were going to stay put, and that was that. So Gravel approached the men guarding the LZ. He asked one of the Quad-fifty drivers, army sergeant Lauver: "Can you help?"

Lauver and his crew had watched the marines being chopped down on the bridge. Their vehicle was largely unarmored, and attempting to cross looked as hopeless for them as it had for Golf Company. But there were downed men lying in the open at the far end. It would be the most difficult moment of Lauver's eighteen months in Vietnam, and he would replay it in his mind for the rest of his life. He felt there was no way he and his men would come back if they started across the bridge. He had not been ordered to do it, so it was up to him. He looked at his men and shrugged.

"Let's go," he said.

With them came a makeshift rescue convoy consisting of a six-by-six with a volunteer driver and Coolican in the passenger seat, another truck carrying Gunny Canley and Father Lyons, and several hot-wired cars.

Struggling back through clouds of yellow smoke, Meadows and his men were still in trouble. Ahead they saw the peculiar caravan of vehicles coming across the bridge. Canley and Father Lyons had pulled to a stop at the north end and returned fire. Lauver realized right away that in his haste he had made a mistake. It was possible to fire the Quad's guns forward, over the cab, but that was like setting off a stun grenade above the driver's head. They should have backed across. Until they reached the other end he could fire only to either side, which was useless.

But once his vehicle reached the far side and turned, he began pouring rounds north. Nolan Lala, a driver on the truck behind him, manned a heavy machine gun in the back and joined in. This provided enough cover for Canley, Lyons, and others to begin carrying and dragging the downed men behind the vehicles. Meadows and his men climbed aboard. During the frantic loading—Coolican would call it a Chinese fire drill—a rocket glanced off the fender of the truck and exploded. Among those knocked down was Murphy. A small shard of shrapnel had angled up under his flak jacket and poked a hole in his chest. The chaplain was hit in the thigh and hand—a cigarette lighter in his back pocket had deflected at least part of the blast. With Private Lala and the Quad-fifty pounding away, the bleeding convoy managed to retreat from the bridge and back to the compound. Lauver's Quad-fifty was the last vehicle off.[59]

As foreseen, Golf Company's attack had been a fiasco. Ten marines were killed, fifty-six wounded. Meadows had lost more than a third of his company, many of them needlessly he thought. On their way back from the bridge, the convoy picked up Dr. Doan Van Ba, an ARVN surgeon who had been hiding, and who ran out to the street to flag them down, wearing his uniform and red beret. He would provide invaluable help in the busy compound dispensary.

It occupied a noisy three rooms near the back end of the compound. Steve Bernie was a bookish twenty-eight-year-old with big glasses. He had recently graduated from The Ohio State medical school, and was now supervising controlled chaos, in a helmet that looked three sizes too big, head down, gloved hands smeared with gore. He had been wounded by shrapnel himself, standing in front of his dispensary when a mortar exploded nearby. Beneath a gauze wrap around his arm there was a bloodstain that kept getting larger, but he worked on. Until the battle started, the work he'd done was mostly limited to dealing with sniffles and stomachaches. Now it was like an emergency ward at a big city hospital in the midst of a ten-alarm emergency. Dr. James Back had come up from Phu Bai, and both young physicians were performing emergency procedures, some major, that they had never before attempted. There were screaming marines with severed or nearly severed limbs. Every few minutes one would stop breathing amid frantic efforts to revive him.[60]

From a cot in the holding area, with a wound that appeared less critical, Major Murphy shouted encouragement to the younger men. He asked for pen and paper and wrote a note to his wife. Murphy signaled to his friend Father Lyons, who had to be carried over.

At intervals, medevac choppers descended in the park. It was hard for the Sea Knight choppers to land safely. They made big targets with their wide body and twin-top rotors. The pilots would hover beyond the range of small-arms fire as the two navy gunboats swung up on the river to spray suppressing fire on the north bank. Then one would swoop in, kicking ammo out the doors and taking aboard the latest batch of wounded, sometimes without touching the ground. The exchange usually lasted only about thirty seconds, and was accompanied by gusts of bullets from enemy positions on both sides of the Huong. When it was fully dark, men on the ground used flashlights to guide the choppers in, being careful to aim them only straight up. Pointing a flashlight anywhere else made you a target. Coolican supervised much of this coming and going, moving back and forth from the LZ to the compound.[61]

He had stopped to check on Murphy shortly before sunset. They had served together earlier in the States, and Coolican had admired the older officer's skillful manner with those both above and below him in the ranks. He could be stern when the situation required it, but he treated even the lowliest grunts as equals. Bill Ehrhart, a corporal, kept a *Playboy* centerfold on which he had drawn a grid that served as his "short-time calendar," marking off each square as the days of his Vietnam tour counted down to March 5, 1968. When a new company captain pointed at the calendar, displayed in Ehrhart's bunker, told him it was "inappropriate," and ordered him to take it down, Murphy immediately intervened. He said, "Captain, that is *my* short-time calendar. Private Ehrhart maintains it for me." They did, in fact, share the same release date. Ehrhart appreciated the gesture. The major was all right. Small things like that built up broad affection in the ranks. Murphy had been at the fore of the fighting nearly all that day, the small hole in his side didn't look too bad, and the major had not acted as if it were serious. Coolican joked that it might be severe enough to get him out of the war, at least temporarily, which did not cheer Murphy.

"I'm good," he told Coolican.

"We've got another chopper coming in," the captain told him. "I'm going out there now. We'll get you out of here."

"Jim, I'm a little uncomfortable here," Murphy said. "Can you roll me over?"

Coolican helped him roll over to one side. What Murphy didn't say was that when he'd sent for Father Lyons, he'd asked him to perform last rites. He'd known his wound was grave. When Coolican returned for him a short while later, the major was dead. He had bled to death internally.[62]

Pressure still came from Phu Bai for Gravel to act. General Truong and his men had bought themselves some valuable time by retreating to concrete bunkers and tunnels and calling down an artillery strike on their own position. This had surprised the attackers, who suffered casualties and had fallen back. Scattered around the city there were still small pockets of stranded Americans, radio operators, administrators, CIA officers, and others. Some, like those at the relay center, were just blocks away from the compound, and in peril. Gravel attempted a move that night to the nearby CORDS office, but even with tanks his marines could make it only a few hundred yards before being turned back. The volume of fire made the streets impassable. Gravel was grief stricken by the loss of his friend Murphy, furious with Adkisson, and dumbfounded by the constant pressure to act against such clearly overwhelming odds. Alpha Company was down to about fifty men. Golf had been wasted. Coolican was ferrying wounded up to the LZ for every chopper that could land. The dead waited. They were stacked outside the dispensary, zippered in black body bags—Marquez, Kinny, Lucas, Kirkham, Murphy, and more—the day's grim toll. Word came back that Frank Doezema had died in surgery.

That night, from buildings around the compound, the enemy shouted insults and threats in English.

"You die, marines!"

"Fuck you, marines!"

Sergeant Gonzalez urged Ligato to answer them.

"You know some Vietnamese," Gonzalez said. "Say something back!"

Ligato's language skills were not up to the task, so he shouted back at them in English.

"Fuck you, NVA!"

The men around him laughed.

"Good," said Gonzalez.[63]

Inside one day, the city of Hue had fallen. No one on Saigon's side of the fight knew yet how fully. By tradition, your first encounter on the morning of Tet was supposed to be a harbinger for the entire year. If that were true, then Hue's fate in the New Year would have been sealed. Its first visitor had been death.

The American chain of command still didn't get it, even as the long and bloody day ended. Captain Meadows got the impression that General LaHue simply could not or would not believe the truth.

To the American command, such a swift and stunning coup was unimaginable. The NVA and VC were not capable of it. The Tet Offensive, a massive coordinated effort, which struck more than one hundred targets throughout South Vietnam, including most of the nation's provincial capitals, had come as a shock, but enemy gains had been quickly reversed in most places. The whole effort was just as quickly dismissed as futile by the MACV leadership. The enemy raiders had held on in most towns and cities for only a few hours, although in a number of other South Vietnamese cities—Kon Tum, Buan Ma Thuot, Phon Thiet, Can Tho, and Ben Tre—fighting would drag on for several days. In Saigon, where the story made the biggest splash, the Front had attacked high-profile targets: the headquarters for the army and navy, the Independence Palace, the US embassy, and the national radio station—from which the raiding party successfully broadcast a message from Ho before they were all killed—but in no case did the invaders make lasting gains. Although a remarkable feat of clandestine planning and coordination, and a demonstration that the enemy could reach almost anywhere in the country it wished, the Tet surprise was regarded by Westy as proof of Hanoi's weakness. Nowhere in his understanding of the war was there room for the size and quality of the force that had taken Hue. So the MACV in Saigon and General LaHue in Phu Bai simply refused to believe it had happened. Reports that contradicted this high-level understanding were dismissed as unreliable, the cries of men facing real combat for the first time, and panicking. Against the certainties of the American command, the truth never stood a chance.

In a secret cable that night, the ever-upbeat Westy sent a summary of the crowded day to General Wheeler, chairman of the Joint Chiefs. Addressing Hue, he wrote: "The enemy has approximately three companies [about five hundred men] in the Hue Citadel."[64]

He was off by a factor of twenty.

PART THREE

Futility and Denial

With the Alliance flag over the Citadel, the victorious commissars begin building their new state, broadcasting propaganda, and hunting down those with links to the Saigon regime. The Tet Offensive sends shock waves around the world. Reporters scramble to get into the city, recognizing that a major battle is taking shape.

The MACV press pass for Gene Roberts, the *New York Times* reporter whose detailed reports were the first to reveal that Hue had been taken.

Jim and Tuy-Cam Bullington on their wedding day in 1968. Both spent days in hiding after the city's occupation.

Marine Captain Mike Downs, commander of Fox Company 2/5, who choppered into Hue on the second day of the battle.

Marine Lieutenant Rich Horner's platoon pinned down on Tran Cao Van Street in another futile attempt to advance a few blocks on February 1, 1968, photographed by Kyoichi Sawada.

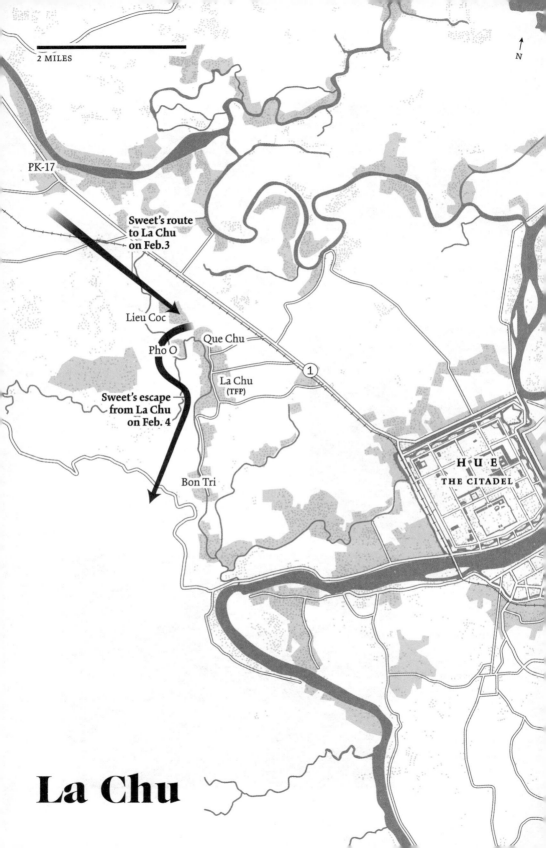

2 MILES

N

PK-17

**Sweet's route
to La Chu
on Feb.3**

Lieu Coc

Que Chu

Pho O

La Chu
(TFP)

**Sweet's escape
from La Chu
on Feb. 4**

1

Bon Tri

H U E
THE CITADEL

La Chu

1

IR8 Rice

Gᴇɴᴇ Rᴏʙᴇʀᴛs ʜᴀᴅ been in Vietnam for just under a month. After stopping in Hong Kong to rent an apartment for his wife, Susan, and children at the end of December, he had flown to Saigon, where he was the new bureau chief for the *New York Times*.

Roberts was a slow-talking southerner, from Pikeville, North Carolina. He was short, with thick dark hair and heavy eyebrows, and had a manner so deceptively shy and shambling it was easy to forget he was present. It was mostly deliberate, a pose he had perfected over a lifetime of working for newspapers. His father, a minister, had published a small weekly paper—sometimes taking his son along as he bartered subscriptions for chickens. After serving a stint in the army, Roberts went to work for the *Goldsboro News-Argus* in Wayne County, where he wandered the farm country looking for stories for his popular column Rambling in Rural Wayne. Roberts had what fellow southerners called a "comfortable way about him." He got people talking, and he would write about anything that interested or amused him. He once wrote a column about a sweet potato that looked like French president Charles de Gaulle. When the *Times* started looking for experienced reporters with southern drawls to help cover the civil rights movement, Roberts was recruited, and then spent years on the front lines of that struggle, often at great personal risk. Journalists working for northern newspapers were considered the enemy by southern segregationists, even those with local accents. Attending a Ku Klux Klan rally, Roberts and a group of other reporters narrowly escaped being attacked by the robed vigilantes. They learned to avoid attracting attention. Roberts once hitched a ride to a civil rights demonstration in a hearse.

At thirty-five, now a seasoned *Times* veteran, he had been tapped to take over the influential Vietnam post the previous year. There were few more prestigious jobs at the paper. David Halberstam had won a Pulitzer Prize for his work from Saigon, and partly because his stories had so continually contradicted Washington's official take on the war, the four-man bureau, which worked out of a tiny office on Tuto Street, had become a point of pride for the paper.

The paper had repeatedly antagonized President Johnson by undercutting his war messages, but it was too important to ignore. Before heading off, Roberts had been given orientation sessions in Washington at the highest levels, most designed to impress on him how much more the country's leaders knew about what was going on in Vietnam than his newspaper did, or likely ever would. That and, of course, how well the war was going. Reporters who played ball got scoops. In that spirit, Roberts was tipped off to an exclusive during a "deep background" session at the White House with Walt Rostow, LBJ's special assistant for National Security.

It was a pretty big scoop, too. Effectively, Rostow told him, the war was over. The United States had won. Sure, there would continue to be "brush fire episodes," he said, but something called IR8 rice had settled the matter; people just didn't know it yet. Rostow had been one of the impossibly brilliant young academics that Jack Kennedy had recruited after winning the White House in 1960. He was an unfailingly polite, considerate man, who epitomized the term "buttoned-down," a man without a hair or an idea out of place, the picture of discipline, confidence, and impeccable grooming. With a broad forehead and thin hair, tightly knotted tie and starched white shirt, its collar pinched with a tie bar, he peered at Roberts pleasantly through glasses with clear plastic frames: a man *in a position to know.* His impeccable academic credentials—Yale, Rhodes Scholar, former Oxford professor of American history—had been grounded by service during World War II with the Office of Strategic Services, a precursor to the CIA. In other words, he was more than an egghead. He was, however, somewhat given to quirky schemes.[1] A strong believer in combating Communism in poor countries through economic development,[2] Rostow explained to the reporter that Vietnam's subsistence-level rice farming was about to explode. The Ford and Rockefeller Foundations had teamed up to sponsor a research and development project in the Philippines, which had produced a genetically engineered strain of rice that with the proper chemical nourishment vastly improved its yield. It was going to sweep the world, but first it was going to transform the economy of South Vietnam. Farmers were going to get rich. They could now grow two crops a year instead of one. Forget the Communist revolution Rostow said. This was the "Green Revolution."

He advised, "Keep your eye on I-R-Eight Rice."[3]

No one else who briefed Roberts believed the war was over. At the CIA he got a more nuanced view. He was accompanied by *Times* Washington reporter Hedrick Smith to a briefing by the agency's section chief for Southeast Asia. There recently had been an intense three-week battle in the Central Highlands near Dakto, and the US military had proclaimed victory; Westy had called it "the beginning of a great defeat for the enemy."[4] Smith asked if the claim was justified.

"There are five reasons for seeing this as a victory," the analyst said. He then enumerated them. During the delay as Smith scribbled notes, Roberts detected a flicker of a smile on the analyst's face.

"Are there any reasons to think it was not a victory?" he asked.

"There are seven of those," the analyst said, without cracking a smile.

When he landed in Saigon in early January, the war was relatively quiet. Being new to the bureau and hardly in a position to direct the three more veteran hands assigned to him, Roberts set out to do some reporting. He decided to check out Rostow's tip. He liked doing stories that no one else was following, and, besides, if the war was indeed won, he wanted the scoop. As the former Rambling in Rural Wayne columnist, he was a natural for the story. He set off for a "pacified" rural area where the Thieu government was holding an IR8 rice festival.

There he found local farmers sitting on their haunches, chewing long stems of grass, waiting for the festivities to begin. With his interpreter, Roberts—who felt right at home—sat on his haunches and began chewing on grass alongside them. They started chatting. Once he had listened for a while without understanding a word, Roberts told his interpreter to ask, "What's your experience been with this IR8 rice? What do you think of it?"

Several of the farmers grew agitated in their response. They went on for a while.

"What did they say?" Roberts asked his interpreter.

"They said they have reservations about IR8 rice," he said.

"No," said Roberts. "Give me an actual translation. They didn't sound that calm about it."

The interpreter looked embarrassed.

"They said, 'Fuck IR8 rice!'"

They had also said, in so many words, that their fathers had grown rice, their grandfathers, their grandfathers' fathers—in fact, every Vietnamese farmer reaching back to the beginning of time had grown rice the way they grew rice, and there was not an expert in the goddamn world who could tell them how to grow rice, and, furthermore, there was not a damn thing wrong with their methods.

"Besides," said the interpreter, "they say the IR8 rice doesn't taste right."

"Well then," Roberts asked. "What are they doing at an IR8 festival?"

The farmers said soldiers that morning had chased them from their rice paddies with guns. They were put on buses and driven to the festival. To them the rice was much like the "freedom" offered by the Saigon regime; it was being imposed on them and it didn't taste right.

Roberts still had more work to do, but the story was off to a good start. He got back to Saigon for Tet Eve, and went with Charles Mohr to a nightclub frequented by South Vietnamese military officers. Mohr, a former *Times* Vietnam reporter, had flown over to help orient Roberts. He explained that the club was a good place to observe the decadent excesses of the regime's privileged few. Also, the drinks were good. They were walking back after midnight when they passed the telegraph office and a reporter, stepping out, told them there had been an attack at Da Nang and that it sounded serious. Roberts left immediately for Tan Son Nhat Airport to get on a plane.

Which is why he was in the air when a daring squad of VC attacked the US embassy in Saigon, in the neighborhood Roberts had just left. An attacking force of about two dozen guerrillas blew a hole in the wall of the embassy compound and tried to get inside the new six-story building, which they intended to blow up. The building was a showplace; it had opened only a few months earlier as a symbol of

America's enduring promise to South Vietnam. The attackers never made it inside. A dozen were killed (along with four embassy drivers and three civilians), and several were arrested. One marine guard and four military policemen were killed, and more were wounded. It was a shock, not a disaster, but with American reporters and cameras nearby, it would be the event that led the next day's stories about the Tet Offensive in the United States. One of many such raids throughout Saigon, some more successful than others, it was enough to give the press corps in the capital plenty of mayhem to cover. Roberts appeared to have flown away from the biggest story of the day.

Reports of the Tet attacks reached the White House on what was still Tuesday afternoon. Rostow stepped into a meeting between the president and his top foreign policy advisers to report: "We have just been informed we are being heavily mortared in Saigon. The Presidential Palace, our BOQs [bachelor officers' quarters], the Embassy, and the city itself have been hit."

"This could be very bad," said Johnson.

"Yes, I hope it is not Ambassador Bunker's residence," said Secretary of State Dean Rusk.

"What can we do to shake them from this?" asked the president.

"In a city like Saigon people can infiltrate easily," explained General Wheeler. "They carry in rounds of ammunition and mortars. They fire and run. It is impossible to stop this in its entirety. This is about as tough to stop as it is to protect against an individual mugging in Washington, DC . . . They are making a major effort to mount a series of these actions to make a big splurge at Tet."

"This is a public relations problem not a military one," pronounced McNamara.[5]

When he got to Da Nang, Roberts learned that stories of a major assault at the air base were overblown. It was business as usual. A few nearby villages had been attacked, but there wasn't much of a story, especially next to all that had happened in Saigon. But Roberts got wind that something much bigger was going on in Hue, farther north. The marines were sending reinforcements. Two companies had already gone, and another was to be flown in that morning. If he could get to Phu Bai he might be able to hitch a ride with them.

2

As Numerous as Ants

For visiting Saigon poet and writer Tran Thi Thu Van, who had come to Hue for her father's funeral, the early hours of Tet were long and frightening. She huddled with her family members in their ancestral home near the tank base at Tam Thai listening to the shooting and explosions. Front soldiers moved in large numbers across her family's property. Then there was a pounding on the front door.

A voice outside cried in Vietnamese: "Open the door! Open the door!"[6]

Tran's husband, Tran Da Tu, had a job with the Saigon government, working in rural development, which meant she might be considered a traitor by Communist forces, but these were not soldiers. When her cousin opened the door, their uncle, his large family, and others from their village pushed in. Their neighborhood had been shelled. They were just looking for shelter.

The now enlarged family group was crowded in the house's large central room when it was rocked by an explosion. Something hit the roof, blowing off tiles and sending pieces of the ceiling crashing down. The family dived to the floor, which was wet and foul. The chamber pot they had used through the night had been overturned. Tran found herself prone in a puddle of excrement, gagging. There were fragments of masonry in her mouth.

Around her, children cried and adults argued. Should they stay or flee? Tran had hoped the fighting would ease by dawn, but it was light and the situation had not changed. They could hear the distant sound of mortar explosions from the American base at Phu Bai. One of her cousins realized, in a panic, that two of his small children were missing. He ran out and returned with both a short time later, having nearly been arrested. He said he was stopped by three VC, two of them wounded. He begged them to let him go find his children. They asked him what he did for a living. He told them he was a carpenter, and they let him go.

Later in the morning the shooting finally slowed and Tran's family was able to leave. The shooting had splintered the trees in their garden and clipped off branches. A bamboo hedgerow between their yard and the railroad tracks in back had been flattened. There was dried blood on the grass. Tran went to the water tank in the garden to drink and clean her mouth, and was there with other family members when an American convoy rolled up Highway 1. It had tanks in front and trucks behind, bringing many American marines.[7]

"Everyone stay where they are," Tran's elder brother said. "Stay quiet. Don't run or they will think you are Viet Cong and they will kill you at once."

The family filed back indoors as the Americans took up positions around their garden. There was no shooting. Two of the soldiers came into the house. One demanded to see "identity cards," mangling the Vietnamese words, so it took a few moments for the family to understand. Tran found hers and tried to hand it over, but the soldiers wanted to see only those of the men. All were in order, and the one who had demanded them thanked them in Vietnamese. As soon as he stepped outside a violent gunfight started.

A brief but furious firefight ensued. Tran heard screams and moaning from the Americans. The family once more pressed themselves to the floor. Rounds slapped off the tile roof and two big trees in the garden outside were blown down by loud explosions. A house across the way went up in flames. Tran's mother cried for everyone to pack up their belongings, fearing the flames would spread to their house. Then the shooting stopped. As the Americans returned to the road and prepared to drive off, one held up several fingers indicating the number of dead people they had left outside.

A short time later they heard sounds of another intense gunfight up the road, and not long afterward two of the American trucks raced back down Highway 1, guns blazing in every direction.[8]

After the storm of Americans passed through, Communist forces returned in great numbers. One of Tran's nephews, an ARVN soldier who had come to spend the holidays with his family, returned breathless from a trip up the road.

"Aunt, they have returned and are as numerous as ants," he said. They were hanging flags up near An Cuu, and through loudspeakers were broadcasting appeals for people to come out of their houses and join them. They had hung a giant flag before the Citadel and taken all of Hue. The city streets were all deserted except for the soldiers.

Tran knew her family would have to leave. The house, built by their father as a place to pray and light candles for the departed, was big, but it was not equipped to house and feed the number who had congregated there. Probably more would be coming. So they scrounged for food and bowls in the servants' quarters, and discussed where to go. The American base was just a short distance south. That meant there very likely would be heavy fighting ahead through their village. They had to get out. They packed their belongings and set off for her older brother's house in Tu Dam, about a mile and a half northwest.

The rest of that day was a template for the nightmarish weeks ahead, as the family walked first in one direction and then the other, chased by gunfire. They first fell in with crowds of other refugees moving to the northwest. They importuned their way past one group of Front soldiers to cross a canal bridge, only to come running back hours later when another group began shooting at them. One angry Front soldier told them they were not allowed to leave their homes. Trying a different way, they walked for the rest of the day with their old and young in tow, passing scenes of death and ruin into the city center, eventually walking up Le Loi Street toward the Truong Tien Bridge, only to be chased back by more shooting. They finally took shelter before dark with thousands of others who were displaced in the Church of the Most Holy Redeemer, the cathedral just a few blocks south of the Huong River. A kindly priest there was doing his best to assign space for everyone inside.

On the afternoon of the first day, Le Van Hoi and his family were asked to take in five Front soldiers. Hoi had a job working for a construction company, a management position, and he made a good living for his wife and four children. They lived near the Bach Ho Bridge in western Hue. Even though he was not directly employed by the regime, his position and the size of his home made him suspicious to the occupiers. But Hoi's younger brother worked for one of the VC's political units, and he was able to help. Instead of being taken away for "reeducation," pressed into one of the guerilla units, or forced to dig trenches or carry food and ammo for the occupiers, Hoi was ordered to help hang revolutionary banners and flags. He did so gratefully. That night he was allowed to return home to his family, where they prepared and served meals for their five guests.

Hoi felt very fortunate. Hundreds of people in his neighborhood were arrested, nearly everyone who had any association with the Saigon regime. If they did not turn themselves in, they were hunted down. Those who had worked as policemen or who held high positions were shot. He and others in his neighborhood who were not enthusiastic about the occupation soon learned to pretend that they were.

After hiding in the stuffy drainpipe all night with his family and neighbors, Le Ngoc Thinh remembered something he had left behind. His family started for a tenement house by the river at sunrise, demanding that he come along, but fifteen-year-old Thinh defied them and went in the other direction. He ran back to their house.

It was even more dangerous than his parents feared. Thinh was shot at and dove for cover. More rounds struck around his hiding place, and then a man called out: "Who's that?"

Thinh recognized the voice. It was an ARVN soldier who lived in his neighborhood. When he called back and identified himself, the man apologized. They shared what they knew. They talked about what had happened with mutual friends. A girl Thinh admired and had fantasized about from a distance had been killed. She was sitting at her desk in her home, studying, when a grenade came through the roof and exploded right where she sat. Thinh had never met the girl, but her death made him very sad. It was too dangerous to go on. He turned around and ran back after his family.

Tran Toi was also fifteen. His father was the head nurse at the military hospital in Mang Ca, and they lived outside the northern walls of the fortress across the Dao River. He and his large family, along with neighbors, crawled into a bunker under their house to escape the shelling and shooting. But when smoke filled the house and crept into the bunker, they fled to a nearby Catholic church. His parents stayed behind with his ailing uncle. When Toi and his siblings reached the church, it was already crowded with people. There was no more room. So they braved the fire in the streets to return to their home, and hid outside it behind trees until sunrise.

That Thursday morning, February 1, a battle was still raging in the areas around Mang Ca, so Toi and his siblings walked west toward an orphanage that might provide a safe haven. The shooting seemed to come from every direction, so it was impossible to know which way was safe. They stayed behind walls and ran to holes gouged in the ground by explosions, dashing from one place of cover to another. As they went, their numbers grew. People were fleeing in great numbers, and Toi's family fell in with them. He was horrified by what he saw. There were dismembered bodies of NVA soldiers caught in the barbed wire fencing around the Citadel walls where they had been killed by remote-controlled claymore mines. There were many more bodies around the gate.

The orphanage was also full. With nowhere else to go, Toi and his brothers turned around and started walking back home.

Nguyen Van Ty saw the Alliance flag flying at sunrise. He had been up all night, awakened by the shooting, listening to the BBC in hopes of figuring out what was going on. Ty's house was outside the Nha Do Gate at the Citadel's southwestern corner, very close to the Ngo Mon flagpole. He lived in a finely built, two-story house, which served as a display home for the construction materials his company sold. Ty supplied concrete and stone for road and building construction, managing fleets of boats and trucks that delivered the material from pits in Phu Bai and elsewhere to construction sites. It was the kind of work useful to everyone, and he had become expert in safely navigating between the two factions, mostly by avoiding work in heavily contested areas. Ty's older sister, Quen, was active with the VC. She worked for one of its regional commanders, so Ty had known that something big was planned for Tet.

On the day the city was taken, his house was commandeered by an ARVN battalion, which used it as their headquarters. Most of the people in his neighborhood fled, but Ty and his family stayed on. Like most in the city, he wasn't sure which was the safest side to be on. So he played it both ways. The ARVN battalion had about eighty soldiers at first, but as the day wore on and more and more reported back its numbers swelled to over two hundred. They held Ty's neighborhood just outside the fortress walls. He stayed with them, but sent a message to his sister, to whom he promised to pass information about his "guests."

Ty hid in his house when the ARVN troops tried to attack the Ngo Mon tower platform and were repulsed. Many of them were killed in the effort. He supervised the preparation of meals for the command staff in his home, feeding them with his own stores. On the second day, his sister came to see him and was arrested by the ARVN soldiers. She complained that her brother was living in the headquarters, so they brought her to Ty's house.

"Mr. Ty, who is this lady to you?" asked General Ton That Dinh, the battalion commander.

"This is my older sister," said Ty.

Dinh let her go. Ty told Quen about everything he had seen, the size of Dinh's force, and its failed effort to storm Ngo Mon. When she left, he warned her not to come back. It was too dangerous for her, he said. Dinh told her the same thing.

"We are fighting and you are coming into this area," he told her. "We have to suspect that you are a revolutionary soldier because the civilians wouldn't do what you did."

Despite these warnings, Quen came back two days later. She was again arrested. Dinh was furious.

"I already told you that you shouldn't come back here!" he told her. "I already suspected that you were a revolutionary soldier. How did you dare to come back?"

"Please, sir, my family was bombed and shot," Quen said. "Many people died up there [she lived north of the Citadel]. One of my children got killed, and two of them were wounded."

Ty asked Dinh if his sister could get some medical supplies to take back with her. Dinh cautioned her again.

"You cannot go up there anymore," he said. "If the revolutionary soldiers see you, they will shoot you," he said. "If the Americans see a person walking across the bridge [she had to cross the Bach Ho Bridge outside the north wall to get to her village] they will also shoot you."

Ty asked if he could take his sister back in a boat. He was given permission, so he loaded a boat with rice and the ARVN guards were told to allow them to pass. Brother and sister then visited the Front's local command post and gave detailed information about Dinh's forces.

Shortly after Ty's return from that trip, Dinh's forces vanished. They had been ordered to find their way up to Mang Ca. Ty was alarmed. He had asked General Dinh to warn him before leaving. Having sheltered and fed them, he was sure to be branded a traitor by the liberation forces. So he and his wife dressed in old clothes and fled with their children. They found a friendly ferry operator, and stayed with him on the water. Their boat was one of about fifteen that anchored in the river off Hen Island for ten days, waiting out the fighting.

After he was gone, his sister returned a third time, most likely under orders to obtain more rice and information from her brother. Caught in a fight along the river by Front troops and US Navy gunboats, she was shot and killed about two hundred yards from his house.

The prospect of Communist troops in the city was especially alarming to the family of Tuy-Cam, the Da Nang consulate worker engaged to Jim Bullington. They had a very impressive house and garden, so they knew they would attract suspicion. Her late father had been a high-ranking Saigon intelligence officer. He was beyond reach now, but her two younger brothers were in training to be ARVN officers. They were hidden in the attic, and their presence, not to mention Tuy-Cam's job, placed them in great jeopardy.

Tuy-Cam had been awakened early in the morning by the sound of a woman crying in the yard outside. She and the rest of her family, in their house by the railroad tracks in southwest Hue, had gone to bed at one that morning after their Tet feast. Her fiancé, Bullington, had gone across the Huong River to the power station, where he was staying with his friend Albert Istvie. The other two Americans, Steve Miller and Steve Haukness, had gone back to Miller's house for the

night. The woman in their yard had fled a nearby village, where she
said Front soldiers had taken away her husband.

"He is only a farmer," she said. "He did not do anything wrong."

Hours later came a loud knock on the family's front door. By then,
with the sounds of fighting raging throughout the city, the rest of
Tuy-Cam's extended family had gathered on the first floor to wait.

Four Front soldiers were at the door, wearing rubber sandals, black
shirts, and pith helmets. They entered and surveyed the group.

"Is everyone here?" one asked.

"Yes," said Tuy-Cam's mother.

"Anybody hiding somewhere?"

"No."

The soldiers demanded that all the women and girls move to one
side of the room, and all the men and boys to the other. The group's
leader told the family that they were reactionaries who had helped sell
Vietnam to the Americans. They had been living well he said, but now
they would suffer. He held a pistol to the head of Tuy-Cam's sister and
forced her to lead them on a search of the house. They looked up at
the attic and asked if anyone was up there.

"No one is there," she said. "If so, you can shoot me." They took
her word.

The women were then led out to the Nam Giao Bridge. Another
group of soldiers came and took the men and boys. A number of
others had also been taken to the bridge, including several Americans,
men and women, who worked for the International Voluntary Services (IVS), an organization that employed recent college graduates to
teach in Vietnamese schools, among other things. They were mostly
pacifists, some of them conscientious objectors, who were engaged
in work much like the Peace Corps. One was a woman Tuy-Cam
had met, Anne Hensley, who seemed, Tuy-Cam thought, remarkably
composed under the circumstances. The soldiers were having trouble
questioning the Americans, and asked if anyone among the assembled
captives spoke English. A woman who knew Tuy-Cam, and who knew
her English was excellent, made eye contact with her and slowly shook
her head, to say: *Don't let them know.* The Americans were then led away.

The family was kept on the bridge with the others for six hours.
One of the young commissars made a speech. He said that Ho Chi

Minh was coming to Hue as soon as the liberation of South Vietnam was complete. He would announce the construction of a large textile plant to bring jobs to the city. There was little enthusiasm expressed. Leaflets were handed out listing the "ten policies" of the new regime. Among the items listed was one that said those who helped the liberators would be rewarded, those who had been working for the puppet regime who surrendered would be forgiven, and those who led the liberation troops to US or ARVN weapons would be "highly praised."

He concluded the oration with: "Okay, you can go back home."

They were informed that each night ten or eleven soldiers would be coming to their house for dinner. It was decided it would be best for Tuy-Cam to go into hiding like her brothers, so she took up residence in the family bunker, hidden under a bed and surrounded by stacks of rice bags. She would spend many days there. The two boys who had been led off, her youngest brother and cousin, were returned the following day.

Across the river at the power plant, Bullington woke in the guesthouse to blasts of incoming mortars. He sat up in bed and heard small-arms fire in the distance. None of it was close, so he went back to sleep. He woke up in daylight, got dressed, and headed out the door. Across a wide courtyard his friend Istvie motioned frantically for him to get back inside.

So he retreated to his quarters and waited. He had no idea what was going on. He had a Chinese pistol, given to him as a gift. He had never fired it; he kept it as a souvenir. Now he reappraised it as a weapon. He figured out how to use it, and loaded it. Then he placed it on the bed next to him and waited, straining to hear what was going on outside, afraid to even peek out the window. After several hours, curiosity and boredom got the best of him. He had to know what was happening. He stepped back outside and crossed the courtyard. Again he saw his friend Istvie in the doorway of the building opposite, gesturing frantically for him to turn back. Bullington ignored him.

"What are you doing here?" Istvie whispered when he got close. "I told you to stay inside. They're here, the North Vietnamese are right here, they're all around us. You'd better get back in that room and stay there!"

The tall American hustled back across the courtyard and back indoors. Istvie was French Vietnamese, and not considered a hostile by the Communist forces. There was no reason for him to hide, but Bullington was in great danger, a fact he only now realized. He stayed in the guesthouse until late afternoon, worried now, waiting for a hard knock on the door. He realized with alarm that the vehicle he had borrowed from the CORDS office the day before displayed the familiar handclasp insignia of the US Agency for International Development. It was like a sign advertising that there was an important American nearby.

Hours later there was a knock at his door. Bullington froze for a moment, but then figured the NVA would probably not knock politely. He asked, "Is that you, Albert?"

It was, with a ham sandwich and a warm beer.

"You are a very lucky man," he told Bullington. The power plant had been completely overrun. There were Front troops in buildings around the courtyard he had crossed—twice!—and if ever a man looked like an American, it was Bullington.

"It seems they've taken everything," Istvie said. "The whole city of Hue. You can't stay here. If they find you, it would be bad for both of us."

"But where should I go?" Bullington asked.

Istvie had not yet worked that out. He said he would return in a few hours, and would knock exactly four times. There followed some dark hours for the American, who now fully understood that his life was in the hands of this French Vietnamese man he did not know all that well. If Istvie was caught sheltering an American, one with an important job like Bullington's, he and his family would be considered traitors. So Istvie was taking an enormous risk. How far could his goodwill be trusted? Bullington felt terrible for placing his friend in such a bad spot.

When Istvie returned it was dark. He said he would take Bullington to a Catholic priest two houses away, Father Marie Cressonier. They decided to wait until the troops occupying the power center sat down to dinner. Istvie would cross the courtyard alone first, and if he turned and signaled for Bullington to come, he should follow.

Istvie noticed the pistol and suggested he leave it.

"It wouldn't do you any good," he said. "There are more than one hundred of them. And if they find it on you, it wouldn't be good for either of us."

At six o'clock, Istvie returned, knocking four times. Bullington waited as his friend crossed the yard. He did not stop.

Istvie returned again a half hour later. There had been a Front soldier in a window of a nearby building, so he didn't want to risk it. A man Bullington's size stood out. This time, after Istvie crossed the yard, he stopped and signaled. The American swallowed panic as he crossed the open space. His heart pounded. He tried to keep a normal, nonchalant stride, as if he owned the place. Maybe he would be taken for a Frenchman. He believed his French was pretty good; he had learned it at a foreign service language school. He was not spotted. Istvie led him through a gate in the back wall of his home. Bullington waited in the family outhouse for a few minutes while his friend scouted ahead, and then the two men crawled through a side window and dropped down into the backyard of the house next door.

Cressonier met them at his back door. He introduced Bullington to a younger priest, Father Pierre Poncet, who had fled the shelling near Khe Sanh. Cressonier, who was also tall, gave Bullington one of his black cassocks. After conversing in French with him for a few minutes, they decided that if confronted by the Front, he would play the part of a visiting Canadian priest. His French was okay, but the accent wasn't. They figured the ruse would have to last only a day or two.

"You're welcome here as long as you need to hide," Cressonier said. "But I'm sure your marines will retake this area by tomorrow or the next day, and you'll be safe."

Many of the Americans and Europeans scattered around Hue were not so fortunate. Steve Miller and Steve Haukness were arrested that morning at Miller's home. Miller's body would be found later, his arms bound behind his back, shot in the back of the head in a field behind a Catholic seminary that the Front used to gather prisoners. Haukness's remains were found six years later.

All foreigners were at risk. Three German doctors who had been teaching at a medical school were executed, along with the wife of one of them. Two French Benedictine missionaries, despite their nationality, were also killed; one was shot and the other was buried alive. Veteran foreign service officer Philip Manhard was arrested at a villa in the city after calling the MACV in Saigon to say his house was surrounded. He and four American employees of a construction company were paraded through the city, interrogated, and taken on a grueling march to Hanoi. With them was CIA employee Eugene Weaver, whose capture was filmed by the NVA and later shown on a CBS News broadcast. All were held until 1973.

Others hung on. More than twenty American military advisers, most of them air force and army technicians, sent word that they were surrounded and trapped. In an office building they had taken positions by the windows and doors, prepared to defend themselves for as long as it took for help to arrive. About three dozen other Americans—civilians, foreign service officers, CIA, and military—found themselves stranded in the occupied city that morning. Chris Jenkins was inside the Citadel. He had flown to Hue to visit friends for the holidays. The twenty-four-year-old Philadelphian worked in Dalat, a city midway between Hue and Saigon, for the IVS. His friends hid him under a bed.

Among the Americans Tuy-Cam saw on the bridge were Marjorie Nelson, a tall, willowy physician who wore glasses, fashionable at the time, with glittery rims that tapered to a point on either side of her face; and Nelson's friend Sandra Johnson, who taught at a Hue high school. Both women spoke some Vietnamese. Nelson had been visiting Johnson. They were marched to a makeshift prison camp in the mountains, where their female guards were shocked that unlike the American soldiers they had captured the women spoke their language. They were peppered with questions from female Front soldiers about their lives in America, about whether they were married or had boyfriends.

"In America, do you cook with wood or coal?" one asked Nelson.

The doctor offered to work. There were many wounded, but she was told there were enough Vietnamese doctors and nurses. Both women were asked to write statements expressing their views about the war; both opposed American involvement and wrote honestly.[9]

3

So You Want
to Go to Vietnam?

Mike Downs, the commander of Foxtrot Company,[10] had worked hard to lead men in combat. He had come to the marines out of Holy Cross College, and at twenty-seven, like most marine officers, he did not want to be left out of a fight. Without combat experience he could not hope to compete for advancement.

Downs had ticked all the right boxes—leading a rifle platoon and a weapons platoon; serving as an assistant battalion operations officer; commanding a rifle company in the quiet regions of Okinawa and Camp Pendleton; attending Amphibious Warfare School in Virginia— but after finishing that he was assigned, not to Vietnam, but to another posting in Okinawa. A kindly superior enrolled him in a recon replacement course back at Pendleton so that he would be unable to report to Okinawa as scheduled. This would effectively cancel that posting, and his reassignment, he was told, would probably be to lead a company in Vietnam. But when he had completed the course—useful training in land navigation and coordination of artillery and air support—he was told by a sergeant that he had once more been bypassed for a combat post. He was assigned again to a job in Okinawa.

"You have got to be shitting me," Downs said. "I came out here for this recon replacement officers' course to get out of an Okinawa posting. I have been to Okinawa. Did that. I want to go to Vietnam."

The sergeant considered this for a moment.

"So you want to go to Vietnam, sir?"

"Yeah."

The sergeant said Downs would have to go to Okinawa first, but promised to work things out so when he arrived, he would be given a change of assignment to Vietnam. And he was as good as his word. When Downs and a planeload of other marines arrived in Okinawa they were given a short administrative briefing, then the captain was summoned by an administrative sergeant, who by the sad look on his face thought he was delivering bad news.

"Your orders have been modified, sir. You are now going to the First Marine Division in Vietnam."

Downs had done all the right things when he took over Fox Company in the fall of 1967. He had gotten all his officers and a few senior noncoms together and told them they knew more about fighting in Vietnam than he did, and that he was going to lean on them heavily for advice. Grunts were always wary of new commanders. They tended to arrive young and fit and eager—and Downs was all those things—qualities that could mean hard work and real danger.

By early 1968, Downs was an old hand. His company was pulled off an active battlefield south of Phu Bai on Wednesday, January 31, just as it was about to help wipe out a trapped NVA battalion. Downs's commander, Lieutenant Colonel Ernie Cheatham,[11] had expertly maneuvered one of his companies, Hotel, in a clash that forced an NVA battalion to retreat. Looking at his map, Cheatham saw they were moving toward the Truoi River, which was too deep and wide for them to ford or swim. The river wound its way in a generally northeastern direction from the spectacular green peaks and waterfalls of the Bach Ma Forest to the South China Sea roughly midway between Hue and Da Nang. Directly ahead of Cheatham's position the river switched back west, which meant if he moved his men fast enough to block them, the entire enemy force would be trapped. Bottling up an entire battalion was too good to be true.

He brought up Downs's Fox Company to help Hotel pin the enemy against the river, and deployed his Echo Company to secure their flank. The NVA battalion was pinned. Cheatham's young company captains felt they were getting a master class in infantry maneuvers. They would now close in and finish the NVA battalion off. The colonel had given them a rare clean shot at an enemy that had been chipping away at them for months with booby traps, mortars, and small ambushes. The marines had far superior firepower, which they rarely got a chance to use. Fighting the VC and the NVA had been like trying to swat a gnat with a sledgehammer. Now they had the enemy cornered. A battalion! Except—then they didn't.

Cheatham was ordered to pull back. He was informed that his fourth company, Chuck Meadows's Golf, had been sent into Hue, and the Task Force X-Ray commanders at Phu Bai wanted to send two more of his companies there, immediately. This would effectively foil the colonel's crushing blow. Cheatham was livid, and got on the radio—his call sign was Rockmat Six—to make that clear.

"Do you realize what we've got here!" he argued, fuming. "We have *got* them!"

"Don't worry, Rockmat Six," came the response. "Where you are going there are more of them than you can count." [12]

His officers were shocked and disappointed, and Cheatham was crestfallen. He would later growl, "Somewhere out there is an NVA battalion commander who will be talking for the rest of his life about the dumbest son-of-a-bitch he ever fought against."

Fox Company would proceed directly to Phu Bai, and then the next day on into Hue to join Golf. Hotel would move off to a bridge over Highway 1 and be picked up and driven north the next day. Cheatham was ordered to leave Echo Company behind to do what it could against the larger enemy force.

Trucks arrived and Downs's men were taken north to Phu Bai. They had left their packs behind earlier that morning—food, ammo, dry socks, personal effects, which would be sorely missed in the coming weeks. Private Ronald Frasier would always remember seeing his pack lined up with the others in perfect parade order at the edge of the field. They would never see them again.

Fox spent one night at Phu Bai, and early the next morning—Thursday, February 1—the company was off to Hue. Downs was told his company would be flown up to the MACV compound for an operation that should last about a day. Air strikes and artillery were out. The city was considered an important historic site, and if anybody was going to start blowing things up it would have to be the ARVN. His men could use the weapons they carried: rifles and machine guns. They were to secure the compound, rescue some of the Americans hiding in the city, and then return. Downs passed the word to his platoon leaders.

"Get your gear," Platoon Sergeant Paul Tinson told the men. "You're going up to Hue City to bail out Golf Company. They hit the shit up there. Just take your flak jackets and some gear because we'll be back for dinner."[13]

They gathered ammo and one can of C rations for the side pocket of their fatigues and assembled that morning on the tarmac, where they would board Sea Knight helicopters[14] for the twenty-minute flight. It would take a series of flights to move them all. On each, the men were lined against both sides of the aircraft, sitting on their helmets to protect their vitals from rounds that might punch up through the floor. As they moved over the city, the choppers hovered high, waiting for the suppressing fire below to start, then swooped in low and fast bearing northwest over the Van Duong River, then hard left where it met the Huong. At that point they banked sideways. On one of the flights, a loud metallic *whang! whang! whang!* sounded as rounds poked through the walls. One marine dived for the deck. The shooting abruptly stopped, and as the chopper leveled off the other men laughed at him.

"What the hell are y'all laughing at?" he asked. "I just beat y'all to it, is all."[15]

The small-arms fire was sporadic, but it spooked everyone. One of the choppers carried a load of journalists, some of whom got off when it landed. The other reporters, to Downs's amusement, stayed right where they were for the return flight to Phu Bai.

Kyoichi Sawada and Mike Morrow were two who got off. Sawada was famous; he had won a Pulitzer Prize two years earlier for his photos from Vietnam. Morrow was a complete amateur. He had effectively stumbled into the battle, a tall, skinny kid with a thick unruly mop of chestnut hair who wore black horn-rims. He had been at Dartmouth College studying the history of Chinese-American diplomacy and trying to learn Chinese when he had wangled himself a summer abroad in Taiwan. When the summer was over, he wanted to stay. He felt his Chinese skills were improving, and he got permission from his professor to remain there a while longer before returning to complete his undergraduate studies. But Morrow had overstayed. A year later, still in Taiwan, he learned he had lost his student status. His parents sent him a ticket home, but he knew that without his college deferment he would likely be drafted.

Morrow didn't know how he felt about the war, but, being immersed in Asian studies, he was fascinated by what was happening in Vietnam. There was a big difference between being curious and being committed. He was not against the war, but neither did he believe in it enough to fight. The truth, he reasoned, was that he didn't know enough to have an opinion. So, on impulse, he had traded his ticket home for a ticket to Saigon, and had flown there the previous summer on a tourist visa with sixty dollars in his pocket. He was petrified. He had the name of a friend's uncle who lived in Cho Lon, but he didn't know where that was or how to get there. At the airport in Saigon he found his English got him further than his Chinese. He said he intended to work as a journalist, and was put on a bus to the Caravelle Hotel, where most American reporters stayed. It was getting dark when he arrived, and he didn't know how safe it was to be on Saigon's streets at night, so he went in. He asked how much it cost for one night. The charge was thirty-five dollars, which was more than half of his funds, but he was desperate, so he took the room. He didn't dare spend anything more, so he didn't eat. He didn't sleep either. Early in the morning he remembered the name of a *Baltimore Sun* correspondent, Bob Erlandson, for whom he had worked as a translator in Taiwan. He looked up Erlandson's Saigon address and found that it was, of all things, at the Caravelle Hotel. So he called him on the hotel phone.

"Come on down," Erlandson said. "Have breakfast with us."

Morrow walked immediately down to the reporter's room and knocked on the door.

"Come on in," Erlandson shouted. There was coffee on the table.

The *Sun* reporter helped orient the kid. He took him to the UPI office, which gave him a letter of introduction. It said he was an official UPI stringer. The wire service gave him free film in return for a promise to bring pictures to them first. If they took anything, they'd pay ten dollars. Then he wrote to the *Dartmouth Daily News*, a paper in Hanover, New Hampshire. He offered to send it occasional letters from Vietnam if it would send him, on official *Daily News* stationery, a letter identifying him as its correspondent. The paper wrote back.

With those two letters he had been able to get a press pass from the MACV, which gave him the same access to military transport enjoyed by all the professional reporters. Because he could speak Chinese, he wrote several stories about Cho Lon, a Chinese enclave, where he went to stay with his friend's uncle. These were published in the *Washington Post*, and just like that he was legit, stringing for a number of American newspapers. Morrow had been in the Mekong delta aboard a navy patrol boat when it was sunk by enemy fire, and had to be fished out of the river. So he had seen a few things by the time he landed in Hue.

But he hadn't seen anything like Hue. He arrived with no idea anything newsworthy was happening. He had gotten stuck at an air base in Quang Tri the day before trying to hitch a ride into the city to spend the holidays with some IVS friends, among them Dr. Marjorie Nelson and Sandra Johnson. On the tarmac there, out of nowhere, a machine-gun round dropped right in front of him and rolled to his feet. It had apparently traveled a great distance before falling. It was still warm when he stooped to pick it up. *You know,* he thought, *that was kind of good luck.* He slipped it into his pocket. He managed to get on a chopper to Phu Bai, and when he got off he saw Sawada—whom he recognized and admired—boarding a helicopter with Downs's company. He asked where they were going.

"We're going to Hue," Sawada said.

He asked the platoon sergeant if he could get on, too, and was waved aboard. He was shocked when they landed under fire.

Gene Roberts also came in on one of the Sea Knights along with more of Downs's men, and he ran off into the shooting with them, quickly covering the two blocks to the compound.

Most of the marines were amazed to find themselves in a city. All they had seen of Vietnam were air bases, rice paddies, and jungle. Here were tall buildings, wide paved streets, cars and trucks parked against curbs, parks, bars, restaurants, fine and spacious homes. They didn't have time to look around. They moved with choreographed discipline, forming a big circle around the chopper to provide suppressing fire, and when it rose they sprinted across Doc Lao Park and Le Loi Street and lined up against a building. Rounds snapped around them, bounced off the pavement with a whining crack and exploded into the wall, spraying small clouds of stone powder that filled their noses and mouths and stung their eyes.

While they waited, Dan Carter saw a photographer point a camera at him. Just as his group was ordered to move down to the compound, he turned to the camera—maybe his parents would see him!—and tripped. His helmet and weapon went flying. He collected himself and tried to catch up. There was a tank on the street outside the compound gate, and as he ducked under its gun, it fired, nearly knocking him out with the concussion. His ears ringing, he staggered a few steps backward.

A crewman in the tank turret looked down at him and apologized. "If you want, you can go in now," he said.[16]

4

Consternation Had
Been Achieved

THE TET OFFENSIVE was a huge story in the United States, but was being portrayed by most news outlets as a series of mostly ineffectual surprise attacks throughout the country. That Thursday morning's *New York Times*, in a story written by Mohr in Saigon, focused primarily on the raids in the capital. It was accompanied by a photo of a dead American soldier on the back of an armored personnel carrier and one of a heap of dead VC outside a local radio station. Mohr wrote of "pockets of resistance" throughout the country, and added, in passing: "The Vietcong still held parts of Hue." [17]

Chris Jenkins, the IVS worker hiding in a house in the Citadel, heard the same "pockets of resistance" report over Armed Forces Radio. His Vietnamese hosts told him the Front soldiers were everywhere.

The official assessment, from the South Vietnamese government and from the MACV, was that the enemy had taken very heavy losses in exchange for questionable "psychological" gains. [18] All the reports insisted the enemy had not captured any territory. Mohr quoted Westmoreland, after the general had toured the bullet-riddled embassy grounds in Saigon, saying the enemy's efforts had failed, and that they had sought "to cause maximum consternation in South Vietnam."

"It was clear that consternation had been achieved," Mohr wrote. [19]

But it was also clear to Gene Roberts, picking up information at the MACV compound in Hue, that something bigger was happening there than anyone knew, or than anyone would admit. He was told the Front's flag was flying over the Citadel, although he couldn't see more than a block or two out in each direction. He saw South Vietnamese planes moving over the city, dropping bombs. Marines on the roof of the compound's main building were occasionally shooting at targets across the streets, and while the place itself was not under attack, patrols that ventured out made it only a short distance before being forced to turn back carrying new casualties. The mood inside the compound was surprisingly calm. He heard how Frank Doezema, at least in the retelling, had single-handedly saved the compound the night before. No one said it, but it gradually dawned on the *Times* reporter that the compound was completely surrounded.

He had expected to spend some days reporting there, but now he felt the need to get his story out immediately. Vietnam was twelve hours ahead of New York, where the Friday paper was already being set in type. In order to make the Saturday paper, Roberts would have to send his story no later than the next morning. If he stayed in Hue, he'd have to dictate the story to the office in Saigon over the phone, but there were only two lines out of the compound, and both were busy with military business. So to tell the world what was happening, he'd have to get back to Phu Bai.

By Thursday, a little more than a day after the offensive began, battle lines had solidified, north and south. The Hac Bao company along with General Truong's men, had stabilized defenses in Mang Ca, and at midday they were reinforced with ARVN troops by helicopter. The American Sea Knight choppers that flew them in did so at great risk. Thick cloud cover blanketed the fortress just two hundred feet up, and below that was a heavy mist. The pilots set down under intense small-arms and mortar fire. After just one run, delivering only half of Truong's reinforcements, remaining flights were scrubbed.[20] The bulk of ARVN troops, their ranks thinned by the holiday furlough,[21] were prevented from entering the Citadel by enemy lines dug in around the gates. By midday Friday, one battalion[22] managed to break through. Aided by American helicopter gunships, it had moved up the Huong River east of the fortress in three junks and fought its way through the northeast gate, Tria.

Before those troops arrived, and with a poor understanding of the Vietnamese general's plight, General LaHue was urging Truong to clear the rest of the enemy forces out of the Citadel. The Vietnamese commander was just getting to the point where he could defend his own base. LaHue nevertheless ordered that operations within the fortress would be left to the ARVN, while the marines he'd sent from Phu Bai would concentrate their efforts south of the river, in the triangle.

"Very definitely, we control the south side of the city," he told reporters, falsely. "I don't think they [the enemy] have any resupply capability, and once they use up what they brought in, they're finished."[23]

In fact, the Front had established supply lines reaching back to their mountain camps to the northwest. They controlled all the western and northern gates of the Citadel, nearly all of southern Hue, and the land around it to the west and southwest. They had hospital clinics up and running, and regular infusions of men, ammo, and food. Their hold on the city had stiffened. The six-hundred-man battalion led by Lieutenant Tang Van Mieu, the commander falsely reported to have been captured, finally made it into the city through the Chanh Tay Gate, and was thrown decisively into the fight for the airstrip. In the triangle, the marines were outnumbered by as many as ten to one.

Captain Meadows, whose company had gotten slammed on the Truong Tien Bridge, probably had the best handle on the size of the mismatch. He and what was left of his battered Golf Company were ordered to launch another attack on Thursday morning. They were to proceed seven blocks west and join the fight for the prison. It was an impossible order. Seven blocks? No one yet had been able to move more than one or two!

It was nearly miraculous that the Front had failed to take the communications center, where the air force personnel were trapped. The equipment enabled secure links between Mang Ca, the compound, and Phu Bai. Unfortunately, the flow of information was going mostly from top down instead of bottom up. Efficient and secure coms like these made Vietnam the first war in which distant commanders could intervene in a battle *as it happened*—not always a good thing. General LaHue and his staff at Phu Bai were looking at maps and deciding what was important and possible with no feel for the level of difficulty. All efforts at the compound to convey the uncertainty of its position were overwhelmed by the steady stream of urgent commands.

Gravel protested the order to send Golf back out, again to no avail. So Meadows and his men went. The two tanks they took were so thoroughly raked with fire just past the gate that the antennas and all the gear stowed on the outside of the vehicles were shot away. In the furious exchange, a small crowd of terrified civilians ran into the street, all of whom raced for the safest place in sight, which was the compound. They were the first of what would become a flood in the coming days.

Golf pressed on. It managed to take several of the buildings directly across the street, and then waged a pitched three-hour firefight across the street north to enter Hue University. Meadows lost still more of his men taking the building, a block-long, two-story structure that enclosed a large courtyard. Occupying the university gave the marines better command of the big intersection at the foot of the Truong Tien Bridge. This made traffic back and forth to the LZ and boat ramp a little less hazardous. One by one, the grunts cleared the many classrooms and offices, looking for remaining Front fighters and booby traps. The building was secure by Thursday night. It rapidly filled with civilians. The enemy had fallen back, but the marines did not yet know how far. Of the 160 marines Meadows had brought with him the day before, fewer than 100 remained. The small American foothold in southern Hue had expanded by one block.

Those up the chain could no longer have been ignorant of what was going on in Hue, but disbelief had progressed to denial. Despite Meadows's experience, Captain Downs's Fox Company was ordered on a fool's errand immediately on arrival at the compound. Downs was told only that there was sporadic shooting in the city from stubborn snipers in the blocks around the compound. Fox's job was to rescue Americans holding out at the coms center, treacherous blocks away. An air force sergeant who had been based there offered to guide them, so Downs attached him to his second platoon, which was led by Lieutenant Rich Horner.

Horner was considered by his men to be too brainy to be a real marine officer. He was from Illinois, and after earning an engineering degree at Bradley University in Peoria, he had gotten a job in California for North American Aviation, working for the moon program. He had literally been a rocket scientist. The job came with a military deferment, but Horner, feeling a patriotic tug and a need for more excitement in his life, had entered the marines. He knew this would be likely to land him in Vietnam. His credentials sometimes worked against him

in leading grunts, many of whom considered book learning an imped-
iment to common sense. He was just twenty-six, but deep lines in his
cheeks gave him a grave, professorial appearance, which added to the
perception of him as more of a thinker than a man of action. This
impression was sealed when he had misread a map early in his tenure
with Fox, and led his platoon a long way off course. It also earned him
the nickname Wrong Way Go Far. It all hinted, unfairly, at ineptitude.

Luckier men had nicknames that grew right out of their actual
names. Horner's friend, for instance, leader of Fox's third platoon,
Lieutenant Don Hausrath, was "Rat" from day one. A stocky, jovial
fireplug from California, four years younger, he embraced it, scrawling
Rat on the front of his helmet on his first day in Vietnam. Rat was a
good name for a street fighter.

Horner's nickname was not emblazoned on his helmet. He was
well liked by his men, but they were not shy about questioning his
orders. As his platoon formed up for this excursion into the streets of
Hue, the air force sergeant told Corporal Chris Brown, who one of
Horner's squad leaders: "You know, I have seen other people try to
get down that street all day and they have been getting the shit kicked
out of them. What makes you think we are going to do any better?"

Brown shrugged.

"It's orders."

But the more Brown thought about it, the more he thought it was
a pretty good question. He took it to Horner.

"Nobody had been able to do it, Lieutenant," the corporal said.
"What makes you think we can?"

"Listen, Brown, that is our order," said Horner. "That's what we've
been told to do and we are going to do it."

His platoon took the lead. They moved in classic formation, two
squads on either side of the street, and one held in reserve. Brown's
took the right side and was led out by Lou Gasbarrini, who always
insisted on walking point. He was followed by Charlie Campbell, and
then Brown and the rest of his squad. Behind them was the reserve
platoon and command post: Horner, his radioman, and the air force
sergeant. The rear contingent included two photographers, including
UPI photographer Sawada,[24] AP reporter John Lengel, and the platoon's
two corpsmen. They marched out into the misty rain and made it

without incident to the corner of Tran Cao Van Street, where they relieved Golf Company. There they turned right and started walking down Tran Cao Van, a street with one- and two-story structures on both sides set back from the curbs. On the right side was a wide brick sidewalk with big trees planted in a row, and telephone poles with wires that sagged down to roof level. There were stone walls before many of the houses. On the left were a curb and grass and low stone walls before a long row of large, impressive homes.

The shooting started about thirty feet down. The enemy had clearly waited until the entire platoon was around the corner, cut off from the compound's machine-gun tower and defensive bunkers. Gasbarrini went down first, and lay motionless on the street. Campbell leaped over a stone wall and took cover behind it. Brown hid behind one of the trees. Behind them, the air force sergeant alongside Horner was hit, and fell. Responding to frantic calls for help, Doc Goose, navy corpsman James Gosselin, went racing up the street. He ran past Brown toward the downed point man, but then he, too, was shot. He fell hard against the base of a stone wall in the limp way dead men fell. His helmet rolled off to the sidewalk. Behind him came William Henschel, a bright private from Ohio who was a member of Brown's squad and had volunteered to carry a corpsman's bag when the platoon found itself shorthanded. Henschel had apprenticed himself to Doc Goose and had been learning all he could in the previous weeks. He made it a few feet past Gosselin before he, too, went down, shot in the head. Then Brown's radioman, Stan Murdock, went down. He was clearly dead.

Brown went looking for cover. He zigzagged up the sidewalk and a tracer round hit his helmet, sending it flying. He jumped over the same wall Campbell had gone over, and thought for a moment he himself might be dead. But there wasn't even a mark on his head. The two of them crouched behind the wall for hours, Brown peeking his head up to see what was happening on the street.

"Hey, don't do that," said Campbell.

"What?"

"Don't put your head up like that. They are on to it."

Above the ear-rattling sound of shooting, Brown called to Gasbarrini.

"Yeah," he shouted back. "I'm okay. I'm hit in the arm. I'm playing dead."

Behind them was another, higher wall, and it occurred to Brown that the right way for them to have moved would have been off the street, not down the middle. His friend Cristobal Figueroa-Perez was doing it the right way, making his way forward, jumping walls, crawling, peeking over, and then advancing, until he, too, was shot in the head.

Horner immediately gave up trying to advance, but there seemed also to be no way back. He had dead and wounded on the street, and men hiding behind whatever cover they could find. They stayed put—for *hours*. Captain Downs was abreast of him, but behind a wall. He could not see what was in front of the platoon. He kept urging Horner to advance. The lieutenant shouted that there was no way. He could see that the enemy had well-hidden firing positions throughout the neighborhood, near and far, in buildings, in bunkers, behind stone walls, and, most effectively, on rooftops and at upper windows in the taller buildings. He had tried maneuvering his men to find a different way, breaking into the houses and hopping walls and trying to advance by staying behind them, but every move, like Figueroa-Perez's, just resulted in more casualties. Horner felt none of them were going to get off the street alive.

Then two tanks rolled up behind them. There was some discussion of how to use them to continue moving forward, but Downs knew this would not work. The tanks by themselves were too vulnerable, and moving men up around them would just get more men shot.

In the middle of the action, Downs answered a question from Lengel, the AP reporter. The captain had been in Hue for only hours, but he could already see what they were up against. "It's going to be like this for every house, every block," he said. "One man can keep a whole unit pinned down. We need air and artillery. We'll get no place without it." [25]

After a consultation with Gravel, it was decided to move the tanks up the street to provide cover, pick up the casualties, and withdraw. It took Horner a few minutes to get the tank commander on the radio, and then the vehicles moved up. As they did, Horner's radio operator, David Collins, was shot through the neck and killed.

When the tanks came even with where Brown and Campbell were hiding behind the wall, one pulled over to the sidewalk and both marines got behind it. They picked up Henschel with his corpsman's bag and put him on top of the tank. Brown thought the kid was dead, but soon learned otherwise. The tank lurched forward and Henschel bounced off to the street. When the vehicle abruptly reversed direction and ran over his foot, he screamed. A tourniquet was applied around his lower leg. Roberto DelaRivaVera, who had been walking point on the left side of the street, was farthest ahead. As the tanks advanced they started getting hit by rocket-propelled grenades. Unlike the smaller, lighter tanks used by the ARVN, the Pattons could take the pounding, but the rockets exploded as they bounced off, spraying the marines with shrapnel. Horner was hit and went down.

The flying shards of metal had shredded his left side, badly wounding his arm and his hand. He felt no pain—*I must be high on adrenaline,* he thought—but he was convinced it was time to get off Tran Cao Van Street. DelaRivaVera looked dead, and Horner, still functioning and feeling no pain, judged it wasn't worth risking more men at that point to retrieve his body. Downs was on the verge of concurring, but then stopped himself. Leaving a fallen man behind violated a basic tenet of the Marine Corps. He directed the tanks to move up close enough for his men to step out and pull the body to cover, which proved unnecessary, because when the vehicle got close enough, DelaRivaVera hopped up and got behind it. Downs vowed he would never again hesitate to retrieve a fallen man.

Horner remained conscious until his platoon limped back to the compound. Then he passed out. His wounds would send him out of Hue. After the doctors patched him up, he spent the night alone in a room on a table. Now and then someone would stop in to check on him. He still felt no pain.[26]

Members of his platoon huddled on the floor of another room in the compound, smoking cigarettes, comparing memories of what had happened, and trying to make sense of it. Why the hell hadn't they been sent out with the tanks in the first place? The men ran through what had happened to them and to each member of their platoon. They all agreed that Cristobal Figueroa-Perez looked bad. He probably was not going to make it.[27]

This was a particularly tough loss for Brown. He and Figueroa-Perez were close. Some weeks back, when they had gotten mail for the first time in weeks, Figueroa-Perez had a letter from his wife—the worst kind. She was leaving him. He had showed it to Brown, who was his squad leader. Most of the guys were too young to be married, but Brown was a little older—he was just twenty-one, but he *felt* older—and he had a wife at home, too. So they had bonded, even though the Puerto Rican's limited English and Brown's nonexistent Spanish made conversation difficult.

It didn't take much explaining for Brown to know that the letter had dealt his friend a terrible blow. Brown had met his own wife, Madeline, in Brooklyn, New York. He was from Ohio and had enlisted in the marines in 1964 right after high school. He initially had been stationed as a security guard at the Brooklyn Naval Yard. Madeline was nineteen and from Brooklyn and working at a desk for a big insurance company in Manhattan, right on Fifty-Ninth and Madison. She felt she had the most glamorous life imaginable. At night she and her friends volunteered at a servicemen's club in her neighborhood, and that was where she met Chris. There were bands that played the latest rock 'n' roll hits, and the girls would usually dance together unless one of the men was bold enough to cut in. Brown was. And he was a good dancer. He had big eyes and thick eyebrows, and he wore his dark hair longer than most marines, swept down over his forehead. They had gotten engaged in December 1965 and were married a year later. Brown had just one more year on his enlistment when he got his orders for Vietnam. It was the worst. They wrote each other three or four times a week.

So Brown could feel his friend's pain.

"You know," he told Figueroa-Perez, "I'll take you up to the chaplain." He figured his friend could use some professional counseling. Once there, he had tried, without success, to talk the chaplain into giving Figueroa-Perez some R&R, just to pull himself together. Now it probably wouldn't matter, except that the faithless Mrs. Figueroa-Perez would be receiving his death gratuity—about ten thousand dollars—which was galling.

All the marines had been both impressed and shocked by Sawada, the Japanese photographer. It seemed odd to them that there were reporters and cameramen calmly at work in the middle of such mayhem.[28] It made them feel all the more that they had stumbled into something big.

Mike Morrow, the freelancer who had in fact stumbled into Hue, went out with another marine foray off the compound that day. They also had not gotten far, but in the middle of the shooting a young Caucasian man came darting up the middle of the street toward them. It was Steve Earhardt, one of the IVS team Morrow had been planning to visit, who had been hiding for two days. He told Morrow that Nelson and Johnson and the others had all been taken away. The reporter realized that if he had made it to Hue in time for the party, he would have been likely to share their fate. He flew back to Phu Bai the next day on one of the medevac choppers, but made plans to return. Morrow wasn't an experienced reporter, but he knew a story when he saw one.

The grunts did not have the option of stepping back. On the compound floor that night, Brown was eventually alone with his own thoughts. He had spent his first day in Hue as scared as he had ever been. The fear had started when they were shot at on the chopper coming in, and had then just stayed at full throttle. He realized he had adapted to it. It surprised him. Fear, because it was everywhere and everyone felt it, receded in importance. It was still there, but when you realized there was nothing you could do about it, it ceased to matter. It just became your new reality. He kept going over the events on the street that afternoon. What could they have done differently? He remembered thinking, as Henschel went down, *Okay, this is it*. And when he had felt too scared to move, for some reason that's when he moved. It was as if his brain and his body traveled in opposite directions at the same moment, the mind saying *stay* and the body saying *run*. The body ruled. And he had survived. It was luck but also instinct. What he felt now more than fear was frustration. How were you supposed to advance under conditions like these? Why were they being ordered to do this? People were getting killed and nobody seemed to know what was going on. He didn't sleep that night. Half of the guys stayed up while the other half closed their eyes, but even when Brown closed his eyes his mind raced.

His commanding officer had much the same thoughts about the way they were being used. Captain Downs had been ordered that evening to saddle his men up for another try at the prison, which was still an impossible seven blocks distant. Even if he hadn't known about Meadows's experience, he had been out on the street with his men that afternoon, and he could read a map. The prison was adjacent to the province headquarters—the approach to the prison went through the site—and Gravel suggested that Downs take his men there and use it as a springboard for the attack. This, of course, ignored the near impossibility of getting to the province headquarters, which was five times farther than anyone had been able to move in southern Hue in the last two days. When Downs talked to some of the military advisers who were getting reports from their ARVN allies, he asked if anyone had consulted with those at the province headquarters about the plan. He was told there were now NVA machine gunners on the roof of that building, and on the flagpole outside flew a Viet Cong flag.

He told Gravel the order was crazy. Like the others, it had originated at Phu Bai, so the colonel felt obligated to obey it. Downs radioed his gunnery sergeant, Ed Van Valkenburgh, and told him to get the men ready.

But the more Downs considered the move, the more convinced he became that it was foolhardy. He sought out Gravel again, and requested permission to draft a formal message explaining the situation in detail and requesting that the order be rescinded. Gravel sent the message and in fairly quick order Task Force X-Ray backed down.

When Downs called his sergeant back and told him to have the men stand down, Van Valkenburgh was relieved. He told the captain: "I was afraid we were going back down the street we were on this afternoon."

"Gunny," said Downs, "where we were going tonight would have made this afternoon look like a walk in a park."

Gravel was instructed to send back to Phu Bai the vehicles that had delivered Alpha and Golf Companies the previous day. The trucks were loaded with dead and wounded, and drove down Highway 1 with an escort of forty marines, with both Quad-fifties. Meadows sent along his most experienced platoon leader, Lieutenant Bill Rogers. If they made it, he told Rogers to meet personally with the Task Force X-Ray command staff and to tell them in the bluntest terms possible what the hell was going on in Hue.

5

Snuffies and the Most Macho
Woman in the World

Gᴇɴᴇ Rᴏʙᴇʀᴛs ɢᴏᴛ out of Hue on the last chopper Thursday evening, February 1, at dusk. There were wounded marines on the floor, and body bags stacked against the walls. He sat on the dead, holding up bottles in each hand with tubes attached to the still living on stretchers at his feet.

Word was seeping out about Hue, but only inadequately. On Friday morning, the *Washington Post* would have a story compiled from news dispatches that reported a stubborn force of one thousand Viet Cong in the city, flying their flag. It was not a report from the scene, and the number of enemy forces was far too low, but it accurately reported that nearly all of the city had been taken. It also suggested that there was little chance that the enemy could hang on to any of it.[29]

Roberts's report would be the first from the scene, and the first to capture the magnitude of what had happened. It ran on page 1 of the *New York Times* on Saturday.

ENEMY MAINTAINS TIGHT GRIP ON HUE

Force Put at 5 Battalions—U.S. Marines
Hold Two Square Blocks of City

HUE, South Vietnam, Feb. 2nd—Enemy battalions weathered repeated attacks by Marine tanks and South Vietnamese aircraft today to maintain a tight grip on the ancient city of Hue.

At nightfall, the Marines held only two square blocks of the smoking city. And seven South Vietnamese Army battalions struggled unsuccessfully to push North Vietnamese and Vietcong troops from the Citadel—a 19th-century fortress built to shield the nation's historic imperial palace.

The strength of the enemy resistance caught the South Vietnamese by surprise. As late as yesterday, Vietnamese commanders in the area were saying that the enemy troops in Hue were weak and ill supplied and would fall with the first major allied push.

But today the assessment has changed. "Enemy forces in the ancient Citadel are believed to number five battalions," the regional Vietnamese command said in a late communiqué that gave the Hue battle more attention than any other engagement under way in the country.[30]

Firsthand reporting lent weight to his account. Relying on official sources, Roberts reported that the enemy presence was "five battalions," roughly two thousand men. It was off by a factor of five, but closer to the truth than anything previous. He captured the growing sense of desperation: "Parents hold their children tightly by the hand, and move sideways with their backs pressed against buildings. When they reach an open space—an intersection or a gap between houses—they run quickly and flatten themselves against the first wall they reach." He made it clear that the battle was far from over: "With the enemy in strong positions, the marines and the South Vietnamese face the prospect of lengthy house-to-house fighting. In several parts of Hue, the line between the allies and the enemy is a narrow one—a situation that could make virtually all of the fighting bitter. The situation was dramatized yesterday when a lean marine sergeant stood by a brick column near an intersection"—this had been the man directing Roberts and Downs's marines as they came off the chopper—"waving his arms like a traffic officer and ordering his men to move behind a low concrete wall. 'Friendlies on the left,' he told each passing marine. 'Enemies on the right.'"

The surprise achieved in Hue was complete. It was not a case of simply being caught off guard. It was so unexpected it triggered not just alarm, but disbelief—*deadly* disbelief. Ordering Meadows to storm the Thuong Tu Gate or Downs to take the prison was just the beginning.

Many young Americans would die or be severely maimed over the weeks it took for the truth to sink in.

It was not that no one saw. On the first day of Tet, Walt Rostow had sent LBJ a note attached to a startlingly accurate CIA report. The note read: "Mr. President, This is a bad report about Hue. We will check it with Westy when he gets on the phone."

The attached report read (emphasis added):

1. The friendly position in the city has apparently deteriorated seriously during 31 January.
2. According to a US official who made a flight over the area late on the afternoon of 31 January and received information relayed from US military officials in Hue, *the city appears to be largely under the control of the communists.*
3. During the flight, the official reported that a major market place on the north side of the Song Huong River in flames, with other smaller fires burning on the south side of the river. A firefight was in progress along the river road on the south side. Ground fire was also coming up from the vicinity of the air strip inside the Citadel area.
4. The official was able to raise several local elements by radio and was told that a provincial reconnaissance headquarters inside the city had been overrun, and that many VC were present throughout the area. The official was unable to make contact with the MACV headquarters, or the CORDS headquarters. He observed an ARVN battalion approaching Hue from the northwest, firing artillery to clear the way.
5. A message from the C-2 advisor's office in the MACV compound at Hue, received at I-Corps Headquarters in Da Nang, stated that *the MACV compound and the 1st Division Headquarters in the Citadel at Hue were the only "known" places still holding out against the VC.* Reportedly a marine company had tried to cross the highway bridge from the south into the northern sector of the city, but had been driven back with heavy casualties.[31]
6. There is no other information currently available here to confirm the above report.[32]

This completely accurate summary, which Westy surely had seen, was apparently dismissed as false. The general continued to maintain publicly and privately that the enemy presence in Hue was minor and completely manageable. In a cable to Washington that same Wednesday, January 31, he reported wrongly that there were only three companies of enemy soldiers (about five hundred to six hundred men) in the city.[33] Later that same day he reported: "The northeast and southwest portions of the Citadel of Hue continue to remain partially occupied with heavy contact reported." In fact, the "northeast," Mang Ca, was the only part of the Citadel not occupied by the enemy. Westy seemed to have, at best, only a sketchy idea of what was going on, despite this agency field report. Typically, such assessments were sent directly to Washington and to Westmoreland, and the commander was known to be unhappy that they were not sent to him alone. He resented analyses that undercut the story he was selling, and would have been unlikely to share them.[34]

In these first two days of Tet, the general continued to stress that the real attack was coming at Khe Sanh.

"I am in constant contact with developments around Khe Sanh," he cabled. "The enemy has major forces in the area which he has not yet committed." And: "Expect enemy initiation of large scale offensive action in the Khe Sanh–DMZ area in the near future." For LBJ's general, the anticipated battle for the isolated marine camp had become such a fixed idea that the actual struggle taking place in Hue, in Saigon, and in dozens of other cities throughout South Vietnam was a sideshow. Ten days into the struggle, in a cable to the Joint Chiefs, he dismissed the idea that his obsession with Khe Sanh was a mistake: "While it is possible that the enemy build-up in the Khe Sanh–DMZ area is a diversion, I consider the possibility remote. He [the enemy] has put too much effort in the build-up to support the diversion theory."[35] Meanwhile Westmoreland seemed almost oblivious to the largest single battle of the Tet Offensive, if not of the entire war, under way in Hue. His forces there were badly outnumbered, struggling, and dying.

The truth became harder to ignore in Phu Bai with every new wave of dead and wounded. They came on the irregular chopper flights, whenever the poor visibility enabled pilots to dip into and out of Doc Lao Park, or they came in bleeding heaps on returning trucks. Doctors set up triage centers on the tarmac and just inside the front gate.

Thursday afternoon, General LaHue handed authority for the fight in
Hue to a regimental commander, Colonel Stanley Hughes, and promised him more men and arms. It would be two days before Hughes
would arrive at the MACV compound. By then, the enclosure would
be jammed with nearly fifteen hundred men. Arriving with Hughes
would be Lieutenant Colonel Ernie Cheatham, whose Golf and Fox
Companies were already there. He would soon have a third, Hotel Company. Their mission would be sweeping the enemy from southern Hue.

But that was still days away.

Roberts started trying to get back as soon as his story went out Thursday night, but by now there was competition. Previous to his story, it had
just been Hanoi trumpeting its major victory over the puppet regime,
but outlandish claims from that source were commonplace. When the
New York Times confirmed the truth about Hue on its front page, word
was definitely out: trapped marines . . . smoking city . . . five battalions of
enemy troops. A huge fight was shaping up inside the old fortress. Suddenly
nearly every reporter in the country was trying to get to Hue.

After three years of escalating American effort, covering Vietnam had
become a scrum, with competing news organizations from all over the
world. Veteran war correspondents fought to break news and capture
the action alongside amateurs, most of them young, some of them
quite talented, and many ambitious and fearless, if not foolhardy. By
Friday morning, February 2, their growing numbers at I Corps Press
Center in Da Nang were getting on the marines' nerves. Whenever a
chopper landed with more casualties, a mob of journalists wanted to
board it for the return flight. They queued on the tarmac alongside doctors doing triage. The marine colonel in charge at the press center got
fed up. He blew a whistle and chided reporters: "Shape the fuck up!"[36]

In the scrum was Sam Bingham, a freelance photographer who
had recently graduated from Yale. He had paid his way to Vietnam in
order to see for himself what was going on. When a chopper landed,
he started capturing images of the wounded men being off-loaded
until the colonel grabbed his camera and chewed him out for "taking
pictures while men were dying." Bingham helped carry stretchers until
the helicopter was empty. The more seasoned journalists were not as
obliging. They felt they had a right and responsibility to record what

was happening. Some responded to the colonel's anger with expletives of their own, and raised middle fingers.

Roberts spent that night in the battalion aid station, and in the morning reported back to the tarmac. The colonel was now so worked up that he announced, henceforth, no reporter was going anywhere in I Corps (which stretched from the DMZ to well south of Da Nang) without a marine escort. Roberts started to protest. There were rules about such things. He was warming to his argument when a very mature-looking master sergeant tapped him on the shoulder. Roberts turned, expecting trouble, but the sergeant advised, "Don't object. Just pick me as your escort."

So Roberts did. When they had a chance to talk, the sergeant introduced himself as John R. King, "night manager and editor of the *Bergen Record*." He was a veteran of both World War II and Korea who had volunteered for a program that sent retired marine noncoms to Vietnam for one year. King fixed Roberts up with a truck convoy that was leaving for Hue shortly. It would be picking up Lieutenant Rogers, his Golf Company platoon, and assorted volunteers at Phu Bai. By the time the four-truck convoy departed, it was jammed with journalists. Bingham, who had been given his camera back, was aboard, along with a cheerfully boastful French photojournalist named Catherine Leroy, who would astonish everyone.

Leroy had the seat next to his. She was a scrawny young woman— she weighed just eighty-five pounds—who stood barely five feet tall, with bright if frequently dirty blond hair she wore braided into a thick ponytail. She had arrived in Saigon two years earlier with no experience and a cheap Leica. She talked fast and moved fast. Pleased to find herself beside an American who spoke French, she chattered amiably. If Bingham felt jittery about racing toward a battle, Leroy seemed delighted. She regaled him with war stories and close calls and pulled up her trousers to show off the shrapnel scars on her legs. Bingham thought she was the most macho woman he had ever met. The marines just saw a blond female in fatigues and combat boots, with cameras draped around her neck and a cute French accent. She was accompanied by Francois Mazure, a blue-eyed, bearded reporter for *Agence France-Presse*.

On the same convoy were two marine "snuffies," or combat correspondents, Steve Berntson and Dale Dye. Both were marine sergeants
with unusual jobs. They were "military journalists," or, rather, public relations reporters in the field charged with writing stories about
their fellow marines. They were assigned to the Information Services
Office (ISO) and covered the war the same way as civilian journalists
but with a mandate to stress the positive. They had a license to go
anywhere and do anything that could be turned into a story, so they
were far more widely traveled than most marines, and they had a
great deal more independence. Like the journalists, whom they came
to know well, they traveled around the country looking for hot spots,
but unlike their civilian counterparts, they didn't just drop in and then
leave. They attached themselves to units, picked up a rifle, stayed with
them, and often fought beside them. This earned them both respect
and better access. Marines in the field were usually happy to oblige
reporters anyway. It was nice to think about getting your picture or
name in the news back home. Maybe their families would see it. But
they tended to regard the civilian correspondents as dilettantes, or war
tourists, who dropped in to sample the deadly excitement of combat,
didn't help, and exited on the first chopper out.[37] And some of the
men were growing skeptical of reporters' motives, particularly those
of the foreign reporters. Marines noted the growing tendency to paint
Americans as losers and bad guys in this conflict. Snuffies didn't bug
out, and they didn't write shit about you, either.

Dye had a drawing of the *Mad* magazine icon Alfred E. Neuman
on the back of his flak jacket, above which he had written the goofy
character's slogan: "What, me worry?" Berntson had two things written on his flak jacket, his name and his nickname: Storyteller. Some
combat correspondents had Snuffy Smith, the hillbilly comic book
character, drawn on theirs—the name "snuffy" often was attached to
junior enlisted men. Because they traveled and wrote continually, within
the ranks some became well known and even esteemed. They saw the
war closer than any civilian correspondent. Some of them, Berntson
included, had been wounded and even decorated. Their stories were
published in the marine newspaper *Sea Tiger*, and often in *Stars and
Stripes*, the independent newspaper devoted to covering the US military.

Berntson looked for sad and funny stories, too. He wrote one about a particularly beloved gunny, Nathaniel Weathers, who had been killed outright when a mortar shell landed on him as he was out checking com lines in Quang Tri. A more lighthearted effort concerned a marine at Phong Dien who got caught in a mortar barrage while he was taking a shit on a honey bucket—a big metal barrel half-filled with diesel fuel that had a board with a hole in it laid across the top. He was blown right off the drum, and landed drenched with its contents. The corpsmen insisted he be hosed off before they would treat him. There were also terrible stories, ones he did not write, like the night a squad leader he knew tripped a booby trap that sliced open his stomach. The man's innards spilled out of him, and shortly before he died he was frantically trying to gather them back, calling to Berntson: "Help me get these in! Help me get these in!"

The snuffies' stories were regularly handed out to civilian correspondents, who sometimes reshaped them and put them on the wire, which meant they sometimes showed up in little newspapers throughout the United States. Mention a marine's hometown—something Berntson was always careful to do—and there was a good chance it would end up in his local paper. There were usually no bylines on these stories, but the marines remembered who wrote them. Berntson would be hailed by a grunt in the bush who said, in so many words: *Hey, Storyteller, you lying sack of shit. You know all that bullshit you wrote about me? You know what? My mom clipped it and sent it to me! They think I'm a hero at home now and maybe they'll buy me a beer when I get back!* That felt better than a byline. Commanders heading off on a hairy patrol would say, "Get Storyteller. We're going out on a romp."

Berntson had started out writing stories as a high school sophomore in Park River, North Dakota, getting paid a nickel per column inch by the *Walsh County Press*. When he didn't head to college right after high school graduation, he found himself confronted by the draft board. He enlisted in the marines to take advantage of their two-year option. He was trained as a machine gunner, but after completing the course and discovering he didn't like it—the work was dirty and the guns were heavy and loud—he raised his hand and asked how he could opt out. He was referred to a reenlistment officer. Turned out if you wanted to be anything more than a gun humper, you had to sign up for two more years. What sort of work did he want to do? Berntson said he knew how to take pictures and write stories. He was told there was no such military occupation specialty in the US Marine Corps. He knew this was not true, because every base had its own newspaper and he had read these papers. He persisted. With a spanking new four-year commitment, he found himself helping to put out the base newspaper in El Toro Marine Air Station in Irvine, California. What he really wanted was Vietnam. He read the stories from there, and they were a lot more interesting than his, which were all too often composed as glorified captions around posed pictures of glad-handing generals. He had visions of writing gripping accounts of battles and sweeping troop movements, but when he finally managed to get to the war, he found that the work was about finding the little private first class with the big rifle who did something unusual—and making sure you spelled his name right and put in the name of his hometown.

Berntson carried a little standard-issue green notebook. On the inside flap he had written his name and, proudly: CORRESPONDENT, VIETNAM 67–68. Under that he wrote the number of his ISO unit, and next to it: ISO, FIRST TO GO! LAST TO KNOW! On the opposite page he recorded the serial numbers of the two cameras he was issued, an Asahi and a Canon, and the serial number of his service pistol. By February 1968, he had been in Vietnam for eight months, and he'd learned to hear the difference between the sound of an explosion that said: *Get down right now!* and the kind that said: *No worries, keep walking.* He was afraid a lot, but it had become a discerning fear.

The Tet Offensive had started just after he arrived at Phu Bai, and true to the slogan in his notebook, even after two days he had no idea what was going on. He had gone to the supply tent, where his friend Roger Doss was the sergeant, and Doss had found him a bunk in the back among all the boxes. He filed a few stories, took a long hot shower, ate some hot food, and drank as much gin as he could stand. He was wandering around the camp on Thursday, hungover, when he noticed things had gotten tense. He saw some marines climbing onto a truck convoy just in from Da Nang, and was told they were heading up to Hue. There was some major sniper fire up there and they needed support. He didn't think anything of it, and spent another night in the supply tent.

The next morning someone stuck his head into the tent and said they were looking for volunteers to fight in Hue. Berntson thought, *What the hell?* He had been to the city once before, with Dye. They had a friend there who had worked at the air force coms office, and they'd had a nice dinner at a restaurant down by the Huong River. He could use a little taste of civilization. Maybe his buddy was still there. He grabbed his gear and climbed onto the truck, where he ran into Dye.

They stopped at a village to pick up two dozen ARVN rangers. The French reporters, Leroy and Mazure, stepped out and greeted the civilians with a hearty "Bonjour!" They were eager to make it clear they weren't Americans. The shooting picked up as they moved into the city, but they arrived at the compound intact and with no one wounded. They had been shot at in a few places, and the marines had fired back aggressively.

Roberts just kept his head down. They sped over the An Cuu Bridge, which, miraculously, the Front had not yet dropped. Past it he could see very little through the wooden slats of the truck, and couldn't tell whether the gunfire was incoming or outgoing. He felt the vehicle pull to a stop, and marines rolled out to assume firing positions. He thought it was just another delay on the road—he had never been driven from Phu Bai to Hue before, so he wasn't sure how long it would take—but as he got out he realized they were back at the compound. He started asking around for Fox Company, the group he had flown in with the day before. He was told that most of them had been shot up and evacuated, which was an exaggeration.

Berntson was shocked by what he saw when he arrived. He knew serious danger when he saw it. There were dead enemy soldiers bloating on the street outside. Inside there were stacks of dead Americans with tarps over their heads; the supply of body bags had run out. The whole place looked shot up and battered. It was now jammed with marines, and more would be coming in a few hours—Hotel Company, led by Captain Ron Christmas. Golf still had about one hundred men, and Fox had over two hundred. With Hotel, there would be three companies from the 2/5 marines in addition to the remnants of Batcheller's Alpha 1/1, now being commanded by Gunny Canley. Then there was

Colonel Adkisson's army contingent and all the marine advisers who had come to spend the holidays.

Tense and urgent efforts were being made to organize all these men. Outside the walls there was still shooting. From the rooftops, where the marines now had sandbagged firing positions, they were still popping off at targets nearby. The men up there had relaxed into the new state of constant battle. They had a big cooler of soft drinks and were listening to the radio, which was about to broadcast a month-old tape of the Senior Bowl, the annual college football All-Star game. They would chat with one another, cheer at something on the radio, and then take aim and shoot.

Other than the crowded conditions and this odd new normalcy, Roberts saw that little about the position had improved over the last two days. The marines were still surrounded and owned very little of the immediate neighborhood. The trucks that brought them turned right around and headed back to Phu Bai to pick up Hotel Company. The marines and ARVN rangers who had just arrived were quickly spread out. With so many concentrated inside the increasingly crowded compound, a well-placed mortar could cause catastrophic losses. So men were sorted and assigned positions on the perimeter.

Bingham no sooner stepped off his truck than he fell in with a group of marines heading out the front gate. They were carrying scaling ladders and hooks. Whatever they were about to do looked interesting, so he followed. He took shelter with them in a trench on the south bank of the Huong, where they were waiting for tanks to roll up and provide covering fire.

Waiting there, Bingham was surprised to find a book, in French,[38] written by the Austrian Stefan Zweig, an author who interested him. So he was bent over the book as the tanks started firing over their heads. With the crashing sounds came a big explosion—he would learn later that it was a mortar—and he saw blood, his blood, splash on the open page. He keeled over. A metal fragment had entered his eye at the bottom of the socket, passed through his cheek and jaw and neck—nicking his carotid artery—and landed in his throat. He felt hands grabbing him, stripping away his camera and clothing, and was thrown onto the back of a truck. He was bleeding profusely and couldn't talk. He felt no pain. A bandage was wrapped tightly around his head to stanch the bleeding. He was conscious, but now he couldn't see. He asked for a piece of paper and a pencil, and wrote down his name, his blood type, and "freelancer."

He was jerked off the truck and placed on a stretcher.

"This guy is in bad shape," someone said. "He can't talk, but he can hear you. If he gets in any trouble he can wave his hand."

Roberts, who had just lit a cigarette—he had not even taken off his backpack—saw Bingham being carried in. He was shocked. He had just met the photographer on the ride up. They had been there only a few minutes. He followed the stretcher, telling Bingham he was there, and the young man wrote out the name and address of his girlfriend and gave it to him. He did not want his parents to know he had been wounded, but he wanted the girl to know. Roberts took the note and promised to deliver the message.

Leroy and Mazure were missing. The two French journalists had slipped away during one of the convoy's stops. They had changed from their fatigues and donned civilian clothes, rented a tandem bicycle, and pedaled into the city on their own. They did not wish to be perceived as military, and announced to everyone they met that they were "*Phap bao chi bale!*" French press from Paris!

People paid them no mind. The few they saw on the street hurried away and would not look at them. They were in a Communist-controlled area, just a few blocks north of the Phu Cam Canal, and people were not eager to be seen with two Caucasians of any nationality. There were sounds of gunfire nearby. The two pedaled to a market and watched South Vietnamese planes drop bombs over the Citadel.

An old man directed them to the Church of the Most Holy Redeemer, an enormous white stone structure with a towering arched veranda and high conical spire. Inside they found thousands of civilians, mostly women, the elderly, and children, families who had been there for days, who were camped out in pews and in the aisles. People were hungry. Some were wounded. Babies were crying. Children shrieked whenever an explosion sounded nearby. There were wounded civilians on the floor behind the church's main marble altar.

Among these refugees were Tran Thi Thu Van, the writer from Saigon, and her family, who had reached the place after their long day of walking on Wednesday. Tran watched the two French journalists with curiosity. To her, Leroy looked dazed, and her companion, Mazure, bearded and disheveled. He looked to Tran as though he had been living in the forest. The two were quickly surrounded by children and the curious, but when Leroy lifted her camera and started taking pictures, the crowd pulled back quickly.

"Press. Press," said Mazure.

When Leroy turned the camera toward Tran and her family, her brother Thai stood up and turned his back.

"What a monkey," he said to the others in Vietnamese. "To take pictures in this situation."

Leroy didn't understand this reaction. She smiled to try to counter some of the scowls directed her way. Minutes later there was shooting outside the church, and people started to panic.

"The Viet Cong are coming!" someone shouted.

There was anxious whispering in the crowded pews. If the liberation soldiers came in, they would think the two French reporters were American, and the refugees would all be killed.

"Get them out of here!" said one.

"Break the camera," said another.

"Don't let them be here with us," one implored the priest.[39]

Mazure kept up his "Phap bao chi bale!" But he encountered only glowers. The church's French-speaking priest explained to Leroy and Mazure that the people were afraid of being seen with any Westerners, even the French, because of how it might look to the liberation forces.

"We have refused to let in soldiers from either side," the priest told them. "We have sent them away every time, telling them that this is a sanctuary for civilians."[40]

He let them spend the night in his room.[41]

6

The Chariot Is Coming

Captain Christmas and his Hotel Company[42] didn't get started from Phu Bai until after two o'clock Friday afternoon, February 2. They were traveling with reinforcements for Batcheller's Alpha Company, along with the wounded captain's replacement, Lieutenant Ray Smith.

Christmas had spoken to a number of the wounded men from Golf and Fox Companies, so he knew the convoy was likely to take fire on the way up Highway 1. He ordered extra ammo for all his men, and they were advised to ride with their weapons pointed out. He said he didn't want anyone from his company riding in the cabs of the trucks, a prime target, except the drivers. They rolled out in twelve trucks, bracketed by the Quad-fifties. The threat in Hue was finally getting the respect it deserved. Christmas was also given two more Dusters and two odd light tanks bristling with six 106-mm guns. These latter would prove to be some of the most useful weapons in the battle.

They were called Ontos, after the Greek word for "thing," in part because they were ugly. An Ontos was a small armored vehicle mounted with an entire battery of recoilless rifles, three long barrels on each side. It carried three men—a driver, a gunner, and a loader—and was originally developed as an antitank weapon by the army. The army had rejected it in part because the back blast made it almost as dangerous to those behind it as to those in front. That and a reloading problem—the crew had to climb out from its lightly armored nest and reload the thing from the outside. The army concluded that it posed more danger to its own side than to the enemy. But the marines had embraced it. The Ontos was faster and more maneuverable than a Patton tank, and it had more firepower. It was capable of firing six high-explosive rounds in rapid sequence, which meant it could collapse buildings and blow big holes through even the thickest stone walls, of which there were many in Hue.

Ron Christmas was a tall, square-jawed, twenty-seven-year-old officer from Yeadon, Pennsylvania, just outside Philadelphia, and he was a man who had seen more than a little death and suffering in his life even before going to war. He was ten when his mother had sent him upstairs to wake his teenage brother, whom he found dead, with bubbles of saliva at the corners of his mouth. He had succumbed to a fatal lung disease. While still in high school he had joined the volunteer fire company, and frequented the scenes of car accidents and house fires. He had once crawled underneath a train after it accidentally ran over two teenagers. Christmas was the youngest man on the fire truck— collecting the body parts. He prided himself on his tough blue-collar roots, and he looked the part; an auto accident had left a deep scar across the right side of his face from the edge of his mouth to his ear. But he had been the first member of his family to go to college, attending the Ivy League University of Pennsylvania on a scholarship. He joined the ROTC program there because it offered a fifty-dollar monthly stipend, which had made him feel rich, and once enrolled he was drawn to the marines. He had begun with no intention of making the military a career. But he discovered he was good at it, and he found himself a few years later watching the sun set into emerald water from the deck of a warship in the Caribbean Sea, asking, *Who are you trying to kid? You really love this stuff.* By the time he was sent to Hue he was a seasoned infantry commander, fully committed to a marine career.

Ray Smith was one of two lieutenants from Alpha Company on their way to Hue. He was an Okie who had volunteered for the marines because he was looking for the quickest way to Vietnam. In boot camp they had noticed something in him, and instead of shipping him off to war immediately, they sent him to officer candidate school. He had been with Alpha Company for a year as a platoon leader, and, with Captain Batcheller down and out, had just been named company commander. The other lieutenant was Donald Perkins, from Winnetka, Illinois, who was not the gung ho officer Smith was, but they were friends. Perkins was more of a character. He enjoyed joking with the men, and had a surprising meditative streak. He had once asked Smith, out of the blue, what he thought would happen to him after he died. It was not posed as a religious question. It was more in the nature of a metaphysical dialogue, and while they didn't resolve the matter, Smith would never forget the conversation. Perkins was the company's artillery forward observer, which meant he was responsible for coordinating air and artillery strikes. He was very serious about his work, but, despite his occasional philosophical rambles, little else.

The convoy ran into the usual rain of fire on its way north. One of the trucks ran into a crater, throwing some of the men to the road. Perkins was thrown from the truck and killed when its back end, which lifted on impact, landed on his chest, crushing him.

On his arrival at the compound, Smith assumed command of Alpha Company's three platoons from Gunny Canley. He would lead Second Platoon, and he put another lieutenant, Rick Donnelly, in charge of First Platoon.

He told Canley: "Gunny, I want you to take over Third Platoon."

"Gonzalez has got Third Platoon," Canley said.

Freddie Gonzalez's exploits in the previous days, when he led a charge across an open field and when he and Canley had crawled forward to destroy an enemy machine-gun position, had made a deep impression. Despite his youth, the wiry Texas sergeant's uncommon poise and bravery had earned him enormous respect. Smith didn't know this, and pushed Canley.

"I know. I know, Gunny, but he is young and I would just feel better if you took command of the platoon."

Canley answered him a little louder this time.

"Gonzalez has got Third Platoon."

"Gunny, I understand, but I want *you* to take command of Third Platoon."

The black sergeant was a man of few words, and was known for strict adherence to procedure, but on this occasion he wasn't budging. He actually made a short speech, which shocked Smith. It was the most he had ever heard Canley say at one time.

"Lieutenant, Gonzalez's got Third Platoon," he said. "If I survive this fight, I am going to see to it he gets the big one for what he has already done. Now, if you want me to go down and follow Third Platoon around I will, but Lieutenant, Gonzalez has got Third Platoon."

Smith realized that Canley knew a lot more about what was going on than he did, and that he, the new company commander, was likely to need Gunny Canley following him around a lot more than Sergeant Gonzalez did. Canley didn't say any of that, but it was implicit. Pointedly so.

Gonzalez kept Third Platoon, and Canley went to work as the lieutenant's gunny.

Captain Christmas had a little reunion with Meadows and Downs. The three young company commanders were friends. They had fought together and they trusted one another's courage and judgment and ability. They were pleased to be together in the biggest fight of their lives. None of them was impressed with Gravel, who at present was their commander. He had, in their eyes, failed them. He had sent Meadows and Downs out on missions that were foredoomed. It wasn't all his fault, because he was getting pushed around from above, and he had complained about it bitterly and consistently. But part of being a leader was being able to push up as well as down. You didn't ask men to risk everything on a mission that you did not believe in yourself. Gravel had been doing this now for several days. The men knew when they were being misused. This was the real deal, not some classroom exercise. These were blood decisions. They were the most important ones a military commander is asked to make. If you knew more because of where you were and what you saw, then you stood your ground. You didn't just protest; if need be, you *refused*. You put your judgment on the line. This might destroy your career—hell, it would certainly destroy your career—but you accepted that, because whatever happened to you, your career, your reputation, these were minor things by comparison. Lives were at stake. A real leader knew his responsibility was not first and foremost to himself; it was to his men, and the mission. What mattered in combat, what really mattered, was not only understanding why you asked men to risk their lives, but making them understand. Men would willingly risk their lives, but they needed to know that it counted. And they needed to know they had a chance. If the commander believed those things himself, he could convince his men. The problem here was that neither the young company commanders nor Gravel held that belief.

Since both Fox and Golf Companies had been badly bloodied, it was decided that Hotel Company would move out and occupy Hue University, which they needed to house the growing number of marines. Christmas moved his men into the university that night.

Inside the MACV compound, Gene Roberts pounded out his story on a portable typewriter with a spent ribbon. The words grew fainter and fainter on the page. Things had settled down enough for him to send this one over the phone lines very early Saturday morning. His second story from Hue finally made clear to the world, albeit in an understated way, exactly what was happening. It ran on the front page of the Sunday *New York Times*.

U.S. MARINES SEIZE
A 3RD BLOCK OF HUE

Reinforcements Enter City
32 American Civilians
Are Listed as Missing

HUE, South Vietnam, February 3—United States marines were in firm control of three square blocks of Hue today, compared with only two blocks yesterday. They steadily increased the lengths of their probes in search of the enemy.

Camped out at the university on Friday night, Christmas got word that their battalion commander would be coming tomorrow. This was the best news possible. What he and the other two 2/5 company commanders saw lacking in Gravel's leadership was exactly what they had learned to expect serving under Ernie Cheatham—*weight*.

Cheatham had it in every respect. He was a big, powerful man from Long Beach, California. He stood well over six feet tall and had a thick neck; a broad, muscled frame with wide sloping, bearlike shoulders; and powerful arms and legs. He was a prodigy of size, with the thickest forearms and wrists any of his men had ever seen. His head seemed to entirely fill his helmet, which swam on most marines. He had a deep, rumbling voice that could be heard even in the midst of a roaring firefight. Some marine officers feel a need to continually prove their toughness, a quality admired above all others in a combat commander. Cheatham had nothing to prove. He had played football for Loyola University in Los Angeles before entering the marines in 1952. And when his two years were up—after service in Japan and Korea—he had played on the defensive line of both the Pittsburgh Steelers and the Baltimore Colts. After discovering that the NFL paychecks stopped coming when the season ended, he rejoined the marines. He had intended to leave football behind, but found himself being traded around by commanders looking to improve their base football teams. He protested to his commanding officer, who had him transferred to Alaska to get him as far away from the game as he could. As physically imposing as he was, Cheatham was more interested in using his mind. But his gridiron past made him something of a star in the Marine Corps, even after he stopped playing.[43] He was and always would be Big Ernie. He used his size and his volume to advantage, playing the role of a big, dumb football player, but cunningly. His young company commanders saw past the act; behind the brawn was a subtle mind. They were awed by Cheatham's tactical skills, and entertained by his lively, mischievous, and often self-deprecating sense of humor. Cheatham had a store of anecdotes from his football days, and, as the years went by, from his soldiering: he had served as a platoon leader in the Korean War. He led with clarity and welcomed candor from his men. When he received an impressively detailed and pointed letter of complaint from a junior officer, Lieutenant John Salvati, he summoned him and promoted him on the spot. He assigned Captain Salvati to his staff. He liked a man who could intelligently disagree. Cheatham gave respect and received it in return. And despite his brawn, he led with a light touch. He made sure his men understood a mission, and then left them to carry it out. He intervened only when necessary. On the other hand, up the chain, he threw his weight around with abandon.

In fact, he had been doing just that all day Friday. Cheatham had assumed command of 2/5 just a month earlier, and was angry as hell about having the battalion effectively taken away from him. He was still furious over being yanked from the fight along the Truoi River, not just because his battalion had missed out on the glory and satisfaction of crushing an NVA battalion he had maneuvered into a corner, but because he had been ordered to leave one of his companies, Echo, behind, outnumbered and in a precarious position.[44] It did not make sense to him. His other three companies had been sent into Hue piecemeal without a clear idea of what they faced. Just before he had left for the city, Christmas had seen Cheatham arrive at Phu Bai ready to explode. He was determined to retake the reins of his battalion. He demanded to be sent to Hue immediately. Three of his companies were there and, he argued, he ought to be there, too. He promptly won the point.

Christmas was thrilled when he got the news. Cheatham would bring clarity. He would pull the disparate parts of this counterattack together, and Lord help anyone who tried to interfere.

Christmas got on the horn to Downs and Meadows to share the news. It felt like deliverance, like a biblical event.

He told them: "The Chariot is coming."

No explanation needed. They both knew what he meant.

PART FOUR

Counterattack in the Triangle and Disaster at La Chu

Saturday–Monday
February 3–5

Three days into the battle, American and South Vietnamese forces have made little progress, despite continued assurances from Saigon and Washington that Hue is under allied control. With the arrival of Lieutenant Colonel Ernie Cheatham, there is for the first time a coherent plan of attack to retake the triangle. At the same time, miles to the north, the US Army joins the battle, sending about six hundred troopers on a march south along Highway 1 toward the Citadel to sever National Liberation Front supply lines.

Big Ernie Cheatham, former NFL lineman and the lieutenant colonel in command of 2/5, directing fire from an Ontos during the battle.

Catherine Leroy, the French photographer who slipped away from American forces on the way into Hue and spent a day photographing Front soldiers.

Army Captain Bob Helvey in a photo taken at TFP hours before he and his company led a harrowing night march through enemy lines to safety.

Lieutenant Ray Smith photographed after receiving the Silver Star for heroism during the Hue battle.

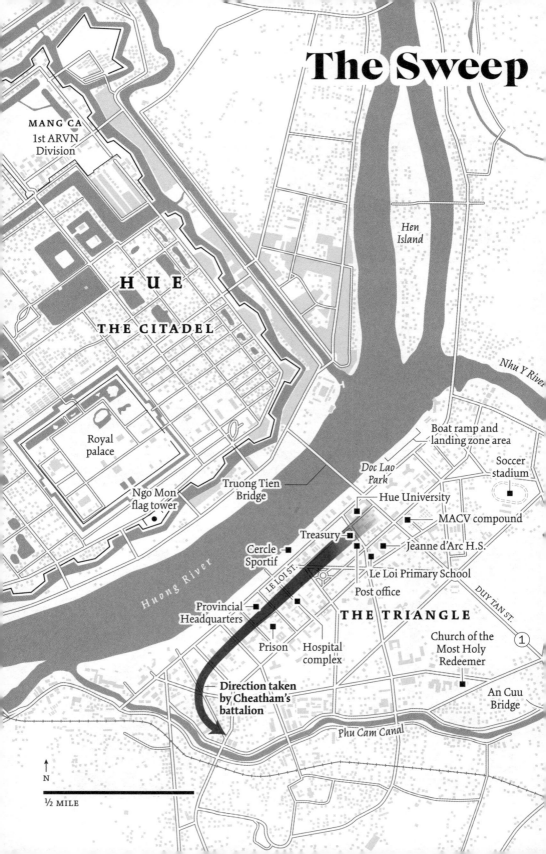

The Sweep

MANG CA
1st ARVN
Division

Hen
Island

HUE

THE CITADEL

Nhu Y River

Royal
palace

Boat ramp and
landing zone area

Soccer
stadium

Doc Lao
Park

Ngo Mon
flag tower

Truong Tien
Bridge

Hue University

MACV compound

Treasury

Jeanne d'Arc H.S.

Cercle
Sportif

Le Loi Primary School

LE LOI ST.

Post office

Huong River

Provincial
Headquarters

THE TRIANGLE

DUY TAN ST.

Prison

Hospital
complex

Church of the
Most Holy
Redeemer

1

**Direction taken
by Cheatham's
battalion**

An Cuu
Bridge

Phu Cam Canal

N

½ MILE

1

Pluses and Minuses

FOUR US MARINE companies had now been fed into Hue. They were getting creamed. It was clear enough to them that the city was in enemy hands, and taking it back was going to be hell.

Denial persisted higher up, however, even with the alarming casualties—about one hundred in three days.[1] When one member of the Task Force X-Ray command staff at Phu Bai suggested to Jim Coolican on the phone that there might be a "few platoons" of enemy in the city, the marine captain rebuked him, "Hell, we've got a platoon of NVA dead on the wire!"

General Robert Cushman, the I Corps commander in Da Nang, forbade American bombing and shelling in the city out of concern for its historic treasures—there was no similar expression of concern for its tens of thousands of trapped residents. He said the use of such heavy firepower should be left to ARVN commanders.[2] This may have been less a reflection of delicacy than further proof that the high command still had not accepted the fact that Hue was in enemy hands; the ban would be lifted promptly as this sank in. General Truong's lack of progress in the Citadel was chalked up to ARVN deficiencies, which in the American command's view were only to be expected, but the marines' inability to advance was judged more harshly. It was seen as a failure of leadership. The forces there were at best a patchwork, units assembled on the fly and poorly coordinated by the compound's ranking marine, Lieutenant Colonel Gravel. His persistent protests against attack orders looked like a classic case of the jitters. The fact that he had been proved right repeatedly didn't seem to matter. Being defeated and dead would have made his point more forcefully, and might have restored Gravel's reputation.

In Saigon and Washington the strategy was to insist that the Tet Offensive had been a complete bust. It had *not* been a surprise. Westy had foreseen it, and it had been a shattering disaster for Hanoi. The Joint Chiefs chairman, General Wheeler, characterized it as "desperation tactics." He said no major city had been taken. He fell back on Westy's all-purpose yardstick: body counts.

"Their losses have been extremely heavy," Wheeler told reporters. "[The Communists] have lost in the last three days some 6,200 men killed. We, too, have suffered some losses, but theirs have been ten times greater than ours."[3]

The defiant Communist flag before the Citadel was portrayed as little more than a publicity stunt.

McNamara, testifying before the Senate Armed Services Committee, argued that Westy's Checkers maneuver had fully anticipated and countered Hanoi's objectives, which he speculated had been twofold: "He [the enemy] may be trying to inflict on the South Vietnamese, the U.S., and allied forces a severe military defeat. I believe we are well prepared for that. Or, alternatively, in the event that such an objective eludes him, he may be seeking to achieve a substantial psychological or propaganda victory."

Sunday morning, on NBC's *Meet the Press*, Secretary of Defense McNamara said, "It's quite clear that the military objective of the attack has not been achieved. It was to divert US troops and South Vietnamese troops from the probable offensive action of the Viet Cong and North Vietnamese around Khe Sanh. And secondarily it was to penetrate and hold one or more district or provincial capitals. In that sense the military objective has not been achieved. Nor have they fully achieved their psychological objective, although I think there have been pluses and minuses psychologically."[4]

In Hue the marines were not weighing psychological "pluses and minuses." The body bags were piling up.

Westy's preoccupation with the vulnerability of Khe Sanh had played perfectly into Hanoi's plans. The buildup of NVA forces there had been a feint.[5] The objective all along had been Hue and the other cities.

Westmoreland had fallen for it so completely that even after Hue fell neither he nor his superiors in Washington could see it, much less admit it. American military commanders had been scoffing at Hanoi's military capability for years.

Recognition of the enemy's remarkable success in Hue failed to register fully in the States because most accounts of the Tet Offensive focused on Saigon, not least because that's where most reporters were. The raids there had been alarming and had disrupted normal life, but they were largely futile. Westy called them "suicidal." He used the same terms to characterize the surprise attacks everywhere else. The offensive had been a disaster—*for them*. Never mind that more than one hundred targets had been struck simultaneously by enemy forces estimated to number more than eighty thousand—so much for Westy's confidence that Hanoi could not muster troops in sufficient strength to mount attacks deep inside Vietnam. In fact, the only major American base that was not attacked on the eve of Tet was Khe Sanh.

And yet, as Westy sold it, the offensive had been nothing more than a treacherous and murderous trick, violating a holiday truce (the one he had urged President Thieu to revoke) by a villainous foe. No cities had been taken. The anticipated "general uprising" had not occurred. His all-important battle metric told the whole story, as far as the general was concerned. The body count leaped higher and higher in each day's cables—it was 5,800 on Thursday, and up to 12,000 by Saturday.[6] And this wasn't just Westy's public line, a calculated attempt to avoid handing Hanoi a propaganda victory; this was his analysis in private, in regular cables to Wheeler.

Writing about Tet years later, Westmoreland backed away from this assessment. He would somewhat grudgingly come to see Tet as a "limited success" amplified by "gloom and doom" press commentary. "One received the impression that the press were gleeful that the VC had finally accomplished something significant and the U.S. and South Vietnamese were in an awkward position," he wrote.[7]

There was no hint of such insight as the battle unfolded. Days after the attacks were made, President Johnson declared them "a failure."[8]

Press reports like Roberts's in the *New York Times*, echoed soon by other newspapers, showed this to be false, but everything in the newspapers was now regarded skeptically by those in power. War correspondents had become so uniformly antiwar that, to those running the war, they appeared intent on painting the worst possible picture. There was some justification for that opinion. In Saigon, for instance, early news accounts had exaggerated the extent of the raids—most had, for instance, reported incorrectly that the Viet Cong raiders had penetrated the embassy itself. And then there was the fixation on a shocking photograph of South Vietnam's national police chief Nguyen Ngoc Loan shooting a hand-cuffed Viet Cong prisoner in the head. It had been snapped at the instant of death, the victim's face contorted in shock and pain. Never mind that this fellow had been busy that morning shooting scores of people in cold blood,[9] the image alone told a simpler, more brutal story, one brandished enthusiastically by the war's opponents.

Press accounts fed the rhetoric of antiwar leaders. Just that week Senator Eugene McCarthy, who was challenging LBJ for the Democratic presidential nomination, cited news reports about Tet to accuse the administration of self-deception.

"We are in a much worse position than we were two years ago," McCarthy told reporters in Washington. "The Viet Cong are clearly getting protection from the population, and the so-called pacification program must be largely a sham." He ridiculed Johnson's claim that the attacks had been a failure. "If taking over a section of the American Embassy [they hadn't], and a good part of Hue . . . constitutes complete failure, I suppose by this logic that if the Viet Cong captured the entire country, the administration would be claiming their total collapse." The senator said that an American victory in the war was "militarily unattainable."[10]

In a Saturday editorial, the *Times* of London stated, "The scale and daring of the Viet Cong attack on South Vietnamese towns seems to have taken the Americans and South Vietnamese completely by surprise, for all of Gen. Westmoreland's unconvincing assurance that the Viet Cong build-up had been under observation for months past."[11]

The war effort still had plenty of supportive journalists. One of the most prominent was Joe Alsop, a longtime *Washington Post* columnist who sometimes used his journalistic credentials as cover to gather intelligence for the CIA. While he was not always a friend to LBJ, Alsop saw no reason why the Tet attacks should discourage American efforts. They were an act of desperation he compared to Japanese kamikaze attacks near the end of World War II. Tet had not been a surprise. Alsop wrote, incorrectly, "Everyone has known that such hidden assets existed."[12]

Whatever mistakes and misstatements were made on both sides of the debate, the stories and pictures from Hue dramatically undercut the claim that nothing of consequence was happening there. The rush of journalists to the city guaranteed that the battle would be independently observed and reported. NBC's Pentagon reporter Robert Goralski told viewers on Thursday night, "The communists may not be winning the war, as the Pentagon claims, but they don't seem to be losing it either."[13]

Even Walter Cronkite was starting to sound uncertain. The avuncular dean of TV anchors, whose CBS Evening News had set the standard, was a warm and familiar presence in American living rooms. He had faithfully reported progress in Vietnam, trusting in official sources, and had played down early contrarian reports as reflecting an antiwar vogue among ambitious young reporters in Saigon. Correspondents like David Halberstam, for instance, saw their reputation swell with every new critical article or book. There was something trendy about the antiwar message that bothered Cronkite. But he had been a war correspondent himself during World War II, and he found it hard to completely dismiss the work of younger reporters under fire. His own network's stories frequently undercut Westy's chipper assurances. So when the first reports of Tet rattled off teletypes at CBS's Broadcast Center in New York on Thursday, February 1, the anchorman tore them from the machine and waved them at his producers.

"What the hell is going on?" he demanded. "I thought we were winning the war?"

That night he told viewers that "bitter" fighting continued in Hue and other parts of South Vietnam. On Friday, Cronkite told his audience of millions, "The allies proclaimed today that they have broken the back of the five-day-old communist offensive in South Vietnam, but dispatches out of that pathetic country tell a somewhat different story."[14]

Publicly, President Johnson pushed the official line.

"We have known for several months now that the communists planned a massive winter-spring offensive," the president said in a Friday press conference. "We have detailed information on Ho Chi

Minh's order governing that offensive.[15] Part of it is called a general uprising . . . The biggest fact is that the stated purposes of the general uprising have failed. Communist leaders counted on popular support in those cities for their effort. They found little or none . . . The ferocity and violence, the deception and the lack of concern for the basic elements that appeal to human beings—they may have shocked a lot of people in that respect. But the ability to do what they have done has been anticipated, prepared for, and met."

In a private, off-the-record session with select reporters later that same day, Johnson doubled down on this confidence. With typically folksy charm, the president admitted that Tet might have surprised, say, as he put it, a sergeant asleep with a beer in his hand and his zipper down, or perhaps even with a woman on his lap, but that he was satisfied that Westy's intelligence and preparation had been superb.[16] He was, however, beginning to wonder why there had been no attack at Khe Sanh.

Max Frankel, head of the *New York Times* Washington Bureau, asked the president if he had underestimated General Giap.

"I always *overestimate* Giap," said Johnson. "You see what he did to the French. He is extremely able. I don't know what will happen. I asked the Joint Chiefs of Staff to give me a letter saying they were ready for this offensive at Khe Sanh."

"What do you think Ho is thinking?" Frankel asked.

"I do not know," said Johnson. "I felt by February third we could have expected the major offensive [at Khe Sanh] to begin. What Ho thinks I do not know. I believe he thought that the people would rally with them. They did not. There has been much sporadic activity. The ferocity was not anticipated."

The president then read out loud to the reporters a famous paragraph from Thomas Paine's *The Crisis*—"These are the times that try men's souls. The summer soldier and sunshine patriot will, in this crisis, shrink from the service of their country . . ." Johnson was given to theatricality, and he was determined to rally the country behind the war, but Paine's stirring words, which had been quoted somewhat histrionically in a cable the previous week from Ambassador Ellsworth Bunker,[17] were hardly apropos. Paine had been rallying Americans to support a war for their own survival as a nation. His ringing words could hardly be expected to resonate in the same way with these seasoned newspapermen. The Vietnam War had been a questionable undertaking from the start. It had been sold as a relatively minor military challenge.

Johnson was correct in stating that the South Vietnamese people had failed to heed Uncle Ho's call for a general uprising, but even the president's faith was flagging. In answer to a question at his formal press conference, Johnson admitted, "I go to bed every night feeling that I have failed, because I couldn't end the conflict in Vietnam. I do have disappointments and moments of distress." His son-in-law the marine captain Charles Robb was soon headed to Vietnam, and Johnson tried to reassure his daughter Lynda that he would return safely. But the worry sometimes woke him up in the middle of the night. To his old friend the retired general Matthew Ridgway, a former army chief of staff, Johnson complained, "Nearly every option open to us is worse than what we are doing." Ridgway went home and told his wife, "The President is a distraught man, a tired man, a very worried man, a very sincere man."[18]

Hue was the one place in South Vietnam that most directly contradicted Westy's assurances. Only small portions of the city were not in enemy hands. Three days into the battle, however, General LaHue felt the tide was turning. General Truong had beefed up his division at Mang Ca and was poised to rout enemy holdouts inside the Citadel. Big Ernie Cheatham would shortly be in southern Hue, where he'd give Gravel's foot-dragging force a much-needed kick in the ass. But there was another piece to consider. Whatever size enemy force was in the city, its supply lines were to the west and north. That would also be the direction of its retreat, once pressure was applied. Before US-led forces could end this battle, they needed to cut off those avenues, close the trap. A full brigade of airborne infantry—about three thousand men—had been moved into position.

This mission fell to General John Tolson, commander of the army's First Air Cavalry Division. Before the Tet Offensive began, Tolson had been in the process of moving to Camp Evans, and one of his battalions had been shuttled on Friday to a small ARVN outpost just off Highway 1 called PK-17. It would march the seven miles down to the city walls on Saturday, destroying any enemy troops it encountered.

This would be fighting in the open rather than in crowded city streets, the kind of fighting at which the army excelled. The movement was expected to last only a few hours.

2

TFP

THE LAND NORTH of Hue was sandy and flat. Highway 1 ran parallel to the shoreline of the South China Sea, just ten miles east. To the west, in the distance, were the green hills and distant mountains of the Central Highlands where the Communists had their hidden camps. On both sides of the elevated road were rice paddies and cane fields, the flatness broken only by occasional berms, dikes, and small cemeteries and, at intervals, by villages surrounded by trees. The graveyards were newly decorated for Tet.

Charles Krohn, an officer in one of Tolson's battalions, would describe Camp Evans, fifteen miles northwest of Hue, as "a dump—treeless, muddy, and just plain ugly."[19] It was also big and noisy, a hub, with choppers coming and going at all hours, radios barking and whining, generators hammering, and trucks and Jeeps moving men and supplies. Most of the time you had to shout to be heard.

This was the new home to lead portions of Tolson's division, roughly fifteen thousand men. The marines had mostly moved out and the air cavalry had moved in. The division consisted of three brigades, each made up of three battalions, which each consisted of four companies of about one hundred and twenty men each.[20] Two of Tolson's battalions would be thrown into the battle of Hue: the Second of the Twelfth Cavalry (2/12), commanded by Lieutenant Colonel Dick Sweet; and the Fifth of the Seventh Cavalry (5/7), commanded by Lieutenant Colonel James Vaught.[21] The third battalion was held back to defend Camp Evans. All three had arrived that week and were busy painting their bright yellow and black horsehead emblem on everything. Over the holiday truce, they had anticipated a few quiet days to dig in and organize. Instead, there had been a rude greeting.

"We got mortared last night," wrote the lovelorn Andy Westin to his wife, Mimi, back in Ypsilanti. Westin's mortar platoon was part of Vaught's battalion.

> *About 40 rounds. They did it just when the early morning fog set in and our choppers couldn't see the guns firing. About 40 people got hurt. The rounds landed on the other end of the LZ. It's a long way from me. I had a good hole last night, but today my RTO and I sandbagged it, deepened it, and strengthened it. Tomorrow we'll put a very thick roof on it. I call it "Chicken's Paradise."*

The lieutenant, who was still decorating his letters home with line drawings of himself sporting ever larger antlers, was very excited that Mimi had sent him a *Playboy* magazine. He and the other men of Charlie Company were put in charge of guarding a "water point," a place where water was sucked from a nearby stream, run through filters to remove bacteria and bugs, and then delivered to makeshift shower stalls. They took turns enjoying their first shower in months. Westin figured there were worse places to settle for a while.

Word of the big fight in Hue had ruined those plans. General Tolson wrote out new orders for his third brigade on a small piece of his personal notepaper:

1. Seal off city on west & north with right flank based on the Song Huong River [cq].[22]
2. Destroy enemy forces attempting to either reinforce or escape from Hue Citadel.

Westin wrote Mimi:

> *On the news tonight you'll probably hear about a big fight in Hue. Well, if it gets any bigger we'll be there, too. Our company is all saddled up and ready to go. We've got armored vests and gas masks, and a lot of ammo. I'm carrying 400 rounds + 2 mortar*

rounds. We're really loaded for bear. I'd just as soon not go. I'm a lover, not a fighter.

That afternoon they had traveled to PK-17, which got its name from the kilometer marker on Highway 1. Tolson had scrapped an air assault any closer to the fortress after one of his Cobra helicopters had been shot down on a reconnaissance mission outside the northern wall on Friday and its crew had barely escaped with their lives.[23] Besides, his refueling and maintenance crews hadn't made it to Camp Evans yet, so he couldn't keep helicopters in the air for very long. His men would move to the city on foot. Sweet's battalion would lead the way.

Colonel Dick Sweet was an army lifer, a Korean War veteran, a man of considerable charm who nevertheless was regarded by some as an arrogant runt, a classic "little Napoleon" type, short and fit, experienced, tactically sound, and brimming with confidence. When he had taken command just weeks earlier, he'd asked his company captains what they would like to do in the future. Captain Bob Helvey, as was his way, came right to the point.

"I'd like to have your job, sir," he said.

Some commanders might have been rattled by that, or at least taken aback, but Sweet just smiled.

"Okay," he told Helvey. "I've got what I needed to know."

Helvey wasn't quite sure what his new commander meant by that, but he clearly wasn't bothered. In war, after all, it was only prudent to assume your subordinates might have to step up and do your job at any time, so Helvey's bald ambition was both frank and even appropriate. Sweet was untroubled by an ambitious junior officer. In short order Helvey saw why. The "arrogant runt" of a colonel knew what he was doing.

From all his time in the field Sweet had a ruddy complexion. He talked fast and a lot, and he was unfailingly decent—at night he could be heard in his quarters dictating loving messages to his wife and children on the audiocassettes he mailed home. But he could, at times, be stern, even a stickler. One day he sent Captain Krohn, his intel officer, on a walking tour of the base to make sure his men were obeying an order against rolling up their sleeves—covering the arms helped cut down on mosquito bites, and hence, malaria. When Krohn suggested that enforcing long sleeves when the temperature and humidity were off the charts might be regarded by the men as chickenshit, Sweet told him that if they refused to obey such a simple order on base, how could they be relied on in combat? If you disappointed him, you heard about it sharply, face-to-face. But Sweet could also be funny, as when he launched into his dead-on impression of Tolson, whom he did not like, mimicking the general's high voice with a ridiculous squeak and his antic manner by waving his arms. With startling irreverence (and reflecting the army's casual institutional racism), Sweet called Tolson "the dumbest white man in the army." He also talked openly about things other officers didn't. He was frank about masturbation, for instance, which he saw as a necessary outlet. He called it "thumping the dummy."

Sweet's junior officers shared his disdain for Tolson, which increased their affection for him. He solicited their ideas and freely shared his own. He thought the Vietnam War, for instance, had evolved beyond the tactics favored by Westy and the rest of the MACV. The highly touted airmobile tactics of their division, inserting small infantry units into hot spots with helicopters, was already outmoded, he said. It was well suited to fighting small fast-moving Viet Cong units by beating them at their own game. The US Army could move men and deliver devastating firepower more rapidly than any other force in the world. The adrenaline rush of swooping down to a hot LZ, guns blazing—Helvey would call it "living on the razor's edge, ten feet off the ground"—was what made life in a cavalry unit exciting. But no matter how effective and cool the tactic was, Sweet had begun to see long before Tet that the enemy was moving toward more conventional land warfare, maneuvering large armies in the field. The revolution, he told his officers, was entering a new phase, a more generalized offensive. More and more regular NVA units were making their way south, and they were experts at large-scale land battles.

Colonel Sweet was determined to be just as good. His predecessor had been killed only weeks earlier when the helicopter from which he had been commanding was shot down. Sweet preferred to lead with his feet on the ground, alongside his men, the old-fashioned way, the way he had led his platoon in Korea. That way he was seeing the same things his adversaries saw, from the same perspective. And battles were about more than maneuvers and position; they were also about men.

A leader needed to know how his men were feeling, what they were thinking. You couldn't look a man in the eye from five hundred feet.

On this mission he anticipated no more than possible light action and a long walk, but he was wary. There had been reports of large numbers of NVA in the area. They had been dismissed as implausible but he kept them in mind. If the reports were true, Sweet believed his battalion was more than capable of defeating whatever popped up in its path. And the need to get to Hue was urgent. The biggest concern Sweet had discussed with his staff was how to avoid friendly fire once they got to the city.

Room on the choppers was tight, so he ordered that packs be left behind at Camp Evans—ponchos, sweaters, dry socks, blankets, air mattresses, entrenching tools, food, etc. It was a decision he regretted right away, because when they got to PK-17 he realized that keeping his large force concentrated on the small base would make them too vulnerable to mortar attack, so they camped a short march away, outside the base. His men spent a wet and very cold night exposed to the elements—the temperature dropped into the forties. One soldier cut a hole in a rice sack and wore it. Others stuffed newspapers and rice straw under their flak jackets, a remedy that came at a price because it itched like hell. Men huddled two to a foxhole and held each other to stay warm. A mortar battery at the ARVN base exploded a white phosphorus shell over their position during the night, and one of the men, Manuel Silva, got a chunk of the burning substance on his nose. He screamed as he tried to rub it off, and was so badly burned he had to be evacuated by chopper before dawn.[24] They set off on Saturday morning carrying only their weapons and ammo, spreading out across the fields in the cool fog. Sweet kept them off the road, figuring that as it was the most likely approach to Hue the enemy might have mined it or prepared an ambush. Overnight there had been an air attack on an enemy force between them and Hue, and it was reported that thirty-seven were killed. So the enemy was around.

The gray sky hung so low they could see only about half the width of a rice paddy in all directions. Sweet had decided to move his men along the west side of the highway. They were heading off without their usual artillery and air support—ideally, a march like this would be preceded by aerial gunships and a moving wall of explosions. The

weather had delayed delivery of the division's gun batteries to Camp
Evans, and many of the choppers were without fuel.

The battalion spread out in a diamond formation, with one company
at each corner, nearly four hundred men covering a wide swath of
soggy rice paddies, their boots making sucking noises as they pulled
them from the mud. Wearing their vests and draped with ammo they
looked bigger, but most of the men were nothing but scrawny teenagers. Basic training, infantry drills, and the rigors of camping and
patrolling had so reduced most of them that their mothers would
have been dismayed. They wore battered green helmets and faded pale
green flak jackets. In addition to their ammunition belts, from which
many strung a sock stuffed with C rations, most carried bandoliers
stuffed with extra rifle ammo and hung with grenades. They walked
at a good pace with their rifles held forward and ready. For a little guy
like Theodore Wallace, who had grown up in Harlem, it was hard to
keep up. His sergeant dropped back alongside him.

"You know, Wallace, the enemy snipers, they shoot the stragglers."

Wallace gained speed, scared now, passing soldiers on the left and
the right until one asked, "Man, where do you think you're going?"

"I got to catch up with the company," Wallace said.

"Hell, I'm the point man," the soldier told him. "The company is
back there."

Carl DiLeo, a tall skinny kid of eighteen from Trenton, New Jer-
sey, was in a mortar platoon. He carried a forty-pound base plate
strapped to his back, which made him walk stooped. He had been
kicked out of high school as a senior less than a year earlier. He was
from a rough neighborhood where the Italians carried on a rolling
rumble with the blacks who lived just a few blocks away, each side
determined to prove how tough they were. DiLeo had a thick crop
of dark hair and sunglasses he wore even on gray days, or especially
when he saw a camera.

Squad leader David Dentinger, slogging forward, wasn't worried
about seeing action on this walk. There were too many of them for the
enemy to challenge. The gooks were all about hit-and-run; you never
encountered them in force. He was pleased to see Sweet walking with
them. Dentinger was cynical about officers. He figured that if Sweet
and his staff were coming along, then the walk was certainly safe.[25]

Sweet had mapped a route that went through small wooded areas and villages, avoiding open ground as much as possible. They walked straight through one village—just a collection of straw huts—that had small North Vietnamese flags everywhere. The villagers had been there moments before—smoke rose from abandoned cooking fires—and as the soldiers moved forward out to the fields they saw some running away. Two of the women shouted back a warning: "Beaucoup VC! Beaucoup VC!" In the distance they could make out the villages of Que Chu and La Chu, which they had been warned might harbor some enemy. Sweet altered their course to swing around. He had his radioman request a smoke round from the brigade's artillery battery at Camp Evans. The smoke would mark the target if they had to order high-explosive rounds. He was told that guns were not yet in place.

What neither Sweet nor Tolson knew was that La Chu was the command center for the National Liberation Front's entire operation in Hue. It was protected by a full regiment of NVA, close to five thousand men.[26] Sweet would have needed a much wider detour to avoid a force of that size. The battalion was walking into trouble.

The overcast turned to a driving rain. In the far distance they could see a dim glow and rising black smoke from Hue. The men were locked into the rhythm of their march, into a kind of half sleep, half wakefulness familiar to infantrymen. Your feet moved on their own, while your mind wandered or even dozed. Krohn snapped at one of his men, a private with bushy red hair, for whistling the tune "(What a Day for a) Daydream." He was not in the mood.

The marching men woke up fast when they heard sniper fire from a line of woods ahead. The point man for one of the platoons was shot in the head and killed instantly. The sniper killed two more men before he was seen to leap from a foxhole and run away. He moved too fast for anyone to get a bead on him.[27] As they pressed forward the volume of fire increased. To Wallace it sounded like bees buzzing around him. He started to swat at them, and then noticed that all of his buddies were flat in the mud. He hit the deck. Soon the lead company reported seeing enemy movement in the woods, and then the shooting rapidly intensified. It was startlingly precise. The enemy had waited until the battalion was well within range and then began laying down interlocking grazing fire, low and deadly. Sweet and his command group dashed for the cover of a nearby clump of trees. There wasn't much else to hide behind. Most of the men just flattened themselves on the ground in the field. The rounds passed overhead with a chilling *zip!* Those in the most exposed places had to keep so low that their faces were in the mud. Juan Gonzales was one of the few men with a radio strapped to his back, and this made him an inviting target. Rounds smacked into the water just a few feet from his face. A sergeant next to him said, "Get rid of it!" Gonzales wriggled free, and they crawled toward a small graveyard, where they curled behind headstones.

Gonzales, a Texan, was an elite soldier, a member of Pathfinder Team 229. Members of his unit usually worked alone. Daring and talented orienteers, they moved stealthily behind enemy lines to scout for landing zones, and then, using the bulky radios they carried everywhere, they would talk the choppers to the right spot. Pathfinders did not belong to any unit in particular—they would be lent to those heading out on missions—so Gonzales and his buddies spent nearly all of their time in the field. Because they wore headsets to communicate on the run, they did not wear helmets. Instead they wore simple black caps that were an emblem of status. They were very proud of those black caps. It was considered bad form, even under intense fire, for a Pathfinder to replace his cap with a helmet. They also hated to be parted from their radios, their primary tool. Gonzales had shed his with great reluctance, and he would not leave without it.

DiLeo pressed himself to the ground and watched the command group nearby with concern. He was not the only one with eyes trained on the officers, waiting for some direction, some way out of this mess. Judging by their body language, the colonel and staff appeared upset and confused. There had plainly been some kind of intel fuckup. Hours passed. DiLeo saw Sweet talking animatedly on the radio, yet no air support came, and no artillery.

Then enemy mortars started to fall. The steady grazing ground fire continued. As more time passed, it became clear to the waiting men that unless they wanted to spend the day as target practice, at some point they were going to have to move.

They were not used to this. American infantry units in the field lived and died by artillery and air support. It was their trump card. There were two big ARVN guns at PK-17, but they were considered imprecise—and no one could speak Vietnamese well enough to guide the gunners. The low clouds made air attacks almost impossible. Sweet even tried calling down to Phu Bai to ask the marine battery there for help but was denied. Fixed-wing pilots were willing but could not get low enough to aim before screaming past. Chopper pilots couldn't see anything until they were almost on the ground. They had to either drop down and get lucky or risk hovering within range of ground fire until they could figure out where the target was supposed to be. Still, Sweet did manage to coax two Hueys down. The men heard them as they approached and felt the first stab of hope. Then the aircraft were directly over them. With his pack out in the mud Gonzales wasn't able to offer his expert guidance. It was frustrating. The aircraft were so low that he felt the heat of the rockets' burners as they opened fire. One accidentally aimed at the wrong tree line, killing one and wounding four at Sweet's position before it was pointed toward the more distant line of trees. But even as rockets fell and machine gunners in the Hueys' open doors strafed the enemy position in the woods, it was clear that this would not be enough. The men were still pinned down.

Sweet spoke on the radio to Colonel Hugh Campbell, the brigade commander, explaining forcefully that any attempt to continue moving forward without sufficient artillery or air support would be ill-advised. For his part, Campbell was under intense pressure from Tolson to get his brigade into the fight at Hue. The general had wanted a second battalion inserted by helicopter southwest of the Citadel, but Campbell had fended off that order for the same reason Sweet was now pinned down—lack of artillery or air support. He had prevailed in that instance only because Sweet's battalion was supposed to arrive shortly. The colonel was adamant that they deliver on that promise.

"You will attack now!" Campbell told Sweet. Then, using his call sign, he said abruptly, "Warmaster out!"[28]

There would be no further discussion. The men around Sweet heard him say, "Roger, out," and knew what was coming. Captain Helvey thought, *If it's possible, we'll do it. If it's not possible the charge will be remembered for a long time and celebrated in the annals of the regiment.* The time to move was now, while the Hueys were still overhead. Sweet ordered his men to prepare to charge the woods. Captain Krohn fought the urge to empty his bladder. He chambered rounds in both his rifle and his pistol. When the order came, he would stand and start running with everyone else.

"Move out," Sweet ordered.

"Let's go!" came the cry.

Four hundred men rose and began running forward. There were too many for the enemy to shoot at once, but many were cut down as soon as they stood. There was no choice but to keep going. Some stopped to pull others up and drag or carry them. These were seasoned soldiers, and there was no panic. Gonzales fired his rifle in three-round bursts as he ran. Dentinger ran and prayed. DiLeo, with that heavy mortar plate on his back, felt as if he were running in slow motion. He assumed he'd get hit. He had spent nearly every day of his months in Vietnam in the field. He was pretty good at math and, given all the death and maiming he'd seen, he'd long ago figured that his chance of getting out of Nam alive, or without a serious wound, was near zero. Paralyzing fear had eroded to grim acceptance. Moments like this drove it home. This was the deal. He ran. He tried to zigzag and he collided with the man next to him. They went down heavily; DiLeo felt as if he'd been chop-blocked on a football field. He got up and resumed running. His immediate hope was that he would be killed cleanly and quickly.

When he and five others made the tree line they saw three big foxholes. These seemed empty, but in the first they discovered three NVA soldiers, who tried to surrender. They were shot dead. Two more leaped from the next hole and ran. They, too, were cut down. The third hole was abandoned. DiLeo flopped into it, exhausted. He was amazed to still be alive. The firing had momentarily stopped.

The gun position that had pinned them down now seemed insignificant. Eight enemy soldiers were dead and four others were prisoners. That was it. Nine of Sweet's men were dead, forty-eight wounded. Gonzales jumped into an empty foxhole and found an arm and part of a brain. He threw them out and settled in deep.

They had advanced just two hundred yards, and were now stuck again. Private Wallace was with a man who'd been shot in his crotch. He'd had morphine for the physical pain but there was more to deal with.

"I should just walk out of here and let them blow me up," he said.

"No, no," said Wallace. "Your life is precious."

"Ted, what am I going to do?" he asked. "I can't go home like this."

"Yes, you can. You're still alive, and life is not just sex, okay? It's only ten percent. People overrate it and make it so important to them, but you just have to learn how to have sex differently. You may be known as the oral man in your neighborhood!"

The man laughed, in spite of himself.

Wallace said, "You'll be very popular."

They immediately began to receive sniper fire from the next line of woods around La Chu. Once again they were pinned down and only slightly closer to the village. They exaggerated the number of enemy they'd killed in their radio report to Campbell, not wanting to admit how little they had accomplished at such cost. As James Vaught's operations officer Charlie Baker would later put it, the enemy "had scarcely been scratched."[29]

Much like the marines in Hue, they had been thrown against an immovable object. It was learning by trial and tragically bloody error. Saturday ended with all three allied forces surrounded and pinned down: the ARVN troops bottled up at Mang Ca, the marines in southern Hue, and now an army battalion in a copse of woods to the northwest.

Mortars continued to drop into Sweet's new position. Dentinger saw one of his squad mates fall, hit in the shoulder. The platoon's medic, a young Chinese-American soldier from Pasadena, California, Hoi Tin "Tony" Lau, ran out to help and was immediately shot dead. He collapsed over the wounded man, who pulled himself from under Lau's body and crawled off the road. Dentinger and two of his team members located the sniper's position in a foxhole ahead. As they crawled toward it, the sniper mysteriously stopped firing at them. They got close enough to hurl grenades at the hole, killing him. When they recovered his rifle they found a round jammed in the chamber.

Gonzales, who was unscathed, found that he didn't feel angry about having had to make the charge, as some of the men did. He accepted risking his life. That was the job. He'd put himself here on purpose. The year before, trapped at a rear base and eager to see some action before his one-year tour ended, he'd bluffed his way into the Pathfinder unit. He'd threatened his battalion commander.

He'd said, "Do you know who Henry B. Gonzalez is?"—Henry Gonzalez was a famous Texas congressman, and, as the slight difference in spelling would suggest, no relation to Juan—"Well he's my uncle, and if you don't transfer me to a Pathfinder company I'm going to write him. I came to Vietnam to fight!"

He never knew if his commander had believed him, but it worked. Gonzales, in his bloody hole wearing his black cap, was exactly where he'd wanted to be.

But it wasn't a good place. They owned a small stand of trees at the edge of a rice paddy, with a significant and well-dug-in enemy force to their front. To make matters worse, they realized soon after establishing a perimeter that the enemy had moved around behind them, closing off the direction from which they'd come.

"How are we goin' to get outa this fucking place?" one of the men asked.

This Fucking Place. Their hard-won patch of woods on the outskirts of La Chu would from that point on be referred to as TFP.[30]

3

Big Ernie

T HE NIGHT BEFORE leaving for Hue, Ernie Cheatham had a rare opportunity for a combat commander. He had time to think. He had bulled his way into headquarters at Phu Bai on Friday afternoon, February 2, and gotten his battalion back. General LaHue told him to move up to the city on Saturday, which meant he had a long afternoon and evening to figure out what was going on, and how he intended to proceed.

What he learned just made him angrier. LaHue had been feeding marines—some of them *his* marines—into Hue piecemeal for three days: first Gordon Batcheller's Alpha 1/1; then three of Cheatham's, Fox (Mike Downs), Golf (Chuck Meadows), and Hotel (Ron Christmas). He'd been hurling them repeatedly at an enemy whose strength and disposition were still unknown. And they were getting cut to pieces. Dozens of Cheatham's men were dead or in the battalion aid station, some of them dying, and more were arriving every few hours. Task Force X-Ray had been insisting that there was nothing more threatening in Hue than a handful of snipers. Now it was said that several enemy companies might be there—about four hundred men.

"I want you to attack through the city and clean the NVA out, and if you're looking for any more [intelligence], you aren't going to get it!" he was told flatly by Colonel Stan Hughes, commander of the First Marine Regiment, who would be going with Cheatham into the city the next day to assume overall command from the disappointing Gravel. "Just get up there and get going, and I'll support you in any way I can. You do it any way you want to, and if you get any heat from above, I'll take care of that."[31]

Under the circumstances, Cheatham thought it wise to assume that the enemy was present in large numbers, well supplied and dug in. He did not know exactly how many, or what kind of arms they had, or even what their intentions were. He knew only one thing for sure—where the fight would take place. So he set out to prepare himself for that.[32]

Neither he nor his marines had ever fought in a city, nor had they been trained for it. The last time the Corps fought a big urban battle had been in Seoul in 1950, a grinding fight that had lasted for almost a month and killed more than four hundred and fifty marines.[33] Cheatham knew there were several footlockers filled with field manuals that traveled around with the Fifth Marines, so he searched them out. Inside he found two pertinent booklets, *Combat in Built-Up Areas* and *An Assault on a Fortified Position*. He gave himself a crash course. The basic idea seemed to be staying off the streets. Walls and buildings were both your enemy and your friend. It was the kind of environment where you could be in mortal danger in one spot and two feet away you were safe. The way to proceed was to secure a starting position, and when you moved, you moved *through* walls, not around or over them. You blasted your way forward, blowing holes in anything that stood in your way. When you encountered the enemy in a building or bunker, you flattened it or gassed it or burned it. Then you sent your riflemen in to clean up. He knew there were tanks in Hue, and that Christmas had taken two Ontos with him, but that wouldn't be enough for the job. So he set off in search of the right weaponry. He enlisted his executive officer John Salvati, now *Major* Salvati, to collect all of the bazookas in Phu Bai's armory, not the lightweight, disposable rocket launchers the marine infantry now carried, but longer, heavier Korean War–era metal tubes that fired a big, nine-pound rocket with a shaped charge that could blow right through some walls or a tank if it hit at the right spot in the rear. He also ordered up every 106 recoilless rifle in the battalion armory. Cheatham wanted all he could get, and Salvati found six. They were the same as the six mounted on the Ontos, rifles as big and heavy as cannons—lifting one took several strong men. The 106 fired an explosive round that weighed nearly twenty pounds, and it delivered a ferocious back blast.

Cheatham rounded up small flatbed vehicles called mules to carry them. These were about the size of a golf cart, fast and maneuverable, and just big enough for the 106s. Both the bazookas and the 106s were old weapons, tried and true, but too heavy to ordinarily be of much use in Vietnam. Men patrolling in rice paddies or in jungles rarely encountered armor or heavily fortified positions, and patrolling mostly on foot they preferred the more lightweight, disposable LAWs (light antitank weapons), or hand grenades. So there were plenty of the heavier weapons in storage. Cheatham also instructed Salvati to round up gas grenades, gas masks, flamethrowers, and as much C4 explosive as he could find.[34] It would take a while, so Salvati stayed behind at Phu Bai for one more day.

This newest relief convoy wasn't ready to leave until well after noon. It was a big one. The ranking officer aboard was Hughes, most of whose regiment had not yet arrived at Phu Bai when the offensive began. When his executive officer had found him days earlier sitting in a small tent with a cot, he asked where Hughes's command post was.

"This is it," Hughes said.[35]

He had only part of one battalion. Another part, Alpha Company 1/1, had been badly mauled on the first day of the battle. Hughes would bring up a second company, Bravo, the next day. When he got to Hue he would assume formal command at the compound, but it was Cheatham and his three companies who would initially handle most of the fighting.

And "the Chariot" was coming in heavy. Returning with him were the Golf Company platoon led by Lieutenant Bill Rogers, the emissary Captain Meadows had dispatched to Phu Bai the night before, and the arsenal of heavy weapons Cheatham had assembled. The six mules, each carrying one of the big 106s, were loaded on lowboy cargo trucks with two more Dusters. The trucks carried lots of ammo, the bazookas, gas masks, and other supplies. At the tail end of the convoy were trucks filled with more volunteers, marines who had relatively safe rear jobs and wanted in on the action.

In the lead truck with Hughes were Alvin Webb, a UPI reporter; and John Laurence, a CBS reporter, with his cameraman Keith Kay, who crouched on the metal bed balancing his big camera and filming Hughes. The marines around them were pleased to have the chance to be in a news report, particularly when they learned that Laurence reported to Walter Cronkite. They also wondered why the network was so interested in this thing in Hue.

"You guys know something we don't?" one asked.

"Yeah, what's going on in Hue?" asked another.

"You know as much as we do," Kay told them.

The marines were amazed that these journalists would head into the battle with them unarmed, and on purpose.[36]

For once the trip north was uneventful. At one point a great volume of fire erupted toward the back end of the convoy, but Cheatham realized it was all coming from the undisciplined troops in the rear trucks. He ordered his driver to speed up, and as the trailing trucks struggled to keep pace the firing fell off. The convoy pulled into the MACV compound at about one in the afternoon.

Gravel got so worked up describing the situation that Cheatham told him, flatly, to get a grip on himself. The beleaguered colonel stayed on as leader of a considerably reduced battalion,[37] which would be further reinforced in the coming days. Hughes ordered him to coordinate with Cheatham, protect the LZ and boat ramp, and continue trying to push out of the compound south along Highway 1 to protect future convoys and to expand the area of the city under American control.

Lieutenant Ray Smith sent a platoon of his Alpha Company west on another mission to rescue the trapped air force coms team, which was still hiding and surrounded. It ran into the same wall of resistance as everyone else and turned back. Two marines were killed and four more wounded. After four days of fighting, they were still being surprised by the stiffness of enemy resistance. Lieutenant Rick Donnelly, whose platoon spearheaded that effort, reported that the stadium alone was defended by a full battalion.

Cheatham set up his base of command at the university. They would push west from there, but they would need a steady flow of ammo and supplies from the compound, and a way to evacuate the wounded. Gravel told Bill Ehrhart, one of his battalion scouts, to find some vehicles. The private and a buddy took a Jeep from an air force officer at gunpoint—sliding a shell into a shotgun for effect. To that they added two ARVN Jeeps, a Volkswagen minibus, a Peugeot, and a Vespa scooter, which was useless for transport but fun to ride. This peculiar fleet, along with the mules, would become a key part of the counterattack in the coming days.

At the university, Cheatham was reunited with his three company captains. The view from the westernmost side on the second floor overlooked the critical stretch of enemy-occupied government buildings along Le Loi Street all the way to the Phu Cam Canal.

Through the gray drizzle Cheatham could see most of it, a swath eleven blocks long and eight blocks deep. The Huong River was to his right. The first objective was directly across the street, the tan-stone treasury building. It had two tall floors and was surrounded by a low masonry wall and an iron fence. With its big steel doors in front, it looked as sturdy as a bank vault. Its tall windows—the ones on the upper floor framed with gentle arches—made perfect firing positions, as did small openings in the wide cornice of ornate masonry under the roofline. Close enough to hit with a stone, it would be the first big challenge. The Front had strongly fortified it, and Cheatham could not push farther west without taking it. Doing so would be a test of the tactics he had planned.

Across the street from the treasury, just south, was the post office building, another large stone structure. Every block behind these two had buildings nearly as imposing, most notably the prison and the province headquarters. All were flying Communist flags, and every one was going to be tough. They were all on the south side of Le Loi Street, and the north side was just the promenade and the Huong River, so that meant Cheatham's right flank would be relatively secure—they were safely distant from the enemy guns across on the north bank. He would sweep west in three company-size columns, with Christmas on the right flank, Downs up the middle, and Smith's Alpha Company on the left flank, taking the smaller buildings in the blocks immediately south. Meadows's Golf Company, which had been so badly mauled trying to fight across the bridge, would be held back in reserve.

The classrooms on both floors of the university looked as if a violent storm had come through. Windows were shattered, desks overturned and jumbled, textbooks and papers scattered. Marines had defaced the walls with graffiti.

"Fuck Communism!"

"Gook Die!"

"Class Dismissed."[38]

Cheatham picked one as his command center, and his captains took seats before him like students. They began to work out the details, how they would use the tanks, the mules, the 106s, the mortars, and the bazookas. None of them had ever done anything like this.

4

I Love Zees
Fucking Marines

AFTER SPENDING THE night in the cathedral, surrounded by wary refugees, the French journalists Catherine Leroy and Francois Mazure were asked to leave. The priest who had sheltered them was apologetic, but their presence was frightening those who had taken shelter in his church.

A boy, one of the priest's helpers, offered to lead them to the American compound, just a few blocks away. Getting there would be risky. Leroy stuffed her MACV credentials in her bra, asking her companion, "Look at my bosom. Does it look strange?" She discarded her boots, which were distinctly military, and the priest gave her his shower sandals. They cut a white flag from one of the priest's robes and made two big signs saying *Phap bao chi bale* ("French press from Paris") and pinned them to their shirts.[39]

They were stopped almost immediately. They repeated that they were French journalists, but the Front soldiers seemed unimpressed. Their cameras were taken and their hands tied. The soldiers were unable to read the letter the priest had written for them, but the reporters weren't harmed. They were led to the house of another Frenchman, a manager at the destroyed electricity plant, who had been directed to stay inside his home by a friendly Front officer. When the officer returned, he had Leroy and Mazure unbound, and their cameras were given back. He told them that the liberation army held the entire city and had been victorious throughout South Vietnam.

He invited them to take pictures of his men. With the sounds of gunfire in the near distance, Leroy and Mazure photographed the happy victors, who adopted staged combat poses, pretending to throw grenades, fire rifles from behind barriers, and storm a captured ARVN tank. Only one soldier objected to having his picture taken. He demanded that Leroy give him the film from her camera, and she coolly handed him a roll of blank film. When they returned to the captive Frenchman's house, Mazure told the officer (their host's wife translated), "We have to get back to Paris with our story, so we'll be running along now."

The boy led them back to the cathedral, where they told their story to the priest. Since they had been so warmly received by the Front, the refugees now warmed to them as well. They were offered food before setting off again for the MACV compound. This time they were found by a squad of startled marines, who escorted them to safety.

Leroy had just arrived when Hughes's big convoy drove in, bringing her friends John Laurence and Keith Kay. She threw her arms around Laurence's neck and kissed him on both cheeks.

"Oh, God, I'm glad to see you guys!" she said in her heavily accented English. "You know, I love zees fucking marines. Zey save my life!"

She told him their story.

"You know, John, I was never so scared so much in my life," she said. "I tell you the truth. Really. Personally, I don't ever think I am going to be so glad to see these fucking marines."

Her dramatic photos would be featured in a cover story in *Life* magazine less than two weeks later, a rare glimpse of the happy enemy, which by then would be fighting desperately to hang on to Hue.

At the compound, several thousand marines were now packed into an area about the size of a city block. There was no running water, and for some reason instead of receiving bottled water they were delivered large pallets of warm orange soda, which everyone grew to hate. The collection of buildings that formed the perimeter were fairly well shot up. There were holes in the rooftops alongside the sandbagged gun positions. The courtyard in the middle hummed with activity, with convoys arriving, quickly unloading, and then hurrying either back down to Phu Bai or out to the riverfront landing zone. The bodies in the streets outside were bloated and so awful they no longer looked human.

Mortars still fell occasionally, so everyone stayed under cover as much as possible. Mike Anderegg, the eighteen-year-old Patton tank driver who had been in the first convoy on Wednesday, spent most of his time inside his tank. Most of the other tankers did the same. They worked, ate, and slept in their steel cocoons. When nature called they urinated and defecated into their helmets, and then just opened a hatch under the seat on the driver's side and dumped it out. The interior was cramped and dirty and it smelled bad, but it felt like the safest place to be. They believed they had it a lot better than the grunts. At least they weren't being ordered to run across streets under fire. From their perches inside, three of the four crew members had periscopes: the driver, the gunner, and the tank commander. The loader had no idea what was going on outside. He just sat on his little seat and moved to reload the gun whenever it fired. The cordite smell and smoke from the blast had to be cleared, so he'd turn on a blower, and the tank commander would immediately bark for it to be switched off because it was so loud he couldn't hear the radio. On most outings the air grew so foul inside that it became hard to breathe. They kept moving as much as possible, because whenever they stopped they drew rocket fire; and B-41 rounds, if they hit the right place, could penetrate the armor and explode on the inside. If that happened they were screwed. The Pattons were the biggest targets on the street. Rounds were constantly hammering against the outside. There were times when the tension, the noise, and the smell made a man want to scream.

Anderegg was miserable. On top of everything else, he felt like a fuckup. He had been driving the tank that ran over Private Henschel's foot, which he felt bad about. It had happened when his tank had moved up to help rescue Lieutenant Horner's platoon on Cao Van Street. The wounded were being lifted and placed on the outside of his tank when they took several rocket hits. Simultaneous blasts bounced the 45-ton vehicle enough to jostle poor Henschel to the street. They rang so loud that they left Anderegg and his fellow crew members dazed. When another blast hit, seconds later, his commander started screaming, "Back up! Back up!" which he'd immediately done, gunning the tank in reverse and inadvertently crushing poor Henschel's foot.

The next day Anderegg himself was wounded. His tank was guarding the LZ, waiting for an inbound chopper. He was bored, so he slipped on his flak jacket and violated his number one rule—he got out of the tank to shoot the shit with one of the grunts. He heard a mortar round hit and felt a stab of pain across his throat. A piece of shrapnel had sliced him open. The marines around him picked him up and threw him onto a mule with another wounded man. Anderegg was in shock. Back at the busy dispensary he was placed on a table. Doctor Ba, the tall ARVN surgeon, didn't even stop to remove his flak jacket or take his weapon. He examined him quickly, calmed him, gave him an injection of morphine, and then removed a chunk of metal from his neck. Anderegg heard it clank into a metal surgical pan. He was bandaged, tagged, and placed in the hallway. The morphine put him in a deep fog and made him feel dizzy. He was told he would be flown out on the next chopper, and after a time he was driven back up to the LZ with the other wounded and lifted into the aircraft. It took off, wobbled, began to fill with smoke, and set back down. He and all of the others were taken off.

"There's another one coming in," a marine told him. "We'll get you on that one. Just wait."

Rattled, the idea of getting on another chopper didn't appeal to Anderegg just then, so he told himself, *Fuck this*, put the tag the doctor had given him in his pocket, and walked back to the compound and crawled back into his tank.

After that the only other time he'd gotten out was when the grunts moving along with him came running out of a building in great distress. One was crying. Another leaned against a tree and vomited. Curiosity got the better of him. There was a family inside, an old couple, two women, and two little girls, who looked as if they had been hacked to pieces. The blood was dry and there was no telling how long they'd been there. The room reeked.

At first the four tanks were useful mostly for shock value and as moving cover. The crews had strict orders against firing their big guns and, in the case of the Zippos, the flamethrowers without high-level approval. But the day after he was wounded, driving with his neck and head still wrapped in bandages like a mummy, Anderegg had broken the rule. The platoon he was escorting had come under fire from a building. The angry lieutenant just a few feet away from him out on the street kept screaming, "Fire your gun! Fire your gun!"

"This is a fucking Zippo!" shouted back the tank commander, Charlie West. The two kinds of tanks looked the same, but at that moment the lieutenant seemed indifferent to the distinction.

"Shoot your fucking gun!" he screamed.

Anderegg, the gunner, hated being trapped between conflicting orders. *Fuck it then*, he thought. On his own he pressured up the napalm tank and lit it, sending out a bright orange spray, two hundred and fifty gallons of liquid flame, splashing the target house from top to bottom. It went up like cardboard. Anyone inside was toasted. The grunts were uniformly happy about it, but when Anderegg got back to the compound his commanders went berserk. He was loudly, profanely, and meticulously chewed out. He didn't try to defend himself, and he found that he didn't much care. It occurred to him, *What more could they do to me? I've already been shot through the neck*—it still hurt like hell—*and I'm stuck in this shithole surrounded by people trying to kill me! How could they make my life worse?* Unless you count the dressing-down, he was never punished for it.

They all grew accustomed to the smell of death. There were dead civilians and enemy soldiers on the streets and sidewalks everywhere they went. The compound smelled of dead marines. It also smelled of live marines, smoke, blood, and cordite. Through all the days of this nightmare so far nobody had bothered to tell Anderegg what was going on, or why, so he didn't have a clue. He just curled up inside his smelly cold tank and waited to be told what to do next. When summoned he would venture forth with the rest of his crew. Everywhere they went they were shot at. And any notion that he was secure inside his tank vanished when his buddy tank commander Bobby Hall got killed. Hall was often in and out of the hatch, and a rocket cut straight down through it from above—the shooter had probably been on a roof. Hall, a twenty-one-year-old corporal from Lynchburg, Virginia, had been studying Vietnamese in hopes of becoming an interpreter. Anderegg had looked up to him.

So had the other crew members. Hall had a way of staying steady and cheerful, even in the worst situations, and was a calming influence. Once when Carl Fleischmann, his driver, looking through his periscope, saw a marine shot in the head, he was momentarily transfixed—the man just fell backward with what looked to be a big smile on his face and then blood poured down from under his helmet. Fleischmann kept staring until Hall told him, gently, "Carl, he's dead." It brought him back to reality. The rocket that hit Hall had torn him apart. One shard of shrapnel had sheared off his face. It left the tank smoking, and, fearing that it would explode, Fleischmann had climbed out. He helped drag Hall and another wounded crew member free. Both the wounded men were placed on a mule. Hall was bleeding profusely, and Fleischmann rode along to hold on to him. Hall gripped him tightly, one hand on his left shoulder and the other grasping his right arm. He could not look at Hall's shattered face. At the compound, the doctor and the corpsman took one look and shook their heads sadly. They couldn't save him.

"Just hold him until he passes," the doctor said.

Hall never released his tight grip. Fleischmann did not want to leave him. He lasted through the night and into the morning. After Hall died, Fleischmann went back to the tank and cleaned out the blood. Then he moved back inside.

Despite the discomforts, the growing numbers inside the compound provided a sense of security. No one was worried anymore about its being overrun. And by the weekend a semblance of order had been restored. Life settled into a routine. Among the marines were a growing number of refugees, and dogs, too, which wandered the streets in hungry packs. A goose waddled in. Marines eyed it menacingly. Even with the arrival of cooks from Phu Bai, without power there was no way to prepare hot food in quantity, and the meat in the freezers was thawing. One of the mess sergeants, Frank Crum, managed to get a stove up and running with a generator and cooked all of the steaks at once. That night men walked around gnawing at chunks of meat in their hands, tossing bones to the dogs. Crum joked that he had cooked the steaks only to spare the goose.[40]

None of this was serious hardship. Marines were accustomed to privation, to living in the field, and there was a steady supply of C rations. The contents would be warmed over a can poked with holes containing a small chunk of lit C4 explosive. The can became a burner, hot enough to boil water over. Each night men would swap out items from the packaged meals—canned pound cake and fruit were premium items; lima beans and ham were scorned.

A portion of the compound had once been a small French garrison, and in one of the buildings there was a large lavatory with metal toilet stalls, urinals, and communal showers. There was no running water for the showers, and with no way to flush the overworked toilets they filled, and they reeked. It was too dangerous to leave the compound to dig sanitary latrines (marines called them "heads"), so the grunts made do. A man would climb up and straddle a stall and add his contribution to the pile. Eventually some of the stalls had mounds of shit five and six feet high.

There were metal bunk beds in many of the upstairs rooms, but few men slept in them. Falling mortar rounds made it safer to stay on the ground floor. They slept in shifts in the mess hall, spreading sheets of cardboard—or air mattresses if they were lucky—to shield them from the cold floor. They smoked cigarettes—tobacco and sometimes marijuana—and compared notes, trying to make sense of what was going on. None of the men were privy to radio coms with the chiefs in Phu Bai, and their commanders were telling them little. Each man had only his own experience that day, where he had gone, what he had seen, what he had heard. Each account was a piece of the puzzle, and at night they tried to put it together. *What the hell happened to us out there? Where are they sending us tomorrow? How bad was it where you were? Why is there no artillery support? Where is so-and-so? What happened to him? Where did he get hit? How bad was it?* The picture remained incomplete, feeding both fear and doubt. Chris Brown, whose platoon had been nearly wiped out on the first day, was convinced that his commanders didn't know what they were doing, and were, as a result, throwing their men's lives away. After all they had lost on Wednesday, the day his friend Cristobal Figueroa-Perez had been killed, they hadn't advanced a foot. *For what?*

Tanker Brad Goodin, who was high much of the time, would lie at night with most of his body under his tank, but with his head out so he could look straight up. One night a radio tuned to the Armed Forces Vietnam Network played "Love Is Blue," a big hit at the time, by French orchestra leader Paul Mauriat. The tune was dreamy and sappy and made, particularly when Goodin was stoned, a surreal accompaniment to the nightly light show in the sky. Illumination flares blossomed from the clouds, falling from high-flying aircraft and then slowly drifting earthward from parachutes like drunken stars, leaving twisty trails of brilliant white smoke. Their slightly bluish, ghostly light splashed on the undersides of the thick cloud cover. Tracer rounds, green and red, zipped overhead like shooting stars falling up, and occasionally backlit by the flash of an explosion. Goodin found such interludes peaceful and restoring.

Reporter Gene Roberts and his escort Sergeant King took turns sleeping with the hundreds of marines in the mess hall. The air in Hue was so wet you never felt completely dry, and the nights were cold. Few slept well. Men tossed and turned and swore and talked through the night. Roberts lay awake listening to these conversations in the dark, sometimes scribbling notes. He was moved by these men. They were so young. They were also remarkably disciplined and bright. Most calmly accepted the discomfort and danger. One marine talked about his girlfriend at home in Battle Creek, Michigan. He went on and on, describing his last day there, and how he and his girl had gone for a long walk in the afternoon.

"It was the best damned hour I ever spent," he said, wistfully.[41]

On their second night back, King found beds for both of them. The correspondent was filing daily stories now from Hue, and he discovered to his dismay that the ribbon for his small portable typewriter was spent. King said there were nearby office buildings that must have typewriters in them, and if the ribbons wouldn't fit his make and model there was nothing to stop them from just carrying one off. So they braved the streets with a grunt volunteer to fetch one, walking along a stretch that was considered relatively safe. They were coming back, Roberts with a typewriter in his hands, when the marine who had come along was shot. The round hit his flak jacket and knocked him over, but he was not seriously hurt. They ran the rest of the way back. Roberts set up the typewriter on a table and threaded in paper to begin work, only to realize that the keys were in Vietnamese. It was worthless to him. For the remainder of his stay in Hue, he wrote out his stories longhand and dictated them over the phone to his bureau in Saigon.

Al Webb, the UPI reporter, produced his first story from Hue Sunday night, February 4, in longhand with a blanket draped over his head, writing with an illuminated pen.

"I was too young for the Second World War but older men have told me about the street fighting in Italy, France, and Germany," he wrote. "It is like that—maybe worse—in this city."[42]

Gradually some of the hiding Americans came straggling in from the surrounding neighborhoods. Donald Bradley, a waterworks supervisor who had hidden in an attic over his apartment, had watched a squad of NVA soldiers fire mortars just outside for three days. When a shell blew a hole in the roof of his building, he had climbed down and made his way in desperation toward the compound. He managed to remain unseen until just beyond it when a bunkered squad of ARVN soldiers shot at him with a machine gun . . . and missed.

Safe inside, sipping a cup of cold coffee, Bradley told Roberts, "God, I was lucky. Everyone had their chance to get me, but none did. I must be bulletproof."[43]

On Monday morning a platoon from Fox Company finally rescued the twenty-two American military advisers and two civilians trapped at the US Air Force coms center. The marines had punched through stiff enemy resistance to recover the grateful men, who had been hiding in a surrounded house for days, keeping the enemy back by firing from the windows, expecting at any moment to be overrun.

The house had been approached warily by a squad of marines led by Sergeant Jim McCoy. They thought it might be the one where Americans were hiding but they weren't sure. McCoy and Dan "Arkie" Allbritton stood to either side of the front door.

"Try the door," McCoy told Allbritton. "If it's unlocked, throw it open and I'll throw something in."

Instead, Allbritton knocked on the door, and with his southern drawl sang out, "Anybody to home?"

"Are you Americans?" came a voice from inside.

Most of the trapped men were air force personnel, but there were also army soldiers and civilians. They had built a bunker just inside the front door. Allbritton's natural politeness had spared them.

Roberts tracked them down at the compound. They were badly shaken by the ordeal, and some had been placed for safekeeping in a dugout bunker. The reporter crawled over the sandbags in front and down into the dark space.

"I'm Gene Roberts from the New York Times, and I've come to get your story," he said.

"Hey," one of the men said. "Didn't you write the Rambling in Rural Wayne column for the Goldsboro News-Argus?"

His name was Roy Jones, and as a boy he had delivered the same newspaper on his bicycle. He was a technical adviser for a development project. "We were running out of food," he said. "We were eating one meal of C rations a day and we found some contaminated water, boiled it, and drank it." [44]

They had gathered water from puddles outside and boiled it to have something to drink.

"Man, were those marines a sight for sore eyes," said Joe Hamilton, an army private. "I thought we had had it."

Nearby, another, smaller group of Americans in hiding was not so lucky. That same day, a marine lieutenant, James DiBernardo, who had run the Armed Forces Network radio and TV station in Hue, tried to make it to the compound with six of his staff members. For five days they had hidden two blocks from their studio in a small compound surrounded by a high wall. Their studio had been overrun on the first night. On Monday morning, February 5, they heard American voices outside, but then they came under attack. The enemy force that came at them was driving an ARVN tank. In the gun battle that ensued, the attackers set fire to the roof of the main house in the compound. An explosion injured DiBernardo's right arm. Realizing they could not hold out, he made a break toward the compound, only to be cornered by about twenty enemy soldiers. Two of DiBernardo's men were shot and killed, and he was shot and wounded again. He and the remaining four, all of them wounded, were marched off. They were taken to a Buddhist temple nearby, where their wounds were tended by the captive American IVS workers Dr. Marjorie Nelson and Sandra Johnson. They would be imprisoned for five years. [45]

5

The Breakout

Word passed from foxhole to foxhole at TFP on Sunday morning that they were completely surrounded. Colonel Dick Sweet's Air Cav battalion was spread out in foxholes that pitted the pointless acre of Vietnam they had purchased at such cost. There were trees and waist-high shrubs throughout the space, so commanders could not take in the whole position at once. Platoon sergeants would run from hole to hole to check on their men and keep the ammo distributed. To the north and west was a curving line of trees. Several small trails and one larger one ran through the center of the position. More enemy were just beyond the tree line to the east. The rice paddy they had charged across opened up to the north and west, where there was now a line of enemy troops.

Inside the Americans' perimeter there was a small stone hut that served as Sweet's command center. He had positioned his men to lay down fields of interlocking fire, so any massed charge toward their position, while likely to be successful, at least would be painful. Captain Krohn estimated that an all-out attack by the NVA would potentially sacrifice a thousand men, a price he hoped the enemy would be unwilling to pay.[46] There were probes, small charges at spots around the edges that produced ferocious volleys of rifle and machine-gun fire, and here and there Sweet's men were driven back. They would vacate their foxholes, retreat a distance, and dig new ones—the soil was sandy and easy to excavate. The enemy settled into the ones they'd abandoned. So their boundary was shrinking.

The mist was so thick that even at midday the two sides could not see each other clearly beyond about twenty yards. Despite this, choppers came in to evacuate the wounded and dead. Major William Scudder, the battalion's executive officer, had scrounged as much ammo and grenades as he could find at Camp Evans, and he'd also collected two hundred and fifty dry socks, not enough to go around but a great comfort to the lucky ones. Scudder defied rules against sending ammo on a medevac mission and delivered them in person Saturday afternoon. All three helicopters were badly shot up, but they made it back to Camp Evans. Krohn had watched the body of Tony Lau, the young medic, being loaded. Before the march had begun that morning, he had been talking to Lau, whom he found to be a literate and cheerful soul, the son of a grocer. They had discussed the best way to prepare beef with ginger, and Lau knew what he was talking about.

Even the small attacks produced prodigious exchanges of gunfire, more than even the most veteran soldiers had experienced before. A probe would start with the pop of an M16, then more and more, followed by the higher-pitched cracks of the AKs, and then the great ripping noise of the machine guns until it reached a volume that compared only to army firepower demonstrations they had seen at Fort Benning. Even with the resupply, the battalion was running out of ammo again by nightfall. The circle kept tightening. Between the snipers, the assaults, and the mortars, they seemed doomed to being whittled away. The wet air smothered them with the smell of cordite.

"I fought the Chinese in Korea," said Sweet, "but I never fought through any shit like this!"[47]

Krohn tried not to think about it. He focused on the tasks at hand, keeping his rifle clean and ready. He busied himself by updating his intel estimate, and he calculated when it would be safe to crawl off and urinate. Taller men didn't dare. They peed into C-ration cans and dumped them outside their foxholes. Alcohol was forbidden, but Krohn carried some brandy—"cough syrup"—in small medicine bottles he tucked into his ammo pouch. At night he dosed the powdered coffee and shared it with the other officers. It helped ease the chill. He was convinced that men lost their nerve in combat when they allowed themselves to think too much. The part movies never got right about war was all the waiting, and all the effort it took not to think.

The plight of Sweet's battalion had not fully registered back at Camp Evans, mirroring the disbelief that had greeted the marines' travails in Hue. Like marine general LaHue, army general Tolson seemed reluctant to believe Sweet's firsthand reports. There was simply no way that the NVA could seriously challenge a full battalion of American infantry in the field! By Sunday afternoon the second of the three battalions in Tolson's brigade, Vaught's, had been shifted to PK-17, and Sweet received a bullish communiqué from his brother battalion commander.

"Drive 'em to us and we'll blow them away!" said Vaught.

Sweet was dumbfounded. How had Vaught or anybody in the rear gotten the impression that they were in a position to *drive* the enemy anywhere? His men were hanging on for dear life!

Camp Evans was having problems of its own. The normal land supply routes from Da Nang were down because of the enemy's hold on Hue, so supplies had to be airlifted. This meant shortages of gasoline, food, and other necessities. The NVA was hammering the base regularly with rocket attacks. Tolson showed signs of wear. He completely broke down after an enemy rocket hit an ammo dump, igniting a series of enormous explosions and fire within the camp. The general appeared in his operations center distraught and babbling incoherently, and he had to be led back to his quarters by one of his staff officers. He emerged later apparently no worse for wear.[48]

The division's artillery battery at Camp Evans was still not up. On Saturday two 105-mm howitzers were flown to PK-17 but, wary of the volume of enemy fire around the outpost, the Chinooks dropped the big guns in a field about three hundred yards away. That's where they had been when Sweet's battalion stormed the tree line and took TFP. Four more were driven to PK-17 the next day by an artillery officer who ignored orders to stay off Highway 1. Captain Dane Maddox, the battery commander at PK-17, borrowed trucks from the ARVN motor pool to retrieve the two guns in the field. By late Saturday the outpost had six howitzers and quickly fired off its full load of about four hundred rounds.

This was hardly decisive, but it was tremendously satisfying for the surrounded men of Sweet's battalion. The fields around them erupted dramatically. The enemy didn't know that this was all they had at that point, so it was hoped the shelling would discourage the all-out attack they feared. Several of the shells exploded inside TFP, but no one was hurt. And things did quiet for a few hours afterward. The men were wet and shivering in their holes. Few slept. Several enemy mortars exploded inside the perimeter shortly before three in the morning, and then, not long after sunrise, came an enormous barrage. Krohn estimated that some two hundred shells fell inside their position, and this time there were casualties.

Private Carl DiLeo was on the receiving end. He and Sergeant Bob Hopkins were in the foxhole where they had killed the three surrendering NVA soldiers the day before. They had dragged the dead bodies a distance away. Then they moved in, huddling together to keep warm. At dawn Sunday they could see that their predicament had grown worse.

The shooting rarely stopped. The lower branches of the trees had all been shot away. DiLeo and Hopkins were in some kind of outdoor patio space. There was a stone table nearby with thick legs and some chairs. Theirs was one in a long row of foxholes spaced about forty feet apart. Their orders were to stay put, to keep close watch on the tree line in front of them, and to shoot at anything that moved.

The enemy made a couple of tries, and each time they were turned back. Hours passed. The Trenton teenager expected the big charge to come at any minute, and he strained to keep his eyes focused on the tree line, but it was dangerous even to put his head up. Judging by the numbers of enemy he could see, their position didn't stand a chance. And that wasn't even the worst thing. The worst thing was the mortars, which rained straight down on them. They were being launched periodically from only a few hundred yards away. DiLeo would hear the *pock* and then the *whoosh* of its climbing. If he looked up he could actually see the thing as it slowed to its apogee. From that point on it was perfectly silent. There it would hang, a black spot in the gray sky, for what seemed like a very long beat, the way a punted football was captured in slow motion by NFL Films, before it plummeted straight down at them. The explosion was like a body blow, even when it wasn't close. All of these were close. You opened your mouth and sometimes you screamed out of fear and it kept your eardrums from bursting. It was hell, a death lottery where all you could do was wait your turn. If you stayed down in the hole you were okay unless the mortar had your number and landed right on top of you.

This is what happened to DiLeo's good friend Walt Loos and the other man in his foxhole, Russell Kephart. They were one hole over. They got *plumed*. They were erased from the earth. DiLeo watched the round all the way down and it exploded right in their hole, vaporizing them. One second they were there, living and breathing and thinking and maybe swearing or even praying, just like him, and in the next second two hale young men, both of them sergeants in the US Army, pride of their hometowns—Perryville, Missouri; and Willimantic, Connecticut, respectively—had been turned into a plume of fine pink mist—tiny bits of blood, bone, tissue, flesh, and brain—that rose and drifted and settled over everyone and everything nearby. It—or *they*—drifted down on DiLeo, who reached up to wipe the bloody ooze from his eyes and saw that his arms and the rest of him were coated too. Then there would come another *pock!* And another *whoosh!*

He knew his only hope was to be lucky and to keep his head down. Even though he could not tell by watching where the next shell would fall, he could not stop craning his neck to watch. Which is probably why DiLeo got shot on the top of his head. The round hit his helmet and knocked him out cold. He folded over, unconscious, and Hopkins, panicking, jumped out. He moved to the stone table before he, too, was shot in the head. This round hit not his helmet but his forehead, killing him instantly.

DiLeo was out for what he later figured to be about two hours. One of the platoon sergeants, moving from hole to hole to check on the men, found him inert but still breathing. A medic was summoned, who revived him. His helmet had a hole in the top but the round had just grazed the top of his skull. His head was swollen and he had a headache, but there was little blood . . . or sympathy.

"You've got to keep the integrity of the perimeter!" the sergeant said, sharply.

A big attack came later Sunday. Fending it off took nearly all of their remaining ammo. Eleven more men were killed, and fifty-one wounded. The battalion was down to half its original four hundred. There weren't enough medics to treat all the wounded. Every few hours for the rest of the day a chopper would brave the intense fire to come in, sometimes hovering just off the ground as wounded men were thrown aboard. Medics had to triage, choosing which to send back; they never knew what Huey would be the last. By dusk, eleven of the unlucky ones lay side by side, some dead, the others judged too severely wounded to make the cut. One man with a sucking chest wound made awful rasping and gurgling noises as his lungs slowly filled with blood. Finally he stopped. Some of the men started to break under the stress. Krohn stopped one soldier who ran off in a panic, claiming he'd been blinded. A round had creased his brow. Krohn cleaned blood from the man's eyes, which were fine; calmed him; and led him back to his position. Sweet observed one unharmed soldier escape by throwing himself into the last chopper on the pile of wounded just as it took off.[49] The already overloaded aircraft wobbled but righted itself and flew away.

As darkness fell Sunday, Juan Gonzales, the black hat, had just one magazine for his rifle and two clips for his pistol. It was so dark he could just barely make out his hand in front of his face.

That darkness would save them. After the last load of treatable wounded were flown away at dusk, Sweet started planning a breakout. His commanders had put him and his men in an impossible situation. Light infantry battalions in Vietnam, like his, relied on air support and artillery. Without these, they were in trouble if they encountered a larger enemy force. This was rare in Vietnam, but it had happened here. The timing of the Tet Offensive worked perfectly for the enemy. It had come just as Westy was shuffling marines out of Camp Evans and the army in, so the camp had been caught in between and was temporarily weakened as a battle center. That and the weather had combined to leave Sweet's battalion stranded.

It was impossible for him to complete his mission—to fight his way through La Chu to the outer walls of the Citadel—but the colonel was reluctant to turn around. How would that look? What message would it send to the marines fighting in the city? That the Second Battalion of Twelfth Cavalry had *chickened out*?[50] Such a thing would be a permanent stain on the regiment annals.

Sweet gathered his officers and laid out the alternatives as he saw them: stay and fight on, retreat to PK-17, or escape and regroup well clear of La Chu to resume their march toward Hue. He asked for opinions. Given the glorious tradition of the US Cavalry, staying and fighting to the last man had a certain mythic ring, but there was little enthusiasm for that option. It was clear to all of these men that they had a better grasp of their situation than Tolson or Campbell or anyone else up the chain. Other than the medevac choppers and the one artillery barrage, the division wasn't helping. And yet the idea of fighting their way back to PK-17 was also unappealing. No matter how justified, a retreat is a retreat. If they were going to break out, the more appealing choice was Sweet's third.

They'd go that night, aiming for the hills to the southwest. That way they would be continuing their march toward the Citadel, albeit much reduced. If they didn't encounter still more masses of enemy in the hills, there was a chance of completing their mission. The decision left them with one sad consequence. There was no way they could carry their eleven dead out. They would have to bury them right there in a shallow grave.

Late that afternoon, Sweet sent a coded message to Colonel Campbell: "If we continue on our present mission and attack toward Hue via . . . La Chu, we'll be cut down. If we defend our present position, we'll be nickel-and-dimed to pieces. If we are exfiltrated to gain a more defensible position, we can flank the enemy stronghold and disrupt him. I recommend we do it."[51]

Campbell mulled this over, consulted with Tolson, and then gave his approval, but he washed his hands of the consequences. As if to say, *Okay, but don't tell anyone this was my idea,* he said he would not be responsible if the move failed, and that if they managed to escape, they'd essentially be on their own. Sweet and his men found Campbell's response galling.[52]

A black-and-white picture was taken by the battalion's chaplain, Dan Clem, of Captain Helvey just after this exchange. The captain's Alpha Company would lead the way out. The picture shows a lean man with a round face and at least a week-old beard. The dirt on his face and hands turns him roughly the same shade as his fatigues. He is squinting into the camera. His rifle is in his right hand. His flak jacket is open and he has a first-aid bandage wrapped around his neck to use as a sweat rag and wipe the dirt from his eyes. There is a rolled-up map resting on his ammo pouch; from his belt hang grenades, ammo clips, and a holster for his pistol; and C rations are draped over one shoulder in a sock. He's wearing a compass on his wrist. He looks calm and determined . . . even happy.

Word passed quickly from foxhole to foxhole that they were going. DiLeo felt . . . what? "Relief" wasn't a strong enough word. He felt a stab of hope, of *exhilarating* hope. He had seen so much in the past two days. He had helped carry the shattered bodies of the wounded to the helicopters for evacuation. He had seen the man whose warmth comforted him in his hole through a freezing wet night lying stiff and dead, a hole in the middle of his forehead. He had seen two men, one of them his good friend, simply *erased* from existence in an instant and been coated with their mortal remains. He had been shot, albeit not badly. It had made him feel—not imagine or think, but *feel*—how temporary was his life, and how, from one breath to the next, it could end. He would be no more. This shift in his thinking was subtle but profound. It moved him from fear to acceptance. At a certain point he stopped fearing death or horrible maiming; he just *expected* it. If not from a football of oblivion overhead, then it would be from a flying chunk of hot metal like the one that tore a hole in the top of his helmet. And now came this: *They might get away!* He might live! It was the first glimmer of hope in two days. He rejoiced. He knew that any attempt to move would be dangerous, probably fatal, but that was okay with him. He had come to grips with that. This was a chance. Anything was better than waiting in that hole trying to figure out what to think about in his last moments on earth, waiting to be plumed or slaughtered. He'd rather die trying to live.

Preparation for the move began before nightfall. Working deep enough in their holes not to be seen, men used twigs and rags to shape some semblance of a person so that enemy troops watching would believe they were still there after they left. It was a flimsy deception, but it might buy them precious minutes. The weapons and equipment of the dead and wounded were gathered and rigged for demolition. All the equipment they carried would have to be tied down to avoid clatter. No one was to shoot his weapon on the march without an order from the company commander, even if they were fired upon. One of the orders was "no smoking," which raised a few chuckles. They had run out of cigarettes the day before. The shallow grave for their eleven dead comrades was dug around a crater left by one of the mortars. They left a note on top of the mound, in poor Vietnamese, explaining that beneath were only dead bodies, no weapons or ammo.

That same afternoon, Captain Lewis Jeffries, the battalion's artillery officer, was finally able to report that his battery at PK-17 was fully up and loaded. Two bigger howitzers had been added to the six that had fired off all their ammo the day before. The bigger howitzers were M110s, whose eight-inch-wide barrels were among the largest in the army's inventory. They fired high-explosive shells that were three feet long, terrifying rounds that arrived with a bloodcurdling shriek and could gouge a hole three feet square in hard ground. Jeffries arranged for the battery to begin firing about ten minutes before the battalion started its move. The initial fire would be intermittent, the kind that a unit in the field would ordinarily order in at night to establish a defensive perimeter. A sudden dramatic bombardment might arouse suspicion. White phosphorus would be mixed with the explosive shells. Because the air was so wet and heavy, this would create a thick white cloud that would linger.

Keeping two hundred men together on a night maneuver was a challenge in itself, but to do so without flashlights in complete silence while threading through enemy lines on unfamiliar ground—ground that might be wired with booby traps and trip flares, ground that was pockmarked with holes from the artillery bombardments—made the attempt so treacherous it bordered on foolhardiness. But there was no quarrel about its necessity. The battalion officers huddled around Sweet to plot the path they would take. This was something Sweet knew how to do. He had taught night tactics at Fort Benning's infantry school. Remaining ammunition and food were distributed evenly among the two hundred men so that everyone carried the same size load.

Just after seven, when it was completely dark, the exhausted men emerged from their foxholes and formed two close columns toward the center of their perimeter, a long line of one hundred men, two abreast. Helvey's Alpha Company took the lead, led by its point man Hector Comacho. Per the infantry manual, the man behind him, Sergeant Henry Paschal, would keep track of how far they had gone by counting his steps and tying a knot for every three hundred, marking one hundred yards of progress. To DiLeo it seemed like a conga line, each man holding on to the soldier in front, moving in quiet unison. They took turns carrying the wounded on their backs. The walk started north, across the rice paddy they had charged through two days before. Sweet had noticed a small gap in the forward enemy line, about seventy-five yards wide. Once they were clear of that, he would turn them southwest. Everyone understood that this first part of the walk was the most risky. The ground was so muddy that sometimes a man's leg would sink to the knee. If he stumbled, others stumbled. The orders were: if you fell down and the column moved away from you, you were to stay down and silent until dawn. Of course, by then, you'd be alone and surrounded by the enemy. Theodore Wallace vowed to himself that he would not, under any circumstances, fall down. If the enemy had set mines or flares, or if they drew attention to themselves in any way, they were done. They'd be lined up in the open field like victims before a firing squad.

For the first dark minutes of the march, the gently sloshing sounds of two hundred pairs of boots emerging from the mud and the occasional scrape or ting of metal on metal sounded like a racket. At one point the men distinctly heard the familiar click of a round being chambered in a machine gun. Just a solitary but distinct *click!* Every man in the column turned his head toward it at the same time, waiting for the slaughter to commence.

DiLeo knew exactly what he had heard, and everyone else's reaction confirmed that he had not imagined it. Some enemy soldier out there in the darkness had spotted them. He put himself in the man's place. What would he do? Before him was a column of hundreds of men. If he fired, he'd alert his own force and the American column would be killed where they stood, but he would also be committing suicide. Every gun on the column would be trained on him. DiLeo figured, if it were him, he wouldn't fire, he'd crawl off looking for help—which is apparently what the enemy gunner did. After an agonizingly long moment of silence the column began shuffling forward again. No one fired.

They moved in fits and starts. When a man stumbled or paused, everyone behind him would be held up, but once he let go of the man in front of him, that man would pass word up to the front of the column to halt. The front part of the column would wait for the detached portion to catch up. None of the men had slept in days, so whenever they stopped, some would fall asleep standing and be jarred awake only when they started moving again. One man accidentally pulled the trigger on his grenade launcher. The grenade was engineered to avoid such an accident. It would not go off until it had traveled some distance. So it did not explode; it just hit the mud with enough force to make a very loud *thwack!* that could be heard clearly across the field. Nothing happened. They kept walking.

When they got to the small cemetery at the far end of the field, they breathed more easily. They had made it past the first enemy line. Sweet turned them toward the southwest. This took them to a river, fifty to sixty feet wide. Comacho waded in looking for a place to cross and promptly dropped in over his head. He came swimming back. Through trial and error he found a point shallow enough, just barely. Anyone on the short side of six feet had to turn his head up and bounce to keep his nose and mouth above the water. DiLeo was tall, and for the first time in days this felt lucky.

When they were safely across the water, their abandoned position, TFP, erupted. Jerry McLain saw first the trip flares they had planted around their position going off, illuminating enemy soldiers moving in. Then came an enormous blast. The explosives they had placed on their discarded equipment detonated, and then came the extended and intense bombardment.[53] Captain Jeffries had contacted the USS *McCormick*, a destroyer with five-inch guns that was a few miles east in the South China Sea. He was informed that the ship was ready to fire as many as five hundred rounds, and noted that this would set a record for the most ever fired by a US destroyer in a single day.[54] It came at a slow-rolling pace at first, and then, after a delay, it accelerated into an all-out roar. Captain Jeffries's hope was that the enemy would have overrun the position by then, placing themselves squarely in his crosshairs. The battery at PK-17 fired off hundreds of rounds. To the men in Sweet's escaping columns the mist far behind them lit up like a circle of hell.

They walked on through the rest of the night, at one point passing within two and a half miles of the Citadel's north walls, close enough so that the descending flares cast shadows. Sweet sent an urgent request that this stop, and, after a few minutes, it did.

At sunrise Monday morning they had reached the foothills. Surrounded by large boulders under a still drizzling, gray sky, the men could at last relax. They had made it. There was no enemy in sight, and the rocks provided cover. Krohn felt a joy that he would later compare to a religious experience. It wasn't a glorious military achievement but it had been a brilliantly executed maneuver. Sweet's men would remain grateful for his skillful leadership. They owed him their lives.

Holding On to the Enemy's Belt

MAJOR JOHN SALVATI arrived at the MACV compound at ten in the morning on Sunday, February 4, on a convoy with more marine volunteers, and with a navy doctor to help the three weary ones at the compound dispensary.

On the way up that morning they were passing an abandoned ARVN ammo dump when something behind the barbed wire caught Salvati's eye. He hopped off for a closer look. On the first night of the assault the dump had been overrun by the Front, but it had lacked either the time or the vehicles to pick it clean. What he'd seen were objects that looked like big plastic backpacks, rectangular containers in a harness with straps. He had seen them in Cuba two years before. They were E-8 gas launchers. Salvati distinctly remembered, because when he'd first seen one he didn't know what it was, so he'd looked it up in a manual. When you opened the lid the launcher looked like a block of hard plastic with sixteen neat holes bored in it. Inside each hole were tear gas canisters. The ones he found that morning were fully loaded, four 40-mm canisters in each bore. When you set the thing up on its pedestal, it could launch a canister from each hole every five seconds, creating a substantial gas cloud three hundred yards distant. If he could figure out how to use them, they would be very useful in the assault of a large building.

When he arrived in Hue, American forces controlled only about one-fourth of a hard-won square mile, centered on the compound and reaching two blocks north to Hue University and Doc Lao Park, with the LZ and boat ramp. Patrols that had pushed south, east, and west of the compound, mostly in an effort to rescue trapped Americans, had made it only a few blocks before pulling back. Within that controlled space it looked as if a titanic struggle had taken place. There were huge chunks of masonry and bricks on the wet streets. Litter from explosions and collapsed office buildings was everywhere, paper and furniture mostly. There were abandoned vehicles, many of them charred hulks. There were bicycles and fallen branches. Here and there lay dead civilians and enemy soldiers, grown stiff and bloated and ashen gray. The smell was terrible. It was dangerous to move in the open because of enemy snipers hidden in tall buildings.

With thousands of marines now occupying this patch, along with a growing number of civilians and ARVN soldiers who had made their way in, traffic was constant between the river and the compound, bringing food and ammo and medical supplies and evacuating the steady stream of dead and wounded. Trucks and Cheatham's extremely useful four-wheeled mules splashed through puddles as they raced back and forth to the LZ, to the boat ramp, and to his command post in the university building, where preparations were under way for the push west. The crackle of nearby gunfire was steady, and now and then came a thunderous blast from inside the Citadel across the river where General Truong was pressing his counterattack from Mang Ca. His men had begun moving toward the west side of the enclosure, along the inside of the north wall. Outside the fortress Major Ton That Dinh's ARVN battalion was making a futile effort to break through near Ngo Mon. But in the triangle that fight seemed a world away.

South of the river, Viet Cong lieutenant Hoang Anh De's battalion[55] was dug in throughout the neighborhood Cheatham planned to take back. While both commanders had roughly the same number of men at that point—there were about two thousand on each side—Cheatham had more firepower, and Colonel Gravel's depleted battalion tilted the balance further to the Americans.[56] But Hoang had huge advantages. His men were defending and behind cover. The city, with all of its buildings, houses, and walls, provided plenty of places to hide. Cheatham's men had to attack, which meant they had to move and expose themselves. Hoang also had fresh troops and, for the time being, enough ammo. He had lost only a handful of men moving in, and his ranks had swelled significantly after the stubborn defenses at the Thua Thien prison caved on Friday night. Most of the freed prisoners were local Viet Cong fighters and sympathizers who knew where to find caches of ARVN weapons and ammo, so there was no trouble arming them. Hoang had machine guns and rocket teams in bunkers high and low, and his riflemen were everywhere.

He called his strategy for resisting the coming counterattack *bam vao that-lung dich* ("hold on to the enemy's belt"). It was how he hoped to overcome the Americans' overwhelming firepower. The marines would typically hammer an enemy line with bombs and shells before advancing. By "clinging to their belt," Hoang meant keeping his men so close to marine lines that it would be too risky for them to shell—he did not believe reports that Americans would not use heavy weapons in the city. His battalion was arrayed in two flexible and irregular defensive lines, one directly across the street from the marines and another two blocks back. During an attack the front line could bend in one place and hold in another. It would hold off an assault for as long as possible, and then fall back to the second line. If the attacking marines failed to occupy and hold the block they had just taken, as had mostly been the case so far, Hoang's men would move back up at night, always staying directly across the street. If things worked out as he planned, this would force the marines to advance with small arms alone, evening the fight. In that kind of fight, Hoang believed his men had the advantage. Most were veterans with far more experience than the marines, and so long as their lines of supply stayed open they could resist for days, maybe even weeks, bleeding the marines for every square foot.

By necessity, military commanders are realists, and to Hoang it was already apparent that the "general uprising" part of the Tet plan was not happening. While some had rallied to the cause, and others seemed willing to follow orders to help dig and carry and cook (keeping their true feelings to themselves), there had been no swell of popular support. The citizens of Hue had either fled or dug in. What he saw were people in shock over the violent disruption of their lives. Refugees ran to the countryside, if they could get there, or huddled in places they hoped would be safe: in churches, behind his defensive lines, or behind the American ones at the compound and now the university. They were not rallying to one side or the other; they were trying to stay alive. They hung close to the front lines for the same reason that he stayed close to the marines, to escape bombardment. So Hoang had no illusions about keeping Hue permanently. But he was going to make the Americans pay to take it back.[57]

For Cheatham, taking back Hue was a professional mandate, and the most significant challenge in his fifteen years of service. He had witnessed the results of the uncoordinated efforts so far. The night before he arrived, Captain Downs made an attempt on the treasury that failed to even make it all the way to the street in front. Downs had been slightly wounded. The captain was just behind Lieutenant Hausrath's lead platoon, in position to observe firsthand and react. The mayhem that ensued on their first try had sent a shard of shrapnel stinging into his right thigh. On Friday night he visited the clinic at the compound to have it cleaned and bandaged, and he was given a tetanus shot, and later Downs dutifully noted himself among the "WIA" in his pocket diary—there were twenty from his company that day.

Gene Roberts had also watched that attempt from inside the university. Sergeant King, his escort, explained that the tactics they were using were like those employed in the Korean War, where he had fought as a young man. One squad would provide covering fire while another ran across the street toward the target building. Only now, instead of charging into the bolt-action rifles used in that war, they were charging at automatic rifles. The AK-47 could be used as either a sniper rifle or a machine gun. A single soldier so armed could barricade himself on an upper floor, and with enough ammunition he could hold an entire company at bay for hours.[58]

Lieutenant Hoang was inside the treasury, with just over one hundred men. There were so many guns firing out, everything from heavy machine guns to rocket launchers and rifles, that it was deadly to approach from any direction. In time the marines discovered there was a heavy machine gun in Le Loi Elementary School on their left flank that could cover the entire street before the building, and more were in the public health complex on their right flank. The big steel door before the treasury was impervious to their grenades and rockets. All of the buildings along the main avenue were the same, extraordinarily sturdy French colonial structures built with masonry walls that were at least two feet thick. The French built them that way to ward off the heat. Vietnam was sweltering in the summer months, and the thick stone walls kept the insides of the buildings cooler. No rifles, light rockets, or grenades could penetrate them.

There were shooters behind the knee-high perimeter wall and iron fencing around the building's yard. There were firing positions on the roof and from those openings in the cornice. There were gun positions in each of the neatly spaced windows on the first and second floors. Beyond all these, as the marines would discover, there were snipers hidden in carefully camouflaged spider holes dug along the surrounding wall, so that men who made it to the yard could be shot at from behind.

Tanks that drove out to the street were rattled so violently with enemy fire that crew members emerged dazed. Cheatham called them "punch drunk."[59] After the first abortive attempt to cross the street on Saturday, February 3, two marines had lain in the open for hours. Wayne Washburn was mortally wounded and slowly dying. William Barnes, who had gone out to try to drag him back, had been shot in the head and killed instantly. Barnes, an eighteen-year-old private from Battle Creek, Michigan, had just arrived that day. He had lasted only minutes in combat. No one knew him. After Barnes was killed the enemy could have finished off Washburn at will. Instead they left him as bait, waiting for someone else to come out for him. Mindful of how shocked he had been to discover Roberto DelaRivaVera still alive in the earlier "body recovery," Downs was not about to leave the two men in the street. He requested a halt to illumination flares over the central part of the city that night, and both men were recovered. Washburn was still alive but he died the next day.

Fighting in the city was unfamiliar and deadly. Perhaps the worst thing was not being able to see very far. You could see across a street or to the next house, but that was it. The Vietnamese built walls around everything. They embedded the tops with broken glass, so it was difficult to climb over without slicing yourself. And you never knew what was waiting for you around a corner. It was hard to tell where shooting was coming from because sound, like bullets, bounced off the walls. In the countryside, you could orient to the crack of a gunshot, or see a distant muzzle flash. Here, you never knew, and if you didn't know where the enemy was it was impossible to feel safe.

It was unnerving. The only time David Tyree felt safe was after his squad had secured a house and he was inside it with his back to a wall while others were fighting in the front. He was a nineteen-year-old private from West Virginia, who had gotten tired of his college classes and quit to join the Corps. He found the tedium of life as a marine far worse than school, and nothing had prepared him for the danger. Here in Hue, his days were reduced to trying to stay alive and not to disgrace himself. Sleep was a distant memory. You were lucky if you could grab two hours here and there. He was cold night and day. Stone walls absorbed the chill, but the only way to stay safe was to stay against one. Tyree got lucky, in a sense, on Saturday. A bit of shrapnel skipped off a wall and sliced across his face, breaking his nose. Another bit punctured his wrist. The marine next to him was more badly hurt, in both legs, and after Tyree carried him out to a mule for evacuation, bleeding dramatically himself, he was ordered to climb on. He rode back in a chopper to Phu Bai with the bodies of Washburn and Barnes and the other wounded. He would spend the next few days getting warm. Then he'd return.

"Charlie," as the marines called the enemy, stayed frustratingly behind cover. The marines would catch glimpses of men moving at the edge of a window frame or wall, but that was it. They seemed to be everywhere. The heavier bazookas Cheatham brought made a big difference. Their bigger rockets weighed nine pounds and could punch holes in walls big enough for men to climb through—sometimes it took two or three shots. When they attacked on Sunday, February 4, under Cheatham's guidance, it meant that in some places they would be able to move forward without stepping out into the open. But there was no way to avoid crossing streets.

The lack of progress that Saturday, after Cheatham's arrival, had made Colonel Gravel feel somewhat vindicated. Both Big Ernie and Colonel Hughes had arrived full of courage and bluster, and they had treated him like a failure. Now they'd had a taste themselves.[60]

The marines of 2/5 settled into neighborhood buildings for the night. Some of the men used university classrooms, commandeering the Bunsen burners in a chemistry classroom to cook C rations. They grabbed a few hours of sleep, cleaned their weapons, and braced themselves for the next day. In the music room some of the grunts picked up drums and tubas and an assortment of other horns and amused themselves into the night by making very bad, discordant music.

Christmas's Hotel Company had managed to occupy two buildings in the public health complex on Saturday afternoon, but Downs's inability to cross the street had left them too exposed to remain there overnight. So at dusk Cheatham ordered them to pull back to the university. Hotel's marines reluctantly gave back the ground and buildings they had bravely purchased. It all illustrated for Cheatham the need for better tactics and coordination.

He and his captains conferred well into the night, reviewing his plans. The young officers were frustrated. What they had been doing hadn't worked. They were eager to try what Big Ernie had in mind. He had brought with him, in effect, a mobile battery. The 106s and the bazookas and four mortar tubes would clobber the treasury beforehand. Tanks would continue to be used to provide cover for advancing men. The mules would move the 106s where they were needed. This firepower would be aimed primarily at the enemy's machine-gun emplacements, or to blow holes in outer walls. The mortars would hammer the roof until it buckled. It was the same principle as aerial or artillery bombardment; it would just take longer. Ideally the building's defenders would be dead, wounded, or too dazed to put up much of a fight when the marines made their charge.

While the commanders conferred, Major Salvati set up the four E-8 launchers he had found on a street just south of the university, tilting them on their pedestals until they were pointed almost straight up—the treasury was only about fifty yards away. He wasn't sure he could make them work, and he sought out Downs.

"I don't want to encroach on your turf," he told the captain, but then he explained that he wanted to give them a try before the initial assault.

Downs was ready to try anything.

"Make sure your men have their gas masks," Salvati said.

The treasury looked invincible but, in fact, overnight its defenses had thinned. This was not apparent to the marines, but Hoang, noting the size of the force massing across the street, had decided to move most of his men back. That morning he had just one platoon, about thirty men, defending both it and the post office.[61] They were still going to put up a fight. Snipers remained on the roof and in the attic and second-floor rooms. Automatic weapons were on the lower floors. Soldiers were still in the spider holes that ringed the inside of the low courtyard wall and iron fencing, each with a rifle and a rocket launcher. The big machine gun at the elementary school was still in place, and Hoang's men had retaken the buildings Christmas had been forced to abandon on the right flank.

Jeanne d'Arc School

CHEATHAM'S SUNDAY MOVE was the first of the three major battles it would take to reclaim Hue—the fight for the Citadel remained stalemated, as did the army's effort to march down to the city from the northwest.

In the three-pronged attack, coordinated by Colonel Hughes, Smith would go first. He was farthest back, at the compound. The idea was for him to push out early and move up to his flanking position on the left, clearing buildings in the blocks south of the treasury. Cheatham's battalion would make the main thrust. Downs would take the center, with Christmas covering his right flank.

Smith's objectives did not appear as formidable as the treasury. The largest structure was the Jeanne d'Arc High School, which consisted of two L-shaped classroom buildings, each two stories, that enclosed an open yard with a large tree at its center. Before these buildings was a quaint Catholic chapel, and beyond that was the elementary school where the enemy's machine gun had wreaked such havoc on Saturday. He was expected to be in position by midmorning, when the treasury attack would begin.

At first light, Smith started his move. His third platoon, led by Alfredo Gonzalez, the wiry young sergeant whose conspicuous courage had earned him command, first attacked the chapel. It was a beautiful structure with a graceful dome and steeple. On the inside its towering walls were lined with fluted columns and high arches. An explosive was placed against the chapel door, and when it blew open several marines charged in . . . and were promptly blown back out the door. Most of the enemy soldiers inside were fleeing out a back door as more marines followed, but some of them stayed high in the church's rafters, tossing down grenades, which were what had chased the first squad out.

Gary Eichler was with those waiting to enter, but his rifle wouldn't work. Just minutes earlier he had lifted it to take aim at an enemy soldier in a second-floor window across the street, and the trigger just clicked. It was his own fault. Some weeks earlier, he had traded the standard-issue bolt in the firing mechanism of his M16 for a fancy chrome one. Turns out, as Eichler now discovered, the chrome bolts, which looked bright and fancy, would become notorious. Bits of them flaked off and chewed up the rifle's works. His had now failed at the worst possible moment. So he had bummed as many LAWs as he could carry.

Across the street, Gravel, a pious Catholic, wrestled with what he had to do. If there were shooters in the rafters, the chapel would have to come down. He reluctantly directed a 106 and his mortar platoon to take aim, and a Patton tank lifted its big gun. When they fired, the top of the steeple came off and the rest crashed down into the dome and spilled out into the street.[62]

Eichler entered the collapsed church firing rockets at anything that looked like a firing position, laying further waste to the interior. The pews were covered with the remains of the steeple and dome. There were gaping holes in the back wall alongside a large crucifix. Blasting away at the statuary and stations of the cross seemed sacrilegious to Eichler, who had been raised Catholic. He decided to choose his targets more carefully, worked his way to a circular space behind the elevated altar, and aimed through the rear door at fleeing enemy soldiers.

The marines soon owned what was left of the chapel. The two L-shaped school buildings were tougher. They formed a square that was open at the north and south. Smith's men were able to occupy the east building without much of a fight, but that was apparently the enemy's plan, because they no sooner moved in than blistering fire erupted from the west building. The two structures faced each other across the school yard with the big tree at its center. The only way to move from one building to the other was to step out into the open. Lieutenant Hoang's men had set up bunkered machine guns that covered the open ends of the buildings and the school yard, placed so they could not easily be targeted from inside the east building.

Smith's men were trapped there for hours. Every time someone tried to establish a fighting position outside, he was shot. Time and again, Gunny Canley would endanger himself to carry the wounded men back inside. Meanwhile, Cheatham was on the radio to Smith's commanders impatient to begin the main attack, wondering where the hell the lieutenant was.

Bombardment of the treasury had already begun, with mortars exploding on the roof. Salvati's first attempt to fire one of his E-8 gas launchers failed. The lanyard attached to the trigger broke. So he sought out the battalion's engineering wizard, Lieutenant Richard Squires, who was known as "Sparks." He came up with a hand-cranked field telephone, which was attached to the launcher's firing mechanism by wire. When he turned the crank the thing went off like the Fourth of July, blowing off all sixty-four canisters in just a few minutes. It created an enormous billowing cloud of tear gas that settled over the treasury and everything else in the area.

Some of the gas drifted south. Smith had only thirty-seven gas masks for one hundred and forty men. It was a nuisance but, as he started across the school yard at the heavily defended west building, gas seemed to be the right idea. He inquired about its source, and Salvati got on the radio to tell him there were more launchers at the compound. Smith sent a man to fetch one. He had the gas masks he'd collected given to his first platoon. He would gas the hell out of the west building and then send the men who had masks across.

The launcher arrived with a small comic book–style manual. Following the instructions, Smith tilted it on its pedestal. He wanted to place it on the yard, but stepping outside would be too dangerous, so he pushed the thing out the door with a long bamboo stick. The yard was paved with ceramic tiles and the launcher slid easily. He positioned it carefully, with the tubes aimed toward the west building. Crouched in the doorway, Smith pulled the lanyard to the trigger and the launcher ignited. He had expected it to fire the canisters all at once, but instead they came in rapid succession from one side to the other. The first two gas rounds went where he had aimed them, but the recoil set the launcher spinning on the smooth tile. One of the next two canisters struck him in the chest, knocking him over backward. The launcher just kept on spinning, throwing gas canisters in all directions. Several flew off toward the compound. More exploded over the east building. When it stopped spinning and firing, the lieutenant had wounded himself and had gassed not only his own men but the command post across the street—Hughes and Gravel and his other superiors in the compound. Those without masks took the soft cover off their helmets, soaked it, and draped it over their faces. Some raced back to the compound, looking for cover.

Fortunately for the lieutenant, the tear gas over the compound was blamed on Salvati's big treasury cloud. It took more time for Smith, bruised in both chest and ego, to regroup his company. He obtained one of the 106s, which his men carried upstairs and set in a second-floor window. They began blasting away at one of the west building's corners, where his first platoon was planning its assault. The third time the big gun was fired its back blast caved in the floor. It was now afternoon. Alpha was stuck and Cheatham was fuming.

Shooting continued across the school yard, and Alpha Company took still more casualties. Bill Huff had his thumb shot off. John Ligato wrapped Huff's hand and, worried that he would go into shock, tried to make him laugh.

"You know, Huff, when you get back to the world, you aren't going to be able to hitchhike," he told him.

This did not make him laugh.

"Yeah, Huff, when you get back, nobody can ever accuse you of having a thumb up your ass, can they?"

Freddie Gonzalez, whose heroism on the way up from Phu Bai had amazed everyone, tried once more to take matters into his own hands. He gathered up a number of LAWs, and holding six under one arm and one more over his right shoulder he moved them to a room on the second floor. Out a large window that looked past the big tree at the center of the yard, he leaned and fired a rocket at one of the enemy machine-gun positions. He then ducked back down as return fire came at the window. A rocket flew in through the window, exploding against the back wall. Gonzalez waited and then leaned out and fired another. He did this three times, creating enough of a disturbance for his men to successfully cross the southern alley and break into one end of the west building. But the return fire on the third shot came back faster, and a rocket struck him squarely in the abdomen and exploded. His wounds were massive.

Corpsman Jim O'Konski was the first to reach him. He knew immediately that Gonzalez would not survive. His intestines were hanging out and he had very nearly been torn in half. He propped Gonzalez's torso against a wall and tried to figure out what he could do for him. His eyes were closed and he was moaning. The corpsman gave him a shot of morphine, leaned in, and started reciting the "Our Father" prayer in his ear. He got as far as the line "Give us this day . . ." when another rocket exploded nearby. O'Konski couldn't do anything more for him, so he left. One of Gonzalez's buddies came in to hold his hand. Another corpsman later gave Gonzalez a second dose of morphine. He died without waking up.

His loss was a heavy blow to the men of Alpha 1/1. He had been an inspirational leader and had seemed to them invincible.

The work went on into the afternoon. Having attained a foothold in the west building, the marines were now fighting Front soldiers at the other end of it. The gunfight raged from room to room. Bodies littered the bloody floors.

Jimmy Sullivan stopped over one dead enemy soldier and started rooting through his pockets and gear. Lieutenant Smith came up behind him.

"Jimmy, what are you doing?" he asked.

"First marines strip their dead," he said.

"Jimmy, we don't have time for this shit," Smith said. "Just kill them."

Going in, they all knew war was terrible, but this was worse than anything O'Konski had ever imagined. There was not a man among them who did not find himself asking, sometimes even out loud, *How the fuck did I get myself into this?* At some point they had agreed to serve, often because there was no other acceptable choice. Nearly all of them were proud of being marines, with the fidelity and toughness that implied, but none could ever have imagined Hue. For O'Konski the entire rationale for fighting in Vietnam was rooted in faith. Faith that his elected leaders and military bosses knew what they were doing and that the calculation that had placed his life at such peril mattered, that it did more than just make sense but *demanded* his suffering and sacrifice.

He hoped that this was all true but, personally, he couldn't see it anymore. He thought America had no business being in this war, that *he* had no business being in this war. He felt like the last person who had any. He was a peace-loving man. He took his Catholic faith seriously, even said the rosary every night. He'd planned on becoming a dentist, but an illness had forced him to drop his college classes for most of a year, making him eligible for the draft. His guiding principle had been to avoid Vietnam. He'd tried for the air force first, but when acceptance there was delayed he'd gone to a navy recruiter. If you were on a ship, you wouldn't be humping a rifle in the jungle, right? But when navy administration noted all those science classes on his college records, he was steered to medical training, and, just months later, here he was, a corpsman, wearing marine fatigues, in Vietnam, in the thick of the fighting, patching up wounded marines. He was even required to carry a rifle, although he'd never used it.

He and the other corpsmen tried to preserve their own identities. O'Konski kept his white sailor's cap in his backpack, and he wore it sometimes to remind the marines that he was not one of them, or perhaps to remind himself. But immersed in the horror of combat all such distinctions fell away. There were too many urgent tasks at hand. He crawled from room to room to avoid the fire coming through the windows, spending most of the afternoon on all fours. He was literally taking a blood bath, soaked first by Gonzalez and then by another of the men he tended, who'd had both legs blown off below the knees. He bound the stumps with tourniquets and gave the screaming victim morphine.

Late in the day he was with a group of marines in a small courtyard, surrounded by walls on three sides, when a mortar or grenade exploded. He went immediately into triage mode, quickly evaluating which men he should help and which he could not. He was pulling a piece of shrapnel out of a marine's neck when one of the other men said, "Hey, Doc, there's blood coming out of your boot."

O'Konski looked down at a slice in his boot and, indeed, his own blood was contributing to the pool on the tiles. For some reason, it was not until he saw it that he felt it.

8

Look at Your Sorry Ass!

CHEATHAM'S MAIN ATTACK didn't kick off until midafternoon. Smith still hadn't moved his company into position, and it had taken much longer than expected to satisfactorily batter the treasury.

CBS reporter John Laurence watched as a group of marines wrestled one of the nearly half-ton 106 rifles upstairs to a second-story classroom and aimed it out the window at the treasury's big steel doors. They set it on a table and with difficulty angled it down. Once they had it balanced and aimed, they fired a tracer round from the gun mounted above the barrel, and then prepared to shoot. Everyone was ordered to back away. Laurence stepped out of the room, watching through the doorway. The crew covered their ears. When it was fired, Laurence heard a sound like a thunderclap that "rocked the floors and ceilings and knocked plaster off walls and brought a shower of debris down on the gun and the men around it." [63]

The size of the blast both scared and delighted the marines. Laurence couldn't see what the shell had accomplished across the street, but the back blast alone had wrecked the classroom. It had blown down the door and torn a hole in the floor. The gun teetered on the lip of it. The crew stood stunned and coated with plaster dust. They pointed at one another and hooted like the teenagers most of them were.

"Oh, man, look at your sorry ass!" one said. [64]

Downstairs, Laurence managed to pull Cheatham aside for an interview on camera as the fighting raged. The massive colonel was conferring with Downs, Christmas, and Meadows about all the enemy spider holes around the building.

"You've got to dig these rats out of their holes," Cheatham told them. "Got it?"

Then he stepped over to field Laurence's questions. Cheatham looked to be in his element. He was unshaven and covered with dust, and he had goggles pulled up and strapped over his helmet. He seemed calm and businesslike. Laurence and his cameraman Keith Kay positioned him before a mule-mounted 106. Behind them was a store with an awning that projected over the sidewalk. Laurence held a microphone under Cheatham's chin.

"What kind of fighting is it going to be?" he asked.

"It's house to house and room to room," Cheatham said.

"Kind of inch by inch?"

"That's exactly what it is."

"Did you ever expect to experience this kind of fighting in Vietnam?"

"No, I didn't. And this is my first crack at street fighting. I think this is the first time the marines have been street fighting since Seoul in 1950."

Cheatham stopped to help direct a squad of marines.

"What's going to happen to civilians who might get caught in there?" Laurence asked.

"Well, we're hoping that we don't run into any civilians in there right now. If they are [there]—I'm pretty sure they are civilians we would consider bad guys right now. We have certain areas in there that we have blocked off, that we know there are friendly civilians, and we aren't gonna take those under fire."

"And the others?"

"The others—if there's somebody in there right now, they're Charlie as far as we're concerned."

When they had finished and stepped back, the 106 fired. The back blast kicked up a huge cloud of dust, shattered the storefront, and sent the awning crashing to the sidewalk.[65] The twenty-pound round blew a hole just under the roofline of the treasury across the street.

When Christmas's company had crossed the street on Saturday they had popped smoke to hide themselves, but they had been hit hard just the same. The big gun in the elementary school, most likely a 12.7-mm

Soviet machine gun (about the size of the American .50 caliber), had produced devastating grazing fire. The enemy gunners hadn't needed to be able to see Christmas's men in order to fire effectively down the street through the cloud. Nothing had changed since then. The gun had been firing at targets of opportunity all morning. There seemed to be no way to silence it. Mortars were too imprecise; it was too far away for the bazookas; and before they could fire a 106 it would have to be moved out from behind cover to be aimed, and aiming, as Laurence had seen up in the classroom, was a production. Its crew wouldn't stand a chance.

Cheatham studied the problem himself. He crawled out to a telephone pole and waited for the gun to fire. It was using green tracers, so he could see the trajectory of its rounds. He noticed that when it shot at things to its left, toward the treasury and the street directly in front, the rounds were low, but whenever the gun shot to its right, on the university side of the street, the aim was high. This suggested that the gunner's field of fire was obstructed by something on that side, something that forced him to aim the gun up. If he was right, Cheatham figured there was a spot near him out on the street where a man could stand up and still be too low for the machine gun.

He went back into the university courtyard and worked out the plan with the weapons platoon leader. Cheatham then bet his life on his calculation. It was the sort of thing that had earned him such respect. He stepped out into the street and fired several tracer rounds at the machine gun. It returned fire with rounds that looked as big as basketballs hurtling toward him, but which cracked harmlessly over his head. Thus assured, the 106 gunners rolled the mule out to the same spot and took several shots with the spotting rifle to zero it in.[66]

At the same time Captain Christmas was assembling his own men for another run across the street. After their experience yesterday, they dreaded it.

"I know what to do, Skipper," said one of the 106 crew. "You know how big the round is. They [the enemy machine gunners] will pull in their heads. And, sir, you know this thing's back blast. You can run the whole company across the street if you want."

Christmas had no better ideas. His men waited as the gun's crew counted down, and with a final chorus of "Fire the one-oh-six!" it popped one round toward the target. The round flashed by so close to

Downs's lead platoon, which was waiting behind a wall down on the street, that it seemed to brush their noses. There was plenty of fire when Christmas's men took off, but the dust kicked up by the back blast hid them. More important, the enemy machine gun stayed silent.

The public health complex was quickly retaken—it also had been under mortar and gas bombardment. Hoang's remaining men retreated when they saw the marines coming, and it was hard for Christmas's platoon leaders to stop their men from giving chase. One squad, led by Corporal Robert Hedger, pressed on past the buildings and blew a hole in a wall with a C4 charge. Hedger was weighted down with bazooka rounds, but no one with him had one of the tubes. He fell hard when he was struck in the chest and neck. His buddy Lyndol Wilson crawled out to him, called for a corpsman, and saw that Hedger, although still alive, was not likely to survive. Infuriated, Wilson emptied his rifle on full automatic toward the enemy positions across the street, even though he couldn't see any targets. When he'd used up all his rifle magazines, he drew his pistol and emptied that. His furious efforts enabled the men behind him to drag Hedger back. One was shot through the leg. Hedger was soon dead.[67]

With Christmas's company now in position to provide flanking fire from his right, Downs ordered the assault on the treasury. The 106 had knocked the steel door off its frame, but it was still upright. A bazooka finished the job, and the lead platoon, all wearing gas masks, led by Lieutenant Hausrath, took off across the street.

Ronald Frasier was in that group. He had lined up with the rest of the men in his platoon behind a wall, waiting. When they were told that they were going to be first across, no one said a word. Frasier, a nineteen-year-old corporal, was petrified. He had been wounded the day before by a rocket fragment. It had torn through his upper right leg and exited his right buttock. He had been patched up. The wound was judged borderline, ugly but insufficient for a ticket back to Phu Bai. Now it hurt. His leg and butt were swollen and stiff. He smelled tear gas and smoke and cordite, and the sound of gunfire and explosions was deafening. The order to charge seemed suicidal but he knew the second he heard it that he would go. There was no way he was not going to go. His buddies were going so he was going too. Having seen what had happened to Washburn and Barnes the day before, the way they both lay on the street for hours, he knew what to expect. But despite his fear and the pain he ran when he was ordered to run. He ran as fire erupted in front of him and behind, no longer even aware of what was going on around him, but especially fearful of the big gun in the distance to his left that had been hurling huge rounds down the street for the last two days. He was wearing a gas mask, which made it harder to look around, so he just kept moving forward. He felt that he was moving faster than he had ever moved, but it was still the longest sprint of his life. To his amazement he made it across the street, along with others from his platoon, and then they all just kept going. There were no tactics. It was just move and shoot.

In the midst of it all, Lieutenant Hausrath climbed to the top of a wall to shout directions to his men, exposing himself needlessly. Jim McCoy, his platoon sergeant, made a mental note. Danger made most men cautious, but with some it had the opposite effect. Hausrath, with his nickname "Rat" scrawled on the front of his helmet, had warmed to street fighting a bit too much for McCoy's liking. That was Hausrath's business, of course, but the sergeant felt it was his own responsibility to keep his men—and himself—from being swept up in the lieutenant's enthusiasm.

Dan Allbritton, the drawling corporal from Arkansas, was first to the treasury door, which was about twelve feet back from the front gate. A Patton tank was blasting the front of the building with machine-gun fire. Allbritton could hardly hear himself think. He threw a tear gas grenade inside and then stepped through, firing his rifle on automatic. There was no one there. The first floor looked like a grand bank lobby, with counters and barred teller stations. It was full of dust and gas and smoke. Dongs, South Vietnamese currency, were scattered everywhere. It was hard to look around with the gas mask on, but right away he saw that the staircase he'd been told would be right in front of him when he got in—it was never if he got in—was not there.

Chuck Ekker, his squad leader, came behind him with the rest. The men spread out, looking for a way upstairs. They had been shot at from the roofline and second floor on every attempted assault, so they had every reason to believe there were enemy soldiers upstairs, but how to get there? Behind a heavy door down the hall, Allbritton heard Vietnamese voices. The door was locked. He shot through it, and another marine came up from behind to spray it with his heavier M-60 machine gun. It still would not budge, even when they threw themselves against it. They placed grenades at its foot, pulled the pins, and ran far back. The explosions blew the door off its jambs, but it was still standing. The top tilted inward but the bottom stayed in place. They threw some more grenades into the room through the opening at the top. When they were finally able to push past the door the room was empty. Big chunks of the stone wall blown away earlier had been piled against it. There was a spiral staircase in the middle of this room. At the far end was an open door. They found only one wounded soldier upstairs.

Ekker had waited momentarily in the downstairs hall to assemble his squad. Through a hole in the ceiling, he saw someone who seemed to be gesturing for him to move back. He thought at first that it was Allbritton, but then the man dropped a grenade, the Chinese variety that looked like a tin can on a stick. It rolled to the floor beneath his feet. Frantic, he tried to move away but ran into a wall. The hallway was narrow, and men were scrambling into each other as they tried to back off. The grenade exploded, disintegrating the handle of Ekker's rifle, and shrapnel cut through the lower part of his left leg. Jerry Dankworth, who was directly behind him, received the blast's full force in both of his legs.[68]

Just across the street, Hausrath radioed Downs to say that Ekker's squad was down and they needed to bring them back.

"No!" Downs shouted into the radio. "Bring back be damned! You get going!"

Ernie Weiss and Mike Sowards were among those poking farther into the hazy mess of the building. Weiss found an abandoned enemy radio pack; inside was an NVA flag, which he took as a souvenir. On one side of the building, in a small courtyard, he and Sowards found a wounded enemy soldier crawling away. Weiss had never seen an enemy up close. He called for help.

"We've got a wounded gook over here," he said.

Another marine lifted his rifle and shot the man dead.

In the end it was almost anticlimactic. When the attack was over, the building was so full of holes that it resembled a worn sponge. Its defenders either were dead or had run by the time Downs and his third platoon fully occupied the building. None of his men had been killed, but eighteen had been wounded. Hoang would report losing seven men.[69] In their haste to clear out, the Front had abandoned weapons and ammo at various firing positions. In one of the outbuildings behind the treasury, the marines found about thirty civilians hiding. One spoke English well and convinced them that they had been trapped there since the previous day. They were let go.

Downs's second platoon then moved on the big post office building next door. That went more easily. Clearly Cheatham's bombardment and Salvati's gas cloud had made a difference. The enemy had cleared out.

Most of them, anyway. On the southwest side of the post office they found a vault with heavy steel doors at both ends. Some of the marines swore they had been fired at from it and that they had seen enemy soldiers just outside it, but by the time they reached the bunker its doors were closed and locked at both ends. It was about twenty feet long and covered with earth and had grass growing over it in a large mound, with concrete porches at both ends. They tried blasting through one of the doors with a bazooka but it didn't budge. One of the men who spoke a few phrases in Vietnamese called for those inside to surrender. There was no response.

Chris Brown, the dancing marine from Brooklyn, had a suggestion. He noticed four small air shafts emerging from the grass.

"Why don't we put some gas in there?" he said.

So as they backed off and covered the doors David Kief ran up the grass mound and dropped a gas canister down one of the shafts. It took a few moments, but then the steel door in front opened a little. The marines didn't wait to see if the men inside intended to surrender. They opened fire. One fired a rocket into the bunker and it exploded. Then came a secondary explosion from inside. After a few moments, those inside who could still move began to emerge from the door at the opposite end. They were shot one by one.

Inside and outside the bunker they found the remains of two dozen men. Inside the marines found a stash of rifles, a machine gun, rocket launchers, and satchel charges. The bodies were laid out in the court-yard, more enemy soldiers than any of them had ever seen at one time, alive or dead. To Brown they seemed oddly young and small and skinny, until it occurred to him that he and his fellow marines were all young and skinny, too, only taller, most of them. All of the dead men had new dark green uniforms. Some of the marines searched them for souvenirs—pistols, rifles, canteens, knives, binoculars, cameras. They would send the loot back to the compound, where friends would tag it and load it on a small trailer for shipment back to Phu Bai.

One, Reymundo Delarosa, opened the dead men's mouths and examined their teeth. He produced pliers from a side pocket and extracted gold fillings, a practice even the hardened men in his squad thought grotesque.

9

The Dismal Strand
of Acheron

THE FIGHTING SLOWED at nightfall. In the ruins of the chapel, Smith's men found two priests, one Belgian and the other French, who were unhurt. They were livid that their church had been destroyed. Gravel was amazed they were alive, particularly because both were cloaked in black, a color his men associated with the VC.[70] They calmed down enough to pose with the apologetic colonel for pictures inside the chapel's remains.

Once Smith's men had taken the school and chapel, they moved up and occupied the elementary school where Cheatham's 106 had already silenced the machine gun. Alpha Company settled in for the night. Its advance that day was supposed to have been the easiest, but it had proved the most difficult. Smith had started his assault with one hundred and forty-seven men. He had lost more than half. After another day of fighting he would have just seven—one hundred and twenty-three wounded, seventeen killed.

Sunday had been a pivotal day, although it was not recognized as such at first. The advance had been small, and it had come at great cost, but the effort had turned the momentum of the battle in the triangle.

Roberts, in the story he dictated over the phone for Monday's *New York Times*, noted the marines' paltry gains: "At nightfall, the marines held eight blocks of the city, a gain of five from yesterday," he reported. "They suffered more than 20 casualties, bringing the total for five days to about 150. Enemy losses were described as heavy."[71] The commanders Roberts spoke with still vastly underestimated the enemy's size and strength. He said, "Fresh intelligence reports showed that the enemy held 10 strategic positions and scattered sniper posts in Hue." One officer was confident that the battle would end swiftly once the weather cleared and they could conduct air strikes. The number of enemy troops in the city was estimated "by several officers" to be two thousand. Despite such gross underestimates, five days after the surprise attacks the MACV was coming closer to understanding the extent of the challenge. Roberts reported, "Some officers said that the stiff resistance by the enemy meant that the battle for Hue could drag on for days, perhaps even weeks."

The ground gained that day—Cheatham had crossed one street and Smith had taken two blocks—didn't seem like much on a map, but it was the first time the marines had actually prevailed. They had pushed the Front back. Cheatham had teamed weapons and tactics that worked. Every block between the treasury and the canal would be bitterly contested but now seemed achievable. The only questions now were how long it would take and how much it would cost.

Miles to the north, Colonel James Vaught had arrived at PK-17 with his battalion, the 5/7, which would begin marching south toward La Chu with what Sweet had lacked: artillery. Out in the South China Sea, ten miles or so east, the navy had moved a cruiser and a destroyer[72] into position, and had already begun using its big guns on positions to the north of the city. That fight to cut off enemy supply lines in the countryside, the second major front in the effort to retake Hue, would soon be joined.

Inside the Citadel, the third major front, General Truong had also made progress. His men had recaptured the Chanh Tay Gate at the northwest corner. He now controlled the less populated north side of the two-square-mile enclosure, and his men had pushed south about six blocks from Mang Ca. Truong now had an impressive lineup of units on paper,[73] but all had been badly depleted. One of his battalions was down to just forty men.[74] They were still overmatched by the enemy, and they were low on food and ammunition. Dug in before them were four reinforced battalions of the disciplined and experienced enemy.

That evening Captain Jim Coolican, who had helped steady the defense of the compound on the first morning, left with several other advisers on a very hairy flight across the river to Mang Ca to rejoin their Vietnamese units. And that same evening, south of the city, Front sappers finally blew up the An Cuu Bridge. This severed Highway 1, which meant the steady train of convoys back and forth to Phu Bai was halted. In the coming weeks, through the worst of the fighting, the main avenue of resupply and evacuation for the marines would be the boat ramp and LZ in Doc Lao Park.

The navy lieutenant Terry Charbonneau was on the last convoy to make it over the bridge. He had even stopped his vehicle to climb down and inspect its underside for explosives before they drove across. He had seen nothing.

Charbonneau had been stuck at Camp Evans for several days since he had traveled through Hue on Tet Eve. He'd hitched a chopper ride back to Phu Bai, and had then persuaded the marine captain in charge of the convoy to take him along.

"You know," the captain told him, "there's fighting up there."

Which was precisely why Charbonneau wanted to go. He craved the experience. What he saw next probably should have given him pause. At the same time he was volunteering, Nolan Lala was refusing to go. It had been Lala, days earlier, who had plunged bravely into battle on the Truong Tien Bridge after Captain Meadows's company had turned back from its futile attack on the Citadel. Lala, a private, had driven a truck out to the north side of the bridge and personally manned a machine gun to cover Meadows's withdrawal. There were men who owed their lives to him. He had been evacuated two days later with a relatively minor wound, and now he was refusing to board the convoy back. He was a tough kid, Lala, a roughneck from Colorado who was a difficult man to handle. He'd been a hero in Hue days before but he'd had enough.[75]

Charbonneau wanted to go.

"Fine, you'll be my trail officer," the captain said.

The naval officer set off for the last vehicle. In one of the trucks were marine reinforcements, newly arrived. They were still wearing cleanly pressed stateside fatigues, and none of them had helmets.

"Why are you men not wearing helmets!" Charbonneau demanded.

Turns out there were none. The supply officer had told them that with the steady stream of dead and wounded they would find plenty of discarded helmets at the compound.

Charbonneau boarded a "wrecker," a tow truck, that brought up the convoy's rear. At first the drive was quiet. After the convoy crossed the An Cuu Bridge, an explosion, either a grenade or a mine, destroyed the captain's Jeep, wounding him and nearly severing his driver's foot—hours later a doctor at the compound would remove it with one snip of his surgical scissors.[76] Charbonneau was now in command of the convoy. They limped into Hue late that afternoon, planning to unload the recruits, ammo, and supplies and then return immediately to Phu Bai. When word came that the bridge had been destroyed, Charbonneau settled in for a longer stay.

Even after Sunday's success, it was still dangerous to be on the street near the treasury and post office. Ernie Weiss was crouched against a wall outside the university building, exchanging shots with enemy positions across the street. When he turned to reach for more ammo a rocket exploded on the wall behind him. At first he thought it had missed him, but then his left arm and left leg suddenly felt as if they were on fire. He was bleeding from both. He crawled inside to warn his sergeant, Willard Scott, and the rest of the platoon.

"Scotty, they have a rocket team out there," he said. "They have us zeroed in."

"Ho, Hoss," Scott replied. "We'll take care of it."

As the sergeant turned to leave, Weiss added, "Do you think if I don't get to a corpsman I won't bleed to death?"

Scott came back and inspected him, and then he called for a corpsman. Weiss was helped out to a Jeep that was taking other wounded back to the compound.

The doctors there cut away his fatigues and inspected the damage. There were nearly fifty puncture wounds up and down his left side, shrapnel but also chips of stone from the building. Most of the wounds had been cauterized, so there wasn't much bleeding.

"We can't cut all this stuff out of you here," the doctor told him. "We'll have to send you back to Phu Bai."

They cleaned him up as best they could and wrapped him in bandages from neck to toe. He was given something for the pain, but over the next few hours his body began to swell and throb. He could no longer bend his left elbow and he could only drag his left leg.

This eighteen-year-old mummy waited by the Huong River at the LZ that night with all of the other wounded, dead, and dying. Men were crying out in pain and groaning. Some wailed. It was like the dismal strand of Acheron,[77] with the departing souls stretched along the riverbank, waiting for transport. Stretcher cases went out on the first Huey. When the second and last one for that night touched down it, too, quickly filled with stretcher cases. Weiss, who had been waiting patiently with the walking wounded, shrugged and turned to limp back to the compound, but then one of the door gunners shouted, "Hey, you! We've got room for you."

"Where?" Weiss asked. The interior was jammed.

"Right here, next to me," the gunner said, standing in the doorway.

"I'll fall out!"

"Don't worry, I'll hold on to you."

Weiss figured it was either that or wait for the next chopper, and *how bad could it be?* So he climbed on. It was bad. The door gunner had a firm hold of his flak jacket, but his legs were hanging out the door as they took off. Then the pilot began evasive maneuvers, and Weiss found himself staring straight down at the dark river, hanging by his flak jacket, his body bouncing with the aircraft's quick turns, breathless. The bandaging around his leg began to unravel and flapped in the wind like a kite's tail. His leg and arm throbbed. Finally the chopper leveled off. As they passed over villages he heard the *pop! pop!* of people shooting at them.

A few hours later at Phu Bai, after a long wait while the doctors methodically worked their way down from the most survivable cases to the worst, with his wounds oozing and throbbing unbearably, Weiss at last found himself unwrapped on the surgeon's table.

"This is an abortion," the doc said.

Which did not sound good. The private had been given a local anesthetic, but he felt it sharply when the first scalpel went to work. The blade made a grinding sound against the metal in his body and he nearly shot off the table. He screamed, and cried, and carried on, trying to get away. He couldn't stop himself. He had reached the absolute limit of his tolerance.

He was given an injection of Demerol then, and the pain eased, and for the first time in days he relaxed. He felt himself happily floating away.

PART FIVE

Sweeping the Triangle

Tuesday–Monday
February 6–February 12

As the battle enters its second week, the National Liberation Front still occupies most of Hue. Civilians are increasingly taking to the streets in search of a safe haven, of which there are few. In the triangle, Colonel Cheatham's marine battalion continues its punishing sweep, battling building by building, block by block. In the countryside northwest of the city, meanwhile, the army has stalled in its effort to march to the Citadel walls. A second cavalry battalion begins retracing the route taken by Colonel Sweet's, which fled the field after being reduced by half. The army is moving toward a climactic collision with thousands of enemy soldiers at the village of La Chu.

Civilians in Hue photographed by Kyoichi Sawada.

Marine Captain Ron Christmas, commander of Hotel Company 2/5, posing with a toy rifle given to him by his men as a joke.

Captain Christmas's marines defiantly raise the American flag over the provincial headquarters building.

Lieutenant Andy Westin, whose daily letters home to his wife Mimi offered a diary of his cavalry unit's mission.

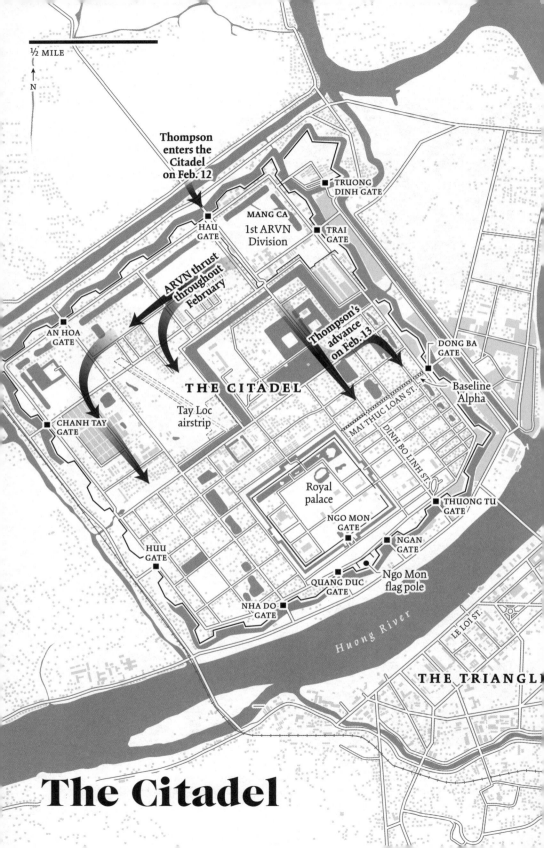

½ MILE

N

Thompson enters the Citadel on Feb. 12

TRUONG DINH GATE

HAU GATE

MANG CA
1st ARVN Division

TRAI GATE

ARVN thrust throughout February

AN HOA GATE

Thompson's advance on Feb. 13

DONG BA GATE

THE CITADEL

Baseline Alpha

CHANH TAY GATE

Tay Loc airstrip

MAI THUC LOAN ST.

DINH BO LINH ST.

Royal palace

THUONG TU GATE

HUU GATE

NGO MON GATE

NGAN GATE

Ngo Mon flag pole

QUANG DUC GATE

NHA DO GATE

Huong River

LE LOI ST.

THE TRIANGLE

The Citadel

1

Flags of Surrender, Flags of Fright

*N*HAN DAN, THE people, had nowhere to go. Far from being liberated by the invading Communist army, they had been trapped by the Tet Offensive in a nightmare of bloodletting. For some it began on the first day, but as the battle entered its second week, it encompassed all.

At first there were enough eager converts to swell the sails of the true believers. The young commissars proclaimed the war all but won. Citizens were rising up not just in Hue, they said, but throughout South Vietnam. Independence and reunification were at hand! For Xuan, the poet propagandist, these first days were like a dream. Small red flags came out and flew from dwellings up and down the crowded streets. Even some of his old friends who had shown no enthusiasm for the revolution were now active recruits. At his political headquarters in the post office inside the Citadel, there were three lines of people waiting to sign confessions about their past sins and to enlist in the righteous cause. Some told him they had been inspired by his rhetoric, that he had spoken to their hearts.

Nguyen Van Quang, the local organizer who had smuggled arms into the city and then led troops through Chanh Tay Gate, moved in with a local family. They prepared celebratory feasts with food they had collected for the holidays and shared freely.

It felt right that the revolution in the city's streets was being led by Hue's own youth. After all, in China the zealous young Red Guards were upending their own society with Mao Zedong's "Little Red Book." All over the world in 1968, like some global fever, young people were challenging authority and demanding change. While in the United States and Europe "revolution" was an excuse to sell pop music, stage protests, and hold festivals, it was being played for keeps in Asia. Young people were not just challenging their elders but pushing them aside, expelling, imprisoning, and in many cases executing them, all the while extolling the young as the righteous vanguard, their very youth a badge of purity. They were, by definition, forward-thinking. And in Hue they were armed.

In stories and songs and lectures the commissars celebrated the people as the wellspring of all power and virtue, but there was, nevertheless, need for instruction and guidance. Some things would have to change. Decadent Western influences were everywhere, and not just in politics. The modish hairstyles and short skirts favored by the more fashionable girls, for instance . . . these were unseemly and un-Vietnamese, as were wealth and corrupting ideas. With an army behind them, the commissars were hastily remaking Hue in their own image.

The first priority was the city's defense, and for this everyone able was put to work. Then there was the business of correcting errant thinking. For this there were public lectures on the seven tasks of all party members and on the slogans of Uncle Ho, which were to be memorized and shouted in unison. The Front had issued stern prohibitions on looting, but the commissars and their local militias had a different understanding. They saw strong revolutionary logic in confiscating whatever was needed—food, shelter, supplies . . . or those things that caught their eye. They took cars, scooters, and bicycles. Boys and girls in Hue were amused by the young rebels trying to ride them. There was prudent acceptance of this plunder.

There was food to be collected, cooked, and delivered to the fighters. When the counterattack came, teams would be needed to evacuate the wounded and bury the dead. Digging began everywhere—trenches, foxholes, and underground shelters. Neighborhoods were soon honeycombed with tunnels and bunkers. There were not enough weapons to arm everyone, so families were told to cut bamboo stems to the length of long guns and paint them black. When the counterattack came, they were instructed to point their sticks at the enemy's planes and helicopters, or at advancing troops. That way the Americans would believe all the citizens of Hue were armed with guns, and see the people as united and indomitable.

This particular tactic sounded like suicide to most. Beyond the initial display of support a more stubborn truth became clear. The people were not resisting their liberators, but neither were they "rising up." After the first days of the occupation, it was apparent that the party's goal of a "general uprising" was stillborn.

Commissars rationalized this. Since the attack depended on surprise, they had been unable to prime the citizenry. They had pinned their hopes on spontaneous explosions of support, but the occupation had produced only shock and disorientation. While some rural villages had rallied impressively, Hue itself stayed lukewarm. Part of this was the effete nature of its citizenry. It was home to many learned, well-traveled people, college professors, scholars, artists, scientists, bureaucrats, and businessmen, among them many who had been infected by foreign ideas or who had profited by exploiting the masses. However the young revolutionaries interpreted it, the educated class of Hue citizens were not impressed by mindlessly parroting Ho's poetry and slogans. Even those who sympathized with the idea of a united, independent Vietnam now found themselves being lectured by dreamy commissars who were younger than their own children. Some joined the cause enthusiastically, but most went through the motions, stayed home, or ran. Many were terrified by their saviors.

Fear spread from the first day. Known "enemies of the people" were immediately rousted from their homes. Retribution was high on the list of Front priorities. Orders called for "a wave of assassinations of enemy thugs, spies, and secret police in the area."[1] Nguyen Quang Ha, the sapper who had taken part in the initial attack on the tank base at Tam Thai, spent the days afterward raiding targeted homes and hunting down enemies. The Front had extraordinarily detailed lists, lists that went way beyond the obvious places and people, the government buildings, radio station, residences of Americans, military and police outposts, high officials, and top ARVN officers. Among many others there were these:

- The Phu Cam Church
- The "Faculty of Law" for Hue University

- Xa, a policeman from Quang Tri, [who] lives on Thong Nhat Street near the Y-shaped road junction about one or two houses from Le Van Duyet Street
- Soi, 1st Lieutenant of Puppet 1st Division, lives on Thong Nhat Street near a stone-house and tailor's shop.
- Cao Tho Xa, a cruel tyrant, native of Phu O. Huong Chu Village, Huong Tra District. He quit his native village and came to live on Thong Nhat Street near the Chanh Tay western gate . . . At night, administrative personnel from the neighboring villages sleep at his house.
- Van, bus driver on the Thuan An Road, lives on Thong Nhat Street (at the side of the Citadel in front of Xa's house). Puppet administrative personnel from the neighboring villages gather to gamble and sleep at his house.
- The clock repair shop on Thong Nhat Street, obliquely opposite the . . . Recruiting Office. Administrative personnel from the neighboring villages sleep there.
- Ho Thi Kim Loan, a member of the Provincial Rural Development Group. Her house is on Trinh Minh The Street near the Nguyen Hoang bus station.
- The Lac Thanh restaurant on Dinh Bo Linh Street, outside the Thuong Tu Gate. Enemy secret agents and policemen usually frequent this place to take meals.
- Viet Tuyen radio shop, No. 3 Tran Hung Dao Street. The shop's owner is Ton That Vu, son of Ton That Ke, member of the Dai Viet Party [the Greater Vietnam Nationalist Party].[2]

The list went on and on, twenty-two typewritten pages in all, single spaced. And once the people caught the spirit, the purges picked up speed. At the start the idea had been to round up only the worst of the *nguy*. To idealists like Xuan and Quang this was not vengeance; it was justice. Young men with megaphones walked the streets demanding that servants of the puppet regime show themselves. Those who did not would be found. There would be reeducation for the redeemable, and revenge for those who owed *no mau*, a blood debt. Soon enthusiastic informers were pointing out the homes of "traitors," and in some cases even dragging them out themselves. Commissars fanned the flames.

And like mob violence everywhere, the purges assumed a life of their own. Hoang Thanh Tung, a commissar who had been working with the VC for four years, entered the city with the lead battalions led by the village girl Che Thi Mung and the other Huong River Squad members, but even with that early arrival he found retributions out of control. Tung specialized in convincing ARVN soldiers to change sides. His methods were education and persuasion. Getting soldiers to switch sides was extremely valuable to the cause. He had expected to have many captives to recruit in Hue, but what he found were VC units and local militiamen busily executing them. At one central location in southern Hue, he came upon large numbers of prisoners awaiting judgment, soldiers and civilians and some foreigners (including a few Americans). The local commissars were working with lists written in English and French, and they didn't understand these. Some of the captive foreigners worked for the Hue Power Station, a project of SIPEA (Société Indochinoise Pour les Eaux et l'Électricité en Annam). Since the acronym on their papers included the letters *I* and *A* and its first syllable was pronounced "See," the captors would immediately declare someone "CIA," bind him, and send him to be shot.

Tung went to see the head of this unfolding travesty, Tran Quoc Phong.

"Brother Phong," he told him, "this is not right. The guerrilla soldiers are shooting the wrong people, and it is not okay."

"What nonsense are you thinking now?" Phong said.

"The guerrilla soldiers can't understand the English and French words on the list," Tung said. "I am a student, so give the list to me."

He secured permission to sort the captives, asking when and where they were born, and where and how they worked, making sure that those punished were the right ones.

After eight days he was sent across the Huong River to Gia Hoi, a neighborhood just outside the Citadel's east wall. There he found long burial trenches with bodies stacked alongside them wrapped in bamboo blankets. Many bodies. He summoned the cadre leaders.

"According to the order from the city party, you are now under my lead," he told them. "You need to take care of the people here. Don't just go and shoot them!"

He met with the ARVN soldiers who had been rounded up.

"Now I am here," he told them. "You will get out of this alive. Nobody is going to kill you."

He divided the captives into two groups: those who had either been drafted or who had been students in military academies, and those who had sought military service. The former he would lecture and release. The latter, designated for reeducation, would be marched off to camps outside the city. No one liked the sound of that, even with Tung's reassurances. The mood in the city was bloody, especially after the Americans began their counterattack and people were dying in droves anyway. Tung offered to escort them himself. Otherwise, he told them, "They [the local people] will eat you alive."

He walked before the prisoners with a megaphone, and when they approached villages he made an announcement.

"Dear people in this liberated area, I suggest that you all applaud the spirit of these brother soldiers who have left their troops to come join us in the forest!"[3]

In some cases, the people seized the opportunity to settle personal scores. The crackdown on Buddhists years earlier had killed and wounded hundreds. Many had seen family members killed, imprisoned, and tortured by the police. They remembered the men and the families of the men who had done these things. And beyond personal grudges, there were deep-seated divisions over religion and politics. There were simple rivalries between villages and neighborhoods that had descended into violence before. There were splits within families over the present war, where one son had sided with Saigon and the other with Hanoi. The "liberation" of Hue suspended law and order and upended basic decency, giving retribution an official stamp of approval. It tapped a deep vein of savagery.

In some neighborhoods, communal meetings were held to pass judgment, since what could be a better expression of the new Vietnam than tribunals where the people judged for themselves? The most notorious of these was the one where Tung had been sent, Gia Hoi, where crowds assembled at the local high school to pass judgment, and where punishment, often execution, was carried out summarily, accompanied by jeers and cheers.[4]

In the area known as Thoi Lai, just outside the northeast walls of the fortress, a notorious criminal joined the cause. Mai Van Ngu was a local crime boss, responsible for robberies, extortion, and killing members of rival gangs. He had been arrested and imprisoned in the past, and held grudges against the local police and ARVN forces who had dogged him for years. With liberation, Ngu became a new man, literally. He changed his given name to Hoa, becoming Mai Van Hoa, and was such a fervent recruit that he led special teams charged with rooting out collaborators. In some cases he didn't bother turning in his targets; he supervised their execution right in their homes.[5]

Nguyen Cong Minh and her family lived in Vy Da. On Tet morning the VC were going door-to-door in her neighborhood looking for traitors. There were three knocks at their front door. Minh's father told her brother and uncle to flee out the back. When he answered the door, the soldiers demanded to see his family's identification papers. They asked Minh's father what his occupation was, and he told them he was old and about to retire, but that he was the deputy district chief of Trieu Phong in Quang Tri, a province just north of Hue. The soldiers wrote down the names of everyone in the house, and left.

Later that morning they came back for him and marched him off. He returned an hour later. He said he had been questioned at Vy Da Elementary School, along with sixty or seventy other people. The soldiers returned the following morning. It was the same thing. More questions at the school, then he was allowed to go home. On the third day they told him to pack food, clothing, and bedding. They informed the family he would be gone for ten days. He had been assigned to a reeducation camp.

He left and never returned.[6] Minh's presumed death and others illustrate the nature of the purges. The killings were official, deliberate, and coordinated.

Nguyen Huu Ai was a high school student, living in Vy Da. His older brother was with the ARVN but was away. When the VC came to his door they took away his uncle and his aunt. They were allowed to return home, then taken away on a second day and allowed to return. On the third day they were taken away and did not return.

Day by day, the terror spread. Those particularly feared were the returned locals like Xuan and Quang, who knew their way around. They knew names, faces, jobs, and family histories. They knew ordinary people who for a variety of reasons might warrant suspicion.

They knew who had done what in their old neighborhoods, and they knew who had prospered from relationships with the Saigon regime and with the Americans, like Tuy-Cam's family. Their appearance in their old neighborhoods struck fear in many households. People felt their lives now depended on the whims of these armed young zealots.

Quang, with a red bandanna tied around his head, was driven through the streets inside the Citadel in a Jeep flying the Hanoi flag on the first day, supervising the arrests of the targeted *nguy* government officials. This was heady work for a man of just twenty. Three years earlier he had been a high school student, preparing for his matriculation exams. Now, still scrawny and undersize, he was in charge. He held court in a building on the grounds of the royal palace.

An ARVN lieutenant attached to the ordnance unit by the airport, Lam Ung, reported and brought his wife and his son, Lam Hai Luong, who also served with the ARVN. Quang sat behind a table in the hearing room, and the accused ordinarily sat before him in chairs, but Mrs. Lam instead stood before the table and folded her arms over her chest, a sign of respect ordinarily shown to elders.

"I have something to say," she said.

Quang asked her to unfold her arms. He was younger than her son.

"I am a wife," she said. "And a mother. These two"—she motioned to her husband and son—"are guilty. It is known. They have done the nation wrong. As a mother and a wife, I am begging you for forgiveness."

Quang let them go. Both father and son thanked him profusely. Puffed up with his own magnanimity, he told the son, "Your mother has just given birth to you for the second time."

Such generosity was the exception, so much so that Quang was later censured for it.

"Since they were aware of their mistakes and reported on their own, it wasn't necessary," he argued in his defense. "What mother isn't hurt if her husband and son are in this position? It isn't about one side or the other, it's about being human."

He forgave a police lieutenant who had nine children. The man had not reported himself; he had been arrested. Under the rules, it meant he had to be sent away. But Quang weighed the fate of his wife and children and told the man, "You have to live to raise your children. I forgive you because your nine kids are still too young. Your crimes are way too clear to forgive, but because of your children I here let you go home."

Knowing that such leniency would be reported by his comrades, Quang decided to report on himself. He sought out Tran Anh Lien, the political commissar who supervised him, and explained what he had done in these cases. Lien hugged him.

"You are twenty years old and very willing to sacrifice yourself to fight out there," said Lien. "But you are also truly a communist. A true communist must be humane like that."

Such instances of mercy might have eased the conscience of those in charge, but in the streets judgments were typically more harsh. Given the penalties for opposition, it's little wonder that the people, as a rule, were eager to show ardor for the new order. Allegiances shifted on the spot. ARVN soldiers renounced the Republic of South Vietnam and took up arms with the liberators. Xuan called such recruits his *Nghia binh,* "Righteous Soldier Division." They led him to many of their comrades who were hiding or trying to pass themselves off as civilians. He also formed a *Nghia binh Canh sat,* "Righteous Police Division" made up of city cops who were offered amnesty and a return to their patrols if they pointed out their old colleagues who had chosen to hide. The purge tribunals were kept busy.

In her memoir of the Tet Offensive, *Mourning Headband for Hue,* Tran Thi Thu Van described a young commissar called "Dac"[7] (whom she later identified as Nguyen Dac Xuan, although he denies it)[8] who interrogated a suspected collaborator, a man named Mau Ty, by having him climb into a foxhole. There he was publicly berated and condemned to death. "Dac" promised to kill him slowly and painfully. As the man pleaded, some of his neighbors also begged "Dac" to show mercy, arguing that "personal hatred" had clouded his judgment.

"No, my personal hatred is also the hatred common to all of my friends," said "Dac." As the instrument of the popular will, if hatred was what he felt, then this was the genuine hatred of the people.

"Dac" toyed with the man. He pointed his pistol at his head, and as the victim closed his eyes, waiting to be killed, he shot just past his ears or shoulders. Mau Ty screamed. Eventually he was led away.[9]

Whether "Dac" was himself or not, Xuan saw his grand vision of the future grow dark. By the second week, more and more of his comrades were falling. Xuan had persuaded a young couple, friends of his, to join the struggle, and the husband was killed by an artillery shell. He had to go to the man's wife, who had just given birth to their first child, and tell her that her husband was dead. Then, as the days grew more bloody, anger and resentment built. Xuan believed in the necessity of some retribution but watched it spin into bloodlust.[10] Suspicion fell on everyone.

Xuan intervened when his own men arrested a civilian who was found monitoring radio signals. He was well dressed and well spoken and had been writing notes in what appeared to be a numbered code. Surely this was a brazen, high-level spy. The arrested man insisted that they take him to the top commander in their area, whose name he knew. Xuan obliged. He turned out to be a communications expert working with the Front's command.[11]

In the face of these hazards, many dug in and tried to wait it out. They guessed that the occupation would not last long. Huynh Van Don lived in Vy Da. He sold gasoline at a depot before the police station at Hung Vuong Street. He was thirty-six years old and had been running the business for thirteen years, working every day from five in the morning until ten at night. He had fallen asleep on Tet Eve and woke up to a city transformed.

He saw two friends who had been in ARVN units who were now wearing the black shirts and helmets and red bandannas of the liberators. Many in his neighborhood who had fought or who had jobs with the Saigon regime fled immediately, and many were captured. Since Don's father had fought with the Viet Minh—he had left in 1945 and had never come back—Don believed he did not have to worry about being labeled a traitor. But despite his family's revolutionary bona fides, Don was summoned to defend himself. He was allowed to go home, but was instructed to return in five days to help the self-defense effort. When he did he was pressed into service digging a long trench from the Huong River to the edge of the town. He and the other local "volunteers" were treated to a show by one of the traveling propaganda troupes. Knowing that a counterattack was coming, Don worried, after days and nights of this, that he would be mistaken for one of the Front's fighters when the Americans came. There were false rumors that South Korean units were assisting the Americans—Koreans were believed to have taken part in massacres of Vietnamese civilians.[12]

Don had started digging a bunker for his family on the first day. In between his shifts with the liberators he dug more at home. His shelter had to be big and deep enough for seven—him, his wife and four children, and his mother. The hole he dug was three feet wide and thirteen feet long. They chopped down a China tree and an apple tree from his family's garden and made planks to place over the top. He covered the planks with soil and leaves. When the fighting came close, he and his family began living underground.

The family of Le Cong Thanh, the boy who was surprised that the VC did not have tails, prepared for a long stay indoors. Their home was near the Dong Ba Market, just outside the gate on the Citadel's eastern wall. Le's father, Le Van May, an ARVN soldier, told his large family—there were twenty of them—that they would have to hide, perhaps for days. They inventoried their food. Because they had stocked up for the holidays, they had enough to last for a week. Water would be a problem. Le's father calmly explained that Saigon's forces and the Americans would be back, and that when they came, there would be a terrible fight.

"We are going to dig a shelter," he said.

Others fled. Getting out of the Citadel wasn't easy. Residents plotted paths around the newly dug defensive positions and checkpoints, and found ways under and over the walls. There were few certainties in this. Flight was considered an admission, if not of guilt, then of a traitorous spirit, and even if you made it past checkpoints and guarded gates and through the shelling and gunfire to the few American- or ARVN-held areas, there was a chance you would be mistaken for VC before you had time to explain. The jumpy Americans in particular, even the few who knew some words of Vietnamese, were notorious for shooting "gooks" before asking questions. Dead civilians were all over the streets; who would question one or two more Vietnamese bodies?

There were too many ways to die. Sergeant Chuck Ekker, whose squad had led the assault into the treasury, was in a second-floor room of a nearby building several nights later with another rifleman when they saw a figure dressed in traditional Vietnamese garb and wearing a *non la* step out of a building carrying a saucepan filled with rice. They concluded that the person—they could not tell if it was a man or a woman—might be carrying food to enemy soldiers, and the marine with Ekker shot the individual on the spot. They did not think twice about it.

Nguyen Dang Khoa and his extended family had been hiding for days in their home near the MACV compound. As fighting intensified, Front soldiers with megaphones demanded that those hiding come out. They were herding civilians into a nearby school building, and culling traitors. One of Khoa's sons worked as an administrator in the local government, so the entire family was at risk. Khoa was the eldest, a grandfather, a slight, stooped man with a white beard. He volunteered to go outside.

"I am old," he said.

He tied a white shirt on a stick and walked out, holding it high. His family watched nervously. Khoa had advanced only a short way when an American marine hiding behind a gate called out for him to stop.

The old man was hard of hearing. He turned toward the marine, saw him pointing a rifle, hesitated, and made a fatal mistake. He ran. He was shot in the back. The wound exited from his abdomen, spilling his intestines down his front. Khoa managed to crawl back to the door. His family rushed out to him.

"I will probably die!" he said.

Those were his last words. The marines seemed stricken by their mistake. They helped carry Khoa into the Jeanne d'Arc High School and laid him on a table. He died there.[13]

Despite these hazards, hundreds, then thousands, took flight, especially as the fighting intensified. There had been 140,000 residents of Hue before the battle started, and it was estimated later that 80 percent of the city's structures were damaged or destroyed in the battle. The displaced ran from one place to another like ants on a hot plate. In southern Hue, thousands of refugees gathered wherever there was the slightest glimmer of safety—in churches, pagodas, and the city's great buildings. They found it nowhere.

Tran, the author of *Mourning Headband for Hue,* who had come to Hue to bury her father and been trapped by the battle, spent days with her family inside the Church of the Most Holy Redeemer. She had been among the multitude there when the two French journalists had wandered in days earlier. As the fighting intensified in the triangle, coming closer each day, conditions in the church became unbearable. There were no toilets. People had no choice but to defecate in the open outside. From time to time the Front's soldiers would barge in with weapons, searching for names on their lists, and bullets and bombs seemed to arrive at random. Fear and grief and privation drove some mad. Tran watched as a dead baby, beginning to rot, was pried away from its mother, who insisted that it was still alive. An older man who had fled his well-appointed home cried out, pleading with imaginary communist soldiers, "Please, sirs, no please, sirs, brother-liberators! Please, sirs, liberators, please, sirs, don't burn the house, don't burn the house!"[14]

As Tran would later describe the scene in her book, the fighting ebbed and flowed around them:

> Now not only small guns but also large guns explode in successive salvoes. And it seems that cannons have joined in. There is a great clanging sound, and a lot of broken pieces of glass fall down. From the front and from the back, it seems that gunfire comes from everywhere. I recognize the sound of B40s, the sound of AKs, the sound of all kinds of guns. From many other directions there are the clattering sounds of falling glass. There are many loud shouts. People call for each other, screaming, "Hey! Hey!" Another crashing sound and glass falls down followed by a loud explosion, and a fiery red mass flies into the middle of the church. Bricks and tiles, smoke, pitch dark. Run, run and don't die.[15]

They fled to An Dinh Palace, an ornate, three-story stone structure that had been the last residence of the emperor Bao Dai, but it, too, came under attack. As part of the roof crashed down they ran from that place in panic, leaving most of the possessions they had carried from their home. Tran later described the scene on the streets:

> The group approaching us consists of about a hundred people; the leaders of the group are several Catholic priests and a couple of Buddhist monks. In their hands they hold white flags made of tattered cloth, flags of unconditional surrender, flags of fright. They walk, then run like children in a hurry. Following the white flags, the leaders and their followers go supporting each other. People carrying loads on their shoulders go at a jog

trot. Thai stands up on the edge of the road and lifts his hand in greeting:

"Venerable Father, what's going on up there?"

The priest shakes his head, his mouth frothing at the corners. A monk carries in his hands a wounded child, blood dripping in small drops on the road; the monk stretches out his hand and waves, giving us a sign to follow them. Don't stop; it's dangerous. But the monk does not say a word. The group of people slowly runs like this in front of us, women carrying children in their arms, men carrying loads on their shoulders, children going at a jog trot. On top of it all, they also carry the wounded. A man wounded in his leg runs, limping and hobbling. From time to time he falls on the ground, then forces himself up again. There is someone with a loose arm connected to his body by only a little bit of skin. Another person has something swelling on his head; still another one has a fractured forehead with small drops of blood on it. They chase after the several pieces of white cloth of which the white flags are made and which flap, leading the way in search of security. The people in the group run, moaning, crying, and praying; a fellow recites a Christian prayer, and another one appeals to Heaven and calls on the Buddha.[16]

Tran and her family eventually took shelter in a bunker under the ancestor-worshipping house of a friend. When the artillery shells from Phu Bai fell close they came together in a group embrace, "so that when death comes, we will die together, in one heap."[17]

Tuy-Cam, the fiancée of foreign service officer Jim Bullington, who was still hiding with French priests, was mostly hiding in the family shelter as her family was put to work cooking meals for the liberation soldiers, sometimes as many as six meals a day for groups of ten to twenty-five. Her older brother, an ARVN officer, and her younger brother, an ARVN aviation cadet, were still hiding in the attic. The soldiers were polite, and the family was told it would be compensated for the food "after the revolution." Several times commissars stopped by to hold hour-long indoctrination sessions. They tried to recruit the family's teenagers to join others working at their new headquarters making placards with party slogans and flags, but the youngsters declined. Although Front troops searched their house several more times, they never ventured into the attic, and did not discover Tuy-Cam's hiding place.

When the American artillery bombardment began—their home was not far from where Bullington was hiding—the family left, aiming for their home village, about four miles west.

"We are on the South Vietnamese side," her older brother said. "We don't want to be killed by the South Vietnamese!"

He put his eighty-year-old grandmother on his back, and they set off. They picked their way through the streets, trying to avoid the fighting and concentrations of liberation troops. They decided to stop and rest at a pagoda, only to wander into a VC patrol. Since these were locals, some of them knew Tuy-Cam's family. One of them immediately pointed out her older brother as an ARVN lieutenant. They scrutinized her younger brother.

"He is not a soldier yet," one of them said, "but I understand that he has joined the Air Force."

Both were led away. Tuy-Cam was terrified for them, but she didn't dare cry or beg or draw more attention to the rest of the family. One of the cadre members stared at Tuy-Cam. Her eyes met his, and she quickly looked away. He had worked as a mason on an addition to their home. She knew him and his family well, and she knew that he knew she worked for the Americans. But he said nothing. He decided not to give her away, and the family kept walking toward the pagoda.

When they arrived they were met by a monk they knew well.

"Where are the two brothers?" he asked.

Her mother explained that they had been taken away.

"The VC, they were staring at Tuy-Cam," she said. "I am so afraid for her life. So we are here."

The monk said that Tuy-Cam would have to separate from her family. They could all stay at the pagoda, but she would be sheltered elsewhere. He hid her in a nearby bunker beneath a large statue of the Buddha. He then left to see what he could do about getting the two brothers back.

He returned hours later empty-handed, shaking his head sadly.

The family was invited to eat with the monks, but none of them were hungry. They huddled and wept, and finally decided to walk back to their house. They retrieved Tuy-Cam, and along the way back they were stopped again, this time by an ARVN patrol. They were told not to return home: it was too dangerous. Instead they went to Hue University, which the Americans were using as a refugee center.

At the center all eleven were assigned a small square of space. They had nothing to eat, and had no room to stretch out and sleep. So they sat leaning back-to-back, waiting. They were there for several weeks, eating whatever food they could scrounge, like everyone else.

It was there they learned from a young man who had escaped the Front soldiers that Tuy-Cam's two brothers had been shot.[18]

2

Something Is Wrong
Over There

PRESIDENT JOHNSON HAD urged Westy to hold daily sessions with reporters while the Tet fighting continued in order to help offset the "gloom and doom." On the first day, the general had told reporters that the real enemy target, the big battle still to come, was at Khe Sanh, and despite all evidence to the contrary, this is what he continued to insist. As for the city attacks, they were nothing more than a desperate, even suicidal act—a distraction.

Hue rarely even came up in these daily briefings. At the start, Westy acknowledged only that "a sizeable force" had entered the city:

> He [the enemy] now holds a portion of the city. ARVN forces
> are now in contact with the enemy attempting to clear that city
> of enemy units . . . In summary, gentlemen, this second phase of
> the [enemy's] campaign was a bold one. It was characterized by a
> treachery and deceitfulness. It showed a callous disregard for human
> life. It has brought considerable destruction in the number of towns
> and cities. The enemy has paid dearly . . . How long will he be able
> to keep up this tempo? I give him the capability of continuing this
> phase of the campaign for several more days. There is, however,
> evidence to suggest that he is about to run out of steam.[19]

Over the coming weeks, Westy was frequently called upon to make sense of the fighting, particularly in Hue, where things were most definitely not ending quickly. But no matter how he looked at it, the general could not see enemy gains. He conceded nothing to Hanoi. There had been no surprise. There had been no accomplishments. No city had been lost. His adversary had tried something desperate and had failed. The losses were catastrophic. He had foreseen the move and had not just countered it; he had crushed it. Why, his prescience alone had apparently forestalled the big attack at Khe Sanh, at least for the time being. This was not an act. By all indications, the general really believed these things, even as the death toll mounted in Hue, even as world opinion collapsed around him, and even as one after another his assurances about the battle failed. Never had a general so effectively willed away the facts.

Two days into the battle the Joint Chiefs asked him to explain the meaning of the Tet Offensive and to assess the current situation. Westy again insisted that the countrywide attacks were a diversion from the big one at Khe Sanh. He had begun sending daily updates about the marine outpost directly to the president. The attack on Hue and other cities "[m]ay be a diversion to confuse friendly forces and draw our attention and possibly troops away from the major area of threat [Khe Sanh and the DMZ]." The city offensives "were not made in sufficient force to permit them to continue over a long period. For example, most of the attacks have petered out." Westy explained that the coming offensive at Khe Sanh was still likely to happen.

Indeed, the attack he expected there loomed so large in his mind that he had entertained the use of chemical and even tactical nuclear weapons. A secret planning group had met in Okinawa the day after the Tet Offensive started to consider such a contingency. The plan was code-named "Fractured Jaw." The purpose was explained by LBJ's military adviser, air force general Robert N. Ginsburgh, in a memo to Wheeler: "If, despite General Westmoreland's best estimate, the situation at Khe Sanh should become desperate, the issue of using TACNUCS [tactical nukes] will be raised."

General Wheeler scribbled a note at the bottom, "Caution that plans should be very very closely held."

Two days later, Westy weighed in. He was fully prepared to employ nuclear weapons if the situation worsened. He wrote to Wheeler:

"The use of tactical nuclear weapons should not be required in the present situation . . . However, should the situation in the DMZ area change dramatically we should be prepared to introduce weapons of greater effectiveness against massed forces. *Under such circumstances I visualize that either tactical nuclear weapons or chemical agents would be active candidates for employment."* [20]

Word of this leaked out when Senator Eugene McCarthy, campaigning as an antiwar Democratic alternative to LBJ, told a reporter at Boston's Logan International Airport that the use of nuclear weapons had been considered—word of Fractured Jaw had reached the Senate Foreign Relations Committee. The revelation caused an international stink and prompted immediate and aggressive lies to cover it up. The president's press secretary, George Christian, described McCarthy's statement as "false, irresponsible, and unfair to the armed services." [21] The Pentagon scrambled. A cable to Westy on the tenth from Admiral Sharp was blunt: "Discontinue all planning for Fractured Jaw. Place all material, including messages and correspondence thereto, under positive security. Debrief all personnel with access to this planning project that there can be no disclosure of the content of the plan or knowledge that such planning was either underway or suspended. Security of this action and prior actions must be air tight."

LBJ did approve the use over Khe Sanh of COFRAM (controlled fragmentation munitions), a devastating weapon that could kill masses of enemy soldiers with an air burst that scattered a large number of smaller bombs over a large area. [22]

As for Hue and the other South Vietnamese cities under attack, Westy was dismissive and even scornful. The city attacks had caused the enemy terrible casualties, he said, and had evinced "an extreme, sometimes even foolish, aggressiveness."

This point of view was backed by a CIA assessment delivered to the president on Monday, the twelfth. Unlike the accurate analysis from Hue days earlier, this one was cast more in Westy's mold. Surprisingly, it found a "massive intelligence failure," not by the Americans and the ARVN, but by the Communists:

> The Communists can be credited with having maintained excellent security for such a comprehensive plan, but they are guilty of a massive intelligence failure. Documents captured over the past four months and interrogations of the prisoners involved

in the recent attacks indicate quite clearly that the VC did intend to take and hold the cities, did expect a general uprising, and did plan to install a revolutionary government, as evidenced by the presence of a standby VC administrative structure in the major cities. It may seem incredible that VC expectations should have been so divorced from reality, but there are three factors which probably explain this. First, the communists are and always have been victims of their doctrine, and in the present case the articles of faith were: "The longer we fight, the stronger we become;" and, "The more viciously the enemy fights, the closer he is to collapse;" and, "The people support us and when the urban people have the chance to rise up, our victory will be assured." Second, the leaders have been consistently and greatly misinformed by the lower cadres . . . Third, the need for a significant victory after two years of drought may have introduced a lack of prudence.[23]

Westy had another possible explanation: "The attacks may have been designed as a show of strength as part of an effort to win back control of the people, a control that has been slowly but surely eroded over the past several months," he wrote. "The enemy may have believed that the psychological and propaganda value of demonstrating his ability to attack so many cities, towns, and installations more or less concurrently would be worth the cost." He rated this explanation as unlikely.

As for the present situation, "The enemy has already had over 12,000 killed in action and this is just for the period between 0600H/29 January and 0001H/ 3 February," he wrote. He said U.S. and ARVN losses were less than one-tenth that number. "Although the enemy is still fighting in and around several cities and installations, *he does not control a single one* and I am confident that he will not control a single one when his efforts subside . . . Whatever its purpose may have been, the surprise attack by the Communists on a dozen cities and military installations in Vietnam is ending in disaster for the attackers. There is still some fighting going on and the Communists may have some uncommitted reserves. But their effort, despite a strong showing in Hue and a few other places, seems doomed."[24]

By Tuesday, February 6, Westy's count of enemy dead had reached 21,000 . . . and it was still climbing.

Despite a concerted effort to spin Tet as a Communist disaster, the press wasn't buying it. Westy's promise at the National Press Club just a few months back of an end beginning "to come into view" now seemed preposterous. The *Washington Star*, citing the complete surprise achieved by Hanoi, the damage to whatever sense of security Thieu's government promised, the big jump in American casualties, and the blow to Westy's rose-colored picture of the war, editorialized on Friday, "What kind of victory is this? By any military standard it has been a crushing defeat." The *Philadelphia Inquirer*, heretofore a solidly hawkish newspaper, wrote that "the cozy assumption that the South Vietnamese government has been winning the confidence of the people has been virtually exploded by the daring Vietcong attacks."

George Romney, the governor of Michigan and a Republican candidate for president, told newspaper editors, "If what we have seen in the past week is a Viet Cong failure, then I hope they never have a victory."[25]

On Thursday, February 8, Senator Robert F. Kennedy gave a widely reported speech at a book-and-author luncheon in Chicago that must have spiked LBJ's troubled blood pressure, calling Vietnam "the deepening swamp." Johnson had, of course, taken up the torch for the war after President Kennedy was killed, and he wasted no opportunity to sprinkle his speeches about the war with references to the near-deified JFK. Now here was the president's younger brother and heir apparent taking up the antiwar banner. Kennedy had so far resisted appeals to challenge Johnson in the upcoming Democratic primaries, leaving the field to McCarthy. Just a week earlier the *New York Times*, in a note on its editorial page, had written that Kennedy had declined to endorse McCarthy because the senator "looks like a forlorn loser."[26] But Tet had improved McCarthy's fortunes. It had spurred campaign donations and volunteers—antiwar students were flocking to New Hampshire to man telephone banks and knock on doors. His was starting to look like a viable candidacy, even a movement. Kennedy's speech suggested to many that he might be keeping the door open for himself.

"It is time for the truth," he said. "It is time to face the reality that a military victory is not in sight and it probably will never come . . . The events of the last two weeks have taught us something," Kennedy said. "For the sake of those young Americans who are fighting today, if for no other reason, the time has come to take a new look at the war in Vietnam . . . and the first step is to face the facts." He said that Tet did not "represent some sort of victory," and then ridiculed Westy's over-the-top body counts. "It would seem that no matter how many Viet Cong and North Vietnamese we claim to kill, through some miraculous effort of will, enemy strength remains the same. [We are told] that of the 60,000 men thrown into the attacks on the cities, 20,000 have been killed. If only two men have been seriously wounded for every one dead—a very conservative estimate—the entire enemy force has been put out of action. Who, then, is doing the fighting?"[27]

In Washington that same week, Dr. Martin Luther King Jr. met with 2,500 religious leaders over a two-day planning session for a march in April that would link the civil rights and antiwar movements. King participated in a silent antiwar prayer vigil at Arlington National Cemetery, and talked of leading protests at both the Democratic and the Republican conventions later in the year.[28] His assassin, James Earl Ray, was already stalking him at that point, and would shoot him in Memphis just a month and a half later.

Skepticism about the war was being expressed not only by the protesters outside security barriers wherever Johnson went. At his regular breakfast meeting with Democratic congressional leaders on Tuesday, February 6, transcribed by a Johnson aide, Senator Robert Byrd, the secretary of the Senate Democratic caucus and no liberal firebrand, asked about the apparent underestimation of VC strength.

"I have never underestimated the Viet Cong," said Johnson. "They are not pushovers. I do not think we have bad intelligence or have underestimated the Viet Cong morale."

"Something is wrong over there," said Byrd.

"The intelligence wasn't bad," Johnson insisted.

"That does not mean the Viet Cong did not succeed in their efforts. Their objective was to show that they could attack all over the country and they did."

"That was not their objective at all."

"You have been saying that the situation with the Viet Cong was one of diminishing morale," said Byrd, who politely backed away from accusing Johnson personally. "When I say you, I mean the administration."

"I personally never said anything of the sort," said the president, clearly irritated. "I am not aware that anyone else has been saying that. What do you think the American people would have said if we had sent in troops and lost twenty-one thousand of them as the enemy has? . . . I am of the opinion that criticism is not worth much. I look at all of these speeches . . . at all the people who are going around the country saying our policy is wrong. Where do they get us? The popular thing now is the mismanagement in Vietnam. I think there has been very little. I wish Mike [Senator Mike Mansfield of Montana, an outspoken opponent of the war] would make a speech on Ho Chi Minh. Nothing is as dirty as to violate a truce over the holidays. But nobody says anything about Ho. They call me a murderer. But Ho has a great image."

Byrd, who was something of an LBJ protégé, said he didn't want the president to think that he was opposing him personally, but felt it was legitimate to ask the questions.

"I do not agree with what you say," said Johnson.

"I do not agree that the intelligence was good," said Byrd, sticking to his guns.

". . . Personally, I think they suffered a severe defeat," said Johnson. "But we knew there would be no general uprising, and they did not win any victory."[29]

LBJ hung tough, but he was disturbed enough by Byrd's attitude that he expressed alarm to his chief foreign policy advisers later that day. He was concerned that such criticism reflected a spreading point of view.

"If the war goes well, the American people are with us," counseled Walt Rostow. "If the war goes badly, they are against us. The only way for us to answer this is for our military situation out there to come out all right. I think the men in uniform now have the burden in determining how much support or lack of support we get."[30]

3

The Sweep

It took Big Ernie Cheatham four days to fight his way to the Phu Cam Canal. These were long and bloody, with a fierce clash at each of the significant municipal buildings along Le Loi Street, but once begun, the advance was unstoppable. It was the first notable American achievement since the city had been taken.

The successful treasury takedown set the pattern. Cheatham would first bombard the target building or complex with mortars—he called them his "sledgehammer."[31] Then came a gas cloud, tanks, Ontos, 106s, bazookas, and, finally, marines.

Lieutenant Hoang Anh De's men would defend each place ferociously until the bombardment began, and would then slip back to form the next defensive line. The rubble produced by the shelling created lots of new places to hide.

The sweep's big prizes fell one by one: the hospital, the prison, and the province headquarters, with smaller fights in the houses, schools, stores, garages, and courtyards along the way. Every step forward was costly. In the first two days, Cheatham's three companies worked abreast, with Fox shifting to the south to take the left flank and Golf moving up into the center. When Lieutenant Smith's company moved up it relieved Downs's Fox Company, which had taken heavy casualties, and it was moved north to fight along the right side of Le Loi Street. Dense cloud cover still prevented aerial attacks, and the closeness of the enemy made the use of heavy artillery too risky, but the weapons Cheatham had brought along, and the tactics he perfected, were getting the job done.

The old football lineman knew a good blocker when he saw one, so that's how he used the tanks. It was too dangerous to position men around them, so he sent them out alone and in front. The Ontos was more vulnerable to enemy fire, but it was smaller, was faster, and had more firepower. Cheatham kept it behind the tanks as each day's advance began. The heavy fire directed at the tanks exposed the enemy's firing positions. Cheatham would then calmly stand on the street alongside the Ontos—with his helmet on he was almost as tall as the vehicle's top hatch—and point out targets for its six big guns. Then the vehicle would speed out in front of the tanks, use tracer rounds from its spotting rifle to zero in, and fire one or more of its guns. The vehicle would rock so far backward it looked as if it might tilt over, but then it settled back and sped in reverse to safety. It was a very useful weapon. Its six big guns knocked down even thick walls completely, or blew big holes in them. In time the enemy was seen to flee as soon as the Ontos's spotting rifle was fired. Few waited for the blast to follow.[32]

After the treasury fell, the fighting was still slow and hard, but the marines did not encounter the same level of resistance. Despite the bonanza of guns and ammo seized in ARVN warehouses and abandoned posts, Lieutenant Hoang's forces were running low. He did not mount counterattacks, nor did he try to flank Cheatham or break the busy flow of traffic between the front line and the MACV compound, the steady outbound flow of ammo and supplies, and the inbound flow of wounded and dead. The ammo shortage forced Hoang into a strictly defensive posture. He was losing men at a rate at least as fast as the marines', but his strategy of hold and retreat was keeping his forces together. He knew that he could not stop the marines. He occasionally would send out probes to harass them at night, which kept him apprised of exactly where they were before each day's advance. The worst part of the attacks was the mortar bombardments and the tear gas. Some of Hoang's men were exposed to so much gas they were blinded and vomited blood.

He had orders to keep fighting. His superiors wanted to make a statement. The Americans had greater firepower, and could rapidly assemble in greater numbers, but his superiors wanted to show that they were capable of meeting the challenge head-on. The oft-expressed disdain of American soldiers for an enemy that refused to stand and fight was felt by the enemy, too. Hit-and-run tactics took a toll on their own morale. Here in Hue they would show once and for all, to themselves and the world, that they were willing and able to slug it out with Americans.[33] As his front line fought each day, behind them their comrades figured out how to best defend the next line, establishing firing positions that took advantage of the layout of the block, rigging new booby traps, digging new foxholes and trenches, setting up on rooftops and at high windows. Increasingly they relied on snipers to slow the marines' advance.

When Cheatham's command center moved, Major Salvati made it a priority to find a new bottle of good Scotch, Cheatham's preferred drink. Most of the nicer abandoned homes in southern Hue had generous liquor cabinets. The only obstacles were dogs. Many families had left their pets behind, which would snarl ferociously at him. He shot them.

Night was a time to regroup, resupply, plan for the next day, and perhaps grab a few minutes of sleep. The predictable battle rhythm produced what Captain Christmas called a "gentleman's war," but there was nothing gentle about it.

Some of the grunts had felt good about fighting in the city at first. They were sick of the bugs and the heat and the dirt and the leeches that plagued them in the bush and rice paddies. City fighting seemed a welcome change . . . until they had been in Hue for a few days. In the field, when you located an enemy position, you would flank it; you would send a squad to the left and another to the right. The center would open fire on the target as the flanking squads attacked from both sides. If you tried that in Hue, in an open courtyard or a city street, the men approaching from both sides would be shot down.

When they had trained to assault a building in their infantry course at Camp Lejeune or Camp Pendleton, they had practiced against a simple one-story plywood structure. They were taught to attack from top to bottom, to come in from the roof. Here this was impossible. The buildings were too high to easily access the roofs, and you couldn't get close to them without being exposed to torrents of fire. Buildings had to be cleared from the ground floor up. Any obvious point of entry was suicide. The doors and windows had been pre-zeroed by nearby gun and rocket positions. This the marines had discovered the hard way. You had to avoid doors and windows. You used a bazooka to blow a hole in the wall and went in through that. Then you cleared the ground floor, room by room, and worked your way upstairs. It was hard on the decor. When you kicked a door open a rifle barrel would immediately be stuck against the frame to keep anyone inside from slamming it back shut. A grenade was tossed in, and after it exploded you went in spraying rounds—usually two grunts, three if it was a big room. The first man in shot center-left, the second shot center-right, and the third punched rounds up through the ceiling in case there were enemy soldiers in the room above. Sometimes they would find a dead enemy soldier in an upstairs room who was full of holes, hit fifteen to twenty times. But that was rare. The enemy nearly always escaped, even from the upper floors. Sometimes they would find blood trails that led to a window. Once the place was cleared you usually had a few minutes to catch your breath, which gave you time to explore.

They never knew what they would find. Booby traps were a concern. Charlie was ingenious. The enemy would place an American hand grenade—they seemed to have an ample supply of these—in a can, pull the pin on it, and release the spoon so that it was held in place by the inside of the can. It was then balanced on top of a door. When the door was opened the can would fall and the grenade would spill out and explode. When the marines found a body they would look for ID cards and, if the dead soldier had a pack, they would send it back to the command post. Fear of traps generated strict orders against moving bodies or searching equipment further. Grunts, who tended to be souvenir hounds, sometimes learned the hard way to obey these orders, but they learned.

Danger did not deter the most avid hunters. Hastings Rigolette was so eager to collect trophies that he sometimes had to be restrained from running out to downed enemy soldiers under fire. In one house he found two beautiful elephant tusks and a bureau he thought was gorgeous. Rigolette came from a family that appreciated beautiful things; his father was a jeweler and model maker. In Phu Bai he had a duffel bag full of things he was planning to take home. He coveted the tusks and bureau, but they were much too big to carry off. So he searched the drawers. He found a very nice heavy blue work shirt that fitted. He put it on right away. It got chilly at night in Hue, and he had only a damp, soiled T-shirt under his flak jacket. He was wearing the work shirt a few days later when he got shredded by thirty-three pieces of shrapnel, and he would still have it almost a half century later, although he had grown wider and it no longer fitted comfortably. Still, he put it on sometimes to see if the holes still lined up with his scars.

Some things found in the houses stayed with marines in other ways. Eden Jimenez was clearing rooms, tossing in grenades, waiting for the blast, then racing inside shooting for all he was worth. He entered one room this way that was empty except for a tall old wardrobe, which he had filled with holes. He opened it gingerly, and inside found a young woman, whom he had mortally wounded, who was holding a baby and a rifle. One of Jimenez's rounds had pierced her throat. She was bleeding and choking to death, and soon died, still holding the baby, which was miraculously unscathed. He handed the child off and it was passed to the rear. When he was on old man, living in Odessa, Texas, he still wondered almost every day about that woman and child. Why was she holding a rifle? Did she think that was going to protect her? Did she think that no one would look inside the wardrobe? Who was she? How would he have felt if he had killed the baby, too? What ever happened to it? Should he have looked before shooting into the wardrobe? These things turned over and over in his mind and gave him a sick feeling.

Bill Ehrhart was clearing a room when he noticed legs sticking out from under a table. He leaned over for a look and found a young couple, or perhaps a brother and sister, who had clearly pulled the table away from the window and crawled under it to take cover. They had been dead a while. Their faces were so bloated that they were no longer even recognizable as human.

The marines were always learning. The 106 crews found they could collapse a house with a single shot by placing the round directly over the front door, where it would shatter the structure's main supports. Men providing covering fire learned that it was smarter to aim at window frames than to shoot through the windows. A round that passed through a window—none had glass in them anymore—would hit against a back wall, but those that clipped the edges sent bits of stone and metal flying in all directions. Sometimes the impact would alter the bullet's trajectory, and it would hit someone hiding off to the side or below the bottom of the frame. Hard as it was, Captain Downs learned to postpone retrieving fallen men from the street until he had taken the opposite house or yard. When they attacked a building, they learned to cover all predictable points of exit before beginning their assault. Marines would compete for dibs to display their marksmanship. On the first day of the sweep, Alpha Company's Josef Burghardt had calmly knocked down four enemy soldiers with four shots as they fled the west building in the Jeanne d'Arc School complex.[34]

Not often, but every once in a while, they got the drop on the enemy. Lieutenant Michael McNeil's men took eight prisoners in one building. Most dropped their weapons and threw their hands up when they were cornered. One did not go as easily. He was a sniper in an NVA uniform who had two rifles—Soviet SKS and an American M-1—and eight grenades. With McNeil pointing a Thompson submachine gun in his face, the sniper lunged at a marine and tried to pull a grenade off his ammo belt. He was wrestled to the ground and his hands were tied behind his back. The prisoner fought all the way as several marines carried him down the steps.[35] They would have admired such fight in one of their own, but dismissed the enemy's as fanaticism.

"It has been a real bear," Colonel Hughes told Roberts on Monday, February 5. "But we are making progress."

The Timesman's story that day said that the marines had made the most progress yet. The wedge-shaped section of the city they now controlled covered less than one square mile. He reported that thirty had been killed and more than two hundred wounded, twenty-four more that day.[36]

Marines were now spread out down Le Loi Street. One group bivouacked in a museum. When Roberts stopped in they were playing at swordfighting with ancient ornate pikes that were part of the collection, and were knocking over vases and other items from its displays. Those who took back the radio station spun records. There were 45-rpm discs with two tracks, often by different artists, on each side. Over the eerily lit urban landscape floated choruses of the Righteous Brothers' "You've Lost That Lovin' Feelin'" and the Beatles' hopeful "All You Need Is Love."

Evacuations and supplies now depended exclusively on the boat ramp and LZ. An attempt to set up a pontoon bridge to replace the downed An Cuu Bridge at the triangle's southern tip had been driven back, so the road to Phu Bai remained cut. Three marine officers, Major O. K. Steele and Lieutenants Allen Courtney and Peter Pace, swam across the Phu Cam Canal on Wednesday night with seventy-five much-needed replacements. Steele had arrived to replace Salvati, Courtney was joining Ray Smith's Alpha Company, and Pace joined Golf Company.

Both sides struggled with the throngs of displaced civilians. The blocks between the treasury and the canal were densely populated. When Cheatham had told reporter John Laurence that he considered anyone before him to be "Charlie," he had neglected to consider this. Many civilians were right in his path, and his regular pounding with mortars had turned hiding into Russian roulette. A direct hit on a house or shelter with civilians inside was catastrophic. So as the line of fighting moved toward them, people calculated the risk. When the danger of staying undercover was judged greater than running, they ran. Civilians seized any opening to race across a contested street, even when they weren't sure which way would lead to safety. Hoang found them useful sometimes. Their presence would sometimes slow and confuse the marines.

With the marines advancing in an orderly way, the fighting had at last assumed a recognizable pattern. Refugees figured out that the safest place in the city was anywhere behind the marines, but getting there was extremely hazardous. While American policy was to protect and help civilians, in the heat of a fight many grunts, tired and angry and frightened, saw any Vietnamese as a potential threat. The refugees came running toward the American lines in abject terror, clinging to each other, carrying crying babies. Stories spread among the marines of civilians dropping grenades as they flowed past, which made them suspect everyone Vietnamese, and less likely to hold their fire when surprised. They had seen plenty of enemy fighters dressed in civilian clothes—indeed, many of the fighters had been freed from the prison just days earlier. Telling the difference between an innocent and a combatant in a few tense seconds wasn't easy, and the wrong choice was often fatal. Images captured by the photographers documenting the fight showed dead civilians, or apparent civilians, in almost every frame.

On Monday night, as Hotel Company was securing its perimeter, Christmas got a radio call from Lieutenant Ken Kromer, his forward platoon leader.

"Sir, we have five or six civilians across the street who want to pass through our lines," Kromer said. He wanted permission to send a squad across the street to escort them.

Christmas knew that his men were visible to enemy troops across the street, but a platoon from Golf Company was on their right flank and could provide covering fire if needed. How long could it take to get five or six people across? Just then the platoon leader called back to say that there were actually closer to twenty-five civilians.

"Fine, let's get them back," Christmas told him.

A few minutes later Kromer called to say that as soon as the squad had started across they had come under fire—none were hit—and that "several hundred" civilians had come running through their lines. This prompted immediate fears that there might be enemy fighters among them. On this occasion the escapees included five Americans who had been in hiding. Brought to the captain, they were pleased to explain the number and location of enemy forces his men would face the next day.

At the university, bodies were wrapped in blankets or sheets and interred in shallow graves. The living, like Jim Bullington's fiancée Tuy-Cam and her family, remained confined to cramped spaces inside and in the courtyard alongside Cheatham's mortar battery. Water and food were scarce, and there were no toilets or latrines. Conditions were shockingly bad. People worked to make the best of it. Lines were strung from tree to tree to hang laundry for families who found enough water to clean their clothes. For most, leaving was not an option. Their homes had been destroyed and it was too dangerous to venture out. Some civilians nevertheless braved the streets to make furtive nighttime visits to the ruins of their homes to scavenge for food, clothing, and supplies. Some died in the effort. Wood from destroyed buildings was used to keep cooking fires burning. Stray ducks were prized catches; served with rice, one would provide meals for an entire family for two days. Hunger spread. The marines were kept supplied with C rations, but the supply wasn't big enough to feed all the civilians, who grew increasingly desperate.

One evening Bill Ehrhart and his buddies were approached by a fellow marine with a proposition: "Anybody wanna get laid tonight?"

A woman trapped with the other refugees at the university had offered to have sex with anyone who would pay for it with a C-ration meal. There was no shortage of takers. A mortar crew by the river had agreed to let them use their gun pit. Only one of the men in Ehrhart's squad opted out.

He went along. He was eighteen. Two years earlier he had been an honor student at his high school in Perkasie, Pennsylvania, and had written an editorial in the school newspaper about the war. At its conclusion, he wrote, "As long as the Vietcong or any other subversive influences exist, there can never be a free country in South Vietnam. This, then, is the cause for which so many Americans have lost their lives. To those of you who feel that these boys are dying for no good reason, we say this: 'What more noble a cause can a man die for, than to die in defense of freedom?'" Ehrhart felt strongly enough about this noble cause that he enlisted. His idealism and his clear statement of principle had prompted the *Perkasie News-Herald* and *Quakertown Free Press* to print stories about him. He had been photographed with his recruiter and his girlfriend standing in front of his school.[37] Now he lined up—to his lasting shame—for his turn taking advantage of a hungry, desperate Vietnamese woman, probably trying to feed her family. She did not appear to be a prostitute—the marines were familiar with those. She was nicely dressed, and seemed grimly resigned. She removed dark silk pants and lay on a piece of cardboard, grunting quietly as one by one the men placed down their C-ration package and then entered her.[38]

Some of the grunts hardly considered the Vietnamese human, much less deserving of sympathy. Corporal Jim Soukup, for instance, part of a 106 crew, had nothing but scorn for the whole country, which he would refer to as "that stinking blood-soaked shithole." He had a slogan written on the back of his flak jacket, *Try Your Luck, Charlie,* and like everyone else was counting down the final weeks of his deployment. He referred to all Vietnamese as "dinks" and viewed every one as a potential threat.[39] He and others were certain that among the throngs of refugees were Front fighters who had thrown down their weapons and joined the multitude. It was impossible to vet them all. Soukup's was not an attitude conducive to rescuing trapped and frightened civilians. A radioman at Cheatham's command post told marine correspondent Steve Berntson that he stopped one platoon from shooting two figures moving toward them on the street one night during a heavy rain. The radioman told them to hold their fire until he could check out the figures for himself. He found an old woman helping a very pregnant younger woman, in labor, down the street to safety. They were shown to a corpsman, who had seen births only in a training film, but nevertheless helped deliver the woman's baby, a girl.

The radioman asked Berntson, "What if I had told them to fire?"

As the sweep proceeded, Christmas climbed into the attics of houses to direct the mortar battery. On the first days the mortars in the courtyard had to fire rounds almost straight up because the enemy was just across the street. As the distance between Hue University and the front line grew, the angle of the tubes lowered, but it was still difficult to aim precisely. To avoid dropping mortars on his own men, Christmas looked for good vantage points to help direct them. When he couldn't find one, he had to aim by ear. Once he recognized the enemy's pattern, holding the line and then quickly falling back two blocks, he would try to aim the mortars to shell them on their way out.

Part of the job of preparing for each day's advance was to position the all-important 106s. A four-man gun crew led by Soukup took two vehicles off the street, an orange Chevy pickup and a black sedan. When they found a suitable firing position for the gun, they would drive it there in the car, followed by the pickup, which carried two of Soukup's team. They would then wrestle the gun out and carry it to the spot, setting it up on its heavy tripod. If they had no prearranged spot, they'd set it up on its stand in the back of the pickup and use it as a mobile firing platform, with one man driving the sedan. When they weren't using the vehicles for this purpose, they used them to collect the wounded and carry them to the rear.

It was dangerous work, because once the 106 was fired, its location was known to the enemy. One day all four men assigned to the gun were hit. Two rockets landed on their firing position. One was killed instantly; the blast took off most of his head. The three others were wounded and evacuated.[40]

Individual marines never had a clear picture of what was going on, just that they kept moving from building to building, from point to point. Often they could not even tell if they were advancing or retreating. They took a building, cleared it, moved in a fire team to hold it, and then moved on to do it all over again. They kept getting shot at,

they kept shooting back, and the men around them kept falling. Eddie
Neas, a nineteen-year-old corporal from Brooklyn with Lieutenant
Smith's company, just attached himself to his platoon sergeant, sure-
shot Burghardt, and followed him everywhere. Neas was nicknamed
"Alfie," because guys thought he looked like *Mad* magazine's Alfred
E. Neuman. He didn't think he did, but the name stuck. He wrote it
on his helmet. Two of his friends had been killed, one shot through
the head, and a third who he thought was dead would later turn out
to have survived. Neas's biggest fear was having to engage in hand-to-
hand combat. He was small and did not like the idea of having to fight
someone to the death, stabbing with his bayonet, so, determined to
do all his fighting with his rifle, he loaded himself down with twenty-
eight magazines of ammo. He considered himself a marksman. When
there was a lull in the shooting he practiced. On the day his platoon
helped take the high school he had shot two chickens. One he got on
the first try. The second one took two. He had seen horrible things.
He had seen a dead NVA soldier with hugely swollen testicles whose
eyeballs were hanging from their sockets. He had seen rats and dogs
chewing on corpses in the street. He started shooting at every dog he
saw. When he got a chance to close his eyes he slept with one hand
closed around his rifle. He found lots of good things in the houses they
occupied—liquor, radios, books, TVs—but there was no sense trying
to carry anything off, as weighted down as he was. He lugged himself
and his rifle and all his ammo wherever he was told to go, keeping low
when he passed a window, running zigzag across open spaces, always
looking for things to shoot.

Some marines seemed to thrill at the danger. Paul Tinson, a popular black sergeant who had taken over Lieutenant "Wrong Way Go
Far" Horner's platoon after Horner was wounded in Fox Company's
first day of fighting, dubbed his platoon "Tinson's Terrors." They all
shaved their heads into Mohawk haircuts. With some men there was
a competition to take risks.

All three of Cheatham's young captains, Downs, Christmas, and
Meadows, stayed close to the fighting, but far enough behind to maintain control. It was a confusing battle space. With so many armed,
frightened, pumped-up men moving in a relatively small area, sometimes inside a single building, there was always worry that two marine

squads would happen upon each other and start shooting. Somebody had to stay back and work to keep order, staying in touch with the adjacent companies in order to coordinate movement. Visibility was poor and communications were iffy. They had military-grade maps of Hue, but the standard scale in Vietnam was 1:50,000 (one centimeter on the map equaled 50,000 centimeters), which was nowhere near detailed enough for close-in urban combat. Cheatham started the battle with a tourist map from a gas station. After a few days some of the commanders got 1:12,500 scale maps. These had a very helpful numbered index of the main buildings, but when they got down to it, in the confusion of a gunfight, explaining exactly where they were was hard.

"Hey, I'm in the pink building," Christmas would say.

"That's fine, I'm over here in a green building," Downs would answer.

Meadows would come on the radio with, "Good! I'm in the brown building!"

Cheatham would growl into their radios, "Where the hell are the green, pink, and brown buildings? Be advised, all the buildings on my map are black."[41]

There was competition among the three to keep up with one another, and they joked about which was Cheatham's favorite.[42] When they took the hospital on Monday, the fifth, a complex that took up a very large city block, Christmas's company was dealt the contagion ward, which, they agreed, settled which was the colonel's *least* favorite.

Downs was summoned by Tinson's platoon to a nearby building, where he found two Vietnamese men spread eagle against the wall.

"Sir, this guy says he's the mayor of Hue," said Tinson.

The man turned out to be Lieutenant Colonel Pham Van Khoa, who actually was both the Mayor of Hue and the Thua Thien Province chief. He and his bodyguards had been hiding in the building's attic for days.

The hospital, prison, and the province headquarters were the last big buildings to be taken on the sweep. Downs's company lost twelve men the next day, attacking additional hospital buildings south of the prison walls. Among them was Tinson. Six others were wounded.

Berntson, the "Storyteller," walked through the hospital after it had been fully secured. The halls and rooms reeked of death. He had given up writing stories for the time being. Since he was not attached to any of the combat units, he could have gone back to Phu Bai if he wished. But he felt compelled to fight. For the first few days he had helped carry the wounded and deliver ammunition, but then had walked back to the compound and picked up a rifle and ammo. Just as he was moved by the bravery of the enemy, he admired the courage of his fellow marines. Several days into the battle it was hard to find one who had not been wounded. Many just patched themselves up and kept going. Only the most severe cases were evacuated.

From inside the hospital, Captain Meadows of Golf Company gazed down in wonder at the prison walls a block over. On the first day of the battle, after his men had been cut to pieces attempting a foolhardy attack across the bridge on the Citadel, he had been ordered to take those he had left to assault the prison. It had taken Cheatham three reinforced companies, including Meadows's, and three days of intense combat to get that far. The original order had been insane.

The last objective on the advance down Le Loi Street was the province headquarters building. The Alliance flag still flew over it. The complex was surrounded by a stone wall and a fence, which enclosed a big courtyard. The main stone building had two tall stories and was L-shaped, angling around the courtyard that faced north, toward the river. Behind it was a Catholic school, another large, solid structure. Both buildings were heavily fortified, with machine-gun positions in every window on both floors and another on the capitol building's porch, which could sweep the entire front courtyard. The first group of Christmas's men who tried to cross it from the outer wall to the main building found themselves fired upon from all directions, even from behind—from spider holes along the inside of the courtyard wall.

The Americans fell back. Christmas was plotting Hotel Company's next move when an errant truck filled with replacements blundered past his position and into a driveway before the main building. The enemy soldiers inside slammed the truck with machine-gun fire, and the driver, when he realized his mistake, threw the truck into reverse and backed to safety. But in his haste he left two wounded marines on the street. One managed to scoot on his back to a hedge, despite a severe chest wound, and was pulled to safety, but the other lay in the open.

Walter Kaczmarek, a private who was called "Chief," was ordered to go get him. Terrified but obedient, he started out by crawling on his stomach, but stopped when a bullet sent a chip of brick into his face, under his left eye. He crawled back, bleeding, but the chip was pulled out and the wound was little more than a scratch. He was deeply disappointed. This meant he'd have to go back out. And so he did, crawling behind a metal door, only to have a round puncture it. The bullet passed close enough to his hand, which had been resting on the door. It stung him badly, but, once again, he looked down and saw no blood. He was hurt but not wounded. He moved along the hedge to a point as close to the downed marine as he could get, set his weapon down, stripped off his ammo belts, and made a mad dash out, throwing himself down beside him. For a moment, the shooting stopped.

The wounded man said he had been shot in the chest. Every time he moved, the shooting started up again. Kaczmarek tried to calm him and then yanked his arm to pull him toward the hedge—this evoked a howl of pain from the wounded man. Kaczmarek let go and dived again for cover. He was amazed that he had not been hit, and decided that under no circumstances was he going to step out into the open again. He had pulled the wounded marine close enough so that he could reach out from the hedge and grab the collar of his flak jacket. He counted to three, jumped up, and pulled the man to cover. When he tore open the man's jacket, looking for a bullet hole, he found none. He was so angry that he was ready to strike the man, until a medic, taking over, quickly diagnosed a shattered collarbone—which explained the agony when Kaczmarek had pulled on his arm. The round had been deflected by his flak jacket, but the impact had done painful damage.[43]

Christmas tried an Ontos—the men had taken to calling it the "Frankenmobile." It came rolling up Le Loi Street toward the front gate. The idea was to blast a hole in the front of the building away from the heavily defended front door. But as it prepared to fire, the vehicle was hit squarely in the front by a rocket. It started smoking. It was still in gear but no longer being steered, so it ran up against the complex's outer wall and got stuck. The treads kept turning in place. The back hatch opened and the gunner and driver dragged themselves out, faces black with smoke and grime, both bleeding from the ears and nose. A corpsman and several marines braved the fire to pull them to cover. The Ontos just kept churning, jammed against the wall, its treads grinding away, its motor running, an annoying symbol of futility. Finally one of the marines ran to it, climbed inside, and turned it off.

So that had failed. Christmas got on the radio and explained his predicament to Cheatham, who sent up a mule-mounted 106, and an E8 gas launcher, which enveloped the building in a cloud of tear gas. Instead of attacking from the front, the marines now eyed a small outbuilding to the side, from which they could approach the main building across a narrower portion of the courtyard. The 106 blasted a hole in the main building's wall. Wind from the river quickly dispersed the gas, but that and the big gun enabled the lead group to make it from the outbuilding to the hole in the wall.

Leading the way in was Kaczmarek, who had been knocked unconscious briefly by the back blast from the 106 and was still unsteady. Wearing a gas mask and unable to see clearly, he entered headfirst, tripping over rubble in the doorway. The rest of the platoon piled in right on top of him. When he looked up he saw enemy soldiers retreating down a hallway to his left and firing back.

An intense indoor firefight ensued, with the marines battling on the ground floor toward the main entrance. The building rang with explosions and gunfire. Clearing of the building ensued, kicking doors, grenades, and gunfire. Outside, men poured fire into the spider holes. Berntson helped drag wounded marines out to the front portico.

A voice cried out, "First floor clear!"

The gunfight then moved upstairs. Lieutenant Hoang had been using the building as his headquarters. He and his staff cleared out.

As the grunts spread out into the building, they found once again that the enemy had melted away. Cheatham sent every available marine from his command post to help with the methodical search of the large building. By dusk it was theirs.

When the search was over, the men moved methodically down the row of spider holes. One by one they kicked them open and shot down into them. The dead fighters were then dragged limp to a growing line in the center of the courtyard. One of them managed to get his hands up before being shot. He was wounded, but not badly. Berntson provided a sock, which was used to blindfold him, and listened while he was interrogated—a CBS camera crew had an interpreter. The man protested that he was neither NVA nor VC. He had been a prisoner, he said, and when he was freed he had been given a rifle and ordered to fight. He said they put a soldier in the hole next to his, so if he had tried to escape he would have been shot. It was a good story. It might have been true.

Cheatham called a halt to the advance at that point. It was Tuesday night, February 6. Five blocks beyond the province headquarters were the canal and some apartment buildings that the enemy still held. But for the moment the battalion rested. Many of the grunts in his battalion had been fighting constantly for six days. The colonel's orders had been threefold: (1) destroy as many of the enemy as possible; (2) keep your own casualties to a minimum; (3) spare as much of the city from destruction as is humanly possible. The battalion had done its best with the first two but had failed at the third. Behind them was a swath of ruin almost eight blocks wide.

"Some South Vietnamese are complaining about the damage to their buildings," army lieutenant colonel Howard Moon told Roberts back at the compound, "but I have no sympathy—not after I've seen what happened to the marines. There have been times when the wounded and the dying have been coming in here every two or three minutes. The marines don't know how to quit. If you can save a marine by destroying a house to get at Charlie, then I say destroy the house."[44]

That had been the rule. Every house and building behind them had its windows blown out and doors torn off. Roofs had caved in. The contents of homes and offices were strewn everywhere. Huge chunks of masonry and stone were scattered in yards and streets. There were big holes in the walls around the structures and in the structures themselves. There were bodies and pieces of bodies, dead civilians and Front soldiers in varying degrees of decay. Hungry dogs roamed. The marines and the Front both removed their dead and wounded when they could—in this the marines had the advantage; they now controlled the ground they took. But dead civilians tended to stay on the streets and rot. There was one that had been killed riding a scooter. It had come to rest upright, and the corpse sat there unattended, day after day, slowly decomposing.

That night the first two Mike Boats[45] from Da Nang slid into the boat ramp in Doc Lao Park, delivering a three-day supply of ammo and supplies. There was still a lot of fighting left in southern Hue, but the worst was over. ARVN forces were at a standstill inside the Citadel, holding the north wall and its four gates, but unable to make much progress into the crowded urban neighborhoods and the royal palace grounds to the south. The big flag flying across the river from Cheatham's position was a reminder that the marines' work had just begun.

Lieutenant Hoang's force had not been destroyed. He had taken losses, but the strategy he'd adopted had preserved most of his men. With the province headquarters gone, he fell back to positions along the river. Cheatham would pivot southeast now and fight them along the canal. Hoang had no intention of withdrawing. They got help from city residents, who brought them food. Nuns at the Catholic churches took in their wounded. As far he was concerned, his men had a lot more fight in them.

Roberts's story in the *New York Times* on Wednesday morning, February 7, summed up what had been accomplished in the first week:

Marines Advance in Hue

14 More Blocks Retaken

Hue, South Vietnam, Feb. 6—United States marines recaptured the provincial capital building today and added 14 more blocks to their growing foothold in this historical city . . .

Their advances were the best in seven consecutive days of fighting . . . Before dusk [they] hauled down the Vietcong flag. The enemy flag continued to fly over the Imperial Palace and over a captured police observation post on a hill on the edge of the city.

According to some intelligence reports received by military advisors here, the Vietcong claim a great psychological victory in Hue. They had planned to hold this city for at least one week, they say, a mission that was accomplished today.

Enemy casualties have been high. Bodies of Vietcong and North Vietnamese soldiers can be seen at almost all the scores of buildings the marines have taken. Marine and South Vietnamese Army spokesmen now say that more than half of the 2,000 to 2,500 enemy soldiers have been killed.

Roberts was told, incorrectly, that the number of American casualties, army and marines, was fifty dead and two hundred and fifty wounded.[46] He reported that there were now thousands of refugees at Hue University—"As many as 150 to a classroom."

"It is difficult to walk in the university building without stepping on a child," he wrote. "Outside, on the campus lawn, hundreds of refugees huddle under trees and cluster around one well, sometimes waiting an hour to lower a bucket or pot into the water. At the corner of one building this morning, a family stood in the drizzling rain, holding a funeral service."

Images of the destruction and death in Hue were having a sobering impact in the United States. Columnist James Reston summed it up: "Here is the dilemma of our military strategy of victory. How do we win by military force without destroying what we are trying to save? The battle is so fierce and the situation so solemn that the impulse to rally round is very strong, but the mind boggles at the paradox of tearing apart what we have undertaken to defend."[47]

These were questions above the pay grade of Berntson, the Storyteller, who sought out Christmas early Tuesday evening to interview him about the day's events. The tall captain with the scar across his cheek had bloodshot eyes and seemed exhausted. He told Berntson the story of taking down the flag and raising the Stars and Stripes before the province headquarters. It was a good one. The marine correspondent found a hole behind the headquarters building with concrete on three sides and climbed into it with two other grunts. One of them pulled out a can of food, which they shared. Then he took out his tattered correspondent's notebook and began scribbling down notes from the day, bits and pieces he wanted to remember for a story he would write later, quotes from the men involved, descriptions of the scene, names, numbers, details:

"Battle for Provincial Building. H 2/5 [Hotel Company] spearhead . . . support G2/5 [Golf Company] . . . attack on NVA stronghold in Hue . . . building taken—NVA flag lowered—US raised."

The flag story is important, Berntson thought. Before the assault was over, Christmas had sent Frank Thomas, his gunnery sergeant, to find an American flag. He knew it was against the rules. This was a war on behalf of the Republic of Vietnam, and the correct flag to run up the pole at its province headquarters would have been Saigon's yellow and red ensign. But Christmas's men had bled and died all the way across southern Hue, not ARVN troops. They had looked up at that enemy flag the whole way. They had taken it down, and they wanted to show who had done it. The Stars and Stripes had earned its place.

Berntson continued jotting down Christmas's words:

"'Proudest moment of my life—to be given opp to do it' . . . 'main thought was getting the flag up—so it would fly and everyone could see that flag flying' . . . Capt. Ron Christmas, 27, 2001 S.W. 36th Ave, Fort Lauderdale, FLA CO for 2/5 Hotel . . . 'street fighting is dirtiest close in. Biggest problem is control—keeping all platoons in line—communication also problem . . . platoons have done extremely well . . . flag. 'inspiration thing I have ever seen in my lifetime—because it was a hard thing. That feeling of patriotism . . . all you could hear are cheers . . . really brings out America Spirit.'"

Hours later, Christmas was paid a visit by two officers, both majors, one army and the other marine. They had been sent by Colonel Hughes from the compound. They said the American flag would have to come down. The South Vietnamese flag was the appropriate one.

The men around Christmas were still loading up the wounded and dead.

"I don't think my men are going to like that," he said.

"That doesn't make any difference," said one. "You are violating protocol."

"Well, I'll tell you what," said Christmas. "If you want to take the flag down, you guys go take it down. But I cannot be responsible for all of my men."

Kaczmarek, who was sitting close enough to overhear the exchange, chose that moment to reposition his rifle. The majors left. The flag remained. Christmas had a gunny sergeant haul it down at sunset, and the next morning a bright yellow South Vietnamese flag flew in its place.

But watching Old Glory run up that afternoon was a sight none of the marines who witnessed it would ever regret, or forget.

4

Staying

Despite the marines' inexorable progress, General Dang Kinh, one of the prime architects and leaders of the Front's effort in Hue, felt that one week in things were still going well. Inside the Citadel, reinforced ARVN troops, backed by air strikes and artillery, had retaken the Chanh Tay Gate and were advancing toward the fortress's most populous neighborhoods, but the Front still held most of it, including the Dong Ba Gate on the eastern wall, the three southern gates—Thuong Tu, Nha Do, and Ngo Mon—and the southwestern gate, Huu. Their big Alliance flag was still proudly flying.

Lieutenant Hoang had been conducting an orderly retreat from the American advance in the triangle. His ammo was low, but that could be remedied. His lines of communications and support were intact. No longer tied down to defending specific buildings every day, he was free to maneuver and, in effect, choose where and when to confront the marines, who Kinh believed were terrified and confused by city fighting. His men could still hurt them. The sapper unit and support battalion that had destroyed the ARVN tank compound at Tam Thai in the initial attack had swum across the Huong River on Tuesday night, February 6, to join the fight in the Citadel. They had fought alongside Hoang in southern Hue, and now they would shore up defenses inside the fortress.

Kinh had lost the important strip of buildings along Le Loi Street, but he had made the Americans pay dearly and he still occupied about a third of the triangle and most of the Citadel. The triangle would gradually be lost, but the Americans would have to fight for every block. With well-established defensive positions throughout the southern half of the fortress, there was no telling how long his forces could hold out there, and as far as Kinh was concerned, every day they did was another victory.

But on Tuesday morning, he received a distress call from his forces there. He sent several staff officers to inspect their defenses and met with them later in the day. They reported that the ARVN was pressing a "ferocious counterattack" and that the commanders in the Citadel[48] were requesting permission to withdraw.

Kinh then called the political cadre leader for his forces there, who described the conflict as "one of tough, back-and-forth fighting for possession of ground, just as it had been over the past few days." The general learned that the party's Current Affairs Committee—the commissars who oversaw military operations—was drafting a recommendation to Hanoi that the Front in Hue, north and south, give up the fight. It was clear that they could not hold off the counterattack indefinitely, the committee argued, and many men would be lost in the attempt.

At that point Kinh reassessed his position. The commissars were his superiors; they could overrule his military judgment. *But,* he thought, *war is fought to support political goals.* There had not been nor would there be a popular uprising. Militarily speaking, the countrywide Tet Offensive had only one major accomplishment: taking Hue. He was not ready to relinquish it.

Holding on paid daily dividends. America was taking a severe beating abroad. In BBC radio broadcasts the Tet Offensive and the occupation of Hue were being portrayed as a major embarrassment for the United States, and the destructive effects of the counterattack were being denounced by war critics. The general believed that the longer his forces held out, the louder this censure would become. He opposed the decision to withdraw but knew he lacked the clout to overrule the party leaders. So he went above their heads.

He called General Tran Van Quang, his military superior, and made an angry request.

"Sir, I request your permission to return to our southern wing [forces in the triangle]."

"Why do you want to go down to the southern wing?" Quang asked.

"Sir, the party Current Affairs Committee has decided to order our forces to withdraw from the city and has already sent that recommendation to the Central Military Party Committee," Kinh explained. "I want to go down to the southern wing to help Than Trong Mot [General Mot commanded the Front's forces in southern Hue] work out a plan for an orderly withdrawal of our forces from the city."

The tone of his voice made it clear that Kinh was not happy about this.

"What do you think we should do?" Quang asked.

"I have just checked on the situation in both the northern and the southern wings," Kinh said. "I believe that with the forces we now have we will be able to hold the city for a while longer, and that will be greatly beneficial for the overall political struggle."

He convinced Quang, and received permission to write a cable, with the general's signature, to Hanoi's top military commanders.

A half hour later Kinh received a radio message from Hanoi "warmly approving" of Quang's (Kinh's) decision to hold on in Hue "for a few more days." It was signed by all three senior military leaders: Generals Vo Nguyen Giap, Van Tien Dung, and Song Hao.[49]

Kinh had outmaneuvered his political overseers.

5

Vaught

AFTER ITS DARING nighttime escape from the trap at TFP, Colonel Dick Sweet's cavalry battalion, now down to less than half strength, had found an ARVN outpost on a hilltop and dug in. From that vantage the men could watch over the main road into Hue from two directions. Sweet had for the time being abandoned orders to march to the city walls. His men were exhausted and had been battered. They needed time to recover. The small band of South Vietnamese soldiers at the camp were thrilled at their arrival. They had been stranded, vastly outnumbered, ever since Tet began, and had survived only because the Front had apparently considered their post too insignificant to attack.

They were there four days. Carl DiLeo, the skinny mortar platoon private from Trenton, was thrilled just to be alive. His platoon, ordinarily about fifty men, was down to just fourteen. He felt they had been put through such a trial that they ought to be pulled from the field and given a break. He felt that LBJ himself in his cowboy hat should have stomped up the hill to shake their hands. DiLeo had been in-country for eight months, and it had been one deadly scrimmage after another. And now this. He felt, *How much more can they ask?* Morale in his group was at an all-time low. Many of the guys he had been close to were gone—either dead or wounded and evacuated. He felt isolated and had lost trust in his leaders. *Who the fuck did this?* He felt he and the others were owed an apology.

He was not the only one. The men were surly. Theodore Wallace, by virtue of attrition, was the radio operator for his platoon. Earlier, before he was given the job, he had seen the lieutenant commanding his platoon kick the radio operator in anger. For that reason he always walked about ten feet away, despite being told to stay close. Finally he was confronted over it.

"Wallace, what the fuck are you always doing to the left or right of me?" the lieutenant complained. "When I get a call, you're always telling the colonel to wait while you walk over to me."

Wallace leveled his most meaningful Harlem street stare.

"Because, sir, if you lift your leg to me, I am going to shoot you. And I don't want to have to shoot you."

Wallace had rapidly soured on the whole Vietnam adventure, although he intended to stay and do his duty. On one patrol he found a pile of what he thought was burning wood. When he got closer he saw that it was the blackened remains of an old woman. She probably had been hit by a grenade they had launched at her village. Wallace wondered what she had been doing when she had been killed like that.

One day he saw an officer casually aim his rifle and try to shoot a Vietnamese boy in the distance.

"Sir, what are you doing?" he'd asked.

"He's probably supplying the NVA," the officer said. "What's he doing out here anyway?"

"It's his country!" said Wallace. "What's he carrying? Did you even look through your binoculars to see if he was carrying anything?"

Wallace had pretty much decided that from then on he wasn't going to shoot at anybody who was not actively shooting at him.

The men were delivered food and warm, dry clothes. General Tolson, the division commander who had sent them marching toward La Chu with inadequate support, now flew in personally. If he had expected to be received as a savior, he was disappointed. He was given a distinct cold shoulder. The men were still digging foxholes, and they kept at it. Some of them stood up to salute him as he passed, but not many. DiLeo felt that instead of offering them goodies and a pep talk, the general ought to have admitted his mistake. *Look, I moved you guys too fast.* If he'd done that the men might have responded differently—DiLeo would have. He just wanted somebody to admit to having fucked up. But the general didn't even come close. He just offered canned army rah-rah bullshit.

"They won't stop digging for me," Tolson complained to Sweet. As they spoke, inside a small hut, some of the men tore off its roof to use as a covering for their foxholes.[50]

The general stopped to chat with pathfinder Juan Gonzales and one of his buddies, asking them if they were okay, if they needed anything. They were polite, but they didn't get up. When the general walked away, one of the officers on his staff confronted them.

"Don't you men know enough to salute a general?" he asked them. "He is a general!"

Gonzalez said, "Sir, we do not salute officers in the field. Would you like for us to salute you?"

The officer walked off mad.

One of the nights when they were camped on the hill, Wallace got a tape from his family. They found a tape player and all of the guys huddled around to listen. It was a sweet, run-of-the-mill message from home, updates on various family members, lots of *love-yous* and *stay-safes* and *can't-wait-till-you-come-homes*, and there was not a dry eye in his unit. For those minutes in the chilly darkness on a hillside in Vietnam, those voices from home were, he realized, the voices of everyone's family.

Then came orders that they were to march back toward La Chu to take part in a pincer move. Colonel James Vaught's battalion had been moving south from PK-17 and planned to attack the village, which at long last had been recognized as an enemy stronghold. Sweet, whose decision to break out of the encirclement was regarded as faintly cowardly in some quarters, was ordered to retrace his steps, get back, and rejoin the fight by attacking the village from the opposite direction.

So DiLeo, instead of getting thanks, an apology, and a break, now found himself humping his rifle and heavy mortar plate *right back into the shit*. Right back to the place where hundreds—hell, thousands!—of murderous gooks[51] had whipped them days earlier, the place they'd been extremely lucky to have escaped! *Jesus*, he thought, *we didn't do too good with four hundred, five hundred men, what are we going to do with less than half that?* He had this vision of commanders like Tolson sitting in an office somewhere behind the lines looking at maps and talking on phones without a clue about what it was actually like to be out in the drizzly fucking muck watching your friends get torn to pieces or turned into goopy pink mist. *Fuck this*, he thought, *nobody is doing this! Audie Murphy himself wouldn't do this! This is crazy!* He felt as if he were serving some terribly brutal penalty for a crime he had not committed. His purpose in life had been reduced to scheming to get an extra can of C rations or a pair of dry socks. *What could he do?* He resolved to be more careful than he had been. He certainly wasn't going to be putting his hand up for anything. As far as the overall purpose of the war, it deserved no further sacrifice from Private Carl DiLeo . . . he was done with that. Nobody seemed to give a damn about him and he could return that outlook with a vengeance.

When the battalion chaplain asked if he might offer a prayer before they embarked, and then asked God to bless "those who were going to die," Captain Helvey nearly threw something at him. He told Sweet to keep the chaplain away from his men.[52]

Farther north, setting off from PK-17 on Thursday, February 8, Vaught had arrayed his full battalion in a diamond formation, with Delta Company in the lead, commanded by Frank Lambert, and two more behind it to the left and the right, Howard Prince's Bravo and Robert Preston's Alpha. Charlie Company commanded by Mike Davison moved behind them in the center. This gave them the flexibility to fight off an attack from any direction without breaking formation. No matter where the enemy approached, the battalion had its flanks covered and had strength to its rear. Vaught and his command staff walked before Alpha Company, stripped of all signs of rank and carrying rifles like everyone else. They moved through rice paddies and villages, retracing the route Sweet had taken days earlier, about a thousand yards to the west of Highway 1.

Andy Westin was walking with Davison's company. The night before, at PK-17, he had written to his wife, Mimi:

> *Things are really hot! We'll probably jump off this
> afternoon. I guess there are a terrific amount of gooks in the
> area . . . Somewhere around here is a gook with a mortar and he
> pops a round or 2 at us every hour or so. I hope somebody spots
> it and can get rid of him. It's a pain in the neck! All of a sudden
> this war has really changed tempo. It was slow and easy. Now it's
> fast and furious. There's something going on all the time. I think*

*the fighting is going to get very heavy before it gets better. I'm glad
I've got the weapons platoon. I'm a little further back, but not far
enough to make me happy. I'd just as soon be home.*

As they started walking, the lieutenant was thrilled—all four companies arrayed in the field! Five hundred American soldiers moving together. Vaught had seen big infantry battles before, in World War II and in Korea, but in Vietnam it was rare to perform such an industrial-strength maneuver. Westin had never seen more than a company together at once. He was dazzled by Vaught, a gruff, thick man with big facial features and squinty eyes under a hard rim of brow, with bushy eyebrows that arched upward even when his face was at rest, so that when he looked at you, even with indifference, it felt significant, like a leveling stare. Down his cheeks he had deep lines that seemed carved from stone, and he spoke with a slow southern drawl—he was from Conway, South Carolina. Westin and the other officers were in awe of him. When he first met Prince he said, "This is my third war so I feel like a fugitive from the law of averages. In other words, I'm scared shitless and I assume you are too so let's just get that out of the way and do our jobs anyway." He exuded confidence. He had a wealth of stories and told them well. He claimed to be a direct descendant of Francis Marion, the "Swamp Fox," the Palmetto State's guerrilla general during the Revolutionary War. He was magnetic. *If war it is,* the young lieutenant thought, *please let me go with this guy.* And so they were going now, marching south in this enormous formation with artillery rounds making a curious buzzing sound like giant insects as they flew overhead, and then shaking the ground when they exploded several hundred yards ahead. It was like walking behind a moving wall of thunder. After what had happened with Sweet's battalion, they weren't taking chances. Westin thought it was the coolest thing he had ever seen.

It did not take them long to find the enemy. A Huey was hit as it flew ahead of them. It was the command-and-control bird and ordinarily would have been carrying the battalion commander, but since Vaught, like Sweet, preferred to lead from the ground, the chopper had just been providing surveillance. Captain Howard Prince, commander of Bravo Company, had spoken to the crew earlier, advising them to move away because there might be antiaircraft batteries in the vicinity. Minutes later the chopper went down.

Vaught ordered Prince to move to the crash site to rescue the crew. He found it, and the chopper was intact, its nose down in the rice paddy, but the crew had gone. They had already been picked up by a rescue chopper. Prince could tell the area where it crashed had been an NVA camp. There were sandal tracks and dugout fighting positions and communications wires.

Bravo, his company, was then sent by Vaught south across the dry rice paddies toward the wood line at the northern edge of Que Chu to look for the enemy. They were drawn straight into an ambush. It was still early afternoon. The point squad made it to the trees—he later realized that they had been allowed to make it that far—and then were cut down. All ten men were either killed or wounded. As the rest of the company moved up, they took heavy fire. There was no cover.

The captain had been in firefights before, and like everyone else in his company, he was scared, but he had learned to keep his own emotions wrapped and, what was sometimes even harder, to accept that when bullets and grenades started to fly there was only so much he could control. A dark-haired, broad-faced, reflective man, Prince had graduated high in his class at West Point and had earned a master's degree from American University. This, and the fact that he had been shot in the foot earlier in his tour, was why his radio call sign was "Limping Scholar Six." Talking to his platoon leaders by radio, he cautioned them to stay calm even when every instinct in their bodies was telling them to panic, as his were now. *Just assess the situation and tell me where the fire is coming from, how heavy it is, how many people are shooting at you, and what kind of weapon you think it is.* This kind of thing was easier said than done. But his job was to piece together the information and decide what he *could* do, which was usually less than what he might like.

In this case he could call down artillery on the enemy positions, which was risky because his own men were down in the woods and the rest of the company was less than a hundred yards away. He called for both high-explosive rounds and smoke rounds, and set off moving through the heavy smoke. They were still being shot at, although the fire was now less accurate. It took his men several hours to move back across the rice paddies and rejoin the company. The fire was so intense that the bodies of those killed had to be left behind—Prince would send a patrol back out after dark and the NVA allowed his men to retrieve the bodies, which were evacuated the next day after the wounded.

At the same time Delta Company was attacked by small-arms fire to its right from a village called Lieu Coc. They, too, had fallen back. Even with the moving wall of fire, Vaught's battalion had not gotten very far. The seemingly invincible marching formation Westin so admired in the morning was now scattered and digging in on all sides, facing forces equal to or possibly stronger than its own.

That night, Vaught, the veteran, gave his command staff a little lesson in digging a foxhole, which would later be described with admiration by his operations officer, Charles Baker, in his memoir, *Gray Horse Troop*. Vaught excavated a trench two feet deep and three feet wide and about a foot longer than his body. The dirt he removed was used to form a lip around the edges, and branches from a nearby hut were stretched across the top. Then he put a thick layer of dirt over the branches. He crawled in feetfirst, with the antenna of his radio sticking out the front end. He bragged that it "could take a direct hit from an eighty-two-millimeter mortar."[53]

Westin, in his own hole with Charlie Company, wrote another letter to Mimi that night:

> Well, we're really in the thick of it and Charlie apparently doesn't want to leave. Our entire battalion is working together as one unit. We're gradually working towards Hue, but it sure isn't the easiest hike I've ever been on. The gooks manage to toss mortar rounds at us about every 15 minutes. Luckily nobody has been killed [in his unit], but we've taken a few casualties. I've got a flak vest and I just about live in it. The weather is really rotten. Day and night it's a cold mist. Not heavy enough to really get you wet, but just enough to make us cold and miserable. Ugh!!
>
> . . . I've moved underground. No kidding. I dug a hole, then tunneled out from there. I have my air mattress and other sleeping gear about 5' below ground. It's cool. No wind or cold gets down here and when Charlie mortars us I don't even have to roll over. The tunnel part is about 3' high and 10' long, with a couple of bends so that if

a round lands in the entrance hole, the shrapnel won't get me. Over my head is about 6' of solid ground. It's a pretty safe spot. I wasn't planning on having it, but I got cold and to keep warm I dug. I dug about all day yesterday and this is what I ended up with.

General Tolson had moved his forward tactical command to PK-17, and as a reminder of how little control of the battlefield he had achieved, the outpost was regularly hit with mortar fire. On Friday night, three rounds landed directly on top of the command bunker. Major Don Bowman was inside with the brigade commander, Colonel Hugh Campbell. It was deafening. It felt like being in a metal drum that someone was whacking hard with a baseball bat. Each hit blew out the lanterns and filled the cramped workspace with dust and smoke. Then their communication lines went down—the explosion cut the antenna cable. They were still alive only because the enemy rounds were exploding on impact. If the mortar crew targeting them decided to try one with the fuse set on "delay," which would give it time to penetrate before exploding, they were done. Surely the enemy had a spotter who would relay this suggestion. Bowman bowed his head and took a moment to silently ask God to please take care of his wife and children. Then he went back to work by flashlight.

"Are you hit bad?" Campbell asked him, alarmed.

"Sir, I'm not hit."

"Oh, I saw your head drop and I thought you were wounded," the colonel said.

Bowman explained about the prayer, and they both laughed.

A week later, the enemy mortar crew did as Bowman feared. Trying to grab a few hours of sleep in his bunker after being relieved at midnight, he had stretched out in his flak jacket under two ponchos, resting his head on a canteen. He awoke abruptly with a loud ringing in his ears, tangled in equipment and bedding, as if he and all of the contents of his bunker had been put in a blender. A mortar round with a delayed fuse had exploded just two feet short of the bunker wall. It blew behind Bowman's head, throwing him clear across the space and slamming him into the wall opposite. He was dazed and slightly concussed, but otherwise unhurt.

Vaught's battalion continued to walk south, now with a pair of helicopters overhead as spotters—the presence of the choppers made the men feel more secure. When forward elements encountered the enemy, they would dial up the howitzer battery at PK-17, which was at that point delivering strikes on request. Once or twice a shell landed in the middle of their own formation, injuring no one but somewhat reducing their enthusiasm for maneuvering with artillery. Ahead were three more villages: Lieu Coc, where they had been delayed; and then Que Chu; and La Chu, which stood in the shadow of the three-story American-made concrete bunker that was the heavily guarded headquarters for the Front's assault on Hue.

The artillery battery at PK-17 was having a hard time keeping up with the demand for fire missions. Ordinarily it was resupplied from Camp Evans by helicopter. The need for new rounds was pressing. The Chinooks, big dual-rotor choppers, generally delivered ammo on pallets suspended in a sling. In order to see they had to stay below the clouds, which were so low that the sling kept hitting trees and hills and even the flat ground. So ammo now had to be delivered in much smaller amounts by truck. And once Sweet's battalion was on the move again, the battery started getting fire missions from it, too.[54]

Vaught solved this problem by calling the navy, which unloaded with five-inch guns from the deck of USS *Lofberg*, which was parked out in Yankee Station, the naval staging area in the South China Sea. This chased the enemy out of Lieu Coc. In the village they found bodies of NVA soldiers, lots of dugout fighting positions, food, and ammunition for a large force. The men who had been fighting from there had apparently retreated to their next defensive line. Villagers who survived the shelling assured Vaught's men that there had been "beaucoup VC" there until hours earlier.

The march continued with daily harassment and delaying actions by the NVA, as it became clear to Vaught that a very large enemy force, much bigger than any of them had imagined, was waiting for them at La Chu, where it had more favorable ground to make a stand. After four days of fighting, his battalion had made it no farther than Sweet's. They continued probing NVA positions the next day, without success. And the next. And the next. Each morning the company commanders would huddle with Vaught in the field, get their orders, move back to their positions, call in air and artillery support, deploy their men, maneuver and engage the enemy, and attempt to push through. That spot in the rice paddy would be Vaught's base camp for the next two weeks.

It wasn't as precarious as it had been for Sweet's battalion. In addition to the artillery, both his own and the navy's, Vaught had the advantage of better understanding. His men had painstakingly cleared his flanks on the way down. So Vaught was in a much more stable position than Sweet had been. Diminished enemy fire now enabled regular helicopter flights, so his men stayed well fed and supplied.

They even got mail.

Westin got a letter from Mimi that really pissed him off. Thirty guys from his unit had been wounded. He was in constant danger. He was living in a fucking hole in the ground. And Mimi was worried about him fooling around with other women.

One of her former boyfriends, a Vietnam veteran, had said something to her about how easy it was for guys to get laid there. Aggravating matters were some photos he had sent her from his brief R&R, when he and his buddies had posed with several scantily clad showgirls. He had not even danced with them! He had taken a few admiring pictures, and some—particularly of Joyce Grayson, "Miss Las Vegas Showgirl"— from admittedly provocative angles, but that was it! He curled into his underground bunker and fired back in thick pencil:

> Just because a guy you used to go with went away and got some, you seem to think that I am. The side view of Joyce is because you had to see her to believe her. I took them primarily for 2 horny bachelors. If I hadn't enjoyed taking them, I would say that I wasn't normal . . . Grow up!

Two days later he was distraught. Men in combat form close ties, but often even more important is the admiration they feel for especially skilled leaders, the kind who, usually just a few years older, seem to know everything and to be immune to fear and danger. You were glad to have these men with you not only because they knew what to do, but because their very presence was reassuring—if you were with them, you felt you would survive. In Charlie Company that man was Lieutenant Winfield Beck, the burly, round-faced, unflappable lawyer from Pensacola, who was on his second tour. He was the platoon leader who had taken reporter Denby Fawcett on that village sweep three months earlier. Beck was the same age as Westin, but his experience and poise made him seem older. He had such a clear, logical way of thinking that he just seemed always to know *exactly* how to handle a problem. The two had swapped jobs a few weeks earlier, Westin leaving his position as company executive officer (XO) and taking over a weapons platoon. When he was killed, Beck had been stretched out alongside Davison—right where Westin would have been if they hadn't traded jobs. They had been assaulting a tree line. Beck lifted his head and was shot through the throat. He choked and bled to death as the captain held him and tried to figure out what to do. There was nothing to be done. Beck's death hit Westin hard.

In his hole, he wrote to Mimi:

> My Darling, For the first time since I came here, last night, I cried. I wasn't the only one. From the CO on down, our men were crying. Our XO, Lt. Beck, got killed in a fight yesterday. He was probably the most liked and respected officer in the company. Our entire battalion got caught in a gook trap. I still don't know how many killed and wounded we took, but there were a terrific amount. It was a slaughter!
>
> All the brass thought the gooks had moved out, so we just went waltzing into this woodline. The gooks had hundreds of grenades and anti-personnel mines. They waited until our people were right on top of them, then cut us down.
>
> We finally got out about 11:00 PM and pulled back. My platoon ran out of ammo (we'd been supporting from the rear) so we made stretchers out of ponchos and went out to help carry wounded. None of my people were killed, but 2 got light wounds. The rifle platoons were really surprised to see myself and my platoon come charging across the field with stretchers on our backs. Once we got our people out, we went to the other companies and helped them. I've never seen anything like it and I hope I never do again. I'm now the XO again.

Positioned near such a large enemy force, Vaught and his men knew that they were vulnerable to being overrun if caught by surprise. Nerves were taut, especially at night. When a trip flare went off suddenly on their perimeter one night, the men panicked. Vaught received an urgent request to fire illumination flares—but this would be like turning on a floodlight over their position.

He refused. He also issued crisp orders that *no one* was to fire a rifle or a machine gun—the barrel flashes would also mark their position. He did allow several small rockets to be fired at the point where the flare had gone off, because the LAW barrels had no muzzle flash.

In the morning they found a very dead pig.[55]

6

Fuck Him,
He's for the Other Side

THREE DAYS AFTER the marines took back the province headquarters, the last and most symbolic of the major structures along Le Loi Street, Gene Roberts left Hue, replaced by his colleague Charles Mohr. Roberts's reporting had been the first and best from the front lines in the city, and he had stayed with the effort through the critical first eight days. Two days before his departure, Wednesday February 7, still dictating over the phone, he reported on substantial progress and also some of the ways marines were adapting to their urban battlefield.

Marine Squad Rides to Battle on Motorcycles

Enemy Driven Out
of a 70-Block Area
in Battle for Hue

Hue, South Vietnam, Feb. 7—Capt. Bacel Winstead of Hot Springs, Ark., gazed out on the debris-littered street of this embattled city today and shook his head in wonder.

"The American military is the damnedest military in the world," said the captain, who is a United States Army adviser to South Vietnamese troops. "Just look out there."

Down the street came a squad of marines zipping off to battle on red, blue and yellow Honda motorcycles they had "liberated" from recaptured middle-class homes.

Each marine had one hand on a handlebar and the other around
an M-16 automatic rifle. Full field packs, complete with blanket
rolls and entrenching tools, hung from their shoulders . . . With
the motorcycles and battered civilian cars, the marines intend to
recapture large areas of enemy-held territory.

They held about 70 city blocks tonight on the south side of
the Huong River compared with about 30 blocks yesterday. This
leaves a little more than a third of the southwest side of this city
of 145,000 in enemy-hands.

On the north side of the river, where eight South Vietnamese
battalions are fighting, the battle for Hue was going more slowly.

The story featured an Associated Press photo of a marine bent under
an enormous pack, riding a small motorcycle. Roberts reported that
the marines had now suffered two hundred and fifty casualties. Officially, they reported having killed a thousand enemy soldiers, but the
number was the usual amped-up guesswork. The marines still in the
fight, Roberts wrote, "are bearded, dirty and tired. Today a marine
'liberated' a case of pastel-colored pocket combs and passed them
around to members of his platoon. 'Damn!' one of them said. 'This
is the first time I've combed my hair for weeks.'"[56]

The city was still socked in with gray clouds and misty rain, wet by
day and cold at night. The low cloud ceiling and poor visibility still
made air attacks infrequent, although South Vietnamese bombers managed to slip underneath and drop two dozen five-hundred-pounders on
enemy positions inside the Citadel—positions that included thousands
of civilians. Even though he now had more freedom to maneuver, Lieutenant Hoang was keeping to his strategy on the south side, holding
his enemy "by the belt," which made it all but impossible for artillery
from Phu Bai to zero in on his forces.

Colonel Gravel's company was reinforced by additional marines by
boat—the marines in fresh fatigues and full backpacks Roberts had seen
were part of this influx. On Saturday they would fight their way into
the soccer stadium, the largest structure in the northwest corner of
the triangle. This provided a second, better-protected LZ and another,
bigger place to put the ever-growing crowds of needy refugees.

Roberts slipped out on Friday. Going by road was out of the question. The last convoy to attempt the drive from Phu Bai had been hit hard. Twenty marines had been killed, thirty-nine more wounded, and all of the vehicles had either been destroyed or turned back. The weather had slowed helicopter traffic to a trickle, and the few that made it quickly filled with severely wounded marines. So the reporter queued up with a crowd of evacuees before a Mike Boat when it berthed at the boat ramp.

The gray metal vessels were now making regular runs past the guns on both sides of the river. Each would ease up to the concrete slab that angled down into the water and lower its wide bow to unload. Behind the vessel was the great steelwork of Truong Tien Bridge, bent down sharply at the middle into the river, the city's broken spine. The Front had finally managed to drop it on Wednesday, the seventh. At its far side green-uniformed Front soldiers could be seen manning bunkers and moving in the streets. They lobbed mortars across the water, trying to hit the boats. This and the occasional sniper rounds from buildings to the south made it daring to wait by the ramp. The incoming marines disembarked at a run, crouching. They were directed toward designated reception points across Le Loi Street. Off-loading of supplies then commenced, one hundred and fifty tons of ammo on pallets, along with stacked boxes of C rations, medical supplies, and other necessities. Marines worked rapidly with forklifts, ignoring the occasional gunshots that cracked overhead or slapped into the water. Mortar shells sometimes came close. When one hurled up dirt and shrapnel, a Filipino woman, wife of an American adviser, scooped up her five-year-old and hid behind a pallet of C rations. There were about fifty people waiting to board, including wounded marines on stretchers and those still upright, grungy and tired in their bloodstained fatigues and bandages—most had been hit in the arms, hands, legs, or feet. Theirs were not life-threatening wounds, but many were stiff, swollen, and painful. Navy crewmen warned them and the civilians that they would be safer waiting back at the compound, but the Mike Boats tended not to linger, and those waiting feared missing their chance if they moved. No one left.

Roberts watched with his usual air of quiet detachment. The woman holding the child told him in a low voice, "We've been through so much these last nine days, it wouldn't seem fair if something happened to my son now."

"The only thing we can do now is hope the bastards are lousy shots," said one of the wounded. He sat lounging against a packing case smoking a cigarette. "There ain't no place to hide."

He was right. A direct hit on any of the ammo pallets would probably have killed them all. But the mortars kept missing. Two fell in the river, "kicking up small geysers of water," Roberts wrote. One hit a packing crate at a distance from where the passengers waited. When it came time to board, women, children, and the stretcher-borne wounded went first. The walking wounded and other passengers were an interesting mix. Among them were two priests who had been held by the Front and then released, several South Vietnamese physicians (who had been searched carefully before being allowed to board), and a six-man team from the International Control Commission (ICC). This was a UN-sponsored group made up of volunteers from Poland, Canada, and India, who were there to monitor adherence to the Geneva Accords, which governed treatment of prisoners and civilians. The ICC teams were always careful to include members with opposing sympathies in the war—the Canadians leaned toward their US cousins and South Vietnam, the Soviet bloc Poles toward Hanoi, and the Indians were hard to read. This delegation had been discovered by marines the day before after hiding in their headquarters for a week. One of the members, Indian colonel G. D. Joshi, said that the Front had rocketed their building and "shot it up with mortars and rifles," but had backed off when informed who they were. Joining them was David Greenway, a reporter for *Time*.

None of the passengers relaxed until the boat pulled away and began moving downriver, but their relief was short-lived. As soon as the destroyed bridge receded, gunfire picked up from both banks. Enemy soldiers could be seen jumping up to shoot rockets at them. The river flowed past the south wall of the Citadel and bent north as it approached Hen Island, a long sliver of land at the center of the Huong, which divided the flow into two greatly narrowed forks. The shores were three times closer no matter which way you went. Both banks were controlled by the Front.

"If you've got weapons, you ought to get them ready," a crewman announced ominously. "It will be a miracle if we don't have to use them."

As they entered the fork, shooting did become more intense. A small patrol boat behind them was hit by a rocket and sank. Bright red tracer rounds cracked overhead and the wounded marines attempted to fire back. Some bit at the bandages on their hands to free their fingers. One who could not manage to pull the trigger on his rifle handed it to another who could. The petty officer skippering the boat called for every man on board to grab a weapon, get to the rails, and return fire. Greenway did as instructed, shooting blindly at the riverbanks first from one side and then the other. Roberts refused—journalists were not supposed to be combatants.[57]

The boat seemed to be just inching downriver.

One of the ICC men asked, "Is this boat moving at all?"

It took hours to reach the South China Sea. Most of the shooting stopped about a half hour after they slipped past the island and then left the Citadel behind. One of the Canadians, an army major, pulled out a bottle of Ambassador Scotch from under his jacket. He gave it to the marines, who passed it around eagerly, emptying it in four minutes—Roberts timed it. The Canadian then gave them another. He explained that he had passed by the Cercle Sportif on his way down Le Loi Street that morning and had liberated all the bottles he could carry. His jacket and cargo pants pockets were all heavy with them. After a while, Roberts and the marines and some of the other ICC members sat in a circle, passing around a bottle.

When they made the South China Sea, the vessel started bouncing and heaving. There were ten-foot swells. One of the Poles wandered over to the circle and asked the Canadian major in broken English if he had Dramamine (motion sickness) pills.

"I saw them on the bureau in your room," he said.

"God, in all the haste I forgot to bring the Dramamine along," the major said.

The Pole stumbled to the other side, hung his head over the rail, and vomited.

Then the major pulled a bottle of pills from one of his many pockets. He flipped it in his hand.

"Fuck him," he said, gesturing toward the sick Pole. "He's for the other side."

Those with more seaworthy stomachs continued with the Scotch until late that night. Seven hours after they had started the fifty-seven-mile voyage they slid up to a dock at Da Nang. The Filipino woman crossed a gangplank to the pier and then reached back to take her boy from one of the crewmen. She hugged him happily. "We're here!" she said. "We're here!"

Roberts didn't realize how drunk he was until he stood up. He made his way to the edge, stepped off the boat, and missed the gangplank. His new friends fished him out of the drink.[58]

7

Hell Sucks

CHEATHAM'S THREE COMPANIES had been fighting with the park and river to their right, and buildings and houses on their left. So most of the shooting at them in the first days had come from their left flank. Now, as they made a left turn and began pushing down the east bank of the Phu Cam Canal, most of the shooting came from the right.

The enemy occupied buildings on both sides of the canal, which was not as wide as the Huong River, so fire from both was effective. The marines would fight block by block down to the southern tip of the triangle and then would turn left again, sweeping back through the less densely occupied neighborhoods south of their original march. Eventually they would meet up with Gravel's battalion, which was pushing farther and farther south and east every day from the compound. It had made it all the way down to the destroyed An Cuu Bridge and was protecting engineers as they stretched a pontoon across to reconnect Highway 1. So the Front was being squeezed out of the triangle. Increasingly it moved across the small tributaries and canals at the triangle's edges. Snipers shot across the water and Hoang's men would launch occasional night attacks across the many small bridges. The fighting was no longer as intense as it had been, but it was constant and deadly. It would remain so for almost two more weeks.

The most important stretch of southern Hue, the south bank of the Huong River, was now secure. The large, important buildings along Le Loi Street were all occupied by marines and, increasingly, ARVN troops. On Saturday morning, Steve Berntson walked down the wide street, picking his way around the rubble, the bodies, and the charred vehicles all the way back to the compound. He had written up some of his stories and was looking for someone to take them to Da Nang. The ARVN forces he saw along the way struck him as undisciplined, poorly trained, and avaricious—they were openly looting. The best South Vietnamese troops were across the river fighting inside the Citadel. These were busily reinforcing the marines' bad opinion of their South Vietnamese allies.

When Berntson got to the compound, Walter Cronkite was there.

Cronkite's nightly news broadcasts reached tens of millions of viewers, so to Americans his face and voice were instantly familiar. That morning he was wearing crisp green fatigues, a flak jacket, and combat boots, interviewing Colonel Hughes in the compound officers' bar under bright lights. Berntson, who was foul and unshaven, listened for a bit, then snagged a few of the olive loaf sandwiches that had been set out for the anchorman's visit. His hands were so filthy that the bread was brown before he took the last bite. It tasted great. Then he helped himself to chicken noodle soup and coffee.

Word that the CBS anchorman was coming had spread the night before. Lieutenant Smith was asked if his area was safe enough to bring Cronkite for a visit—his Alpha Company was now up in the northeast corner of the triangle where the Nhu Y River met the Huong, before a narrow bridge to Dap Da, where the Front was still dug in. Colonel Gravel came up to inspect the site firsthand that morning. He and Smith were running together across a narrow road when there was a burst of white smoke across the water, and then a rocket, initially just a black dot in the distance, came straight at them. It looked as if it was just floating but getting bigger. Smith, in midstride, thought, *That thing is going to hit me!* It flashed past him, nicking his lower leg with one of its fins. That slight impact deflected it upward. It performed a slow arc across the street, where it exploded on an old woman, killing her instantly.

Smith's wound was minor, so he and Gravel kept going, seeking out a platoon commanded by Lieutenant Allen Courtney, who nights earlier had swum across the Phu Cam Canal bringing reinforcements. Courtney was the kind of man for whom war seemed invented. He was considered a wild man even by the marines. Tall and fair-haired, with a smile always edging toward laughter, he liked blowing things up. He had once filled a heavy roll of barbed wire—it came in tight rolls about the size of beer kegs—with C4, rigged with a claymore mine, and rolled it out to a small hill on the base's defensive perimeter. Every time there was even slight movement beyond the line—like, say, a squirrel—the lieutenant would ask permission to blow it.

"No," said his commander, who did not want to encourage this sort of thing.

Eventually, Courtney detonated it without permission—"an emergency," he swore, with that grin. The thing was so loud and so powerful it blew off the top of the hill.

If Courtney had not been such an effective combat officer, he'd have been stripped of his command for such stunts. As it was, his men loved him.[59] When Smith and Gravel reached his position that morning, they were met by a platoon sergeant who told them excitedly that they had fought back an attack across the bridge the night before. One of the men they had killed was so much bigger than the others they suspected he might have been Chinese, perhaps an adviser.

"Do you have the body?" Gravel asked.

"He's out there on the bridge," the sergeant said, pointing. He was, indeed. Courtney had arranged the body upright on a chair facing the other bank. It was out there still, one leg crossed over the other, a cigar in its mouth, with a copy of *Playboy* draped across its lap.

The devout, dignified Gravel was furious. Desecrating corpses was obscene, and a violation of Marine Corps policy and the Geneva Convention. He demanded that Smith send him court-martial papers for Courtney immediately.[60] The colonel also decided that bringing Cronkite out for a look-around was ill-advised.

The anchorman was in Vietnam to add a personal touch to a network documentary that would assess America's progress in the war. There had been a remarkable stream of frontline video reports on the CBS nightly news, the work of John Laurence, Don Webster, Bert Quint, Dan Rather, Robert Schakne, Morley Safer, and other hardworking network crews. It was the best frontline reporting on TV. Cronkite wanted to pull all of it together and add his personal stamp. After complaining in New York the week before about the disparity between news reports and official accounts, he had decided to come see the war for himself. He had been a frontline reporter in World War II, one of the first to go along on a dangerous B-17 bombing mission over Germany. He was part of a generation that instinctively respected the military. But now Cronkite felt misled. He believed he had been fed disinformation by official sources, and he had gone to CBS News president Dick Salant to pitch a personal documentary that would set the record straight. It would focus on the Tet Offensive but give Cronkite a chance to assess the entire war effort, which would mean departing from his ordinary approach to presenting the news. The company president was less concerned about his anchorman taking a stand than he was about sending him into harm's way.

"I think it's foolish to risk your life in a situation like this, risk the life of our anchorman," Salant said. "But if you're going to go, I think you ought to do a documentary about going, about why you went, and maybe you are going to have to say something about where the war ought to go at that point." Salant said that the network had been criticized in nearly equal measure for being pro-war or antiwar. He felt they had played the story fairly, down the middle. "So, if we've got that reputation, maybe it would be helpful, if people trust us that much, trust you that much, for you to say what you think. Tell them what it looks like, from you being on the ground. What is your opinion."

The anchorman had not criticized the war. He had no moral qualms about it, and he tended to believe the reports that he read on the air. He thought the effort was overly ambitious—trying to win a war not just militarily but *politically*, trying to win the peace and the battle at the same time—but he felt the effort was a worthy one, and while skeptical, supported it. He also, of course, read the newspapers, and was aware that many of the print reporters in Vietnam were regularly contradicting the official line. He could also see that opposition had become fashionable, particularly among young people and intellectuals. But the pictures and stories his own reporters were sending back were often disturbing. He had, for instance, been as shocked as everyone by Safer's report from Cam Ne showing marines calmly setting fire to Vietnamese huts. But neither CBS nor any other broadcast network had pulled all these accounts together into a coherent counternarrative. They had troubled him, but they had not changed his mind.

Tet, however, threatened to do just that. Was it possible that the line he had been fed, the one he had for years been delivering nightly, was a lie? If so, it was a betrayal both personal and professional. His reputation had been used. It made him angry. If it had happened, he needed to correct it, even if that meant abandoning strict journalistic neutrality, one of his core beliefs.

And right away on his visit to Vietnam Cronkite's worst suspicions were confirmed. If the United States had things completely under control, as Westy claimed, why were all the airports in the country shut down? His flight had trouble finding a place to land. Why were he and his producers, Ernie Leiser and Jeff Gralnick, forbidden to even visit Khe Sanh? Too dangerous, they were told. And then, when he interviewed Westy in his crisp fatigues and with a chrome-plated AK-47 in his office as a prop, the general seemed even more cocksure than usual. He repeated the official line that Tet had been a big success for his forces. He declared the battle of Hue over. He said that US forces and ARVN troops had soundly defeated ten thousand NVA and VC troops there—blithely contradicting his earlier assertion that there were no more than a few hundred enemy soldiers in the city. Then Cronkite flew to Hue, where ten minutes on the ground was enough to show none of it was true. The battle was still raging.[61]

The men caught up in the battle were pleased, even delighted, to see him. Just the day before, in an informal meeting with his staff where they were musing about famous people they would like to meet someday, one of Gravel's officers, Captain Jim Gallagher, had said, "Walter Cronkite." He was bent over a map when Gravel walked in with the anchorman.

"Excuse me, Jim, there is someone here I want you to meet," Gravel said.

The captain was so stunned he could hardly stutter a greeting.

Most of the hard-core war reporting that would flesh out the documentary, which would air at the end of the month, was done by Laurence, Webster, Keith Kay, and others. Their work in the midst of the fight, showing weary, dirty marines risking their lives and capturing the scenes of death and destruction around the city, provided a realistic backdrop to the anchorman's commentary and analysis.[62] Cronkite himself was kept away from active combat and ugly scenes like the posed enemy corpse. His interviews were conducted in relatively safe areas, but those who spoke with him on camera, particularly Hughes and Gravel, were not inclined to sugarcoat the challenge. The enemy in Hue had not been defeated. The Citadel loomed across the river like death itself. After two days Cronkite flew out on a chopper with body bags and wounded marines. He had seen enough to be convinced that he had not been told the truth.

By then every journalist in the world with an interest in the war was trying to get to Hue. One of them, a short, slight, twenty-seven-year-old man with thinning hair, a wide face, and very large glasses that made him look bug-eyed, was Michael Herr, a correspondent for *Esquire* magazine who would probably do more than any other writer to frame the story for American readers—the story not just of Hue, but of the whole war. Unlike most reporters bumming rides around Vietnam, making their way into war zones, Herr was not filing regular stories and pictures. He was taking notes, meeting people, watching, listening, and soaking it up. His work was self-consciously literary—he had contributed to a literary magazine at Syracuse University edited by Joyce Carol Oates. He had never worked as a newspaper reporter, and he shared none of the profession's mania for nailing down the verifiable details that ground stories in reality. Herr was dreamy. He had arrived in Vietnam the year before, recently divorced, with a ticket purchased by the magazine and five hundred dollars. Harold Hayes, the editor who had agreed to send him, would later say he forgot completely about Herr after he departed, but the truth is they were still corresponding. Hayes was eager for someone to begin writing about the war in the style then popular in highbrow journalistic circles. Dubbed "the New Journalists," writers like Tom Wolfe, Gay Talese, Norman Mailer, Joan Didion, Gloria Steinem, and others were turning out incendiary nonfiction riffs in magazines like *Rolling Stone, Harper's,* the *Atlantic Monthly,* and *New York,* and occasionally in *Esquire*, that ignored all the conventions of newspaper journalism. Their stories and essays were infused with their own perspectives—they often put themselves in the center—and featured artfully drawn characters, setting, action, and dialogue, and were often less concerned about facts than *feelings*. Every magazine was looking for the next great New Journalist, and every young writer with a yen to write true stories wanted to be it.

Herr rode into Hue on a convoy from Phu Bai—the pontoon bridge had at last reopened the road. He would later write that the mood in the truck where he sat with other marines was "like a locker room before a game that nobody wanted to play." [63] On the same truck was Dale Dye, the marine combat correspondent, returning for his second visit to the battle. Herr would describe Dye in his report "Hell Sucks."

"[He] sat with a tall yellow flower sticking out of his helmet cover, a really outstanding target. He was rolling his eyes around and saying, 'Oh yes, oh yes, Charlie's got his shit together here, this will be *bad*,' and smiling happily. It was the same smile I saw a week later when a sniper's bullet tore up a wall two inches above his head, odd cause for amusement in anyone but a grunt." [64]

To Dye, Herr seemed like a hippie.

In a letter to Hayes that day, Herr wrote:

> *The last ten days have been incredible. Even the most experienced correspondents here have been shattered by the offensive and, even more, by the insane American reaction to it . . . I have passed through so many decimated towns and cities that they get all mixed up in my mind. Here in Hué . . . the destruction has been incredible, air strikes knocking out whole blocks of the one really lovely city in Vietnam, destroying the university,* [65] *the walls around the Citadel and, probably tomorrow, the Citadel itself. Yesterday morning, in Cho Lon, I was riding on the left side of an armored jeep when a mortar round exploded ten yards away. I had my field pack slung over my shoulder and a four-inch piece of shrapnel burned into it, and another fragment hit the driver, blinding him in the left eye. [The Vietcong] fight at least as well in the cities as they do in the jungles, and I think they could, eventually, take Saigon. Right now, with about 1,500 men,* [66] *they have crippled the city, and no American with any power will admit it, will even give the Vietcong the respect they've earned by this offensive. Where we have not been smug, we have been hysterical, and we will pay for it.* [67]

As the journalists unloaded from the convoy, Colonel Adkisson complained, "Who the hell are all these civilians?"

"Media types," answered Captain George Smith, the information officer.

"Well, tell them to stay out of the way," the colonel said. "And get their names. I want to know who they all are and if they should be here."

Smith walked around with his notebook and got everyone to sign in.[68] Adkisson decreed that henceforth all journalists who arrived at the compound should be prepared to help defend it. They were to be issued weapons. As John Laurence wrote in his book *The Cat From Hue*, the captain handed a rifle to Dana Stone, one of the war's most celebrated photographers, and took him to a firing position at one end of the compound.

"[Smith] pointed out the window to the wall of a building about fifty yards away . . . and told him to aim for a powder burn the size of a frying pan on the wall. 'Let's see if you know how to hit anything,' he said. In one smooth movement, Stone flipped off the safety with his thumb, put the carbine to his shoulder, took aim and fired the clip at the wall, one quick shot after another. . . . All the shots hit the center of the powder burn."

The shots provoked a furious volley in response, which ended such demonstrations.[69]

8

The High Weirdness

On the same Saturday morning Cronkite was making his rounds, a big Sea Knight helicopter landed at the riverside LZ carrying two "four-deuces." These were much bigger mortars than those Colonel Cheatham's battalion had been using. The four-deuce was so named because its bore was 4.2 inches wide. It had a rifled barrel, which meant it was much more accurate than the smaller, smooth-bore mortars. The weapon weighed six hundred and fifty pounds, and could hurl a thirty-five pound shell four miles.

Each four-deuce came with a crew of six, so there were a dozen men who accompanied the two that morning. Among them was Ed Landry, a twenty-year-old marine from Lynn, Massachusetts, who kept a diary.

February 10th, Hue . . . The chopper skimmed the rice paddys weaving as it roared its way toward the city. What a ride! Better than any roller coaster you can imagine. We were getting shot at to boot. The door gunners answered back with their machine guns. The CH-46 suddenly zoomed up, did a half turn, and landed at a small LZ near a huge railroad bridge with its center laying in the water of the Perfume River. We piled out of the chopper as the machine-gun nearby banged away at a target across the river. Small arms fire greeted us as we hurriedly unloaded our guns.

Landry and the other members of his team,[70] along with their two big weapons, were driven by truck across Le Loi Street to the university. Landry was shocked to see the thousands of refugees living there, most crowded into the central courtyard. They were then taken to what would be their permanent position near the river's edge, a big pit that had been excavated beside the boat ramp. Before them was the impressive ruin of the Truong Tien Bridge, and beyond that were the towering walls of the Citadel. Black smoke rose from inside it. To their right was Hen Island. Their radio call sign was "Whiskey X-Ray." They were given space to bunk in a two-room stone house directly across the street from their firing position. It had a big hole in its red tile roof from an artillery round.

> *Artillery is impacting all around the area, mostly across the river . . . The city is shot to hell. Every building is burned or blown up. Bullet holes and shell holes mark every building . . . I have a bad feeling about this city. I don't think I will get out of here alive. I can't shake this feeling. This is a bad place. Death is all about us. I can feel him. That sounds crazy, but that's how it is. I want to get out of this place as fast as possible. Lets kill the bastards and leave! Airstrikes going on across the river as I write. An island to our right as you look across the Perfume River, is being pounded by mortars. The island is close and the sound of the explosions is very loud. Sniper rounds go by your head if you go outside. There are dead NVA in the streets and floating by on the river. The place smells of death.*

That first night they received a delivery of tear gas rounds, gray shells with red markings. With the steady glow of flares overhead, they did not even have to turn on the night lights around their position in order to see their aiming stakes. Landry had guard duty until shortly before midnight. He lay on his back and watched the illumination flares twist slowly down. The reverie ended when enemy soldiers who had crept out as far as they could on the bridge started shooting . . . *at him!*

> *Their machine guns opened up and the yellow tracers were flying. The marines on the LZ opened up with machine guns and*

*rifles and the red tracers of their guns were bouncing off the steel
bridge. The NVA started dropping mortars all over the place.
They make a high whistling sound as they fall. I got down on the
ground and watched the show. I couldn't fire as the boat ramp
was between me and the line of fire. While all this was going on,
up the river from behind the island came two small Navy boats
firing machine-guns at the bridge. They in turn started to draw
fire from the Citadel. Tracers were landing all around the boats
and around me! I crawled to the gun parapet, which we had made
out of ammo boxes filled with dirt, to get out of the line of fire
and watch the show. Suddenly, and I mean suddenly, the shooting
stopped. No firing, no sound. It was over that fast. The Navy boats
went back down the river.*

Whiskey X-Ray got its first fire mission that night.

*The 5th Marines were calling in a mission. We fired five or six
rounds into the Citadel for them. The guns make a loud noise when
they go off. The sound is magnified by the close proximity of the
houses around us. So passed the first night in Hue.*

The advantage in arms was gradually shifting to the Americans. They
now had two LZs and the secure boat ramp, and the pontoon bridge
had resumed traffic from Phu Bai, so the flow of men, weapons, and
ammo picked up pace. While there was no public about-face by the
MACV, the sheer volume of American men and armaments now flowing into the city was a tacit admission that its pronouncement about
Hue had been wrong. The enemy was present in very large numbers.
Gone was the assumption that the city could be retaken easily.

Downs's Fox Company occupied an apartment complex on the east
bank of the canal. As they settled in, Lieutenant Hausrath, the officer
with "Rat" written across the front of his helmet, arrived with reinforcements. He pulled the new and old men together to speak with
them but was interrupted. There were snipers across the river placing
accurate fire at their position. The lieutenant set to work as a spotter,
talking to the 81 mm mortar crew on the radio, trying to direct them
to where he saw muzzle flashes. He would go to the window and look

through his binoculars, then duck back to relay coordinates. As the mortars started to zero in, he grew excited. He was in the window, binoculars pressed to his eyes, when a round struck him square in the chest. It knocked him over backward, and he died fast. The round had pierced his heart.

"Hell, and I was just getting attached to him," said Tom "Bernie" Burnham, a corporal.

McCoy had warned him to stop, and the lieutenant had ignored him.

"Well, at least zip up your flak jacket!" McCoy had said.

Captain Downs took the news hard. He came to see Hausrath's body and then gathered together all the members of his third platoon. There were only twelve of the original fifty. Downs had tears in his eyes.

"You men have done fantastic," he said.

As the sweep continued, Hotel Company found Jim Bullington, the foreign service officer who had been hiding with two French priests. Several times Front cadres had come to the rectory door—Bullington was prepared to pretend he was a visiting Canadian priest—but they never entered. As Christmas's men were working their way south, getting help now from Phu Bai's artillery battery, the two-story rectory took a direct hit that blew off its upper floor. Bullington and the priests were hiding under the staircase and were unhurt. They heard American voices outside and Bullington joyfully called out to them. To avoid revealing to the priests' neighbors that they had been sheltering an American, he was wrapped in a blanket and carried out as if he were a wounded marine. The priests were offered a chance to leave, but opted to stay.

Peter Braestrup, a reporter for the *Washington Post*, interviewed Bullington not long after his escape. He described him as a "husky" man "in white shirt and dark slacks," who was disappointed by the setback the Tet Offensive had caused America's pacification efforts in the province.

"It was really showing progress in Quang Tri until this happened," Bullington said. He declined to discuss the details of his eleven days in hiding. He did not want to make those who helped him a target for reprisal.[71] He was flown to Da Nang, where he was debriefed on his experiences, in part by Ambassador Bunker himself. Bullington told the ambassador that the Frenchman who had saved his life, Albert Istvie, had had his office at the power plant and that of his boss vandalized and looted by marines, who took whiskey and money. Bunker cabled to General Cushman and demanded that the incident be investigated.[72] The rescued foreign service officer then began a determined effort to locate his fiancée, Tuy-Cam.

The same day Braestrup spoke to Bullington, he found Colonel Cheatham in a boastful mood.

"I must have a bunch of Chicago or Detroit gangsters," he said. "They are really good at street fighting."

The reporter also found Captain Christmas relaxing, smoking a cigar, and watching from an upstairs window as a group of his men blasted into a house with C4 explosive. There were few advantages to fighting in the city, but one of them was being able to find a roof or high balcony or window from which officers could clearly observe their men.

"It's a squad leader's war, this kind of fighting," Christmas said. Braestrup thought the captain looked bored, and walked with him as he went down to the street into the gray drizzle to confer with his lieutenant on the radio.

"You need more C4 to breach walls?" Christmas asked. "Can you go ahead without it? Okay, then go ahead. We'll try to get it up fast as possible."

Down the street a group of Vietnamese civilians appeared, and Christmas directed that they be taken back to the rear. One of the men, guarded by a "grimy marine," Braestrup reported, was wearing an ARVN uniform with pajamas underneath.

"Is he VC or what?" the marine asked the captain. "You never know."

"Treat him as a POW until we turn him over to battalion," said Christmas. "Let them handle it."

Christmas moved up the street to confer with his lieutenant personally. Some of the grunts were not happy about him being in the open.

"If the Skipper gets blown away, then we get left without our ruler," one of them complained to the reporter.[73]

With the reinforcements arriving daily came Lonny Connelly, a corpsman. He arrived on a harrowing flight that skimmed the waters of the Huong before pulling up and landing at the park LZ. At the compound he was introduced to a fellow corpsman.

"What unit is this?" Connelly asked.

"This is Second Platoon in Fox Company," the man said. He explained that he was on loan from Golf Company.

"Why?" Connelly asked.

"Because Fox lost three corpsmen already."

Now that Connelly was here, the veteran corpsman said he'd be going back to Golf. "They just lost another corpsman," he said.

Connelly stopped asking questions. The next morning, heading out with Second Platoon, the marines told him truthfully, if with a touch of cruelty, that corpsmen lasted on average just three days.

At that point Connelly began to retrace the series of missteps that had landed him in Hue. He had joined the navy specifically to avoid Vietnam. He had been a nineteen-year-old stock boy in a Baltimore grocery, saving to buy himself a car, when the draft board sent him a notice. Connelly figured that if he were drafted he'd probably end up in Vietnam, and since it was a land war, he'd be safe working on a ship. So he'd joined the navy, even though he had to sign on for twice as long.[74] At boot camp he was given a form to fill out that asked him to list his military job preferences. He liked to draw and paint, so he put down first the job that seemed closest to art: "photographer's aide." He had experience stocking shelves, so he next selected "storage" as a career choice. For his third preference he selected "yeoman," meaning office work—Connelly was a high school grad and imagined himself eventually going to college and studying business administration. There were five choices, so by the time he got to the last one he selected, since it was just a throwaway, "hospital corpsman" because his mother was a nurse, and he had occasionally helped out around the surgical center where she worked. He'd learned that he was not freaked out by the sight of blood, so if it came to that, he figured, a shipboard clinic job would do.

The ink had not dried on the page before his fate was sealed. Connelly didn't know it, but he had just bought an express ticket not just to Vietnam but to one of the most dangerous jobs there. The marines needed corpsmen at that point a lot more than the navy needed apprentice photographers, storage workers, or yeoman . . . or anything else for that matter. He did field training at Camp Lejeune, trained for six months at the Philadelphia Naval Hospital, and in short order was landing in Doc Lao Park.

Another of the newbies went to the squad led by Chris Brown, the marine who'd impressed his Brooklyn wife with his dancing. It was down to just two men, so the squad was presented with a spanking-new private from Brunson, South Carolina, named Wayne Crapse. Everything about the kid—he was just eighteen—was fresh: his fatigues, his helmet, his flak jacket, even his rifle. He had been in Vietnam for nine days; six months earlier he had been in high school. Brown didn't know where to begin.

"Look, just stay close to me," he said.

Two hours later they were moving in the middle of a column, passing through courtyards and houses, when a shot rang out and Crapse went down beside a row of low shrubs. He had been shot through the right temple. Blood was pooling rapidly on the pavement.

"Corpsman up!" Brown called as the shooting intensified.

Connelly responded. He had squatted behind a wall when the shooting started, so scared that he had to wrap his arms around his knees to keep them from shaking. But when called he went. He crouched beside Crapse, who was unconscious but still alive and breathing. Connelly knew that even with a bad head wound like this there was a chance. He felt completely exposed. He realized that the victim had been standing when hit, and since they were both now close to the ground, it calmed him a little. He and Brown dragged Crapse to a courtyard and Connelly went to work. It was the first time he had treated a wound in combat, and he felt like all eyes were on him. If he saved the man he would prove himself a good corpsman; if he lost him, a bad corpsman. He applied a field dressing to the hole in Crapse's temple and wrapped his head tightly to stanch the bleeding, then fumbled for a few moments trying to get an IV started. He handed a bottle of albumin to Brown. "You're the IV post, so hold this bottle," he said. Then he went back to work finding a vein, and finally succeeded. Crapse was still alive when he was carried off on a stretcher, which made Connelly feel good. He had done all he could. He felt he had showed that even with a bad wound like that, so long as he got there fast, the man had a chance. In Crapse's case, he lasted until he got to an operating table in Da Nang, where he died.

This would be the first of many wounded men for Connelly. After a few days his fatigues were so brown and stiff from being soaked with blood that they felt starched. Blood got into the stem of his watch and dried, killing it.

For the grunts, lacking an overview of the battle, each day resembled the last. They started moving in the morning, advancing on new streets and into new houses. Each day more of them fell. At night they gathered in a cleared house to rest. Booze was still plentiful. A few swallows of brandy or vodka or whiskey helped drive off the oppressing and constant chill and calm tattered nerves. Brown found a camera, and he and his buddies posed for pictures, looking very ragged and dirty. They smiled. He also found a microcassette tape recorder. He had a bigger recorder in his gear back at Phu Bai. He and his wife, Maddy, made tapes and sent them to each other every few days, but ever since he'd been parted from his gear he hadn't been able to do one. So he used this one to make a recording for her. When there was an explosion and machine-gun fire as he was talking, he quickly reassured her, "Oh, don't worry about that; it's away from me."

Connelly also made tapes for his mom and dad, for whom he did the opposite. His father wanted all the gory details. Connelly held up the microphone to capture the sounds, and, showing off his newfound battle savvy, offered a running commentary about which explosions came from which weapons. His buddy, Gordon Broadfoot, another corpsman, made a tape for his mother. As Brown did for his wife, Broadfoot did for his mother, constantly reassuring her that he was perfectly safe. Back home, he learned later, his mother was talking regularly on the phone to Connelly's mother, and the two had a hard time squaring the reports. Later Connelly's dad sent him a tape recording with "The Battle Hymn of the Republic," the "Marines' Hymn," and also the navy's "Anchors Aweigh." Some mornings he would get the platoon's radio operator to put his handset to the recorder and pipe out both songs.

Men slept sitting up against walls because the rooms were crowded and it was more comfortable than stretching out on a cold, hard floor. They tore curtains off the windows in finer homes and used them for blankets, until Captain Downs chewed them out for it—something that did not endear him to them. Platoons in different houses would check in with each other on a set schedule throughout the night, not by talking, but by clicking the radio handset. One platoon had a three-click sign, another four clicks. It was just to signal that they were okay.

No one talked much. There were none of the card games marines usually played in downtimes. They were too tired to concentrate, and poker was serious business.

They were numb, physically and emotionally, worn down by the constant need for vigilance—their lives depended on it—the fear; humping heavy weapons and ammo or dragging or carrying wounded men; the constant moving, stooping, crawling; the unending chill and drizzle of February in central Vietnam . . . They were all running on adrenaline, which cannot just be turned off. So even when they had silent hours and felt reasonably safe with their backs against a wall, most could not fully sleep. They would nod off with their head between their knees, a rifle in one hand and a grenade in the other. It was more like being temporarily *not awake* than sleep. The radiomen—company commanders had two, one for communicating to their platoon leaders, the other for talking with the battalion commander—would sleep sitting up, back to back. They would put their radios on "squelch," which meant there was a constant white noise of static that would be interrupted by a moment of silence whenever someone at either end pressed the button to say something. They slept so lightly that any break in that squelch, an instant of silence, was enough to wake them. At the slightest irregular sound a man's head would jerk upright and he would realize that for a few minutes he had almost been asleep.

Bill Ehrhart, whose short-time Playmate calendar was down to its last row of squares, had been driving the motley assortment of vehicles he had assembled back and forth from the compound for several days. Having survived a full year in Vietnam, even these terrible days racing through gunfire in the streets of Hue, he had begun to surrender a little to wishful thinking—to allow for the possibility that he would survive. The battalion command post had moved out about two blocks west of the compound and set up in an abandoned, grand, three-story residence. There they found warm beer in the kitchen, brown bottles with yellow labels featuring a drawing of a tiger, which they duly dubbed "Tiger Piss." Ehrhart was relaxing in a large overstuffed chair in a second-floor bedroom with his buddy Kazunori "Kenny" Takenaga, a Japanese national serving in the US Marines. They had been assigned security, helping to keep watch out of a barred window at a row of enemy-occupied houses across the street. Gravel had ordered a

Zippo up to burn it. While they waited for the tank to arrive, Ehrhart had pulled the chair over to the window and pointed his rifle out. He pulled the trigger now and then when he caught a glimpse of someone moving. Takenaga sat on the bed cleaning his rifle.

At some point, Ehrhart got lazy. He got so relaxed that he stopped looking out the window and went to work instead boiling water in a can for a cup of instant coffee. Then he found himself face-first on the floor. It felt like something had taken off the back of his head. *This is really bad.* He reached up to feel it . . . and his head was intact! He had expected to feel blood and brains. He got up on his knees and only then noticed that he was bleeding from a number of other places. A rocket had come through the bars of the open window and passed between the back of his head and the wall behind him, missing him by inches. The explosion had thrown him forward, blown both of his eardrums—he would be stone deaf for weeks—and so walloped the back of his head that it dented his helmet: the metal had such a crater in back that it no longer fitted on his head. The blast destroyed the chair he was sitting in and peppered his flak jacket with metal, concrete, and wood. He had cuts on his right arm and right leg and in the right small of his back, beneath the jacket. Takenaga, who had not been wearing his helmet or jacket, was far more seriously wounded. His right arm was nearly severed, and he had a huge cut on his head.

They could never let up, and forgetting that could be fatal. Men retreated into themselves. They were reluctant to form strong ties or even rag on each other. The portent of every exchange made it hard to converse. When you are mindful that every word might be your last, or that the man next to you might be gone in the next moment, banter becomes difficult. And, increasingly, they did not really know each other. The constant toll of death and injury, in addition to the policy of rotating marines out promptly when their thirteen months were up, meant that squads were always changing. There was no such thing as unit cohesion. Each marine had the friends he'd made before the battle started, and having them close was a comfort but also a worry. Most had seen friends killed or badly wounded and carried off to an uncertain fate. All had had close calls. They lived in what combat correspondent Dale Dye would later call "the high weirdness of survival when the odds say you should be stone dead."[75] On some nights a man would say something like, *I'm not going to make it out of here alive,* and if he was then killed the statement would be remembered with awe, as if he had foretold his own death, but the odds were such that there was no prescience in it. In Hue you did not have to be a pessimist to believe something bad was going to happen. It was likely.

They were all sick of seeing men die. The day after Hausrath was killed, Allbritton spotted a high-ranking officer walking down the middle of a street with a battalion sergeant major. They seemed to think the area was much safer than it was.

"Get your butts out of there!" shouted the twenty-year-old Arkansas corporal, trying to deepen his voice to sound more authoritative. "I don't want to get my men killed dragging your bodies off the street!"

The two men hustled for cover, and Allbritton bolted—he didn't want them to see who had chastised them. But he'd been right.

Allbritton got new fatigues on Sunday, trading in the stinking rags that hung on him. A shower was rigged from a water tanker and they got to scrub off the accumulated layer of sweat and dirt and blood and plaster dust. His new fatigues were three sizes too big, but they were clean. A Gillette razor was passed from man to man until it got to him. He shaved off two weeks' growth. In his new oversize fatigues and shaved face, he was transformed. One of the newer men in the platoon pointed him out and asked, "Who's the newbie?"

"That's Corporal Arkie," one of the veterans said, and explained that Allbritton had been fighting with them for weeks.

"My gosh, he looks so young and angelic!"[76]

No matter who died, there was no time or energy to grieve. This haunted them. There was also something shameful about violent, shattering death. It wasn't rational. How you were killed was rarely your fault, but part of the horror was the humiliating display—bodies ruptured, insides horribly spilled. No matter how dignified or admired or liked a man had been in life, here he was, very suddenly and publicly dead, sometimes left in some ridiculous splayed posture or missing a part. One moment you were an inspiring leader, like Sergeant Alfredo Gonzalez, and the next you were nothing more than dismembered, bleeding remains. And while each death would echo loudly halfway around the world, hurling families and even whole communities into grief, often with shattering consequences for generations, in Hue there wasn't even time to stop and look, much less grieve. The body was reassembled and recomposed by corpsmen, covered, and removed. One less cold, wet, scared marine. There was no such efficient removal of the Vietnamese dead. There wasn't time to even bury them all properly. The men were instructed to just cover the corpes' heads with dirt to stave off the flies and vermin.[77]

Many men felt misled. Resentment percolated quietly. Their leaders— the officers, not the gunny sergeants and squad leaders who stood with them side by side—were relentless. They would issue orders for the grunts to move forward into danger, and when they emerged intact, feeling that they had narrowly escaped a terrible fate, they were ordered to do it again, and again, and again. You could press your luck like that for only so long. As their numbers were whittled down, they came to feel that more was being asked of them than ever should be asked of anyone. Why weren't they rotated out? Why was it always them? Was it because their officers were glory-seekers, looking for medals and promotions? They noticed that the officers were never the ones out front. Were they dying and bleeding to further these men's careers?

Corpsman Connelly found himself a target for men trying to escape. There was hardly a man who hadn't been wounded once or twice. The story circulated about a visiting honcho making the rounds of the wounded at the compound, stopping to ask a grunt how many times he'd been hit. The man answered, "You mean today?" The perfect wound was one that was not mortal, debilitating, or disfiguring, but that was bad enough to get you out. Some looked bad and hurt plenty and even bled a lot until they were cleaned and bandaged. It would fall to Connelly then to shatter the hopeful look on a marine's face with "You're good to go," which meant, *No ticket home this time.* Everyone came to him with even the smallest scratch, to document it, because three wounds meant three Purple Hearts, which meant you would be taken off the firing line. It was not uncommon for men to reach their hands up from cover during a mortar barrage, hoping to catch a piece of shrapnel. The corpsman was the one who kept score.

Some were shameless.

"Hey, Doc, look how swollen my knee is," said one who came to him. "I have water on my knees. I can't squat down, I can't crawl, I can't run down the street anymore."

Connelly sympathized. He wanted out himself. But he had the man stretch out his leg, and then palpated his kneecap with two fingers. If there had been fluid in the joint, he would have felt resistance. He did not.

"No," he said. "No fluid. You're good to go."

Connelly's platoon leader insisted that he personally examine every man slated for evacuation.

Men learned firsthand how to gauge the severity and type of wounds. Shrapnel burned. It was hot metal. If you were hit by shrapnel it felt like someone touching you with fire. With a bullet the first thing you felt, after the shocking impact but before the pain, was wetness. Shrapnel cauterized the wound instantly, but bullets made you bleed. You tried not to think too hard about it. Thinking about it was tempting fate. And fear? Fear was just the air you breathed.

Most kept going. The sun would rise and they would form up and wait to be told to run across another street, climb through another wall, barge through another door, knowing each time it might be their turn to pay the price. Art Marcotte, a private from Boston, would feel sick to his stomach with fear when he was ordered to step out into a street or run across a courtyard under fire. But he went.

Hygiene was a memory. Since many had been plucked from the field and sent directly to Hue, they had not washed in weeks. At night they shared a toothbrush. All of the men gave off a pungent odor. One of Connelly's jobs as corpsman was to find a safe spot to dig a latrine, a trench. He would find a chair and knock the seat out of it to serve as a commode. One day in his second week Fox Company passed through a wastewater treatment facility near the canal. It had large circular vats made of concrete divided into reeking pie-shaped segments where human waste settled out before the water was drained off for the next step in its purification. A rocket blast knocked three marines into one of them, and because they were loaded with gear, there was a danger they might drown. Connelly and another corpsman had to plunge in to pull them out. They hadn't thought it possible for men to smell worse, but after that, they did.

In the middle of everything were the tankers. They called themselves the Bandits. They were H&S Company, Third Tank Battalion, and were in Hue by accident. The unit consisted of the four Pattons, two gun tanks, and two Zippos that had been en route to the boat ramp in Hue when the offensive began. They had been co-opted by the marines into the fight, and were too valuable to lose. They were always getting hit and damaged and losing crew members. Only one had been killed so far—Bobby Hall—but over the course of the battle, three-fourths of them would be wounded. Charlie West, a Zippo tank commander, was so sure he would be killed that he wrote a letter to his wife telling her to go ahead and find another man. The crews changed but the battered tanks kept coming back out for more.

The Bandits mostly stayed to themselves, sleeping in the compound at night when they could; repairing, refueling, and reloading their machines; and drinking . . . for the most part in moderation. There was plenty of booze, lifted from stores and homes, but it was too dangerous to drive out into the city drunk. Marijuana was different. Few of the tankers smoked, but those who did found that the tank was a perfect smoking chamber, sealed up tight. Sometimes you could see vapor rising from the vents. The inside of the tanks smelled terrible, every kind of human odor mixed with diesel and cordite and exhaust and dope, but it didn't smell bad enough for them to prefer being outside.

After the rare occasions when the Zippos were allowed to spray flame—or they did so unauthorized—their crews would cook up napalm in big steel drums, sprinkling Styrofoam flakes into gasoline, and then reload their pressurized tanks. They were on call. As soon as they rolled out of the compound, they were the most popular targets on the street.

Ray Smith, the Alpha Company commander, thought the tankers' attitude was cowardly. For the first few days, he could not get Sergeant Dailey to even open the turret hatch of his gun tank. Smith would climb up, knock, and shout in to him, but the hatch stayed closed. Dailey had earlier blown the top off a church steeple without permission, so he wasn't timid when properly motivated. But it seemed to Smith that every time he wanted the gun tank to blast something now, the buttoned-up sergeant would send an Ontos to do the job instead. He was thinking about citing Dailey for cowardice. But then he saw a change. The lieutenant attributed it to whiskey and, indeed, Dailey had managed to obtain an ample supply of Cutty Sark. Smith never saw him drunk, but after the whiskey showed up, for the remainder of his time in Hue, Dailey was never completely sober either. Thus fueled, he became bold.

Locked in a firefight at the soccer stadium, Smith's men were pinned down by fire from a gas station. He called for tank support, and two tanks came forward, Dailey's and the Zippo commanded by West. Placing his tank between the gas station and Smith's downed marines, West turned it sideways to protect them. As he did so the tank was hammered by small-arms fire, machine guns, and rockets. The Front had been preparing for this fight for weeks. They had dug trenches right through the pavement, deep enough so that when they stood only the tops of their heads were above ground level. The tankers did not like to drive over the trenches because the enemy could thrust a grenade or satchel bomb into their treads. Rounds pinged and rang and boomed off West's tank like a fired-up timpani section. When a wounded enemy soldier before them on the street trained his rocket launcher toward the tank's more vulnerable rear, West tried to back over him. In the heat of that effort he opened the top hatch halfway and poked out his head to better direct his driver, and a bullet caught him. It had come from a rifleman on a roof or upper-story window, because the shot angled downward, entering his side and exiting his back. West crawled out and lay on the rear of the tank, still wearing his helmet with its radio connection and trying to steer it with voice commands, when the wounded enemy put a rocket through its armor. Marines killed the man. The Zippo caught fire. It got off one more round before the rest of the crew bailed. They dragged West off with them as the tank and then the gas station erupted. Flames shot high into the air with machine-gun rounds popping off like a top-dollar fireworks display. It burned for several days.[78]

After that the Bandits were down to just three tanks. Carl Fleischmann and the entire crew of the remaining Zippo were wounded the next day by a mortar when they risked getting out in the city to load ammo. Fleischmann was cut in the face and the right leg. After he was treated, he went back to his tank to spend the night. His three crew members were evacuated, and the next morning he and the other remaining tanks drove back to the compound to pick up replacements.

There was a batch of newbies there, among them John Wear, a skinny three-year veteran with glasses who was assigned to be gunner on a

tank driven by a diminutive Jewish lance corporal from Texas whom
everyone called "Scooby." He'd gotten the nickname after receiving a
Dear John letter from his girlfriend, who said she had begun seeing
someone she called "Scooby." After that, of course, the hapless corporal had a new nickname.[79] Wear, a full corporal, slightly outranked
Scooby and had logged more time in tanks, but Scooby had been, as
they say, "eating the elephant's ear," meaning he knew the ropes in
Hue. So Wear swallowed his pride and assumed the subordinate role.

After the wild chopper ride he'd had in that morning, he was just
glad to be on the ground and alive. Its evasive maneuvers had left him
shaking. When he jumped off, down by the boat ramp, there had been
a mortar barrage and a lot of shooting. As he ran across Le Loi Street
toward the compound he blundered into the path of a marine calmly
firing a heavy machine gun—sheer luck alone preserved him. To Wear,
Hue seemed like bedlam, with workers at the boat ramp racing around
on forklifts through the barrage, loading and unloading, marines firing
steadily across the river, and civilians moving in the streets begging for
food. *Man, this is real. I'm not watching this on the news!*

The newbies were not handled with care. One of them, Al Esquivel,
was Mexican American but he had grown up in Texas and could not
speak Spanish, while Wear, who was unmistakably Caucasian, had
grown up in Colorado around Spanish-speakers, and could *habla español*
reasonably well, so poor Esquivel was razzed mercilessly by the other
Hispanic marines—"*Ey, ese cuatro ojos* can speak Spanish better than
you; you're *desgraciado!*" The Bandits also took perverse pleasure in
frightening the new guys. They were shown the Zippo tank that had
been destroyed just days earlier.

The husk of West's tank was scary. It was black and had two big
rocket holes in it. They were also shown the mask Bobby Hall had been
wearing when the explosion tore off his face. Inside were clumps of
hair and dried scalp and blood.

"Don't be surprised," warned Lieutenant Jim Georgaklis, their platoon leader. "You're going to take RPGs and all kinds of weapons fire
from either side as you go down the streets. Be careful."

On their first night, someone—an ARVN soldier was blamed—threw
a can of gasoline on some Front prisoners in a pen at one end of the
compound and then set them on fire. It was a ghastly scene, and with

large pallets of ammo nearby, potentially an even worse disaster. There was a general panic as the tankers—it took two of them to lift a single box—had to run all of their ammo to the other end of the compound.

Wear and Scooby's tank had a slogan painted on the barrel of their flame gun, *Anh yeu em*, or "I Love You." They spent their days rolling out to lead marine advances, then driving back with the wounded and dead draped on top. They would get a call, and Georgaklis would shout, "Tankers, mount up!" He led them out in a Jeep, driving straight into gunfights. His uncle had been a highly decorated marine, and the men were convinced Georgaklis was trying to outdo him. Already he had been awarded two Purple Hearts. Sometimes he would mount the back of a tank and ride into a scrape that way.

The rules of engagement governing the use of the tank's big guns were still in place, and still resented. The gunner had to ask the tank commander, who in turn had to radio his commander back at the compound seeking permission. When this was first explained to Esquivel, he said, "You're shitting me, right?"

He really did think it was part of the general razzing. But then on a mission into the city he was looking through the periscope when a tree directly in front of them exploded. He could see where the shot had come from, a window in a building straight ahead. There was a large enemy weapon in that window, either a recoilless rifle or a rocket launcher. He started shouting to his commander, Sergeant Dailey, for permission to fire.

"Wait, I've got to call this in first," Dailey said.

You are out of your mind, thought Esquivel.

Permission came back rapidly. "Yeah, you can go ahead and fire," said Dailey.

Before he had finished the sentence Esquivel put an explosive round in the window, turning it into a large hole. Half of the building's front was missing.

In battle, the rule was often forgotten . . . deliberately. On Wear's first ride out, he was scanning the street by slowly panning his periscope from side to side. Scooby was in the cupola above, so he had a wider and better view.

"Wear, bring it over to the left," Scooby said urgently. "There are gooks."

Wear started to rotate the turret.

"Shoot them! Shoot them!" shouted Scooby. He had an override on the turret controls so he turned it to face the enemy soldiers. Through the periscope Wear could only see black shapes and the sparkles of their muzzle flashes, but he clearly heard the *bing! bing! bing!* of rounds hitting the outside of the tank. So he let loose a stream of napalm. They caught hell for that—the commanders were worried about setting the city on fire—and afterward their tank had to stay empty. They became just a machine-gun platform and a rolling cover for marines on the street. They did a lot of "cleanup duty," meaning they would arrive immediately after a gunfight, and the grunts would hand up the wounded and dead. Wear would get out to help haul them aboard and would ride back with them on the outside, keeping them from rolling or bouncing off. He'd finish those rides soaked in blood. He learned that gaping wounds were often fetid.

It took a few days of overindulgence for Wear to get used to the nighttime drinking. He and his crewmate, Brad Goodin, got sick, with vomiting and diarrhea. They learned to pace themselves.

At an ARVN armory, Fleischmann's crew found a stash of Thompson submachine guns and .38 revolvers. They scooped up as many as they could carry, thinking they might trade them, but ended up handing them out to any marine who wanted one. Fleischmann, who had been in Hue from the beginning, picked a nifty rifle with a grenade launcher attached, which was his favorite weapon until a gunny sergeant saw him with it.

All he said was, "Time to give that up."

One day they robbed a bank. Carl Fleischmann's Zippo was sitting outside a Bank of Hue branch and, seeing it was abandoned, he decided to see what was inside. It was clear they were not the first ones with the idea. Grunts had tried blowing open the steel door with grenades and C4, to no avail. The Zippo crew asked one of the gun tanks to shoot, and with a single high-explosive round it blew open not just the door but the whole side of the building. Money floated down, lots of it, dollars and dongs. They filled six duffel bags. Grunts showed up and started grabbing everything they could carry. Later, at the battalion aid station in Phu Bai, the medical staff were shocked to find wounded men with their pockets and packs jammed with cash.

An army officer put a scare into them before they got away with the loot. The crews, most of them teenagers, were warned that they could be charged with looting and imprisoned. He confiscated their duffel bags—all but one which they managed to hide. It was filled mostly with dongs. They took a picture of the officer in front of the destroyed bank building before he made off with the others.

They laughed about it later. *Hey, we knocked off a bank and didn't get a penny out of it!*

They would wonder for a long time about who that army officer was.

9

Like Men Who
Fell Out of the Sky

THE FIGHT THAT took back the soccer stadium was not one of the major ones in the battle. Most of the battalion defending it had departed in the face of the marines' buildup. One of those who remained behind was Che Thi Mung.

It had been a hard ten days for the village girl who had helped spy in the city as part of the Huong River Squad. For the first week, she and the other girls were kept out of the fighting. They carried the wounded to medical stations and delivered food and supplies. But as the counterattack intensified, and losses mounted, they had joined the fight.

The squad was divided in three. One went to fight at Dap Da, across the Nhu Y River just east of the triangle. Another fought in the Cong Market, which was on the west bank of the Nhu. With this group was Hoang Thi No, one of the girls from Che's village. The third group, Che's, was sent to the soccer stadium. At first she was given an old M-1 carbine. Pham Thi Lien, their squad leader, had a rocket launcher. Eventually Che was given an AK-47.

The Front had been preparing for this fight for weeks. They had dug trenches right through the pavement, deep enough so that when they stood only the tops of their heads were above ground level. The main intersections around the stadium were cut with them.

The trenches in which Che fought were L-shaped, which gave fighters a place to retreat if American guns zeroed in on them. Dressed in VC black pajamas, she lived in them for days at a time, helping to turn back American probes with tanks and infantry. She had a wet cloth to cover her face when tear gas was used, but it was only partly effective. When there was no water to wet the rags, the fighters grew so desperate that they urinated on them. She gagged and her eyes and sinuses stung terribly. There was a terrible smell of burning buildings and flesh in the air.

Che spoke no English, but she had been warned that when she heard the Americans shout "VeeCee," it meant they needed to move fast, they had been spotted. She exchanged fire with the marines but never took careful aim. There were too many of them coming. When she used the rifle, she would just spray fire in the general direction of the enemy. After one skirmish she recovered a newer, more lightweight American rifle, an AR-15, which she preferred. Teams of the young people brought her ammo for it, looted from ARVN depots.

Whenever Lien fired her B-40 they would immediately run to a different trench, because it gave away their location and drew a hail of return fire. It took seven seconds for the launched grenade to explode. For some kinds of grenades it was only three seconds. For days they shot and ran, shot and ran. They moved so fast they rarely had a chance to see if they hit anything.

At the nearby Cong Market, her friend Hoang Thi No was engaged in a similar running street fight. She found the marines easy targets, because they were big and because they did not move confidently in the streets the way she and her team members could. She was very familiar with the blocks where she fought, so she knew which way to run when the shooting came close. To her, the Americans with all their heavy equipment were like men who had fallen from the sky to a strange planet. She picked them off individually, and when she found them in a group, she and her comrades threw grenades. The carnage she saw around her did not so much frighten as enrage her. Hoang resolved to fight to the death. She expected she would be wounded or killed because so many others had been. She didn't think about it. She just fought. She was seventeen and excited and filled with pride and she did not tire easily. At night she and the others in her squad took turns sleeping for an hour or two. Four of those in her group were killed before they were finally ordered to withdraw to the forest and regroup.[80]

Hoang's team lasted longer than Che's, which was in the path of Lieutenant Smith's company. It held its own until the air and artillery bombardments started, which were unlike anything the girls had ever experienced.

On Friday morning, February 9, a Vietnamese man in civilian clothes made a dash toward the marines' line. He was very lucky not to have been shot. He asked to see Smith and then explained that he was a major in the ARVN, an operations officer for General Truong, and he had been trapped in a bunker under his house ever since the first night of the offensive. The Front had moved into his house and had been using it as a battalion headquarters. He urged Smith to call in an attack on his own house.

"We can't do that," Smith told him, and explained the reluctance to employ big guns in the city.

The ARVN major was incensed.

"Can you get me back in touch with my command?" he asked.

He was escorted back to the compound, where he spoke directly to Truong. Within the hour, he had secured permission. What ensued would be first major air and artillery barrage in southern Hue— afterward, getting permission eased across the board. Fighter bombers hit the ARVN major's house and neighborhood, and an unholy torrent of artillery shells descended shortly thereafter. More than seven hundred howitzer rounds—eight-inch and 155-mm—were fired from Phu Bai, everything they had.[81]

Just one of those bigger 155-mm rounds could tear a crater four feet deep and thirteen feet wide. Trenches collapsed. Che ran with the others to take shelter behind a wall, but then the houses and walls crumbled, too. There was no place to hide. Che at first could tell by the sound of an approaching shell whether it would land close or fall short or pass overhead, but then one landed so close that it deafened her. For long afterward she could hear only a ringing in her head. All she could do was hide and try to make herself small and hope. Those that landed close shook the earth and hit her like a punch to the gut. They left her dazed. The people in the neighborhood hid in underground shelters beneath their homes—during the worst of the fighting they lived in them around the clock—but a direct hit would collapse the shelter and kill those inside, sometimes burying them alive. Many people died this way. Che was so shaken and disoriented by the shelling that she had to be evacuated for several days to recover. Then she returned.

They held on at the stadium for four days. The neighborhood people who had brought them rice balls and water no longer came. They either were dead or had run away. By Monday, February 12, Che and Lien and the others were isolated and starving. They had no way of knowing what was happening elsewhere. They had received no order to retreat, so they stayed.

The shells kept coming, and the marines followed. Two of the girls in Che's group, friends she had grown up with, were killed at twilight when a shell exploded over their trench. One's head was partly taken off. The other had her body torn into two pieces, her torso crashing into another fighter and wounding him. It was dark when Che got hit. She was down in the trench when a rocket exploded near her. Initially she felt only slight pain, mostly a strange, sudden half consciousness. When she reached up to her shoulder she saw that she was bleeding. She had been hit in the head, arm, and upper back.

Che's wounds were dressed and she was moved to a medical clinic and then after a week to a camp in the forest. She was in pain and sad, sad for the loss of her friends—six of the original eleven girls in her squad were killed—and sad for all the death and destruction in the city. It felt like a defeat. Che had entered the battle with the highest of hopes, but now the more seasoned soldiers told her that they had done better than they imagined they could. It was not cheering.

So many had been killed. As far as Che could tell, the hopeful Front forces she had helped guide into the city on the night of the attack had been mauled. Civilian losses were far greater than she had believed possible.

It was almost painful to remember the excitement she had felt racing barefoot through the dark fields on the eve of Tet.

10

War Is Hell

ONE NIGHT AS the campaign to clear the triangle wound down, the three remaining tanks parked at the soccer stadium. There was a wide track around the field, so the two gun tanks raced the remaining Zippos. It was like watching the Indy 500 in slow motion. The gun tanks won.

With the triangle increasingly secure and the fight for the Citadel looming, the Bandits feared they would be sent north to continue the fight. They had come through a harrowing ordeal, and dreaded another like it. On Sunday, February 13, they were ordered to report to the boat ramp, but before departing they learned to their enormous relief that another tank platoon would be taking over. They were leaving the city.

Putting the tanks on the Mike Boat was difficult; they had to back them on. Mortars, as usual, were falling. An officer ordered them to get off and help guide from the outside, so Scooby and Goodin stepped out. They were immediately knocked down by a mortar blast. Both were flown to Phu Bai. Scooby was severely wounded.

In the nearby four-deuce mortar pit by the river, crewman and diarist Ed Landry could hear shooting and explosions from inside the giant fortress across the river and sometimes see flashes of gunfire from positions on top of its great black stone walls. Landry had lost some of the fright of his first nights and become more discerning about being shot at. On Monday he wrote:

> *Hue City is constant noise. Rifles and artillery are going off or*
> *impacting almost constantly. Airstrikes in the distance across the*

river have been going on since we got here. The snipers across the Perfume are still active. We have learned an old trick that I read about, that the Marines used in the Pacific during World War II. When a sniper's bullet comes close, don't duck! That way he will keep his aim over you and miss. When he is way high over your head, then duck! That way he will keep his aim over you and miss. These random shots at us from across the river are just a form of harassment. It is a good 500 yard shot between the far side and our position.

We are digging in the gun with sandbags and building fighting holes near the guns. Today we cleaned out the house we are staying in. The place was ransacked . . .

After two weeks of fighting, Art Marcotte, one of Fox Company's grunts, amazed to still be alive and uninjured, found a typewriter in a building his platoon occupied and banged out a letter to his sister Katy in Michigan on stationery he had taken from Hue University.

. . . War is hell. As you can probably see I can't type too good. I've been sitting here for two days trying to learn. How is everybody? I hope you are all fine. I'm doing okay. Have you been reading anything in the paper about Hue? It is supposed to be big news in the states. Well that's where I am. It is supposed to be some of the worst fighting that has been fought in the war. If it isn't it will be plenty for me. I can't really say how bad it has been. We've lost a hell of a lot of people. . . . This house to house fighting is a son of a bitch. I've never been so scared in all my life.

Most of the triangle was in ruins. The dead were everywhere. Bloated bodies floated down the Huong River under the destroyed Truong Tien Bridge. Marines began uncovering mass graves. Dale Dye, the combat correspondent, was drawn to one by the unbearable stench. He stood over a large pit containing hundreds of bodies, all jumbled together. They had been buried beneath a thin covering of dirt, and now the stench was nauseating.

Hundreds of Vietnamese civilians, handkerchiefs pressed to their faces, were picking through the remains, looking for loved ones, occasionally crying out in horror or grief. Some of the dead were found with their hands bound behind their backs, with a bullet hole in the head. These were clearly victims of the purges, which had continued up until the marines chased the "liberators" from the neighborhood. But some, too, were probably victims of the intense artillery bombardments like the one experienced by Che Thi Mung. Some had no doubt been caught in the crossfire, or were shot out of fear, or anger, or boredom, or hatred of the natives—gooks—or maybe out of sheer meanness.

Dealing with all these bodies had been too big a challenge for the Front, which in the days before being driven out had taken to bulldozing them into common pits. There was plenty of blame to go around for all this killing, and neither side had the time or the means to sort it out.

And worse was in store.

PART SIX

Taking Back
the Citadel

Sunday–Sunday
February 11–February 25

After nearly two weeks of intense combat, most of the southern Hue triangle has been retaken. The army is preparing to attack the Front's command center at La Chu northwest of the city. The "liberation forces" still hold most of the Citadel, where ARVN troops have been unable to advance. That effort is about to be joined by a battalion of US Marines, under the command of Major Bob Thompson.

Walter Cronkite (center rear holding microphone) interviewing Col. Stan Hughes on the CBS anchorman's reporting trip to Hue during the battle.

Marine Major Bob Thompson, who was given the mission of taking back the Citadel with his battalion, 1/5.

Steve "Storyteller" Berntson, the marine combat correspondent, wrote stories that ran in *Stars and Stripes* and other military publications.

Marines assaulting the Dong Ba Tower on February 15, 1968.

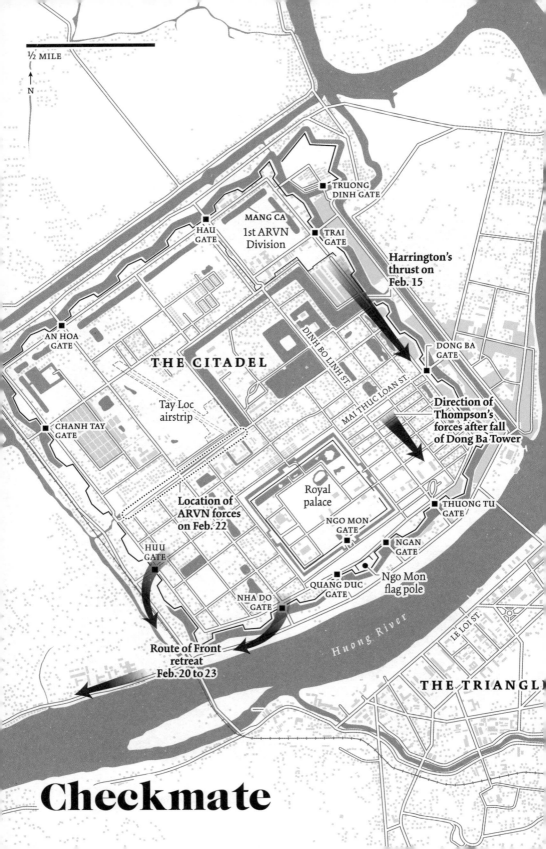

½ MILE

N

TRUONG
DINH GATE

HAU
GATE

MANG CA
1st ARVN
Division

TRAI
GATE

Harrington's
thrust on
Feb. 15

AN HOA
GATE

THE CITADEL

DINH BO LINH ST.

DONG BA
GATE

Tay Loc
airstrip

MAI THUC LOAN ST.

Direction of
Thompson's
forces after fall
of Dong Ba Tower

CHANH TAY
GATE

Location of
ARVN forces
on Feb. 22

Royal
palace

THUONG TU
GATE

NGO MON
GATE

NGAN
GATE

HUU
GATE

QUANG DUC
GATE

Ngo Mon
flag pole

NHA DO
GATE

Route of Front
retreat
Feb. 20 to 23

Huong River

LE LOI ST.

THE TRIANGL

Checkmate

1

Clusterfucked

MAJOR BOB THOMPSON got his first glimpse of the Citadel on Sunday, February 11, from the south bank of the Huong River. It looked fearsome. Taking it back was now his job.

There had been fighting inside the Citadel since day one. The Front had owned most of it now for twelve days, setting up a revolutionary government, rounding up enemies of the people, recruiting fighters, digging trenches, and erecting barricades. They were fully prepared to hold it, and this was a structure designed for defense. Surrounded by a wide moat, it could be entered only across the narrow bridges that led to its eleven gates. Above most were stone towers from which guns could completely cover any approach. Thompson's way in would have to be through one of the four northern gates controlled by General Ngo Quang Truong. During World War II, when the city was occupied by Japan, the occupying army had honeycombed the wide expanse at the top of the walls with foxholes, trenches, and tunnels. From that height, the enemy could observe any movement of men and vehicles inside and out, and rain ruinous fire. Rooting them out would be nasty work. Below, in the tight grid of its streets, lived more than half of the city's population in row after row of one- and two-story homes. Most were surrounded by stone walls or fences and were planted inside and out with trees and vegetation, so in most places the farthest you could see in any direction was about ten yards. At the south center there was, of course, the historic royal palace and its grounds, a protected area surrounded by its own high stone walls, from behind which the enemy could launch rockets and mortars with impunity, at least for now—Thompson would be barred from shelling or bombing it. As he pondered the layout of his objective and the time the enemy had had to prepare, he realized that his men would face hundreds of naturally camouflaged, mutually supporting, well-fortified gun positions. There were also several four- and five-story buildings inside that would have gun positions on the upper floors and rooftops. As of yet, there was no chance of waiting or starving the enemy out, because his supply lines were still intact. The army was stalled in the countryside. Still flying from the monumental platform in front was the galling red-and-blue-striped Alliance flag, with its defiant yellow star. Hanoi still owned the old city.

The imagery was potent. The flag announced Hanoi's claim, not just to the Citadel but to the city of Hue and, in a sense, to all of Vietnam. The Front professed to be the only authentic nationalists in the field, so the tricolor flag, which they had taken pains to make different from their own or the VC's, promised a Vietnam for all Vietnamese—*our* fortress, *our* royal city, *our* country. And the fact that it was going to take a foreign army to dislodge them proved their point. The battle was all too real, but it was also theater, as surely as the plays enacted by the Front's traveling propaganda troupes. Hue was a metaphor for the whole struggle.

A key part of this narrative was the undeniable inadequacy of the ARVN. General Truong's men had fought bravely to retain their hold on Mang Ca and had, at great cost, taken back almost a third of the Citadel. Truong held several blocks immediately south of Mang Ca and had pushed out along the north side all the way to the west wall, taking back both gates in the northwest corner. His force had fought down the west side to retake the airstrip at Tay Loc but then had lost it again after an enemy counterattack. The most densely populated part of the fortress, its southern half, was still owned completely by the Front, and Truong, having lost much of his force, lacked the strength to drive them out. Even the fierce Hac Bao unit, now reunited with its marine adviser, Jim Coolican, was down to only a fraction of its men. No matter how sincere the ARVN forces were about defending a separate, free South Vietnam, and no matter how few of the residents of Hue had rallied to the Communist cause, AVRN was no military match for the Front. Taking the fortress back required American help, and Truong had asked for it repeatedly.

The recovery effort had fallen to Thompson, a tall, slender, extremely fit[1] thirty-seven-year-old career marine officer from Mississippi. He had majored in physical education at Union University near his hometown of Corinth before enlisting. Unlike Cheatham, the giant who had steered the thrust in southern Hue, Thompson had nothing flamboyant about him. He was a serious man who had proved he was good at moving large numbers of men and vehicles and supplies efficiently, a worthy skill, but he had no claim to talent in combat and lacked utterly the bluster and presence that often marked such men. Thompson had an advanced degree in public administration from Pennsylvania State University, and for his first six months in Vietnam he had been an embarkation officer, a glorified cargo supervisor, for the Third Marine Amphibious Force in Da Nang. But he had been given command of First Battalion, Fifth Marines the day after the Tet Offensive started. Thompson had flown to battalion headquarters at Phu Loc that day and landed in a mortar barrage. He spent his first fifteen minutes in command with his luggage at the bottom of a muddy hole with several marines lying on top of him.

He had flown to Phu Bai with three of his companies that Sunday, February 11; there, he was briefed by the commanding general. LaHue told him that General Truong was useless. He had "circled the wagons" on the north side of the fortress and "was just holding on to his ass." No consideration was given to Truong's disadvantages. The South Vietnamese general was the victim of the same surprise that had left the MACV compound stranded and the marines at such a disadvantage, and against very large odds he had held on and expanded his position. LaHue was not impressed. Thompson's point of entry would be the Hau Gate on the east side of the north wall, which opened into Mang Ca. To get there he would have to put his men on Mike Boats (landing craft mechanized, or LCMs) at the boat ramp on the south bank of the Huong and move upriver—the same route that Gene Roberts had taken days before. Anything that moved along that water route would take fire from both banks. One boat had been lost delivering the first of Thompson's companies, Bravo, to the Citadel the day before. Despite that sinking, the company had arrived intact, along with five Patton tanks and two Ontos.

LaHue, with his unfailing aptitude for selling the enemy short, told Thompson that the "mop-up" shouldn't take more than a few days. He and his men were under no circumstances to take orders from General Truong, despite the fact that Truong was the ranking officer and the one with the most experience fighting inside the Citadel—quite apart from the fact that it was *his* country the United States was defending. The innate superiority of the US Marine Corps was a given. Thompson was to take charge. Concerned that Truong (whom LaHue did not know well) might balk at taking orders from a mere major, the general considered making Thompson a brevet colonel on the spot. The major demurred, modestly arguing that since he would not be wearing any sign of rank anyway—it was sniper bait—he could simply present himself as "Colonel Thompson."

That afternoon Thompson and his three other companies were driven from Phu Bai to Hue, where he met at the MACV compound with Colonel Hughes. The onetime way station for military advisers was now a crowded, busy military base, with traffic roaring in and out at all hours and reasonably secure accommodations. Hughes reiterated that Thompson was to report to him, not Truong—he shared LaHue's estimation of the South Vietnamese general.[2] Thompson was to take his Alpha and Charlie Companies with him into the Citadel to join Bravo. His fourth company, Delta, would stay behind in southern Hue. Once inside, Thompson's men were to push out of Mang Ca and fight their way to the south wall, then pivot west to take back the royal palace and its grounds. Truong's men, thus relieved of having to defend the southern perimeter and reinforced by two more ARVN battalions, would devote their efforts to the fortress's west side, driving the enemy forces back out the gates they had entered, where, with any luck, they would collide with the US Army's First Air Cavalry Division. That was the plan.

Thompson and his men were sent that night to the soccer stadium, which had become a supply depot and transit center. Most of the field was covered with pallets of C rations and ammunition. The men each grabbed a week's worth of ammo, stuffing their packs and draping themselves with bandoliers, and each was given a gas mask. They were then moved into homes in the surrounding neighborhoods to spend the night.

In the ones still occupied, residents simply made room or cleared out. They had grown used to hosting uninvited soldiers. The marines were impressed by the modernity of the homes, many of which were nicely furnished and filled with appliances, refrigerators, radios, and TVs. Only the toilets disappointed. They consisted in most houses of a hole in the floor, over which one squatted. Unlike the Vietnamese, for whom squatting was as natural as walking, the marines found the posture challenging. But for a lucky few, the houses provided their first chance to sleep on a mattress in months, even if they did have to share it with one or two others.[3]

As Thompson prepared to turn in, the battalion chaplain came to see him. He said he preferred to go back and minister to troops at Phu Bai.

"No, you're going with us," Thompson said.

The preacher broke down.

"I can't do it," he said.

Thompson fired him on the spot. The preacher was not the only one overcome with dread. The upper ranks of the American military may still have been in denial about Hue—just three days earlier General Wheeler had told LBJ that the major enemy threat "is still posed north of the DMZ and around Khe Sanh," and that Hue would be completely cleared in "several days"[4]—but the rank and file had sized up the coming fight inside the Citadel as the shit storm to end all shit storms.

Later that night a Jesuit priest, Father Aloysius McGonigal, stopped in to see Thompson. A slight, middle-aged man from Philadelphia with a receding hairline and glasses, he wore the uniform of an army officer, complete with a pistol strapped to his hip. He had a cross on his collar, which was the only thing that identified him as clergy.

"I understand you don't have a chaplain," he said. "I have permission to go with you. May I do that?" Thompson was glad to accept him, and the two men became friends.

The battalion queued up glumly at the boat ramp on Monday morning, February 12. The first of the Mike Boats, loaded to the gunwales with supplies and ammo (including high-explosive mortar rounds and grenades), and filled to capacity with about fifty marines, received such intense fire that it turned back shortly after shoving off.

By late afternoon the volume of fire diminished enough for them to get under way, but they were targeted by enemy guns for the whole trip. The leader of Charlie One, Charlie Company's First Platoon, was Second Lieutenant Nick Warr, who would later spell out in vivid and often bitter detail his experience in Hue in a memoir titled *Phase Line Green*. He was twenty-two, a newly minted infantry officer who had attended the University of Oregon before joining the marines with hopes of becoming a pilot. He had been leading Charlie One for about three months. Pressed into the Mike Boat, Warr was so nervous that he felt his testicles retracting before they even got underway. When they did, first one, then two, then three mortar rounds splashed into the river and exploded around them. The boats zigzagged where the river narrowed in the north fork around Hen Island.[5] The marines on board could only hope, or pray. A hit would blow them to oblivion before they even heard the blast. But the mortars stopped falling and the shooting eased once they cleared the island. They arrived unscathed before dusk north of the Citadel, sliding up to a ramshackle ferry landing—not much more than a collection of tall sticks jutting from the water and draped with drying fishnets.

They were unopposed as they off-loaded—more boats coming up behind them would deliver the remainder of Thompson's men. When Warr assembled his squad leaders to go over the route they would take to the gate, he asked if there were any questions and got one.

"Do they expect us to get back in them fucking boats after we're done in here?" asked Ed Estes, a lance corporal. "Like shit. Ain't no way I'm getting back in one of them fucking boats, even if I have to swim across that fucking river and hump all the way back to Phu Bai all by myself."[6]

The march was short to Hau Gate, with Thompson and his command group leading the way. This was unusual. Commanders ordinarily stayed back from the point. Warr thought it was foolish, with the long antennas on their radios waving over them like "aiming stakes."[7] Friendly villagers had warned them that the Front had prepared an ambush on the direct route, so they went around it. They passed a burned-out ARVN truck with charred and stinking bodies in and around it. They made a wrong turn at one point, and Warr raced to catch up with Thompson to redirect him, but they arrived at the gate without incident. They were met by several ARVN officers and the commander of Bravo Company, Captain Fernandez Jennings. The Vietnamese objected to bringing so many men through at once, fearing it would draw enemy fire.

"If you don't let us in," Thompson said, "we're going to knock down this gate."

They relented.

Mang Ca was stately by comparison with the crowded MACV compound. There was lots of green space, a parade ground, rows of palm trees, and big buildings in the French colonial style. A canal passed through the center with water so chilly that mist curled from it in daytime. There were bullet holes in the tree trunks and chips on almost every stone surface, testament to the recent intense fighting.

Thompson found Truong with Colonel Adkisson, his adviser, in a command bunker. Both appeared enormously relieved by the battalion's arrival. Truong showed no concern for Thompson's rank—he never even asked—and was delighted to turn over the reins of the battle. The marine commander outlined the plan to push directly south. They would set off the next morning.

That night, the major consulted with Coolican. After his heroic efforts in defense of the compound on the first night, the captain had rejoined the elite Hac Bao unit as soon as he could get a chopper into the fortress.

Coolican had stayed despite frightening news from home. Soon after he got there, he was told that he needed to call home immediately. Such a message could mean only bad news. Patched from Truong's headquarters through the MACV to Hawaii and then to Camp Pendleton, Coolican was linked to his wife, Jean, in a radio call—only one could speak at a time. Jean told him that their seventeen-month-old son had just undergone emergency brain surgery. She heard shooting and explosions in the background when her husband spoke. She had no idea exactly where in Hue he was, but it sounded like a tough spot, and she knew from watching the evening news that fighting in the city was fierce. She had already received official notice days earlier that her husband had been wounded there—a minor injury, but the marines had their protocol. Given the crisis with their son, she knew that he could probably qualify for emergency leave, but she made a decision on the spot to urge him to stay. Given the intensity of the battle, she worried that trying to get out might be more dangerous than staying. The surgery was done and their son, while still in critical condition, was recovering. Her husband was due to come home in just six weeks anyway.

"I'm dealing with this situation here," she told him, "and I don't want to be dealing with another situation there."

Which was good, because Coolican didn't want to leave. It was a critical time in the battle. He'd invested so much of himself in it, and expected the Hac Bao to be in the thick of things at the finish. The ARVN had been unable to push back very far, but Coolican knew that they were far more experienced and skilled at city fighting than the newly arrived marine battalion.

His assessment was confirmed in the meeting with Thompson. The new battalion commander seemed to be starting over from scratch, ignorant even of the lessons learned by Cheatham south of the river. It wasn't all his fault. There was confusion high and low. The major's orders from Task Force X-Ray were to avoid destroying the culturally valuable structures inside the fortress, so he was barred from calling in artillery and air support (even if the infernal monsoon clouds ever lifted), and his tanks were prohibited from using their big guns—they were to provide cover on the streets and support fire with their machine guns.

This denial of heavy firepower was especially surprising since Cheatham had gotten around it from the start by using his own version of a mobile battery—tanks, Ontos, mortars, bazookas, and 106s—and was now regularly drawing on the First Marine Field Artillery Group (FAG) at Phu Bai. The FAG had even shifted four of its 155-mm howitzers to Gia Le, a short distance west, in order to have a better bead on targets in the city. Days before Thompson arrived, one of the group's officers, Lieutenant Alexander Wells, had choppered into the Citadel under heavy fire, landing at the tenuously held Tay Loc airstrip—where he was taken in by a group of Aussie advisers in a Quonset hut who were coolly playing cards and drinking Scotch. Wells had been sent to direct artillery and naval gunfire. He had been instructed by General Truong that the only no-fire zone inside was in the royal palace enclosure.[8] The RVN Air Force had been hammering at Front positions inside the fortress for weeks, whenever their Skyraiders could get beneath the clouds. Nevertheless, Thompson's instructions were to push ahead with small arms alone.

Like most American officers, the major expressed a dim view of the fighting abilities of the ARVN. Coolican urged Thompson to consider coordinating closely with them, but the major just wanted them to stay out of his way. Truong had had his chance; now the marines were going to show him how things were done. This attitude—and the detachment it fostered—was about to contribute to a tragic misunderstanding. Thompson believed—he would always insist he had been told this by Truong—that a battalion of South Vietnamese airborne troopers were holding a defensive position several blocks south of Mang Ca, along Mai Thuc Loan Street. He intended to march his men south in the morning to that line, marked on his map as "Baseline Alpha," where he would relieve the ARVN force before mounting his own attack. The street ran straight west from the Dong Ba Gate, with its ornate tower.

In fact, the ARVN battalion along that street, which was being advised by marine captain Ty Cobb,[9] had departed the previous day. They had been ordered out. The battalion had assembled at the compound that day in broad daylight, boarded helicopters, and flown off to Phu Bai. It was just one move of many in what had been a busy stretch of days, but surely Truong would have known about it. For whatever reason, Thompson believed it was still there, and Coolican didn't know enough about all the troop movements at that point to correct him.

"So here is what we will do," Thompson told the captain. "We will jump off at eight hundred hours."

He pointed out on the map the streets his two companies would march down, and where he wanted ARVN troops to stay, off to their right side.

"No," Coolican told him, bracing himself—he was outranked but clearly more experienced. "That is not going to work. First of all, do not go down the road at any time because you will get killed, because every house is occupied. Second, we fight at night, because when you are moving you want to move in the dark. You do not want to move in the daytime."

"Well, if you are afraid," Thompson said, "then I will take the road," meaning that he would cover his own flank.

Coolican was insulted, but he knew better than to argue. He had wasted his breath often in the previous week trying to talk sense to Task Force X-Ray. He and the Hac Bao would not wait for morning. They moved stealthily down and into position while it was still dark. They would be waiting when Thompson's men came down the street in the morning.

The grunts who would carry out Thompson's plan knew nothing of troop movements or even the overall strategy, but they were also unhappy with it. Why were they being sent forward without any prep fire? Why had they never been given any training on fighting in city streets like this? Their counterparts south of the river had built valuable experience in urban fighting, but this battalion had not. It was all new to them.

"Fuck, we're more likely to blow each other away than the gooks," said Corporal Estes when Warr outlined the plan that evening. There were lots of questions but the lieutenant had no good answers. He shared their misgivings. What little training he'd had in house-to-house combat, and it was minimal, was that small-unit coordination was essential to avoid marines killing other marines. He spent much of that night trying to recall what else he learned and relaying it to his men. You held a grenade for a few seconds after releasing the spoon before throwing it into a window in order to prevent the enemy from picking it up and tossing it back out at you. Glass should be broken or shot out of windows immediately for a host of reasons, not the least of which was that grenades sometimes bounced off glass and back at you. Inside a building, it was critical that squads keep calling out loudly to each other to make sure they knew exactly where each one was.

On Tuesday morning, February 13, it finally stopped raining. The battalion moved out right on schedule, expecting no resistance until they reached Baseline Alpha. But during the night the Front had moved up to reclaim the positions vacated by the withdrawn ARVN battalion the day before. So instead of walking down the street to relieve a line of friendly troops, Thompson was walking his men straight into the enemy's guns. They went in two columns: Alpha Company on the left in the front with two tanks down Dinh Bo Linh Street, which ran parallel to the treacherous inside wall. Bravo and Charlie companies would trail. It started out as a nice walk, with beautiful homes, even mansions, on both sides surrounded by lawns and gardens and high stone walls.

The enemy waited until Alpha Company was well down before opening fire. In minutes the entire unit was down. Thirty men were hit, including all of its officers.

Grenades pelted down on Vic Walker's squad. It was part of the First Platoon, to the left of the formation, the one closest to the eastern wall, and had turned left three blocks shy of the baseline, walking toward the Dong Ba Tower. Then the gunfire and explosions started. His point man went down. Walker took a shred of shrapnel in his hand. He and his men scrambled for cover, firing up at the three-story tower, but they couldn't see anyone to aim at, and the grenades just kept coming and coming. They finally took shelter in buildings near the base of the wall, dragging their wounded with them. They were stuck there. Machine-gun fire echoed off all the stone walls so it was impossible to tell exactly where the shooting was coming from.

Thompson ordered a retreat, and the riddled company came running back into Mang Ca dragging and carrying their casualties. The company's executive officer, Frank Wilbourne, limped back alone, stiffly, as if the joints in his arms and legs were locked, covered with blood from head to toe. He had been riddled with shrapnel. Two dead marines were still out on the street. Wilbourne told Warr, whose platoon was several blocks back with Charlie Company, that they had been "cluster-fucked." He said the commander of the tank with them had had his head blown off. He told Warr, "Get your head out of your ass and move your men off the street."[10]

Up and down Baseline Alpha and the streets that fed into it, marines were being cut down. Dennis Martin, who was driving a Patton on the right side, watched as a driver sped past him on one of the four-wheel-drive mules. Martin thought, *Oh, shit, he's lost.* The driver was shot and killed and his vehicle ran off the road. It came to rest squarely in front of the tank, where it seemed to Martin that the enemy was using it for target practice. The driver's body jerked every time a round hit home. No one dared leave cover to go after him. So Martin rolled his tank up and placed it between the dead mule driver and the enemy guns. With rounds pinging off his tank, he waited until the body was lifted from the vehicle and carried back.

In the hasty retreat, another of the tanks backed over and killed a wounded marine. Driver Joe Graham's commander was wounded by a rocket that exploded against the side of the tank. He fell from the top hatch and ordered Graham to back up. Marines on the street screamed for it to stop, and Graham did, but too late. They dragged the dead, mangled grunt's remains from the tank treads.

Thompson ordered Charlie Company to move up. This took several hours. It was already afternoon when Warr's platoon, Charlie One, moved gingerly forward, surveying the wreckage. Warr walked in the front door of an abandoned house on one side of Mai Thuc Loan Street, pleased to hear his men calling out to each other loudly as they moved, just as they had discussed the night before. When he stepped back out of the house he saw them arrayed down the street, some of them crouching behind trees too small to provide adequate cover. *Why were they not being shot at?* He realized at once that the enemy, just across the street, was holding fire deliberately, waiting to see how many more Americans would show up. His men were sitting ducks.

"Get the fuck outta the street!" he shouted.

Gunfire erupted from the front and from both his left and right flanks. The enemy was shooting from first- and second-floor windows and from the rooftops. In the chaos that ensued, several of Warr's men went down on the street—two of them dead; the third, Charlie Morgan, wounded, alive, and fully exposed. Morgan called for help. When his team leader tried to retrieve him, he was shot through the leg. Then Ed Estes, Morgan's squad leader, the corporal who had so vigorously disliked the boat ride, paced violently for a few seconds and then abruptly raced out toward Morgan and was immediately cut down, shot through the throat. Both Estes and Morgan died.

Despite this carnage, Charlie Company's commander, First Lieutenant Scott Nelson, kept ordering the First Platoon to advance. Warr resisted, trying to explain that they didn't have a chance against such massed enemy fire, but Nelson was insistent. Warr then argued that his men were completely exposed on their left flank, from which the enemy could pour down fire from the tower, but Nelson wasn't buying it. He said that Major Thompson had assured him that Bravo Company had moved up far enough to cover the left flank, which Warr could see was not true. There was a tank to his left that could have moved up to help cover an assault, but its commander refused to budge. Despite having these things pointed out to him, Nelson reiterated that they were going to drive the enemy back across Baseline Alpha before the day was done. It was an order.

Feeling numb and helpless, Warr withdrew. He found a rocking chair in the house where he had taken shelter and began rocking, stirring only when his platoon sergeant took him by the shoulder and insisted he had to get back on the radio with his superiors. Finally, resigned to the implacable stupidity of the order, he set about launching several futile attacks. On the first, with one fire team from each squad attempting to cross the street while the others covered them, the men did not make it halfway. This left several more downed marines in the street, one of them dead. Nelson ordered another attack, and again they were forced back, leaving yet more wounded and dead.

After this try, the ranking sergeant from another of Charlie Company's platoons, Robert Odum, came running to tell Warr that one of his men was down on the street in front of the tank. This the lieutenant already knew. He could see the man's inert form. Warr strongly suspected that he was dead. He had been shot in the head. The lieutenant argued that it was foolish to send more men out to get shot trying to retrieve a dead body, but Odum insisted, and did so in a way that seemed to challenge Warr's commitment to his men. Young lieutenants were loath to earn the disdain of seasoned noncoms, so against his better judgment he acquiesced. Odum adjusted his helmet chinstrap and set out to perform the rescue personally. He crept out to the front of the tank and then jumped into the street to grab the downed man. An enemy round took off the bottom of Odum's face. The round entered just below his left eye and exited below his chin, exploding through his mouth and jaw.

He fell back to the tank without the marine, who was in fact dead. His wound was horrible. He had no more mouth or jaw. He calmly poured water from his canteen over the shattered remains of his face, as if, Warr would later write, "he believed that he could simply wash out this nightmare," and, stubborn to the last, refused to be carried off on a stretcher. Bandaged, Odum walked alongside the wounded on stretchers toward the rear.[11] After that, Warr ordered his men to retrieve bodies only at night.

Nelson ordered a third attack, and this time two marines actually made it across the street. Two more lay dead, and several more were wounded. The two who had made it were stranded, unable to move without drawing fire. They waited until dark and then ran back.

Nelson finally came to inspect the situation himself. He was built like a linebacker, tall and thick, and made an impressive show when angry. He was angry now. Charlie One had failed repeatedly. Warr walked him down and showed him the position of the tank, still in the same spot, and the location of Delta Company. His left flank, contrary to Major Thompson's insistence, was completely exposed. Nelson didn't say anything, but he did seem surprised that Warr had been right and his commander wrong.

The debacle of the first day in the Citadel would live with Thompson the rest of his life. He spent the remainder of the day trying to get his men back to Mang Ca in one piece. More were killed and many more wounded in the effort.

Alpha Company was so badly mauled that it was no longer an effective combat unit. The fight would be pressed the next day with Charlie and Bravo. Both had been hard hit as well. Charlie One alone, with eight dead and twenty wounded, had fewer than half of its original complement of fifty-one men. Warr was effectively demoted. His men would be distributed to other units, and he would take charge of the company's weapons platoon, functioning primarily as its forward observer and radio operator.

Charlie One was no more.

2

We Do Not Doubt
the Outcome

THREE DAYS BEFORE Thompson's disastrous first foray in the Citadel,
Bernard Weinraub, a *New York Times* correspondent in Saigon, assessed
the significance of the ongoing Tet Offensive. He made only a passing
reference to Hue but reported that, contrary to official assurances, the
surprise attacks had shaken South Vietnam to its core. Relying mostly
on unnamed American sources, Weinraub found a widespread sense
of panic.

"There is an opportunity here to be seized or lost," an American
official said today. "If the [South Vietnamese] Government moves with
decision, they'll wind up in a strong position. If not, they're in trouble."

". . . The people are frightened and they want some kind of leadership—maybe the word is protection," said another official. "And this
is the time for the Government to act and show what they can do."

Although couched as opportunity instead of disaster, the unnamed
official was conceding a lot more than the MACV would. Beyond
the impact in South Vietnam, Weinraub reported that the American embassy was losing confidence in President Nguyen Van Thieu's
regime. The story cited its concerns with corruption, patronage, and
Saigon's lack of control over its generals, who ruled their own armies
and regions like warlords. In the past, the relatively small VC presence
in most parts of the South, particularly in big cities like Saigon and Hue,
made it easier for citizens to simply acquiesce to Thieu's government
as the better bet. Tet had changed that.

Weinraub quoted an anonymous Saigon journalist who said, "Now, with the war brutally and unexpectedly brought to their doorsteps, most city people are forced to think over their traditional indifference and make a choice between the Government and the Viet Cong."[12]

While that choice may still have been academic in Saigon, in Hue it had become a matter of survival. Either you dug in and played Russian roulette with American shells, or you braved the cross fire and murderous commissars in the streets in a frantic search for safety. The great tragedy unfolding in Hue seemed not to register with those in charge. Neither Saigon nor the MACV—nor the press, for that matter—expressed concern for the masses of people trapped by the fighting. The only concern expressed about collateral damage concerned Hue's historical treasures, and after Thompson's debacle the last vestiges of that vanished. None of the stories written about the fierce fighting in the city mentioned mounting civilian casualties, and yet there was hardly a marine fighting in the Citadel who had not encountered underground bunkers filled with civilians, alive and dead. Avenues of escape were few in the fortress, so the crisis there was particularly dire. The lucky ones who emerged alive from the shelling and fighting did so with their hands up, bowing submissively, and were led back to the growing numbers of refugees encamped around Mang Ca. When civilians did make it into stories filed from the battlefield, it was only to describe the mounting logistical challenge of dealing with them.

President Johnson evinced few pangs about killing Vietnamese. As the battle for Hue began its third week, he reiterated his support for bombing the North—the very policy his own advisers had judged ineffective.

"Let those who would stop the bombing answer this question," he said. "What would the North Vietnamese be doing if we stopped the bombing and let them alone? The answer, I think, is clear. The enemy force in the south would be larger. It would be better equipped. The war would be harder. The losses would be greater. The difficulties would be greater. And of one thing you can be sure: it would cost many more *American lives*."[13]

Johnson was increasingly frustrated by both Vietnams, North and South. On Wednesday he told Clark Clifford, whom he would soon name defense secretary, that the current secretary, McNamara, "deeply feels that Teddy and Bobby [Kennedy] are right, that the South Viet-namese are no god damn good and that they ought to do more and that we ought to have a confrontation." Using a political metaphor for the current crisis in South Vietnam, he added, "I think it's a hell of a poor time though, just before the day of election for you to divorce your wife!" As for Hanoi, Johnson had tried repeatedly and unsuccess-fully to draw it into peace talks, stopping and starting the bombing campaigns. United Nations secretary-general U Thant, whom Johnson called Hanoi's "agent almost," was just then pressuring him on the matter. The Tet Offensive, which LBJ referred to as "this murder," had made such a renewed offer impossible.

"We went just as far as a human could, and they come up and they haven't moved one inch!" he complained to Clifford. "We know that. Therefore, since they have answered it with this murder we cannot reward this kind of stuff. And therefore we're gonna clean this thing up before we do anything . . . the Vietnam cities and the Khe Sanh battle. Old U Thant is going to be here tomorrow morning to demand we stop the bombing."

Clifford agreed and outlined the talking points for a "backgrounder" with the press to clarify the administration's reading of Hanoi: "We've now extended in the past six bombing pauses," he said. "Not one of them has been productive of anything at all. This last time we made an all-out effort . . . which would have required minimum from them . . . more than we had ever done before, we extended the *mini-mal* requirements—all they had to do was start talks going promptly and not increase the flow [of soldiers to the south]. That's absolutely minimum . . . everybody agrees to that. They don't accept it. What they do is they come back with this ferocious attack, both militarily and on civilians, murder thousands of them and so forth, and that's their answer to us . . . This discussion about the bombing is just part of their propaganda strategy."[14]

Johnson was feeling increasing pressure from Congress, too. Sen-ator William Fulbright was holding hearings about the 1964 Gulf of Tonkin resolution, in which Congress had authorized LBJ to escalate the war after two American warships were fired upon by the North Vietnamese. The hearings were examining whether that provocation had been faked or exaggerated by administration hawks as an excuse to widen the war. Senator Eugene McCarthy was also pressing his antiwar challenge on the campaign trail in New Hampshire.

And the Battle of Hue ground on. Every report of further marine casualties added fuel to antiwar criticism. Former president Dwight Eisenhower had advised Johnson to avoid a protracted war, one where losses mounted slowly over years. Better, the great World War II commander argued, to finish the war in a move that might lose twenty-five thousand men a day and "get it over with, than to fight a war where you lost 2,500 men every month for years." [15] What was happening now was the worst-case scenario; the pace of the killing had accelerated at the same time as its end seemed ever more distant.

This was, of course, deliberate. North Vietnamese prime minister Pham Van Dong had explained, "Our purpose is, through a program of all-out attacks, to cause many US casualties, and so to erode the US will that antiwar influences will gain decisive political strength." [16] By this measure, the Tet Offensive was a major victory for Hanoi.

Time reported that week, "As the ancient capital of Viet Nam, Hue was a prime piece of captured real estate for propaganda purposes." It faulted Westmoreland not just for inflated body counts but for his bloodthirsty embrace of them:

> Less than two months ago, he was reporting publicly that the Viet Cong had been so bloodied that some U.S. troops might be able to start home in 1969. Last week, he speculated that heavy Communist losses during their attacks on the cities "may measurably shorten the war." If the losses are indeed as heavy as claimed, he may be right. But the White House found his optimism in the midst of carnage a trifle embarrassing. Privately, Johnson last week ordered the general to tone it down.
>
> There is no indication, however, that Westmoreland's reports to the White House have been less exuberant than his public pronouncements. Presumably, he was misled by his intelligence unit. Nearly all military experts agree that Westmoreland has underestimated Communist strength—or overestimated the effectiveness of [South] Viet Nam's regular army and paramilitary units. His own command admits that the strength of the enemy *Tet* offensive came as a shock. [17]

Johnson flew to California on Saturday the seventeenth to help send off men from the Fifth Marine Division who were to reinforce the troops fighting at Hue, Khe Sanh, and elsewhere.

"This is a decisive time in Vietnam," he told the ranks as they stood at attention for his remarks. "The eyes of the nation and the world—the eyes of history itself" were on them. "We do not doubt the outcome," he said. "The duty of peace is burdensome. It is a duty many generations of Americans have chosen as their own. It is a duty many other young men have borne as you bear it now. In the discharge of that duty, none have honored themselves—none have honored their nation—so nobly, or so bravely, as the United States Marines."[18]

Random Agents of Doom

Hᴀɴɢɪɴɢ ᴏɴ ᴡɪᴛʜ the thousands of other refugees at Hue University, Tuy-Cam and her family learned that her fiancé, Jim Bullington, had been rescued.

"Mr. Jim is alive!" said one of the family's servants. "A man told me he saw the US soldiers who entered the electric plant and took an American with them. Mr. Jim stayed there, didn't he?"

"Yes, he did," said Tuy-Cam. "It must have been him!"

The good news about Bullington was just one of the tidbits gathered by Tuy-Cam and her sisters and their servants, who set off each morning from the university trying to find food and information. Most of the news was bad. One of those who had been killed was their late father's cousin, a senator, who was said to have been buried alive. Many more—the exact numbers would be hard to pin down—had been rounded up and executed.

In her wanderings, Tuy-Cam found one of her colleagues from the US consulate in Da Nang, who, distressed about what had happened to her, arranged for a flight out on a chopper the following day. Waiting in a crowd at the park landing zone (LZ), she was thrilled to see Bullington step off a helicopter, wearing a heavy coat. He passed right by the crowd, not seeing Tuy-Cam at first. Over the previous weeks she had lost weight, and she looked haggard. She was certainly not dressed or made up the way Bullington was used to seeing her.

"Jim! Jim! It's me!" she cried, but he kept walking. Her friend also called after him and he turned around. He stared back, not recognizing them at first.

"It's me, TC!" she shouted.

Bullington swept her up in his arms.

"Thank God you're alive!" he said. "Don't you know I was looking for you? I am here to look for you!"

Life was slowly returning to normal south of the river, but on the north side, inside the Citadel, the battle was full-on. Mike Morrow was one of many reporters in the thick of it. The former Dartmouth student, who was ironically ducking the draft by visiting battle zones in Vietnam, had hopped another flight to the city and was now inside the fortress, sleeping nights on a floor at Mang Ca. He stuck out like the collegian he had recently been, a tall mop-haired American in thick black-rimmed glasses wandering around the battlefield unarmed. He wasn't filing stories or selling pictures. He wasn't even sure what he was doing. In later years he would marvel at his stupidity, but he was certainly seeing the war up close. One day he was furious and ashamed because a wounded Front soldier was left to bleed to death on the street. The marine unit Morrow was with ignored the dying man's pleas for help. The grunts were unremorseful and seemed confused by his anger. Then there were times when he saw the same marines risk their lives to help each other, or even to carry wounded civilians to safety.

Morrow was a halfhearted journalist. He told everybody that he was in Vietnam just to try to figure out what the war was about. He spent a lot of time with *Washington Post* reporters Peter Braestrup and Lee Lescaze—he got along well with Lescaze; less so with Braestrup, whom he considered hawkish. He had changed from a questioning college kid into a cynical and frustrated old hand. He had started smoking—in part struck by the absurdity of Saigon's antismoking campaign in the midst of this disastrous war. He was up to three packs a day. He'd also started drinking a pint of whiskey a day. He assumed he wasn't getting out of Vietnam alive anyway. Going home meant being drafted to fight in a war he judged immoral and pointless. He believed the United States was simply wrong to view Vietnam's struggles as part of some global Communist threat. Its people deserved to be considered, simply, as Vietnamese. He had met people on both sides of the civil war whom he respected, and he believed the nation's split might be resolved through negotiation. The longer he stayed, the more the war seemed tragically wasteful and surreal.

He had attended a reception at the Independence Palace in Saigon in November for Vice President Hubert Humphrey. Morrow was standing in the back of the room, there just to observe, when Humphrey stepped out from behind a curtain and reached out to shake his hand. Just then there was an explosion outside. A mortar had been lobbed at the embassy, no doubt in honor of the vice president's visit. It had landed in the courtyard. Morrow turned his head to look, and when he turned back Humphrey was gone. Vanished. Morrow's hand was still extended.

Weeks before the battle began he had gone on a walking tour with an ARVN ranger unit outside the Citadel with army captain George Smith, the public relations liaison who would be in the MACV compound the night of the initial assault. They had hiked completely around the fortress, a two-day trip. The ranger commander had a case of beer, which was carried for him by one of his men, and he walked with an open bottle in his hand. At one point he stopped and interrogated a Vietnamese civilian, whom he beat with his pistol. Morrow took a picture. Smith gently took him by the arm and drew him away.

"Come with me and stay close to me," he said.

When they had walked off a distance—Morrow didn't witness the Vietnamese man's fate—Smith said, "You should not have taken that picture. These guys will kill you."

Morrow was glued to Smith for the rest of the day. They camped with the rangers at an abandoned villa, inside which they found liquor. The rangers all got drunk. Morrow had a few drinks himself. He and Smith talked into the night. Morrow was a few years younger than the captain. He explained why he opposed the war. Smith wrote later, "It was not that he was against the military or his country, he just did not believe that the United States had any of its national interests at stake in Vietnam. He believed that his country was throwing away its youth in a venture that was not only ill-advised but impossible to win. The cost in lives, which he had seen firsthand too many times, was particularly troubling to him, as it was to everyone. The military had the politicians hoodwinked, he argued, and the politicians were conning the public."

Smith could see his point, but, like a lot of Americans who had come to fight, he was not prepared to surrender South Vietnam to a one-party Communist state. He felt those who opposed the war had no concern for the Vietnamese people, some of whom he had come to know and respect.

"The trouble with you, Morrow, is that you don't have any experience in wearing a uniform. Do you think if the US military packed up its weapons and went home, all the killing would stop? There are a lot of people who think if we leave it will only get worse. Once South Vietnam falls into the hands of the Communists, who's next?"

"It's all none of our goddamn business," said Morrow.[19]

They were attacked in the early morning. Morrow awakened to explosions and bullets flying through the windows of the villa. Mortars crashed. Morrow called them "random agents of doom," which made the captain laugh.[20] They hid behind a rockery in a garden. The rangers sobered up fast and were putting up a spirited fight. Smith handed Morrow a pistol.

"You may need this before the night is out," he said.

It would be the only time he held a weapon in Vietnam. The attackers were few and were driven off quickly. Morrow gave Smith back the pistol. Later that same day they were attacked again. Morrow dived into a bed of daffodils. He savored the absurdity of the moment, gazing up through the yellow blossoms at a blue sky as bullets whizzed overhead. When the shooting moved off and then died down, he poked his head up and found himself alone. It struck him that none of the men he was with cared what happened to him; he did not belong to either side in this fight. It gave him a sinking feeling. He followed a path out of the garden and soon found Smith, who, it turns out, had been worried about him.

By the time Tet came he had stopped even trying to sell his photographs. He gave up after snapping a picture of an ambushed Jeep full of dead journalists, who turned out to be his friends—it sold for thirty dollars. It made him sick. Before coming north to the Citadel, where he was reunited with Smith, he had spent a few nights inside Hue University, where thousands of refugees were being housed. There he first heard Trinh Cong Son, a young Vietnamese folksinger, poet, painter, and composer. Trinh was a small, skinny man whose broad forehead and big glasses were well known in his country. He had been called the "Vietnamese Bob Dylan." He was from Hue, and his pacifist protest songs had upset both regimes, North and South. Morrow befriended him and at night would listen with hundreds of others who crowded into the university library for Trinh's performances. Word of his presence had drawn other singers, so every evening, against the backdrop of gunfire and explosions, there was this Vietnamese hootenanny. Morrow would remember Trinh's performances under those circumstances as deeply moving and beautiful.[21]

Inside the fortress now, Morrow wandered with his camera, still shooting pictures but only for himself. He took one of a truck loaded with dead marines and was waved away angrily. On the western side of the fortress he was shocked to see piles of dead Front soldiers, hundreds of them. They had been killed around the Tay Loc airstrip. He had never seen that many dead at one time. He was told that they had been killed in an artillery barrage. On his way back to Mang Ca, moving through the sparse green blocks at the far north of the fortress, he encountered a uniformed NVA soldier, unarmed, moving in the other direction. The man was apparently separated from his unit. Morrow had caught a glimpse of him jumping behind a building, and their eyes met. The soldier then stepped out to stare at him. They both warily moved on.

Michael Herr, the *Esquire* correspondent, was also in the middle of the fighting, taking notes light on specifics but rich with insight and feeling.

> Between the smoke and the mist and the flying dust inside the Citadel, it was hard to call that hour between light and darkness a true dusk, but it was the time when most of us would open our C-rations. We were only meters away from the worst of the fighting, not more than a Vietnamese city block in distance, and yet civilians kept appearing, smiling, shrugging, trying to get back to their homes. The Marines would try to menace them away at rifle point, shouting "Di, di, *di*, you sorry-ass motherfuckers, go on, get the hell away from here!" and the refugees would smile, half bowing, and flit up one of the shattered streets. A little boy of about ten came up to a bunch

of Marines from Charlie Company. He was laughing and moving his head from side to side in a funny way. The fierceness in his eyes should have told everyone what it was, but it had never occurred to most of the grunts that a Vietnamese child could be driven mad too, and by the time they understood it the boy had begun to go for their eyes and tear at their fatigues, spooking everyone, putting everyone really uptight, until a black grunt grabbed him from behind and held his arm. "C'mon, poor li'l baby, 'fore one a these grunt mothers shoots you," he said, and carried the boy to where the corpsmen were.[22]

Herr captured the offbeat pugnacity of the grunts. He recorded the defiant, sometimes funny, and sometimes inscrutable slogans they scrawled on their flak jackets: FAR FROM FEARLESS, MICKEY'S MONKEY, AVENGER V, SHORT TIME SAFETY MOE, BORN TO LOSE, BORN TO RAISE HELL, BORN TO KILL, BORN TO DIE, HELL SUCKS, TIME IS ON MY SIDE, JUST YOU AND ME GOD—RIGHT?[23]

After leaving Hue, the dean of an older school of reporting, Walter Cronkite, stopped on his personal fact-finding tour at Phu Bai to visit Westy's deputy, General Creighton Abrams, an old friend. They had met in World War II, when Abrams was a young tank commander. In the Battle of the Bulge, he had famously remarked about the enemy, "They've got us surrounded again, the poor bastards."[24] Both men had grown grayer, thicker, and more august, and they had been friends for too long to bullshit each other. Abrams was far more candid than his boss about the scope of the enemy's accomplishment, particularly in Hue. He spoke of the Front's complete tactical surprise and the magnitude of the impact.[25]

For Cronkite, the trip had confirmed his worst suspicions. When he returned to Saigon, just before flying back to the States, he invited all of the CBS men there to a dinner at the Caravelle Hotel's rooftop restaurant. They sat around a large round table covered with white linen. With him were his producers, Jeff Gralnick and Ernie Leiser; and reporters John Laurence, Bob Schackne, George Syvertsen, and Peter Kalischer, who had covered the early years of the war and had recently returned for more. Kalischer and Leiser got in a heated argument over the war (Kalischer against; Leiser for), and Laurence joined in on Kalischer's side, only to feel Gralnick kick him hard under the table—the producer later told him that the vehemence of the discussion had more to do with bad blood between the two men than policy differences. Cronkite played the role of the dispassionate journalist throughout, asking questions and listening. Kalischer, in particular, seemed intent on convincing him that the entire American effort was wrong.

After dinner a bottle of brandy was opened. Cronkite bore in on Laurence for details about the US pacification program. The reporter had covered it extensively and told story after story of corruption and bureaucratic failure, of hungry children and warehouses filled with American-donated rice that was not being distributed.

"How could this happen?" Cronkite kept asking.

He and Laurence stood outside late that evening on the rooftop balcony. They watched fighting in the distance through binoculars, taking turns watching for muzzle flashes and artillery fire, and Cronkite, the old war hand, tried to estimate how far away it was. Laurence had scorn for the reporters who covered the war from the hotel in Saigon and was proud of his own work, risking his life to see the war up close. Cronkite said how grateful he was for the work Laurence was doing. He told Laurence about some of his own experiences covering war and recalled how hard it had been to convey the import and urgency of events to editors who watched from thousands of miles away.[26]

When Cronkite got back to New York, the anchorman and his producers would put together their documentary for airing at the end of the month. Before his TV audience of millions, he would present his first try at what he termed "advocacy journalism."

The White House was not going to like it.

4

The First Annual
Hue City Turkey Shoot

T HOMPSON WAS so low on ammo and had taken so many casualties, and his men were so beaten down, that on Wednesday, February 14, he rested them. He was down to about half of his strength. Some of his men had not been fed for two days. The enemy remained dug in along Mai Thuc Loan Street, which the grunts had dubbed Rocket Alley. The enemy still held the Dong Ba Tower, which commanded the street. It was clear that before any progress could be made, the marines would have to take it. While there were now regular chopper flights from Phu Bai to southern Hue, hostile fire made it difficult to land in the Citadel. Because the wounded had the highest priority, they went out on the few that did. The dead were left behind, stacked in body bags like cordwood outside the battalion aid station.

The battalion used the relatively quiet day to regroup. Lieutenant Warr, who had lost his platoon in the disastrous first assault, was enormously relieved to leave his position on Rocket Alley. His appetite for the battle was gone. The weapons platoon he took over consisted of two mortar crews, ably led by an experienced gunnery sergeant, which suited Warr fine. He relegated himself to opening crates and keeping the teams supplied. He felt numb, as if he had been, he would later write, "immersed in a vat of novocain." [27] He suspected that his commander, Lieutenant Nelson, was aware of his mental state because Nelson kept looking at him funny. Warr didn't care. Nelson could eyeball him all he wanted. As commander of the weapons platoon Warr had a radio, but no one called him. He later wrote, "It was just as well, because if anyone had asked my advice at that point, I'm certain that I would have been immediately charged with cowardice in the face of the enemy. I would have advised them all to withdraw, to leave this city in the hands of the enemy who obviously wanted it so badly, and to tell the goddamned politicians who had gotten us into this mess and then tied our hands behind our backs so securely to go fuck themselves."[28]

The failure of Thompson's first foray was reported by Thomas Johnson in Wednesday's *New York Times*. "In their first ground battle in the northern part of Hue, an American Marine battalion advanced 500 yards today after meeting stiff resistance from enemy forces . . . ," Johnson reported. "Marine casualty figures were not disclosed here, but there were estimates that at least 15 men had been killed and 40 wounded."[29]

One consequence of the fiasco was that Thompson had a clear idea of what he was up against. His men weren't going anywhere until he took the tower.

Steve Berntson, the marine combat correspondent, rode up that day from southern Hue with a boatload of reinforcements. A black marine from Philadelphia, who called himself "Philly Dog,"[30] had spotted him in the MACV compound.

"Hey, Storyteller, you gonna go with us up the river?" he asked. He explained where they were going. He said, "We're gonna kick the shit outta some gooks up there."

Berntson knew that the Hue story was shifting north. On the southern side there were marines joyriding in cars they had hot-wired, and he'd heard about the tank crews racing inside the soccer stadium.

"There's a bunch of ARVN up there and they ain't done diddly shit," said Philly Dog, "and they're getting overrun all the time, and we're going up there and take over their building for 'em."

Philly Dog carried a "blooper," an M79 grenade launcher. He sweetened the invitation for Berntson by getting him one, too, and on the ride up they sat on opposite sides of the junk and fired off rounds at the riverbanks.

When he arrived in the Citadel, the lull in the fighting gave him a chance to wander around looking for more stories. He had not been writing, but he had been filling his battered green notebook with names and interviews and observations, planning to pull some of them together when the battle was over. Picking his way through a flattened neighborhood controlled by the marines, he was drawn to the sound of rifle shots. It was not the crazy, hurried shooting typical of the fighting along the forward line, just an occasional volley of what sounded like four rifles. He found two snipers, spread out on the roof of a blue bus in the middle of the street, and two others leaning on its front fender.

"Hey, man," said one of them, David Morales, cheerily. "Welcome to the First Annual Hue City Turkey Shoot!"

Far down the street there were bodies. Enemy soldiers would occasionally try to sprint from one side of the street to the other, giving the snipers targets, which, by the look of it, they hit frequently. Berntson jotted two of the names in his notebook, Morales and Eric Henshall, and watched as a small figure suddenly darted across the street. All four men fired, but the runner made it. Minutes later, three others darted across. One made it, another went down, and the third hesitated, turned around, and started back. He was shot down. Then two more soldiers ran out to recover the downed men, and one of them was shot.

"How long have you guys been doing this?" Berntson asked.

They said they'd been at it for hours. He wrote "3?" in his notebook.

"They just keep running back and forth," said one of the marines. "They don't fire at us. You want to take a shot?"

Berntson lifted his rifle and leaned against the fender. He tried to remember his firing discipline from boot camp, *slow breath out . . .* he held that pose, sighting straight over the bodies on the street, until his eyes started to water. Then another figure darted out . . . *squeeze.* He had neglected to put his rifle on single shot so the gun jumped and he emptied his magazine. The man made it across.

The snipers teased him about what a bad shot he was.

"You want another shot?" one asked him.

Berntson declined. "I'd only miss again."

He left them wondering why the enemy, otherwise so smart, would keep exposing themselves like that.

He stopped to talk to Sergeant Tom Birch of Minneapolis, who three days earlier had passed his twenty-fourth birthday, his second in Vietnam. He had celebrated by washing his face, shaving, and brushing his teeth. He'd eaten a C-ration dinner of ham and eggs and beef and had shared a fruitcake from his wife and daughters. He told Berntson he planned to spend his twenty-fifth at home quietly, with a home-cooked meal.

During the lull in the fighting, General Truong flew down to Phu Bai to meet with South Vietnam's vice president, Nguyen Cao Ky, who had come up from Saigon to confer with General Abrams. With him were General Cushman (the I Corps commander who had initially ordered his men to avoid destroying significant buildings in the city), and all of the rest of Task Force X-Ray's top leaders. General LaHue briefed Ky on the battle. More than two weeks after the city had been taken, Hue finally had the full attention of Saigon and the MACV. Abrams told reporters after the meeting that Ky had characterized Hanoi's effort in Hue as doomed, a demonstration of its willingness to sacrifice "thousands of men to win a slight political gain." He also announced that Ky had accepted full responsibility for the destruction of churches, temples, pagodas, and other culturally significant structures in the city. There was no mention of civilians trapped by the fighting. Any restrictions on force levels were formally lifted—although the marines and ARVN had already done a fair job of destroying most of the city anyway.

When Truong returned he found his command beefed up with another seven hundred men, a full battalion of South Vietnamese forces led by Colonel Pham Van Dinh. The Hac Bao had its pick of these reinforcements. Lieutenant Tran Ngoc "Harry" Hue and Coolican were back in business with a force of 150.[31] Pham's men joined those fighting on the west side of the fortress, where progress had halted for days.

The Front still had about three battalions in the Citadel, just under two thousand men, but the growing strength and numbers of the allied effort had begun to tell. It was getting harder for the Communists to send troops into the fortress. On Friday night, February 16, an ARVN forward observer spotted a battalion-size Front force moving toward the Huu Gate. Alexander Wells, the marine battery's forward observer, summoned an artillery bombardment that decimated it and killed a regimental commander. Radio intercepts later that evening overheard the enemy's command center at La Chu refusing the replacement commander's request to withdraw. He was ordered to proceed, with whatever men he had left, into the fortress to dig in and fight.[32]

Ten more days of heavy combat were ahead, and for the time being, Thompson's battalion was stuck. His rate of progress was unacceptable to General LaHue, and it didn't help that the major was requesting more men, ammo, and supplies. During one testy exchange on the radio, Thompson offered to resign. He was exhausted mentally and physically. At that point losing command would have been a relief. His offer was not accepted.

5

The Tower

LIFTING THE FORCE restrictions had little immediate impact on Thompson's push. Until the weather changed, aerial bombardment was only occasionally possible. Naval gunfire, while it was enormously loud and impressive, arrived at a trajectory too low to be effective. Shells roared above the clouds over the east wall and flew straight across the fortress to explode against the west wall. Artillery batteries at Phu Bai and Gia Le, south and southeast of the city, had difficulty aiming. They had to place shells *in front* of Thompson's line. They were good at shooting over the heads of their own men toward enemy positions beyond, but it was far more difficult to aim at their own troops and have the rounds fall slightly short. It was too risky.

The marines did what they could with what they had. They fired mortars, worked the 90-mm guns of the Patton tanks, and blasted away with the Ontos whenever they dared to bring it close to the enemy line. The tanks were so much in the thick of things that crew members were knocked silly by the force of the explosions against their armor. They came back unconscious, dazed, or dizzy, some so badly concussed that they had to be evacuated. Nearly all had headaches. It was to little avail; the enemy didn't budge. Tanks aimed their big guns up at the Dong Ba Tower but succeeded only in obliterating its fancy masonry.

Thompson sought and received permission to call up his fourth company, Delta, commanded by Myron Harrington, a captain. It had been left in the triangle to assist with the continuing mop-up efforts there, in keeping with Task Force X-Ray's estimation that Thompson ought to be able to do in days what General Truong had been unable to do in weeks. Now, having effectively lost one company, the major was allowed to bring the last of his rifle companies forward.

Harrington spent all day Wednesday trying to get his men upriver. The lead Mike Boat, which carried him and his command group and a few of his men, took such heavy fire from Hen Island that its navy skipper refused to make the return trip to pick up the others. It took hours to arrange for Swift Boats to pull South Vietnamese navy junks loaded with the rest of the men. Despite these delays, two of Delta's platoons were at Mang Ca before dark. The final junks did not arrive until very early Thursday morning. Much to Harrington's chagrin, a good portion of one of his platoons—twenty men—had been held back by Colonel Hughes to help with convoy security in the triangle. The captain had resisted. Given what Thompson had encountered on his first day, he felt the need inside the fortress was greater, but Hughes thought otherwise, and Harrington had lost that fight. Two of his platoons were under strength, and his third was still stuck back at the boat ramp. It would not arrive until the next day. But as soon as he checked in with Thompson, he was given the job of taking the tower first thing the next morning.

As he left the meeting, he told his radioman Steve Wilson, "Steve, hell is coming tomorrow. You've got to be ready."

The captain was a trained and experienced infantryman, but he was new to combat. He had taken over Delta Company only weeks earlier, coming from a supply job, which had made his more experienced men wary. But he had impressed them. Days earlier he had pulled them back from chasing an enemy squad. "They may be leading us into an ambush," Harrington had said. To his men, such prudence was a welcome sign. Their new captain had something they valued more than swagger. He solicited advice from his experienced men, listened to it, and acted on it. He also led from the front, exposing himself to the same risks his men faced.

That night he sought out Maury Whitmer, one of his squad leaders, a corporal six months into his second Vietnam tour. They had known each other for about three weeks. Whitmer was a slender, sandy-haired young man with a world-weary manner—when he'd told his father, a navy veteran, that he was going to join the marines, his old man had said, "It's your life. If you want to fuck it up, fuck it up." Not much bothered Whitmer. He had impressed Harrington with his poise and natural leadership; the other men looked up to him.

"We're making a company attack first thing in the morning," Harrington told him.

"A *company* attack?" said Whitmer. He reminded the captain that they did not have their full company.

"Yeah," Harrington said. "I have to get up on this wall and attack this tower."

"What tower?" Whitmer asked.

"I don't know," Harrington said. "I haven't seen it. Alpha Company got hit hard out there. Bravo Company went to help them, and they took heavy casualties. Now it's our turn. What do you need?"

"Men," said Whitmer.

"I don't have any more men," Harrington said. He reminded Whitmer that his third platoon was still on the other side of the Huong River. "They might never get here," he said. "What else do you need?"

"A corpsman."

"What happened to your corpsman?"

"He got shot the other day, so I don't have a corpsman."

Harrington noted that.

"Okay, I'm going to need you to get up on the wall first, and then I'll give you a radio call to tell you when to attack."

"I don't have a radio," said Whitmer.

"What do you mean you don't have a radio?"

"I mean, my radio operator was shot through the chest and the bullet went through the radio and destroyed it. We turned it in when we got to Phu Bai, and nobody had a radio to give us in Phu Bai."

"Jesus," said Harrington. "You don't have anything!"

He suggested that they coordinate the attack with their watches, and Whitmer said his watch wasn't working anymore. What's more, none of his men's watches were working either.

"You know, Captain, the weather over here, it just destroys them."

The captain caught Whitmer's drift. He and his squad wanted no part of what they were being asked to do.

"Now, you're a marine," Harrington said. "You'll follow orders. I'll get you up on that wall and you're going to attack the tower. We have to take that tower and clear it."

"We'll do what we can," said Whitmer.

"I know you'll do it."

Illumination flares cast their spooky silver light on both men. The captain put his hand on Whitmer's shoulder.

"Good luck, Whit," he said. He had tears in his eyes.[33]

A brief break in the clouds allowed aerial attacks on the tower that night. It was such a startling break in the status quo that it made Thursday's *New York Times* in a story Gene Roberts wrote from Saigon. "United States jets bombed Hue's historic Citadel repeatedly yesterday in an effort to destroy the enemy's last major stronghold in a South Vietnamese city."[34]

The tower was also targeted by the artillery battery at Phu Bai and shelled from two warships, the destroyer USS *Manley* and the cruiser USS *Providence*, which fired a total of two hundred rounds. Captain Smith, Adkisson's public affairs officer, braved sniper fire to watch from the roof of Truong's division headquarters. He would describe it as a "symphony of sound and fury."[35] By morning, the stone walls at the tower's base had crumpled into a steep gradient of rubble. The upper floors were just charred shells. But the stubborn structure still stood. Its lower level had high arched openings on all four sides, and the top floor had rectangular openings that remained secure fighting positions with a commanding view of the streets below.

One of the Front units on the receiving end of this pounding was the sapper battalion that had destroyed the tank base at Tam Thai. Bazooka gunner Le Huu Tong, who had come to Hue on the long march through the mountains, weathered it somehow. There was nothing he could do to defend himself. He came close to being killed several times. Twice he was knocked out cold and awoke disoriented. He dreaded the sound of more incoming fire; once begun, it had continued relentlessly. Getting ammo for his bazooka became difficult. More and more he would fight only with his rifle, saving his rocket rounds for times when he had a clear and appropriate target.

As the sun rose over the South China Sea on Thursday morning, February 15, Harrington set off with his men down the inside wall of the fortress. It was still quiet. They managed to pass a few blocks without being discovered. At street level, staring up at the battered tower for the first time, Harrington thought it looked so bad that for a fleeting moment he allowed himself the hope that it had been abandoned. He quickly learned otherwise. Lieutenant William Conrad, leading his second platoon and moving up behind him, climbed to a second-story balcony to get a better look. Conrad and his radioman and one of his squad leaders were immediately hit with a rocket; all three were wounded and out of action. The platoon's radio was destroyed. Its men, out of contact and not knowing the way, would not rejoin Harrington until midafternoon.

The captain had found a radio for Whitmer. They stopped together at a stile that led up to the top of the wall. A squad from Bravo Company had secured a small position just north of the tower two days earlier and was holding it.

Whitmer took ten men. He found the Bravo Company sergeant, who showed him around their small position. There was a parapet where you could look down the high wall to the moat below. Just to the south was the narrow bridge before the Dong Ba Gate. It reminded Whitmer of something from a Robin Hood movie. The sergeant pulled him back as he leaned out from the parapet.

"One of my guys was killed leaning out of here to take a look," he warned.

Whitmer told him that they were going to help attack the tower.

"Where's the rest of your men?" the Bravo sergeant asked.

"There's only ten of us."

"You want us to stay here and help you?"

"You've got orders to go someplace else, don't you?" Whitmer asked.

"Yeah."

"Then you better go."

To help with the assault, Harrington had a tank, which had initially stayed back in order to preserve surprise. But very soon any chance of sneaking up on the tower was blown. First, there was the blunder of his lieutenant exposing himself on the balcony, and then Harrington gave away his own spot. He stepped away from the wall with his radioman to get a better look at the tower and drew a torrent of fire. One of the marines behind him was hit. The captain sought cover, feeling stupid. He had not even begun to fight and his force already had been reduced by half. Still, he was determined to justify Thompson's faith in him. The terrible bombardment the night before had, if nothing else, underscored the importance of their mission. He called for the tank to come forward and spent the rest of the morning standing behind it, directly across the street from the tower, trying to get his second platoon back and to maneuver his roughly one hundred men into attack positions. By late afternoon his lead platoon, led by Sergeant Bob Thoms, a gung ho career marine who would later receive a battlefield commission, was on the north side of Rocket Alley with another led by Lieutenant Jack Imlah. They had been exchanging small-arms fire with the enemy across the street.

It was a long day of waiting for Harrington's men. At his position on top of the wall, Whitmer was summoned by one of his men, Randy Romine, who was standing at the parapet.

"Whit! Come over here," he said.

"Don't be looking through there," Whitmer told him. "That guy just told me a sniper shot and killed one of his guys looking through there!"

"Yeah, but there's a bunch of NVA down there!" Romine said.

Whitmer crept over and peered down. There was a whole squad of enemy soldiers at the base of the high wall. It looked like they were practicing wall-climbing exercises. Whitmer assembled his squad. Romine carried a grenade launcher.

"As soon as Romine pops off a round, you guys drop grenades down at them," he said. They did as instructed, felling all of the men below. The squad immediately came under fire and backed away from the parapet.

It was four in the afternoon when Harrington attacked. Whitmer's squad was about the length of a football field away. They moved forward, clearing the burned-out houses, trenches, and foxholes as they went—they killed six enemy snipers. They stopped a good long stone's throw from the tower. Up ahead they could see there was an L-shaped trench before the tower itself that had been covered by tin roofing, dirt, and bricks. There was also a bunker aboveground surrounded by bricks. The shelling and bombing the previous day had left debris scattered everywhere, which afforded the enemy lots of places to hide. Whitmer could hear them talking and could see some of them aiming down toward the street where Harrington had set his command post.

With Whitmer's squad close enough, the captain called for covering fire and he sent more men up to the top of the wall. They scaled
two stiles, one immediately north and the other south of the tower's
crumpled base.

The tank opened up, and the marines rushed the tower from both
sides. Along with Imlah's platoon, Whitmer came forward with his
men from the north, shooting three or four more enemy still in their
foxholes. One popped up screaming with a homemade bomb in his
hand, wrapped in bamboo leaves with a lit fuse protruding. He was
apparently waiting for the fuse to burn down before hurling it. Whitmer shot him in the head. He was still yelling when he was shot three
more times from the other direction. He crumpled and the bomb
exploded.

There were not that many enemy soldiers left in the tower itself,
but all of Harrington's men were exposed to fire from rooftops and
upper floors in the neighborhood around it: rockets, rifle fire, and
grenades. One explosion lifted Thoms into the air in a ball of flame.
He and several of his men landed hard in the slope of rubble. Thoms
had several pieces of shrapnel in him, and the flames burned off his
shirt and the cover of his helmet. The blast also had torn his trouser
leg from the crotch to the top of his boot. Since few marines wore
underwear, Thoms was a startling sight.

Whitmer came back down to the street to confer with Harrington,
who was directing the tank's gun. They were shouting to each other
when a rocket bore down. The corporal dived to his left, the captain
to his right. It flew past the tank and exploded against a wall nearby.
Neither man was hurt.

"Get back up there!" Harrington screamed to the corporal. "Take
the rest of that tower!"

Whitmer found a mule loaded with ammo, grabbed some grenades,
and recruited more marines to carry as much as they could back up
the slope. Near the top he jumped through an opening at one end of a
trench and, in the darkness, could make out eyes. He fired his rifle on
automatic and then felt it come apart in his hands. He was hit several
times in his flak jacket and knocked over backward. Two of his men,
Dave Schultz and Ray Sexton, dragged him out of the hole.

"Throw some grenades in there!" he told them.

Grenades were thrown, and several of his other men ran up and shot down through the tin covering.

"Where are you hit?" Sexton asked.

"Man, I'm hit all over," Whitmer said, except . . . he wasn't! The only blood he found was on his hand. He had three or four small cuts on it and on his little finger. He had bruises on his chest under the vest. He assumed the rounds must have come from farther down the trench and may have passed through the men immediately in front of him, so they lacked the force to penetrate. He joined his men as they sprinted up the ramp toward the tower itself . . . and in the next instant he found himself again at the bottom of the wall. He was on his back covered with dust and plaster. He tried to move, but someone took hold of his leg. An enemy soldier in a spider hole beneath him had slid out another bamboo-wrapped explosive and was now holding Whitmer so he could not scoot away. The corporal used his other foot to kick the bomb back into the hole. The grip released, Whitmer scrambled back and the bomb went off, pelting him with the enemy soldier's remains.

When he got to his feet, Whitmer was so blood-splattered that he could not tell if he was wounded. To his surprise, it all seemed to have come from the man killed in the hole—he would later discover shrapnel fragments in his legs. He didn't feel any pain. He rejoined his men, who were now in the lower level of the tower. Whitmer looked in such bad shape that his men now led him.

"Are you ready to go?" asked Don Hammons.

"Okay," said Whitmer.

"Okay, follow us," said Tony Meggs, a private.

Bricks and chips of stone were flying off the walls around them. There was another explosion directly in front of them.

Once more, Whitmer came to twenty feet down the ramp, again on his back. Beside him was Hammons, his helmet blown off, calling, "Whit! Whit! Help me!"

Corpsman Alan Kent arrived at the base of the tower in time to see the men sprawled on the rubble. He had come down from Mang Ca on a wild mule ride with a driver named Ray Howard, who for some reason wore his helmet backward, and who had HOWARD IS

MY NAME / TROUBLE IS MY GAME scrawled on his flak jacket. Kent had stretched himself flat on the back bed of Howard's vehicle, hanging on to the rails for dear life. Howard kept bellowing, "Keep your head down!" as he steered the mule through gunfire. He had dropped Kent off and then waited as the corpsman climbed toward Whitmer and Dave Schultz, who also had been blown off the tower. Those two were trying to pull Hammons to cover when Schultz was shot. The corpsman and the corporal managed to pull both men down. Schultz had been hit in the lower leg; Hammons looked worse off. He had a hole in his back by his shoulder blade, and blood was pumping out of it rhythmically.

"I'm hit bad," Hammons kept repeating. "I'm hit bad. Whit, I'm hit bad. My family, my family." His wife had given birth months earlier, and he seemed panicked to be letting her down. Then he passed out. He didn't look good.

Kent patched them up quickly and they were placed on Howard's mule. He roared off with them back to Mang Ca.

Whitmer went back up the slope. Most of the tower was now held by marines, but they were running out of ammo. Some of the men were hurling rocks and bricks. Enemy soldiers would duck, expecting a grenade, and that would stop them from shooting for a few moments.

This intense fighting lasted almost thirty minutes. By four thirty Harrington's men had the tower. It was little more than a high pile of rubble, but it was theirs . . . temporarily.

Whitmer was back up the hill looking for a member of his squad who was missing, Tom Zwetow. Thoms was helping. The two were talking quietly when they heard a muted voice calling out, "Corporal Whit! Corporal Whit!"

The voice was coming from underground. Zwetow had taken cover in an underground bunker vacated by the enemy, and an explosion had caved it in over him. It had knocked him out, and when he revived he was trapped. All of his body was buried except for his head, which, remarkably, remained uncovered in a pocket below the surface. There was space enough for him to breathe, but that was it. He had heard Vietnamese voices talking around him, so he had stayed still and quiet for hours. Then he heard Whitmer.

Everyone started digging. After they removed several large stones, Thoms spotted a helmet cover. They dug deeper and uncovered Zwetow's head and part of one arm. Thoms removed his helmet and poured water into it from his canteen, then he dipped his bandolier in the water and tenderly washed the dust and dirt from Zwetow's eyes. He patted him on the head, encouraging him. Both men were crying, but Zwetow smiled. He said the enemy had literally stood on top of him, yelling to each other as they fired down at the marines. For Thoms, it was the most joyful moment of a difficult day. Zwetow had a few bruises and scrapes, his face looked like someone had beaten him up, he had clearly been concussed and had been frightened terribly, but he was otherwise okay.

Harrington's men were hungry. A trip back to Mang Ca to collect C rations would have been too dangerous, so he sent some of his men to scrounge. Whitmer and two from his squad went through some of the empty houses on the block. They opened cupboards and drawers and found nothing. Whitmer remembered seeing fat colorful koi in an ornamental pond behind one of the houses on the way in. Fish are fish, Whitmer thought. They found the pond . . . and it was empty! Days later Thoms confessed: "Whit, I want to tell you something. I ate your fucking fish."

Thoms and his seven remaining men shared the small amount of water they had left and passed around one box of C rations. They helped patch each other up—all of them had shrapnel wounds. There was a pack of Salem cigarettes in the box, so Thoms opened it and passed one to everyone. They all smoked, the cigarettes cupped in their dirty hands to keep the light from giving away their position. Zwetow whispered to Thoms loud enough for all to hear, "Hey, Sarge, didn't you hear smoking can be hazardous to your health?" That produced a healthy round of muffled laughter.

The fight wasn't over. At about four in the morning, the enemy counterattacked, chasing the marines back down the gradient. Damien Rodriguez had been in the tower's lower level, shooting down at the enemy, when a rocket exploded in the room. He must have seen it flash, because he jumped just as it went off. He was hurled out of the structure and came down in the rubble with what turned out to be twenty-two pieces of shrapnel in his body. Half of his left calf muscle was gone, and one piece had torn straight across the top of his right wrist. He crawled down alongside another marine, passing dead and wounded men. They heard someone nearby calling for help but didn't see anyone. Rodriquez and the other marine crawled around until they were directly over the voice.

"He's right here, man," said the other marine.

"Help me!" the buried man called.

They began pulling off bricks, Rodriguez using his one good hand. He saw a photographer nearby, squatting behind cover—John Olson of *Stars and Stripes*. The photographer had come up with Kyoichi Sawada just in time to witness the Front retake the tower.

"Hey, motherfucker, get over here and help us!" Rodriguez said.

Olson stayed where he was. They uncovered half of the man; he was alive and sitting up straight. Rodriguez was now feeling his blood loss. He recognized his symptoms; he was going into shock.

"You know what, man," Rodriguez told the half-buried marine, "you better lean down because there are snipers here all over the place."

Rodriguez crawled across to where Olson was. A corpsman found him and began to patch him up. He pulled out a needle with morphine.

"Save that shit," Rodriguez said. "There are a lot of guys back there—I don't know if they're alive or what—they are going to need all the stuff you've got."

Harrington was still at the base of the tower, once more taking fire from above, urging his men back up. The marines' best chance of killing the enemy soldiers above them was to get close enough to throw grenades through the tower's windows, but when they stood to throw they were vulnerable, not only to the enemy back in the tower but to those on rooftops across the street.

Olson kept shooting pictures. He caught dramatic images of Thoms starting back up the rubble. The sergeant had taken shirts from two dead enemy soldiers and cut off the sleeves to have something to ward off the chill, and his torn trousers made it look like he was wearing a skirt. One of the men with him was Selwyn Taitt, a marine from New York whom everyone called "S-Man."

Thoms and Taitt managed to climb high enough to hurl grenades at positions in the tower, but the angle was bad, so the sergeant slid over and up to a better spot. Taitt had brought up a pouch filled with grenades. He would pull the pin on a grenade and toss it like a hot potato to Thoms, who would catch it and throw it up into the opening. When they made it to a flat spot on the wall, Taitt demonstrated a pretty good arm himself. He was small but athletic, and he could hurl a grenade a good distance. Photographer Don McCullin snapped a picture of him from behind, standing up amid the ruins of the huts and houses on top of the wall, just as one left his hand. In the lower right-hand corner of the frame, hiding under a piece of tin roof, was an enemy soldier who fired at him. Taitt saw the muzzle flash and heard the round crack past. He hit the ground, found his rifle, and was able to shoot before the man could fire again.

By early morning Harrington's marines owned the tower for good. They pulled twenty-four dead enemy soldiers from it and threw their bodies off the front of the tower. They had suffered badly themselves—six men killed and fifty wounded. Harrington had lost 40 percent of the men he'd brought into the Citadel. A few blocks back there was also heavy fighting, and fighter-bombers moved low over the city firing and dropping bombs. In the next day's New York Times, reporter Johnson wrote, "Shell casings from machine guns fell like rain on hundreds of Vietnamese spectators who swarmed out on the streets to watch the air action." He noted that the effort, while taking the tower, had advanced the marines' position by only two hundred yards.[36] But they were a critically important two hundred yards.

Whitmer was evacuated with the other wounded that evening. His injury was minor. When he got back to Phu Bai, one of the walking wounded, he was ordered to look through nearly a hundred body bags and identify those he recognized.

It took him two days to complete the job, unzipping the bags and looking at the pale, lifeless faces. He found Don Hammons, who had died from his wounds. It did not surprise Whitmer. Hammons had looked dead when they carried him away. But on the second day of this grim assignment he got a shock. He found the body of a friend whom he had left alive and well in Hue.[37]

6

Lefty

THESE DAYS IN the third week of the battle were the worst. Both sides were bloodied and many of the city's residents were dead or hurt or in hiding. The marines were using flamethrowers to burn bodies on the street, mostly in an effort to control the stench. Hue had become a city of the dead. It was still damp and cold and gray and was choking on its incinerated remains. The wet air absorbed the smoke and the foul odors of close combat until you not only breathed it; you wore it and tasted it—ash and cordite and the stench of rotting flesh. There were corpses everywhere, twisted and in pieces, in every stage of decay. On the littered city streets they rotted where they had fallen or where, in some places, they had been hastily tossed or bulldozed into heaps. Dead dogs, dead cats, dead pigs, dead people. In addition to those in the open, there were the dead in bunkers and enemy spider holes, and under rubble. The cool gray mist turned to a downpour from time to time, but mostly it just smothered everything and drained the city of color. The look of the place differed only slightly from the black-and-white photos on the front pages of American newspapers, a gloomy palette that ranged from the chalky white of pulverized plaster to the rich, oily black of dried blood. At American field hospitals, the dead were zipped into bags, numbered, and stacked, so that as the days passed they formed black walls of mortal remains.

The margin between life and the hereafter was tissue thin. You could die by lifting your head at the wrong moment, or by taking a step in any direction, or by doing nothing at all. Any piece of wall or house or chunk of debris large enough to hide behind was as precious as life itself but offered only the illusion of safety. You tried to cheat the odds by making yourself small and still, but the round that killed you might come at any time, from any direction. If you had to move, to step into the open, you did so in a mad dash toward some new lump of concrete or plaster that might be a refuge.

There was a steady roar of gunfire and explosions that would be eclipsed at intervals by the sound of a shell fired from one of the warships anchored fifteen to twenty miles east in the South China Sea. The biggest of their guns were sixteen-inchers, a term referring to the width of the barrel's bore. The gun itself was fifty times that long. It could hurl a projectile as heavy as a small car twenty-five miles. This would emerge in the general din as a low whistling that grew louder as it approached until it became a thing felt as much as heard, passing above the opaque ceiling of clouds like an airborne locomotive. The hurtling projectile moved with such force that it pressed on the grunts' eardrums, and when it hit the ground, even at a great distance, the earth shook. Walls crumbled.

It felt like the end of the world to Richard "Lefty" Leflar, who was deposited into this maelstrom on Friday, February 16, joining Harrington's Delta Company the day after it took the Dong Ba Tower. Leflar was eighteen. He had no idea what was going on. He had never heard of Tet, or Hue—which he pronounced *Hyoo* instead of *Hway*. He knew nothing of Ho Chi Minh, could not have pointed out Vietnam on a map, and could not define what the word "Communism" meant, other than something bad, something his country—*he*—was obliged to fight.

Just months earlier he had been a tough guy. Small, scrappy, and fearless—or so he thought—he was a white delinquent from a big Catholic family in Conshohocken, an industrial town northwest of Philadelphia where the land rises steeply from the Schuylkill River. Mills and factories along the bank defined the character of Leflar's hometown, but he was too young for a union job and too rambunctious and unruly for school. His father didn't work; he drank. With a brood of six, his mother had more than she could cope with. So Leflar ran wild. He had discovered that a boy didn't have to be big to win a fight, just willing. The key was to fear pain less than the other guy. This gave him, despite his size, a swagger in his neighborhood. Life had been shaping up just fine until the local magistrate, a barber, eyed the surly teenager dragged into his shop by the police for the umpteenth time, and between snips of his scissors, said. "You again. You have two choices, my man. They really want to put you in juvie. I have to put you somewhere."

And just like that, Leflar was a marine. Rather than ask his mother, he had forged his father's signature on the enlistment papers. Didn't know where the old man was. With the name Leflar, the marines probably would have called him Lefty even if he hadn't been left-handed. They sized him up as a shit bird from the get-go, but boot camp was built for tough guys, and America needed marines. So they whipped him into enough shape to wear a single crooked stripe on his dress greens and marched him out on graduation day. He turned eighteen in the summer of 1967 as a private first class. After Parris Island it had been Camp Lejeune for some light seasoning, then off to California, Okinawa, and Vietnam. He embraced it all. Marine Corps training instilled a reverence for the country's long history of warfare, for the men down through the generations who had lost or risked their lives in the nation's service. It initiated him into a proud tradition at the same time that it channeled Leflar's appetite for mayhem. Beneath that pugnacity was faith in his elders, one that had survived his father's drunken example. It was tribal, this faith, something so deep that it would never have occurred to him to question it, at least not yet. The big decisions, the ones that sent young men to war, were surely made with care by wiser heads who had his best interests at heart, like the magistrate who had rescued him by sending him to the Corps. That had been life-changing. Private First Class Leflar was ready. He was hard. He believed. He was all marine. Never mind the fine points of infantry maneuvers. He thought, *Cool. Just show me who to shoot.*

He landed with a shipment of recruits in Da Nang, the busiest American air base in South Vietnam. Leflar and the other newbies—to the marines they were "FNGs," Fucking New Guys—camped out for a night and a day inhaling diesel fumes and exhaust by the loud runways. Jets and helicopters came and went.

Among those waiting with Leflar was Calvin Hart, a private from Oakland, California, who was so tall and skinny that—according to a saying he liked—when he stood sideways and stuck out his tongue he looked like a zipper. Hart had been disappointed by the lack of promotion at his first post in Hawaii, the Marine Barracks Naval Ammunition Depot in Oahu. He was black and ambitious and was under the thumb of a commander he thought was racist, so he had volunteered for Vietnam, thinking that service there might speed him toward his goal of becoming a military policeman—his military occupation specialty (MOS). Only out on the runway in Da Nang there was no discussion of MOS, no consideration whatsoever of the career goals of Private First Class Calvin Hart. You just waited with all the other poor sumbitches until your name was called and you learned which infantry unit you would be joining.

By then the Battle of Hue was already notorious. It was more than two weeks old and the word was out: this was the last place on earth you wanted to go. Among the brothers it was *Oh, man, DO NOT go to One Five* (as if any of them had a say) . . . *the Fifth Marines up there in Hue City are gettin' their ass whipped . . . least of all do you want Delta Company One Five.* And of course, when they called Hart's name he was assigned to Fifth Marines, as was Leflar. Now, Hart was an optimist and he figured to himself, *Might not be so bad, . . . maybe . . .* there were thousands of men in the Fifth and only a few hundred were with Delta Company, but after the men were all sorted, Leflar and Hart and thirteen other unlucky bastards were given used helmets and flak jackets for the short flight north, cast-off gear just for the chopper ride, and, sure enough, the tags on them read "D 1/5," and, underscoring the true *fucked-uppedness* of their fortunes, the gear came complete with bullet holes and bloodstains.

They were choppered up to Phu Bai, and then trucked north into Hue on Thursday, February 15. They were deposited just outside the black stone walls of the Citadel, which was an astonishing thing for these newbies to behold, like something displaced in time. Nothing had prepared Leflar for it. He had envisioned rice paddies and jungle. Instead, this was a massive fort city, or the remains of one. The grunts already there, the men they joined, looked terrible. The rumors had been true. Delta had been through hell. They had taken heavy losses. They stank. They were covered with dirt and dried blood and, weirdly, powdered plaster—white or pale pink or yellow. They were sullen and silent. They were unshaven. Weariness hung on them as heavily as their bandoliers of ammo. Their fatigues were limp and in tatters. Lefty and the other FNGs practically shone in their crisp stateside greens, complete with starched caps. They had washed up clueless in the land of lost hope. Around them were high walls, ruined houses, and a huge Buddhist church of some kind with big bites taken out of it. The streets were strewn with rubble and dead bodies. One of the dead civilians—to the grunts, he noticed, all the locals were "gooks," the same as the enemy—had been placed in a macabre pose, sitting up with one cigarette jutting from its teeth and another wedged between two stiff, outstretched fingers.

The battle was raging. The squad they joined was to advance again at first light. They prepared that night. Considered useless for anything else, Leflar and Hart were designated ammo humpers. In addition to his rifle, Leflar was handed a second rifle and a helmet. Two light anti-tank weapons (LAWs) were hung across his back from straps over his shoulders. Then someone draped him with long bands of machine-gun ammo. He was a little fellow and, weighted down like that, he could barely move. And the guy in charge—Leflar had no idea who any of these men were and nobody wore symbols of rank—explained that they were going to move through a ruined archway in the great stone wall beside them and attack across the street. One group was to break left; the other was to break right.

It was a long wait until sunrise, and then, abruptly, it was, "Go! Go! Go! Go!" and everyone started running like mad. The squad passed under the arch and the world around Leflar erupted with gunfire and explosions. His instructions vanished with his wits. He stood in the open, frozen. A loud blast nearby knocked him down. He saw a car and crawled under it. He could hear the other guys shouting, "Come on! Come on!" urging him, but he dared not move. He had somehow already lost the helmet, the rifles, and the LAWs. Finally he started crawling as fast as he could in the direction of the voices. He reached a doorway and came face-to-face with a dead grunt, one who had been alive just moments before out on the street beside him.

"Where is your weapon?" another marine shouted at him.

"I don't know!"

"Just take this fucking one," he said, handing him the dead man's rifle and squaring his helmet on Leflar's head.

He sat immobilized in the roaring fight. His world shrank to the wall he crouched behind, the street just outside, and the dirty, angry men all around him trying to do what they were told and to stay alive. Leflar, the tough kid from outside Philly, shook uncontrollably. It was deafening.

"Shoot your fucking weapon!" one of the grunts screamed at him over the din, so Leflar lifted it and let fly a whole magazine of rounds out the doorway, aiming at nothing in particular. Then he loaded another and ran through that in the same way. He felt useless.

He lost track of time. It seemed like a long time that they were in the house, a big one with high ceilings and a second-floor balcony. Leflar was amazed that Vietnamese people even had houses like this. They stayed until more marines arrived. Someone Leflar took to be an officer, the kind of man who exudes authority by his bearing, loomed over them, his face smeared with white powder. Beneath his flak jacket he was wearing a non-marine-issue shirt with the sleeves cut off, and his trousers were torn and flapping from crotch to ankle.

"All right, men," he announced, "we are going to go across there," pointing to the street Leflar and the others had recently escaped. "We are a team; we are marines; we are going to do this."

Leflar thought he was out of his mind. *Who the hell is this guy?* He guessed the man was a colonel or a general. Whatever his rank, Leflar resolved to go no farther. Orders or no.

The "general" was, in fact, Sergeant Thoms, who had been in the thick of this fight for days and who was running hard on adrenaline and fear and, perhaps, the sheer exhilaration of somehow, improbably, still being alive. He exhibited the kind of courage that shames other men. The grunt beside Leflar counseled, "Do what he says."

So when Thoms bellowed, "Move!" the men moved, including Leflar.

As soon as he stepped outside the world again turned into deafening chaos, with the crack of small arms and the numbing blast of rocket grenades that sent men and the surrounding walls flying into pieces. He heard a wounded man behind him screaming, "Corpsman!" Up until this moment Leflar had bet his teenage life on the conviction that no matter what he did, nothing seriously bad would ever happen to him, and here the United States Marine Corps had taken him up on it. He thought, *Oh, my God. What did I get myself into? I've really messed up here.* He ran blindly.

He made it across the street. The carnage behind him was terrible. In movies, when a man got shot, they would sometimes show a small hole in his body. Leflar saw a grunt shot in the arm, and it was like the guy's limb had exploded. There was blood, lots of it, and glistening shredded strands of muscle and tendon and protruding ghastly white ends of bone. The man's arm just flapped weirdly at his side as he screamed. Some of those pleading for corpsmen were beyond help. One had been shot in the belly and his guts were spilled forward across his legs. The ones who made it across intact rested in this new spot, a corner hut painted pink. The ones nearest Leflar were a white marine and two black marines. Around them were the crumbled brick and mortar remains of houses and walls. The ground was thick with smaller flinders of construction. Then came the airborne locomotive passing invisibly overhead and a blast so big that they were all knocked flat. There was a great juddering and pieces of roof and wall crashed down. One of the black marines looked at Leflar, horrified, clutching his bleeding throat. He stood and ran. Leflar did not see the white marine. Then came another eardrum-shattering blast. The wall behind him cracked, the ground opened, and Leflar slipped into it.

The hole was about five feet deep and pitch-black. His pants had been blown off and his shirt was ripped and he was bleeding from several places. His feet hurt. He had lost his weapon again. He was dazed. His ears rang. It was so putrid that he gagged. When he came to his senses he groped in the dark, feeling for his weapon, and everywhere he reached it was wet and mushy. It took him a few moments to realize that he was lying in the rotting remains of dead people. He had no idea how many. They either had been killed in the hole or had been pushed into it afterward. He recoiled and moved to escape, but overhead were the sounds of intense shooting and bombs, which petrified him even more. Suspended between revulsion and terror, he leaned against the side of the hole and wrapped his arms around his bare, shaking legs. He shook with fear and he cried. He may have screamed, but it was so noisy above him that he couldn't hear himself. He had given up. Curled in a fetal position, Lefty Leflar wailed like a baby.

In time, he calmed down. The shooting directly overhead eased. He gently maneuvered the pile of debris over his head and peeped out.

He saw no one. Where were the marines? He guessed they had pulled back. He was not about to stir from his hiding place, no matter how ghastly it was, until he knew where they were.

An hour or so passed before he saw two grunts picking their way down the block. Knowing how easy it would be to get shot, he waited until they were close and then sprang out of the hole with his hands up.

"I am here!" he shouted. "Don't shoot!"

"Who the fuck are you?" one of the marines asked. Leflar was quite a sight. The explosion that had thrown him into the hole had ripped his shirt and blown his pants and boots off. He had lost his pack, his helmet, and his weapon. He was scraped up and bleeding and was covered with dust. He was so overcome at having been found that he wept. His feet hurt.

"Weren't you guys looking for me?" Leflar asked. "I was stuck in this hole."

"Get the fuck out of here," the marine said.

"There are dead gooks in the hole," he said.

"There are dead gooks everywhere," the marine said. "Get the fuck out of here."

Leflar made his way two blocks back to where he found a collection of dead and wounded marines on the ground, and a busy corpsman at work sorting them.

He sat down there and watched. The corpsman finally asked him, "What's going on?"

Leflar explained what had happened to him.

"Well, you are a fucking mess," the corpsman said. He directed the shaken young marine to a pile of boots and clothing taken off the wounded and dead and told him to suit up. Leflar found boots that were too big but he was happy to have them. He lifted a filthy shirt that looked about his size, but there was blood on the back of it, still wet.

"Just be glad it's not your blood," the corpsman told him. Then Sergeant Thoms appeared—he was the man who had ordered the attack that had put Leflar in the hole.

"Get yourself some fucking gear," he barked at Leflar, and he began riffling through the pile and tossing more pieces of clothing to the private.

"Jesus Christ, I don't want to do this," Leflar complained.

"Look, a marine dies, you honor him by splitting up his gear," said Thoms. "Never forget that."

"Okay," said Leflar.

"If you die, I split up your fucking gear; if I die, you split up my fucking gear."

"Fine," said Leflar.

Thoms saw Leflar eyeing his own trousers, which were still split from crotch to boot. He told the private, modeling one bare leg, "These are better than what you've got on; your fucking balls are hanging out . . . come on!"

Leflar fell in again with Thoms's squad. He got to know two of their names, Ken Blair and Bob Anderson. They seemed like wild men to him. They would run across contested streets with their guns roaring at their hips, screaming at the top of their lungs. It was like they didn't care about getting hit. They acted like they were *loving* it! They shot at everything. Most of the time they didn't look long enough to know what they were shooting at; anything across the street on the enemy side got blasted.

Leflar stayed behind them and tried to avoid the crazy risks they took. He would stay outside the buildings they ran into, as if standing guard. Once they were inside, he would find a place with some cover and wait. At one of these houses, with Blair and Anderson inside, a Vietnamese man stepped through a side door. They saw each other. Both froze. The man was not in a uniform. He wore brown pants and a lighter brown shirt and had a rag tied around his head. He was turned to the side, looking back at Leflar. He had no weapon. It looked like he wanted to run but didn't dare. He was about twenty-five yards away.

Leflar shouted into the window, "Yo! There's a fucking civilian out here!"

"That ain't no fucking civilian!" shouted Blair. "Kill him! Kill him!"

What the fuck? thought Leflar. He leveled his rifle, and, just as the marines had taught him, took a breath, let out slowly, taking aim. The man hadn't moved—only seconds had elapsed. He seemed to be waiting to be waved off. Leflar fired. He hit the man in the buttocks and he went straight down.

"I got him!" Leflar yelled, excited. He had never shot anyone before. Blair looked out to see.

"He's still fucking moving!" he shouted. "Kill him! Kill him!"

The man was trying to raise himself. He was on one knee. Leflar emptied his magazine into him.

His squad mates hooted their approval.

"You killed that motherfucker!" said one.

Leflar was shaking like a leaf. They congratulated him on his first kill, and they passed along their own approach to fighting in Hue: *A gook is a gook. Kill them all.* This struck Leflar as a reckless policy, but that same day, as he was crouched on the street with the others scanning the terrain before them, they saw a man who looked to him like a civilian pop his head up from the tin and debris of a collapsed roof. The man had not seen them. Several men from the squad crawled back and returned with handfuls of grenades. Then they started shooting at the place where the man showed his head and tossed a few grenades at it. After the explosions, they stopped and listened. A Chinese Communist (ChiCom) grenade came hurtling at them from the hole. Blair swore later that it hit his helmet. It exploded. The concussion blew them back a little but none of them were hurt. They reopened fire. Leflar thought he had been hit. He was afraid to look down, but he felt his pants, and they were wet. His squad mates dragged him to a wall.

"Are you all right?" asked Anderson.

"No, I'm hit!" Leflar said. "I'm hit!" He felt like something had hit him in the stomach. He was afraid to look down.

"You ain't hit," Anderson said, laughing. "You pissed your fucking pants!"

Through these humiliations, Leflar gradually felt he was getting the hang of it. They would attack a position, a house across the street, and the enemy would throw and shoot grenades at them, blast away at them with rifles and machine guns, and they would come back with more and better firepower, with the tanks and the Ontos. Mortar squads would set up not far behind them and drop 60 mm rounds on them— the marines called them, fondly, "sixty mike-mikes"—with uncanny precision. Thoms's men would move forward a little and the enemy would move back a little. Then everybody would set up to do it again.

Leflar was disappointed that Thoms would not write him up for a Purple Heart—all he would need were two more! He showed Thoms all the cuts and scrapes he'd gotten from the explosion that first day. Thoms just told him, "Suck it up and go away."

It was hard to argue with the sergeant. He had been hit in both legs, in the arms.[38] None of the wounds was life-threatening, and he swore he wasn't in pain, so he refused to be evacuated and the remnants of his squad did not want him to go either—near the end of the battle his men were carrying him around with them. He had kept them alive. He was more than smart; he was lucky. If he left, they'd get some fresh-scrubbed lieutenant who'd be sure to get them killed.

Bill Eshelman, a marine major attached to Colonel Dinh's forces as an adviser, was impressed by the cornered enemy's skill and resolve. He had never seen such well-designed defenses. They had interlocking bands of fire at every intersection, the cross fire covering the streets from all directions, and were also dug in on top of the west and south walls, so they could shoot down. His job was to figure out how to advance against this.

Air support was iffy, but he was able to draw on the marine batteries and naval guns. His Vietnamese troops, who could listen in on the enemy's radio communications, had learned that the Front was using the grounds of the Royal Palace, long off-limits to big guns, as a place to regroup. They had a hospital there, and it functioned as their forward command center. Eshelman began raining shells on it. Although nothing like the outer walls, the ones around the palace grounds were formidable, but the steady bombardment wreaked havoc inside.

The ARVN troops received mortar fire in return. One strike, right after Eshelman arrived on Friday, wiped out the aid station, killing five medics. The neighborhoods where they fought were all residential, but civilians were nowhere to be seen. The going was very slow. For days at a time they made no progress while losing large numbers of men.

Eshelman's counterpart, whose job it was to direct the South Vietnamese artillery, came to him in the evening of the third day and threw up his hands.

"We can't get across that street," he said. "What more can we do?"

The two sat over a map and plotted the artillery strategy anew. There was nothing they could see to do differently. They had tried to drop troops on top of the wall by helicopter, but the men were cut down immediately. Over the next five days, the ARVN forces lost two hundred men.[39]

On the same day that Eshelman arrived, an enthusiastic young lieutenant named Pat Polk showed up at Mang Ca with more reinforcements for Thompson, and he was immediately given command of the demoralized and depleted Alpha Company. Polk had served as a corporal before going back to school to become an officer. He had nearly finished his rotation in Vietnam and, after being wounded twice, had been given a job in the rear to finish out his tour. He had volunteered to go to Hue and had swum across a moat with a case of grenades on the way up, earning the nickname "Hand Grenade," which captured his personality. Thompson saw Polk as the cure for what ailed Alpha Company. The night he arrived, he personally led a daring mission with a handful of volunteers to rescue a squad that had gotten cut off, and returned to cheers and congratulations from his new command.

As the marines pressed in on them, the Front defended an ever-decreasing ground and fought, if anything, with even more intensity. They would shelter as best they could from the bombing and shelling, and then use the rubble created to set up new fighting positions. Civilians were being flushed out in increasing numbers. The top Front commander inside the Citadel, Lieutenant Tang Van Mieu, believed the Americans were using civilians as shields. He saw so many moving in and immediately behind enemy lines that it was impossible to fire on marines without hitting civilians. But the same was true on his side of the line, and if the Americans were playing that game, he could, too. He and his men stayed close to the crowds when they could.[40]

7

Why Are You Guys Doing This?

Nguyen Van Quang, the former student organizer who had been setting up the liberation government in his sector of the Citadel and deciding on the guilt of traitors, gave up these efforts and went back to fighting, digging in with what was left of his militia in the southwest corner.

When he had burst through Chanh Tay Gate at the vanguard of the Front's armies on the first morning of Tet, Quang believed he was spearheading the victorious final battle of the war. Now those hopes were dashed. Each day he and his squad would fall back to a new block into long trench lines that sometimes ran right through people's homes. These enabled them to shift forces around without being seen. Their most important and final line of defense would be the Huu Gate, which was also going to be their way out. It was clear they would be leaving. His dreams of helping to rule his home city as political commissar had collapsed. Every day more of his comrades fell. They scarcely had time to bury the dead in shallow graves. The wounded were carried off by bearers whose shoulders and hands were blistered and raw from the work.

Quang lost five members of his unit in one day, fighting in a bunker just two hundred yards from the flagpole at Ngo Mon. Skyraider bombers appeared overhead and he shouted for everyone to get out. Before they did, a bomb knocked him off his feet and battered him with falling rocks. He was not seriously hurt, but he found two of his female fighters dead just outside the bunker. They had been shot as they emerged. The blast had collapsed the shelter and buried three others. He dug frantically but found only one body. Two of them were so new to his squad that he did not even know their names. This haunted him, because it was his job to eventually notify the families of those killed. Here they had sacrificed everything for the cause, and it would never be known or honored.

He tried to keep as close to the enemy lines as he could. To Quang, it felt like a deadly game of tag. If the Americans or *nguy* moved, he would shoot at them. If he or his men moved, they would be shot at. Their losses mounted hourly, especially once the heavy shellings and bombing started.

There were so many ways to die in Hue that it became impossible to sort causes. The South Vietnamese and the Americans blamed all the deaths on the purges. Mayor Khoa, who had been rescued days earlier, told *New York Times* reporter Johnson that in one day, Friday the ninth, three hundred had been executed by the Front. The victims were "government officials, civil servants and technicians," he said. They had not yet found their common grave.[41]

But there was blame enough for both sides. The storm of war blew flat all semblance of law, logic, and decency. To soldiers there was a kind of order—causes and lines to be defended, soldiers who were either friend or enemy—but to civilians it was just savagery.

Tran Thi Thu Van, the writer from Saigon, spent those weeks wandering in the wasteland of the battle trying to stay alive. She would later record scene after scene of horror in her book *Mourning Headband for Hue*. Her uncle, Doi Hoa, a kindly elder and musician who lived in a small hut near the royal palace tending antique musical instruments, and who used to give her music lessons when she was a child, was killed by a fragment from an artillery shell that pierced his temple. His house and his collection were destroyed.[42] Near the Gia Hoi School, where the most notorious of the purges was being orchestrated, an entire family, including children, had been killed because a VC soldier believed their TV set was a method of communicating with the Americans.[43] Vietnamese-American toddlers in one house were killed by VC soldiers who swung them by the heels and crushed their heads against a wall—"These are children of an American imperialist who are left here to harm the future of the nation," their leader explained.[44] Tinh

Hoa, a bookstore owner, left his house to look for food and water and was shot dead—"Some people guess that it was the Viet Cong who shot him, and other people are absolutely sure that it was the Americans, but whoever fired the shot, Mr. Tinh Hoa nevertheless got killed," Tran wrote.[45] American soldiers at a bridge shot a dog that had fallen into the river. As it struggled to swim back to the shore, the men continued shooting, not to kill the animal but out of sheer cruelty, to prolong its suffering by keeping it from reaching the bank—"The dog gradually gets farther and farther away from the shore, howling plaintively; it's absolutely heartrending."[46]

> So, this is the end, from the eldest person, the most ancient one like my uncle, to the little crossbred Vietnamese-Americans—they all have been killed in the whirlwind of war. How many tons of ammunition are pouring down on the heads of people in the city of Hue? These several days the airplanes flying over the city are countless. Standing by the National Highway [Highway 1] we can see jets flying swiftly like lightning and dropping load after load of bombs, followed by the sounds of explosions, which even though reverberating from far away are still endlessly terrifying. We go out farther and stand on this side of the river looking across: Dong Ba market has become flat ground; houses in the downtown area seem to be tightly wrapped in smoke and dust. With each explosion, dust and bricks and tiles fly up in bits and pieces, as if a gigantic firecracker explodes, throwing corpses up into the air . . . I think about the people still trapped in Tu Dam and in the Citadel. The entire Citadel is enveloped by high walls . . . bullets from airplanes, American bullets, fall like rain. How many people are nervously struggling with this? The sturdiest underground shelters can withstand guns of only small caliber; how can they withstand the penetration of missiles and tons of bombs dropped down each day?[47]

The dead were on the sidewalks and streets, in shattered buildings, in shrubs where they had been tossed out of sight, or beneath heaps of bricks that covered their decay but not their stench. The mounting toll weighed heavily on Nguyen Dac Xuan, the hopeful poet and commissar who had entered the Citadel so overjoyed, and who was now bent and sore and spent from digging graves. He fought during the day and spent all night trying to inter the dead. Nighttime was the only safe time to dig, and the scene was nightmarish, lit by explosions and the glow of the Americans' descending flares. Because there were so many dead, the graves were shallow, just enough to cover rotting flesh. Sometimes they put two or three bodies in the same hole. Heavy American artillery killed Front soldiers and civilians alike, and there were times when there were so many bodies that they just shoved them into a bomb's smoking crater and filled it back in.

And still, as if there was not dying enough, the purges continued. There was no longer any pretense of building a new society. The culling of enemies had its own unstoppable logic.

As Xuan was digging one night, in the rain, a new group of five or six arrestees were being led past with their hands tied behind their backs. A flare lit the sky, and he noticed that among them was one with long hair, whom he immediately recognized. It was his friend Le Quang.

He stopped the officer leading the queue, a Major Hai, and asked, "Why did you arrest Le Quang?"

Hai told him that Quang was a traitor. He had been sending intelligence to the enemy at Mang Ca that enabled them to zero their artillery in on the command posts of liberation forces.

Xuan took up his friend's defense. He told the officer that Le Quang was a photographer and that he lived in a village far outside the Citadel. He had helped the liberation by taking pictures for Xuan's unit.

"He does not know the neighborhoods or the people here. How could he inform on anyone? Mr. Le Quang is a patriot. Why are you guys doing this?"

Le Quang was set free and thanked Xuan profusely for saving his life.[48]

8

There It Is

Jᴇʀʀʏ McCᴀᴜʟᴇʏ sᴛʀᴀɴɢʟᴇᴅ an enemy soldier with the chinstrap of his helmet. He managed to step aside and avoid the man's bayonet thrust and then grabbed his helmet, which was strapped under the chin, and, with a tremendous surge of adrenaline, twisted the strap violently around his neck, held him down, and choked him to death. It took an agonizingly long time to do. Afterward he hardly gave it a second thought. It had been a life-and-death struggle, and if he felt anything, it was amazement that he'd had the strength and presence of mind to prevail. Not all of his kills left him that untroubled.

After the tower was taken, McCauley helped stand guard. It had been reduced to four tall heaps of charred brick and mortar, but it was still the highest point on the east wall. His machine-gun squad, part of Alpha Company, would creep up after dark and choose a new position every night at about ten o'clock. There were still enemy guns close enough to mortar them if they were discovered. They usually settled into existing spider holes, one dug by the Front before the marines arrived, or in between large chunks of what had been the tower. The wall below had crumbled, so the Dong Ba Gate was now impassable to vehicles. People, however, could still slip through.

The view from McCauley's position was panoramic. The falling flares sketched the city in tones from silver gray to black. Roofs and walls had crumbled into piles of wood lathing, plaster, tile, and stone. Some of the outer walls still stood with empty black windows and doorways that opened on littered hollows. Here and there were shattered bamboo gardens with jumbled piles of scorched stems that looked like discarded pipes. In the middle of the night the ruins became spookily silent. There was the occasional pop of a rifle, but men on both lines did their best to stay still and quiet, so close to each other that it wasn't safe to reveal exactly where they were. Sometimes enemy mortars would rise from outside the Citadel, arc over the walls, and crash into the neighborhoods inside. They were anything but precise. Some would explode against the wall; some skipped off the top and landed by pure chance inside, as likely to hit the Front's own lines as marines. There was never a minute when death could not arrive without warning. McCauley spent those hours behind an M60 machine gun. They had strict orders to shoot anything or anyone—even any Americans—who tried to pass through the ruined gate.

"Anyone who tries to come through, you are to consider them the enemy," they were instructed. "You are to shoot and kill them."

There was cause to be suspicious of everything, and also to shoot without warning. Calling out gave away your position. And anyone exiting the fortress could be delivering useful intelligence to those mortar batteries outside.

But there were also civilians still trying to escape. Those in the killing zone faced a maze of gun positions, manned by fighters on both sides, all of them jumpy. One night up on the wall, McCauley and his assistant gunner spotted what looked like a Vietnamese couple with two children approaching the gate on the street below. It was two o'clock in the morning. The squad hesitated.

"Our orders are to kill them," one of the men said.

They went back and forth about it, and one of the men said, "You have the gun, McCauley, you do it."

He shot them down. He was relieved to learn later that the woman had a carefully drawn map of where the gun positions were on the streets leading to the gate. McCauley took that as confirmation that the couple were delivering intelligence, so he felt better about killing them. The map, of course, was also exactly what people would make before trying to pick their way out of a dangerous spot.

Chris Jenkins, the International Voluntary Services (IVS) worker from Philadelphia who had been hiding in a house just south of the tower ever since the first night of Tet, got back under his bed when his Vietnamese friends heard firing close by. Then someone knocked on the door.

An American voice shouted, "Are there any VC in there?"

Jenkins got up and identified himself. It was one of Thompson's marines.

"You're lucky we didn't throw a grenade in the window before asking questions," he said.

He was escorted to Captain Jennings, who asked with disbelief, "Did the marine really walk up and ask, 'Are there any VC in there?'"

Jenkins nodded.

"It's a great war," said Jennings.[49]

The battle sputtered to a near halt again on Friday, February 16. After taking the tower, Thompson's battalion had nine blocks between it and the fortress's south wall. General Truong's troops, which would soon be heavily reinforced, had about the same distance to cover on the west side. That would leave only the royal palace, which they knew was now the command center for Front troops inside the Citadel. With the triangle now almost fully recovered, if the army could do its job in the countryside to the west and north, the battle would at last be over.

Alvin Webb, the veteran United Press International (UPI) war reporter, wrote a personal account on Saturday, from the front lines inside the Citadel:

> This is getting tough and terrifying. I don't mind admitting I'm scared. I wish we knew what was going on on the outside. It is nine blocks from where I am sitting on the south side of the wall around the Citadel.
>
> It may become the bloodiest nine blocks for the men of the U.S. Marine Corps since that other war in Korea when they fought and died in the streets of Seoul.
>
> "Seoul was tough," an old top sergeant who was there told me a few minutes ago. "But this—well, it's something else."
>
> There is a kid marine on a stretcher about 10 feet from me. There isn't much left of his left leg.
>
> . . . "Five snipers," Capt. Scott Nelson of Jacksonville, Fla., said. "That's all it takes to tie us down completely."

You can hear the whine of the snipers' bullets and the eerie whoosh of B-40 rockets and feel the thunder of mortar rounds chewing up houses.

"This all looks terrible," Cpl. Frank Lundy of Gravette, Ark., said. "We're being eaten up. They gotta get out of here."[50]

Progress was painfully slow. The big guns on the tanks and the Ontos and the skill of the marine artillery batteries had made progress inevitable—the marines could now batter enemy positions mercilessly before attempting to cross streets. Artillery would unload first, and then, following the pattern Cheatham had developed across the river, the tanks would roll out, drawing fire from every quarter. This would reveal the major enemy gun positions. Then the Ontos would race out in front and unload with all six barrels before scooting back to cover. The tactics worked by destroying everything in the marines' path. The Front retreated to ever-shrinking ground.

Michael Herr, the *Esquire* writer, described Major Thompson at his command headquarters, just a few blocks behind the forward line:

At night in the CP [Command Post], the major who commanded the battalion would sit reading his maps, staring vacantly at the trapezoid of the Citadel. It could have been a scene in a Norman farmhouse twenty-five years ago, with candles burning on the tables, bottles of red wine arranged along damaged shelves, the chill in the room, the high ceilings, the heavy ornate cross on the wall. The major had not slept for five nights, and for the fifth night in a row he assured us that tomorrow would get it for sure, the final stretch of wall would be taken and he had all the marines he needed to do it. And one of his aides, a tough mustang first lieutenant, would pitch a hard, ironic smile above the major's stare, a smile that rejected good news, it was like hearing him say, "The major here is full of shit, and we both know it."[51]

The enemy was tenacious. The marines paid for every block, sometimes for every house. On one of these days, Calvin Hart, the marine who had volunteered for Vietnam in hopes of becoming a military policeman, faced a wrenching dilemma. Doc Rhino—Michael Rein-hold—one of the platoon corpsmen, a man whose selfless acts of courage under fire had made him revered, finally tempted fate once too often. He was shot down as he ran from cover to reach two downed men. Reinhold was a tall, red-haired man from Arizona, a big target anyway, and he had gotten himself an army backpack that was twice the size of the ones issued to marines just so he could carry more medical supplies. The guys loved him. And now he was down in the open. He got up on one knee and was trying to pull himself upright when he was shot again. This time he lay motionless, clearly dead. He stayed there until dark, about twenty-five feet in front of them. A platoon sergeant then asked for volunteers to go out and bring Doc and the others back.

Hart desperately did not want to volunteer. It was a rule he'd embraced in boot camp that had been strongly reinforced by experience—*never volunteer for anything*. But on the other hand, he wanted to do the decent thing. If he were out there, he sure as hell would want somebody to come get him. Not raising his hand was a moral failure that he knew would haunt him. Why should somebody else have to do it? He was new. He had taken nowhere near the same number of risks these other men had. How could he *not* volunteer? It was quiet, but they had all learned during the day that the enemy was dug in all around. The sergeant's challenge hung there for a long, excruciating moment. Hart kept his hand down and was grateful when three others raised theirs. As they prepared to go out, he waited behind his gun for all hell to break loose again and prayed that it would not. All hell did break loose, and Hart fired back with everybody else. Doc Rhino and the other two dead marines were dragged to cover without any of the volunteers getting hit, which was an enormous relief. Hart knew he would not have wanted to carry that around with him.

He was horrified from the first moment he entered Hue to the last. The things he saw! The Front's snipers were extremely accurate, and they aimed for the head. Guys would be sitting on the floor and not even realize that the tops of their heads were visible through the window, and the next second they were dead and the tops of their heads were gone. One marine was hit in the head and toppled out of a second-floor window, except his foot was tangled on something so he hung upside down while the inside of his skull emptied. There was this one dead Vietnamese woman in the street. Both of her legs had been crushed flat by a tank. When Hart's squad walked past her the first time, she was sitting upright, dead, with a surprised look. When they came back that way she had been run over so many times that you could no longer even tell she had been a person.

"There it is," said one of the men in his squad. It was a sentence they nearly wore out.

Hart had come to Vietnam expecting to fight amateurs, little men in black pajamas and conical hats who were no match for United States Marines. But the enemy encountered in Hue was tough and professional, every bit their match. These fighters were uniformed and well-equipped, and they set up defensive positions and fields of fire as good as anything taught by the Corps. And they sure as hell seemed to believe in their cause. In his first few days Hart had seen some dragged live from spider holes where they had stayed behind to fight to the death. As tough as the marines were, they didn't feel that kind of commitment. He and the other grunts, as far as Hart was concerned, at least half of them, had no clear idea why they were even there. None of them knew enough to write a paragraph about Vietnam. Maybe the officers did, but most of the grunts, it seemed to him, didn't even really care to know more. They had enlisted, they were trained to fight, the country had sent them. Enough said. As far as Hart could see it, they fought mostly to finish out their tours and get their asses home intact. That was it. Still, there were situations like Doc Rhino's that seemed to demand something heroic, even from him.

Who lived and who didn't live, who got hurt and who seemed immune . . . it made no sense. Every day some of the smartest, most salty guys got hit, and others, well . . . take Leflar. He'd been in trouble since the day they came. The first days in particular, Leflar had seemed almost comically lost. But other than those scratches he kept whining about, the kid seemed invincible. In the middle of one grinding street battle a Patton clanked out into the street and slowly turned and then raised its big gun to aim at a house on the edge of their line. Hart knew that Leflar was upstairs on its second floor. And just as the realization hit—BOOM!—the gun blasted away half of the building. Hart and the rest of his squad found Leflar in the rubble, coated with pulverized mortar and dust but otherwise unharmed. A squared-away guy like Doc Rhino was dead, and Leflar? He seemed to have nine lives!

Captain Harrington's company fought down the top of the wall in tandem with the marines advancing on the streets below. Harrington was surprised that the Front did not launch any counterattacks. With the pressure being put on the southwest sector, they could not have been getting much ammo or replacements anymore. The killing of the Front's regimental commander in the artillery barrage had apparently created some confusion. But the fight didn't get easier.

Webb, moving with Harrington's men, wrote:

> I am alive and intact, for the moment. But when I look around me I get the sinking feeling I am among a rapidly diminishing number of Americans in Hue who can say that.
>
> The monsoon drizzle woke us this morning. It fell gently, making little puddles. There was a warming fire and the leathernecks sat around chatting in the wet gray dawn.
>
> A marine stepped briskly into the circle. "Charlie is getting resupplied. They just advised us."
>
> He was followed by another, "Okay. Saddle up. We're moving out."
>
> We moved out . . . We are in Finh Street.
>
> On our right, Bravo and Charlie companies had pulled even with us.
>
> "Let's go!" somebody screamed.
>
> The sky was suddenly filled with lead, steel, and explosions from both directions. [Greg] Jenkins was not with us this morning. The platoon leader lost some fingers on his right hand on Saturday. He will have a Purple Heart to go with his Silver Star. Neither was [John] Carlson here today. A concussion from a communist grenade had blown his ear drums.
>
> A lot of others are not here this morning either. They were men whose faces I had come to know well. Their bleeding and dying in this war is over.
>
> We went terrace by terrace . . . I timed my moves between rockets and dashed across the street and up a flight of broken stairs over a 2 ft high stretch of barbed wire. Bullets sang over my head.[52]

When the marines got to within four hundred yards of the south wall, the enemy was about as compressed and dug-in as it could be. That day marines found two dead enemy fighters chained to their heavy machine guns.[53] Fred Emery, a reporter for the *Times* of London, was shown the bodies and the chains. It was the only instance of its kind, and the men may have been prisoners released weeks earlier and forced to fight, but the story quickly made the rounds, reinforcing the notion that the enemy was made up of soldiers who would fight to the last, not because they believed in their cause but because they were being compelled to do so.

Firepower made all the difference. When it could, the air force now dropped napalm over neighborhoods still occupied by the enemy. It was more effective than bombs, which left piles of rubble into which the enemy could crawl and set up new firing positions. With napalm, the flames sucked all of the oxygen out of underground bunkers, suffocating anyone inside, while incinerating everything above that wasn't made of stone. There was no ducking the onslaught.

And Harrington was right about resupply. By the third week of the siege the Front was depleted of both men and ammo. It could not compete with the marines' ceaseless reserves of guns and bombs and men. Le Huu Tong, the bazooka gunner, had seen seven members of his squad killed by one tank round. Their bodies were torn into pieces and scattered so badly that his squad could not bury the men individually. His squad especially feared the Ontos. It came close and its aim was more precise. It could kill men hiding behind thick stone walls. During daylight they now spent as much of their time moving as fighting, saving their ammo, picking their shots.[54] The Front's tactics impressed the veteran marine officers. Under terrible conditions it maintained order and was still conducting disciplined maneuvers.

Grunts who had been eager for combat were sorely disabused. The conditions were hellish. Tommy Brown, who arrived a day or two after Leflar and Hart, joining Harrington's company, had been so eager to get to Vietnam that when he was told it might be months before he shipped out he went AWOL out of disgust. He got caught six months later and spent a month in the brig before they gave him what he wanted.

Brown was now bewildered and revolted by what he'd sought. He spent the first night in Hue scared, damp, and cold, listening to the gunfire in the distance. His squad leader kept moving them. They would settle into a building, doze off, and an hour later be roused to move someplace else. But once the sun came up he relaxed, followed orders, and felt safer, surrounded by ruins that reminded him of photographs he had seen of European cities during World War II. They moved amid the detritus of everyday lives, vitamin bottles, a child's backpack filled with homework smeared with blood, American candy bar wrappers, the contents of someone's shattered wardrobe. It was nothing at all like what Brown expected—the Corps had prepared him for Vietnam by giving a course in jungle fighting. The city itself, the parts of it still standing, reminded him of Nashville, where he had grown up. He was struck by the images of the swastika he saw everywhere, not knowing that it was an ancient Buddhist sign for good fortune (and not noticing that it was an inverted form of the Nazi symbol).[55] There were cars and trucks everywhere. The tops of the trees were nearly all blown away.

One of the first buildings Brown entered was a spaghetti factory. It had been blown up and everything inside was draped with strings of pasta. One of his squad mates exclaimed, "Mamma mia!" The factory was infested with rats. Another night they camped out at an abandoned Esso gas station.

All of this was just strange. What really shook Brown was the unremitting horror and cruelty. He watched as an enemy soldier who refused to come out of a spider hole voluntarily was blown out of it in pieces. In one very big, well-appointed house they found two dead children who had not been killed in an explosion; each had been shot multiple times. *Who would be deliberately shooting kids?*

"There it is," one of the men said.

Dogs were shot by reflex—after you'd seen one rooting into a dead body it wasn't hard to do. Brown watched a tank run over a big hog, which got caught up in the treads and carried along a distance before it fell out, its remains completely flattened by the tank behind it. People were run over, too, civilians mostly. He was walking behind Harrington and his squad leader, Sergeant Richard Morris, when they came upon a dead enemy soldier whom rigor mortis had frozen with one arm pointing up. Morris walked over to the body and kicked it, then turned to Harrington and said, "He won't talk, sir." Brown thought it was funny but the captain did not.

Every night there was booze. Bottles discovered in empty houses were opened and shared. Brown was just eighteen and had little experience with alcohol. Whenever they moved a few blocks behind each day's firing line, there were children peddling beer in sixteen-ounce bottles. The men had been drinking brackish well water dosed with iodine pills or Kool-Aid packets they had received in letters from home mixing it in their canteens to cover up the bad taste, so even warm beer looked good. Brown discovered the wretchedness of a hangover. He saw marines looting; one ran out of a jewelry store with watches up his forearms to the elbow. Later, when the fighting inside the Citadel was over, Major Thompson declared that any object for which a marine had no proof of purchase would be destroyed. Men started smashing radios and watches and other loot against the walls, much to the dismay of Vietnamese civilians looking on.

Rick Grissinger came to Hue on the same day as Brown. A small, skinny eighteen-year-old from Clearwater, Florida, Rick was a religious young man who didn't drink, smoke, or swear. He'd been eager to come to Vietnam, but the war turned out to be a lot different from what he'd imagined. He was repulsed by the bodies floating in the Huong River. He reeled at a stack of partly burned Vietnamese bodies, soldiers and civilians. Someone had doused them with diesel fuel and set them on fire, but the effort had just left them charred. In the pile were also body parts. He could not sleep. An older sergeant, a large black man, took him into a bombed-out house on his first day and showed him a Vietnamese family, man and woman and children, all dead. They had been wired together before being shot and set on fire.

"I know what you learned in high school, but this is what Communism really is," the sergeant said.

He watched bulldozers moving great piles of bodies into mass graves. The stench was so horrible, his stomach would turn just thinking about it years later.

"There it is," he said.

On every block they found people hiding in holes. The marines were amazed that people could survive crowded together underground in spaces so small. In one, they found ten family members who said they had been there for two or three days. The family emerged screaming, terrified, with their hands over their heads. The marines checked them for weapons and sent them to the throngs now being managed by Truong's forces.

It had become an enormous job. In order to avoid being infiltrated by the enemy, Truong's men had to question every civilian. Those deemed true civilians were herded into several school buildings where they camped. Those deemed prisoners were bound and roped together. They sat squatting on their haunches, blindfolded or with their heads covered by burlap sacks, silent and stoical, waiting to be carried off by choppers to an uncertain fate. Some of the ARVN soldiers abused them, spitting on them, slapping them, kicking them, or poking at them with rifles.

Surrendering could get you killed. Felix Bolo, the Agence France-Presse bureau chief, described a scene he witnessed:

> Hue. Feb. 21—He was waving a white flag, but it did not stop the bullets.
>
> I watched him today, one of four civilians who emerged from houses burning after a napalm attack by United States Skyhawk fighter-bombers. The houses were in the bullet-riddled Sporting Club zone between two American positions.
>
> One of the civilians ran to hide but the other three walked slowly, waving what appeared to be a white flag. From the United States marine sector came a hail of fire. Two of the civilians dived for shelter. The third stopped short at the top of some stone steps, turned slowly around, dropped the flag, and collapsed. He did not get up again.
>
> Some 150 Vietnamese refugees, including 50 terrified children, hiding in the Sporting Club cellar watched through the cellar windows. "How sad. It was a civilian," one of the refugees commented to me.
>
> The Skyhawk attack was the first time since Friday that aircraft had intervened in the battle of Hue. The Skyhawks dropped bombs and napalm on the Citadel a few yards away from the Imperial Palace where the Vietcong flag continues to wave. Because of the bad weather the bombs hit a rocket dump from which enormous blue and green flames shot up.[56]

Washington Post reporter Lee Lescaze was with a group of Bravo Company marines as they camped in an affluent home. There was a Buddhist altar on one side of the first-floor living room, and on the other wall were *Playboy* centerfolds.

"He's the Hugh Hefner of Vietnam," one marine said, settling into an armchair.

They had found a full liquor cabinet and beer, much of which was gone the following morning when some of the owner's servants came by. The civilians, eager to reoccupy their homes, seemed to know as soon as the marines had cleared them. These servants brought a note, in English, from the house's owner.

"Let us take back my things and come back to the safe region," it read. "Thank you very much. We wish you a happy new year and a complete victory."

"The note said that rice and salt and other 'precious things' were to be salvaged," Lescaze wrote. "Bravo company watched as the servants carried out the television set first, then the refrigerator, then several lamps, plates, and small decorations, then the radio, phonograph and finally a one hundred pound bag of rice. It took four of them three trips before they were finished. They took the Johnny Walker, but the Seagram's bottle had been broken and the Marines had taken care of the beer."[57]

The chaplain, Father McGonigal, failed to show up at Thompson's quarters Saturday night, February 17. He had been all over the battle-field those first days, heedless of risk, rushing out to help carry the wounded, comforting them, and giving last rites to the dead. Marines in the worst of the fighting would find him at their shoulder, encouraging them. It was heroic, but also, Thompson thought, suicidal.[58] The priest stayed with Thompson every night, and they talked.

"Chaplain, you'd better stay back a little bit," Thompson advised him. "You're going to get killed."

When he failed to show up, there was a search. He was found alone in a building near that day's front line with a hole in the back of his head. A bullet or a piece of shrapnel had found him.

Nineteen-year-old Donny Neveling was put in charge of a ten-man squad when his lieutenant, Moe Green, was shot in the neck. He was proud but quickly learned that with status came responsibility. When a small pig wandered into their camp one afternoon and his men attacked it with bayonets, for fun, the butchery was witnessed by a disgusted battalion master sergeant, who bellowed, "Who's in charge here!" Neveling, who had dozed off, poked his head out of a window and said, "I am, Lance Corporal Neveling."

He was summoned that night by Captain Harrington, who chewed him out royally and fined him twenty-five dollars.

The marine Whitmer found in the body bag at Phu Bai, Dennis Michael, had been with Berntson when he died. The combat correspondent had interviewed him days earlier about the second and final assault on the tower. The twenty-year-old private from Vacaville, California, described sitting in a hole with another marine when two ChiCom grenades landed between them. One had rolled off his leg. They had piled out in a panic, but both grenades were duds.

"They're lousy grenades," Michael told him. "A lot of times they don't go off. But when they do, they'll kill you."

On Monday, February 19, Berntson was running down the street with a platoon of marines, helping with cover fire, pushing farther down the east wall, when Michael, who was on top of the wall, was shot through the throat. Berntson heard a corpsman calling for help, and ran up the stile to find him kneeling by Michael, who was choking and gasping for air. Rounds were chipping stone around them and kicking up clots of dirt.

"We've got to get him down off this wall," the corpsman said.

They lifted Michael and were trying to carry him down the narrow stairs to the street, when three civilian correspondents, Webb, Charlie Mohr, and Dave Greenway (who had returned to the city after leaving with Roberts), came running. The five of them ran with Michael to a truck that had been blown over on its side and set him down behind it. The corpsman began to perform an emergency tracheotomy. Michael was still choking and gasping. There was lots of blood.

Berntson stood. He saw a wooden shutter blown off a tall window that might work as a stretcher, announced he was going to fetch it, and . . . woke up with ringing ears flat on his back several yards away smelling cordite and burned flesh. Then he felt a searing pain in his arms and back. He tried to get up, but his legs wouldn't move. The taste of blood was in his mouth. He looked down and saw a large piece of shrapnel projecting from his right arm. The corpsman and the correspondents were still back beside the truck, and Berntson screamed, "For God's sake, get me off the street before they shoot me!"

He was pulled back to cover. The corpsman must have given him a serious shot of morphine, because the next thing Berntson knew he was at the battalion aid station at Mang Ca, flat on his back in the cold drizzle surrounded by other wounded men. One of his arms was badly mangled. The other was strapped down and connected to an IV tube. He could move neither. He felt stoned, spacey from the morphine. Around him was a world of misery and death, marines groaning and crying in pain, some dying, some already dead. There were not enough body bags for the dead, so doctors would pull the poncho up and over the head of those who expired, and they would be carried off to the dead pile. Every once in a while a gust of wind from a helicopter rotor would blow the ponchos up and their pale, vacant faces would stare across the tarmac.

Michael was near Berntson at the LZ, still alive but dying. He wasn't going to be evacuated. Triage had sorted him; there were too many others badly wounded with a better chance of making it. The man alongside Berntson already had his face covered.

When a gust of wind blew his poncho up and over his own face, he panicked. He could not move his arms to pull it off. One of the surgeons nearby was complaining bitterly that there were badly wounded Vietnamese soldiers being left to die because his orders were to tend to Americans first. Berntson called to him pitifully, "Captain, don't let them put me on the dead pile!"

Greenway and Webb were also wounded in the blast.[59] They rode back to Phu Bai with Berntson, the Storyteller, in a helicopter.

Army Colonel James Vaught on the road to La Chu, where he would lead the final assault on the Front's command center.

John Olson's photo of marines wounded in the Citadel. In the foreground, shirtless, is Alvin Bert Grantham, who had been shot through the chest.

2 MILES

N

PK-17

Lieu Coc

Vaught's attack from north

Que Chu

Pho O

Two battalions attack from the west

La Chu
(TFP)

1

Sweet's attack from the south

Bon Tri

H U E
THE CITADEL

La Chu

9

La Chu

THE LONGER THE battle went on, the more apparent it was that Westy
had been wrong. From the beginning, he denied that the enemy had
won any significant ground in South Vietnam. He had portrayed the
Front's presence in Hue as no more than a few companies. At no point
had he acknowledged that the city had fallen into enemy hands or that
his men were fighting a monumental battle to reclaim it.

Even as the fight stretched into its third week, Westy persistently
downplayed it. Hue was rarely even mentioned in his daily dispatches
to Washington, and when it was, it was only to say that the enemy was
about to be crushed—on February 4 it was "in the next few days"; on
the ninth it was "several more days"; on the twelfth it was "a couple
of days"; and on the twenty-first it was "by the end of this week."[60]

At the same time, Westy continued to send minute accounts of developments at Khe Sanh. He detailed the number of enemy mortar attacks
and kept count of the daily B-52 sorties blasting away at the base's
outskirts, noting both the number and the kind of bombs dropped.
He scrupulously recorded the seemingly endless train of resupply. All
of this for a battle that beyond enemy shelling had yet to begin.

Meanwhile, the real battle, the one actually joined, stubbornly
refused to go away. To collapse the Front's defense of the Citadel
required severing its line of supply and, ideally, retreat. Both of the
army battalions General John Tolson had marched south from PK-17
had failed to get past the heavily defended villages of Que Chu and
La Chu. Colonel Dick Sweet's, the Second Battalion, Twelfth Infantry

Regiment, had been mauled, reduced by half, and escaped by slipping off in the night. For almost two weeks Colonel James Vaught's, the Fifth Battalion, Seventh Cavalry Regiment, had been stalled just north of the villages. So long as he remained there, it was likely the enemy flag would continue flying over the Citadel.

On Friday February 16, seventeen days into the battle, the second-highest American commander in Vietnam, General Creighton Abrams, visited Tolson at PK-17. Major Don Bowman, the brigade operations officer, took two minutes to summarize for Abrams the events around La Chu, and then Major Earle Spry, its intelligence officer, briefed him on revised assessments of the enemy's strength—the experience with Sweet's and Vaught's battalions had confirmed that it was far greater than had been thought. When they were finished, Abrams stepped out of the bunker to confer privately with Tolson. Bowman couldn't hear what was being said, but he could tell that the visiting general was exceedingly displeased. Then Abrams got back in his chopper and flew away.

Bowman immediately went to work, writing furiously in his note-pad. A staff colonel asked what he was doing, and the major said, "I'm making a wish list." If he'd read the scene correctly, he said, "We are going to get called in to see General Tolson in about fifteen minutes, and we're about to get everything we need."

The only thing on Bowman's list that he didn't get was a tank pla-toon. The bridges to La Chu were not sturdy enough to support them. Two more full cavalry battalions, approved. Two Quad-fifties and two M42 Dusters, approved. Additional air strikes, approved. Additional artillery batteries, approved.[61]

Que Chu and La Chu were in a thick stand of trees surrounded by rice paddies. The northern portion of the trees, where Que Chu began, had been dubbed the T-T Woods, for "Tough Titty," because it had resisted everything thrown at it. A string of bloody skirmishes had been fought before Vaught had fallen back and dug in around the adjacent, smaller village of Lieu Coc, convinced he needed more of everything. Vaught had lost eighty-four men, including most of his junior officers. Most of their ammo was gone, and their mortar crews were down to an emergency supply, enough to maintain their own defenses but not enough to attack.

Gradually, intel reports confirmed the Front's enormous strength. Two prisoners taken on the previous Sunday night, both NVA regulars, confirmed they were from units that the MACV had believed to be near Khe Sanh. They had been outside Hue since the first night of the offensive. These clues and others made it clear that Que Chu and La Chu were not just an obstacle on the road to Hue but the hub of the entire enterprise. The Front's command post was in the virtually indestructible three-story concrete bunker at the center of La Chu, and it was defended by thousands of NVA regulars.

Getting at it would be hard. Vaught's probing had established that the village was protected by lines of trenches and fortified bunkers in the T-T Woods, which had survived intensive bombardment. There were thousands of NVA regulars in the village, perhaps as many as three thousand—there never would be a complete account. As many men were defending the outer entrenchments as Vaught had brought to attack them. The trenches were deep and irregular. Americans dug linear trench lines, either at the front of a position or along a well-defined perimeter. The NVA, who unlike American troops were accustomed to being attacked from the air, had adopted a far less predictable pattern, digging L-shaped trenches that were sometimes set at odd angles to each other. Most were connected, so the outermost trenches could be quickly reinforced, and defenders could fall back rapidly if necessary. They were set in dense thickets of trees, shrub brush, and bamboo, so it wasn't possible to map them from above—they threw up torrents of fire at any aircraft that came close. But if it had been possible, the map would have resembled the web of a drunken spider. Its unpredictability meant that an assaulting force could be trapped between two or even three trenches and be fired upon from several directions at once. To prepare for the assault, Vaught resurrected a World War I–era technique for attacking trenches, instructing his men to improvise bangalore torpedoes, long tubes packed with explosives that could be fed out from behind cover deep into an array of trenches and exploded. Bamboo stems were perfect for this, being long and straight and hollow.

To soften the enemy position, the US Air Force began hammering it with bombs and napalm. It used a new technique called Sky Spot, which did not require bombers to get beneath the clouds. Two radar sets at different bases would calculate a line from their position to the target. The intersection of those two lines gave a fairly accurate reading. Then, considering the angle of descent, they adjusted the point of release to account for the bomb's trajectory. Guided by radar, a bomber would fly out along one of the radar vectors and release its load at the designated point. It was not precise enough when friendly troops were close, but Vaught was far enough back to use it. These bombs arrived without warning. The jets flew too high to be heard above the clouds. Many targeted the big bunker, but none apparently scored a direct hit. When the bombardment was over, there was no way to tell how badly the enemy had been hurt, but the NVA let the nearby American forces know it was still there. Its soldiers blew whistles and sounded bugles at night, which unnerved Vaught's troopers and kept them on constant alert.

After Abrams's visit, two more cavalry battalions were moved up to join the ground attack. The final assault was set for Wednesday morning, February 21. Sweet's was coming north from the hills near Bon Tri, west of the Citadel, where it had taken shelter. He would be attacking La Chu from the south. The two other battalions would close the ring around the village to the east and the west. The primary attack would still be made by Vaught.

His final plan was complex and risky. Directly before their position was a dry rice paddy. About three-quarters of the way across was a dike. A stream roughly defined the enemy's western and southwestern trench lines. Vaught and his operations officer, Charlie Baker, determined that this was the best place to hit. But getting there meant crossing a lot of open ground. Once their men stepped out from cover they would be under heavy fire all the way across. The tanks Bowman had on his wish list would have made a big difference, but there were none.

Vaught meant to approach the T-T Woods from several directions at once. Davison's Charlie Company would occupy Phu O, a small hamlet in a stand of bamboo immediately to the west, from which it could provide covering fire. Alpha Company would provide the same from the north. Delta Company would swing south and make a looping approach from the west, taking advantage of the bamboo thickets outside Vaught's position in Lieu Coc. The central attack, the most dangerous one, fell to Howard Prince's Bravo Company.

When Prince briefed his platoon leaders on the plan on Monday night, they were not enthusiastic. The T-T Woods were not new to them. They had been probing it without success from various angles for two weeks. Prince had lost four of his five junior officers. All but one of his platoons were being led by noncoms. The remaining lieutenant was very young and very green. The entire company was worn out and scared. Its men had spent most of their time in Vietnam on search-and-destroy missions. That was bad enough, but it was familiar and they were good at it. They were not used to being maneuvered in the field like conventional infantry, particularly mounting charges on an entrenched enemy, and they didn't like it. They were unfamiliar with bangalore torpedoes and satchel charges—which were dangerous to handle and could get them killed. The attack plan required a lot of preliminary positioning in noisy bamboo thickets in the dark—which could get them killed. They hated the idea of charging across open ground—which was certain to get some of them killed. And, even if they made it to the enemy's trenches, they were going to have to fight their way single file between narrow walls at close quarters with the enemy—which could get them killed.

After Prince briefed his platoon leaders, the new lieutenant left to explain the plan to his more experienced men, who would be in the vanguard. He returned, troubled.

"Sir, they're not going to go," he told Prince.

The captain was stunned. This had never happened to him. There was nothing wrong with the plan tactically, legally, or morally. He didn't know what to do. He went to Vaught's operations officer, Baker. The attack was due to kick off in a few hours. He explained that his men might mutiny.

Baker was no help.

"I don't know what to tell you, Howard," he said.[62]

Prince stomped around in the darkness trying to figure out what to do. He was both scared and angry. He was furious at the men for balking, and he was scared about what he might have to do if they refused his orders. All he could do, he thought, was the thing he was supposed to be good at. He could explain. He was the most educated man in the battalion—Limping Scholar Six—so he could teach. The plan was risky, but it made sense. He had to make his men see that.

When he approached the balking platoon, the men refused to make eye contact.

"What's going on?" Prince asked.

"Sir, we think you're trying to get us all killed so you can get a medal tomorrow," one of the men said.

That floored him. He hadn't imagined that their refusal was *personal*, that they believed he would put his own career before their lives. It was insulting. But he ignored it. He got down in the dirt and drew up their position, the location of the enemy positions, and how they intended to attack. Realizing that they were unfamiliar with conventional infantry tactics, right there in the dirt he taught them a class on fire and movement, how one squad would fire at the enemy while the other tried to move up, and then the lead squad would halt and provide covering fire while the one behind them moved up closer still. They weren't going to charge blindly into machine guns; they were going to cover their own advance—in addition to having the supporting fire from the other companies—effectively leap-frogging their way across the open rice paddy.

There was silence when he finished. Finally the same man who had made the accusation said, "Okay, sir, we'll do it."

That same night Andy Westin—since Winfield Beck's death he was once again Davison's XO—noticed that Charlie Company was being issued huge amounts of ammo, along with a new supply of stretchers. That gave him pause. He took five hundred rounds for himself, even though his job was going to be running the medevac pad well behind the front line.

It was still dark on Tuesday morning when the three companies moved out to their assigned positions. Charlie Company set off through a thicket of bamboo to the right, pushing down toward Phu O, tasked with silencing guns that could sweep across the rice paddy. Prince's Bravo Company edged up to the point in the bamboo thicket on the edge of the open rice paddy.

They were glum. They believed that many of them would be killed or wounded. Prince felt this way, too. His guts were in an uproar. He found a spot to the side, slid off his pack, dropped his pants, and violently emptied his bowels. Despite lingering worry about his men's willingness to fight, they were all in their jump-off position when the artillery barrage began shortly before sunrise.

And when it started, they took off across the rice paddy, a swarm of men in muddy green, moving forward as he'd instructed, leapfrogging their way toward the exploding tree line. The enemy trenches were deep, so it was hard to see exactly where they were. The lead platoon, the one led by the green lieutenant, made it all the way past the dike and close to the edge of the woods when it came under intense fire from several directions. In addition to machine-gun and rifle fire, the enemy started hurling grenades and lobbing mortars into their ranks. Some of the trenches were now behind them and others to the front and side. The lieutenant panicked.

"We're under heavy attack!" he radioed Prince, who was watching from behind, still inside the stand of bamboo across the paddy. "We can't see the enemy. They're going to kill everybody! We've got to come back!"

"Stay where you are," Prince ordered.

He took off with his small command group: two radio operators, Jim Wilson and Dennis McGuire; his forward observer, Lieutenant Bob Childs; and Childs's radioman, Henry Winston. They made it to the dike, where there were small burial mounds raised up just under two feet. Prince paused there to get a better fix on the trenches that were blistering his forward platoon. He was doing this when he heard and felt an enormous blast to his right. Prince and McGuire were closest to it; Childs was behind them, about ten feet away. Childs felt a few pieces of shrapnel ping off his helmet, but that was it. Prince's right side was torn up from head to toe. McGuire was down with shrapnel wounds to his right arm and shoulder.

With all of the shooting and explosions, Childs was too busy calling in artillery strikes to help either of the wounded men. Prince had also been shot in the knee, although with all his other more severe wounds he wouldn't realize it until much later.[63] He managed to crawl back toward his original position before passing out.

Medevac choppers were orbiting behind the fight. One of those watching the attack unfold was Juan Gonzales, the pathfinder in the black cap who had been with Colonel Sweet's battalion weeks earlier. Always moving to the point of most action, Gonzales had left Sweet's battalion to join Vaught's days earlier. Following the radio traffic, he heard a chopper called in when Prince and his command group were hit. Gonzales was in a copse of trees adjacent to the rice paddy.

One of the other radio operators called to him, "Hey, Black Hat. That medevac, he is turning back."

Guiding choppers in was his specialty, so Gonzales got the pilot on the radio.

"I understand you're turning back," he said.

"That's right," the pilot said. "There is no communication from their position and I understand it's a hot LZ."

Gonzales, who could see the chopper overhead, said he was going to lead it in himself.

"I will be coming out of the tree line at your eleven o'clock," he said. "Just follow me."

He started running. He had the radio on his back, the handset in one hand, his rifle in the other, and the chopper flying low right behind him. Bullets kicked up at his feet. *Damn, with this black hat and this chopper following me they must think I'm somebody really important*, he thought. It was a long run and he started to zigzag. He threw himself down, exhausted, beside the wounded men. The chopper passed directly over his head, swung around, and landed between him and the enemy guns. Gonzales helped carry McGuire and Prince to it. When he picked up Prince, whom he had been with the night before, he reeled. He liked the captain. Now he was covered in blood, cut up from head to toe, unconscious, and his skin going gray from shock. Gonzales thought he was dead. *And we were just talking a few hours ago!*

Major Baker took over Prince's company. He regrouped them and determined where the NVA trenches were. The frightened lieutenant had fled the field, so Baker put two experienced sergeants in charge of his platoon. One of the newly authorized Dusters rolled out from the bamboo thicket toward the dike and directed its enormous firepower in a stream at the targets, while soldiers crept up to the edge of the trench lines. A satchel charge rigged at the end of a ten-foot bamboo pole was dropped into the first one, killing the two enemy soldiers at the near end. A third was shot and killed when he popped out of the back side. The Americans had broken into the first trench.

What followed was hard, gradual work. A squad of men would crawl down the trench toward a firing position. They would mark the bunker with smoke, and the Duster would hammer away at it. Then they would move on to the next one. The woods were laced with them.

One squad cleared a trench only to face another inside a dense stand of bamboo. Even the Duster's two big guns could not penetrate the thick stems around it. A private carrying a flamethrower was called forward. He reported to Baker, and forthrightly told him, "I can't do this."

It was easy to see why. To attack the bunker with the flamethrower meant standing up before the enemy's guns with a huge tank of napalm strapped to his back.

"Sure you can," said Baker.

The private, who looked to Baker as if he was all of sixteen, reluctantly edged down to the end of the trench, and when the signal was given he did what he felt he could not. He stood up, lit his flamethrower, and hosed the bunker with fire. A single gunner immediately jumped out and fled.[64]

Back at the LZ, Westin waited until the steady stream of casualties reached enough for a chopper load, and then he would call the next one in.

"I've got three guys for you," he would say.

"Do you have any incoming?" the pilot would ask.

"No," Westin said.

Then, as the chopper descended, rounds would zero in, dinging off its metal frame.

"You told me there was no incoming!" the pilot would complain.

"There wasn't until you showed up!" said Westin.

He particularly enjoyed watching the Duster. He was dazzled by its firepower. A weapon designed to shoot at aircraft, the Duster would lower its twin 40-mm guns to spray its extremely rapid fire at ground level. It looked like it was throwing flame and chewed up almost everything in its path. He hadn't seen one of the Quad-fifties yet, but he'd been told those were even better.

The lieutenant had a clear view of the battlefield across a wide expanse. He was relatively safe, far enough from the action to get hungry, but when he pulled out one of the two cans of C rations from his pants pocket—peaches—he found that it had been punctured by a piece of shrapnel. The juice had all leaked out. He was, first, shocked that the metal shard had hit so close to him without his even knowing it; second, delighted that he hadn't been hit himself; and third, disappointed because the chunk of metal had come to rest inside the can and fouled his peaches. The other can held pound cake, which Westin felt was the finest item on the C-ration menu. He had planned on eating it with the peaches, but he settled for eating it plain. He was on his knees watching the Duster do its thing, taking bites out of the delicious cake, when his elbow was whacked with what felt like a three-wood.

The pain was blinding. His arm went completely numb, like when you hit your funny bone . . . times ten. His pound cake was in the dirt. His ears were ringing. A mortar had landed about fifteen feet behind him in a furrow of loose dirt, which had fortunately absorbed most of the blast. His radio operator, who was next to him, had gotten hit with a piece of shrapnel that passed through his cheek and out his mouth somehow without touching his teeth. The men around him were lying as flat as they could make themselves. One's backside looked as if it had been scraped hard with long fingernails. It dawned on Westin then that he'd also been hit.

"Medic!" he shouted. "Medic!"

"Shut up, Lieutenant, I'm right here," the medic said. "Where are you hit?"

Westin tried to move his arm. Blood poured out the cuff of his sweater. A piece of shrapnel had hit his elbow and just exploded, sending tiny bits of hot metal up and down his arm. Nearly a half century later, whenever he lifted that arm, the fourth and fifth fingers of that hand would go to sleep.

Captain Davison called on his radio.

"Anybody hurt over there?" he asked.

"Yeah," Westin said. "Me."

It was a blow to the captain, who had already lost several of his officers.

"See you later, boss," Westin said.

He went out on the next bird.

The four-pronged assault on Que Chu and La Chu was successful but proved anticlimactic, as so much fighting in Hue did. After the attacking cavalry units broke through its outer defenses, NVA melted away. Nguyen Duc Thuan, the veteran NVA commando who had been shot through the knee on the first morning of the offensive inside the Citadel, had to be carried out during this quiet retreat. He had been fighting in La Chu ever since the night of the assault on Hue, enduring hellish aerial attacks and shelling, with his wounded knee all the while becoming more and more swollen and painful. On the night before Vaught's assault he was evacuated with the rest of his men to their old mountain camp. There was no one inside the three-story bunker when Vaught's forces reached it later that day. Seeing the forces arrayed around them and closing in, and feeling the heat of increasingly precise aerial and artillery bombardment, the NVA had quietly pulled up stakes, perhaps as many as three or four days earlier. It was hard to tell.

Tolson's troopers were now less than five miles from the gates of Hue, and the command center for the enemy's armies had fallen.

Andy Westin was in a hospital room on clean sheets in Cam Ranh Bay that evening. He had flown there inside a C-130. The walking wounded, like himself, were seated along the edges of the plane's body, while those in worse shape were strung up in heavy canvas stretchers suspended from overhead. The guy directly in front of Westin, who was up high enough so that he could just see the underside of his stretcher, began leaking blood through the canvas shortly after they took off. Westin pondered how much blood there would have to be for it to soak completely through such heavy material. He doubted that this fellow would make it.

He wrote to Mimi en route:

> *My Darling, The helicopter is an amazing thing. It only took 20 minutes for me the get to Bn aid-station and another hour to get to a big hospital. Tonight I'll be in Cameron Bay* [sic].
>
> *Oh yes. I get a purple heart, too. Before you panic, I'd better give you the details.*
>
> *Our Brigade (not Bn) attacked this morning and I had our second platoon (the usual plt ldr is on R&R) and actually was (should have been) in just about the safest place around.*
>
> *Well, anyway, to make it short. A gook mortar round hit about 15′ behind me. We're in a freshly ploughed field and it dug in*

before going off. As it was, I took 2 chunks of shrapnel in the left elbow and a nick in the right one (it now sports a band-aid).

The doctors X-rayed and probed and couldn't find a piece big enough to pull out. The metal disintegrated when it hit. It didn't hit the bone or anything else that could mess me up.

In short, I got a $100,000 wound. Bad enough to go to Cameron Bay, but not bad enough to due [sic] anything permanent.

Actually, except for a damn sore elbow, it's a good deal. Cameron Bay is far, far from the fighting and I figure it will be at least a month before I get back to work. By then, I should be getting a staff job anyway.

Westin was given a pass to recuperate in Japan. He flew to Tachikawa, on the western edge of Tokyo, where he reported to North Camp Drake. There he was placed in a bed alongside Prince, who had lost a lot of blood but survived. Prince's right arm was useless, so Westin wrote letters for him—"I'm your right-hand man!" he told the captain. Shortly after Westin arrived, an officer came to present him with his Purple Heart.

"What's your rank?" he asked.

Westin said he was a lieutenant, and what his last job was, and how long he had been in Vietnam, which was six months.

"I'll give you a choice," the officer said. "You can go home or you can go back."

"Excuse me?"

"Look at it this way. If you're going to stay in the army, go back. You're certainly not going out in the field again."

Westin knew that "not being in the field" did not necessarily mean he'd be somewhere safe.

"If you go home," the officer continued, "what you've done does not count as a full tour."

Westin didn't think long. Mimi popped into his antlered head.

He said, "I think I'll go home."

10

Checkmate

On Tuesday, the twentieth, Major Thompson was publicly relieved of his command. General Abrams said he considered the effort inside the Citadel to have been "inadequate."[65] General Cushman announced to reporters that Thompson's command would be assumed by Colonel Hughes, who had been commanding the overall effort from the MACV compound.

When this decision was relayed to Hughes, however, he said he would resign before he would accept an order to replace Thompson. The major stayed and the matter died.[66]

Very early the next morning, Thompson assembled his officers. They were closing in on the southern wall, but each advance seemed harder and more painful than the last. The battle had been terrible, and now it had also turned tedious. Each day was the same, an attack by mortars and artillery and planes, if they could make runs, then the tanks and Ontos followed by hunched-over marines braving the street. Their fight would then progress house to house, room to room, followed by the enemy falling back and retrenching. Thompson felt his men, those that remained, were wearing out. But they were close. Ahead were the southern wall and the Thuong Tu Gate, which opened toward the river, the downed bridge, and southern Hue.

But as the marines advanced those final blocks, the Front's remaining forces were compressed into an ever-smaller area and their defenses became, if anything, more desperate and more robust. Across the street from the current battle line was an especially difficult objective, a tall building that had been giving them fits. It was the biggest building they had encountered inside the fortress. From its upper floors and roof, enemy guns commanded the blocks below.

Thompson reconsidered what Coolican had advised him on his first night in the Citadel. The young captain, who had been fighting with the Hac Bao, had argued that night was the best time to move. The major asked his officers if instead of going after the building in the morning, as usual, they might consider a surprise move in the dark. If they could seize it before sunrise, then they would own the high ground for the final push to the wall.

All three of his frontline company commanders—Harrington, Nelson, and Fern Jennings—liked the idea, but none was eager to volunteer his men for yet another risky undertaking. It was hard enough to ask them to keep hurling themselves across vicious battle lines. How would you convince them to undertake something even more daring? Sensing their hesitancy, "Hand Grenade" Polk offered his Alpha Company.

Thompson admired Polk. He thought the young officer had breathed fresh bravado into his haggard command. It had lifted his own sagging spirits, and he was hopeful that the cocksure young officer's spirit would have a similar effect on the others. As the lieutenant led his small raiding party across the street, Thompson told his three captains to keep their radios tuned to Polk's frequency throughout. He wanted them to hear the lieutenant at work.

But when the team left, with Polk in the lead, they found no one to fight! Just an old man and three terrified children were in the building. The Front apparently had grown so accustomed to the battle's rhythm that they had left their forward positions for the night. It made sense. Farther back they could sit out the morning mortar barrage at a safe distance. So when dawn came, Polk and his men were looking down from an upper floor when numbers of enemy soldiers began to emerge from buildings to the rear. They came strolling across the street and through the building's wide courtyard, returning to take up their fighting positions like men reporting for a morning work shift.

Polk's radio operator called Whiskey X-Ray across the river, gave them the coordinates, and urged them to start firing immediately. The mortar crew checked with their battalion commander, who judged the target too close to the marines' position.

"Don't fire," he said.

The mortar crew stressed that it was Alpha Company itself requesting the fire mission. Then came another call from Polk's man.

"Hurry up, for chrissakes, hurry up! Danger close! Fifty meters!"

With Polk pressing the issue, permission was granted. In the riverfront mortar pit, Ed Landry heard a ferocious exchange of gunfire start up inside the Citadel before they started. Polk's men were shooting down at the enemy soldiers by the time the first big rounds lofted across the river and over the walls. They scored direct hits with three rounds. Three more quickly followed. With Polk's men picking off targets from above, the remainder of Thompson's forces moved across the street to grab the enemy's forward line. A tear gas shell from Whiskey X-Ray exploded over the blocks farther ahead. The battery would send twenty rounds in all, racing to clean their tubes between each firing. Along the battle line, for once the marines owned the high ground. The surprise move broke the Front's last line of resistance before the southern wall. Thompson achieved all of his objectives by noon.

It was just the start of a long day for the mortar crew, which continued to receive fire requests—roughly one every fifteen minutes. Two Phantom jets screamed low over them at one point and loosed two five-hundred-pound bombs that exploded inside with such force that Landry felt the percussion all the way across the river like a great gust of wind.

With the capture of the southern wall, and the fall of La Chu, the Battle of Hue was all but over. General Tolson's reinforced brigade, having moved past La Chu, now closed rapidly on the Citadel's western gates, and the Front troops that remained inside were in danger of being bottled up. That night they slipped away through the only two gates they still controlled, those at the southwest corner of the fortress, the Huu and Nha Do. Major Eshelman, who had been so frustrated trying to advance with the Vietnamese marines on the fortress's west side, was shocked Wednesday morning, February 21, to discover enemy lines only lightly defended. There was still some shooting from the enemy's rear guard, but the impenetrable fields of fire that had stymied them for days had vanished. As if to prove you get what you need when you no longer need it, on the same day they were reinforced by a fresh company of US Marines.[67]

There was still fighting here and there, but life sprang back into the city at an astonishing pace. Sensing the end was near, crowds of civilians filled the streets. *New York Times* reporter Thomas Johnson took a ride in a marine truck making its way through the crowds. "They're crazy," the driver said. "Bullets zing up and down these streets all the time and these people think it's a side show."[68]

Life began to flow once more in and around the ruins. Sampans and fishing boats once more plied the Huong, scattering whenever gunfire erupted—usually around US naval vessels—but returning when it died down. Families again sold greens, celery, and mangoes from boats along the canals, and, Johnson noted, marines moving through the streets were offered soda, peanut brittle, dried fish, soup, and candies.

The enemy's hold on the Citadel had been reduced to the royal palace and its grounds, before which still flew the Alliance flag. A few weeks earlier, the *Times* of London had referred to it as "mocking them [the marines] from the top of the 123 ft. mast on the Citadel waterfront."[69] It had flown twenty-three days. The grounds around the palace had sheltered troops that had been launching mortars and rockets at the allied forces for weeks.

When a terrible battle is almost over, the men who have survived regard with special dread the final assault—one last chance to catch a fatal or maiming round. There was talk of a possible suicidal last stand by Front fanatics. Lieutenant Polk joked about it with his men the night before, strumming a guitar he had found in the ruins.

"Gee, Lieutenant, can I go first up on the wall?" asked a marine, facetiously.

"Only if you carry a bayonet clenched in your teeth," said Polk.[70]

Choosing which unit to lead the final assault was made easier by the insistence of Harry Hue, the Hac Bao commander. The week before he had urged Thompson to "just blow a hole in the palace walls and we'll rush in and kill everybody." It wasn't realistic at the time, but now that it was, Thompson felt the aptly named Hue was the man for the job. So on Friday morning, February 23, the palace grounds were bombarded and the Hac Bao broke in, accompanied by its American adviser, Jim Coolican—he had helped man the tower at the MACV compound on the first night and was now present for the battle's final act. The Hac Bao were followed by Colonel Dinh's soldiers.

Like so many of these final assaults, this one was anticlimactic. The enemy was gone. Only a few rear-guard soldiers fired on them, and these were quickly killed. The Hac Bao discovered the bodies of sixty-four enemy soldiers on the palace grounds—the Front had been using the relatively safe haven as a hospital and had left in too big a hurry to finish burying their dead. The invading force also found a supply of weapons and ammo, and the remains of a horse and dog that had evidently been slaughtered for food.

A nearly naked, emaciated man staggered from the underbrush to greet them. A member of Truong's First Division, he had been cut off in the original siege of the Citadel and had spent the previous weeks half submerged in foliage in one of the palace's ceremonial lagoons, sneaking out at night to scrounge for food. He was Colonel Dinh's older brother.

Le Tu Minh, the chief of the party's Central Committee for Hue, had seen the end coming. The leaders of the Front's forces had assembled at a village just west of the Huu Gate eleven days earlier. They noted their mounting losses and the gradual buildup of American and ARVN troops. During the meeting American planes dropped bombs on the village. General Kinh shared a foxhole with the political commissar for the Hue city front, Le Kha Phieu. Neither was hurt, but the futility of holding Hue was driven home dramatically.[71] The last of the Front's forces to leave the city were those in the fortress's southwest corner guarding the Nha Do and Huu Gates.

The phased withdrawal had begun three nights earlier. On the last night, it became a chaotic rush. The final days of the battle had been excruciating. Lieutenant Tang Van Mieu had one of his company commanders killed right beside him by an American sniper; the bullet took out the man's eyeball and sent it smacking into Tang's face. A smaller man than his subordinates, Tang surmised that the sniper, seeing a group of enemy soldiers conferring, must have assumed that the larger man was the more important. His NVA regulars maintained order on the way out but, anticipating a crushing last blow, the VC and local fighters broke ranks and ran. Students who had been pressed into service carrying the wounded threw their stretchers down on the road and wept. They pleaded that they could go no farther. Tang's Seventh Battalion had begun the offensive with six hundred men. At the end only fifty would walk out.[72]

There was an aspect of the battle that the Americans missed. Throughout, the opposing Vietnamese sides eavesdropped on, heckled, and threatened each other over the radio. At one point, one of General Truong's officers, named Chot, had broken into the Front's radio frequency and demanded to talk to Tang, who took the call. Chot told Tang he was going to offer a ransom for his capture.

Tang told him to go ahead.

"I dare you to defeat and capture me!" said Chot.

"I *dare* you to try to defeat and capture me!" replied Tang. "I am going to capture *you*. You will be defeated."

As hard as the fight had been, Tang was distressed when the order came to retreat. He believed it would have been worthwhile staying and fighting on, even if they were all killed. As he moved his men out Nha Do Gate, he worried about the local militias; they had been recruited from inside the city, and many would stay behind hoping to blend back into the civilian population. What would happen to them now? Surely their neighbors would know them and point them out. Was he just supposed to desert them? He felt his men, if reinforced, might have carried on for days more. But orders were orders. Tang had them pick up the wounded dropped by the students and had the students carry weapons and ammo instead. The frantic exit of these broken units stood in stark contrast to the proud and happy ranks that had entered the city on the first morning of Tet. One entire battalion had been reduced to just six men.

Mai Xuan Bao, whose sappers had launched the attack on police headquarters on the first night, had received the order to withdraw on Tuesday night, before Thompson's men had taken the south wall. The company he was with had been cut down to thirty men and had moved to a position outside the Citadel. There were newly arrived ARVN troops between them and their escape route south. When the withdrawal order came, the political commissar assigned to Bao's company urged him to attack the enemy position immediately.

"No, we can't," Bao told him. "If we attack now, we'll suffer even more casualties. We have to be patient."

They waited through the night, trying to lull the enemy into thinking that nothing would happen until morning, which was the usual pattern. Bao's men attacked well before sunrise and broke through. They retreated, leaving many of their wounded behind and taking ARVN soldiers who had surrendered. They marched to the lowland liberated areas, pounded by artillery as they passed east of Phu Bai. The shelling killed even more of Bao's men and some of the prisoners.

Nguyen Quang Ha's sapper unit, which had assaulted the ARVN armored compound at Tam Thai on the first night with 150 men, was down to just 20. Ha himself had received six minor wounds before a piece of shrapnel cut into his intestines. He had begun wearing his backpack in front in hopes of warding off just such a wound, but the shrapnel sliced through. He and what was left of his unit had been running from house to house for days. They would build shelters in each place to shield them from constant bombardment. Ha left the Citadel in a hammock strung from a pole carried by two of his comrades.

Sergeant Cao Van Sen, the Viet Cong regular who had prepared the Alliance flag and delivered it on the first day, left with his unit on Wednesday night. Sen and his men had fought for three weeks around the Tay Loc airstrip, taking it, losing it, retaking it, and ultimately losing it as the ARVN built up enough power to hold them off. The approach of the marines in the final days, along with more and more shells and bombs, was finally too much. Sen was amazed at the firepower beating down everywhere and on everything, so much that sometimes the Americans hit the ARVN troops.

Le Huu Tong, the bazooka gunner, had been nearly deaf for weeks. He could no longer distinguish the noises made by bombs or grenades or rifles. He had a constant buzzing in his ears, and he could not bear the horrid odor that hung over everything in the Citadel. The smell was worse during the day because at least at night, if they were near a rotting corpse, they could drag it away or bury it. He had forgotten what it was like to go to sleep. He was sad but relieved when his unit was ordered back to "the green," its base camps in the mountains. His battalion, which had helped assault the tank compound, was one of the last to leave the city. They hung on outside the Citadel until Sunday, February 25, traveling by boat to the train station in southern Hue and then overland to the west. They were bombed badly on the way.

When they returned to the camp they had nothing because they had thrown everything away when they departed, expecting never to return. Hoang Thanh Tung, the commissar who specialized in converting captured ARVN troops, felt a great sadness on returning to his unit's old mountain camp. It was a place he had never expected to see again, but, looking back, he realized that, even camping there, they had enjoyed some pleasures. Now they had nothing. They had to search, scrounge, and beg for food, seeking help from Montagnard tribesmen. It was a month before regular food supplies resumed. For the first time since he joined the VC, he felt pessimistic about the war. Perhaps they would not prevail. They had briefly tasted victory, but it was the smell of death in Hue that would never leave him.

The young militia leader Nguyen Van Quang, who had been one of the first to enter the Citadel, was one of the last to leave. He got the order the night before the storming of the royal palace. He led the remainder of his unit out of the city that night through the Huu Gate. A machine gunner inside the royal palace had begged to be allowed to stay.

"I know my way around," the young man told him. Quang learned later that the man had fought until he had run out of ammo and had been killed.

Lieutenant Hoang Anh De, whose men had fought for southern Hue in the first week, and had gradually fallen back to the outskirts of the triangle to continue harassing the growing numbers of Americans, did not receive the order to leave until Sunday, February 25. He had moved all of his men into the suburbs in the days before, and from there they retreated south to the lowlands of Phu Vang.

For the symbolic final act, Major Thompson had been told there would be no replay of the American flag raising at the province headquarters. The flag before Ngo Mon Gate was the final and most visible prize. The major wasn't happy about it, nor were many of his marines, who felt they had paid dearly for the privilege of running up Old Glory, but the Alliance flag would be replaced by the big yellow-and-red-striped flag of South Vietnam.

The cords on the flagstaff had been cut, so two nimble Hac Bao scaled the pole. Portions of it had been blown away, leaving only twisted strands of rebar, but the men climbed over the gaps to the top and finally cut down the hopeful symbol of Hanoi's Tong-Tan-cong-Noi-day. The ARVN troops then tied their own yellow and red banner to the top.

The battle for Hue had ended, but the bloodletting had not. After more than three weeks of hard fighting, the city was finally, from a military standpoint, where American officials had said it was on the first day—clear except for pockets of enemy resistance. Now that Saigon was back in charge, there would be further hell to pay. Phan Van Khoa, the mayor who had been rescued weeks earlier by Captain Mike Downs's marines, issued an order for public execution of looters and of those who had sided with the Front. An unnamed American official had seconded the order in a statement to an Associated Press reporter.

"There will be summary executions, public executions of VC and hopefully some of the infrastructure," the official said, referring to those who had cooperated in forming a "liberation government" in the previous weeks. He said he was encouraging Khoa to include as a prominent victim the former Hue police chief, Nguyen Chi Canh, who had left the city after the Buddhist uprisings in 1965 and returned to assume the role after the city was overrun. Khoa told reporters that his men would begin culling refugees, looking for those who had sided with the Front in the previous weeks.[73]

General Nguyen Ngoc Loan, the top police official who had been made infamous weeks earlier when cameras caught him shooting a bound Viet Cong prisoner in the head, left Saigon for Hue Thursday night. He would supervise the interrogations.

11

The Toll

As is usually the case, the brunt of the battle was borne by civilians. For Hue residents the death toll is usually set at fifty-eight hundred, which is almost certainly less than the true number. Many civilians were killed in bombings, shelling, and crossfire, or died in bunkers beneath their homes—likely interred in the rubble. Over the roughly four weeks of fighting, more than 80 percent of the city's structures were either destroyed or sustained serious damage.[74] As for bodies found in mass graves, without careful examination it would be impossible to say with certainty how they perished. The sheer number of dead necessitated hasty mass burials.

To those thousands lost accidentally we must add those who were put to death. The Front, in its purges, executed anywhere between three hundred and 4,856—a ridiculously disparate range. The first is the official estimate of the Socialist Republic of Vietnam, which would clearly like to minimize its culpability. The second impossibly precise count was given by the ARVN, which had every reason to inflate the number. Douglas Pike, an American foreign service officer and analyst who during the war was employed by the US Information Agency, made a study of the matter at mass burial sites immediately after the fighting and came up with the number 2,800. Pike was a serious scholar, and his count is probably closer to the truth than the others, but given his war role, his figure, too, must be considered suspect. We will never know for certain how many were shot, but without any doubt, the Front engaged in a systematic effort to find and punish those allied with the Saigon regime, just as that regime undertook its own reprisals when the battle ended—no one has offered an official count of those victims. A conservative guess of those executed would be two thousand. This brings us to a combined civilian death toll—those killed by accident and those put to death—of about eight thousand. It's not an exact figure, but to the degree it's off, it's off by being too low.

Two hundred and fifty American marines and soldiers were killed, and 1,554 wounded.[75] Another 458 ARVN soldiers were killed and an estimated 2,700 wounded. The Front's losses are estimated to have been between 2,400 and 5,000—the difference between the official counts of both sides, both known to lie about such numbers. When you add the numbers of combatants killed to estimates of civilian deaths, the final toll of the Battle of Hue numbers well over ten thousand, making it by far the bloodiest of the Vietnam War. Over six months, the shellings and bombings in and around Khe Sanh accumulated a comparable total, perhaps even more, but no other single battle came close. Even Americans who supported the effort, and most still did, would never think about the war in the same way again.

While the American public recoiled from such heavy fighting and losses, the Johnson administration doubled down. The headline of the *Philadelphia Inquirer* on Saturday morning, February 24, read, VIET CONG FLAG LOWERED AT HUE; 48,000 ARE CALLED IN APRIL DRAFT. The subhead read, PLAN TO TAP RESERVES ALSO PUSHED. The troop surge came even though some at the highest levels of the Johnson administration had lost confidence.

When Westy originally requested more than one hundred thousand men soon after the Tet Offensive started, there were many, even in the White House, who viewed the request sardonically, in light of his proclamations of complete victory. Doubts about him had begun to spread early in the struggle for Hue.

"There is a very strange contradiction in what we are saying and doing," said Clark Clifford in a meeting on February 9 with the president and his top military advisers. Clifford had been named as McNamara's replacement at Defense and would take over as secretary on the first of March. He noted that ever since Westy's "End-in-View" publicity tour in November, the general had downplayed the threat posed by

Hanoi, and then, after the shocking attacks over Tet, professed to have been expecting them all along.

"We now know the North Vietnamese and Viet Cong launched this type of effort in the cities," said Clifford. "We have publicly told the American people that the communist offensive was: (a) not a victory, (b) produced no uprising among the Vietnamese people in support of the enemy, and (c) cost the enemy between 20,000 and 25,000 of his combat troops. Now our reaction to all of that is to say that the situation is more dangerous today than it was before all of this. We are saying that we need more troops, that we need more ammunition and that we need to call up the reserves. I think we should give some very serious thought to how we explain saying on one hand the enemy did not take a victory and yet we are in need of many more troops and possibly an emergency call-up."

"The only explanation I can see is that the enemy has changed his tactics," said Johnson. "They are putting all of their stack in now," echoing the rationale he had heard from Westy himself—"going for broke" was the general's most recent take on the enemy's strategy, spelled out in conversations and cables to the president. "We have to be prepared for all that we might face," said LBJ. "Our front structure is based on estimates of their front structure. Our intelligence shows that they have changed and added about 15,000 men. In response to that, we must do likewise. That is the only explanation I see."

"I have a question," asked Secretary of State Rusk. "In the past, we have said the problem really was finding the enemy. Now the enemy has come to us. I am sure many will ask why we aren't doing better under these circumstances, now that we know where they are."

The next day, at a meeting with his top foreign affairs advisers, LBJ asked, "Where is all this criticism of Westmoreland coming from?"

"Not out of the Defense Department," said McNamara.

"I have heard no criticism of Westmoreland at the State Department," said Rusk.

"What's causing the enemy to delay its attack on Khe Sanh?" Johnson asked.

"The bombing affected their schedule," said McNamara.

"I doubt if a second wave of attacks will be as great as the first," said Rusk.

"Should we just sit and wait?" asked the president.

"I think so," said McNamara, who then outlined four steps that could be taken: they should (1) get back all the ARVN soldiers who had gone on leave for Tet; (2) try to get the South Vietnamese to fight better; (3) get President Thieu to authorize the drafting of nineteen-year-olds; and (4) move ARVN soldiers performing less critical jobs to fighting units.

But they all knew the answer wasn't going to come from the ARVN. More American troops would have to be sent. Tet had exposed Westy as an untrustworthy source of information, not just to the press and public but even in his secret communications to the White House. Each day without a major attack at Khe Sanh ate away his repute for foresight. In fact, no matter how impressive the general looked and sounded, he was clearly less in control of events than he claimed to be. Doubts about him and the war had spread from a handful of journalists and academics to the mainstream.

Senator McCarthy, running as a write-in antiwar candidate, would come within seven points of defeating LBJ in the New Hampshire primary just a month later. But at the same time as the clamor grew to put on the brakes, the war machine was accelerating. Division over it would soon reach nearly every household in America.

When the Battle of Hue entered its second week, and fighting continued in Saigon and other places hit by Tet, it was time for President Johnson, at least, to shed Westy's strategy of denial. On Thursday, February 8, Rostow sent the president a long memo and the draft of a new speech he had written for him.

"In the next day or so you have a unique opportunity to slay the credibility-gap dragon with one blow—or rather with one speech," Rostow wrote. "The correspondents and the public know in their bones that we and our allies sustained a heavy blow last week. Yet there is a growing feeling that the administration is attempting to pretend otherwise. It will do us no harm to tell them what they already know—and it will do us much good to do it in so unvarnished a way that the wonder will be at your candor and frankness . . . It is, I think, also the time to say plainly that hard fighting and heavy casualties lie ahead. They do, and the way to minimize their impact on American public opinion is to acknowledge them in advance and set the national tone by a call for steadiness and resolution."

The draft speech ended with a ringing call to arms:

> We are going to give them [the North Vietnamese] the fight that they want—and more than they want. We are going to mete out the measure that they ask for—and more than the measure. We will not do this with any joy—for we are a people who hate war. But we are also a people who are willing—and not for the first time—to do what is necessary to preserve our freedom and the freedom of our friends . . . last week was a hard week and other hard weeks will come . . . This is a time for steadiness—and for resolution—and for determination.[76]

Johnson never delivered the speech, but he continued to believe in the war. He considered antiwar protests to be un-American, suspecting that they were coordinated and underwritten by the Soviet Union.[77] When he announced the much-reduced troop buildup, he visited the aircraft carrier USS *Constellation*, which was leaving for waters off Vietnam. One of the reticent young sailors invited to dine with the president asked him, bitterly, about growing antiwar fervor, saying "hippies" were giving servicemen like him "a hard time."

"It doesn't seem right and it makes us all feel bad," said Johnson. "Like when there is an outlaw in town [who] tears up the town." He said there were draft dodgers and resisters in every American war. "In World War II they indicted fifteen thousand for treason and disloyalty . . . Some think I should let the communists take South Vietnam. We think that it would be one step right after the other, just like Hitler . . . We are going to have these dissenters and disbelievers . . . Just thank God it is not you or your brother who is a hippie or burning his draft card. You ought to take pity on them. The best thing to do is just realize that in every period of history you separate the men from the boys—some can't take it and as you go along the harder it gets to climb the hill; you will have the neurotics who will drop out . . . You are helping to keep the country free. Be tolerant. You are so much bigger and stronger and doing so much for your country—so much more than these hippies."

Johnson's assertion of manliness might have been enough to buck up a young sailor, but it wasn't just "hippies" who were turning against the war. The stories and pictures from Hue, in particular, had a profound impact. They depicted battle on a scale reminiscent of the world wars, with a proud city reduced to ruins and ashes, with the dirty faces of wounded and frightened marines caught in merciless conflict. At the very least such pictures gave the lie to Westy's unfailingly upbeat, rose-colored view of the war. The commander appeared increasingly clueless.

Clifford, the new man in the room, seemed to have reached that conclusion. He treaded carefully; Westy was greatly admired by the president. But it's easy to see Clifford's jaundiced assessment in his words to the president as early as February 10:

"On one hand the military has said we had quite a victory out there . . . , on the other hand, they now say that it was such a big victory that we need one hundred and twenty thousand more men."

A few weeks later he was secretary of defense, and one of his first acts was to deliver a stern dressing-down to his commanding general. Disgusted with Westy's flair for minimizing failure and exaggerating success, he said so in a heart-to-heart with Joint Chiefs chairman General Wheeler, who summarized the talk in a cable to Westy that night. It must have stung:

> I had a most interesting and informative conversation today with our new Secretary of Defense . . . He is a man of stature and achievement, one whose views must be accorded weight. The two main points he made with me this morning were the following:
>
> 1. The Tet Offensive mounted by the enemy came as a great shock to the American public. He believes that this shock was the greater because of the euphoria engendered by optimistic statements in past days by various spokesmen supporting administration policy in South Vietnam.
> 2. He is concerned at the lessening support for the war effort . . .
> 3. He thinks the American public cannot stand another such shock as that administered by the Tet Offensive. He believes

that we have laid ourselves open to the possibility of an additional setback with the American public by playing down the effects of th.e Tet Offensive on the GVN [Government of Vietnam], the RVNAF [Republic of Vietnam Air Force], and on the South Vietnamese public.

One government spokesman (who shall remain nameless) was ridiculed a couple of weeks ago for what the press considered to be wild overstatements in minimizing the strength and cunning of the enemy and the impact on the GVN . . . I must admit that Secretary Clifford's assessment is shared by me . . . The secretary continued that he believes our best course of action is to be conservative in assessments of the situation and enemy capabilities. Otherwise, we could have the American public subjected to a second shock.

1. Do not denigrate the enemy.
2. Do not indulge in forecasting enemy plans or our plans.
3. Do not make predictions of victory.
4. Do express the view that there is tough fighting ahead.[78]

Clifford had noted with particular displeasure quotes in a story that would appear in the next day's *New York Times*, in which a "senior military spokesman" in Saigon explained to Gene Roberts that the MACV was "less worried now that at any other time during the last five weeks about a general 'second wave' of attacks against Saigon or other population centers." The spokesman went on, "I don't believe the enemy has any great capability to assume any general offensive in the near future. He has been hurt and hurt badly. He is tired. His logistic efforts have been adequate to support his campaigns thus far, but there is evidence of developing logistic problems."[79]

The spokesman was, of course, Westy himself, as he promptly confessed in his response to Wheeler, "I am the 'senior military spokesman' referred to by Gene Roberts in his article." He confirmed the accuracy of the story and explained, "You know of my efforts to attempt to reverse this defensive attitude and get on the offensive, which action is necessary if we are to take advantage of the opportunity presented

by the enemy . . . Apropos to the secretary's guidance, I will do my
best to conform to it, consistent with intellectual honesty as to my
appraisal of the situation and in consideration of an essential attitude
of command requiring a reflection of confidence."

Intellectual honesty was the point. There were growing doubts about
everything coming out of the MACV, including Westy's favorite statistics, those body counts.

Newsweek wrote:

> Westmoreland [claimed] . . . that, in a week and a half of
> fighting, the enemy had lost a staggering 31,000 men killed—
> some 14,000 more than the total number of American troops
> who have died in Vietnam since 1961. Yet even if this enemy
> body count was accurate—a matter deeply doubted both in
> Saigon and Washington—many Americans thought that it
> represented the sort of "victory" the U.S. could ill afford. For
> one thing, U.S. casualties during the same period—920 killed and
> 4,560 wounded—were a record high for the war. But even that
> fact, painful as it was, did not disturb the U.S. psyche as much as
> the puncturing of countless official claims, made over a period
> of years, that the U.S. was winning.
>
> Just how misguided those claims had been was demonstrated
> with each passing day last week.

Noting the "savage" fighting in Hue, the article concluded, "At this
late stage of the war, ballooning body counts and promises that the
enemy has 'bet his last stack' are no longer convincing."[80]

And it wasn't just statistics and tactics that were being questioned.
The fundamental premise for being in Vietnam was under attack.
Emmet John Hughes, a former speechwriter for President Eisenhower
who was then working with Republican presidential hopeful Nelson
Rockefeller, wrote in *Newsweek* that it had been a mistake to consider
the struggle in Vietnam as part of global Communist expansionism:

> The fateful basis . . . has been a false analogy—the
> dogged insistence that the war in Vietnam signaled
> precisely the same political commitment as all U.S. actions

since WWII . . . deterring communist aggression. On the
contrary, the intervention in Vietnam has been unique and
unprecedented . . . *No* previous conflict cast America in the
role of an effective heir to hated colonial authority, alienating
rather than arousing national pride. And *no* previous conflict
engaged America in the audacious labor of *creating* a new
sovereignty . . . A policy disdainful of such historical differences
could have but one end. You cannot truly win a conflict that you
cannot truthfully define.

This growing chorus of dissenters doubted the truthfulness of military leaders, questioned the wisdom of national strategy, and increasingly emphasized the futility of staying the course.

The biggest blow was struck by Walter Cronkite on Tuesday night,
February 27, when he delivered to his huge audience the findings of his
sojourn in the war zones, "Who, What, When, Where, Why: Report
from Vietnam." He had written the narrative himself, brushing up his old
chops as a radio reporter in World War II. The show opened with battlefield images over which came his familiar, emphatic, singsong cadence:

These ruins are in Saigon, capital and largest city of South
Vietnam. They were left here by an act of war, Vietnamese
against Vietnamese. Hundreds died here. Here in the ruins can
be seen physical evidence of the Vietcong's Tet Offensive, but far
less tangible is what these ruins mean, and like everything else
in this burned and blasted and weary land, they mean success or
setback, victory or defeat, depending on whom you talk to.

Anyone who has wandered through these ruins knows that
an exact count is impossible. Why, just a short while ago a little
old man came and told us that two VC were buried in a hastily
dug grave at the end of the block. Had they been counted? And
what about these ruins? Have they gone through all of them for
buried civilians and soldiers? And what about those fourteen VC
we found in the courtyard behind the post office at Hue? Had they
been counted and tabulated? They certainly hadn't been buried.

We came to Vietnam to try to determine what all this means
to the future of the war here. We talked to officials, top officials,

civilian and military, Vietnamese and American. We toured
damaged areas like this, and refugee centers. We paid a visit to
the Battle at Hue, and to the men manning the northernmost
provinces, where the next big communist offensive is expected.
All of this is the subject of our report.

During the next half hour, contradicting Westy's assurances, Cronkite
reviewed the totality of the holiday surprise: "Intelligence people,
American and Vietnamese, agree on the same story. They figured the
enemy might launch a big attack on Saigon or another South Vietnamese city, but they admit they grossly underestimated the enemy's
ability to plan, to provision, to coordinate, to launch such a widespread
full-scale attack as this."

Turning to Hue, he summarized the monthlong struggle, and, showing images of the smashed city, he said, "The destruction here was
almost total. There is scarcely an inhabitable building in the whole of
Hue. Whatever price the communists paid for this offensive, the price
to the allied cause was high. If our intention is to restore normalcy,
peace, serenity to this country, the destruction of those qualities in
this, the most historical and probably serene of all South Vietnamese
cities, is obviously a setback."

He noted that Hanoi's hope of triggering a popular uprising had
failed, but he quoted Nguyen Xuan Oanh, a critic of President Thieu,
explaining that the disruption of life in the South had made the effort
"very successful." Cronkite detailed the failure of the pacification program and the clear evolution of the conflict from small-scale encounters
with a furtive, relatively powerless enemy to "large armies locked in
combat, moving toward a decision on the battlefield."

Then he wrapped it up, delivering the commentary that he had
conceived even before his trip to Vietnam, and which he now felt he
had confirmed firsthand:

Tonight, back in more familiar surroundings in New York,
we'd like to sum up our findings in Vietnam, an analysis that
must be speculative, personal, subjective. Who won and who
lost in the great Tet Offensive against these cities? I'm not sure.
The Vietcong did not win by a knockout, but neither did we.

The referees of history may make it a draw . . . On the political
front, past performance gives no confidence that the Vietnamese
government can cope with its problems, now compounded by
the attack on the cities. It may not fall, it may hold on, but it
probably won't show the dynamic qualities demanded of this
young nation. Another stand-off.

We have been too often disappointed by the optimism of the
American leaders, both in Vietnam and Washington, to have
faith any longer in the silver linings they find in the darkest
clouds . . . To say we are closer to victory today is to believe, in
the face of the evidence, the optimists who have been wrong
in the past. To suggest that we are on the edge of defeat is to
yield to unreasonable pessimism. To say that we are mired in
stalemate seems the only realistic, yet unsatisfactory conclusion.
On the off chance that military and political analysts are right,
in the next few months we must test the enemy's intentions, in
case this is indeed his last big gasp before negotiations. But it
is increasingly clear to this reporter that the only rational way
out then will be to negotiate, not as victors, but as an honorable
people who lived up to their pledge to defend democracy, and
did the best they could.

This is Walter Cronkite. Good night.

LBJ probably never said the line that has been widely attributed to
him after the broadcast—"If I've lost Cronkite, I've lost middle America."[81] Nor is it true, as David Halberstam would later write, that "it
was the first time in American history a war had been declared over by
an anchorman."[82] But Cronkite's cautious pessimism had tremendous
impact and made it much harder to dismiss those who opposed the
war as "hippies" or un-American. It was hard to imagine an American
more conventional and authentic than Walter Cronkite.

The anchorman may not have declared an end to the war, but he
had declared the end of something far more significant. For decades,
certainly since World War II, the mainstream press and, for that matter, most of the American public, believed their leaders, political and
military. Tet was the first of many blows to that faith in coming years.
Americans would never again be so trusting.

Clifford, in office as secretary of defense for less than a week, just days after the Battle of Hue ended, advised the president to begin scaling back.

> If we continue with our present policy of adding more troops and increasing our commitment, this policy may lead us into Laos and Cambodia.[83] The reserve forces in North Vietnam are a cause for concern as well. They have a very substantial population from which to draw. They have no trouble whatever organizing, equipping, and training their forces. We seem to have a sinkhole. We put in more—they match it. We put in more— they match it . . . I see more and more fighting with more and more casualties on the U.S. side and no end in sight to the action . . .
>
> We can no longer rely just on the field commander. He can want troops and want troops and want troops. We must look at the overall impact on us, including the situation here in the United States . . . Now the time has come to decide where do we go from here . . . We should consider changing our concept from one of protecting real estate to protecting people. We need to see if these people are really going to take care of themselves eventually. I am not sure we can ever find our way out if we continue to shovel men into Vietnam.

Westy was relieved of his command in June. Officially, the move was a promotion—he became army chief of staff—but it was correctly seen as a rebuke. His projected big attack at Khe Sanh never came. The outpost was dismantled and abandoned in July by the new MACV commander, General Abrams. Hanoi had baited Westy with an imagined replay of Dien Bien Phu, all the while moving great numbers of troops under his nose for the surprise city attacks of Tet.[84]

President Johnson remained stymied by the war. At one point he lamented to his wife, Lady Bird, "I can't get out, I can't finish it with what I have got. So what the hell can I do?"[85]

He abandoned neither the war nor Westy, but one month after the battle ended he announced he would not seek reelection.

12

Why Should
They Keep Fighting?

Two days before the Alliance flag was taken down, a wounded VC
private was captured. He was interviewed six weeks later at a prison
camp in Da Nang by an unnamed Rand Corporation analyst.

Rand (Research and Development) is a think tank that operates as a
brainy adjunct to the Pentagon. It attempts to provide a deep, independent perspective on American military operations, one that looks past
the immediate concerns of strategy and tactics to context, a broader
sense of the history, culture, and attitudes behind any conflict. At the
time of the Tet Offensive, Rand had been at work in South Vietnam
for years. One of its analysts was Daniel Ellsberg, who at the time was
back in the States compiling the report that—after he leaked it to the
press in 1971—would become known as *The Pentagon Papers*. The study
showed that American leaders had been systematically lying about the
scope and progress of the war for years and had consistently enlarged it
despite doubts that the effort could succeed. Ellsberg was not the only
Rand employee whose work in Vietnam turned him against the war.

The captured private was a medic. It is likely that something about
him suggested an unusual measure of poise and intelligence, because
he had made it past the soldiers who found him wounded near the
royal palace and had been spared for further questioning—not all were.
He might first have taken his place among the stoical, squatting, blindfolded men at Mang Ca who would stoically endure the taunting, slaps,
pokes, and spit of ARVN soldiers while awaiting a helicopter flight to
imprisonment and interrogation. The analyst who interviewed him

did not record his name or his age, and noted that the private was not very well informed about military plans or politics. He was described as cooperative and sincere, "gentle and pleasant."

He was from Quang Tri, the northernmost province in South Vietnam, and had marched south toward Hue with his unit on Wednesday evening, February 21, the same day that Thompson's marines had finally taken the south wall. The medic didn't know it, but the battle was nearly over. He was, at best, part of a rear-guard effort to protect the Front's final retreat. It took his unit six hours to walk from their camp in the Gio Linh jungle. He was one of four medics in his company. They were all given more supplies before leaving.

They walked through the night and arrived on the outskirts of the Citadel at three in the morning on Thursday. They rested, ate, and moved inside to join the battle around the royal palace at six that morning. He had been led to believe that the Front was victorious, that it had seized the city, and that the people of the city had warmly embraced the revolution. He had been told that the Americans had suffered defeats throughout the country and that "the enemy's prestige had been much reduced." He was surprised to find the interior of the Citadel in ruins. His company was hit hard immediately from the air—by bombs and artillery.

They fought through that day, until five o'clock, and as his unit fell back he was wounded.

"My comrades told me they would come back to get me out of that place," he said. "I don't know what happened; they did not. I lay on a pile of bricks all night, and the next morning I tried to find a way out. Unfortunately, I did not know the way. I got lost and then I was captured."

The analyst got the medic talking about the battle. He was strikingly articulate, and despite his being wounded and getting captured, he was still hopeful and defiant. For a private second class, he demonstrated remarkable—if somewhat distorted—insight and understanding:

> Of course, our side suffered casualties during the attacks, but our casualties were much lower than those of the enemy. In fact, when we entered the inner citadel in Hue, our battalion killed thirty paratroopers and a number of Vietnamese marines. Only

two of our men were sacrificed, several others were wounded, and three were captured, two other men and myself. Politically speaking, we have been able to show world opinion that we are able to attack all over Vietnam at the same time and will have sufficient forces to win this war. Psychologically speaking, we were able to gain the people's support. People realized that we were the ones who fought for their freedom, and the GVN [the South Vietnamese government] always caused them miseries. The GVN destroyed their houses and killed their people with bombs. The more people realize that, the more support we will have from them.

The medic was convinced that the Battle of Hue had undermined support for the Saigon regime, even among its own soldiers. His unit had captured one soldier from the ARVN's Fourth Battalion, whom the medic described as very frightened and afraid of being killed. According to him, the captured soldier had said, "I wanted to surrender when I first encountered your unit, but I did not have an opportunity. You people fought more violently. My battalion commander has already been killed by your troops and all of his men are now just like a snake without its head."

Encouraged by his Rand questioner, the medic went on:

In my opinion the general offensive has had a great effect on the war's situation. This war should not be fought for much longer because the people are not like stones and things. Since the people feel sorrow, feel pain, they should not keep killing each other. The Americans should be made to understand that the Vietnamese people are fighting against them for their own interests and for the independence of their country. I don't think that the Americans are earning anything from the war in Vietnam, so why should they keep on fighting? Why should their government keep sending young Americans to this country? The Americans should understand that their government is sending them to their deaths. After the general offensive, I believe the American government will realize its mistake, and if it does, of course the war will have some big changes.

The Americans landed in Vietnam, were killed in Vietnam, and others have continued to come here without having good reasons. It simply means that they want to commit suicide. We are not warlike, but we are fighting for our nation. We have just cause, and we won many battles . . . With the fighting spirit of the men in our ranks, I strongly believe that there will be many other waves of well-coordinated attacks in the future. I am now in prison, but I still have strong confidence in our people. I will always think that our people will win the war.[86]

Reports like this by Rand employees were rarely even read. The military considered them to be an expensive waste of time and of little use.[87] This one went into the file with all the others.

13

Krystal Burgers
and the Truck

O<small>N THE FIRST</small> week of the push inside the Citadel, photographer John Olson was with Charlie Company in the thick of the fighting. Officially he was shooting for *Stars and Stripes*, but he carried four other cameras to take pictures he hoped to sell elsewhere.

One of the frames he shot that week was a common sight in those days of terrible street fighting, a Patton tank carrying wounded marines. The picture would become emblematic of the Battle of Hue, one of the most famous photographs from the Vietnam War, and one of the great shots in the annals of combat photography (see page 472).

With an artist's eye for composition, Olson captured seven marines in a tableau worthy of Rembrandt. The palette is dark, muddy greens and blues and browns in a grayish light, with shocking splashes of blood. Under their helmets, the eyes of the men who face the camera are wide and anxious. They are looking past the photographer fearfully. One man has his entire face wrapped in a thick bandage and his arm in a sling. Behind him sits a marine whose face isn't visible but whose bare leg out of torn trousers is smeared with blood. At the center of the shot, in the foreground, the most striking figure is supine and has been shot through the center of his chest. He is pale, limp, and half naked. His shirt has been stripped away and his wound roughly bandaged with a compress and a tan wrap tied around his neck and torso. He is speckled with blood. A worried marine leans over him, one hand draped protectively over his body, the other resting on his bare shoulder. In the left edge of the frame sits another man in a green poncho with an anxious look on his dirty, unshaven face. He is holding upside down a bottle that is feeding clear liquid into a tube that curls down to the limp man's left arm. The limp figure's head is the closest thing to the viewer in the frame. We see him upside down, his eyes closed beneath dark eyebrows, his head resting on a wooden door that had been used as a makeshift stretcher. He has a full head of wet black hair and a lean, handsome face with a long aquiline nose and a faint, youthful attempt at a mustache. He looks dead, or nearly so.

The photograph would appear on March 8 in *Life* magazine, part of a six-page color display of powerful images from Hue.[88] It included shots of Sergeant Thoms, clearly identifiable in his torn trousers, assaulting the ruins of the Dong Ba Tower with his squad, and three compelling shots of a terrified wounded marine crawling toward safety, being pulled in with one hand tightly gripping the barrel of a proffered M16.

But it was Olson's amazing shot of the marines on the tank that got the biggest play. It was splashed over two full inside pages. The remarkable pictures came with no story line or detailed captions. The scenes were not described; the marines were not identified. In the brief text that ran alongside, the magazine noted that the Hue battle "demonstrated the sickening irony into which the war has fallen—the destruction of the very things that the U.S. is there to save."

As stunning as they were, the photographs did not make the cover of *Life* that week. A crying black child was on the cover, part of a special report called "The Cycle of Despair: The Negro and the City." Olson's images were sandwiched between ads for color TVs, Volvos, Best Western Motels, and "The amazing FOTRON color camera," and pictures of movie stars (Richard Burton), politicians (George Romney and Nelson Rockefeller in a golf cart), Joe DiMaggio, the vice president and newly named batting instructor of the Oakland Athletics, and dazzling showgirls from the Folies Bergère. The placement of Olson's pictures suggests a nation at war but preoccupied with other things—there's a two-page spread some pages later on the film version of the soft-porn satire *Candy*. More words were given to a profile of the actor George C. Scott, speaking of his "courage" as a performer.

The pale figure shot through the chest on top of that tank was Alvin Bert Grantham. He was from Mobile, Alabama, and he was eighteen years old. A year earlier he and his friend Freddie Thrift had joined the marines. They had been working as bricklayers. Both had dropped out of high school, and when the draft board came calling they decided to join the marines because the marines were reputed to be the best fighters, and if they were going to go to Vietnam anyway, they might as well go with the best. They knew nothing about the country or the war, except that the Communists were trying to take over and had to be stopped. They were led to believe, Grantham and Thrift, that they could stay together if they enlisted together, which sounded good. That way in battle they could look out for each other. Neither this nor the war turned out the way they'd imagined.

They were separated before they even got to boot camp. Thrift was pulled off the bus at a rest stop along the way because his sister had been in a bad car wreck. He was sent home and wound up finishing at Parris Island two weeks behind Grantham. In Vietnam, Thrift went to the Third Marine Regiment farther north. Grantham went to the Fifth in Hue and joined an M60 machine-gun squad.

Grantham found the marines he was with to be cruel. After a while he understood why they were that way, but it never stopped bothering him. It did not take some horrible atrocity to make him feel this way. It was little things. Things he saw nearly every day. The way the grunts hated the Vietnamese, whom they called gooks. They also hated having to be there. They called Vietnam the Asshole. "We just need to kill everything we see and then go home" is how it was explained to him. The normal rules of human feeling and behavior seemed to have been suspended. Grantham watched one member of his squad repeatedly bat an elderly Vietnamese man on the head with the steel handle of his knife. The beating was prolonged and deliberate. The old man was crying. Blood was pouring down his face, and he was pleading, but the marine wasn't happy with his answers so he kept rapping him hard on the same spot on the top of his head. Grantham hated to watch it. He had never seen anyone treated that way before and it didn't seem right, but he didn't dare speak up. The three rules that mattered were these: You followed the leader, you did whatever he told you to do whether you liked it or not, and, most important—an admonition enunciated repeatedly—"Don't fuck up."

In Hue, where they were never sure whether a Vietnamese was an enemy or a civilian, the default decision, particularly with men, was enemy. This was a life-and-death matter. The gooks were hated and they were killed. The marines were all scared and angry. The more they were shot at, the more their friends were killed or wounded, the angrier they got.

Grantham's unit was nearly always directly across the street from the enemy, and each morning rang with action. They were repeatedly ordered to send squads across the street, and every time the men were mowed down. Then they'd spend excruciating minutes, sometimes hours, trying to drag the downed men back. Grantham watched as a sergeant walked out alongside a tank to try to retrieve one man. When they got close, he took off his helmet and leaned down to place his ear on the man's chest, to see if his heart was still beating, and he was shot through the head—the bullet entered by his left ear, just below the temple, and it exited through his right jaw. Almost a half century later Grantham could still hear the sound the bullet made as it passed through the sergeant's head, the *pop!* it made as it hit bone. The sergeant, improbably, was still alive. He fell over and rolled around and the men behind him, Grantham included, shouted for him to crawl back. He made it to a ditch in front of the house where the rest of his squad was hiding, and a corpsman went to work on him there.

This went on for days. Grantham would later be unsure how many days, but it seemed like forever because it seemed like a death sentence. The moist air was thick with smoke and the smell of diesel fuel and rotting flesh. It was awful, and you did not get used to it. Every time they moved they were shot at. It seemed there were no safe places anywhere.

On the day he was wounded, all four of the other members of his machine-gun squad were hit by shrapnel. He was the only one unhurt. He had dragged them, one by one, to cover. When he returned for the last one, a bleeding and incapacitated man he knew only as "Snow," he refused to let Grantham pull him from the room.

"Take the gun first," he said.

Grantham could not carry both him and the gun.

"I ain't got time to come back," Grantham said.

"Take the gun first," said Snow. "You can't let them get the gun."

So Grantham did as he was told. He carried the gun out and then went back for Snow, whom he picked up and carried out to the others.

Then someone down the street started yelling that they needed the gun. Grantham picked it up and ran with it toward the house on the corner, which was set back farther from the street than the others. He stopped behind the last house before that one, looked to his left, and saw an enemy soldier pointing a rifle at him. Grantham ducked through a back door just as rounds hit it behind him. He set up the gun in a rear window and started blasting toward the shooter.

Another marine ran into the house, screaming for him to stop firing. "There's marines in that house!" he said.

"Well, there might be, but there's gooks all over the outside of it!"

More enemy soldiers came running across the street toward the corner house and Grantham started shooting at them. He ducked back out of the window just as return fire came through, waited for a few moments, and then peeked out again. That's when the rifle round hit him square in the chest.

It felt like being hit by a bus. It knocked him backward off his feet and he landed on his back. He still had the machine gun in his hand when he hit the floor. He threw it off to the side and yelled, "I'm hit!"

Then he felt it, like a hot poker had been stuck through his chest, just to the right of center. It felt like it was still there. It burned badly all the way through him. He started to have trouble breathing. Someone, the marine who had been in the room with him, leaned over him and started to work on him. His shirt was torn off and he could see blood spurt out of the hole when he exhaled and suck back into him when he tried to inhale. The marine took the cellophane off a cigarette pack and stuffed it over the wound, poking it in to line the edges of the bullet hole. Then he placed a compress over it and bound it to him tightly with a bandage wrapped around his chest and neck.

Now he could breathe better, but the wound still burned terribly. Several of his ribs were shattered. Grantham was turned on his right side so that his good lung wouldn't fill up with blood. The marine kept slapping him, trying to keep him awake, trying to make him talk. Grantham felt an overpowering need to go to sleep. When a corpsman came, he fumbled with Grantham's arm and started an IV. There was a discussion about morphine.

"We can't give him too much," the corpsman said. "I don't want him to pass out."

He was placed on the wooden door and four marines carried him from the house. He felt that he was going to roll off, that they were going to drop him, but they didn't. They lifted him up to the tank. When it started to move, the pain was excruciating. He thought he would die from the pain.

He drifted into and out of consciousness. They stopped at one aid station, which couldn't take more wounded—it was overwhelmed—so they had to drive farther, toward another. Every shudder and bounce stabbed him with blinding pain. At the second station he was lifted from the tank and zipped into a body bag.

He was still semiconscious. He could hear people yelling, screaming in pain, but there was not enough help for everyone. He heard someone say, "Wait, this one's not dead yet." Grantham felt sorry for that person, whoever he was, only to realize that the corpsman must have been talking about him, because the body bag came unzipped.

Then he was sure he was dying . . . *not dead yet*. He was not going to make it back alive. He would never see his family again. A whirl of sad thoughts went through his head, the people and things he would miss, his parents, his friend Freddie, a girl he liked . . . and then he remembered the truck.

He had fallen ill when he was five years old. He had a rare enzyme disease, porphyria, which had affected his kidneys. He was frightened of the hospital where his parents took him to stay, and he was confined to his bed, so one day his father had brought him the truck. It was a miniature tow truck made of metal, with real rubber tires. It had a hook on the back. You could change the tires and lower and raise the hook. The doors would open and close. He loved that truck. It gave him something to play with in bed in the hospital and it had come home with him when he was released. The memory of that truck cheered him a little. He missed that truck.

And then he remembered Krystal burgers. He and Freddie, after they'd worked a long morning laying bricks, would drive together to the restaurant Krystal, where they sold small square hamburgers for ten cents each—you could eat one in two bites. They would order a dozen each, two large fries each, two big Cokes each, and two pieces of pie each.

"Who's going to eat all this food?" the counter girl asked.

"We are," he said.

They took the food out to the car and sat there and feasted until it was time to go back to work. Grantham remembered those burgers as, perhaps, the happiest moment of his life. They tasted that good.

His reverie ended abruptly. He was taken to an operating room—he wasn't sure anymore where he was or how much time had elapsed—but it was a huge room with lots of lights. There were many people in the room and a lot of noises, shouting. Some were screaming. He was stripped naked and turned over on his side. A nurse jabbed him with a needle. The doctor lifted one of his arms up over his head and started cutting. He was still conscious and the blade stung like hell.

When he next opened his eyes he was on a hospital ship. He was in a tiny room with a number of other beds. The man in the bed next to him was screaming. This is what woke him. The screaming man had just awakened to discover that he had lost both of his legs. Grantham went immediately back to sleep. The next time he woke up, he was being loaded onto a plane, a C-130, and he was told that he was being taken to the 106th Army General Hospital in Yokohama, Japan.

He would learn more about his wound later. The rifle round had left a small hole in his chest and a larger one under his right shoulder blade. It had shattered his ribs and passed through his lung, but it had not ruptured any major blood vessels. At first they didn't stitch up the hole in his chest. The wound was allowed to dry up and heal from the inside out. He had an incision that went from his right nipple all the way around to the exit wound in his back. There were tubes in his torso and his arm and up his penis.

By the end of March he was able to get up and walk around. He learned that he had contracted malaria in Vietnam, and while he was recovering in Japan he came down with typhoid fever. He dropped fifty pounds, down to 119. They told him he could not be flown back to the States until his fever subsided, so he started taking the thermometer out of his mouth when it reached 98 degrees. They flew him to Pensacola, where, when they learned he still had typhoid, he was placed in quarantine.

He was there when his sister's former husband, who had also served in the marines, visited him and showed him the picture in *Life*. He had been at a barbershop, flipping pages in the magazine, when he'd seen it.

Grantham stayed sick for a year. He had lost so much weight and his body was so depleted that he kept getting sick. Doctors discovered that he had an amoeba in his liver—a leftover from dysentery in Vietnam—that had formed an abscess. He did not feel normal again until April 1969.

He got married when he left the marines in 1970, went to work for Scott Paper Company in Mobile, and fathered three children. Twelve years later he got a job with a company that built circuit boards for computers. In time he was the head of manufacturing. He divorced and remarried, and adopted his second wife's youngest son, who grew up and joined the marines, serving two tours in Iraq.

As with most of those who fought in Hue, the slightest glimpse of a photo or scrap of video shot there in February 1968 is enough to bring back the awful smell; the shattering noise; the days of gray, cold rain, of smoke and cordite; the days of fright and feral anger and pain. Something about the grayness of that month is the battle's spooky signature, as if Hue for nearly a month had literally fallen into the shadow of death.

Grantham never talked about Vietnam. At first it was a difficult subject. The war was ever more unpopular in the years that followed, until it ended, from America's perspective, not just badly but disgracefully. It was the war we lost. There was no shortage of people to blame. The war divided two generations and, nearly a half century later, still shapes our politics and foreign policy to an unhealthy degree. Grantham didn't want to talk about it at first, and in time not talking about it became a habit. He got on with his life. He reset his moral compass. He hid his scars. The Olson picture became famous, but the marine at its center did not. He is like a model who sat for an artist who produced a painting that resonated in the world for larger reasons, for reasons that had nothing to do with him. In that sense, and in that sense alone, the picture is not about him, and yet, because it is a photograph, because it was real, it will always be very intimately, very painfully about him. But no one outside his immediate family and friends ever recognized that the stricken marine with the hole in his chest on that tank in *Life* magazine was Alvin Bert Grantham, and that he, unlike so many other of his fellow marines and soldiers, lived to tell the tale.

Epilogue

THE BATTLE OF Hue has never been accorded the important position it deserves in our understanding of the Vietnam War, or what the Vietnamese call the "Resistance War Against America." By January 1968 public support for the war in America was eroding, but actual opposition remained on the fringes of American politics. It had entered the mainstream by the end of February. The pivot point was the Tet Offensive and this battle, its most wrenching episode. After Tet, there was no more conjecture that the war could be won swiftly or easily. The end was not in view. The debate was never again about how to win but about how to leave. In a larger sense, Tet delivered the first in a series of profound shocks to America's faith in its leaders.

The takeover of Hue was so unexpected that, even during the month it took to wrest the city back, the MACV seemed reluctant to believe it had actually happened. General Westmoreland continually and falsely assured political leaders in Washington and the American public that the city had not fallen into enemy hands. This refusal to face facts was not just a public relations problem; it had tragic consequences for many of the marines and soldiers who fought there. If the extent of the challenge had been weighed realistically at the outset, if commanders had heeded the entirely correct CIA assessment on the first day, and if they had listened to their own field commanders, they might have held off the counterattack until they had readied an appropriate level of force and more effective tactics. There would have been a price to pay for the delay—not the least of which would have been giving more time for the National Liberation Front's commissars to conduct their purges—but a better-prepared counterattack might well have saved both American and civilian lives, and ended the battle sooner. As it was, relatively small units of young Americans were thrown repeatedly against impossible odds, enabling the enemy to drag out its defense and run up the cost.

The conspiracy of denial around Hue also helps explain why this terrible battle has remained, for most Americans, so little known. It has been remembered as just another passing episode in that long war. The director Stanley Kubrick, no doubt attracted by the unusual visuals of urban combat, set *Full Metal Jacket* in Hue, although in his film the battle is just a backdrop. For what we have known of it, we are indebted to the handful of journalists who braved those streets to send back stories and pictures. It has been conscientiously remembered by the US Marine Corps, albeit with more emphasis on the glory than on the leadership blunders that cost so many lives. The books that have been written about it—*Fire in the Streets* by Eric Hammel, *The Siege at Hue* by George Smith, *Battle for Hue* by Keith Nolan, and a few others—have uncritically celebrated the valor of Americans who fought, with little interest in how they were used. They were used badly. In that sense, the Battle of Hue is a microcosm of the entire conflict. With nearly half a century of hindsight, Hue deserves to be widely remembered as the single bloodiest battle of the war, one of its defining events, and one of the most intense urban battles in American history.

Both sides, American and Vietnamese, view the outcome as a victory, the Americans because their immediate objective of retaking the city was achieved; the Vietnamese because the battle had such a damaging impact on American public opinion. It did not, of course, end the war, but it was the point at which everything changed. A month after it ended, President Johnson decided not to seek reelection, and Westmoreland would shortly thereafter be removed as its commander. Richard Nixon was elected president eight months later mendaciously promising not victory, but a secret plan to bring the war to an "honorable end."[1]

The secret plan prolonged the conflict seven more years, spreading misery and death throughout Indochina. Nixon began gradually drawing down the number of Americans fighting there in 1969, and—catastrophically, as it turned out—began shifting the military burden to Saigon. General Abrams threw greater and greater responsibility for prosecuting the war to the ARVN, shifting his efforts to disrupting and destroying Hanoi's delivery of troops and matériel. This is what prompted the raids into the neighboring countries of Laos and Cambodia, where North Vietnam had long sheltered troops and supply routes. The bombing of Communist sanctuaries in Cambodia destabilized that neutral country, leading to the overthrow of Prince Norodom Sihanouk in 1970 and the rise of the murderous Khmer Rouge, which would be responsible for the deaths of millions of Cambodians in ensuing years. In January 1973, President Thieu reluctantly signed his name to a peace agreement in Paris that ended America's direct involvement in the war, although it continued to support his regime as the fighting dragged on for two more years. Eventually the weight of Vietnamization became too much for the Saigon government to bear.

Through these years, opposition to the war swelled, with hundreds of thousands of protesters marching in the streets demanding its end. These protests fueled the great counterculture movements of the 1960s, and they occasionally turned violent. Four students were killed at Kent State University in Ohio in May 1970 when National Guardsmen opened fire on protesters. The incident accelerated the antiwar movement's efforts, deepening the country's division. The 1972 presidential election turned almost entirely on the question of the Vietnam War, as Nixon, summoning support from Americans who were troubled by the rise of antiestablishment feelings and by violence in the streets, soundly defeated Senator George McGovern to win reelection. The president's illegal efforts to undermine McGovern's campaign led to the Watergate scandal and his resignation in 1974.

Under President Gerald Ford, the United States continued to provide substantial assistance to Thieu's government, but its military was no match for Hanoi's. An offensive launched in 1975 quickly routed the ARVN. The city of Hue fell again and for good in March 1975, and Saigon followed a month later, as US helicopters scrambled to evacuate remaining American personnel and as many South Vietnamese officials as they could carry. The final images of desperate civilians clinging to the skids of American choppers as they lifted off framed the futility of the decade-long effort.

Nevertheless, in the nearly half century since, some American military historians and many American veterans have insisted that the Battle of Hue was won, and that, indeed, the entire Tet Offensive was an unqualified American victory. Westy certainly felt that way. Eight years later, in his autobiography *A Soldier Reports,* he was still insisting that he had not been surprised by the Tet attacks—he said he had forecast the attacks on the city but that word apparently did not reach the MACV compound in Hue. He conceded at long last that on the morning of January 31, 1968, "the MACV advisory compound was under siege and most of Hue was in enemy hands, including much of the Citadel." Yet the battle to win back the city warranted only two pages in his 566-page book. He portrayed it in perfunctory terms, complimenting the American and South Vietnamese commanders on their excellent leadership, exaggerating enemy deaths, and underreporting the number of Americans killed by nearly a third.[2] He lamented the destruction of the historic city, and effectively lay blame for all civilian losses on Hanoi, citing only those killed in the purges. He makes no mention of civilians killed by American and South Vietnamese bombing and shelling. If your knowledge of the Battle of Hue came from Westy alone—from his public statements at the time and from his memoir— you would view it as a thumping American victory.

You have to give the general credit for consistency. On the day after the Saigon flag was run back up the pole at Ngo Mon, he gave a long interview to reporters in Saigon, in which he again declared that the Tet Offensive had been a "military defeat" for Hanoi. He was still anticipating the big attack at Khe Sanh and did not even mention Hue. Even the fact that the enemy had surprised him (slightly) by the number of forces they deployed, to him this was not a setback but an opportunity: "In a very real sense, when he [the enemy] moved out of his jungle camps he made himself more vulnerable and gave us an opportunity to hurt him severely." He denied that his official casualty estimates were inflated and said that the enemy's offensive was a sign of desperation. Westy added that many NVA and VC had fought "halfheartedly."[3]

This was certainly not the experience of those who fought them in Hue. To a man, the American veterans I interviewed told me they had faced a disciplined, highly motivated, skilled, and determined enemy. To characterize them otherwise is to diminish the accomplishment of those who drove them out of Hue. But taking the city back qualifies as a "victory" only in a narrow sense—they achieved their objective. In any larger sense the word hardly applies. Both sides badly miscalculated. Hanoi counted on a popular uprising that didn't come, while Washington and Saigon, blindsided, refused to believe the truth. Both sides played their roles courageously, and to terrible effect. In sum: Hanoi's troops seized the city and were then forced at tremendous cost to relinquish it, while the city itself was leveled in the process. The status quo was upheld but greatly diminished, and it lasted for only a few more years. How is this victory? It takes a determined act of imagination for either side to make that claim. It makes more sense to consider the ways both sides lost.

If we use Westy's favorite measure, the body count, the battle's clearest losers were the citizens of Hue. In the city today, where memories of that nightmarish month are still bitter, it is said that there is a victim under every square meter of ground. It remains a shameful fact in the Socialist Republic of Vietnam that many hundreds, perhaps thousands, of its citizens were dispatched deliberately by their "liberators." The ruling Communist Party labors to promote national unity by remembering the conflict not as a civil war but strictly as a struggle for independence, so reprisals against its own countrymen are an inconvenient memory. The party has never named or punished those responsible, not least because they were following clear orders from above. Many of those who carried out the purges have been celebrated as heroes of the state. The official position is that while there were some excesses, some "mistakes," the numbers have been exaggerated by Vietnam's enemies.

Of those who perished, by far the greatest number were killed by accident, either in the cross fire or by allied shelling and bombing. Accidental deaths do not equate morally to mass execution but, as the writer Tran Thi Thu Van has pointed out, the effect is the same. Today we rightly weigh the cost in civilian lives whenever violent action is taken, but I found very little concern expressed in 1968, not in any of the official papers I reviewed, not in contemporary press accounts or the dozens of books and papers written since, and not, for that matter, in any of the interviews I conducted. Vietnamese civilians, when they do come up, are described as a nuisance, even though the battle, like the war, was ostensibly *about them*. Nearly every marine I interviewed recalled seeing dead civilians in the streets, inside buildings, and in bunkers underneath those buildings. The Citadel, in particular, was a confined area, where escape was all but impossible. Nearly all the civilians I interviewed who survived the battle described losing family members, most often to shells and bombs. The survivors described, without hesitation, bombardment as the most terrifying memory, even those who'd had family members executed. If Hanoi did not win many new friends by taking Hue, neither did the allies in taking it back.

Death tolls for combatants clearly show more Front soldiers killed than Americans, by a factor of five to one, so by Westy's favorite measure the battle was an unqualified success—by that measure, of course, the United States won the Vietnam War. But losses weighed more heavily in the United States than in North Vietnam. There's no doubt that an authoritarian state can more easily absorb battlefield deaths than a democracy, where every one is a blow to public support. It is to democracy's credit, and benefit, that casualties dampen enthusiasm for all but the most vitally important conflicts. Hanoi, on the other hand, had millions of men at its disposal, and could justify its suffering and sacrifice by asserting the noble cause of independence—more inspiring than some abstract theory about the balance of power.

Journalism has long been blamed for losing the war, but the American reporting from Hue was more accurate than official accounts, deeply respectful, and uniformly sympathetic to US fighting men. Reporters in Hue listening, watching, and taking pictures and notes at great personal risk, such as among others Gene Roberts, Al Webb, Catherine Leroy, John Olson, and John Laurence, were performing a vital public service.

Because Hanoi ultimately won the war, it's tempting to ascribe greater wisdom and foresight to its leaders and generals than they deserve. The entire Tet Offensive was driven by grandiose misconceptions. Hanoi hugely overreached when it took Hue. More pragmatic North Vietnamese leaders including Ho Chi Minh and General Vo Nguyen Giap tried to stop it, and professional soldiers down the ranks saw right through the party's propaganda. They knew they could take the city but that they could not hold it for long. They lost the argument but were proved right. A top Communist general, reflecting on the whole Tet Offensive years later, wrote, "We did not correctly evaluate the specific balance of forces between ourselves and the enemy," and called its objectives "beyond our actual strength . . . in part on an illusion based on our subjective desires."[4] The dreams broadcast by the party songbirds were embraced by romantic young recruits like the village girl Che Thi Mung and the Buddhist poet Nguyen Dac Xuan, and when they were driven from Hue, broken and bleeding, they felt crushed. Their defeat was sealed in the first days of the city's occupation, not by allied guns but by the tepid response of Hue's citizens. I suspect anger over this did a lot to fuel the purges.

The takeover of Hue was a huge success for Hanoi in only one way: it achieved complete tactical surprise, despite Westy's claims otherwise. Conversely, it represents perhaps the worst allied intelligence failure of the war. That's true of the entire Tet Offensive, and particularly true of the attack on Hue. Hanoi spent months amassing an army around the city without attracting notice. And although it is true that after three weeks of heavy fighting the enemy was driven off, it was the impact of the initial blow that resonated most loudly. Bringing the war to city streets deeply undermined the faith of middle-of-the road Vietnamese in President Thieu's government. Nonideological citizens—read, *most* citizens—were concerned primarily with survival. They wanted to be on the winning side when the war ended. Tet lowered the odds on Saigon as the safer bet. Hanoi may have aimed too high, but in the long run its effort succeeded in ways its leaders could not have fully foreseen.

Alternative history enthusiasts promote the preposterous idea that the United States might have won the war if it had thrown itself more heartily into the conflict. It is possible, of course, that a severe, expensive, long-term commitment by the United States, one with the full backing of the American people and a far greater investment of men and treasure, might have been able to prop up Thieu and his successors indefinitely. But the suppositions are not viable. America had no more appetite for colonial adventures or "third world" conflicts in 1968 than it has today. As some of the nation's more recent wars have helped illustrate, "victory" in Vietnam would have been neither possible nor desirable. It would have required a massive and sustained military presence, and very likely a state of permanent war. Hue illustrates just how bitter that war would have been.

From the perspective of nearly half a century, the Battle of Hue and the entire Vietnam War seem a tragic and meaningless waste. So much heroism and slaughter for a cause that now seems dated and nearly irrelevant. The whole painful experience ought to have (but has not) taught Americans to cultivate deep regional knowledge in the practice of foreign policy, and to avoid being led by ideology instead of understanding. The United States should interact with other nations realistically, first, not on the basis of domestic political priorities. Very often the problems in distant lands have little or nothing to do with America's ideological preoccupations. Beware of men with theories that explain everything. Trust those who approach the world with humility and cautious insight. The United States went to war in Vietnam in the name of freedom, to stop the supposed monolithic threat of Communism from spreading across the globe like a dark stain—I remember seeing these cartoons as a child. There were experts, people who knew better, who knew the languages and history of Southeast Asia, who had lived and worked there, who tried to tell Presidents Eisenhower, Kennedy, Johnson, and Nixon that the conflict in Vietnam was peculiar to that place. They were systematically ignored and pushed aside. David Halberstam's classic *The Best and the Brightest* documents this process convincingly. America had every right to choose sides in the struggle between Hanoi and Saigon, even to try to influence the outcome, but lacking a legitimate or even marginally capable ally its military effort was misguided and doomed. At the very least, Vietnam should stand as a permanent caution against going to war for any but the most immediate, direct, and vital national interest, or to prevent genocide or wider conflict, and then only in concert with other countries.

After Tet, the American antiwar effort spread from pacifists and principled religious leaders into a broad youth movement, one that galvanized a growing spirit of youthful rebellion. Opposition to the war became cool. It rapidly joined recreational drug use, rock music, and greater sexual freedom as an emblem of the youth counterculture. Youthful idealism—painfully naive in many respects—was also a big reason why many of those who fought in Vietnam had enlisted. Their motivations were every bit as pure. I was moved by the heroism and dedication of those who fought on both sides of the battle. Nearly all the veterans I interviewed—on both sides—are understandably proud of their service. The Americans had a wide range of feelings about it, but there is no question about their bravery and patriotism. In the worst days of this fight, facing the near certainty of death or severe bodily harm, those caught up in the Battle of Hue repeatedly advanced. Many of those who survived are still paying for it. To me the way they were used, particularly the way their idealism and loyalty were exploited by leaders who themselves had lost faith in the effort, is a stunning betrayal. It is a lasting American tragedy and disgrace.

Because Americans were plucked off the battlefield on the day their tour ended, or whisked away when wounded, most of these men lost contact with one another when they left Vietnam. Their shared ordeal became thousands of individual memories, which, in isolation, seemed all the more futile and meaningless. The growth of the Internet has enabled many of them to reconnect. They have formed organizations and hold reunions that keep alive memories of the war—good and bad. These networks made it a lot easier for me to piece together this story than those who did so in the past.

The Vietnam I visited in 2015 and 2016 is an exciting, thriving nation, full of industry and promise. It has become a popular tourist destination for Americans, particularly for those who fought in the war. I was privileged to take a walking tour of southern Hue with Chuck Meadows, one of Big Ernie Cheatham's company commanders, who now leads veterans on regular excursions to the city. Given the wholesale violence the United States visited on it, part of the living experience of at least half of its population, it is extraordinary how little resentment is shown toward Americans. To the contrary, I was met with warmth and generosity wherever I went. Government restraints on the economy have eased enough to allow a vibrant private industry, which is evident everywhere you look, from cranes over big construction projects to family restaurants to stores selling the latest Apple products to the swarms of scooters that crowd every street.

Still, there is no question that the Vietnamese people lost something precious when Hanoi won the war. One young woman from Ho Chi Minh City, born decades after the war ended, told me that her generation looks at Seoul and at Tokyo and asks, "Is this what we would have been if we hadn't chased the Americans away?" And while the Communist Party has relaxed its hold on the economy, to great effect,

Vietnam remains a strictly authoritarian state, where speaking your mind, or even recounting truthful stories from your own experience, can get you in trouble. Researching the Battle of Hue was tricky. In telling the story I was revisiting a heroic chapter in the national struggle, but I was also reopening old wounds. The purges in 1968 left many citizens with profound grievances against the state that they remain frightened to voice. Many were reluctant to speak candidly to me, particularly those with sad stories.

On my first visit I worked with an independent translator and guide, Dang Hoa Ho, a former Vietnamese military officer (he is too young to have fought in the American War and served in Vietnam's modern army), who was skilled at putting people at ease and who fully understood my desire for uncensored memories. On my second trip, against my expressed wishes, Hoa was nudged aside by Dinh Hoang Linh, deputy director of Hanoi's Foreign Press Center, part of the country's Ministry of Foreign Affairs. Linh proved to be unfailingly helpful and charming, and a skilled translator, but his presence had a chilling effect.

The following exchange illustrates my point. I was interviewing Doang Thanh Xu, a former VC leader whose men fought north of the city during the battle. Both Doang and Linh were speaking Vietnamese, which I do not understand (the recording was later transcribed and translated for me by my own assistant).

"I'm talking so that you can record to the Party Committee and the Ward Committee later about this interview between me and the writer," said Doang. "Because I am working as a member of the Ward Committee, I have to make sure I am following the policies."

"Yes, exactly," said Linh, "and that's why I'm here. If there is something not right, I will let you know. I am responsible for press and info. I am from the Foreign Affairs Department. So, Mr. Doang, don't worry about this. If there is something worth the notice, I will give you a warning."

Hardly something to give a reporter confidence. In most cases, answering the kind of questions I asked posed little "worth the notice" of Linh. I was not asking people to explain their political views or to offer sweeping judgments about the past—although on many occasions these were offered. My own concerns were mostly granular: Where were you born? When did you join the liberation forces? What did you see? What did you hear? What did you do? How did you feel? It is the accumulation of these individual stories that provides an overview and informs my perspective in this book.

There were, despite Linh's presence, instances of surprising, even painful candor. Nguyen Dac Xuan, a noted historian in Vietnam, played a role in the purges as a young commissar, and he has been labeled by some a "butcher." I was particularly eager to talk to him. He is a practicing Buddhist and has written extensively about his own experience during the war, in no small part defending himself against specific charges of cruelty raised by Tran Thi Thu Van in her book *Mourning Headband for Hue* (see Part Five, chapter 1). He admits he did play a role, albeit an indirect one, and said he has called repeatedly, without success, for formal apologies to be made.

"In a war, it is impossible not to make mistakes," he told me. "If we did wrong to one person, we have to make an apology to one person. If we did wrong to ten persons, we have to make an apology to ten persons. If it was one hundred persons, we have to do the same for one hundred persons. We have to do that for people to forgive us. But from then until now, from 1968 until now . . . nobody made any apology. They consider everything in the past. And people are still puzzled and in tremendous pain. The people can understand that the mistakes in the war were due to naïveté, due to the lack of information, and so on. Therefore, I always talk about this again and again, in every meeting . . . Today, when Tet is nearby"—we spoke in early February 2016—"I have to repeat one thing, that in my life I did many good things in the war, but I am also partly responsible for whatever mistakes happened in Tet Mau Than, too. I also take responsibility for the mistakes though the mistakes were not caused by me. But because I was there, in the Front, I still take part of the responsibility with my people."

The Vietnamese veterans I interviewed had their decorations and honors displayed prominently in their homes and spoke of the battle as a difficult but righteous effort. Most admitted to having been discouraged when they were forced to leave Hue, and described their horror at the catastrophe rained on the city, but they saw the battle as just one episode in a long heroic fight against a foreign power over which they ultimately prevailed. The professional soldiers in particular were puzzled by my focus on this one event, when their careers were spent fighting so many battles—some had fought also against the French, the Chinese, and the Cambodians. It brought home to me how much the Vietnamese perspective on modern history differs from America's. To them Hue, the entire American War, was just one chapter in a much longer story.

The Americans I interviewed had opinions too various to be summarized, but three major themes predominated: (1) most (but not all) were proud of having served; (2) nearly all were angry over the betrayal of their youthful idealism, mostly at American leaders who sent them to fight a war that was judged unwinnable from the start; and (3) all felt sorrow for the friends they lost and the horror the war inflicted on everyone involved, particularly because, for most (but not all), it appears that the death and suffering served no purpose. Many described their difficulties in adjusting to normal life after returning home, some because of lingering physical wounds and many because of less tangible ones.

Richard Leflar, for instance, the Philly youth who was sent to the marines to avoid juvenile detention and found himself terrified in a hole in the middle of the Citadel fight, returned home from his tour in Vietnam in what he now describes as a state of ferocious anger. Hue was his introduction to Vietnam, and in the remaining eleven months of his tour he changed from a terrified teenager into an enthusiastic killer. He described to me, with deep remorse, witnessing some weeks after Hue a terrible act of gang rape and murder by his own squad—most of whom were later killed. When he returned home, he said, he wore on a strap around his neck a dried ear he'd cut off a dead VC, and went out every night to drink heavily and provoke fights. He is proud of his service as a marine but deeply troubled—he has sought help to reconcile himself to the things he did in Vietnam, and the kind of man he became.

Bill Ehrhart, who was wounded by a B-40 blast in the fight for southern Hue, said, "I am most definitely *not* proud of it. I am ashamed of having served in Vietnam." A poet and teacher at the Haverford School in Pennsylvania, Ehrhart became an antiwar activist when his service ended.

He had joined the marines when he was seventeen after writing an editorial in his high school newspaper in support of the war. In a more recent essay, he objects to being frequently thanked for his service, a gesture that has become common in the years since 9/11, when the country rediscovered the heroism and sacrifice of its soldiers. Ehrhart spurns the gratitude.

"How could a nation built upon 'Give me liberty or give me death,' 'all men are created equal,' and 'of the people, by the people, for the people' have ended up waging a shameful, disgraceful war against a people who had done us no harm nor ever would or could?" he wrote.

In his classroom he has posted blown-up photographs he took from a VC fighter he killed, two pictures of pretty young women holding rifles, probably part of his victim's squad. Ehrhart said the victim was, like him, no more than a teenager, scarcely older than his students today. The VC was wearing the thin black cotton *ao ba ba* that Americans called pajamas and was carrying a 1936 vintage rifle with a stock held together with tape and with a bamboo strap replacing the leather one that had long since rotted away. He had a few balls of rice in his pocket. Ehrhart contrasted that with the comfortable, well-equipped— even pampered—ARVN soldiers he observed, soldiers who took off on weekends and holidays and, to his eyes, left the serious fighting to him and his fellow marines. He has ever after felt more admiration for his enemy than for his allies.

Ehrhart wrote a poem in 2011, "Cheating the Reaper," about a reunion in Hue with his fellow marine Kazunori Takenaga, who was injured with him in the same rocket blast. It reads, in part:

Who would have thought
the day that RPG exploded
we'd live to see this day,
this house, this city, Vietnam?
Who would have thought
we'd ever want to come back
or be happy because we lost?

This is the very building, Ken.
This is where we almost died
for nothing that mattered,
but didn't.

Jim Coolican, on the other hand, regards such disdain for ARVN troops as self-defeating and unwarranted: "The Americans went in there, and they believed [the ARVN] was just a kind of little colonial military that really could not do much, and they would just step aside and we would take over and show them how to do it."

With unshaken conviction about the rightness of America's mission, he was convinced when the Battle of Hue ended that the United States would follow up on its hard-won victory by launching a major offensive into North Vietnam itself.

"So much so," he told me, "that I got my unit [the Hac Bao] reoutfitted with gear. My points to the Vietnamese were that we were going north. I told them, 'The South Vietnamese will lead the attack, and our unit will lead the South Vietnamese.' I was convinced of that."

When President Johnson gave a prime-time televised address on March 31, millions of Americans were watching—and in Vietnam, many were listening. The president, looking grim, wearing a dark suit and steel-rimmed glasses, reviewed his earlier efforts to end the war. He cited his September 1967 offer to stop the bombing of North Vietnam if Hanoi would agree to "productive discussions" about ending the war.

"Hanoi denounced this offer, both privately and publicly," he said. "Even while the search for peace was going on, North Vietnam rushed their preparations for a savage assault on the people, the government, and the allies of South Vietnam. Their attack—during the Tet holidays—failed to achieve its principal objectives. It did not collapse the elected Government of South Vietnam or shatter its army—as the Communists had hoped. It did not produce a 'general uprising' among the people of the cities, as they had predicted. The Communists were unable to maintain control of any of the more than thirty cities that they attacked. And they took very heavy casualties. But they did compel the South Vietnamese and their allies to move certain forces from the countryside into the cities. They caused widespread disruption and suffering. Their attacks, and the battles that followed, made refugees of half a million human beings."

This was the furthest the administration had gone in acknowledging the impact of Tet. Coolican believed the president was about to announce that he was going to repay this treachery with a bold countermove, a full-scale invasion of North Vietnam.

"So tonight, in the hope that this action will lead to early talks, I am taking the first step to de-escalate the conflict," Johnson said. "We are reducing—substantially reducing—the present level of hostilities, and we are doing so unilaterally and at once . . . I call upon President Ho Chi Minh to respond positively, and favorably, to this new step toward peace."

Coolican was stunned.

"I realized then that we had just lost the war," said Coolican. "Because the North Vietnamese, they were slammed during the Tet Offensive, and we could have gone after them. We did not do it, and then my thought was . . . we had no intentions of winning the war."

Johnson went on: "Fifty-two months and ten days ago, in a moment of tragedy and trauma, the duties of this office fell upon me. I asked then for your help and God's, that we might continue America on its course, binding up our wounds, healing our history, moving forward in new unity to clear the American agenda and to keep the American commitment for all of our people. United we have kept that commitment. And united we have enlarged that commitment . . . What we won when all of our people united just must not now be lost in suspicion and distrust and selfishness and politics among any of our people. And believing this, as I do, I have concluded that I should not permit the Presidency to become involved in the partisan divisions that are developing in this political year.

"With American sons in the fields far away, with America's future under challenge right here at home, with our hopes and the world's hopes for peace in the balance every day, I do not believe that I should devote an hour or a day of my time to any personal partisan causes or to any duties other than the awesome duties of this office—the Presidency of your country. Accordingly, I shall not seek, and I will not accept, the nomination of my party for another term as your President. But let men everywhere know, however, that a strong and a confident and a vigilant America stands ready tonight to seek an honorable peace; and stands ready tonight to defend an honored cause, whatever the price, whatever the burden, whatever the sacrifice that duty may require.

"Thank you for listening. Good night and God bless all of you."

Mike Downs, on an R&R break in Australia, saw a headline that read, "Johnson Quits." He thought it was a joke.

The words that mattered for Coolican were "to seek an honorable peace." Not victory, but "peace."

He left Vietnam at the end of his tour deeply disillusioned. He retired from the marines as a colonel. Downs considers it a "damn shame" that Coolican was never made a general, and speculates it is because he intimidated his senior officers—"not because he tried to but because he knew so much more than many of them and he was so confident in his knowledge." Coolican worked as the superintendent of the Peninsula School District in Gig Harbor, Washington, before moving to Michigan with his wife in order to be closer to their children and grandchildren. His son was a marine Harrier pilot, and his daughter teaches at the University of Michigan in Ann Arbor. When he moved to Michigan, he finally made good on his promise to his old friend Frank Doezema, killed defending the MACV compound on the first day of the battle, by visiting his family in Kalamazoo. At his friend's grave site, he noticed that the information on the headstone was wrong and got the VA to replace it with one that was correct.

Quy Nguyen, the twelve-year-old Vietnamese boy befriended by Doezema in Hue, joined the South Vietnamese army and then spent six years in a prison camp after the war ended. In 1991 he moved his wife and family to Everett, Washington. He established contact there with the Doezema family, writing to share his memories of Frank and his grief over his loss. He still has the camera his friend gave him.

When Saigon fell, Coolican's good friend "Harry," the fierce Hac Bao commander Tran Ngoc Hue, fought on for years. He was wounded attacking NVA troops in Laos and was imprisoned. He slowly recovered as his country and his cause went down to defeat. Hue spent thirteen years in prison, and another eight years unemployable and under watch in Saigon until his old American friends, including Coolican, managed to secure him a visa to the United States. He now lives as an American citizen in Arlington, Virginia, with his family.

"History is not easy," Hue told me. "People are still confused why a huge force like the United States was defeated. But if you don't know your enemy, you will lose every time."

Che Thi Mung, one of the Huong River Squad, was sent for medical training when her wounds healed. She worked as a nurse for the revolutionary forces and was then sent to the north for more schooling to become an ophthalmologist. After the fall of Saigon, she served in the Vietnamese army another four years. When she at last returned home, in 1979, her mother was dead. One of her younger brothers had been killed in the war. She took over as mother to her family. Che married when she was forty, and she has a daughter, who is now twenty-two, four years older than Che was when she fought in Hue. Today Che works as an ophthalmologist in Hue and lives in a house not far from where she was wounded. There is a marker on the street now, outside the soccer stadium, in honor of her and the other eleven girls of the squad. Six of the eleven were killed. Che's daughter is studying English, and she told me she hopes to attend a university in the United States.

Nguyen Van Quang, the student revolutionary who smuggled guns into the city and then led the Front's forces through Chanh Tay Gate, retains all of the charisma that enabled him to recruit young people to his cause half a century ago. I met with him twice in Hue, where he has been a long-serving member of Thua Thien–Hue's party executive committee and the secretary of Hue City—he became, in other words, the mayor of Hue. Actually, he was the superior of the mayor, given the primacy of the party in all aspects of Vietnam's government.

"If things had gone smoothly, we would have had an uprising throughout the South," he said. "More than one hundred cities and towns in the South . . . The first target was Saigon, and the second target was Hue. Imagine that if we could have succeeded, taken over Ho Chi Minh City [Saigon], Da Nang, Can Tho, Da Lat, Nha Trang, just as we did with Hue, the war would have ended much earlier. There would have been less loss for both sides. I believed so. According to the plan, it should have been that way.

"To be honest, after getting out of Hue, in my opinion, I believed that the Americans had no chance of winning militarily in Vietnam. The faith that I had in the party was even stronger after I saw the power of the people during the battle. The people did everything. They transported the armaments, they fed the soldiers, they carried the dead ones out and buried them, they continued working on the next missions. The power of the people was the power of patriotism, of ones who love their country. And whoever could raise the flag of patriotism and had the right policy that followed the path of patriotism would absolutely win."

Andy Westin, who wrote almost daily to his wife, Mimi, stayed married to her for a long time, but they divorced in 2006. Westin went back to school and earned an MBA. He worked in the health business for thirty years and then earned a nursing degree. He worked as a nurse for another decade, attending to patients in long-term care until he retired.

Jim Bullington and Tuy-Cam married and he enjoyed a long career in the foreign service. He served as US ambassador to Burundi, and later as the State Department's senior seminar dean.

Mike Morrow, who wandered the streets of the Citadel during the worst of the fighting as a halfhearted journalist, stayed in Asia. As a member of the Dispatch News Service, he was involved in the publication of Seymour Hersh's story about the My Lai massacres, was captured and held by North Vietnamese forces in Cambodia, and was later thrown out of Vietnam by the South Vietnamese government. After the war he specialized in economic journalism in Asia. I interviewed him (by Skype) where he was living and working in Mongolia.

Steve Berntson recovered from his wounds and went back to school, ultimately earning a master's degree in American history, specializing in the twentieth century. Through a roundabout process he ended up spending most of his working career first as a technical writer, then as a manager for the Trident Nuclear Submarine Missile Program. Before all that he spent a long time in hospitals recovering from the wounds he received in Hue. His transition to civilian life was difficult.

"There were times when I would wake up in the middle of the night almost wishing I was back [in Vietnam], to tell you the truth," he told me. "I know that sounds strange. But once you are accustomed to such an environment where you are living on adrenaline and you are basically—you are thinking you are outsmarting death. I think it is honest to be locked in."

Berntson also found it hard to adjust to the way Americans felt about the war when he got back.

"By 1968, 1969 feelings were running pretty hard subject to Vietnam," he said. "And I remember very well the experience when I got to Long Beach Naval Hospital, which was not on the navy base. So it was in what you would call the civilian world. We were told when we finally got to go on liberty . . . they would tell us make sure that somebody brings you a set of civilian clothes. We do not advise you wearing your uniform going out on Fridays and Sundays, because there would be an antiwar contingent that stayed across the street that yelled at you. And of course they always made sure that we left the hospital from underground parking. That was really kind of a shock to me because here they were telling us not to wear our uniforms because it would just draw too much unpleasant attention. So that is what we did. And I always thought it would be kind of fun to wear my uniform after coming home. But it was quickly understood that in polite company you did not bring the subject up that you were in Vietnam. And the only time you really relaxed and admitted to being in Vietnam was when you were with other people who had had similar experiences. A lot of times, people would ask, 'What happened to you?' Because I was in a wheelchair or on crutches for a long time. Well in the early years, I just said it was an industrial accident."

As for Hue: "Well, we won the battle, but we lost the war," Berntson said, but added that he wasn't sure the word "won" applied. "We were losing the war before that. I mean it was obvious from everything that had been written, intelligence reports and everything else, that the North Vietnamese realized that the longer they could keep the battle in Hue going the more successful it would be for them. The whole issue there for them was, we will spend whatever it takes as long as we can hang on and retain all the attention of the world press. And the fact that they were holding the most sacred city in South Vietnam and the second-biggest city, I think, outside of Saigon, the fact that they would hang on for twenty-five days altered the whole concept of the war, not just in the United States but the rest of the world, I think."

Big Ernie Cheatham became a general. He died in 2014, alas, before I had a chance to meet and interview him for this book. He was interviewed about his experiences in Hue for a Marine Corps oral history project, and his comments have greatly informed my portrayal of him here. Captains Downs and Christmas and Lieutenant Ray Smith all stayed in the marines and rose to the rank of general before retiring, as did two other officers from 2/5, O.K. Steele and Peter Pace—a truly remarkable showing from one battalion, and a tribute to Cheatham's leadership.

Howard Prince retired from the army as a brigadier general and became a professor at the University of Texas, holding a chair in the ethics of leadership at the Lyndon B. Johnson School of Public Affairs. Forty years after the battle he experienced sharp pain in his right knee. Tests showed that he had an AK-47 round lodged beneath his kneecap. It was removed. He walks just fine. He remains angry about the way he and his men were used in Vietnam. He is a judicious man and has studied the matter.

"I spent a lot of time thinking about it after I came home, because I was nearly killed, and my body was injured in a way that has affected me for the rest of my life," he said. "And I went through a lot of soul-searching over what happened to me. Was it worth it? [It was] very much an extension of the Cold War and policy of containment. It was a place where we could fight and the enemy was a totalitarian police state in the north that was going to impose itself and eventually did. But we had a [South Vietnamese] government that did not serve its people, did not have the support of its people, but that did not justify turning our backs and letting a police state take over, which is what happened.

"I fault our political leadership more than anything else. Vietnam was a place that nobody ever heard of. Ho Chi Minh was a nationalist who reached out to the West more than once and was rebuffed, and who then sought support from the Comintern from both Moscow and China. But China is traditionally Vietnam's enemy. [Vietnam] had been kicking [invaders] out for millennia. And we were just the latest. And I do not think we really understood much . . . Our policy makers, I do not think really had any grasp at all on what was going to happen."

Gene Roberts went on to become the national editor of the *New York Times,* then left to become editor of the *Philadelphia Inquirer,* where he hired me in 1979 as a staff writer, still the most significant event in my career. He left the *Inquirer,* in 1990, after leading it to seventeen Pulitzer Prizes in eighteen years, an accomplishment unmatched by any comparable newspaper in American history. He later became managing editor of the *Times*, and then taught at the school of journalism at the University of Maryland. He and my former colleague Hank Klibanoff won a Pulitzer Prize of their own in 2007 for *The Race Beat,* a remarkable account of the role played by the press (including Roberts) during the civil rights movement.

I knew Roberts as a brilliant editor, one whose skills in that role not only benefited me, but are known far and wide. He was once dubbed, deservedly as far as I'm concerned, "the Best Newspaper Editor in America" by the *Village Voice*. I had a general notion that he'd also been a great reporter, but I knew little of his work covering the civil rights movement and then Vietnam. His book helped me understand the former. The latter I didn't learn more about until I ran into him at a memorial service for our late friend and colleague Richard Ben Cramer in 2013.

"What are you working on?" he asked me.

"I've started work on a book about the Battle of Hue," I told him.

"I was there," Gene said.

His was the first interview I conducted for this book, over several days at his home in Bath, North Carolina.

I learned only subsequently—and not from him—that he had not only been there; he was the first reporter on the scene. His well-reported and -written stories were the first and only true accounts of what was happening in Hue.

It was a serendipitous discovery. I owed Gene a great deal for his support when I was a young reporter. Indeed, as I have written elsewhere, he and other editors at the *Inquirer* greatly enlarged not just my experience but my ambition. It was in doing research for this book that I realized what an exceptional newspaper reporter Roberts had been. I know of no better example. For all these reasons, this book is dedicated to him.

Acknowledgments

THIS BOOK WAS Morgan Entrekin's idea. It has been almost twenty years since he agreed to publish my book *Black Hawk Down* after every other major publisher in New York had turned it down. We have since worked together on every one of my subsequent books, with Morgan as editor as well as publisher.

He proposed the idea years before I agreed to undertake it. He was convinced that the battle was one of the most significant of the twentieth century, and a way of writing about the entire Vietnam War. It was a good insight, and a great idea, and, of course, I declined. I had already written a book about a battle, and had no strong desire to return to the subject.

But his idea grew on me. Vietnam was the first major international event to capture my interest as a child. It was my fascination with the swirling debate around the war in the 1960s that prompted me, as a high school student, to begin reading newspapers and magazines, and eventually to seek out books on the subject. I was sixteen when this battle was fought. My father would challenge my opinions about the war, asking always, "How do you know that?" "Where did you read that?" "Why do you trust that source instead of another?" It was this experience, I believe, that started me down the road to a career in newspapers, and ultimately to one as an author. So revisiting the story, approaching it as an experienced reporter and writer, was a way of exploring my own intellectual roots.

But what tipped the scale was that Morgan told me he had another writer in mind for it, one whose work I admired. I slept on it, and called him back the next day. In so many words I said, "Not him, me."

Many people helped me on what turned out to be a five-year effort. I have already written about Gene Roberts, whose stories got me started. I am grateful to him and to everyone else who agreed to sit down and answer my questions, often repeatedly. When I listen to some of those old interviews now, and realize how ignorant I was in the beginning, I am all the more grateful for the patience of those who took time to help me understand, pointing me to books, to articles, and to others who shared their experience.

Cullen Murphy, who has worked as my magazine editor for years, first at the *Atlantic* and now at *Vanity Fair*, gave the book a careful first read and offered several very helpful suggestions. Gene Roberts also agreed to give the book an early read.

I owe thanks to all my great friends at Grove Atlantic, particularly to Allison Malecha, to Julia Berner-Tobin, and also to Hilary McClellen, who undertook the task of checking the ocean of facts in this volume. She caught as many of my mistakes as she could.

I am particularly indebted to Mike Downs, who spent many hours working chapter by chapter to improve my stubbornly civilian understanding, and whose corrections, arguments, and suggestions immeasurably enhanced this book. I likewise received considerable help from Chuck Meadows, Ron Christmas, Ray Smith, Jim Coolican, Charles Krohn, John Wear, and Howard Prince. All of these sources have heard from me repeatedly over the years and have always responded with warmth and insight. Each agreed to review the book prior to publication and make corrections and suggestions, most of which I have taken. Andy Westin was kind enough to share his correspondence for the weeks of the battle, as did Mel Bourgeois, Art Marcotte, and others. I am indebted to Lynn Novick and Sarah Botstein of Florentine Films, who were at work with Ken Burns on his much-anticipated documentary series about the Vietnam War, and who helped steer me to Dang Hoa Ho, who worked as their fixer and translator in Vietnam before undertaking the same services for me. Lynn and Sarah also shared some of the early rushes of the documentary and some of their organization's superb reporting, which helped in my understanding of the story. I am eager to see their finished work.

Hoa was invaluable. He arranged my schedule when I first traveled to Vietnam, and steered me through one interview after another. He made several trips to Hue to interview subjects on his own, sending me recordings. I could not have begun to understand the Vietnamese side of this story without him. Although I was disappointed not to be able to work with Hoa on my second trip, I am grateful to Dinh Hoang Linh, who did an excellent job arranging a full slate of interviews for me on my second trip, and translating. While Linh's involvement brought an inherent conflict of interest, given his government position, I believe he did his best to give me what I needed. He and his sister also produced translations of various memoirs and articles that were also valuable.

I am also very indebted to Xuyen Dinh, a PhD linguist candidate at my University of Delaware (UD), who began working with me several years ago, painstakingly transcribing and translating the interviews I brought back from Vietnam. Xuyen's work informs every chapter of this book, and not just her translations. She did research of her own, accessing Vietnamese websites that I could not read, and fleshing out the accounts gathered by me and by Hoa to provide essential context and cultural understanding. I came to see Xuyen as a partner in this project. To the extent that the book accurately reflects the Vietnamese experience of the battle, credit Xuyen.

Jordan Howell, another PhD candidate at UD, agreed to compile a digital file of newspaper reports during the battle, which I drew upon liberally, both for details of the battle itself and for indications of how the event was being perceived in the United States and elsewhere. It made it easy for me to dial up what various newspapers were reporting each day of the battle. Since all modern war is as much about perception as about reality, the database he assembled forms an important part of this story.

My son, Daniel, conducted dozens of interviews for me, going at least a short way down the path that I took. I could see his understanding of the story grow with each one, and every time I thought, *God, I hope Dan asked a follow-up question here*, he did. What can I say? The boy has solid reportorial genes. I am also indebted to my brother,

Andrew J. Bowden, for his generous work as my lawyer on this and other contracts.

Tim Nenninger was my guide at the National Archives, and John Wilson at the LBJ Library, turning what would have been a random process into something very directed and efficient. Matt Ericson, with whom I worked many years ago at the *Philadelphia Inquirer* when he was a young artist, has evolved into one of the preeminent experts in the field of graphic presentation of news. He was the person I went to when we needed maps for *Black Hawk Down*, and he did the same for *Guests of the Ayatollah*. Today he is an associate editor of the *New York Times*, with lots more on his plate than drawing maps for me. But I went to him first, and he kindly agreed to keep the partnership alive.

I would also like to thank UD for the sabbatical in the fall of 2016 that gave me the long stretch of uninterrupted time to concentrate on finishing the book.

Vietnamese Glossary

PEOPLE

English format	*Vietnamese format*

Bao Dai — Bảo Đại
The last emperor of the Nguyen dynasty, which was the last ruling family in Vietnam

Bay Khiem — Bảy Khiêm
First name: Khiem
Nguyen Dinh Bay: VC, the newly anointed head of "security" for the southern half of the city

Cao Tho Xa — Cao Thọ/Thơ Xa/Xá
First name: Xa
A cruel tyrant who had administrative personnel sleep at his house on Thong Nhat Street

Cao Van Sen — Cao Văn Sen
First name: Sen
A VC regular who took care of delivering the Alliance flag

Che Thi Mung — Chế Thị Mừng
First name: Mung
VC, a member of the Huong River Squad

Chot — Chột
ARVN, nickname of a South Vietnamese soldier who was Le Quang Truong's officer. He challenged Tang Van Mieu by radio

English format	Vietnamese format

Dac

Đắc

A young commissar whom Tran Thi Thu Van, "Nha Ca," the author of *Mourning Headband for Hue,* identified as Nguyen Dac Xuan

Dang Dinh Loan

Đặng Đình Loan

First name: Loan

VC, a political officer whose battalion approached southern Hue from the west

Dang Hoa Ho

Đăng Hòa Hồ

First name: Hoa

VC, an officer

Dang Kinh

Đặng Kinh

First name: Kinh

VC, general assigned to the entire zone of Thua Thien–Hue

Doan Van Ba

Đoàn Văn/Vân Ba

An ARVN surgeon whom Meadows picked up and who treated Anderegg

Hai, Major

Hải

First name: Hai

The VC officer who was leading the queue that had Nguyen Dac Xuan's friend Le Quang

Ho Thi Kim Loan

Hồ Thị Kim Loan

First name: Loan

A member of the Provincial Rural Developmental Group

Hoang Anh De

Hoàng Anh Đế

First name: De

VC, the major of the battalion that took part in the attack on Tam Thai

Hoang Thanh Tung

Hoàng Thanh Tùng

First name: Tung

A propagandist who had been working with the VC for four years, later helped with sorting out the captives

Hoang Thi No

Hoàng Thị Nở

First name: No

VC, a member of the Huong River Squad

Huynh Van Don

Huỳnh Văn Đồn/Đôn

First name: Don

A civilian who sold gasoline in front of the police station on Hung Vuong Street, Vy Da

English format	Vietnamese format
Major Khoa, Mayor First name: **Khoa** The mayor who was rescued by Captain Ron Christmas	**Phan Văn Khoa**
Lam Hai Luong First name: **Luong** An ARVN officer who was also the son of Lam Ung	**Lâm Hải Lượng**
Lam Ung First name: **Ung** An ARVN lieutenant	**Lâm Ứng**
Le Cong Thanh First name: **Thanh** Civilian, a twelve-year-old boy who lived near the Citadel	**Lê Công Thành**
Le Huu Tong First name: **Tong** VC, one of the forty-six men carrying rocket launchers	**Lê Hữu Tòng**
Le Kha Phieu First name: **Phieu** Political commissar for city Front	**Lê Khả Phiêu**
Le Minh First name: **Minh** VC, deputy secretary of Quang Tri, Thua Thien–Hue	**Lê Minh**
Le Ngoc Thinh First name: **Thinh** Civilian	**Lê Ngọc Thịnh/Thỉnh**
Le Quang First name: **Quang** A friend of Nguyen Dac Xuan who was saved by him	**Lê Quang**
Le Quang Truong First name: **Truong** General Truong	**Lê Quang Trưởng**
Le Thi Mai First name: **Mai** The woman who sewed the Alliance flag for Sergeant Cao Van Sen	**Lê Thị Mai**
Le Tu Minh First name: **Minh** Chief of the party's Central Committee in Hue	**Lê Tư Minh**

English format	Vietnamese format
Le Van Hoi First name: Hoi Civilian	**Lê Văn Hội**
Le Van May First name: May Civilian, father of Le Ngoc Thinh	**Lê Văn May**
Mai Van Ngu First name: Ngu A local crime boss in Thoi Lai who later changed his name to Hòa	**Mai Văn Ngụ**
Mai Xuan Bao First name: Bao VC, a commando	**Mai Xuân Bảo**
Mau Ty First name: Ty A student killed by Dac, who was a VC officer. His full name is Tran Mau Ty (Trần Mậu Tý).	**Mậu Tý**
Ngo Dinh Diem First name: Diem President of South Vietnam 1955–1963	**Ngô Đình Diệm**
Ngo Quang Truong First name: Truong Commander of the ARVN First Division at Mang Ca	**Ngô Quang Trưởng**
Nguyen Cao Ky First name: Ky South Vietnam's vice president	**Nguyễn Cao Kỳ**
Nguyen Chi Canh First name: Canh The former Hue police chief	**Nguyễn Chí Cảnh**
Nguyen Cong Minh First name: Minh A civilian who lived on Vy Da Street	**Nguyễn Công Minh**
Nguyen Dac Xuan First name: Xuan VC, a poet/propagandist who came through the northeastern passage into the Citadel	**Nguyễn Đắc Xuân**

English format	Vietnamese format
Nguyen Duc Thuan **First name: Thuan** VC, a Commander	**Nguyễn Đức Thuận**
Nguyen Huu Ai **First name: Ai** A high school student who lived on Vy Da Street	**Nguyễn Hữu Ái**
Nguyen Ngoc Loan **First name: Loan** The national police chief who shot a handcuffed VC prisoner in the head	**Nguyễn Ngọc Loan**
Nguyen Ngu **First name: Ngu** The civilian whose family helped Nguyen Van Quang bring the weapons into Hue	**Nguyễn Ngữ**
Nguyen Quang Ha **First name: Ha** VC, a member of the City Unit	**Nguyễn Quang Hà**
Nguyen Van Ty The owner of a construction materials company whose home near the Ngo Mon Gate was commandeered early in the battle by an ARVN battalion	**Nguyễn Văn Tý**
Nguyen Thu **First name: Thu** VC, a major who was the field commander for north of the Huong River	**Nguyễn Thu**
Nguyen Van Lem **First name: Lem** A member of the NLF who was executed by Nguyen Ngoc Loan, was also referred to as Bảy Lốp or Ew Tu	**Nguyễn Văn Lém**

Nguyen Van Quang
    First name: Quang
VC, the local cadre chief who smuggled the weapons into Hue
	Nguyễn Văn Quang
	    First name: Quang

Nguyen Van Thieu
    First name: Thieu
President of South Vietnam 1965–1975
	Nguyễn Văn Thiệu
	    First name: Thiệu

Nguyen Thi Quen Nguyen Van Ty's sister, who was spying for the VC, and who was later killed	**Nguyễn Thị Quên**
Nguyen Xuan Oanh **First name: Oanh** A critic of Nguyen Van Thieu	**Nguyễn Xuân Oánh**

English format	Vietnamese format
Nguyens	**Nguyễn**

The last Vietnamese dynasty

| **Nha Ca** | **Nhã Ca** |

Civilian, author (pen name) of *Mourning Headband for Hue*

| **Pham Thi Lien** | **Phạm Thị Liên** |
| **First name: Lien** | |

VC, the leader of the Huong River Squad

| **Pham Van Dinh** | **Phạm Văn Đính** |
| **First name: Dinh** | |

The colonel of the ARVN unit Hac Bao

| **Pham Van Khoa** | **Phạm Văn Khoa** |
| **First name: Khoa** | |

A lieutenant colonel who was mayor of Hue and the Thua Thien Province chief

| **Phan Huu Chi** | **Phan Hữu Chí** |
| **First name: Chi** | |

ARVN, lieutenant colonel

| **Phan Ngoc Luong** | **Phan Ngọc Lương** |
| **First name: Luong** | |

Captain of ARVN First Battalion, Third Regiment

| **Quy Nguyen** | **Nguyễn Quy/Quý/Quỳ** |

Civilian, a twelve-year-old Vietnamese boy who was Doezema's friend

| **Soi** | **Soi/Sối** |

The first lieutenant of Puppet First Division

| **Song Hao** | **Song Hào** |

The nickname of Nguyen Van Khuong (Nguyễn Văn Khương), one of the three senior military leaders who approved Dang Kinh's decision to hold on in Hue

| **Tang Van Mieu** | **Tăng Văn Miêu** |
| **First name: Mieu** | |

VC, a lieutenant who was the field commander of everything south of the Huong River

| **Than Trong Mot** | **Thân Trọng Một** |
| **First name: Mot** | |

VC, Southern area commander

English format	Vietnamese format
Thich Don Hau	**Thích Đôn Hậu**

First name: Hau

A Buddhist monk who joined the NLF

General Ton That Dinh	**Tôn Thất Đính**

The ARVN battalion commander who seized Nguyen Van Ty's home near the Ngo Mon Gate

Ton That Te	**Tôn Thất [...]**

First name: Te

A member of Dai Viet Party. The name was recorded wrongly. Instead of Te, it must be Ke (Kế)

Ton That Vu	**Tôn Thất Vũ**

First name: Vu

The son of Tot That Te. He was the owner of Viet Tuyen shop in Hue

Tran Anh Lien	**Trần Anh Liên**

First name: Lien

VC, the Hue City Party Committee secretary

Tran Da Tu	**Trần Dạ Từ**

First name: Tu

Tran Thi Thu Van's husband

Tran Ngoc Hue	**Trần Ngọc Huế**

First name: Hue

Nickname: Harry the lieutenant of Hac Bao (the Black Panthers)

Tran Quoc Phong	**Trần Quốc Phong**

First name: Phong

The head of Hoang Thanh Tung's unit

Tran Huy Chung	**Trần Huy Chung**

An eleven-year-old boy who played games with the VC soldiers when they occupied his neighborhood

Tran Thi Thu Van	**Trần Thị Thu Vân**

First name: Van

Also known as Nha Ca

Tran Toi	**Trần Tới**

First name: Toi

Civilian

English format	*Vietnamese format*
Trinh Cong Son **First name: Son**	**Trịnh Công Sơn**

The famous Vietnamese folksinger, poet, painter, and composer who was known as "the Vietnamese Bob Dylan"

Truong Sinh **First name: Sinh**	**Trường Sinh/Trương Sinh**

VC, a commander

Tuy-Cam	**Túy/Thúy/Thủy Cầm/Cẩm**

Civilian

Van	**Vạn/Văn/Vân**

A bus driver on Thuan An Road

Van Tien Dung **First name: Dung**	**Văn Tiến Dũng**

One of the three senior military leaders who approved Dang Kinh's decision to hold on in Hue

Vo Nguyen Giap **First name: Giap**	**Võ Nguyên Giáp**

VC, the legendary general

Vo Suu **First name: Suu**	**Võ Sửu**

A cameraman for NBC

Xa	**Xa/Xạ/Xà/Xá/Xã**

A policeman from Quang Tri

PLACES

English format	*Vietnamese format*
An Cuu	**An Cựu**

A bridge in Hue, north of Phu Bai

An Dinh	**An Định**

The palace where the last emperor, Bao Dai, stayed. It is located on the bank of An Cuu River

An Hoa	**An Hòa**

The northwestern gate into the Citadel

English format	Vietnamese format
Ba Trieu	**Bà Triệu**

A street that runs through the center of Hue

Bac Ninh	**Bắc Ninh**

A village north of Ha Noi

Bach Ho	**Bạch Hổ**

A railroad bridge that was one mile to the west of Hue

Bach Ma	**Bạch Mã**

The national forest, located near Hue, which contains the highest peak between Hue and Da Nang

Ben Ngu	**Bến Ngự**

A market in Hue

Ben Suc	**Bến Súc**

A village that was the main pillar of the Viet Cong's dominance over the Iron Triangle

Can Tho	**Cần Thơ**

The largest city in the Mekong delta

Cao Van	**Cao Vân, short for Trần Cao Vân**

A street in Hue

Chanh Tay	**Chánh Tây**

The north gate on the Citadel's west wall

Chia Voi	**Chìa Vôi**

A mountain; many books and maps have this mountain's name misspelled as Chi Voi

Cho Lon	**Chợ Lớn**

A market in Sai Gon

Church of the Most Holy Redeemer	**Nhà thờ Đức Mẹ Hằng Cứu Giúp/ Nhà thờ Dòng Chúa Cứu Thế**

A Catholic church in Hue, often referred to by the name Church of Our Lady of Perpetual Help

Church of Our Lady of Perpetual Help	**Nhà thờ Đức Mẹ Hằng Cứu Giúp/ Nhà thờ Dòng Chúa Cứu Thế**

A Catholic church in Hue, often referred to by the name Church of the Most Holy Redeemer

English format	*Vietnamese format*

Con Dao **Côn Đảo**
The islands located in the Southeast region of Vietnam, Site of the infamous
Tiger Cages

Con Tien **Cồn Tiên**
Often misspelled as Con Thien

Da Nang **Đà Nẵng**
The largest city in Central Vietnam, often spelled as Danang

Dai Viet **Đại Việt**
A nationalist and anticommunist political party in Vietnam. Its full name is *Đại
Việt Quốc dân đảng*

Dao **Đào**
A river in Hue

Dap Da **Đập Đá**
A town in South Central Vietnam

Dinh Bo Linh **Đinh Bộ Lĩnh**
A street in Hue

Dinh Mon **Định Môn**
A village near Gia Long tomb

Doi Cung **Đội Cung**
A street in Hue, a block south of the riverfront

Duong Hoa **Dương Hòa**
A village near Gia Long tomb

Duy Tan **Duy Tân**
The stretch of Highway 1 that passed through the city

Gia Hoi **Gia Hội**
A neighborhood located immediately east of the Citadel

Green, the **xanh**
A term referring to the forest and mountainous areas where the VC units were
based

Ha Noi **Hà Nội**
The capital city of Vietnam, often spelled as Hanoi

Hau **Hậu**
The main north gate into the Citadel

English format	*Vietnamese format*

Hen — **Hến**
A long sliver of land at the center of the Huong River. It was usually referred to as *Con Hen (Cồn Hến)* by the Americans. The word *con (cồn)* has the meaning "islet" and therefore is not part of the proper name

Highway 1 — **Quốc lộ 1/1A**
National Route 1A, often referred to as National Road 1A

Ho Chi Minh — **Hồ Chí Minh**
The famous Vietnamese Communist revolutionary leader, or the current name of a city in South Vietnam; often spelled as Hochiminh

Hue — **Huế**
The city in Central Vietnam

Huong — **Hương**
The famous river in Hue   Can also be called Hương Giang and is often referred to as the Perfume/Fragrance River

Huong Giang — **Hương Giang**
The hotel right on the bank of Huong River

Huu — **Hữu**
The gate located in the southwestern side of the Citadel

Jeanne d'Arc School — **trường Jeanne d'Arc**
A high school in Hue, now known as Nguyễn Trường Tộ High School

Khe Sanh — **Khe Sanh**
A district in the northwestern part of Quang Tri Province

Kim Do — **Kim Đô**
A fishing village northeast of the Citadel

Kim Phung — **Kim Phụng**
A mountain west of Hue

La Chu — **La Chữ**
A village in Thua Thien Province. Referred to in many maps and books as *Thon La Chu*, which is actually a misunderstanding. In Vietnamese, the word *thon (thôn)* means "a small village." The name of this village is only *La Chữ*.

Lac Thanh — **Lạc Thạnh**
A restaurant located on Dinh Bo Linh Street, Hue

Le Loi — **Lê Lợi**
A street in Hue that runs parallel to the Huong River

English format	*Vietnamese format*

Le Loi   **Lê Lợi**
An elementary school in Hue. It was also known by the name Chaigneau

Le Van Duyet   **Lê Văn Duyệt**
A street in Hue

Lieu Coc   **Liễu Cốc**
A village located in Huong Tra (Hương Trà) district, Hue. Referred to in many maps and books as *Thon Lieu Coc*, which is actually a misunderstanding. In Vietnamese, the word *thon (thôn)* means "a small village." The name of this village is only *Liễu Cốc.*

Ly Thuong Kiet   **Lý Thường Kiệt**
A street that leads toward the vital center of southern Hue

Mai Thuc Loan   **Mai Thúc Loan**
A street in Hue

Mang Ca   **Mang Cá**
The area where the headquarters of ARVN First Division were located

Nam Giao   **Nam Giao**
A bridge in Hue, often misspelled as Nam Gio

Ngo Mon   **Ngọ Môn**
The two-story platform that stood just outside the royal palace, before the Citadel's southern wall. It is also the name of the gate before the royal palace.

Ngu   **Ngự**
A river built of an old branch of Huong River. It runs from west to east in the Citadel. The full name is *Ngu Ha (Ngự Hà)*. People often call it *song Vua (sông Vua),* which means "Emperor River"

Nguyen Hoang   **Nguyễn Hoàng**
A bus station in Hue

Nhu Y   **Như Ý**
A branch of Huong River that runs by Dap Da

Phan Dinh Phung   **Phan Đình Phùng**
The street that paralleled the Phu Cam Canal

Phong Dien   **Phong Điền**
A rural district in Thua Thien–Hue Province

Phu Bai   **Phú Bài**
A city located just south of Hue

English format	Vietnamese format

Phu Cam — **Phủ Cam**
The canal that forms the western side of the Triangle, and also an important Catholic church in Hue

Phu Loc — **Phú Lộc**
A rural district of Thua Thien–Hue Province

Phu O — **Phú Ổ**
A small hamlet to the west of the T-T Woods

Quang Tri — **Quảng Trị**
A province in the North Central coast region of Vietnam, north of the former imperial capital of Hue

Que Chu — **Quế Chữ**
A village in Thua Thien Province. Referred to in many maps and books as *Thon Que Chu*, which is actually a misunderstanding. In Vietnamese, the word *thon* (*thôn*) means "a small village." The name of this village is only *Quế Chữ*.

Sai Gon — **Sài Gòn**
The former name of Ho Chi Minh City. Sai Gon, which used to be the capital city of South Vietnam, is often spelled Saigon

Soccer Stadium — **Sân vận động/sân bóng**
The stadium located in the center of Hue City. It was also called Long Bao (Long Bảo) or Tu Do (Tự Do) Stadium

Song Lo — **Sông Lô**
Translated as "Lo River," this is the name of Regiment 8, later Regiment 3 in the North Vietnamese Army

Ta Trach — **Tả Trạch**
One of the two main branches that merge into the famous Huong River in Thua Thien–Hue

Tam Thai — **Tam Thai**
Where the City Unit camped, southeast of the Triangle

Tan Son Nhat — **Tân Sơn Nhất**
An airport in Sai Gon. Can also be spelled as Tân Sơn Nhứt and was often misspelled as Tan Son Knut

Tay Loc — **Tây Lộc**
An airstrip located within the Citadel in Hue

Thoi Lai — **Thới Lai**
The area just outside the northeast walls of the fortress

English format	*Vietnamese format*

Thong Nhat — **Thống Nhất**
A street in Hue

Thua Thien — **Thừa Thiên**
A prison in Thua Thien–Hue Province, often referred to as Thua Phu jail

Thua Thien–Hue — **Thừa Thiên–Huế**
Zone

Thuan An — **Thuận An**
A road in Hue

Thuong — **Thượng**
A village located in Thuy Xuan (Thủy Xuân) district, Hue. Referred to in many maps and books as *Thon Thuong*, which is actually a misunderstanding. In Vietnamese, the word *thon* (*thôn*) means "a small village." The name of this village is only *Thượng*.

Thuong Tu — **Thượng Tứ**
The southeastern gate into the Citadel

Thuy Thanh — **Thủy Thanh**
A district located southeast of Hue

Trai — **Trài**
One of the two entrances of Trấn Bình Đài that open directly at the wall without a watchtower above

Tran Cao Van — **Trần Cao Vân**
A street in Hue, often referred to as Cao Van Street

Tran Hung Dao — **Trần Hưng Đạo**
A street that is parallel to the river on the north side

Treasury, the — **Kho Bạc**
One of the targets that the NLF Army aimed for

Trinh Minh The — **Trình Minh Thế**
A street in Hue. It is now a part of Le Duan (Lê Duẩn) Street

Truoi — **Truồi**
A river in Phu Loc district, Thua Thien–Hue Province

Truong Tien — **Trường Tiền**
A bridge in Hue. Can be written with a different spelling: Tràng Tiền

English format	Vietnamese format
Tu Dam	**Từ Đàm**
A pagoda located in southwestern Hue	
Van Duong	**Văn Dương**
A river that flows into the Huong River	
Van The	**Vân Thê**
A village in Thuy Thanh district, hometown of Che Thi Mung	
Vi Da	**Vĩ Dạ**
A ward of Hue City, often spelled as Vy Da (Vỹ Dạ)	
Viet Tuyen	**Việt/Viết Tuyên/Tuyển/ Tuyền/Tuyến**
A radio shop on Tran Hung Dao Street, owned by Ton That Vu	

MILITARY UNITS/POLITICAL ORGANIZATIONS

English format	Vietnamese format
Dai doi	**Đại đội**
The City Unit of Hue	
Dai noi	**Đại nội**
The Royal Palace/Imperial City	
Hac Bao	**Hắc Báo**
Often referred to as the Black Panthers, an elite ARVN unit led by Lieutenant Tran Ngoc Hue, known as "Harry"	
Huong River Squad	**Hương River Squad**
Often referred to as *Những cô gái sông Hương,* which means "The Eleven Girls of the Perfume River"	
Nghia binh	**Nghĩa binh**
The Righteous Soldiers Division, a unit formed by Nguyen Dac Xuan	
Nghia binh Canh sat	**Nghĩa binh Cảnh sát**
The Righteous Police Division, a police unit formed by Nguyen Dac Xuan	
Young Pioneer Organization	**Đội Thiếu niên Tiền Phong Hồ Chí Minh**
The Ho Chi Minh Young, a communist youth organization operating in Vietnam, named after former Vietnamese president Ho Chi Minh	

VIETNAMESE TERMS/PHRASES

English format	*Vietnamese format*

Anh yeu em — **Anh yêu em**
The Vietnamese equivalent of "I love you," but specifically said by males only

ao dai — **áo dài**
Vietnamese traditional clothing

bam vao that-lung dich — **bám vào thắt-lưng địch**
A strategy that Hoang Anh De applied to overcome the Americans' overwhelming firepower. The literal translation is "hold on to the enemy's belt"

Chien-tranh Chong My — **Chiến-tranh Chống Mỹ**
The Resistance War Against America / The American War

dong — **đồng**
Vietnamese currency

Hoc Sinh — **Học Sinh**
A paper formed by Nguyen Van Quang

Hong Bang — **Hồng Bàng**
One of the early Vietnamese dynasties

hot vit lon — **hột vịt lộn**
Half-hatched duck eggs, a Vietnamese dish

Mau Than — **Mậu Thân**
The name of the year 1968 according to the Chinese calendar; 1968 was the Year of the Monkey

nguy — **ngụy**
A derogatory term used against anyone who worked for the South Vietnamese government

nhan dan — **nhân dân**
The people

no mau — **nợ máu**
"Blood debt"

non la — **nón lá**
Vietnamese conical hat

Ong Tao — **Ông Táo**
The Kitchen God

English format	*Vietnamese format*
Phap bao chi bale	**Pháp báo chí Ba Lê**

Means "French press from Paris": Pháp = France, báo chí = paper, press, Ba lê = Paris. This broken wording is not grammatically correct in Vietnamese

Tet	**Tết**

Lunar New Year

Tong-Tan-cong-Noi-day	**Tổng Tấn công Nổi dậy**

General Offensive, General Uprising

Viet Cong	**Việt Cộng**

VC = Vietnamese Communist

Viet Minh	**Việt Minh**

A Communist front organization founded by Ho Chi Minh in 1941 to organize resistance against French colonial rule and occupying Japanese forces; often spelled as Vietminh

Source Notes

For a journalist interested in history, the sweet spot is about fifty years. Enough time has gone by for a measure of historical perspective, and yet there remain many living witnesses.

While some of the key participants in the Battle of Hue have died, most are still living, and since Vietnam welcomes visiting Americans, it was possible for the first time to fully report the story from both sides. Most American veterans were pleased to share their experiences with me, and the sheer number of those interviews gave me multiple perspectives on nearly every event described. In telling the American side of the story, I am indebted in particular to five previous accounts: *Battle for Hue* by Keith Nolan; *Fire in the Streets* by Eric Hammel; *The Lost Battalion* by Charles Krohn (which focuses on the experience of the army's Second Battalion, Twelfth Cavalry); *The Siege at Hue* by George Smith, who combines memories of his own experiences there as an army information officer attached to the ARVN First Division, and interviews Smith (a newspaperman in civilian life) conducted with a variety of others involved in the fight; and *Phase Line Green* by Nicholas Warr, who served as a platoon commander for Alpha 1/5 during the fight inside the Citadel. Each of these books has a narrower focus than this one, but they all provided me with a solid backstop for my own reporting.

I learned a great deal from reports that were written at the time, and even more by talking to some of the reporters and photographers who produced them, particularly Gene Roberts, John Olson, Mike

Morrow, and John Laurence, whose excellent book *The Cat from Hue* relates some of his experiences there.

I relied on official marine and army records of the battle from the National Archives, and on documents from the archives of the Socialist Republic of Vietnam in Hanoi (researched for me by Dang Hoa Ho), and on analyses by Merle Pribbenow and by Lien-Hang T. Nguyen in her book *Hanoi's War*. The papers of Walt Rostow and of William Westmoreland, and notes of the National Security Council at the LBJ Library at the University of Texas in Austin, were extremely useful in detailing the thinking of the Johnson administration during the weeks-long fight and in fleshing out its relationship with Westmoreland. The Library of the US Marine Corps at Quantico had oral interviews with key participants who were no longer around to answer my questions. I also drew on the Presidential Recordings Program of the Miller Center at the University of Virginia, which has helpfully placed thousands of hours of recorded Oval Office phone conversations online.

That said, this book is mostly the work of a journalist, in that it is primarily based on interviews, conducted over four years, in person and on the phone, in the United States and in Vietnam. Memories are not entirely reliable, of course, even immediately after an event, and are hardly so decades later. In conducting interviews for this book I was mindful of the written records compiled at the time and personal accounts given closer to the time of the battle—in previously published accounts and in the source material for them. The sheer number of sources also works to cross-check and validate individual accounts. In most cases, the events described in this book are based on accounts from multiple sources. Where they are not, the details of individual stories line up correctly with the record of the battle and with accounts of related events. Things like the exact date and location of an event, where they could be independently verified, add credence to personal memories. Very often an interviewee would remember an incident without being able to recall exactly where and when it happened. Where I was able to fill in those missing details on my own, it boosted my confidence in the original story. Often interviewees, when prodded with additional information, are able to more fully recall their experience. Memory is imperfect though, and the account here is only a best effort at reconstructing a very complicated story. Where there is no video or audio evidence, all history has to offer are memories and written records.

My son Daniel helped me with these, enabling me to collect the stories of many more participants than I would have been able to accumulate on my own. At the National Archives I found notes from interviews Nolan conducted for his book and detailed letters written to him by various participants. The Archives also had the source material for Shulimson's account of the battle, including documents captured from Viet Cong and NVA soldiers, and the on-the-scene reporting of Douglas Pike, who gathered material concerning the massacres of civilians by the National Liberation Front. In Vietnam, Dang Hoa Ho not only arranged for interviews on my first visit to Hue and provided on-the-spot translation, but also returned to the city twice to find and interview people on his own. Hoa also translated portions of various memoirs and histories that were invaluable to me in sorting out the Front's plans and actions. Dinh Hoang Linh did the same for me on my second trip and also provided translations of various memoirs and articles pertinent to this story. Xuyen Dinh, who translated all of the interviews from Vietnam, also conducted an interview for me and provided invaluable insights about the others.

Where chapters or passages of the book have been drawn from interviews, the sourcing is obvious. In cases where it is not I have added a source note. I have also added notes to provide unessential but interesting details, such as to more precisely describe a weapon, vehicle, or military unit. Such names, numbers, and designations, while important to military readers, make it slow going for most of us. I have also used notes to identify a published account or recorded source.

AMERICAN INTERVIEWS

Dan Allbritton, Mike Anderegg, Jim Arend, Gordon Batcheller, Richard Baughman, Paul Becker, Steve Berntson, Roger Billings, Sam Bingham, Joe Bolt, Mel Bourgeois, Don Bowman, Frank Breth, Walter Brock, Chris Brown, Madeline Brown, Tommy Brown, Jim and

Tuy-Cam Bullington, Dan Carter, Richard Carter, Conwill Casey, Ben Casio, George Cates, Terry Charbonneau, Bob Childs, Ron Christmas, Lonny Connelly, Jim Coolican, Clyde Coreil, Mike Davison, Brad Devitt, Carl DiLeo, Danny Donnelly, Mike Downs, Fred Drew, Dale Dye, Bill Ehrhart, Gary Eichler, Chuck Ekker, Bill Eshelman, Al Esquivel, Bill Fite, Carl Fleischmann, Ronald Frasier, Juan Gonzales, Brad Goodin, Alvin Grantham, Rick Grissinger, John Griswald, Myron Harrington, Calvin Hart, Rich Horner, Lewis Jeffries, Eden Jiminez, Bob Johnstone, Keith Kay, Michael Ker, Larry Kibbon, Charles Krohn, Frank Lambert, Ed Landry, Bob Lauver, Richard Leflar, John Ligato, Merril Ludwig, Art Marcotte, Dennis Martin, Tom Martin, Jerry McCauley, Jim McCoy, Chuck Meadows, Tom Mitchell, Larry Mobley, Mike Morrow, Eddie Neas, Don Neveling, Jim O'Konski, John Olson, Carnell Poole, Merle Pribbenow, Howard Prince, Bill Purcell, Hastings Rigolette, Marcelino Rivas, Gene Roberts, Damien Rodriguez, Tim Rogers, Jack Rushing, John Salvati, Dennis Selby, Jeff Shay, Bobby Smith, Ray Smith, Terry Strassburg, Mario Tamez, Selwyn Tate, Bob Thompson, Jim Thompson, Bob Thoms, David Tyree, Theodore Wallace, Bob Warren, Herbert Watkins, John Wear, Ernie Weiss, Charlie West, Andy Westin, Maury Whitmer, Steve Wilson, Dan Winkel, and Luke Youngman.

VIETNAMESE INTERVIEWS

Che Thi Mung, Cao Van Sen, Dang Dinh Loan, Doang Thanh Xu, Duong Van Xuan, Duong (middle and first name not given), Ho Ban, Hoang Anh De, Hoang Phu Ngoc Tuong, Hoang Thanh Tung, Hoang Thi No, Huang Bao, Huynh Van Don , Le Cong Thanh , Le Huu Tong, Le Ngoc Thinh, Le Thi Mai, Le Thi Thu Hanh, Le Van Hoi , Mai Xuan Bao, Nguyen Manh Ha, Ngo Dinh Diem, Ngo Quang Truong, Nguyen Dac Xuan, Nguyen Duc Thuan, Nguyen Huu Ai, Nguyen Quang Ha, Nguyen Quoc Sinh, Nguyen Thanh Tung, Nguyen Van Quang, Nguyen Van Ty, Quang Ha, Tang Van Mieu, Than Trong Dzung, Thanh Trong Hoat, Tran Anh Lien, Tran Hung Le, Tran Huy Chung, Tran Ngoc Hue, Tran Thi Thu Huong, Tran Toi, and Truong Thi Thuy Hong.

PART ONE
The Infiltration
1967–January 30, 1968

Introduction

1. Rather than try to distinguish in every instance whether the troops engaged with Americans were NVA, VC, or local militias, I will refer to them as the National Liberation Front, which is what they called themselves, or the "Front." On occasion, where the distinction is important, I will refer to the factions specifically.

1. The Huong River Squad

2. https://cherrieswriter.files.wordpress.com/2013/02/vietnam.jpg.
3. The word *nguy* is borrowed from Classical Chinese 偽. It has the meaning of "fake, pretend." When combined with the word *chinh-quyen* (government) to form the compound word *chinh-quyen nguy*, it has the meaning of a government that is supposedly independent but is in fact dependent upon an outside power, similar to the metaphor "puppet state" in English. By itself, *nguy* can be used to refer to soldiers or anyone who works for that government. It was used during the period of French colonialism in Vietnam when the Viet Minh also called the French Foreign Legion *nguy*.
4. In Vietnamese it was called: *Doi Thieu nien Tien Phong Ho Chi Minh*.
5. The *Doan Thanh nien*.

2. Thirty-Nine Days

6. The Second Battalion of the Third Regiment of the ARVN First Division.

3. Spizzerinctum

7. "Commander in Vietnam," *New York Times*, March 4, 1967, p. 2.
8. William Westmoreland, *A Soldier Reports*, Dell, 1980, pp. 304–305.
9. According to Mike Downs, in later years there would be a joke prize at the US Army Command and General Staff College called "the Westmoreland Award," given to "the best-looking mediocre officer" of the class.
10. Excerpts from Westmoreland's speech published in the *New York Times*, October 25, 1966.
11. R. W. Apple, "A Split Is Denied by Westmoreland," *New York Times*, July 24, 1967.

12. "War Gains Called Very Encouraging by Westmoreland," *New York Times*, November 16, 1967, p. 1.
13. Dwight Eisenhower, *Mandate for Change*, Doubleday, 1963, p. 372.
14. John W. Finney, "U.S. Denies Shift on Troop Policy in Vietnam War," *New York Times*, June 9, 1965, p. 1.
15. Tom Wicker, "In the Nation: Into the Quicksand," *New York Times*, November 27, 1966, p. 269.
16. Hanson Baldwin, "Manpower for Vietnam," *New York Times*, November 12, 1966, p. 6. Johnson said the war might require as many as 750,000 men.
17. Thomas A. Johnson, "Logistics in War: Arms, Food, Soap/50,000-Man American Unit Is Largest in Vietnam," *New York Times*, January 25, 1968, p. 13.
18. Roy Reed, "Gen. Abrams Gets Post in Vietnam," *New York Times*, April 7, 1967, p. 1.
19. H. R. McMaster, in *Dereliction of Duty* (hereafter McMaster), Harper Perennial, 1997, p. 333, writes that attrition was "an absence of strategy," one that substituted a tactical goal, killing the enemy, for any clear overarching military objective.
20. Manila speech.
21. The Miller Center of Public Affairs, The University of Virginia, Presidential Recordings Library (hereafter, "Miller Center").
22. "No measure of success was as important to the military command as the enemy body count. Competitions were held between American units to produce the highest 'box score' of enemy KIAs or the best 'kill ratio' (the most enemy killed in relation to American casualties). Some units even awarded a few days of R&R to soldiers who had an exceptional number of 'confirmed kills,' and infantry officers knew their opportunities for advancement were largely dependent on the size of the body counts they reported." Scott Sigmund Gartner, "Body Counts and 'Success' in the Vietnam and Korean Wars," *Journal of Interdisciplinary History* 25, no. 3 (Winter 1995): 377–395.
23. Harrison Salisbury, "Attacks on North Disrupt Economy," *New York Times*, January 1, 1967.
24. Oleg Hoeffding, "Bombing North Vietnam: An Appraisal of Economic and Political Effects," Rand Corporation, December 1966, pp. v–vi.
25. *The Effect of the Vietnam War on the Economies of the Communist Countries*, CIA Directorate of Intelligence, Intelligence Report, July 1968, p. 36.
26. Don Oberdorfer, *Tet! The Story of a Battle and Its Historic Aftermath* (hereafter, Oberdorfer), Doubleday, 1971, pp. 92–93.
27. *The Pentagon Papers*, as published by the *New York Times*, Bantam Books, 1971, Memo #118, p. 554.
28. *The Pentagon Papers*, IV. C. 7.(b), vol. 2, *The Air War in Vietnam: 1965–1968*, "Systems Analysis Study on Economic Effects," pp. 128–129. https://nara-media-001

.s3.amazonaws.com/arcmedia/research/pentagon-papers/Pentagon-Papers
-Part-IV-C-7-b.pdf.

29. Indeed, the administration had been advised by its own experts in 1964 that bombing North Vietnam would not work. The Johnson Report, named not for the president but for Robert Johnson of the State Department's Policy Planning Council, concluded that a bombing campaign would not weaken Hanoi's resolve, would not drive Hanoi to negotiate or compromise, and would not be likely to alter the military situation in the South. The report was not widely distributed and was ultimately ignored, in part because of a misguided belief in the efficacy of bombing (which was believed to have won World War II), and because President Johnson's desire to succeed in Vietnam inclined him to listen more to his military advisers, who were full of certainty, than his civilian ones, who expressed doubts. "The elephant was great and powerful and preferred being blind." David Halberstam, *The Powers That Be* (hereafter, Halberstam), Knopf, 1979, p. 358.

30. Oberdorfer, p. 93.

31. Ibid., p. 195.

32. Martin Luther King Jr., "Beyond Vietnam," a speech at New York's Riverside Baptist Church, April 4, 1967.

33. *Pentagon Papers*, Memo #118, p. 557.

34. Years later, in 1995, far too late to make a difference, McNamara wrote that the United States should have exited Vietnam in late 1963, following Diem's assassination, or in late 1964 or early 1965. "Political stability did not exist and was unlikely ever to be achieved; and the South Vietnamese, even with our training assistance and logistical support, were incapable of defending themselves" (McMaster, p. 373).

35. The same criminal irrationality was still at work five years later, as President Nixon noted privately to his aides that years of bombing Vietnam had accomplished "zilch" and yet continued bombing and continued publicly defending the tactic.

36. Richard Harwood, "The War Just Doesn't Add Up," *Washington Post*, September 3, 1967, as reprinted in *Reporting Vietnam*, vol. 1 (hereafter, *Reporting Vietnam* 1), Library of America, 1998, p. 484.

37. William Prochnau, *Once Upon a Distant War*, Mainstream Publishing, 1996, pp. 171–172.

38. Neil Sheehan, *A Bright Shining Lie*, Random House, 1988, p. 697.

39. US officials claimed that the marines had taken repeated fire from the village and had warned that they would destroy it if such shooting continued, which they did. Safer later said that the only marines injured in the operation had been shot "in the ass," indicating friendly fire. http://www.pbs.org/weta/reportingamericaatwar/reporters/safer/camne.html.

40. Papers of William Westmoreland, LBJ Library.
41. *The Pentagon Papers*, Quadrangle Books, 1971, p. 555.
42. Thomas Ahern, *Vietnam Declassified*, University Press of Kentucky, 2010, pp. 281–282.
43. To Johnson, Asians were Asians. He complained, partly in jest, to the CIA that they ought to be able "to get some coolies from a San Francisco laundry shop and drop them over there and use them" to spy on Hanoi. David Halberstam, *The Best and the Brightest* (hereafter, *B&B*), Fawcett, 1972, p. 512.
44. Charles DeBenedetti, *An American Ordeal: The Antiwar Movement of the Vietnam Era* (hereafter, DeBenedetti), Syracuse University Press, 1990, p. 179.
45. Westmoreland, *A Soldier Reports*, p. 378.
46. DeBenedetti, p. 199.
47. Ibid., p. 177.
48. Stewart Alsop, "Will Westmoreland Elect Johnson?" *Saturday Evening Post*, January 13, 1968. Enough of the old McCarthy-era feeling remained for Alsop's brother, the conservative columnist and war supporter Joe Alsop, to magnanimously assure a group of correspondents at a dinner in Saigon that when they were all indicted for treason for their Vietnam reporting, which they surely would be, he would speak in their defense, arguing that they were not traitors, only "fools."
49. Thieu's closest opponent, the dynamic and eloquent lawyer Truong Dinh Dzu, was arrested and sentenced to five years of hard labor after he complained of voting fraud. A committee from South Vietnam's Constituent Assembly, after investigating Dzu's claims, voted 16–2 to throw out the election results. It was ignored. James McAlister, "A Fiasco of Noble Proportions: The Johnson Administration and the South Vietnamese Elections of 1967," *Pacific Historical Review* 73 (2004): 650.
50. Transcript of Westmoreland's speech in Peter Braestrup, *Big Story* (hereafter, Braestrup), Westview Press, 1977, vol. 2, pp. 3–10.
51. *B&B*, p. 647.
52. Cable from Westmoreland to General Wheeler and Admiral Sharp, January 25, 1968, Westmoreland Papers, LBJ Library.
53. Gregory A. Dadis, *Westmoreland's War*, Oxford University Press, 2014, p. 140. "These border battles also reinforced a widely-held belief that the North Vietnamese simply did not have the capacity for a countrywide offensive. Westmoreland believed Hanoi had shifted its strategic aims but possessed only limited means to achieve them."
54. The line between North and South Vietnam was originally set at the seventeenth parallel by the Geneva Agreement ending World War II. It was decided that China would accept the surrender of the occupying Japanese forces north of that line and that France would accept the surrender south of it.
55. Miller Center.

4. The Royal Capital

56. Oberdorfer, p. ix.

57. The correct spelling of the city, now Ho Chi Minh City, would be "Sai Gon." Because Western readers are so familiar with "Saigon," I'm using it in this book, as well as "Hanoi" for "Ha Noi." All other cities are spelled the way they would be in Vietnam.

58. The Phu Cam Canal widened and sculptured the An Cuu River and helps to keep the Huong from overflowing its banks. It was an enormous project, almost nineteen miles long, undertaken in the early nineteenth century by Emperor Gia Long. Many Vietnamese still refer to the canal as the An Cuu River, or Song An Cuu, and it is designated as such on many maps, partly because the word for "river" in Vietnamese is *song*, and the words for "canal" are *song dao* (literally, "river dig"), so the Vietnamese words for "Phu Cam Canal" repeats *song*—Song Phu Cam Song Dao, which sounds awkward.

5. Moonshine and Half-Hatched Ducks

59. Because the Vietnamese have so many surnames in common—there are at least five unrelated Nguyens in this book—I have elected in some cases, like this one, to go with the given name, Quang, which is how these individuals are commonly known.

60. In most accounts of the battle, the village's name is cited as "Thon La Chu," which means "the Village of La Chu."

61. Erik Villard, "The 1968 Tet Offensive Battles of Quang Tri City and Hue" (hereafter, Villard), Center of Military History, United States Army, 2008, pp. 26–27; and Jack Shulimson, Leonard A. Blasiol, Charles R. Smith, and David A Dawson (hereafter Shulimson), *U.S. Marines in Vietnam: The Defining Year, 1968*, History and Museums Division, Headquarters, U.S. Marine Corps, 1997, chapter 9, pp. 164–167.

62. *Ao ba ba*, the loose-fitting black cotton clothes, well suited to Vietnam's climate, that the Americans called pajamas.

63. Captain Paul N. Gray, who commanded the navy's River Patrol Force, as reported by Glenn E. Helm, "Surprised at Tet: U.S. Naval Forces in Vietnam, 1968," Naval History and Heritage Command, http://www.history.navy.mil/research/library/online-reading-room/title-list-alphabetically/s/tet-offensive-vietnam-1968.html. Helm calls the NVA/VC effort to prepare for Tet "one of the greatest intelligence lapses of the post WW2 era."

64. Villard, p. 27.

6. Nhan Dan

65. Dang lao dong Viet Nam, founded in 1951, which later became (in 1976) the Communist Party of Vietnam.

66. Dang Kinh, *The Famous Guerrilla General* (hereafter, Kinh), Lao Dong Publishing House, 2013 (translated for me by Dang Hoa Ho), pp. 225–228.

67. It began: "'All men are created equal. They are endowed by their Creator with certain inalienable rights, among them are Life, Liberty, and the pursuit of Happiness.' This immortal statement was made in the Declaration of Independence of the United States of America in 1776. In a broader sense, this means: All the peoples on the earth are equal from birth, all the peoples have a right to live, to be happy and free."

68. Marilyn B. Young, *The Vietnam Wars, 1945–1990*, Harper Perennial, 1991, p. 172.

69. Merle L. Pribbenow, "General Vo Nguyen Giap and the Mysterious Evolution of the Plan for the 1968 Tet Offensive" (hereafter, Pribbenow), *Journal of Vietnamese Studies* 3, no. 2 (2008): 13.

70. Ibid., p. 12.

71. Ibid., p. 10.

72. Ibid., p. 5.

73. Lien-Hang T. Nguyen, *Hanoi's War*, University of North Carolina Press, 2012, p. 113.

74. Pribbenow, p. 15.

75. http://giaoducthoidai.vn/thoi-su/ba-chuyen-dang-suy-ngam-ve-dai-tuong-vo-nguyen-giap-3000.html.

76. Pribbenow, p. 19.

77. William J. Duiker, *Ho Chi Minh*, Hyperion, 2000, p. 557.

78. "History of the Sixth Regiment (the Phu Group) 1965–2005." Official record of the Thua Thien Hue Military Command and Party Committee. Emphasis added.

79. He would return to his duties as supreme commander in mid-February, after the offensive was a fait accompli.

80. All references to Nguyen Dac Xuan's experiences are from my interview with him and from his memoir, Nguyen Dac Xuan, *From Phu Xuan to Hue* (hereafter, Xuan), Tre Publisher, 2012, translated for me by Dinh Hoang Linh.

81. Kinh, p. 234.

82. "The Tri-Thien-Hue Theater During the Victorious War of Resistance and National Salvation Against America (a draft)," ed. Kieu Tam Nguyen (hereafter, Kieu), Committee for the Final Report on the War in the Tri-Thien-Hue Theater, Thuan Hoa Publishers, 1985.

7. Andy and Mimi

83. The siege of Khe Sanh.
84. The brigade's three battalions were the First of the Seventh, the Second of the Seventh, and the Fifth of the Seventh. Westin's was designated 5/7.
85. UH-1s.
86. CH-47.
87. Tad Bartimus et al., *War Torn: Stories of War from the Women Reporters Who Covered Vietnam*, Random House, 2002, p. 26.
88. Ibid.
89. The assault on LZ Colt was carried out by sappers who infiltrated the camp through its perimeter defenses, not through a tunnel. Lieutenant Craig Pinchot was killed by a grenade sitting in the same chair Westin would likely have occupied if he had not been transferred back into the field.

8. Banh Chung and Gio Cha

My interviews with Jim and Tuy-Cam Bullington.

9. Palace Soldiers

90. My interviews with Tang Van Mieu, Le Huu Tong, and others. Also Nguyen Manh Ha, deputy head of the Vietnam Military History Institute, Hanoi.
91. My interview with Nguyen Manh Ha, who heard Phieu tell the story at a party conference, to much laughter.
92. Kinh.

10. Hatred in Blood

93. Eric Hammel, *Fire in the Streets* (hereafter, Hammel), Pacifica Press, 1991, pp. xxiv–xxv.
94. George W. Smith, *The Siege at Hue* (hereafter, Smith), Lynne Rienner, 1999, pp. 57–58.
95. Kinh.
96. H. Norman Schwarzkopf, *It Doesn't Take a Hero*, Bantam Paperback, 1992, p. 140.
97. Westmoreland Papers, LBJ Library.

11. A Pretty Night

My interview with Jim Coolican.

PART TWO
The Fall of Hue
January 31, 1968

1. Fireworks

1. The ARVN Seventh Armored Battalion.
2. Le Minh, "Hue in Mau Than Campaign" (hereafter, Minh), *Song-Huong Journal* 29 (1988): 1–2.
3. My interview with Nguyen Thu.
4. Smith, frontispiece.
5. Truong Sinh, "The Fight to Liberate the City of Hue During Mau Than Tet (1968)" (hereafter, Sinh), excerpts from the journal of Truong Sinh, *Hoc Tap* (a Communist Party journal in Hanoi), no. 12 (December 1974): 80–93.
6. Villard, pp. 28–29.
7. Ibid., p. 28.
8. Sinh.
9. Ibid., pp. 80–93. Also Minh, pp. 1–2.
10. Sinh, p. 93.
11. Ibid.
12. NLF soldiers carried Soviet-made B-40 and B-41 rocket-propelled grenade launchers. American soldiers carried LAWs (light antitank weapons) or bazookas (World War II–era weapons that fired a 3.5-pound shaped charge). All were effectively airborne grenades, which for my purposes here will be referred to as "rockets."
13. Minh, p. 6.
14. Villard, pp. 31–32.
15. Nguyen Duc Thuan.
16. Quang would not tell me this man's name because, he said, the man eventually rose to a high position in the party, and his former service with the ARVN is not widely known.
17. Tran Thi Thu Van, *Mourning Headband for Hue* (hereafter, Tran), Indiana University Press, 2014, p. 12. Tran writes under the pen name Nha Ca and would become one of South Vietnam's most famous writers. *Nha Ca* means "gentle song." All accounts of her and her family's experiences are drawn from this book. She and her husband, Tran Da Tu, were arrested and imprisoned by the Hanoi government after the fall of Saigon, and this book was used as evidence of her "war crimes."

2. The Compound

18. Americans had M60 machine guns.
19. Hammel, p. 36.

20. Ibid., p. 39.
21. Smith, p. 37.
22. Ibid., pp. 34–35.
23. As noted in Shulimson: Sinh, translated from *Hoc Tap*, December 1974, Hue
    Folder, Tet Box, A&S Files, Indochina Archives, pp. 93–94.

3. A Mighty Python

24. Transcript from the National Security Council files at the LBJ Library.
25. Hoang Anh De.
26. Nguyen Ta Thanh and Nguyen Quang Ha, *The Fire at the Citadel* (hereafter,
    Thanh), translated in summary for the author by Dinh Hoang Linh, chapter 7.
    Thanh was an officer with the NLF who wrote this memoir years later.
27. Ibid., chapter 9.
28. Ibid., chapter 7.
29. In the North Vietnamese army, a lieutenant might command a battalion, unlike
    in the American military, where rank is roughly commensurate with the size
    of command—a battalion in the marines, under ordinary circumstances, would
    be commanded by a lieutenant colonel.
30. My interview with Lieutenant Tang Van Mieu. He was commander of the
    Seventh Battalion of the Eighth NVA Regiment. The NLF's order of battle
    has been reported in a baffling variety of ways in previous American accounts,
    most of them wrong, including Shulimson's official US Marine Corps history.
    Some of the confusion has been sown by Vietnam. Hanoi had various code
    names and numbers for its regiments and battalions, and frequently changed
    them in order to make tracking their movements difficult. To give some idea
    of the complexity, Dang Hoa Ho, a former Vietnamese military officer who
    helped me with research there, wrote: "Take the three regiments referred
    to today as Regiment 6, Regiment 3 (then Regiment 8), and Regiment 9. To
    maintain secrecy and create confusion in the adversary, they had the code
    names of Phu Xuan Group (Regiment 6), Song Lo Group (Lo River, Regi-
    ment 8, which was changed to Regiment 3 in 1969), and Group Quang Trung
    (Regiment 9). Bigger units often had subordinate units with the same code
    number: Regiment 8 had Battalion 7, 8, and 9; so did Regiment 9; and these
    subordinate units could be shuffled occasionally. Regiment 8, which later
    was referred to as Regiment 3 or Song Lo Group (Lo River), is typical. It was
    founded in 1959 as a battalion, Battalion 929. In 1965 it became a Regiment,
    Regiment 29 of Division 325. There were several Divisions 325, 325 B, and 325
    C, engaging in battles in Quang Tri and in the Central Highland during the
    years 1965–1969. When it was annexed to Division 325, Regiment 29 received
    a new code number—it became Regiment 8 with the new code name of Song

Lo. After the Tet Offensive it became Regiment 3 of Division 324. After the war the Regiment 3 was dissolved. I think the history of this Regiment alone is enough to give you a headache!"

31. *Washington Post*, February 1, 1968, p. A4. The report came from "News Dispatches," which means it was assembled from wire services. Hanoi was making the same claim for Saigon, which was clearly untrue.

32. Thanh, chapter 7.

33. Xuan. This and what follows are from both his memoir and my interview.

34. Thanh, pp. 197–198 (she reports an interview she did with a dying young man she identified only as Kham).

35. Ibid., chapter 11.

4. An Afternoon of Street Fighting

36. First Battalion, First Marine Division, Company A—Alpha 1/1.

37. Indeed, Batcheller was caught in Westmoreland's Operation Checkers, so named because it involved reshuffling marine units all over the map.

38. In this case, temporary wood frame housing.

39. Ferguson was awarded the Medal of Honor.

40. Part of Westmoreland's Operation Checkers. Shulimson, p. 105.

41. Ibid., p. 106.

42. The marines called them Dusters, but they were not the M42 tracked vehicles in standard army use. These were trucks outfitted with the same guns as the M42.

43. M48, a larger, heavier, more modern tank than those used by the ARVN.

44. Zippos were M67 A2 tanks that, instead of the 90-mm cannon standard to the M48 A3 Patton, had a flamethrower that could project a stream of napalm 150 yards or so. It carried a drum of 250 gallons of napalm.

45. Unlike the army, which had its own medics, the marines relied on navy hospital corpsmen. They were not technically marines, although they wore marine uniforms. Some were conscientious objectors who had opted for this nonviolent way of serving.

46. "Marines Under Fire," Kenneth N. Jordan, Sr., PublishAmerica, 2008, Kindle edition, location 4014.

47. Ibid. One of the rounds had passed through Moore's chest, but he survived. He said later that the round missed his heart because his heart was in his throat.

48. Ligato. Gonzalez would later be awarded the Congressional Medal of Honor. Canley would receive a Navy Cross.

49. Batcheller was awarded the Navy Cross.

50. Ligato. Fraleigh survived to undergo sixteen surgeries. As was often the case in Vietnam, men evacuated from a combat scene were never seen again by their

squad mates. Ligato assumed his friend was dead until he stood up in a dark banquet room at a reunion twenty-five years later and offered a toast to his fallen buddy. "That's me, asshole," a voice spoke up from the darkness. "I did not die."

5. An Idiotic Mission

51. Gravel later used the words "stupid and idiotic" to describe the mission in a personal letter to Batcheller, cited in Shulimson, p. 173.
52. Shulimson, p. 173.
53. The Sea Knight was a Boeing Vertol CH-46, known to the marines as a "phrog," with rotors in the front and rear. It was the prime transport helicopter used by the marines in the Vietnam War.
54. Wrongly, as it happens. The guards at the prison held out until the next night.
55. Jan K. Herman, *Navy Medicine in Vietnam: Oral Histories from Dien Bien Phu to the Fall of Saigon*, McFarland, 2009, p. 218.
56. Lucas, twenty-one, from Jackson Heights, New York, died.
57. Kirkham, twenty-two, from Brookfield, Wisconsin, was posthumously awarded the Silver Star.
58. Meadows was awarded the Navy Achievement Medal for his actions, an honor so beneath what it warranted that Downs characterized it to me as "a miscarriage of justice."
59. Lauver received a slight wound to his calf and was flown back with the other wounded to Phu Bai. He was awarded the Silver Star for his actions that day.
60. Ligato.
61. Smith, p. 54.
62. Coolican. Murphy was posthumously awarded a Silver Star.
63. Ligato.
64. Shulimson, p. 174.

PART THREE
Futility and Denial
Wednesday–Friday
January 31– February 2

1. IR8 Rice

1. Rostow had once proposed stationing twenty-five thousand troops along the Vietnam-Cambodian border to stop infiltration by North Vietnamese troops, not realizing that in the heavily mountainous terrain a force of that size would be "completely swallowed up and ineffectual." *B&B*, p. 152.

2. Rostow had written a book, *The Stages of Economic Growth, a Non-Communist Manifesto*, which argued that investments in poor countries that spurred economic growth would steer them naturally toward capitalism and democracy.
3. Rostow was right, in the long run, although the introduction of the new technology would not have any effect until after the war, when multiplied yields would turn the then Communist country into a major rice exporter.
4. Hedrick Smith, "US Officials Say North Vietnam Also Gained at Dakto," *New York Times*, November 29, 1967, p. 14.
5. Notes of LBJ meeting with Democratic congressional leaders, January 30, 1968, LBJ Library Collection.

2. As Numerous as Ants

6. Tran, p. 16.
7. This was very likely Batcheller and Alpha Company making its way up to the An Cuu Bridge.
8. Tran wrote that the returning vehicles were "very few," and given the location and timing of the incident, these were very likely the two trucks loaded with wounded and dead that were sent racing back to Phu Bai.
9. Excerpts from their statements were later broadcast by Radio Hanoi. Both women would be released a month later, deemed friends of the Vietnamese people. Mary Hershberger, *Traveling to Vietnam: American Peace Activists and the War*, Syracuse University Press, 1998, pp. 150–154.

3. So You Want to Go to Vietnam?

10. Foxtrot Company, Second Battalion of the Fifth Marine Regiment.
11. Commander, Second Battalion of the Fifth Marine Regiment.
12. Tom Martin says he vividly remembers this: "And the words I will never forget coming back, 'Don't worry Rockmat Six, where you are going there is more than you can count.'" But Mike Downs said he doubts at that point anyone knew enough about what was going on in Hue to say this.
13. Chris Brown.
14. Sea Knights were Boeing Vertol CH-46s, midsize twin-rotor choppers used by the marines.
15. Danny "Arkie" Allbritton.
16. Dan Carter. The moment is also recorded in Keith Nolan, *Battle for Hue: Tet, 1968* (hereafter, Nolan), Presidio Press, 1983, p. 32.

4. Consternation Had Been Achieved

17. Charles Mohr, "Vietcong Press Guerrilla Raids; Martial Law Declared by Thieu" (hereafter, Mohr), *New York Times*, February 1, 1968, p. 1.
18. Lieutenant General Frederick C. Weyand, press briefing, February 1, 1968.
19. Mohr.
20. Shulimson, p. 176. He cites one of the marine pilots, Captain Dennis M. Dunagan, who delivered parts of the ARVN Fourth Battalion, Second Regiment.
21. The Second and Third Battalions of the Third Armored Regiment.
22. ARVN First Battalion, Third Regiment.
23. Shulimson, p. 175.
24. Sawada would later be captured and killed by Communist forces in Cambodia.
25. "Allied Attack Stalls in Imperial Capital," *Washington Post*, February 3, 1968, p. A1.
26. Lieutenant Richard Horner was awarded the Silver Star. He recovered from his wounds and returned to Fox Company after the battle ended.
27. He died the next day at the triage center at Phu Bai.
28. One of the pictures, taken just as the tanks were moving up the street, was published in *Life* magazine, February 16, 1968 (hereafter, *Life* 2/16/68), pp. 26–27. Chris Brown's wife, Madeline, was horrified to learn that he was in the middle of it. It showed Corpsman Gosselin and Henschel down on the sidewalk, and a row of marines crouched behind the tank. She clipped the photo and sent it to him, and Brown labeled it with the names of everyone in the picture and sent it back to her. Many years later he visited the photographer's studio in New York and was given prints of the entire horrifying sequence.

5. Snuffies and the Most Macho Woman in the World

29. ". . . But Not in Hue/ VC Repulse Attacks in Hue, Retain Partial Control," *Washington Post,* February 2, 1968, p A1.
30. Gene Roberts, "Enemy Maintains Tight Grip on Hue," *New York Times*, February 3, 1968, p 1.
31. This was clearly Golf Company.
32. Papers of Walt Rostow, LBJ Library.
33. Westmoreland Papers, LBJ Library.
34. Gene Roberts had regular access to the CIA station chief in Saigon and occasionally spent time with Westmoreland. It was his impression that the general was consistently trying to sell him a more optimistic view of the war. "When Creighton Abrams replaced Westmoreland it was clear that he distrusted the traditional up the chain of command military reporting system that had a tendency to tell the brass what it thought they wanted to

hear," Roberts wrote to me. "Abrams, I found out, invited sergeants from the field to dinner once a week or so, plied them with booze and got them to tell him what was really going on. I was impressed. I never asked Abrams about his relationship with the CIA, but my general impression was that he was not hostile to it; and liked to get as much information—even conflicting information—on ongoing operations as he could possibly get. That was not my impression of Westmoreland."

35. Westmoreland Papers, LBJ Library.
36. Roberts.
37. Some of this was misunderstanding. Reporters, like Roberts, had to get their stories and film out quickly for timely publishing or airing, and could not do so from the field.
38. Stefan Zweig, *Marie Antoinette: The Portrait of an Average Woman*, trans. Eden and Cedar Paul, Garden City Publishing Co., 1933.
39. Tran, p. 50.
40. Francois Mazure, "Cathedral Sanctuary in Hue," *Times* of London, February 5, 1968.
41. Catherine Leroy, "A Tense Interlude with the Enemy in Hue" (hereafter, Leroy), *Life*, February 16, 1968, pp. 23–29.

6. The Chariot Is Coming

42. Company H, Second Marine Battalion, Fifth Regiment.
43. He is in the Pro Football Hall of Fame in Canton, Ohio, as the highest-ranking military officer to ever play in the NFL (he retired as a lieutenant general).
44. The NVA battalion failed to take full advantage of the opportunity. It melted away without attacking Echo Company.

PART FOUR
Counterattack in the Triangle and Disaster at La Chu
Saturday–Monday
February 3–5

1. Pluses and Minuses

1. Captain Jim Coolican, quoted in Richard Oliver, "Battle of the Perfume River," *Times* of London, February 3, 1968, p. 8.
2. Shulimson, p. 176.
3. Braestrup, vol. 2, p. 152. This quote from Wheeler echoed peculiarly the famous warning by Ho Chi Minh to the French, delivered twenty-two years earlier:

"You will kill ten of our men, and we will kill one of yours, and in the end it will be you who tire of it."

4. Transcript of the interview published in the *New York Times*, February 5, 1968, p. 15.

5. Nguyen Manh Ha.

6. Westmoreland Papers, LBJ Library.

7. Ibid.

8. Carroll Kilpatrick, "LBJ Calls Uprising Failure; Viet Enemy Holds On in Hue; Thieu Asks Heavier Raids," *Washington Post*, February 3, 1968, p. 1.

9. General Loan executed the prisoner, an insurgent team captain named Nguyen Van Lem, after Lem was caught near an open grave with thirty-four bodies. Lem had earlier killed a South Vietnamese lieutenant colonel and his family, including his eighty-year-old mother. The famous photograph was taken by AP photographer Eddie Adams, who was awarded a Pulitzer. The execution was also captured by NBC cameraman Vo Suu. The image became iconic, symbolizing the brutality and unfairness of America's ally and the war. Adams later expressed regret for its notoriety.

10. *New York Times*, February 4, 1968, p. 11.

11. *Times* of London, February 3, 1968, p. 9.

12. Joe Alsop, "Red Raids on Cities Are Sign of Weakness, Not Strength," *Washington Post*, February 2, 1968, p. A18.

13. Braestrup, vol. 2, p. 156.

14. Ibid., pp. 157–158.

15. In retrospect, this comment by the president reveals how little the White House knew or understood the machinations in Hanoi, since Ho Chi Minh was at that point a peripheral figure, ill and recovering in China, who was hardly in a position to "order" the attacks, and whose support for the Offensive was halfhearted at best.

16. Oberdorfer, p. 169.

17. Bunker included the passage at the end of a detailed, multipage rebuttal to an antiwar speech given by Senator Ted Kennedy.

18. Oberdorfer, p. 172.

2. TFP

19. Charles A. Krohn, *The Lost Battalion* (hereafter, Krohn), Praeger, 1993, p. 55.

20. There were also artillery units, helicopters, and a support component attached to the division.

21. Tradition trumps simplicity in the numbering of these units, so they were formally known not as the First, Second, and Third Brigades, but as the Seventh, Eighth, and Twelfth Cavalries.

22. In Vietnamese, Song Huong meant "the River Huong," so Song Huong River meant "the River Huong River."

23. Charles Baker, *Gray Horse Troop* (hereafter, Baker), Powder River Publications, 2013, p. 80; Krohn, p. 60.

24. Gerald McLain, *A Vietnam Tour Through My Eyes* (hereafter, McLain), Independent Publishing Corporation, 2014, p. 277.

25. Dentinger memoir: http://www.12thcav.us.

26. The Twenty-Ninth Regiment of the 325C NVA Infantry Division.

27. McLain, p. 278.

28. Krohn, p. 72.

29. Ibid., p. 74.

30. Ibid., p. 75.

3. Big Ernie

31. Shulimson, pp. 179–180; Smith, p. 95. Interview with Cheatham by the US Navy Bureau of Medicine and Surgery, October 2005, https://archive.org/stream/CHEATHAMErnest/CHEATHAM%20Ernest_djvu.txt.

32. Marine Corps Oral History Program; Vietnam Field Interview on the Battle for Hue City, September 24, 1968, Field interview Number 2511; Lieutenant Colonel Ernie Cheatham (hereafter Cheatham).

33. Fought in September of that year, it was the first of two major battles to retake the city. Communist forces overran the city twice. A force of about forty thousand marines and army infantry took it in less than a week of intense fighting, leaving 280 Americans killed and over 7,000 wounded. The Communists retook the city later that year, and another, much larger battle was fought between December 31 and January 7 by US Army, British, Thai, and South Korean troops numbering almost 150,000 men. Well over 800 allied troops were killed.

34. Cheatham.

35. Shulimson, p. 110.

36. John Laurence, *The Cat from Hue* (hereafter, Laurence), PublicAffairs, 2002.

37. First Battalion, First Marines.

38. Laurence, p. 19.

4. I Love Zees Fucking Marines

39. Leroy, p. 24.

40. Gene Roberts, "Attacks on Hue Fail to Rout Foe," *New York Times*, February 5, 1968, p. 1.

41. Gene Roberts, "U.S. Marines in Hue Drive Wedge into Enemy Units" (hereafter, "Wedge" story), *New York Times*, February 6, 1968, p. 1.

42. Alvin B. Webb Jr., "Struggle for Hue Is Deadly," *Philadelphia Inquirer*, February 5, 1968, p. 1.

43. Gene Roberts, "U.S. Marines Seize a Third Block of Hue," *New York Times*, February 4, 1968, p. 1.

44. "Wedge" story, p. 1.

45. Stuart I. Rochester and Frederick Kiley, *Honor Bound: American Prisoners of War in Southeast Asia, 1961–1973*, Naval Institute Press, 1999, p. 452. DiBernardo and the other four men—Army Sergeants John Anderson, Donat Gouin, and Harry Ettmueller; and Marine Corporal John Deering—would be held as prisoners of war until 1973.

5. The Breakout

46. Krohn, p. 77.

47. My interview with Lewis "Budd" Jeffries.

48. Krohn, p. 132.

49. According to Krohn, the man was never disciplined. He was granted leave to return home when his mother died, and deserted. Krohn, p. 103.

50. Ibid., p. 105.

51. Ibid., p. 77.

52. Krohn, in an e-mail to the author.

53. McLain, pp. 282–283.

54. It accomplished this. The 2/12 Cavalry sent the ship a guidon from one of its companies as a token of appreciation.

6. Holding On to the Enemy's Belt

55. The 804th of the NVA's Fourth Regiment, which also included Viet Cong elements (many released prisoners) and local militiamen.

56. Hoang told me that Cheatham's force also had a South Korean battalion and an ARVN battalion, but there is no evidence to support it.

57. Hoang Anh De.

58. Gene Roberts, "Enemy's Soviet-Designed Rifle Slows Marines' Drive in Hue," *New York Times*, February 6, 1968, p. 17.

59. Smith, p. 96.

60. Shulimson, p. 180.

61. Hoang Anh De.

7. Jeanne d'Arc School

62. Hammel, p. 99.

8. Look at Your Sorry Ass!

63. Laurence, p. 25.
64. Ibid.
65. Keith Kay.
66. Hammel, pp. 158–159.
67. Ibid., pp. 161–162.
68. He looked to be badly wounded, but the shrapnel had missed his bones, too, and left him bloody, with shredded trousers, but otherwise not severely hurt. Another marine, John Griswold, took shrapnel in both his legs but also escaped serious injury. His wounds were enough to get him out of Hue.
69. There is a small memorial at the building today honoring the seven who were killed.

9. The Dismal Strand of Acheron

70. Shulimson, p. 182.
71. *New York Times*, February 5, 1968, p. 1.
72. The light cruiser with the call sign "Northampton," which Budd Jeffries, the battalion's fire support officer, could not identify (there was no USS *Northampton* in service), and the USS *McCormick* (a destroyer).
73. The ARVN's First and Third Regiments, the Hac Bao, the Seventh and Ninth Airborne Divisions, and the 3/7 and 4/5 Cavalry. Smith, p. 122.
74. The ARVN Third Battalion, Seventh Regiment.
75. Charbonneau.
76. Nolan, p. 92.
77. Dante's *Inferno*, Canto 3: *There sighs and wails and piercing cries of woe / reverberated through the starless air . . .*

PART FIVE
Sweeping the Triangle
Tuesday–Monday
February 6–February 12

1. Flags of Surrender, Flags of Fright

1. The official count from this initial wave of killings was three hundred. Kieu, p. 142.
2. A pages-long list of these targets was captured during the fighting. I found a translated copy, "Location of a Number of Objectives in Hue City," in the National Archives.
3. Hoang Thanh Tung.
4. According Cao Van Sen, the decorated Viet Cong regular who had delivered the Alliance flag to the Citadel pole, the reprisals got badly out of hand: "It was a mistake, really. They punished many civilians who were Christians. They killed them, actually, because they considered those people traitors, who helped the ARVNs. Those soldiers were harshly criticized later . . . They were personally driven, caused by some individuals who were enraged."
5. Interview with Nguyen Co Thanh. Mai Van Ngu (Hoa), now deceased, fled with Communist forces after the city was retaken. He was later captured by ARVN forces and imprisoned at Con Dao Island, location of the infamous "Tiger Cages." He returned to Hue in 1975, a "hero" of the revolution.
6. Interview with Nguyen Cong Minh by WBGH, http://openvault.wgbh.org/catalog/V_A871CFC59DC1460DA8775733E0AD8D15.
7. Tran, pp. 213–215. Tran (pen name Nha Ca) identifies this "Dac" as Nguyen Dac Xuan. He has denied the incident in writing and to me personally in my interview with him in Hue in February 2016. Xuan has devoted a great deal of time and energy trying to refute Tan's accounts and others accusing him of direct responsibility for atrocities in Hue during February 1968. He admits that killings of guilty and innocents occurred, and that the purges got out of hand, but denies any direct involvement.
8. Despite his denials, it seems plausible that "Dac" and "Xuan" are one and the same. Given the implication that he participated in the murderous cruelties of those days, Xuan, today a well-regarded historian at Hue University, would understandably not be tied to such things. In his memoir, Xuan relates that as a youth he disliked the name "Xuan" and was reluctant to use it: "Previously, I really hated my name—Xuan. As this name often coincided with those of the girls who were servants of rich men in the city. During this historic time, I suddenly felt excited with such a strange name. I discreetly thanked

my mother for having chosen the name of Quang Trung's ancient capital, where I was born, to name me. Those thoughts flickering in my mind made me miss my footing and roll down the gravel slopes or rice-field many times" (chapter 5, p. 2). While he did not say specifically that he used his other name, "Dac," it would be a likely alternative. In another work recounting events in this period, "A Star on the Top of Phu Van Lau," the author Hoang Phu Ngoc Tuang refers to Xuan throughout as "Dac." Tran is certain that "Dac" was none other than Nguyen Dac Xuan.

9. Tran, p. 214.
10. Xuan, in my interview with him (February 2016): "I wasn't a general, I was only a civilian, but I myself considered the leaders in the events of Mau Than [Year of the Monkey] naive . . . I'm very sorry that in the war, we couldn't avoid many mistakes . . . There is cruelty that happened due to naïveté . . . I am very sorry that in the war we couldn't avoid many mistakes."
11. Nguyen Dac Xuan diary, chapter 11, pp. 7–8.
12. There is no record of South Korean soldiers fighting in the Battle of Hue, although I heard this rumor many times from Vietnamese soldiers and civilians.
13. Le Cong Thanh. Khoa was his great-uncle.
14. Tran, p. 52.
15. Ibid., p. 56.
16. Ibid., p. 75.
17. Ibid., p. 77.
18. Tuy-Cam and James Bullington.

2. Something Is Wrong Over There

19. Westmoreland Papers, LBJ Library.
20. Cable from Westmoreland to Wheeler, February 3, 1968, Westmoreland Papers, LBJ Library. Emphasis is mine.
21. John W. Finney, "Anonymous Call Set Off Rumors of Nuclear Arms for Vietnam," *New York Times*, February 13, 1968, p. 1.
22. Notes of NSC meetings, the papers of Walt Rostow, and the papers of William Westmoreland, LBJ Library. Over the first four months of 1968, more than one hundred thousand tons of explosives were dropped on the five-square-mile area, one of the most concentrated aerial bombardments in history, according to George C. Herring, *America's Longest War*, McGraw-Hill, 1979, p. 145.
23. Presidential Papers, LBJ Library.
24. Cable from Westmoreland to General Wheeler and Admiral Sharp, February 3, 1968, Westmoreland Papers, LBJ Library. Emphasis is mine.
25. Oberdorfer, p. 175.

26. *New York Times*, February 1, 1968, p. 26.
27. Excerpts from RFK speech, *New York Times*, February 9, 1968, p. 12.
28. Walter Rugaber, "Civil Rights, Strong Challenge by King," *New York Times*, February 11, 1968, p. E4.
29. Presidential Papers, LBJ Library.
30. Rostow Papers, LBJ Library.

3. The Sweep

31. Shulimson, p. 188.
32. General Hughes, the overall commander in Hue, said, "If any single supporting arm is to be considered more effective than all the others, it must be the 106 recoilless rifle, especially the M50 Ontos." Shulimson, p. 186.
33. My interview with Hoang Anh De.
34. Hammel, p. 186.
35. Shulimson, p. 189.
36. "U.S. Marines in Hue Drive Wedge Into Enemy Units," by Gene Roberts, *The New York Times*, February 6, 1968.
37. W. D. Ehrhart, *Vietnam-Perkasie: A Combat Marine Memoir*, University of Massachusetts Press, 1983, pp. 9–10.
38. Ibid., pp. 263–264, and my interview with Ehrhart.
39. Soukup, in a letter to Nolan, July 24, 1980.
40. Ibid.
41. Shulimson, p. 185.
42. Smith would retire as a major general, Christmas as a lieutenant general, Downs as a brigadier general, and Meadows as a colonel.
43. Hammel, p. 227.
44. "Wedge" story.
45. Navy LCUs—landing craft utility.
46. These estimates were low. Army Colonel Dick Sweet's battalion alone, which had been trapped northwest of the city, had been halved—nearly two hundred casualties.
47. James Reston, "Washington: The Flies That Captured the Flypaper," *New York Times*, February 7, 1968, p. 46.

4. Staying

48. Tu Minh and Nam Long.
49. Kinh, pp. 241–243.

5. Vaught

50. Krohn, p. 120.
51. My use of the slur "gook" in presenting the thinking of marines or soldiers is based on their use of the term in interviews with me. In these instances, drawn from their own words, I am trying to capture what they thought and felt, which includes their sometimes offensive attitudes toward the Vietnamese.
52. Krohn, p. 126
53. Baker, p. 88.
54. My interview with Don Bowman, the 5/7 executive officer.
55. Hammel, p. 316.

6. Fuck Him, He's for the Other Side

56. Gene Roberts, "Marine Squad Rides to Battle on Motorcycles," *New York Times*, February 8, 1968, p. 14.
57. H. D. S. Greenway, *Foreign Correspondent: A Memoir* (hereafter, Greenway), Simon & Schuster, 2014, p. 65. Greenway writes that he was later disappointed in himself for picking up the gun. "I am not proud of that afternoon . . . Years later, Gene and I were having dinner together in New York and he told me he thought I had done the right thing under the circumstances. But I believe it was he who did the right thing."
58. Gene Roberts, "Hue to Danang: A Perilous Boat Ride," *New York Times*, February 11, 1968, p. 1. The story is supplemented by my interview with Roberts.

7. Hell Sucks

59. Courtney was so beloved by his men that one of them, Merril Ludwig, has a big tattoo on his back in remembrance of him.
60. Instead, Smith had Courtney evacuated. He had been injured days earlier and had insisted on staying. Now Smith told him he needed to take advantage of the wound to get out of Hue "by sundown," he said, which amused Courtney, the Texan. He returned less than a week later after Gravel had cooled off. The colonel did not follow through on the demand for court-martial papers.
61. John Laurence; notes from David Halberstam's files (kept at Boston University) for his book *The Powers That Be*, and from the book itself, p. 512; and from Douglas Brinkley, *Cronkite*, Kindle edition, chapter 22, loc. 6290.
62. The actual battle sequences shown in the broadcast were the work of John Laurence and Keith Kay, Don Webster and John Smith, George Syvertson and Kurt Volkart, along with a number of Vietnamese crew members who assisted with sound. Cronkite apparently wrote the narrative himself, according to an

interview David Halberstam did for his book *The Powers That Be*, with Ernest Leiser, the show's executive producer. Laurence notes that the narration "sounds" like Cronkite. Who else, he asked, would have in 1968 still been referring to himself on the air as "this correspondent"?

63. Michael Herr, *Dispatches* (hereafter, Herr), Knopf, 1977, p. 73.
64. Ibid., pp. 73–74.
65. Herr either confused his buildings or was exaggerating. Hue University was not significantly damaged during the battle.
66. Herr was faithfully reporting the contemporary, incorrect MACV estimates.
67. *It Wasn't Pretty Folks, But Didn't We Have Fun?*, Carol Polsgrove, W.W Norton, 1995, page 174.
68. Smith, p. 111.
69. Laurence.

8. The High Weirdness

70. The 4.2-inch Gun Platoon, Mortar Battery, First Battalion, Eleventh Marines, First Marine Division. They were part of Operation X-Ray and were known as "Whiskey X-Ray" on the radio.
71. Peter Braestrup, "Weather and Thin Ranks Slow Marines' Tough Fight in Hue" (hereafter, Braestrup 2/12/68), *Washington Post,* February 12, 1968, p. 1.
72. Cable from Bunker to Cushman, February 16, 1968, Westmoreland Papers, LBJ Library.
73. Braestrup 2/12/68.
74. Draftees ordinarily were conscripted for two years; those who enlisted usually bought into a full four years.
75. Dale A. Dye, *Citadel*, a novel, Diamond Books, 1994, p. 147.
76. Nolan, p. 178.
77. Lonny Connolly.
78. West was evacuated to Phu Bai and lived. He received a Bronze Star with a V for valor, even though Smith had recommended a higher decoration. The marines did not look kindly on the fact that he had lost his tank.
79. So much so that no one later could recall the man's real name. He was called "Scooby," he was wounded near the end of the battle and evacuated, and none of the members of his tanker unit ever saw him again.

9. Like Men Who Fell Out of the Sky

80. Hoang Thi No fought in Hue until the twenty-sixth of February. Afterward she joined an all-female platoon of Viet Cong called Vo Thi Sau, which fought until the war ended. She returned to her village in 1975 as a celebrated member

of the then famous Huong River Girls. She became a prominent party official and served in that capacity until she retired.

81. Hammel, p. 248.

PART SIX
Taking Back the Citadel
Sunday–Sunday
February 11–February 25

1. Clusterfucked

1. He would later serve as director of the marines' Physical Fitness Academy at Quantico, which trains the Corps's physical fitness instructors.
2. Smith, p. 129.
3. Nicholas Warr, *Phase Line Green* (hereafter, Warr), Naval Institute Press, 1997, p. 87.
4. Memo from Wheeler to the president, February 9, 1968. LBJ Library.
5. Warr, p. 89.
6. Ibid., pp. 91–92.
7. Ibid., p. 92.
8. Shulimson, pp. 194–195.
9. No relation to the Hall of Fame baseball player.
10. Warr, p. 109.
11. Ibid., pp. 113–128.

2. We Do Not Doubt the Outcome

12. Bernard Weinraub, "Saigon's Authority Believed to Be in Critical Stage," *New York Times*, February 11, 1968, p. 3.
13. "Hanoi Attacks, and Scores a Major Psychological Blow," *Newsweek*, February 12, 1968, p. 23. Emphasis is mine.
14. Miller Center.
15. Ibid.
16. Braestrup, vol. 1, p. 190.
17. *Time*, February 14, 1968, pp. 1, 34.
18. "Viet-Bound Troops Get LBJ Sendoff," UPI, *Philadelphia Inquirer*, February 18, 1968, p. 1.

3. Random Agents of Doom

19. Smith, p. 139.
20. Ibid.

21. Morrow would later try to take some of Trinh's music to Joan Baez, in California, but he was turned away by the guards at her gate.
22. Herr, p. 79.
23. Ibid., p. 74.
24. *Time*, February 16, 1968, p. 20.
25. Halberstam, p. 512.
26. Laurence's letter to Halberstam, June 1, 1974.

4. The First Annual Hue City Turkey Shoot

27. Warr, p. 133.
28. Ibid., p. 135.
29. Thomas A. Johnson, "Vietcong Continue to Hold Out in Central Hue Despite Marine Attacks," *New York Times*, February 14, 1968, p. 3.
30. Years later Berntson could not remember the marine's real name.
31. Shulimson, p. 205; and Smith, p. 145.
32. Smith, p. 146.

5. The Tower

33. Whitmer and Harrington.
34. Gene Roberts, "Jets Hammer at Hue Citadel," *New York Times*, February 15, 1968, p. 3.
35. Smith, p. 142.
36. Thomas A. Johnson, "U.S. Marines Gain 200 Yards in Day at Hue's Citadel," *New York Times*, February 16, 1968, p. 1.
37. It was Dennis Michael, whose death is described in Part Six, Chapter 8.

6. Lefty

38. Captain Harrington was later chewed out for failing to remove Thoms from the battle after he had received wounds entitling him to three Purple Hearts.
39. Eshelman. According to Nguyen Quang Ha, a battalion inside the Citadel suffered so many casualties—150 in one day—that they attempted to withdraw that evening, only to be bombarded (Ha attributed this to a B-52 attack) so severely that the entire remainder of the force was wiped out.
40. In his interview with me, Tang Van Mieu first accused Americans of using civilians as shields and then later admitted to doing the same thing. Each side has accused the other of this practice, and while it was not the official policy of either, it is easy to imagine individual soldiers or units taking advantage of the proximity of civilians under the circumstances.

7. Why Are You Guys Doing This?

41.   Thomas A. Johnson, "Hue's Mayor Says Foe Executed 300," *New York Times*, February 12, 1968, p. 1.

42.   Tran, pp. 265–266.

43.   Ibid., p. 279.

44.   Ibid.

45.   Ibid., p. 276.

46.   Ibid., p. 268.

47.   Ibid., pp. 266–267 and 270.

48.   See my comments about Xuan in the Epilogue. In my interview, he said that he believed Le Quang was going to be killed, but earlier he had told me that many of those arrested were not condemned to die, but only sentenced to undergo reeducation. "Then why did you assume in this case he would be killed?" I asked him. Xuan said that because of intensive fighting and shelling, it was reasonable to assume that Le Quang would be killed, but that he did not necessarily believe it would be at the hands of his captors. It sounded to me, given the extreme gratitude expressed by the photographer, that neither he nor Xuan was concerned primarily about the danger of a random shell. It sounded to me like Xuan saved him from execution.

8. There It Is

49.   "18 Days Under the Bed, He Eludes Foe in Hue," *Washington Post*, February 20, 1968, p. 14.

50.   Alvin B. Webb Jr., "Marines Face 9 Hue Blocks of Death, Terror," UPI, *Philadelphia Inquirer*, February 18, 1968, p. 1.

51.   Herr, p. 81.

52.   Alvin Webb, "Fearful Price Paid for Four Blocks," *Times* of London, February 21, 1968, p. 6.

53.   Fred Emery, "N. Vietnamese Die Chained to Their Gun Posts," *Times* of London, February 16, 1968, p. 1.

54.   Nguyen Quang Ha and Le Huu Tong.

55.   The Buddhist tetraskelion is an ancient symbol of good fortune. Its legs are bent in a clockwise direction, while the Nazi symbol's legs were bent counterclockwise.

56.   Felix Bolo, "White Flag That Brought Only Hail of Bullets and Civilian Deaths," *Times* of London, February 22, 1968, p. 6.

57.   Lee Lescaze, "Hue Marines, Bitter as They Are Brave," *Washington Post*, February 20, 1968, p. 1.

58.   After the war Thompson paid a visit to McGonigal's brother in Philadelphia, who agreed that the priest had gone to Vietnam with a "death wish."

59. Both correspondents, along with Charles Mohr, were later awarded Bronze Stars.

9. La Chu

60. Westmoreland Papers, LBJ Library.
61. Bowman.
62. Baker, p. 125.
63. Very much later, as it happens. Almost forty years later, he began having intense pain in his right knee. He went to an orthopedist, who found an AK bullet lodged in the joint.
64. Baker, pp. 130–131.

10. Checkmate

65. Smith, p. 154
66. Hammel, p. 303.
67. Lima Company, Third Battalion, Fifth Marines, commanded by Captain John Niotis.
68. Thomas A. Johnson, "Wary Hue Civilians Live Around the Battle," *New York Times*, February 21, 1968, p. 3.
69. "Vietcong Fight to the Death," *Times* of London, February 16, 1968, p. 10.
70. Charles Mohr, "U.S. Marines Gain a Hue Objective, but Foe Fights On," *New York Times*, February 23, 1968, p. 1.
71. Kinh, p. 244.
72. Tang Van Mieu.
73. "Hue Chief Issues Execution Order," *New York Times*, February 21, 1968, p. 1.

11. The Toll

74. Ibid., p. 216.
75. Marine losses were 142 dead and 1,100 injured (Shulimson, p. 213). The 2/12 Air Cavalry lost 81 killed and 251 wounded (Krohn, p. 140). Krohn updated this figure in a 2008 edition saying on page ix "First, let me correct the casualty figures. During the six-week period described in the book, the foxhold strength of the 2/12th fell from five hundred to fewer than two hundred. I originally said this included 60 killed in action and more than 250 wounded. . . . I now know the KIA figure was eighty-one, not sixty." The 5/7 Air Cavalry lost 27 killed, 203 wounded (Baker, p. 157).
76. Rostow Papers, LBJ Library.
77. Notes of the President's Meetings, January 23, 1968, LBJ Library.

78. March 6, 1968, cable from National Security Council files at the LBJ Library.
79. Gene Roberts, "U.S. Command Sees Hue, Not Khesanh, as Foe's Main Goal," *New York Times,* March 7, 1968, p. 1.
80. *Newsweek,* February 19, 1968.
81. Louis Menand, "Seeing It Now, Walter Cronkite and the Legend of CBS News," *New Yorker,* July 9, 2012.
82. Halberstam, p. 514.
83. Which, under President Nixon, it did.
84. Kieu: "The high command ordered that this attack [on Khe Sanh] should take place about one week before Tet 1968 (i.e., between 20 and 23 January, 1968). The attack would be launched before our nationwide attack in order to draw enemy forces away from other theaters of operation."
85. Betty Boyd Caroli, *Lady Bird and Lyndon: The Hidden Story of a Marriage That Made a President,* Simon & Schuster, 2015, p. 312.

12. Why Should They Keep Fighting?

86. The notes from this interview are in the National Archives in Washington, DC.
87. Mai Elliott, *RAND in Southeast Asia,* Rand, 2010, p. 12.

13. Krystal Burgers and the Truck

88. Olson won the Robert Capa Award for the series.

Epilogue

1. Nixon speech, May 3, 1968, in Indiana.
2. In typical Westmoreland legerdemain ("A Soldier Reports," page 434), he correctly reports the number of American marines killed at 142, but does not mention the 80 Cavalry troopers killed in the battles around La Chu (87). He does, however, add the estimated number of Front troops killed around La Chu (3,000) to the highest estimate of enemy soldiers killed in the city (5,000).
3. "Outlook Assessed by Westmoreland," Associated Press, February 26, 1968.
4. Tran Van Tra, as quoted in Karnow, p. 544.

Index

Abrams, Creighton
  about, 423
  ARVN and, 521
  battle for Hue, concluding weeks, 477
  Ky and, 428
  made MACV commander, 506
  sent to Vietnam, 24
  Tolson and, 475, 486
  Westmoreland and, 423
Adkisson, George, 115, 140, 142, 148, 367–368, 405
Agence France-Presse, 199
Ali, Muhammad, 35
Allbritton, Dan "Arkie," 252, 284–285, 379
Alsop, Joe, 222–223
Alsop, Stewart, 35–36
An Cuu Bridge, 4, 44, 96, 99–100, 131, 290
Anderegg, Mike, 130, 137–138, 245–247, 248
Anderson, Bob, 450
Andrews, George, 28
An Hoa Gate, 83, 102, 111, 296
Armies of the Night (Mailer), 35
Army of the Republic of Vietnam (ARVN). *See also* Hac Bao (Black Panthers); Mang Ca (ARVN base); Truong, Ngo Quang
  Abrams and, 521

American nickname for, 14
civilian bunkers, 6–7
counterattack by, 267
flirting with, 10–11
military capability, 15, 219, 400–401, 406, 407
number of dead and wounded, 496
presence in Hue, 46
strengthening of, as Phase Three of "Success Offensive," 38
Tam Thai Tank Base, 4, 97–98, 99, 102, 104–105, 340
Tet Offensive, 106, 107, 340, 341, 452–453
VC attempts to turn soldiers to communism, 301–302, 305, 306
Arvin. *See* Army of the Republic of Vietnam (ARVN)
An Assault on a Fortified Position, 239

Ba, Doan Van, 149, 247
Bach Ho Bridge, 45, 99
Back, James, 149–150
Baker, Charles, 349, 477, 478, 481, 482
"Ballad of the Green Berets" (Sadler), 75
Bao, Mai Xuan, 100–101, 105, 491–492
Bao Dai, 44
Barbush, Ernie, 17
Barnes, Barney, 146
Barnes, William, 270, 271

Batcheller, Gordon, 95
    about, 126
    battle for Hue, beginning of, 126,
        128–132, 136
    wounded, 136–137, 138, 140
BBC radio broadcasts, 341
Beck, Winfield, 68, 352–353
Ben Hai River, 81
Bernie, Stephen, 116, 149–150
Berntson, Stephen, "Storyteller," 397
    after Vietnam War, 536–537
    Tet Offensive and, 203, 328–329,
        331–332, 335, 337–338, 361–362,
        426–428, 470–471
    as writer, 200, 201–203
Berrigan, Philip, 34
The Best and the Brightest (Halberstam),
33–34, 526
Bingham, Sam, 198, 199, 204–205
Birch, Tom, 427–428
Blair, Ken, 450–451
Bolo, Felix, 468
Bowman, Don, 350, 475
Bradley, Donald, 252
Braestrup, Peter, 372, 419
Breth, Frank, 115–116, 117, 140, 143
Broadfoot, Gordon, 376
Brockwell, James, 131
Brown, Chris, 187–191, 192, 250, 286, 375,
376
Brown, Madeline, 191, 376
Brown, Tommy, 465–467
Buddhists, 53, 64–65
Bullington, Jim, 77–79, 157, 170, 172–174,
372–373, 418–419, 536
Bullington, Tuy-Cam, 157, 170–172,
310–312, 418–419, 536
Bunker, Ellsworth, 33, 224
Burghardt, Josef, 325
Burnham, Tom, "Bernie," 372
Byrd, Robert, 318–319

Cam Ne round up, 32
Campbell, Charlie, 187–188, 189–190, 260
Campbell, Hugh, 234, 350
Camp Evans, 4, 77, 128, 226, 256

Cam Ranh Bay, 69
Canley, John
    battle for Hue, beginning of, 132, 133,
        137, 139, 140, 142–143, 148–149, 203,
        209–210, 276
    as fearless, 139, 276
Cao Tho Xa, 300
Caravelle Hotel, 78–79
Carter, Dan, 182
Catholics, 45, 53
CBS Evening News, 223
Chanh Tay Gate, 54, 84–85, 106, 112, 185,
289, 340, 398
Charbonneau, Terry, 75–77, 290–291
Chattanooga Times, 78
Cheatham, Ernie, "Big Ernie," 322
    after Vietnam War, 537
    all civilians as enemies, 326
    arrival at MACV compound, 241
    battle for Hue, beginning of, 134, 135,
        177–178, 198, 212–213, 225, 241–242,
        267, 269–272, 274, 276, 277, 280–281,
        282, 286, 289
    battle for Hue, second week of, 217,
        320–321, 331, 332, 334, 335, 373
    described, 211–212
    orders given to, 238–239
    tactics, 239–240, 406, 461
"Cheating the Reaper" (Ehrhart), 531
Che Thi Mung, 3
    about, 5–6
    after Vietnam War, 534–535
    battle for Hue, 388–389, 390–391
    preparations for Tet Offensive, 88, 100
    as VC spy, 7–8, 10–11
    waiting for attack, 87–88
Chien-tranh Chong My (Resistance War
        Against America), 41. See also Viet-
        nam War, Communist perspective
Childs, Bob, 480
China, 63
Chot (ARVN officer), 491
Christian, George, 315
Christmas, Ron, 295
    about, 208
    after Vietnam War, 537

American flag raised over provincial
headquarters and, 337, 338–339
battle for Hue, beginning of, 203, 207,
211, 242, 272, 274, 281–283
battle for Hue, second week of, 322,
329, 330–331, 333–334, 373
opinion of Cheatham, 213
opinion of Gravel, 210
Chung, Tran Huy, 110
The Citadel, 4, 98, 398. See also specific
gates to
America bombing of, 433
described, 42, 43, 44, 399–400
fall of, 119
Front's retreat, 488, 490–493
map of, 96, 296
palace in, 43, 44, 52, 86, 96, 99,
107–108, 112–113
primary targets in, 98, 99–100
Civil Operations and Revolutionary
Development Support (CORDS),
31–32, 33, 68, 78
Clem, Dan, 260
Clifford, Clark, 414, 415, 496–497, 500,
501, 506
Cobb, Ty, 88, 407
Coffin, William Sloan, 34
Collins, David, 189
Comacho, Hector, 262, 264
Combat in Built-Up Areas, 239
Connelly, Lonny, 373–374, 375–376, 380–381
Conrad, William, 434
Con Tien, 126, 127
Cook, Jimmy, 138
Coolican, Jean, 405–406
Coolican, Jim, 95
about, 13, 15
assessment of Tet Offensive, 532–534
battle for Hue, beginning of, 115–116,
118, 140, 141, 142–143, 148–149,
150–151, 219, 289–290
battle for Hue, concluding weeks, 400,
405, 407–408
Doezema and, 13–14, 16, 114, 534
with Hac Bao, 15, 91, 110–111, 400, 408,
428, 489–490

holiday in Hue, 91–92
night fighting, 487
opinion of ARVN, 15, 406
prison mission, 144–145
Courtney, Allen, 326, 362–363
Crapse, Wayne, 375
Cressonier, Marie, 173, 174
The Crisis(Paine), 224–225
Cronkite, Walter, 223, 362, 363–366, 397,
423–424, 503–505
Crum, Frank, 249
Cushman, Robert E., 128, 219, 428, 486

Dailey, Eddie, 139, 382–383, 385
Da Nang (American base)
press in, 198–199
road to, 60
R&R in, 73
Tet attack on, 162, 163
Dang Hoa Ho, 528
Dankworth, Jerry, 285
Davison, Mike, 72, 346, 353, 477
Delarosa, Reymundo, 287
Dentinger, David, 231, 235, 236
DiBernardo, James, 253
Diem, Ngo Dinh, 22, 44, 46
DiLeo, Carl
about, 231
battle for Hue, beginning of, 233, 235,
257–258, 261, 262–264
battle for Hue, concluding weeks of,
343, 344, 345–346
Dinh, Ton That, 169–170
Dinh Mon, 49
Doang Thanh Xu, 528
Doc Lao Park, 96, 118, 197, 218, 266
Doezema, Frank, 3
about, 12–13, 17
battle for Hue, beginning of, 114–115,
116, 118, 143
Coolican and, 13–14, 16, 114, 534
friendship with Vietnamese, 16
at MACV compound, 15–16
Doi Hoa, 455
Don, Huynh Van, 306–307
Dong Ba Gate, 296, 398, 458

Donnelly, Rick, 209, 241
Doss, Roger, 202
Downs, Mike, 157
 about, 176–177
 after Vietnam War, 533, 537
 battle for Hue, beginning of, 178–179,
  186, 189, 190, 192–193, 211, 242, 269,
  270, 272, 281, 283
 battle for Hue, second week of, 320,
  324–325, 330–331, 371, 372, 376
 Coolican and, 534
 opinion of Gravel, 210
draft resistance, 34, 35
Drew, Fred, 119, 140, 146
Dung, Van Tien, 63
Duong Hoa, 49
Duy Tan Street, 114
Dye, Dale, 200, 203, 367, 378, 393

Earhardt, Steve, 192
Egan, Terry, 102
Ehrhart, Bill, 150, 241, 324, 327–328,
  377–378
 after Vietnam War, 530–531
Eichler, Gary, 275
Eisenhower, Dwight, 22, 416
Ekker, Chuck, 284, 285, 307
Ellsberg, Daniel, 507
Emery, Fred, 465
Erlandson, Bob, 180
Eshelman, Bill, 452–453, 488
Esquire, 366, 422–423, 461
Esquivel, Al, 384, 385
Estes, Ed, 404, 408, 410

Fawcett, Denby, 68, 353
Ferguson, Frederick, 127–128
Figueroa-Perez, Cristobal, 189, 190–191
Fire Dragons, 129
Fitzgerald, Mike, 132, 136
flags, 52–53, 54, 86, 124, 295, 337–339, 400,
  493–494
Fleischmann, Carl, 248, 249, 383, 386
Floyd, Donald, 133
Ford, Gerald, 521
"Fractured Jaw" plan, 314, 315

Fraleigh, Patrick, 137, 139, 140
France, 22, 39, 44
Frankel, Max, 224
Frasier, Ronald, 178, 283–284
the Front. See also La Chu; North Vietnamese Army (NVA); Viet Cong
  (VC)
 actions against civilians by, 171–172,
  299–307, 308–309, 310, 455–457,
  495–496
 advance signs of, 88, 89–90, 102–103
 Checkers strategy and, 84
 commitment of, 463, 464, 465
 in control of Citadel, 399, 400
 counterattacks against, 267–269,
  275–276, 283, 285–287, 452, 453
 discipline of, 465
 execution of civilians by, 455–457,
  495–496
 execution of members of, and those
  who aided, 494
 field headquarters, 4, 106, 121
 flag for Tet Offensive, 52–53, 54, 124,
  400
 general uprising expectation of, 42,
  57–58, 60, 86, 268, 299, 524–525
 Highway 1 severed by, 290
 Huong River Squad, 8–9, 87, 388–391
 lessons for liberation of Hue, 83
 number of dead and wounded, 496
 number of troops, 51
 recruitment, 47, 51, 53
 reinforcement of, 428
 remaining in Hue as civilians, 491
 retreat from Citadel, 488, 490–493
 supply and support lines, 185
 takeover of most of Hue, 120–122, 152
 troops for Offensive, 41–42, 51–52, 54,
  98
 uniforms, 51, 83
 US military opinion of abilities of,
  221, 321–322
Fulbright, William, 415–416

Gallagher, Jim, 365
Gasbarrini, Lou, 187–188, 190

Geneva Accords, 22
Georgaklis, Jim, 384, 385
Giap, Vo Nguyen, 59, 60, 63–64, 84, 224
Ginsburgh, Robert N., 314
Goldsboro News-Argus, 159
Gonzales, Juan, 233, 234, 235, 236–237, 259,
    345, 480–481
Gonzalez, Alfred, "Freddie," 95
    battle for Hue, beginning of, 133,
        134, 139, 151–152, 209–210, 274–275,
        277–278
    death, 278
Goodin, Brad, 250–251, 386, 392
Goralski, Robert, 223
Gosselin, James, "Doc Goose," 188
Graham, Joe, 410
Gralnick, Jeff, 365, 423–424
Grantham, Alvin Bert, 472, 512–518
Gravel, Marcus
    about, 135, 275
    battle for Hue, beginning of, 134, 136,
        137, 138, 140, 142, 144–145, 147, 148,
        151, 185, 189, 193, 219–220, 241, 275
    battle for Hue, second week of, 356,
        377–378
    Cronkite and, 362, 363, 365–366
    replaced, 238
    soldiers' opinion of, 210–211, 225
Gray Horse Troop (Baker), 349
Green, Moe, 469
Green Berets, 76–77
Green Revolution, 162
Greenway, David, 358, 470, 471
Grissinger, Rick, 467

Ha, Nguyen Quang, 97–98, 102, 299, 492
Hac Bao (Black Panthers)
    battle for Hue, concluding weeks of,
        489–490
    battle for Mang Ca, 99, 111–112, 119,
        184
    Coolican with, 15, 91, 110–111, 400, 408,
        428, 489–490
    described, 15
    prison mission, 144
    Tet holidays, 18, 90

Halberstam, David, 30, 31, 33–34, 160, 505,
    526
Hall, Bobby, 248–249, 382, 384
Hammons, Don, 437, 438, 441
Hanoi. *See* North Vietnam
Harrington, Myron, 430–436, 440, 441,
    466, 470, 487
Hart, Calvin, 444–445, 446, 461–464
Harwood, Richard, 29–30
Hau Gate, 102
Haukness, Steve, 78, 170–171, 174
Hausrath, Don, "Rat," 187, 269, 283, 284,
    285, 371–372
Hayes, Harold, 366
Hedger, Robert, 283
Heidel, Lou, 148
"Hell Sucks" (Herr), 367
Helvey, Bob, 217, 228, 229, 234, 260, 346
Henschel, William, 188, 189–190, 246
Hensley, Anne, 171
Herr, Michael, 366–367, 422–423, 461
Heston, Charlton, 70–71
Higgins, John, 146
Highway 1, 4, *158*
    area around, 114, 226
    battle for Hue, beginning of, 129–132,
        136
    importance of, 44, 45, 60
    severed by the Front, 290
Hoang Anh De
    battle for Hue, beginning of, 105–106,
        118, 127, 267–269, 272, 273, 275–276,
        283, 285–286, 320, 321, 334, 336, 340
    battle for Hue, concluding weeks of,
        493
Hoang Thanh Tung, 301–302, 493
Hoang Thi No, *3,* 8–9, 388, 389–390
Ho Chi Minh
    Bao Dai and, 44
    independent Vietnam, 22
    nationalist credentials of, 32–33
    opinion of Tet Offensive, 63
    as symbol, 61
    Tet Offensive and, 64
    view of war, 61–62
Hoc Sinh (the *Students*), 49

Hong Bang, 43
Hopkins, Bob, 257, 258
Horner, Rich, 157, 186–188, 189, 190, 330
Ho Thi Kim Loan, 300
Howard, Ray, 437–438
Hue, 4, 96. See also The Citadel; Tet
    Offensive; Tet Offensive, civilians
    during
  described, 44–45
  destruction of, 335
  final fall of, 521
  history, 42–43, 44, 86
  holiday preparations for Tet, 74–75, 76,
    78–79
  importance of, 42, 59–60, 101
  popularity of Thieu government,
    45–46
  primary targets in, 98, 99–100
  as target for propaganda purposes, 416
  urban warfare, 239–240, 322–325,
    329–330
Hue, Tran Ngoc, "Harry," 90, 91, 110–112,
    428, 489–490, 534
Hue University, 186, 312, 337, 421–422
Huff, Bill, 277
Hughes, Emmet John, 502–503
Hughes, Stanley, 397
  battle for Hue, beginning of, 198,
    238–239, 240, 241, 274, 275
  battle for Hue, second week of, 325
  Cronkite and, 365–366
  Harrington and, 431
  opinion of Truong, 402
  refused Thompson's command, 486
Humphrey, Hubert, 420
Huong Giang Hotel, 10, 75
Huong River, 4, 44, 45, 60
Huong River Squad, 8–9, 87, 388–391
Huu Gate, 106–107, 398, 428, 454, 488, 493

Imlah, Jim, 435
intelligentsia, 53
International Control Commission
    (ICC), 358, 359–360
International Voluntary Services (IVS),
    171, 175, 253

IR8 rice, 160–162
Irvine, Jerry, 143
Istvie, Albert, 79, 170, 172–174, 372–373

Jeanne d'Arc High School, 274–279
Jeffries, Lewis, 262, 264
Jenkins, Chris, 175, 183, 459–460
Jenkins, Greg, 464
Jennings, Fernandez, 405, 460, 487
Jimenez, Eden, 324
Johnson, Lyndon Baines, 3
  bombing of North Vietnam, 23, 29, 37,
    414, 498
  Byrd and, 318–319
  challenges to, in Democratic
    presidential primaries, 35, 222, 315,
    317, 416, 498
  characteristics, 416
  Congressional pressure on, 415–416
  on Cronkite report from Vietnam, 505
  decided not to seek reelection, 506
  increase in troops, 23, 496
  kill ratios/body count, 24, 39
  McNamara and, 29, 414–415, 496
  notified of Tet Offensive, 163
  opinion of Giap, 224
  peace talks/offers, 415, 532–533
  press and, 29, 32
  racist view of North Vietnam, 34
  remarks to troops departing for South
    Vietnam, 417
  Rostow report on Tet Offensive, 196
  "Success Offensive" assessment of
    progress, 36–37
  on Tet Offensive, 221, 223–225, 497
  as trapped by war, 22–23
  view of antiwar protest, 499
  weapons approved for use, 315
  Westmoreland and, 20, 37, 313, 416, 498
Johnson, Sandra, 175, 181, 192, 253
Johnson, Thomas, 426, 441, 455, 489
Jones, Roy, 252
Joshi, G. D., 358

Kaczmarek, Walter, "Chief," 333, 334, 339
Kalischer, Peter, 423–424

Kay, Keith, 240–241, 245, 281
Kennedy, John F., 22–23
Kennedy, Robert F., 21, 317
Kent, Alan, 437–438
Kephart, Russell, 258
Ker, Michael, 136–137, 138
Khe Sanh, 39–40, 197, 220–221, 314,
    497–498
Khoa, Nguyen Dang, 308, 455, 494
Kief, David, 286
kill ratios/body count
    as bogus, 24–25, 39, 502
    Johnson and, 24, 39
    McNamara and, 27
    Tet Offensive and, 220, 221, 316–317
    Westmoreland and, 21, 24, 220, 221,
        316–317, 502
Kim Phung Mountain, 4, 102
King, John R., 199, 251, 269
King, Martin Luther, Jr., 28, 318
Kinh, Dang, 59, 60, 84–85, 103, 340–342,
    490
Kinny, Gerald, 148, 151
Kirkham, Donald, 147
Komer, Robert, 33
Krohn, Charles, 226, 228–229, 232,
    234–235, 254, 255, 259
Kromer, Ken, 326–327
Ky, Nguyen Cao, 428

La Chu, 4, 158, 473
    American attempts to get passed, 474
    breakout from, 259–265
    destruction of, 264
    importance of, 121, 232, 475, 476, 488
    nickname, 237
    probe attacks, 254–255, 256–259
    Vaught and, 474, 476–482
LaHue, Foster
    about, 128
    battle for Hue, beginning of, 141–142,
        152, 184–185, 198, 225, 238
    briefing of Ky, 408
    opinion of Truong, 401
    Thompson and, 401, 402, 428, 429
Lala, Nolan, 149, 290

Lam, Mrs, 304
Lambert, Frank, 346
Lam Hai Luong, 304
LaMontagne, Ed, 130, 139–140
Lampo, Steve, 116
Lam Ung, 304
Landry, Ed, 369–371, 392–393, 488
Laos, 80, 81
Lau, Hoi Tin "Tony," 236, 255
Laurence, John, 240–241, 245, 280–281,
    363, 423–424
Lauver, Bob, 140, 148–149
Le Cong Thanh, 109, 307
Le Duan, 58, 62, 63
Leflar, Richard, "Lefty," 443–444, 445–452,
    463–464, 530
Le Huu Tong, 433, 466, 492–493
Leiser, Ernie, 365, 423–424
Le Loi Street
    American advance along, 320, 325,
        332–334, 340
    American flag raised over provincial
        headquarters, 337–339
    Front headquarters, 334
    location, 5
    Thua Thien–Hue Province headquar-
        ters on, 75
LeMay, Curtis, 26
Lengel, John, 187–188, 189
Le Ngoc Thinh, 167
Leroy, Catherine, 199, 203, 205–206, 217,
    244–245
Lescaze, Lee, 419, 469
Le Thi Mai, 54
Le Tu Minh, 84, 104, 121–122, 490
Le Van Hoi, 166–167
Le Van May, 109, 307
Liberation Radio, 120–121
Lien, Pham Thi, 8, 87, 388, 389, 391
Lien, Tran Anh, 47, 51, 56, 84–85, 305
Lieu Coc, 158, 349, 351
Life, 245, 472, 512
Ligato, John, 129, 136, 138–139, 146, 152,
    277
"light at the end of the tunnel"
    invitations, 38

Linh, Dinh Hoang, 528, 529
Loan, Dang Dinh, 101
Lofland, Jack, 88
Loos, Walt, 258
Lucas, Glen, 147, 151
Lundy, Frank, 461
Lyons, Richard, 134, 136, 147, 148–149, 150
LZs (landing zones), 71, 72, 143–144, 148, 325

Maddox, Dane, 256
Mailer, Norman, 35
Mai Van Ngu, 302–303
Mang Ca (ARVN base), 96, 296
    battle for, 98, 101, 102, 104, 106, 111, 112, 119, 168
    counterattacks from, 267, 289
    defenses stabilized, 184, 225
    described, 405
    reinforcement of, 134, 142–143, 144, 151, 170, 184, 428
Manhard, Philip, 174
Marcotte, Art, 381, 393
Marquez, Marty, 133, 151
Martin, Dennis, 409
Mau Ty, 305
Mazure, Francois, 199, 203, 205–206, 244–245
McCarthy, Eugene, 35, 222, 315, 317, 416, 498
McCauley, Jerry, 458–459
McCoy, Jim, 252, 284, 372
McCullin, Don, 441
McGonigal, Aloysius, 403, 469
McGovern, George, 521
McGuire, Dennis, 480, 481
McLain, Jerry, 264
McNamara, Robert
    dismissed by Johnson, 29, 496
    DMZ barrier plans, 78
    insistence on Checkers strategy as success, 220
    offensive against Khe Sanh, 39, 497–498
    opposition to escalation, 26–27
    on pacification program, 32

    protesters and, 35
    replaced, 496
    support for war and, 21
    on Tet Offensive, 163
McNeil, Michael, 325
McNeil, Mike, 146
Meadows, Chuck, 95
    after Vietnam war, 527
    battle for Hue, 330–331
    battle for Hue, beginning of, 134, 135, 136, 137, 138, 140, 145–149, 152, 185–186, 242, 281
    opinion of Gravel, 210
Meet the Press, 220
Meggs, Tony, 437
Michael,Dennis, 470, 471
Mignemi, Bob, 17
Military Assistance Command Vietnam (MACV), 96
    change of commanders, 506
    civilians during Tet Offensive and, 414, 428
    Civil Operations and Revolutionary Development Support, 31–32, 78
    compound conditions during Tet Offensive, 114–119, 143, 248, 249–251, 266
    compound described, 10
    failure of Strategic Hamlet Program, 31
    refusal to believe in seriousness of Tet Offensive, 88–89, 141, 142, 144–149, 151, 152–153, 183, 185, 192–193, 195–198, 219, 238, 256, 289, 402
    refusal to believe in seriousness of Tet Offensive, consequences of, 519–520
    tacit admission of error of initial Tet Offensive assessments, 371
Miller, Steve, 78, 170–171, 174
Minh, Nguyen Cong, 303
Mohr, Charles, 162, 183, 355, 470
Moon, Howard, 335
Moore, Donald, 133
Morales, David, 427
Morgan, Charlie, 410
Morris, Richard, 466
Morrow, Mike, 179–181, 192, 419–422, 536

Mot, Than Trong, 98, 122
Mourning Headband for Hue (Tran), 308,
    309–310, 455–456
Mueller, James, 117
Murdock, Stan, 188
Murphy, Walter, 134, 135–136, 142–143, 146,
    149, 150, 151

National Liberation Front. *See* the Front
Neas, Eddie, "Alfie," 330
Nelson, Marjorie, 175, 181, 192, 253
Nelson, Scott, 410–411, 412, 425–426, 460,
    487
Neveling, Donny, 469–470
Newsweek, 502–503
New Yorker, 30
New York Times, 25, 30, 159, 183, 194–195,
    198, 211, 288–289, 317, 336–337,
    413–414, 426, 433, 441, 455, 501
Ngan Gate, 296, 398
Ngo Mon flag pole, 54, 96, 99, 123–124,
    296, 398, 493–494
Ngu, Nguyen, 55, 56
Nguyen, Mrs, 55–56
Nguyen Chi Canh, 455–457
Nguyen Duc Thuan, 483–484, 529
Nguyen Huu Ai, 303
Nguyen Ngoc Loan, 222, 455–457
Nguyen Ngu, 50
Nguyen ruling dynasty, 42–44
Nguyen Xuan Oanh, 504
Nha Do Gate, 296, 398, 488, 491
nhan dan (the people), 57. *See also* Tet
    Offensive, civilians during
Nixon, Richard, 520–521
Nolting, Fritz, 30, 31
North Vietnam
    as able to control pace of war, 33–34
    American bombing of, 23, 25–29, 414
    announcement of new revolutionary
        government in Hue, 123
    capital, 22
    definition of victory, 62–63
    demarcation line with South, 81
    economic development of, 27–28
    flag, 52

government, 58
    Johnson's opinion of, 34
    morale in, 25–27
    name for war, 41
    peace talks/offers to, 415, 532–533
    as in propaganda bubble, 60
    racist view of, 34
    strategy of continuous bleeding of
        American troops, 416
North Vietnamese Army (NVA)
    battle for Hue, beginning of, 102–103
    battle for Hue, second week of,
        347–348, 350, 351–352
    became members of the Front, 81–84
    conditions endured by soldiers, 80–81,
        97
    infiltration in South Vietnam by, 13
    at La Chu, 232, 476
    preparations for Tet Offensive, 39
    regiments involved, 98
    retreat from Hue, 490
    tactics, 476, 483–484
    troops involved in Tet Offensive, 98
    uniforms, 51, 82–83
    VC forces attached to for Tet
        Offensive, 41–42, 51
nuclear weapons, use of tactical, 314–315

Oberdorfer, Don, 28, 29, 41
Odum, Robert, 411
O'Konski, Jim, 278–279
Olson, John, 440, 472, 511–512

Pace, Peter, 326, 537
pacification program, 31, 32
Paine, Thomas, 224–225
Patterson, John, 78
The Pentagon Papers (Rand Corporation),
    507
Perfume River, 5
Perkins, Donald, 208–209
Pham Van Dinh, 428
Pham Van Dong, 416
Pham Van Khoa, 331
Phase Line Green (Warr), 404
Phieu, Le Kha, 83, 490

Philadelphia Inquirer, 317, 496
Philly Dog, 426
Phong, Tran Quoc, 301
Phu Bai, 4
    communications with Truong, 144
    described, 128
    misunderstanding of Tet Offensive,
        141, 142, 151, 152–153, 193, 197–198,
        219
Phu Cam Canal, 44, 96, 242, *318*, 320,
    361
Pike, Douglas, 495
Plainsman, 78
"pockets of resistance," 183
Polk, Pat, "Hand Grenade," 453, 487–488,
    489
Poncet, Pierre, 174
press, 240–241. *See also* specific journal-
    ists; specific media
    "advocacy journalism," 424
    assessment of significance of Tet
        Offensive, 413–414
    attempts to get to Hue, 198–199
    British, 341
    coverage by, regarded skeptically in
        Washington, 221–222
    coverage of battle for Hue, beginning
        of, 160, 183, 191–192, 194–195, 198,
        223, 280–281
    coverage of battle for Hue, concluding
        weeks of, 426, 460–461, 468–469
    coverage of civilians, 205–206, 414
    Cronkite in Hue, 362, 363–366
    development of credibility gap, 30–31
    disbelief in American military pro-
        nouncements about Tet Offensive,
        317, 501–502, 503–505
    as enemy, 29–30
    Johnson and, 29, 32
    "military journalists," 200–201
    "New Journalists," 366
    questions about Vietnam as part of
        global Communist expansion,
        502–503
    in Saigon, 179–180

supporters of war, 222–223
with troops on village sweeps, 68
war as eroding soul of America, 29
Westmoreland and, 29–30, 32, 37–38,
    313–314, 416
Preston, Robert, 346
Pribbenow, Merle L., 63, 64
Prince, Howard, 346, 347–349, 477–480,
    481, 485, 538

Quang, Le, 457
Quang, Nguyen Van
    after Vietnam War, 535
    battle for Hue, beginning of, 84–85,
        106, 108
    battle for Hue, concluding weeks of,
        454–455, 493
    battle for Hue, second week of, 297
    civilians and, 304–305
    preparations for Tet Offensive, 47–52,
        54–56, 78–79
Quang, Tran Van, 341–342
Quang Duc Gate, *296*, 398
Quang Tri zone, 84
Quang Trung, 86
Que Chu, 178, 232, 348, 351, *473*, 474, 476
Quy Nguyen, 16, 534

racism
    by American soldiers, 14–15, 30, 328,
        344, 446, 513
    Johnson and, 34
Rand Corporation, 507
Reinhold, Micheal, "Doc Rhino," 462
Republic of South Vietnam
    capital, 22
    civilians and, 32, 414
    corruption, 424
    as de facto American colony, 23–24
    demarcation line with North, 81
    division into geographic zones for
        war, 84
    fighting Communism through
        economic development, 161–162
    importance of place in culture of, 31

insistence on Tet Offensive as enemy
  failure, 183, 220
number of targets in, hit during Tet
  Offensive, 152
popularity of VC and, 33
Tet armistice, 87
VC in villages, 30, 32, 49, 68
Reston, James, 337
Ridgway, Matthew, 225
"Righteous Police Division"(Nghia binh
  Canh sat), 305
"Righteous Soldier Division" (Nghia
  binh), 305
Rigolette, Hastings, 323–324
Robb, Charles, 225
Roberts, Gene, 157
  about, 159–161
  after Vietnam War, 538–539
  coverage of battle for Hue, beginning
    of, 181, 183–184, 194–195, 198, 199,
    203, 204, 205, 211, 251, 269, 288–289
  coverage of battle for Hue, conclud-
    ing weeks of, 325, 336–337, 355–365,
    433
  departure from Hue, 355, 357–360
  IR8 rice story, 161–162
  reporting on possible other attacks,
    501–502
Rocket Alley (Mai Thuc Loan Street),
  407, 425, 435
Rodriguez, Damien, 439–440
Rogers, Bill, 193, 240
Romine, Randy, 435
Romney, George, 317
Rostow, Walt, 160–161, 163, 196–197, 319,
  498–499
La Rue Sans Joie. See Highway 1
Rushing, Jack, 132, 133
Rusk, Dean, 35, 163, 497

Sadler, Barry, 75
Safer, Morley, 32, 363, 364
Saigon, 22, 152, 162–163, 180, 503
Salant, Dick, 364
Salisbury, Harrison, 25

Salvati, John
  battle for Hue, beginning of, 239, 240,
    266, 272, 276, 277, 286
  battle for Hue, second week of, 322
  promotion, 212
Sawada, Kyoichi, 179, 181, 187–188, 191
Schackne, Bob, 423
Schell, Jonathan, 30, 31
Schultz, Dave, 436, 438
Schwarzkopf, Norman, Jr., 89
Scooby, 384, 385–386, 392
Scott, Willard, 291
Scudder, William, 255
Sea Tiger, 200
"secure hamlets," 31, 32, 51
Sen, Cao Van, 52, 53–54, 112, 492
Sexton, Ray, 436
Sharp, Ulysses S. Grant, 21
Sheehan, Neil, 31
Silva, Manuel, 230
Sinh, Truong, 101–102, 104
Smith, George (information officer),
  367–368, 420, 421, 433
Smith, George W. (combat officer)
  battle for Hue, beginning of, 117,
    274–275, 276–277, 278, 280, 288, 289
  battle for Hue, second week of, 320
  Cronkite and, 362, 363
Smith, Hedrick, 162
Smith, Ray, 208, 209–210, 217, 241, 382,
  383, 537
"snuffies," 200–201
A Soldier Reports (Westmoreland), 522
Soukup, Jim, 328, 329
South Vietnam. See Republic of South
  Vietnam
Sowards, Mike, 285
spizzerinctum, 20–21
Spock, Benjamin, 35
Spry, Earle, 475
Squires, Richard, "Sparks," 276
Stars and Stripes, 200
Steele, O. K., 326, 537
Stone, Dana, 368
Strassburg, Terry, 132, 133

Strategic Hamlet Program, 31, 32
Students for a Democratic Society (SDS), 34–35
"Success Offensive," 36–39
Sullivan, Jimmy, 278
Sweet, Dick
  about, 228–230
  breakout from La Chu, 259–265, 343, 474–475
  march to and taking La Chu, 226, 230–231, 232–235, 236, 254, 255, 256, 259
Syvertsen, George, 423

Taitt, Selwyn, "S-Man," 440–441
Takenaga, Kazunori, "Kenny," 377–378, 531
Tam Thai Tank Base (ARVN base), 4, 97–98, 99, 102, 104–105, 340
Tang Van Mieu, 112, 122–123, 185, 453, 490, 491
Task Force Oregon, 31
Task Force X-Ray, 128, 134, 140, 238
Tay Loc airstrip, 98–99, 127, 406, 492
Tet
  beliefs about, 91
  holiday preparations in Hue for, 74–75, 76, 78–79
  traditional celebration of, 41, 46
  US "Success Offensive" policy phase planned for, 38–39
Tet Offensive
  American disbelief in seriousness of, 141, 142, 144–149, 151, 152–153, 183, 185, 193, 195–198, 219, 238, 256, 289, 314, 315–316, 402, 403
  as American victory, 522
  arms brought into Hue, 47–48, 55–57
  battle for Hue, as "gentleman's war," 322
  battle for Hue, beginning of, 119, 241–242, 267, 269–292
  battle for Hue, concluding weeks of, 401–412, 430–443, 446–453, 458–470, 486–494
  battle for Hue, lull in, 425–429

battle for Hue, primary targets, 98, 99–100
battle for Hue, second week of, 320–327, 328–339, 361–362, 369–379, 382–386, 388–393
China's opinion of, 63
CIA assessment, 315–316
command center, 102
destruction of Hue during, 495
entrance into Hue, 83–84
as expression of people's will, 58
Front's flag for, 52–53, 54, 124, 400
Front's preparations for, 9, 39, 47–52, 54–56, 64–65, 76, 78–79, 80–83, 88, 100–101
Front's takeover of most of Hue, 120–122, 152
Front troops, 41–42, 51–52, 54, 98
Giap's opposition to, 63
Ho and, 63
as intelligence failure, 525
launch decision, 64
lessons US should have learned from, 526
as "logistical miracle," 54
misinformation about, 142
number of target struck, 152
as pivot of American support for, 496, 500, 519, 526
plans, 41–42, 52, 54, 58–59, 63, 82, 98
relying on support of the people, 57–58, 60, 66, 122
in Saigon, 152, 162–163, 503
South Vietnamese reporting of seriousness of, 183
as stand-off, 504–505
training for, 53
US prison mission, 144–149, 185, 192–193, 332
Tet Offensive, civilians during, 295
  American, 171, 172–175, 310, 372, 459–460
  Americans and, 307–308, 326–329, 414, 428, 468
  battle for Hue, beginning of, 109–110, 164–172, 186, 245, 252, 268–269, 288

battle for Hue, second week of, 297,
    298–299, 308–312
conditions endured by, 327–328
converts to the Front, 297
dead, 335–336, 393–394, 495, 523–524
departure from Hue, 357–360
Front's actions against, 171–172,
    299–307, 455–457, 495–496
Front's expectation of general upris-
    ing by, 42, 57–58, 60, 86, 268, 299,
    524–525
hiding attempts by, 467–469
non-American foreigners, 174–175,
    244–245, 358, 372
press coverage of, 205–206, 414
racism of US soldiers and, 328, 446
refugees in Hue University, 186, 337,
    421–422
refugees in soccer stadium, 356
Republic of South Vietnam and, 414, 428
treatment of, 468
TFP. See La Chu
Thanh doi Hue (NVA Fifth Regiment),
    97
Thich Don Hua, 53
Thieu, Nguyen Van, 44, 45–46, 48, 89–90,
    413
Thinh, Le Ngoc, 109
This Fucking Place, 237. See also La Chu
Thoan, Than Trong, 98
Thomas, Frank, 338
Thompson, Bob, 397
    battle for Hue, concluding weeks of,
        399, 402–405, 406–410, 412, 425–426,
        429–431, 461, 486–489
    looting and, 467
    McGonigal and, 469
    Polk and, 453
    shelling of Citadel, 400
Thoms, Bob, 435, 436, 438–439, 440–441,
    447, 449–450, 451–452
"Three Nos," 33
Thrift, Freddie, 512–513, 516–517
Thruong Dinh Gate, 398
Thu, Nguyen, 98, 99, 106
Thuan, Nguyen Duc, 107–108, 112–113

Thua Thien Province, 59, 84
Thua Tien zone, 84
Thuong Tu Gate, 96, 296, 398
Time, 416
Times (London), 222, 465
Tinh Hoa, 455–456
Tinson, Paul, 179, 330, 331
Toi, Tran, 167–168
Tolson, John J., 225, 256, 260, 350
    battle orders of, 227, 228, 234
    forces under, 128, 226–227
    La Chu and, 475
    soldiers' opinion of, 229, 344–345
Tong, Le Huu, 80–84, 104
Tong-Tan-cong-Noi-day (General
    Offensive, General Uprising).
    See Tet offensive
Ton That Dinh, 267
Ton That Ke, 300
Ton That Vu, 300
Trai Gate, 296, 398
Tran Da Tu, 164, 308–310
Tran Thi Thu Van, 109, 164–166, 205–206,
    455–456, 523
Tria Gate, 111, 184
The Triangle, 4, 218
Trinh, Nguyen Duy, 62
Trinh Cong Son, 421–422
Truman, Harry, 22
Truong, Ngo Quang, 102. See also Mang
    Ca (ARVN base)
    American opinion of, 89, 401, 402
    battle for Hue, concluding weeks of,
        400–401, 405
    estimate of attacking force, 88–89, 90
    Hac Bao and, 15
    LaHue and, 184–185
Truong Dinh Gate, 296
Truong Tien Bridge, 10, 45, 88, 96, 99,
    143
Tu Dam Pagoda, 4, 106, 121
Tully, Lester, 146
Tuy-Cam, 77
Ty, Nguyen Van, 168–170
Ty, Quen, 168, 169–170
Tyree, David, 271

United States Armed Forces
  Alpha Company, 161, 203, 209–210,
    260, 262, 277, 278, 288
  Bandits, 381–382, 383, 384–387, 392
  Civil Operations and Revolutionary
    Development Support, 31–32, 33, 68
  command disbelief in seriousness of
    Tet Offensive, 141, 142, 144–149, 151,
    152–153, 183, 185, 192–193, 195–198,
    219, 238, 256, 402, 403
  consequences for soldiers of MACV's
    refusal to face facts, 520
  current opinions of soldiers, 526–527,
    530–532
  Echo Company, 177
  First Air Cavalry Division, 128, 226–
    227, 254–255, 343, 344–352, 353–354
  flag raising over provincial headquar-
    ters, 295, 337–339, 493
  Fox Company, 177, 178–179, 186, 198,
    203, 211, 252, 320, 371
  Foxtrot Company, 176
  fraternizing with Vietnamese, 14
  Golf Company, 134, 140, 145, 161, 178,
    185–186, 188, 198, 203, 211, 240, 320
  hangouts, 10
  Hotel Company, 177, 178, 198, 203, 211,
    272, 372
  importance of AirCav, 67
  increase in numbers of, 23, 496
  Information Services Office, 200
  insistence on Tet Offensive as enemy
    failure, 220
  Johnson's remarks to, 417
  land mines, 81
  listening devices, 81
  Long Range Reconnaissance Patrol,
    76–77
  looting by, 466–467, 470
  Marines, 397
  morale, 378–381, 403, 404, 423, 426, 432,
    445–446, 478–479, 513
  North Vietnamese strategy of
    continuous bleeding of, 416
  number of dead and wounded, 496
  Ontos, "Frankenmobiles," 207, 333

  opinion of military abilities of the
    Front, 221, 321–322
  Pathfinders, 233, 236–237
  patrols described, 70, 71, 72–73
  racism towards Vietnamese by, 14–15,
    30, 328, 344, 446, 513
  radio relay station, 143–144
  R&R described, 73
  Seventh Cavalry, 67
  sky spot technique, 476–477
  staff jobs described, 71–72
  Task Force Oregon, 31
  Task Force X-Ray, 128, 134, 140, 141, 193
  troop arrivals in Cam Ranh Bay, 69
  village sweeps described, 68
  Westmoreland's request for more
    troops, 62
USS Constellation, 499
USS Lofberg, 351
USS Manley, 433
USS McCormick, 264
USS Providence, 433
U Thant, 415

Valkenburgh, Van, 193
Vaught, James, 472
  about, 347
  battle for Hue, beginning of, 226
  La Chu and, 236, 256, 289, 345, 346,
    347–349, 351–352, 353–354, 474, 475,
    476–482
Viet Cong (VC)
  arms brought into Hue, 47–48, 55–57
  attempts to turn ARVN soldiers,
    301–302, 305, 306
  battalions involved in Tet Offensive,
    98
  beginning of war of resistance, 22
  casualties and morale, 60
  CORDS sweeps of, in South Vietnam-
    ese villages, 68
  difficulty of separating from other
    South Vietnamese, 31, 32
  flag, 52
  forces attached to NVA for Tet
    Offensive, 41–42, 51

NVA soldiers as, 81–82
political infrastructure in South, 32
popularity of, by default, 33
reasons for fighting, 508–509
recruitment methods and organization, 49, 50
retreat from Hue, 490
treatment of captured, 30
uniforms, 51, 82–83
villagers and, 30, 32, 49, 68
Youth Union, 8
Viet Minh, 22, 39
Vietnam War, American perspective
   containment of Communism as goal, 34, 78
   current opinions of soldiers, 526–527, 530–532
   election of Nixon, 520
   as "limited war," 36
   narrative of weak enemy with little popular support, 90
   as spreading democracy, 76
   as stalemate US would lose, 33–34
   support for, 34, 35–36
   Tet Offensive as pivot, 496, 500, 519, 526
   war as eroding soul of, 29
   winnability of, 525
Vietnam War, American perspective: antiwar
   draft resistance, 34, 35
   Johnson's view of, 499
   King and, 318
   as not business of US, 420
   overview of, at end of 1967, 34–35
   political opposition, 35, 222, 315, 317–319
   violence, 521
Vietnam War, Communist perspective
   current view, 527–528
   escalation as necessary, 61, 62–63
   Ho's patience, 61–62
   name for, 519
   official history, 65–66
   as struggle for independence, 48
Vietnam Workers Party, 58, 63–64, 65

Walker, Vic, 409
Wallace, Theodore, 231, 232, 235–236, 263, 343–344, 345
Walsh County Press, 201
"The War Just Doesn't Add Up" (Harwood), 29–30
Warr, Nick, 404, 408, 410–412, 425–426
Washburn, Wayne, 270
Washington, 271
Washington Post, 29–30, 194, 222, 469
Washington Star, 317
Wear, John, 383–384, 385–386
Weathers, Nathaniel, 201
Weaver, Eugene, 175
Webb, Alvin, 240–241, 251, 460–461, 464, 470, 471
Webster, Don, 363
Weinraub, Bernard, 413–414
Weiss, Ernie, 285, 291–292
Wells, Alexander, 406, 428
West, Charlie, 247–248, 382
Westin, Andrew, 295
   about, 67, 68–69
   after Vietnam War, 536
   battle for Hue, beginning of, 227–228
   battle for Hue, concluding weeks of, 479
   battle for Hue, in field before, 68, 70–73
   battle for Hue, second week of, 346–347, 349–350, 352, 353, 482–483
   promotions, 70, 73
   wounded, 483, 484–485
Westin, Miriam, "Mimi," 68–69, 352
Westmoreland, Kitsy, 19–20
Westmoreland, Margaret, 19
Westmoreland, William, "Westy," 3
   about, 19, 20
   appointed in charge of war, 20
   Checkers strategy, 59, 67–68, 75, 84, 220
   declarations of winning war made by, 20, 21, 29–30
   "End-in-View" publicity tour, 496
   "Fractured Jaw" plan, 314, 315
   importance of Hue, 101
   Johnson and, 20, 37, 313, 416, 498

Westmoreland, William, "Westy,"
    (*continued*)
  Khe San as real Tet Offensive target,
    39–40, 197, 220–221, 474
  kill ratios/body count, 21, 24, 220, 221,
    316–317, 502
  loss of confidence in, 498
  opinion of protesters, 35
  press and, 29–30, 32, 37–38, 313–314, 416
  relieved of command, 506
  request for more American troops,
    62, 496
  Rostow report on Tet Offensive, 197
  in Saigon, 183
  on seriousness of Tet Offensive, 183
  "Success Offensive" Press Club
    speech, 37–39
  Tet Offensive as American victory, 522
  Tet Offensive as major Hanoi blunder,
    183, 315, 316
  Tet Offensive as proof of enemy's
    weakness, 152, 153, 220, 497, 522
  Tet Offensive attack on Hue seen as
    diversion, 314, 474
  Thieu government and, 89–90
  understanding of Tet Offensive battle-
    field conditions, 197

Wheeler, Earle, 163, 220, 403
  Westmoreland and, 21, 314, 500–502
Whitmer, Maury, 431–433, 434, 435–437,
    438, 439, 441, 470
"Who, What, When, Where, Why:
    Report from Vietnam" (Cronkite),
    503–505
Wilbourne, Frank, 409
Wilson, Carl, 35
Wilson, Jim, 480
Wilson, Lyndol, 283
Winkel, Dan, 133, 140
Winston, Henry, 480

Xuan, Nguyen Dac, "Dac," 3
  about, 64–65, 124
  ARVN soldiers recruited by, 305
  battle for Hue, beginning of, 123–125
  battle for Hue, concluding weeks of,
    457
  civilians and, 124–125, 297, 300, 303,
    305–306
  infiltration of Hue, 86
  Tet Offensive, preparations for, 66

Zippo tanks, 130
Zwetow, Tom, 438–439